# PLANS FOR A DREAM HOME

)06

7
9

*Also by Murray Armor*
*Building Your Own Home (15th edition)*
*Home Plans (5th edition)*
*Heat Pumps and Houses*

# PLANS FOR A DREAM HOME

Selected and introduced by

## Murray Armor

EBURY PRESS · LONDON

First published in the United Kingdom in 1986 by Prism Press under the title 'Plans for Dream Homes'

1   3   5   7   9   10   8   6   4   2

Second edition 1988
Third edition 1991

This fourth edition published in 1996 by Ebury Press
Random House
20 Vauxhall Bridge Road
London SW1V 2SA

Random House Australia (Pty) Limited
20 Alfred Street, Milsons Point, Sydney,
New South Wales 2061, Australia

Random House New Zealand Limited
18 Poland Road, Glenfield,
Auckland 10, New Zealand

Random House South Africa (Pty) Limited
PO Box 337, Bergvlei, South Africa

Random House UK Limited Reg. No. 954009

A CIP catalogue record for this book is available from the British Library

ISBN: 0  09  181039  6

ACKNOWLEDGEMENTS
Colin Spooner
Derek Spence
Jenny de Villiers
Janet Parker
Myra Giles
Sally Edwardes
and design copyright holders

Typset by RTS, Worksop
Printed and bound in Singapore

# *Contents*

# *Introduction*

Today's housing market is a consumer market, driven by consumer choice. After decades of being offered only homes that the architects and planners thought we deserved, which the developers thought profitable to sell and which builders found easy to build, we can now buy new homes in a bewildering range of styles to suit almost any living pattern. The ultimate in this consumer choice is to decide to build your own home by buying a building plot and arranging to have the home of your dreams built on it. Many thousands of families do this every year, and this is a book to help them decide on the design of their dream home. It is one of a series of three books that, happily for the author, have established themselves as the standard consumer guides.

Together with its companion volumes *Building Your Own Home* and *Home Plans, Plans for Dream Homes* does not promote any particular housing fashion, but looks at 400 houses and bungalows built in recent years in all parts of the UK in all price brackets. It describes how the designs are related to the living requirements of the families who commissioned them, to their surroundings and, most importantly, to their budgets. They are not show houses or architectural concepts but the real homes of people who had freedom of choice and knew what they wanted. The text is written to explain why they made their choices, and the influences and constraints that affected their decisions.

All the designs shown are copyright, and plans for them, or for variations of the designs shown, are available from the designers. However, the enthusiastic reception given to earlier editions of this book show that it is particularly useful in explaining what is involved in choosing a design for a new home, and as a source of design ideas.

It is not written to enable the home builder to dispense with the services of an architect or designer, but rather to provide a background against which the home builder can explain his or her own ambitions to the professional who they will need to engage to draw up the plans. It must be emphasised that amateur house plans are not a good idea, invariably leading to delays and other problems when seeking statutory consents, and rarely demonstrating the best way of meeting a design requirement. On the other hand, a new home that completely achieves the aspirations of the family which builds it depends on their ability to analyse and describe their requirements to the professionals who they employ. This book is written as an aid to doing just that.

# Choosing a Design

## The Choices

Houses are for people. Unfortunately most of the people get little say in the design of the house that they live in, and their choice of a new property is limited to buildings already designed by others. However, every year about 20,000 families move into newly built homes where they have had some say in the design, and this book presents 400 typical homes for which they commissioned the plans. How did they decide what they wanted, and how did they set about getting it? Of course, they all had professional advice from the designers who prepared the drawings, but they all had to make up their own minds what sort of home they wanted before the first line was drawn, either with a pencil or a CAD programme.

The decisions are best made by considering the three functions of any new dwelling. First of all it is a contribution to the landscape. It will affect the appearance of the place where it is to be built, will require services ranging from the obvious water supply, to the less obvious medical services that we also expect to be on tap, and it will still be there in two hundred years time. Forty years ago it was decided that, because of this, all development should be regulated and controlled, and the planning acts were born. Today everyone agrees that planning controls are necessary, and just about everyone building a new home finds them an intolerable restriction of their desire to do their own thing. Whatever you may feel about this, the blunt fact is that whether or not you can build a new home at all, and if so every detail of its size, appearance and materials is controlled from the Town Hall. Every choice that you make in these matters is going to be subject to the approval of others, and it is essential to understand what is likely to be approved, and what is not.

The second function of a new home was described by the French architect Corbusier as a house being a machine for living in. This is a very convenient description of the part of the design for a new home where the individual and not the planner makes the decisions. Open plan living, or separate rooms? A small kitchen with an adjoining utility room, or a big family kitchen? A fireplace or not? All these are decisions that you will make to suit your own particular pattern of living, and it is easy to assume that you will decide to specify exactly what appeals to you, and that the interior of the home will be designed to meet your families specific requirements.

In practice this is rarely the case, as when the decisions have to be made a third consideration has to be taken into account — the home as an investment. This is not simply a matter of the cost, but of how worthwhile an investment you are making in bricks and mortar. At some stage of the decision making process virtually every home builder stops to ask himself what the resale value of the property will be, and starts considering how he can be sure that it always remains at the top of the market for its size and position. Invariably this aspect of the whole business comes to play a larger and larger part in his attitude to the alternatives, and tends to become the most important consideration.

When these three factors are put together the question to be answered can usually be expressed as "what design shall I choose which is:

★ the best investment for my money,

★ will be acceptable to the planners,

★ and will suit my family's living requirements."

It is very unusual to find anyone arranging their priorities differently, although there are a few, and they add a little variety to the architect's life and to the sort of houses and bungalows that get built. Apart from these rare exceptions, all the pressures are to conform to the conventional, which is why avant garde new homes are more often seen illustrated in magazines than on the ground.

Fortunately, conventional houses and bungalows these days are better designed and better looking than ever before, largely because consumer choice has returned to the housing market after three decades of housing shortages. (Now it is money to buy houses or to pay for mortgages that is short). Today's new homes are built in a wide variety of styles, and only the 'modern' homes of twenty years ago are out of fashion. All are represented among the four hundred designs in this book, and the following pages describe in greater detail the factors that you will have to consider when choosing between them.

# Choosing a Design

## The Planners

Planning consent for a new home is a subject dealt with at length in the other books in this series, and here we only look at the way that the Planning Acts control the design and the materials for a new home. However, it is important to remember that the regulations also determine whether or not any building of any sort can be erected at all, and if so what the access arrangements shall be, and how it will inter-relate with the environment in every possible way. Planning consents may also impose conditions, such as saying that the garden gates must be set back a certain distance from the road, or even requiring that in rural areas the householder must be employed locally. Consents often have a whole list of 'reserved matters' that require further approval at an appropriate stage.

All this can sound very frightening, particularly when one hears or reads of other people's adventures with planning appeals or other confrontations with the planners, but in practice all is quite simple. First of all, discover what sort of a building the planners would like to approve. Invariably this will be in the style and materials that are typical of the other new homes in the local area. Consideration of the investment value of the new property will usually lead to you wanting a house or bungalow in the same style, and presumably you want to build there because you like the local style anyway. It is probable that your view and the official view will coincide. In this case all that is required is for your plans to be presented in a way that makes it clear that your proposals meet the usual requirements, and deserve automatic approval!

If your understanding of the local planning scene leads you to suspect that your plans are not exactly what the planners are going to be looking for, then it is essential that your application is submitted in a way that gives it the best chance of success. The arguments for your proposals must be put forward properly, seeking a meeting to discuss the proposals on site, perhaps lobbying the local councillors, and certainly setting up the original application in a way that gives you the best opening for an appeal if it is refused.

All this requires that your application should be handled by a professional unless you are very sure of what you are doing, and the professional should be someone who has handled hundreds of planning applications like yours, not just someone who knows how to fill in the forms. In practice it is usual for the person who prepares your plans to submit your planning application on your behalf, so the initial choice of designer has to be made with this in mind. You will certainly want to discuss the pros and cons of the planning application with him, and reading the other two books in this series will help you to know what questions to ask.

In matters of design and the approval of materials there has been some relaxation of a very authoritarian approach adopted by planning authorities in the early 1980's, and successive planning appeal findings and Department of the Environment directives have emphasised that the approval must be of what is acceptable, and not of an ideal which a planning officer may consider desirable. Nevertheless, the system operates in a way that makes it very difficult to get consent for buildings or materials which do not conform to an established local style, and a key element in this is the time factor. The overwhelming majority of people who want to build are in a hurry, and they are usually prepared to compromise on design details in order to hurry up the paperwork. In theory a decision has to be given on a planning application in eight weeks, but the national average decision time on an application is nearly twice this time. Those who have borrowed money to buy a building plot, and who do not wish to lose a prospective purchaser for their existing house, will usually agree to changing a window or the style of the new home if this cuts through an argument and hastens the start of the work on site.

The rigour with which the planning acts are used to control the design of new home varies enormously in different parts of the country. In attractive rural areas and picture book villages the design of a new home may be reported on by three or four different experts before it ever reaches the planning committee, and it is not unusual for drawings to be revised half a dozen times before consent is obtained. By this time the applicant will be convinced that the pace of the deliberations is related to keeping the deliberators in employment. Be that as it may, the accepted routine is discussion, compromise, and redraw the plans until honour is satisfied all round. To adopt other tactics will probably involve even more lengthy delays, and if you want to force issues you must be sure that you have the time to spare.

Virtually every county has a published design guide of some sort, and these are readily available at District Planning Offices. An alternative way of understanding the sort of styles which the planners regard with favour is to look at the new homes being built on plots like yours in the local area. This means buildings actually under construction following a recent planning approval, and not properties built a year or two ago. Planning fashions change, and do not make the popular error of assuming that a planning consent in the past is a precedent for other similar applications. For instance, full bar or 'Georgian' windows are quickly moving out of fashion and in some rural areas the planners will suggest that they are inappropriate to the surroundings. The fact that three years ago they gave consent for windows of this sort in a house across the road is no precedent at all. You will be told that the house across the road merely 'demonstrates the way in which this type of window is adversely affecting the street scene' and this becomes an argument used against you. All of this has a jargon of its own — find out enough about it to be able to discuss it with your own expert, and make sure that he really is an expert.

# A Design Style

## What will your new home look like?

Any consideration of the various styles in which new homes are being built in this decade must start with a little architectural history. The earliest houses of which any number survive in this country are from the 16th century and were built in stone, brick or wood depending on the availability and relative costs of these materials. Over most of the country homes were built from locally cut wooden frames with infill panels in any convenient material, usually lath and plaster or brickwork. The framing timbers were sometimes left exposed, and in some parts of the country the timbers and panels were painted in contrasting colour, sometimes, not always, in black and white. Today we call this the Tudor style.

With the coming of the industrial revolution, cheap transport and a shortage of cheap timber as forests disappeared, this system of construction was abandoned in favour of loadbearing brickwork or stone masonry. This coincided with the classic revival and an appreciation of architecture as an art form. Public buildings and the houses of the great and wealthy were built in classic styles, and the homes of yeomen and merchants imitated them as far as was possible. The essence of this architecture was a feel for proportion, both of the whole building and of individual rooms, with careful consideration of the role of entrances and windows to give a feeling of elegance, inside and out. This classical influence dominated all architecture until the start of the Victorian era, when concern for materials and using them to show off technical virtuosity became as important as the shape of a building.

This reached its climax when the romantic movement arrived, fuelled by the novels of Walter Scott, and leading to buildings designed in a popular version of our gothic heritage. The Victorian Gothic architectural style appeared, bringing with it the towers and spires seen on many of our town halls today. As a part of this there was a limited enthusiasm for tudor style homes as shown in the plate from a 1891 book of plans on the opposite page.

*Genuine Tudor*
*— Halls Croft, Stratford on Avon*

The Gothic style did not last long, but tudor homes grew in popularity and became an important style – in numbers if not in influence – for individually designed detached houses built in the first 30 years of the 20th century. To the aesthetes it was a dishonest style: the half timbering was a decorative feature and was not the essential framework of the building. To those who believed that form should follow function the tudor features were unnecessary and bizarre ornaments, and the style was 'pretty' or 'chocolate box'. This ignored the fact that those who were going to live in the homes liked pretty things and that chocolate boxes were an expression of popular taste. Architects believed that it was their role to be the arbiters of taste, and that they alone understood what was appropriate for our built environment. The avant garde houses of the era were built in plain functional styles that were very different from the public taste, but their influence was out of all proportion to the number actually built.

1939 saw the end to house building for a decade, and then the housing shortages of the fifties and sixties, together with the controls inherent in the new planning acts, gave the fashionable architects of the day the opportunity to dictate what was built. Functional architecture became the rule, partly because its stark economy was in keeping with an age of austerity. For the whole of the fifties, sixties and early seventies all new homes right across the country were in the same 'modern' style, with few concessions to regional design features or to what homebuyers really wanted. As a result the price of good 1930s houses rose above the prices of equivalent new homes, and it is surprising that no one realised that the public actually preferred the pre war designs. Still, remember that this was the time when the experts hypnotised town councils all over the country into believing that council house tenants would prefer to live in tower blocks.

The national developers liked to build these post war homes because they were cheap and could be built to the same plans from one end of the country to the other. The houses were as box-like as possible, usually built in the cheapest walling materials with panels of contrasting materials to 'add interest'. Bungalows had low pitch roofs, picture windows, and were advertised as being 'ranch style' to cash in on a vogue for anything American. Dormer bungalows with flat roofs to the dormer windows had the ugliest profile of any homes ever built in Britain.

Fortunately these homes were built for a race of gardeners, and the splendid front gardens of our suburbs largely distract from the shortcomings of a million of these stereotyped homes. At the time that they were built a few architects were still designing homes in other styles, and a few local authorities built council houses using traditional local materials, particularly in stone areas, but all the attention was focussed on functional designs that cut costs. They often seemed to use new materials simply because they were new, and these were not always successful.

In the mid 70s all this started to change. Once the housing shortage was replaced with a shortage of cash to buy houses, the building industry started to listen to its customers for the first time for as long as anyone could remember. The result was a dramatic return to both regional and 1930 styles. Neo-Georgian homes took the lead, followed by a surprising return to mock-Tudor designs. In the town halls the strong new planning departments formed after the local government reorganisation of the early seventies got into their stride and promoted regional styles with enthusiasm. Most authorities printed design guides with specific advice on what would be considered acceptable features of designs submitted for planning approval, and although the authority of these guides has been undermined by ministerial directives and planning appeal findings, their influence has been far reaching.

Today the planners are more than ever concerned with *where* a building can be constructed, but less dictatorial about its style. They look for a design that does not conflict with the character of the local area, and that is a good example of its type. (Buildings in conservation areas and similar places are an exception). Planners are concerned with what is acceptable rather than dictating a perceived ideal, and public disillusion with tower blocks, modern city centres and other buildings of the 60s makes it likely that it will be a very long time before any significant proportion of new homes will be built with purely functional or non-traditional design themes. The result of all of this is that those building for themselves are currently building in a huge range of traditional styles. Let us look at some of them.

Georgian homes led the movement away from modernism at a popular level, and the popular use of the name covers a whole range of architectural styles and excesses. At its best it describes homes accurately in the style and proportions of domestic architecture in the 18th and early 19th centuries, but this is usually in town houses built on high value sites. In the suburbs the name is attached to any house with a hip roof, full bar windows and a centrally placed front door. If the doorway has a fibreglass portico and the windows are of the sash type the house will command a premium price and will be much admired, even though the Georgians never built detached homes at six to the acre. They also kept their carriages at the back, not behind 'Georgian panelled' up and over garage doors. But it is inappropriate to make fun of this style: it is much admired by homebuyers, and lends itself to well proportioned comfortable rooms.

Regional styles became popular very soon after the Georgian home and are much more significant. They are difficult to define, and easy to identify. The name is used to describe any house which demonstrates as many as practicable of the pre-Victorian features of an area. This means half hip roofs in Hampshire, complex clusters of gable roofs of different spans in the West Country, tile hanging in Kent, colour washed brickwork in Essex and the use of interesting local materials everywhere. Casement windows without top lights are de rigeur, although they are often made in hardwood and are stained, which would be a novelty to those who originated the styles. Even the ubiquitous up and over garage door is increasingly found with vertical or chevron boarding so that it looks something like a pair of coach house doors. All this is matched by a renewed interest in detailing: brick corbels at eaves, stone laid in the appropriate way to suit the grain and texture of the material, chimneys that once more seek to be decorative as well as functional. It is a splendid revival, and examples of it all are found on the pages that follow.

Tudor style homes mark the hugely popular extreme of this personal choice. Between 1950 and 1980 they were unthinkable and even today the architectural establishment derides the style in no uncertain terms. So how is it that 75% of all new homes advertised in the Sunday Times are in a style disapproved of by contributors to the Architects Journal? It is simply consumer choice. Although they have little in common with houses built in the 16th century, which, incidentally usually had the timber framing covered with plaster or brightly painted, they are a cheerful return to the appearance of some homes built in Edwardian England, which is when our version of the tudor style established itself. They are pretty houses, and with the elaborate front doors and use of leaded lights, they make a centrepiece for the Englishman's garden, which for far too long served only to disguise an ugly functional home.

Victorian, Edwardian and Thirties houses are now also being built, and because there are so many originals to be examined, the current versions are usually very accurate copies. However, current building regulations to make new dwellings more energy efficient inhibit the use of large glazed areas like picture windows and limits the potential for replicating the more interesting of the houses built in the 50s, 60s and 70s.

Bungalows are a special case. The word is Hindi, brought home from India by tea planters in the closing years of the last century, and the whole concept is wholly alien. Certainly the Welsh long house and the Scottish bothy have a long history, but in most parts of the country the yeoman's home was two storeys high just as soon as he could afford anything more than a hovel. However the convenience and utility of the bungalow has now given it its own place in our domestic architecture, and it is here to stay. In many areas, particularly in Wales and in the South West, bungalows are now well established and will be accepted without question by the planners in appropriate areas. Elsewhere the rule is that unless you are building among other bungalows you will have to argue your case. The number of bungalows built every year shows that it is often a perfectly good case.

For the family that hopes to build a new home so that they can decide on the design themselves this is all very good news. They have more choice of design styles than ever before, and unless they want to build in a very sensitive area they will find the planning authorities sympathetic to any reasonable ambition provided that the resulting building will not be out of place. Not being out of place is usually a question of fitting in harmoniously neighbouring properties, neither dominating them nor detracting from them. People with a good eye for these things will know instinctively what is appropriate, but it is invariably a very good idea to start off your first meeting with an architect or designer by discussing the style and feel of the property that is required before launching into details of your requirement for a drawing room that will suit your grand piano!

You should also keep in mind that most people want a new house to be the best possible investment, and that this will most readily be achieved if the new property is a restrained but perfect example of the local style. If the house is to have distinctive features, like an elaborate front porch or stone window surrounds, they should have every detail right. To give the new home the maximum market appeal when it is sold – as it will be one day – it is also important that the interior style should match the external appearance. If you mix an exterior in one style with an interior in another you will definitely limit the appeal of the property, even though it may suit you and your family very well.

# Choosing a Design

## To Suit Your Site

Any new home has to suit the site on which it is to be built, and this is why any serious choice of a design can only be made after considering where it is going to be built. This may sound obvious, but it is surprising how many people run around looking for land on which to build a specific home for which they have already chosen the design. Daydreaming about a specific design irrespective of where it is to be built is fine, and daydreams keep up morale while you are searching for the right plot, but the real world is rather different.

A site for a new home will have its own fixed characteristics — the position of the access, the direction of the principal views, the path of the sun at different times of the day, and the slope of the land.

To these must be added the fixed requirements of the new building, and the need to meet them at an acceptable cost. The drains must flow downhill unless they are to be pumped. The drive must have a maximum slope of one in seven. Regulations specify clearances between the buildings and the boundaries, and the distances between foundations and established trees. All of these factors and fixed requirements are unchanged whether you build a house or bungalow in any particular shape, style or material. Let us look at some of them in detail.

First of all, do not be too surprised or disappointed if your dream site for your dream home has a major problem, particularly if it is an isolated infill plot in a rural area. If you think about it, there has to be some reason why any plot with the potential to get outline planning consent has not been built on. Perhaps it is because the owner simply did not want it developed, or because there was no demand for it to be developed, but very often it is because there is a snag of some sort. The access may involve a deep cutting into a bank at the roadside, or the drains may have to be pumped, or there are foundation difficulties. All these are engineering problems which can be overcome, and it will be possible to estimate the cost involved. The price of the land should reflect the special cost of building on it, but obviously the problems should be examined in detail at an early stage. It is a useful rule always to ask yourself why a building plot with outline planning consent has not yet been developed by others.

One characteristic of every plot that is self evident is its orientation in relation to the sun, and the views that it enjoys. A generation ago a 'south facing site' where the sun would warm the principal rooms was considered very important, but today, with central heating and double glazing, this is given a far lower priority. Most people consider that the views are far more important — the nice views to be enjoyed and the unfortunate views to be obscured. Remember too that the views from the first floor rooms are often as important as those through ground floor windows, and that many housewives consider the view through the kitchen window to be at least as important as any other.

The role of any existing trees on the site has got to be settled at an early stage. If they are the subject of a tree preservation order they become part of your negotiations with the planning authority. If you do not know if there is a tree preservation order, remember that enquiries at the town hall may lead to an order being issued straight away. A nice catch twenty two situation which you will have to play by ear. At any rate, if existing trees are retained they are going to be a major factor in your design as they will affect the views from the windows as well as possibly complicating the foundations. They will certainly also affect your landscaping, limiting what will grow beneath them, providing huge areas of shade, and giving barrow loads of leaves to be swept up in the autumn. In spite of all this, few attributes of a site are more pleasing than mature trees of the right species.

*Would suit the suburbs anywhere.*

*Rural areas, South East England.*

*Rural areas, the West of England.*

19

# Choosing a Design

## Building on a slope

If a site slopes significantly, you must consider your approach to building on the slope as a first stage in establishing the design concept

*Option One. Build up above the slope. Involves suspended floors, some additional foundation costs, and the need for very careful landscaping to conceal the large area of brickwork below floor level. Will improve the view, especially from the balcony.*

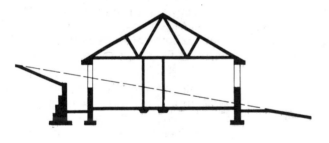

*Option Two. Build into the slope. Permits a cost effective solid floor on natural ground, but may require a retaining wall or steep garden to the rear. Excavated material will have to be carted away unless it can be used for landscaping on stand.*

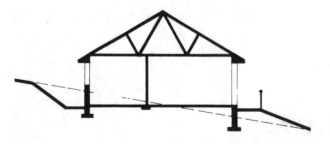

*Option Three. 'Cut and Fill'. This is the usual approach, combining the minimum foundation costs with the look of being built into the hillside. Care required with landscaping.*

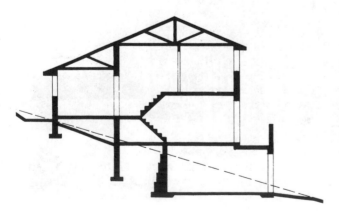

*Option Four. Multi level. Garage below with living accommodation above, following the slope. Gives interesting layouts with opportunities for balconies to take advantage of views, but construction costs will be high. Inevitable steps outside and changes of level inside may limit resale potential.*

The next consideration is the slope of the land. Here again, regional practice is paramount. In the West Riding of Yorkshire, homes are commonly built on sites with one in five slopes, and local styles and local building practice are geared to this. In other parts of the country any slope at all is deemed to merit special consideration. Wherever you build, there are two approaches to be considered; should you arrange to remove the slope, or design a home to make use of the slope?

If the site permits it is invariably cheaper to excavate a level plinth for a new home, adjusting the levels and spreading the surplus soil as part of your landscaping. This involves either digging into the slope or else digging out part of the plinth and using the excavated material to raise the level of the other part. This is called "cut and fill" and the sketch shows what is involved, as do many of the plans on the design pages.

Digging out a level plinth is not always possible, sometimes because the site is too steep or the ground too rocky, but usually because the plot is too small to allow for the necessary changes of level. Remember that you cannot excavate close up to your neighbour's fence: in law his land is entitled to support from your land. In this case you have to consider a building designed to make use of the slope, and sometimes those who like this style of home will deliberately alter the ground levels on their land to be able to do this.

Invariably a multi-level home of this sort is more expensive to construct than providing the same living accommodation on a level plinth, and changes of a level in a home are more attractive to the younger generation than to the elderly. This may affect the re-sale potential, and it is generally true that while split level homes are often exceptionally attractive and lend themselves to exciting decor, they often have a limited re-sale market. There are many examples of multi-level homes in the design section of this book.

The slope also affects the drains. Ideally drains should slope down to the sewer or septic tank at a regular slope of one in forty, about two feet below the ground, and should all leave the house at one convenient point. This is the ideal: lots of new homes have drains emerging at various points, with a pump to move the effluent up-hill to a private septic tank, which itself requires special sub-soil drainage. All things are possible, and all the solutions cost money.

If the slope is at all steep it will also involve the design of a drive. This is always a more complicated issue than it seems to be. First of all the local authority will want a visibility splay at the point where the drive joins the road, and will insist that any gates are set back a car's length from the road. They will probably want your drive laid out so that a car can turn round in it, and will insist that rain water from your drive should not cascade across the pavement. There is obviously a maximum slope that your car can negotiate, but long before you reach this limit, problems will arrive in designing the drive so that your car does not 'hang up' when making the change of gradients as it gets onto the road, or into the garage. Finally, the appearance of the drive is important. It will almost certainly be the largest feature in your front garden, and has to be designed with your landscaping proposals in mind.

The actual ground conditions as far as the foundations are concerned are usually less important than many other considerations, as long as they are understood by all concerned at an early stage. The value of a new house has now risen to a point where the additional cost of specially reinforced raft foundations is not a prohibitively expensive element in the total cost. Even complicated piled foundations are often cost-effective in the overall scheme, particularly if the purchase price of the land reflects the potential foundation difficulties.

All these considerations are discussed at length in the other books in this series. As set out briefly here they should help you to identify the characteristics of any building plot which you need to have in mind when thinking about a home to be built on it.

# Choosing a Design

## The Layout

So far we have discussed the factors that are likely to affect your choice of the style of a new home, and the way in which the site will influence your decisions. The internal layout gives you far more scope for having exactly what you and your family want, although as already explained, it is likely that you will be very concerned that you build a property that is the best possible investment, and this will put a brake on flights of fancy that are too exuberant. How do you make sure that you get what you want?

First of all, the council of perfection. This is that you should think hard about your pattern of living and your likes and dislikes, and write them down in the form of concise notes. Look carefully at the designs in this book, and make notes of the features in some of them that particularly appeal to you. Then explain all this to the architect or designer who is to prepare your plans, give him your notes, and wait to see what his draft design looks like. Avoid giving him your own design drawn up on pages from a pad of graph paper that you have bought specially from the local stationers. In this way you will benefit from his professional training and experience, and will not let him slide into the easy course of simply drawing up the client's sketch. If you have drawn your own sketch — and why not — keep it to yourself so that you can compare it with his proposals in due course. You will probably find that he has approached the design in a different and interesting way, and the odds are that you will recognise that it is a better way. The first draft is only for discussion anyway, and two alternatives to look at are better than one.

I have described this course as a counsel of perfection because it is unlikely that you will take this advice. Although you have a lifetime's experience of communicating with words, and very little experience of drawing plans, most clients approach architects with the inevitable sheet of squared paper in their hands. The choice is yours. Whether you are going to brief a designer and leave him to work out a layout for you, or whether you are going to initiate the design concept yourself, the rest of this chapter should help you.

The best way to make a start is to consider each room of your dream house in turn and to decide what sort of a room you want it to be, what features you want in it, and what features you do not want. Once you have a clear idea of all these ideal rooms you can think about fitting them in a shell of the right shape and size. Start with the hall. Do you think a hall is a very important feature of a home, or is it not very important? If the former, would you accept that all the other rooms should be slightly smaller so that the hall can be really imposing, perhaps with room for a circular table in the centre of the room for a super flower arrangement? Or does the size not matter at all, and you see the only job of the hall to be to connect up the different rooms in the house? Should the front door open directly into the hall, or via a storm porch? Should the hall give access to the lounge through imposing double doors in the centre of a wall, or through a discreet door at one side?

Any staircase is likely to be in the hall; should this be as imposing as practicable, with a half landing and elaborate balustrades, or should it be an unobtrusive and functional single flight? Should the space under the stairs be boxed in, or left open as somewhere to put the pram? Do not worry how all the features that you want can be fitted into the design as the purpose of the exercise is not only to list everything that you hope can be arranged, but also to convey to your designer the feel of the sort of home that you want.

If you carry on like this through all the rooms you will cover a fair number

of pages. Remember that you should also think about views from windows, about whether you want to enjoy the best view from your own bedroom window, or whether this is immaterial. Decide whether you want any particular view from the kitchen. And so on. If two members of a family draw up their own list separately, the debate when they compare them will go on for days. All to the good: the whole point of this is to make sure that you are getting exactly what you want, and to make sure that nothing is built without being carefully considered.

Kitchens and bathrooms are areas where it is particularly important to think carefully about the essentials of what you require, and not to get tied down with detail. These rooms have in common that the fittings can be specified in detail when the house is actually being built, but the basic decisions have to be made at an early stage. Starting with the kitchen area, ignore the relative merits of oak versus melamine cupboard fronts and instead think what size and shape of room you need. Kitchens can be divided into three types: 'farmhouse kitchens' with room for a free standing table and space for other activities, 'breakfast kitchens' with room for a breakfast bar or a table in an alcove, and 'cooks workshop' kitchens with space for nothing but food technology. Your view on which will suit your own living pattern can be complicated by consideration of whether you want a separate utility room, or no utility room and the washing machine and chest freezer in the kitchen. And if the latter, where will the dog sleep? Identify the essential concepts, make decisions on them, and only then move onto the detail.

Bathrooms offer a similar series of options. Fashions change: until a few years ago the w.c. tended to be in a cubicle of its own if space permitted. Now it is invariably back in the bathroom, and the five fittings bathroom with bath, basin, bidet, separate shower and w.c. is usual in larger homes. The latest trend is for this luxury bathroom to be built as the private bathroom of the master suite, with a simpler bathroom for the family and guests. Big en suite bathrooms like this are often associated with small dressing rooms, or a dressing alcove. These are a throwback to Victorian living, and are also somewhere to put fitted cupboards so that the bedroom looks as little like a hotel bedroom as possible. On the other hand, fitted cupboard manufacturers now promote built-in furniture that fits all round the bed-head with a wealth of bedside cupboards, shelves, lights and other supposed aids to a night's sleep. Which approach do you favour?

Both of the other books in this series carry a check list for use in making these decisions, but neither have the number of actual layouts that are shown in the design pages of this book. These are all the actual plans drawn to meet the real requirements of real clients, and the details can be as useful a source of design ideas as the overall concepts.

# Choosing a Design

## House or Bungalow?

In spite of the rude things written about bungalows on an earlier page, and although some county design guides refer to there being 'a presumption against single storey construction', the inescapable fact is that bungalows are an established part of our housing scene and are very popular with home buyers. What are the pros and cons of the house versus bungalow options?

To start with, you will only have this choice of homes on a relatively small proportion of building plots. In most situations it is obvious that planning consent is only going to be granted for a house. In a few other areas only a single storey design will be acceptable. Again, only a small proportion of building plots on the market have the frontage for a large bungalow, so if you want four bedrooms it is likely that you will be obliged to build a house unless you find a plot at least sixty feet wide. Even so, there are plenty of situations where the option is available, and these are the facts to consider.

★ A bungalow is likely to cost marginally more to build than a house of the same floor area.

★ In most parts of the country a bungalow is usually worth rather more than a house of the same size. If this is an important factor you should check this out with a local estate agent.

★ A bungalow will take up more of the plot area than a house, and this can lead to it looking cramped between the boundaries. If your frontage is limited, a bungalow may not have the feel of gracious living that comes with a bigger garden around a home.

★ Bungalows usually have less waste space than a house, — if you regard the staircase well as waste space.

★ Bungalows generally permit more flexible layouts as fewer walls have to be loadbearing.

★ Split level and multi level homes are more easily arranged as bungalows. So are changes in ceiling height and sloping ceilings.

★ If provision is to be made for a home to be extended at a later date, the ease with which this can be arranged, and how much room on the site is available for it, is often a key factor in deciding whether to build a house or a bungalow.

★ Routine maintenance work like painting and cleaning gutters is more easily dealt with by the average householder if he is working on a bungalow. This often appears to be a major consideration to those faced with making a choice.

★ Finally, the 'no stairs' factor is enormously important to many elderly persons.

Consideration of this house/bungalow option invariably leads to discussion of dormer bungalows, and of building a bungalow that is designed for extra rooms to be put in the roof at a later date. This is rarely as straightforward as it may seem to be.

The rectangular dormer bungalow with first floor windows in the gable walls and a flat roofed dormer window in one roof slope had a enormous vogue twenty years ago. At that time statutory requirements and low labour costs combined to make this a particularly cheap way to provide four bedrooms on a narrow plot. Besides this bungalows commanded premium prices over houses, and the functional shape was fashionable. All of these circumstances have changed, and unless a building with dormer windows and low eaves relates to a traditional style it will invariably be better in every way to build a conventional house. Incidentally, flat roof dormers are now very unusual. Unless covered with lead they present maintenance problems, and they rarely look attractive. Pitched roof dormers appear in many places in the design pages, and are often discussed in the descriptions of the designs. A bungalow which is designed so that rooms can be put in the roof at a later date does make sense in some circumstances. It must be realised that this must be a design requirement from the start, and that it is not possible to ask for arrangements to be made for rooms in the roof while the building work is under way — and this is a common request! Provision has to be made for a stairwell, and current building regulations require heavy ceiling joists and other features that will not be used until the first floor rooms are fitted out.

# Choosing a Design

## Garages

If you consider only the basic economics of building a home, a garage is a very expensive luxury. It costs a great deal, probably as much as the kitchen, and is only used to accommodate a car which is itself perfectly weatherproof, and which will not depreciate in value any faster if kept out of doors. Looked at in this way, you are paying a large sum of money so that your car is marginally warmer to get into in the mornings, and so that you can unload groceries from the car under cover when it is raining. None of this is likely to dissuade you from having a garage, but it is interesting to consider just how much a luxury it is. If you have a tight budget this may encourage you to build a larger house and leave the garage until later.

However, there is more to this than the simple utilitarian view. A garage adds another element to the building, or if it is detached, it turns one building into a group of buildings. This adds to the complexity and interest that we look for today in the design of a new home, makes it all look more impressive, and probably a better investment. A garage can also be built large enough to provide storage space for garden equipment and other things, or if you wish it can be further extended into a workshop. If you build a detached double garage, with a roof pitch of over 45° there will be space for a room in the roof, which can be anything from a simple loft to a self-contained flat.

The pros and cons of detached versus integral garages are often irrelevant, as the size and shape of your site may make the choice for you. Given the option, remember that a detached garage can be positioned in relation to the house so that each complements the other, perhaps with link wall to give a courtyard effect. It will be cheaper to build a detached rather than an integral garage as it will not require complex foundations, a fire proof ceiling or other expensive features, and it can be built after the house is completed if this is more convenient. On the other hand it is more expensive to provide electricity, water, or an outside W.C. in a detached garage. An integral garage provides somewhere to put a central heating boiler or an extra freezer, and in many ways is useful simply because it is part of the main building. Finally, an overwhelming advantage of an integral garage for the elderly or infirm is the opportunity to get in or out of a car 'out of the weather'.

Virtually all new garages are built with up-and-over garage doors, and these are now available in a very wide variety of styles and materials, including wooden doors that look like traditional coach house doors. If you want a double garage it is preferable to have two single doors with a masonry pillar between them rather than one double door, although this will take up a little more space. It looks better, is more convenient, and gives more room for car doors to be opened. Electric door openers with remote control arrangements which enable up-and-over doors to be opened from inside a car are now well established and very reliable. They are also addictive: once you are used to them you will not readily go back to opening a garage door by hand. There is something very satisfying to the ego in pressing a button in your car as you drive in the gate and seeing the light come on and the garage door open, and this becomes even more important than practical considerations.

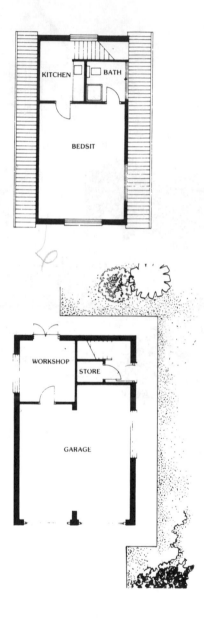

*A double garage with a 45° roof pitch has space for rooms in the roof.*

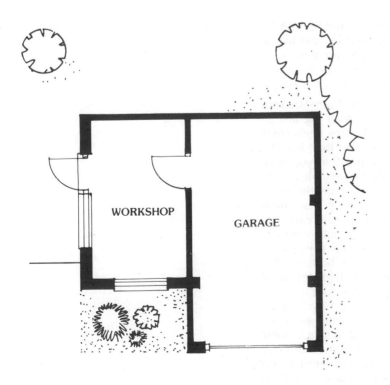

WORKSHOP

GARAGE

*If you want to have a garden store or workshop as part of your garage, you have an opportunity to get away from the conventional garage shape.*

# Energy Saving

The importance of insulating our homes and choosing the right appliances so as to minimise our heating costs is now well understood, and having an energy saving house with the lowest practicable fuel bills is now a priority for most families planning for a new home. For those who are concerned with the environment, energy usage that has the minimal effect on the ozone layer and conserving our natural resources are also major considerations.

Until 1995 the Building Regulations specified the levels of insulation that were required in a new dwelling by describing the 'U values' of the different parts of the structure. Walls had to meet a specific insulation standard, roofs another, and there were regulations for windows and for the insulation of hot water cylinders and piping. These requirements were regularly changed to be more demanding from the 1960's through to 1995, and as a result most people are well aware of the advantages of cavity insulation, loft insulation, double glazing, etc.

In July 1995 all this changed when the whole basis of the relevant part of the Building Regulations was altered. Section L, Conservation of Fuel and Power, now requires that energy usage in the whole house should be assessed and given an arbitrary numerical value using a Standard Assessment Procedure. This is called the SAP rating. It takes into account the design of the property, as a long, thin house with a greater wall area than a more compact house of the same volume is inherently less energy efficient. The area of windows, the insulation provided, the type of heating appliance, the heating controls and much else are all taken into account.

For those building a new home this is very good news, because it means that they can easily find out what the effect on the SAP will be if specific design elements are changed. The example in the box explains this, and how the SAP enables the effect of different energy saving arrangements to be compared.

SAP ratings are calculated using computer programs, and should be obtained for you by your architect or designer who should be able to use them to demonstrate the combination of energy saving features for your own new home that suits your particular requirements. This is now a complex matter, and is dealt with at length in Building Your Own Home.

In considering all of this there are some general points that must be kept in mind. First of all, the changes in Building Regulations over the last 20 years have hugely improved the energy efficiency of our homes. Fuels costs for a house built to meet current SAP requirements are less than half the fuel costs of a house built to 1970 standards, and if homes that you have lived in up to now are more than 20 years old you will be very pleasantly surprised how cosy your new home will be. Secondly, any expenditure on a new home to improve the SAP rating above the Building Regulation requirement may not be cost effective unless chosen with great care. For conservation enthusiasts this may not matter, but most people want the cost of specific energy saving features to be justified by the cost saving over a specific period, usually five to ten years. Finally, there can be both benefits and penalties involved with special appliances or very high levels of insulation. For instance, some heat recovery systems in the roof may not be strictly cost effective, but they provide ventilation that is valued by asthmatics or by non-smokers who share the house with smokers. Sophisticated heating controls may require regular setting to give of their best if you do not have a fixed life style. Triple glazing may not improve your SAP, but may provide welcome sound insulation. Making decisions on the features of a new home that will affect the fuel bills is not an easy matter, but the SAP rating system and the more complex NHER system, are a great help in getting it right.

# SAP Ratings

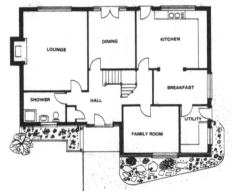

## SAP RATINGS TO COMPLY WITH THE BUILDING REGULATIONS

| Dwelling floor area m² | SAP Energy rating |
|---|---|
| Under 80 (860 sq ft) | 80 |
| 80 to 90 (968 sq ft) | 81 |
| 90 to 100 (1076 sq ft) | 82 |
| 100 to 110 (1184 sq ft) | 83 |
| 110 to 120 (1294 sq ft) | 84 |
| Over 120 | 85 |

The reason for the lower requirement for smaller dwellings is that they have a lower ratio of volume to envelope area than larger houses, and it is not reasonable to expect those building small low cost dwellings to incur higher unit charges for wall insulation than those building larger homes

## THE HOUSE ILLUSTRATED BUILT TO ACHIEVE THE MINIMUM SAP RATING OF 85 WHICH IS REQUIRED BY THE B. REGS. FOR A HOUSE OF THIS SIZE

* *25 mm underfloor insulation*
* *Brick and aerated block walling with 25mm slab insulation in the cavity*
* *150mm roof insulation*
* *6mm cavity double glazing throughout*

* *Ordinary gas boiler with zone controls*
* *Flame effect gas fire*
* *110 litre cylinder with 37mm insulation*
* *Gas cooker*
* *Ordinary light bulbs*

### FUEL USE AND COSTS

| | Energy required Giga Joules (GJ) | Cost per year at 1995 prices | $CO_2$ emission per year, tonnes |
|---|---|---|---|
| Central Heating system | 73.2 | £345 | 4.3 |
| Fireplace appliance | 1.9 | £9 | 0.1 |
| Domestic hot water | 19.1 | £90 | 1.1 |
| Cooking | 5.4 | £25 | 0.3 |
| Lights and appliances | 22.0 | £508 | 4.5 |
| Standing charges | 0.0 | £86 | 0.0 |
| TOTALS | 121.6 | £1063 | 10.3 |

## BUILT WITH A TIMBER FRAME TO A TYPICAL TIMBER FRAME SPECIFICATION GIVING A SAP RATING OF 91

* *40 mm underfloor insulation*
* *Typical walling system, 100mm timber*
* *150mm roof insulation*
* *6mm cavity double glazing throughout*

* *Ordinary gas boiler with zone controls*
* *Flame effect gas fire*
* *110 litre cylinder with 37mm insulation*
* *Gas cooker*
* *Ordinary light bulbs*

### FUEL USE AND COSTS

| | Energy required Giga Joules (GJ) | Cost per year at 1995 prices | $CO_2$ emission per year, tonnes |
|---|---|---|---|
| Central Heating system | 60.1 | £283 | 3.5 |
| Fireplace appliance | 1.6 | £8 | 0.1 |
| Domestic hot water | 19.1 | £90 | 1.1 |
| Cooking | 5.4 | £25 | 0.3 |
| Lights and appliances | 2.9 | £507 | 4.4 |
| Standing charges | 0.0 | £86 | 0.0 |
| TOTALS | 108.1 | £999 | 9.5 |

## BUILT IN BRICK AND BLOCK TO THE STANDARD RECOMMENDED BY THE GOVERNMENTS ENERGY EFFICIENCY OFFICE GIVING A SAP RATING OF 100

* *50 mm underfloor insulation*
* *Brick and aerated block walling with a 100mm cavity fully filled with insulation*
* *200mm roof insulation*
* *6mm cavity double glazing with K glass*

* *Gas condensing boiler with zone controls*
* *Flame effect gas fire*
* *110 litre cylinder with 50mm insulation*
* *Gas cooker*
* *Low energy light bulbs*

### FUEL USE AND COSTS

| | Energy required Giga Joules (GJ) | Cost per year at 1995 prices | $CO_2$ emission per year, tonnes |
|---|---|---|---|
| Central Heating system | 42.6 | £200 | 2.5 |
| Fireplace appliance | 1.0 | £5 | 0.1 |
| Domestic hot water | 15 | £70 | 0.9 |
| Cooking | 5.4 | £25 | 0.3 |
| Lights and appliances | 19.1 | £441 | 3.9 |
| Standing charges | 0.0 | £86 | 0.0 |
| TOTALS | 83.1 | £829 | 7.6 |

Computation by the ECD Partnership by arrangement with the EEO

# Building a Home

## Traditional Construction or Timber Frame?

Anyone contemplating building for themselves will quickly hear of timber frame construction, and will find there are lots of companies offering special services for building timber frame houses and bungalows. As is to be expected, this advertising suggests anyone who is not building with a timber frame is missing the boat. There is no equivalent promotion of traditional construction. This is an area where prospective home builders often feel confused, and there are always more questions on this topic than any other at seminars and advice centres at selfbuild exhibitions.

First of all, a few facts. Traditional masonry construction usually involves composite walls built of brick or stone together with lightweight concrete blocks, and usually have partition walls of concrete blocks between the individual rooms. These walls support the roof and provide the structural strength of the building. Timber frame construction involves some system or other for giving the building a timber skeleton which provides its structural strength, and which is clad with stone, brick or in some other way. Modern roof construction techniques are the same for both systems. Timber frame has accounted for between 5% and 18% of all new homes, up and down for 40 years, and is promoted as being the house building system of the future. This market share has depended more on the price, availability and labour costs associated with masonry products than anything else: when these were high in the early 80's the timber frame market was nearly 20%, but in the recession it dropped to about 5%. The actual figures are hotly disputed, but in the very long term the future will probably lie with timber frame as timber is a renewable resource, and extravagant amounts of energy are required to make cement and bricks.

This is the background. As far as the home builder is concerned there is very little difference between building in masonry or with a timber frame. They are alternative systems of construction, and neither is better or worse than the other. It is virtually impossible to tell which way a finished house has been constructed without a careful investigation, and neither construction costs nor the finished property values depend on how it has been built. Mortgages and insurances for a new home do not depend on the system of construction, fire risks are negligible in all new buildings, and NHBC claim records slightly favour timber frame construction in spite of stories to the contrary. All new homes in Britain have to conform to very high construction standards, and the way in which they are built does not affect their investment value, or their utility as dwellings. However, there are four different areas where comparisons are worthwhile: insulation, sound insulation, speed of construction and the ease in which alterations can be made after a house is completed and occupied.

A very high level of thermal insulation has to be built into all new houses. Additional insulation above the government mandatory standard is relatively easily provided with timber frame systems, and most timber frame manufacturers provide extra insulation. However, extra insulation can also be arranged for a masonry building. Timber frame buildings have a low thermal mass and will heat up from cold more quickly: masonry buildings with the same level of insulation have a higher thermal mass and will cool down more slowly. You can take your choice. Masonry walls offer inherently higher sound insulation levels, but timber frame buildings can be designed to match these levels if required. Anyway, sound insulation depends on many other factors. Speed of construction is less equivocal: once the ground floor slab is constructed a timber frame house can be roofed and water tight in less than a week, while a masonry home will usually take four to six weeks. If saving about four weeks in your total programme for building a new home is valuable to you, then timber frame has clear advantages. For some home builders this is very important, but for most it is irrelevant. Finally, it is generally easier to arrange for major alterations to a masonry home than for a timber frame one, especially if the original design drawings for the latter are not available.

All of this has to be considered against the far more important need for home builders to arrange to get the design of house that suits them best, at the right cost, and designed and built by people in whom they have total confidence. Most of those who use a timber frame package company do so because they like the design and management services offered, and because they simply feel that it is the best way for them to get the home that they want. Those who build with masonry walls usually make their decisions on the same basis. These are certainly the best criteria on which to base any decision unless you positively enjoy an obsession with evaluating technical details that are largely irrelevant to the finished product.

Finally, a brief explanation of the different types of timber frame. There are many proprietary systems and all of them are different. Most involve walling panels built from relatively light timber, with the whole frame deriving its strength from the sum of its parts, rather like the body of a modern car. The panels may be anything from whole walls to relatively narrow units: they are hugely over-engineered and the assembled structure is very stong indeed. Most of the designs in this book were drawn for traditional construction but can be built with walling panels if required.

An alternative is the Potton aisle frame system, which is based on an internal skeleton of massive posts and beams using technology that dates from medieval times. Potton homes are specifically designed for the aisle frame system, and there are many designs for them in this book. In Tudor times the aisle frame internal skeleton was replaced by similar massive timbers which framed the walls of the houses built at this time, and this type of framing is also now available for those wanting a house with a genuine period feel. To confuse the issue, a modern version of post and beam construction called after the architect Walter Segal is promoted by the influential Segal Trust, mainly for low cost housing association use. The brochures from all the timber frame manufacturers explain their own systems very fully: when reading them it helps to realise that not all the systems are the same.

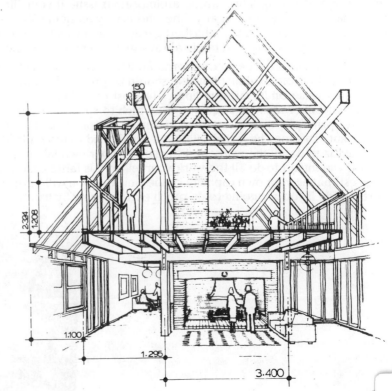

*Aisle frame construction.*

3

# Building a Home

## Landscaping

This chapter is not about designing a garden, or about gardening, but looks at some of the basic considerations involved in relating the house or bungalow to its garden. If you are an experienced and enthusiastic gardener you have probably always thought of your new home in relation to its garden, and you are looking for the right design for a house to suit the dream garden which you can visualise. Most people put things the other way round, and choose a dream house first, and then think about a garden to occupy the space around it. It is important that those in this second group find a little time to give the same careful, analytical thought to the garden that they will give to considering room sizes, window positions and the colour of the bathroom suite.

First of all, how much time are you going to want to give to looking after your garden? At one end of the scale you may think that the less bother the garden is, the better it will suit you. Fine — carefully chosen shrubs, the right grass, no borders, no edges, paths set flush in the grass, and you will have a minimum maintenance garden which can look very attractive indeed. At the other extreme, you may intend that the garden will be a very important part of your life. If so, it is even more important that you analyse what you are going to be able to do, and plan accordingly. If you are fortunate enough to be able to afford to pay someone to look after your garden for you, careful consideration of the labour requirement is just as important, as you will want a perfect garden for your money, and an acre can be laid out either to need only half a day a week to maintain, or to occupy someone nearly full time.

The next thing to consider is your timetable. This is important, and is often overlooked. Do you look forward to watching the garden slowly taking shape, and hope to see your dreams come true in three or four years, or do you want visitors to be admiring it in six months' time? Remember a wisteria will take seven years before it makes a show but a cherry will be in flower next spring. This can be an important issue if your life style is such that you might move at any time, and need your home always to be a good resale prospect. An established garden may or may not add to the value of a property but it certainly always makes it more saleable.

This leads on to the next consideration, which is that of cost. It used to be said that anyone building a house should be prepared to spend at least 10% of its value on its surroundings. The cost of building is now so high that this would require a large plot on which to spend the sum involved, but the principle that the garden deserves its place in the budget is important. This may be a cash budget if you intend to have a landscaping contractor to do all the work, or a budget for your own labour plus some cash if you intend to do all the work yourself. In this latter case, beware of over-estimating your own capacity or the time that you will have available, particularly if you are going to do much earth moving by hand.

Finally, having made a realistic appraisal of the amount of time you wish to give to the garden, of how soon you want it to look established, and of the budget, you can think about what you hope it will all look like. This involves a plan. However unimportant your garden is to you, and however simple you want it to be, it is worth while making sure that your plan is for it to be as little trouble as possible, to show your new home off to the best advantage and to enhance its value.

If you are building on an eighth of an acre in a built-up area, your choices are limited, and you will almost certainly have a marvellous opportunity to look at all your options by simply going for a walk to see what all your neighbours have done with their own plots. Look at their gardens in winter as well as in summer, take local advice on what takes time and trouble, and what is easily looked after, sort out your own masterplan, and away you go. Your garden can set off your house very well, but its size will dictate a limit to what you can do.

With anything over a quarter of an acre the challenge is much more complicated. At this size your garden can be given a distinct character, and house and garden can complement each other in a very special way. If you have this opportunity, then you need to be a very experienced gardener to be confident that you can design a garden like this. Even if you are, it is worth spending a relatively small sum in buying someone else's ideas as well, if only so that you can be absolutely sure that your own are the best. Unfortunately, the right garden designers are as hard to find as the right people to design the house itself.

Local landscaping contractors, nurserymen and garden centres usually offer to design gardens, but this is inevitably linked to their own services. If you are wanting to place a single order at a lump sum price for all the work, materials and plants involved, then contacting them is one obvious way to make a start. Ask for a detailed quotation, which should come with an attractive lay-out plan, lists of plants, details of how the ground will be prepared and of any top soil to be provided, arrangements to replace trees and shrubs that do not take, and proposals to maintain lawns for a fixed period. Everything should be as detailed as possible, so that you can get friends who are keen gardeners to advise you on the proposals.

However, landscaping is one area where the cost of a package service is likely to be far more than the cost of the component parts, and where many people prefer to make their own arrangements for all the various elements involved. If this is what you are likely to want you can ask your local landscaper if he will provide you with a design for a fee, with the option to use his services or not as you wish. Keep in mind that all landscaping contractors make their livings from supplying plants and making gardens and not from designing gardens. There are pressures on them to design what they would find it most profitable to handle, and your only safeguard in this is their local reputation. It is well worthwhile going out of your way to find out what this is, and to look at other gardens that they have made. Do not just visit the one "show garden" that they suggest to you.

An alternative is to use the services of a garden designer. This makes the whole business more complicated, but need not cost very much in relation to the total cost of the garden, and you will know that the advice that you are getting is free of commercial pressure. A garden designer's proposals can be used to get competing quotations from landscaping contractors, or will be your blueprint for managing the job yourself. The problem is to find a designer.

Personal recommendations are invaluable but most people will have to resort to the yellow pages or similar directories. The best initial approach is made by letter, explaining that you are wanting a new garden designed on a plot of xxxx sq. yds. (or x acres) and will be interested to know what the designer can do for you and the costs involved. After that, leave them to sell their services to you and evaluate the proposals very carefully. Again, ask to be put in touch with previous clients. Finally, in explaining your requirements to a designer, make sure he or she understands your own situation with regard to maintenance, timetable and budget.

Some gardening magazines offer a garden design service and these are usually so cheap that it is fun to sign up for one or two of them anyway. The proposals are invariably for an enthusiast's garden with something of everything — lots of quarts in a pint pot. This will give you plenty of ideas, and if you have explained your maintenance/timetable/budget proposals firmly you may even find that they have been given consideration.

All of this needs to be done at an early stage, just as soon as you have settled on the house or bungalow plans themselves. Certainly you want to know exactly the shape and contours of your new garden whilst the builder still has earth moving plant on site, so that you can get him to dump soil where it will be required and to leave the site with the ground at levels that will suit the landscaping work. If you have a large site it is a very good idea to fence off the builder's theatre of operations and to start making the garden on the rest of the land while the house is being built. In this way you will almost certainly be able to get one season ahead, and having part of the garden finished will encourage you to make a start on the area left by the builder as soon as you move in.

To be realistic, if you are managing the building of a new home yourself, it is unlikely that you will have the time or energy to spare to give any of this the attention it deserves, but even so it is important that you do have a landscaping scheme and try to give it consideration, in spite of the over-riding priority to be given to getting the roof tiled on schedule. On the other hand, if you have placed a contract with a builder, then involvement with planning the garden will serve as an outlet for all your frustrations whilst the building work proceeds so slowly. You will have time for visits to garden exhibitions, garden centres, and a great deal of reading and can even venture to plant trees amid the builders confusion if you protect them properly! However much time you have for this, or however little, the important thing is to have a plan at an early stage, and to ensure that it is suited to the long-term relationship between you and the garden which is going to be outside your window for as long as you live in the house.

Given the determination to make an effective plan for the new garden,

preferably before the builder moves his earth-moving equipment away from the site, what are the features to be considered? Many of them are the physical characteristics of the ground from the gardener's viewpoint, such as the soil type, the aspect, and the local climate. These are specialist matters, but others are common to all gardens everywhere. Among the more important are the following.

**THE DRIVE.** Unless you have a very large garden indeed, the drive is the largest single feature at the front of the house, and once it is built it is very difficult to move. It is likely that your planning consent will require that the gates, if any, are set back a fixed distance from the road, that the slope for the first few yards should not exceed a certain gradient, and that there is provision for a car to be able to turn on the drive without backing out into the road. If you can meet all these requirements and still have alternative alignments for the drive, do consider how they will look, and the feel that they will give to the garden, as well as thinking about them simply as a way of getting the car to the garage. If you have a very large garden you may wish to consider a bend in the drive to slow down vehicles using it, but make sure that the oil tanker and the council refuse vehicle can negotiate it.

A tarmac surface or paving brick drive is expensive, and how long it lasts without costly repairs will depend on how the edges are retained to stop it spreading sideways. If it is only to take cars it can be edged with 8" x 2" path edging set in concrete, but if it will be used by heavy delivery vehicles it is well worthwhile using road curbing. The specifications for the construction of the drive itself should be drawn up by your architect, or should be a standard specification from a source that you trust, and should certainly not be left to a contractor. If the cost of a tarmac drive is beyond your budget, then have the curbing installed to retain gravel or chippings and let your car act as a roller for a year or two until it suits you to lay tarmac.

**TREES.** If you are lucky enough to have mature trees on your site you are probably determined to retain them if this is possible. There are a lot of factors involved in this. Tree preservation orders are mentioned on an earlier page, but it is also likely that steps will have to be taken to preserve the house from being damaged by the trees. Tree roots affect foundations in a number of ways, and precautions against damage can involve deepening the foundations or digging a deep trench between the building and any trees, and filling it with concrete. Conversely the building work may have an effect on the trees by altering the sub-surface drainage as well as by interfering with the roots. If a tree is a key element in your landscaping, or is subject to a tree preservation order, it is a good idea to get it surveyed by a qualified tree surgeon. He should be able to advise on the size it will reach, its probable life, and any work necessary to keep it healthy and safe.

If you are planting trees that will grow to any size it is important to take advice on the appropriate clearance from your buildings to avoid problems in the future. This only applies to trees of forest species like beech, cedar, and particularly poplar, and not to fruit trees or ornamentals like flowering cherries or weeping willows.

**HEDGES.** If you have an existing field hedge on a boundary of your land you are very lucky, but it may need a great deal of work to put it in good order. First of all, check with your solicitor whether it belongs to you, or to your neighbour. If the latter, all that you can do to it without his agreement is to keep it trimmed from your side 'in accordance with good practice'. If it is not regularly trimmed on the other side it is worth considering whether you want to try to arrange to take on this work, because a hedge that is regularly cut on one side only will soon become mis-shapen and unattractive. Again, this is a matter on which to get expert advice, particularly if your hedge is of mixed species.

Planting a new hedge always presents a difficult choice of exactly what to plant. Fast growing hedges like privet and leylandii require frequent trimming, and are very greedy, starving neighbouring plants of nutrients. More attractive hedges, like beech and yew, which require little maintenance, take some years to become established. If you can take the long term view and plant a slow growing hedge you will probably never regret it.

**WALLS.** Old walls around a garden are invariably very attractive, a good wind break, and splendid for climbing plants of all sorts. They also have a tendency to start to fall down the moment that you assume responsibility for them, especially if the ground is higher on one side than on the other. The worst potential problem is in the foundations. If a wall leans at all you should consider finding old bricks or stone to match the original material, and have a buttress or buttresses built to support the wall before it becomes unstable. This is cheaper than rebuilding, and if the buttress is really massive and in character, and quickly clothed with climbing shrubs, no one will know it is not original.

The stone coping or coping brickwork is another weak point: fortunately it is easily replaced and it is important to get this done before rain gets down into the masonry. Repointing is less essential than dealing with water getting in at the top, but if it needs to be done, make sure that the work is carried out in exactly the style of the original, with mortar made from the same sand so that the colour matches. If the original wall was built with lime mortar, use lime mortar for the repairs. Walls are a lot of work, but if you are lucky enough to have one, it is worth it.

**FENCES.** The only type of fence which is in any way suited to today's regional architectural styles is a timber post and rail fence. This is attractive, lasts a very long time, and can be fitted with wire mesh at a low level to keep your dog at home. All that can be said about close boarded or chain link fences is that the sooner they are hidden by creepers, climbers, and appropriately planted shrubs the better. If they are unavoidable, and they sometimes are, consider if you can arrange for garden features to give them additional support. A brick built cold frame or compost bay half way along the fence, firmly fastened to it, will help it to still be standing up to the wind long after it would otherwise have needed replacing.

**PATHS, PATIOS AND FEATURE WALLING.** There are many garden books with lengthy chapters on the design and construction of masonry garden features and garden paving, and they are well worth reading. However, they are written by enthusiasts for enthusiasts, so let us look at the snags. Starting with paths, keep in mind that all types need maintenance to some extent or other, and that if they are not laid on properly made foundations they will become uneven and dangerous. Some stone flags become very slippery in wet weather, particularly if they are in the shade, and if you intend to walk around your garden paths at all times of the year it is important to ask about the non-slip characteristics of the surface.

Patios are features that need to be as large as possible, as they invariably manage to look mean and skimpy unless they are big enough to set off the building to which they relate. Unless a paved area has a diagonal dimension of at least a third of any adjacent building it is unlikely to look attractive. It is also important to consider carefully the use to which the patio will be put. If it is principally a feature to be seen and admired, but not used, then the slabs can have gaps to be filled with alpine plants, dwarf walls can be of a height to suit the outlook, and everything arranged for the visual effect. If it will be used for sitting out, or for parties with lots of guests, it is important that there are no gaps to trap high heels, and it will help informal gatherings if any walls are at a convenient height for sitting down.

Masonry features, from simple low walls through to flights of steps and pergolas, are all subject to one over-riding design rule: they must look substantial. Single skin brick walls and nine inch pillars may be structurally satisfactory, and will save on materials, but will always look flimsy and cheap. The same walls at thirteen inches and pillars that are twice as thick as they need to be, will look solid, dignified and established. This is particuarly true of any timber used in a garden feature as in a pergola.

Many people take a great deal of pleasure in carrying out this sort of building work themselves, and it is a very good way to exercise a talent for D.I.Y. bricklaying. What is poor workmanship in a building becomes charming rustic brickwork in a surround to a raised flowerbed! However, foundations, drainage holes and damp courses are all important, and not all types of bricks or stone are suited to garden use, as some are affected by damp and frost. Marshalls of Halifax, who sell cast stone for landscaping have an excellent free booklet about all of this.

**POOLS.** Water in a garden involves a maintenance commitment and if you intend to swim in it you can expect to spend as much time looking after the pool as you are likely to spend actually in the water. If you are an enthusiast you already know this, and will enjoy it. On the other hand, a pool as a status symbol requires careful consideration of the long term commitment, and of the effect on the value of the property. Except in a few areas where high value properties are expected to have pools, they can make a house difficult to sell.

If this does not discourage you, then make your plans for your pool at an early stage. If it is to be built at the same time as your house, it is up to the pool contractor to arrange an effective liaison with your builder. If it is to be built later, then it is important to ensure that an excavator will be able to get round to the site of the pool in due course. You will probably want to retain the excavated soil in your garden, piling it up as a bank to be planted as a shrubbery, so you should allow for this in your landscaping plan. It is probably a good idea to make all the arrangements for pipe runs for a future swimming pool while the house is being built, particularly if the pool is to be heated using your domestic boiler.

**ELECTRICITY.** Electrical sockets in the garden can be very convenient for electric garden tools, garden lighting, and barbecue accessories, and if they are arranged when the contract is placed for wiring the house the cost will be very reasonable. Special circuit breakers and weather-proof sockets will make everything safe. Garden lighting, and any lighting or pumps used with an ornamental pool usually operate at a safe low voltage, and the transformers and cable for this are supplied by the manufacturers of the lights used. Security flood lighting, which is becoming quite common these days, invariably requires mains voltages. All of this requires discussion with an electrician, and it is important to remember that the work involved is little trouble at the time the house is being built, but will be a nuisance to carry out afterwards.

# Making it Happen

## Placing a Contract

There are two ways of building a house or bungalow on your own land, and it is important to distinguish clearly between them. The first is to place a single contract with a builder for the construction of the building. The contract will make it clear that he is responsible for everything from site insurances and arranging the water connection before he moves onto the plot, through to cleaning the finished building before he hands it over to you. You are responsible for paying him in stages as work progresses and warrant to him that the land belongs to you and that the appropriate planning consents have been granted. The contract may or may not provide for him to be supervised by your architect and may or may not involve special arrangements for matters like you buying the kitchen units yourself, or employing your firm's electrician for the wiring, but essentially the responsibility for managing the job rest with the builder.

The alternative is to manage the job yourself, employing firms or individual craftsmen as sub-contractors. In this case you have the final responsibility for the work on site, the liaison between the different trades, and a thousand and one things like services, insurances, contracts with the authorities and much else. If you manage the job this way, whether or not you actually do any of the work yourself, you are what is called a 'self-builder'. The distinction becomes very clear when you look at the VAT position, as a self builder reclaims the VAT paid on materials by filling in forms and receiving a cheque from the VAT authorities, even though he is not VAT registered, while a builder who has a contract to build a house reclaims the VAT himself and has to be registered. The difference is very fundamental. Everything in this chapter is for those who wish to place a contract with a builder. Arranging for this is a very large subject, dealt with at length in *Building Your Own Home.* These are some of the ways of going about it.

**USING AN ARCHITECT.** An architect in private practice will prepare plans to your instructions, obtain all the consents you require on your behalf, find you a builder, prepare a contract for you to sign, supervise the work and approve bills before sending them on for you to pay. He will be concerned to see that you get good value for your money, but he does operate at the top end of the market. His fee will be around 9% of the cost of the work, plus expenses. He should have professional indemnity insurances. Find an architect by personal recommendation, or by asking the R.I.B.A. to recommend a practice in your local area which specializes in individual houses of the size which you propose to build.

**USING A LOCAL DESIGN CONSULTANT.** A design consultant may offer the same services as a registered architect, or a more limited and informal service. His fees are negotiable and he may not carry insurances — both are something to check in advance. Reach him by personal recommendation or through yellow pages, and make sure that he has the experience you require.

**USING A 'PACKAGE COMPANY'.** Various national companies offer comprehensive services for those building on their own, and the five design practices whose plans are featured in this book will all provide whatever assistance their clients may require, from site appraisals and preliminary design studies, to involvement with the actual building contract and supply of materials. As the size and scope of this book demonstrates, their strength is their enormous experience. All work is done against fixed quotations, which many find reassuring. There are many package companies and with any of them check on their resources and ask to see other homes under construction, particularly when they are agents for imported kit houses.

**USING A BUILDER.** Another way of having a house built is to approach a builder, who you already know, and whose work you particularly admire and to ask him to handle everything for you including the design. With the right existing personal relationships this can be a very good way of doing things, but make sure that you have the right contract.

**QUOTATIONS, SPECIFICATIONS AND PRIME COST SUMS.** An architect, designer or package company will obtain competing quotations from builders for you, and will know the builders who they should approach. However, there are probably one or two builders known to you who you would like approached as well and you should not hesitate to ask for this to be arranged. A builder who is invited to quote to build a house is sent a set of drawings and a specification. The specification sets out exactly the materials to be used, the standards of workmanship required and who is responsible for what while the work is being done. It is a lengthy and complex document, but there are ways in which it can be condensed and Building Your Own Home has a whole section about this including a specimen contract which is essential reading before you start negotiating a contract.

A builder will not want to quote for the particular fixtures and fittings that you require and so will allow a 'prime cost sum' for the items concerned. A p.c. sum of £2,500 for a kitchen means that the builder has allowed for kitchen fittings to this value: if you want to spend less than this the contract price will be reduced; if more, it will be increased. Typical features covered by p.c. sums are kitchens, bathrooms, central heating, fitted furniture, fireplaces, feature staircases, wall tiling and floor tiling. It is a very useful arrangement but make sure you know the basis on which p.c. sums are calculated — list price, trade price, special offers or what.

**WARRANTIES.** Virtually all house builders belong to the N.H.B.C. which issues ten year warranties on new houses built by its members. An N.H.B.C. warranty is normally required by banks and building societies as a condition of granting a mortgage, but is not generally available to selfbuilders, who have other alternatives set out in *Building Your Own Home*. The usual alternative for them is the similar Custombuild warranty from the Zurich Mutual Insurance Company.

**CONTRACTS.** Whoever is handling your design is the best person to advise you on a contract with a builder. An architect will write a formal contract for you. Make sure it is a fixed price contract, without inflation escalation clauses and that any extras to be charged have to be authorised by you as well as by the architect before the expenditure is incurred.

If you are using a large building firm, they may present you with one of the various standard forms of contract used in the building industry. You will quickly see that 90% of the clauses protect the builder and not the client and it is important to take advice before signing one of these contracts.

A quotation from a small local builder may well be hand written on one side of a piece of lined paper. This may seem to you to be casual in the extreme, but if the price is right, and the builder is right, it can be the basis of an excellent contract. What you do is send him a letter accepting his offer which *refers to an attached specification and drawing.*

In any arrangement to build a new home it is essential never to pay in advance for any work. Progress payments should always be for rather less than the actual value of the work done, and usually there are retention arrangements in the contract or in the specification to allow for this. Work that is extra to the contract should be costed and authorised in writing before it is put in hand. If these rules are followed you will always be in control of the contract. 99% of disputes on contracts arise from situations where clients have lost control of the contracts by ignoring the terms in them!

# Making it Happen

## Managing the Job Yourself

Building for yourself using subcontractors and managing everything yourself is the single most popular way of arranging for a new owner built home, and as described in the last chapter, these *selfbuilders* are identified because they reclaim the VAT which they spend on materials and fittings, which distinguishes them from those who place a contract with a builder for the whole job. Building in this way has achieved something of a cult status among those concerned and nearly everyone knows someone who has either built a house for themselves, or is planning to do so. They do not necessarily do any of the physical work themselves, and they need not have any building skills or experience, but they have to manage the whole project, engaging sub-contractors to do the work and buying all the materials. Essentially they have to manage the job, although nearly all get involved in some of the actual building work at some stage or another.

What has caused this boom in DIY housebuilding? It has a lot to do with encouragement from both banks and building societies, which are now much more helpful than they used to be to those who want to do without a builder. Provided that you can persuade them that you have a viable proposition, and that you are the sort of person who will make it all happen, they will readily help with bridging finance, and will give you a mortgage when the new home is finished. They will want you to arrange architects progress certificates and special insurances, but this is all part of managing the job.

No-one ever pretends that building for yourself is easy, or that it does not involve an enormous amount of hard work, but the advantages are really impressive. First of all, the saving, expressed as the difference between the open market value of the finished property and what you have spent on land and building work, is usually at least 25%. Besides this, you make sure that you get exactly the home that you and your family want, and you will certainly find the whole project challenging and exciting. How do those who want the challenge set about things?

There are two different ways of being a self builder, and they are quite different — you either join a self-build housing association or else you build on your own. The essential difference between them is that the individuals who go it alone have either got a building plot to start with, or manage to borrow the money to buy a plot (which is not easy), or else they find a plot sold by a council or a development corporation on a 'build now, pay later' basis. They use the title to the plot as security to borrow the money for the building, and when the home is finished they get an ordinary mortgage to repay the loan. In order to arrange this finance it is essential that they really know what to ask for, know what the bank or building society will be expecting of them, and manage to convince all concerned that they really understand what they are doing.

If you have ambition to be a solo self builder, the key to all of this is to make yourself an expert on the subject before you raise the matter with your bank manager or with anyone else whose support you will need. You will have to know something about what it will cost to build your dream home on any particular site, what the optimum ratio of plot cost to building cost should be, and on what basis finance is usually made available. You must be able to discuss the certificates that you will be expected to provide, the insurances that you will be expected to arrange, and to have worked out the costings. There are books that you can read about all of this, and some companies offer special services to help you, but essentially your management of the job starts with you learning everything that you are going to need to know. All on your own.

Being on their own is one problem that the group self builders certainly do not have. They start by finding between twelve to twenty people to form an association to build as many homes as there are members, all working together under an elected foreman, with all the arrangements made by an elected committee. They get loan funds from a specialist source of commercial loan finance to pay for the site and all the building work, and when all the houses are finished they take up ordinary mortgages that have already been arranged for the new homes, use the mortgage money to pay off the loans, and then wind up the association. Unlike individual self builders who usually employ others to do most or all of the building work, group members do a very high proportion of the work themselves, and tend to be involved for rather longer periods than the individuals. Eighteen months to finish a scheme is considered good going for an Association, while most people who build on their own have everything buttoned up in less than a year. This part of the selfbuild scene boomed in the late eighties when two thousand families were building a home in this way at any one time, but in the mid eighties group selfbuilders were down to a hundred or two. It all depends on the availability of relevant finance, and this is now becoming easier to arrange again.

And the risks in all of this? Strangely, virtually none. It is very difficult to get started at all, and to do so you need the assistance of a great many other people. All of them come to have a stake in your success in one way or another, and between them they will make sure that you never get to start unless you have set everything up in a way that makes sure you cannot fail. Among them are the bank, the building society, the inspecting architect, building inspectors, electricity board inspectors, the water board, the planning authority — you will have a host of others involved. Their bureaucratic requirements will seem to hold you back at every stage until you actually get started. From that point on they all have a vested interest in making sure that you finish, and everything then works to urge you on. In some ways building on your own is like pushing a wheel up a steep hill. Everything conspires against you until you are able to start, but when you do start the job gains its own momentum that pulls you along as if the wheel is running down the other side of the hill. The result is that there are virtually no self builders' disaster stories. Even if you die while you are building there are special insurances to enable your executors to hire a contractor to finish the job!

How do you find out more about all of this? The best way to start is with the companion volume to this book, which is called *Building Your Own Home* and which is up-dated regularly. It is not concerned with laying brick on brick but with the infrastructure of the world of self building, and deals with finding a site, choosing designs, planning, finance, costings, using sub-contractors, joining associations and making it all happen. There are case histories with photos, plans, the actual cost of the jobs, and the values of the completed homes. Details of where to get it are at the back of this book.

Other sources of advice and help are the package companies, who offer a special range of services to self builders. Involvement with them enables you to go it alone with access to the advice of professionals, and if they supply you with a complete kit of structural materials it takes the whole business of placing orders, and arranging deliveries off your hands.

# The Designs

## Choosing a design

The designs on the pages that follow are grouped by size, or by function, although the arrangement is arbitary. A three bedroomed house with a granny flat can easily become a four bedroom house with a study, so that the categories are only a guide. The categories are shown on the page heads, while at the bottom of each page is the name of the copyright holder.

The collection of designs can be used in many ways. For those establishing a budget for building a new home and who are using costs per square foot as price guidelines, it serves to show the accommodation that can be available in homes of different sizes, as the area of each design is stated. Those who have found a site on which to build will be able to list all the plans which suit both their budget and the charactersitics of the site, so that they can then consider which of them might be the basis of their own design. Finally, the plans are a source of design ideas which can be incorporated into other design concepts.

Remember all the homes illustrated were built to the specific requirements of a family that had bought a specific plot, and your own new home must suit *your* own circumstances.

Dimensions are shown in both Metric and Imperial units in the plans, but generally Imperial dimensions and areas are used in the text, following ordinary conversational practise as far as possible. The typical homebuilder explains the energy requirements of his new home in kilowatts, but describes the plot on which he hopes to build it as being half an acre. This book follows suit.

The various styles in which the plans are drawn are those of the various designers. Some of the illustrations are to the opposite hand of the plans. This can be disconcerting at first, but serves as a reminder that any of the designs shown can be built to either hand.

All of the plans are copyright, and may not be copied or used in any way without the consent of the copyright holders. Their details are given on page 459 and they will all be pleased to discuss the use of their designs either as published here, or modified to readers requirements. They are equally interested in discussing commissions to design homes specifically to clients wishes and the challenge of their plots, and are only a phone call away.

# Designs with Home Offices

Working from home is growing in popularity and for some people who build for themselves the top priority is getting exactly the home office that they require. To achieve this they need to analyse exactly what their requirements are. This will start with consideration of whether or not the office has to project an image to promote the business. If a consultancy practice will involve meetings on the premises, or if an executive working from home feels that his office must give the right impression on the occasional visits from his superiors, then this is a major factor. Another is whether local staff will be employed to work in the office, either as soon as it is built or in the future. If so the statutory work place requirements have to be considered. On the other hand, someone working wholly on their own can be much more flexible.

An office that has to give the right impression to visitors must be easily accessible from the front door, usually with its own cloakroom facilities, proper storage for records, and above all a layout that will inspire confidence in the professionalism of the business activity. The alternative is to revel in the confusion of a work place where untidiness would deter visitors, but which does not matter as there will not be any, and where the chaos encourages creative thought! Such an office can be hidden away at the back of the house, or even built into the roof.

Remember that you probably want your new home to be the best possible investment. If you ever sell it, you will want the best possible price. If an integral office will not affect the sale potential, or even enhance it, then it is a wise investment. If not, then you must think very carefully.

You will be concerned to gain any tax advantage from working at home. Other homeworkers may tell you that they get a tax allowance for a proportion of the running expenses of their home, and this is certainly possible in many cases. However, there is a hidden time bomb in doing this, as if you establish that, say, 15% of your home is really an office, and you then sell it, the revenue will want capital gains tax on 15% of the proceeds. This would be subject to indexing and the exemptions allowance would be taken into account, but this could easily outweigh many years of tax allowances. You may hope to be able to finance part of the cost of the house from your business, but if you do you should be aware that the revenue authorities are most unlikely to allow capital allowances against this expenditure, and that any ideas of this sort should be cleared with an accountant.

One issue that is important is how the work place is described. The many books written about working from home refer to 'the home office'. Whatever the facts, this name can be associated with planning consent for commercial use, breach of covenants, commercial rates, work place regulations and much else that is often unwelcome. On the other hand, an office activity carried out in a domestic study can usually be properly considered a domestic activity. The image may not be as trendy, but the possibility of future problems is much reduced.

The home designs on the following pages nearly all incorporate an office or study which is near to the front entrance or has its own entrance. They all have adjacent cloakrooms, and are of at least 90 square feet. This area is the absolute minimum for an office with room for the desk space, information technology equipment and the storage usually considered essential. In many cases the storage arrangements are crucial: computerised business procedures usually generate more paper than they save, and managing this paperwork is a major ingredient of business success.

**Ref: 96255**

**328 sq.m.    3533 sq.ft.**

A really large house with an outer office for staff and an inner office for the proprietor. If no longer required for business this would make a family room suite with the study becoming a television room, or alternatively could be the basis of a self-contained granny flat.

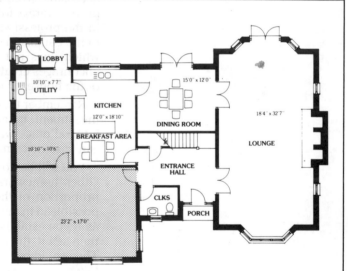

| | | |
|---|---|---|
| Dimensions overall | 59'3" x 37'6" | 18.07 x 11.44 |
| Lounge | 18'4" x 32'7" | 5.60 x 9.93 |
| Dining | 15'0" x 12'0" | 4.56 x 3.65 |
| Kitchen/Breakfast | 12'0" x 18'4" | 3.65 x 5.60 |
| Utility | 10'10" x 7'7" | 3.30 x 2.30 |
| Master Bedroom (ex. Wardrobes) | 18'4" x 14'11" | 5.60 x 4.55 |
| Bedroom 2 (ex. Wardrobes) | 18'4" x 13'4" | 5.60 x 4.07 |
| Bedroom 3 | 20'1" x 14'3" | 6.10 x 4.34 |
| Bedroom 4 | 18'5" x 12'3" | 5.61 x 3.74 |
| Bedroom 5 | 14'0" x 15'3" | 4.25 x 4.65 |
| Outer Office | 23'2" x 17'0" | 7.05 x 5.18 |
| Inner Office | 10'10" x 10'6" | 3.30 x 3.20 |

**REPRESENTS OFFICE SPACE**

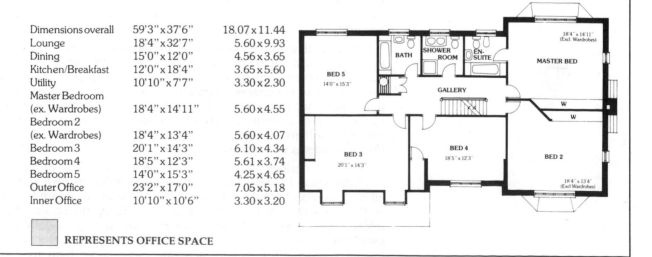

*©Design & Materials*

44

**Ref: 95100**

**348 sq.m.   3753 sq.ft.**
**(inc. car port)**

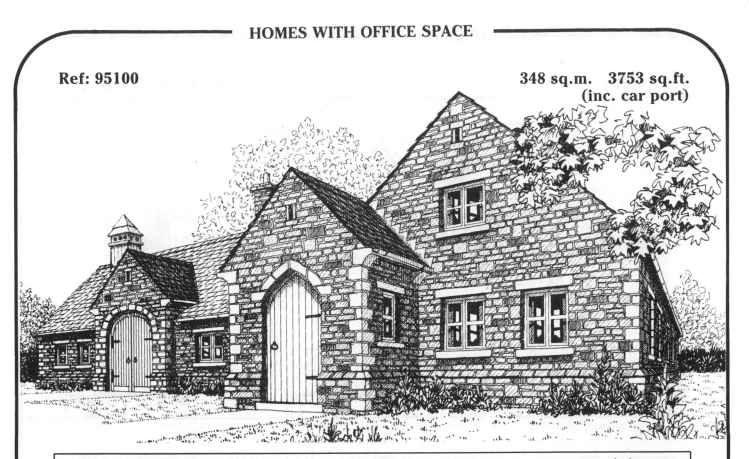

This deceptively large house was designed for a gap in a village street, where it now looks as if it has been there for ever. The garage, with a period door to the street and an open car port arrangement to the courtyard behind, separates the main house from the office in an interesting way.

This is a really large home as will be appreciated by looking at the room sizes, and in particular the very large bedrooms. In spite of this the overall appearance is of a period village street property, which enabled planning consent to be gained in a conservation area where many previous applications had failed.

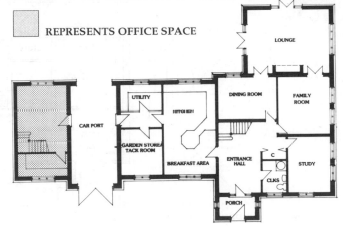

REPRESENTS OFFICE SPACE

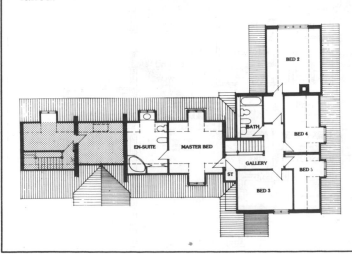

| | | |
|---|---|---|
| Dimensions overall | 81'4" x 47'8" | 24.80 x 14.52 |
| Lounge | 20'5" x 16'0" | 6.22 x 4.88 |
| Family Room | 14'6" x 12'10" | 4.43 x 3.91 |
| Dining Room | 15'0" x 10'7" | 4.57 x 3.22 |
| Study | 14'0" x 10'6" | 4.26 x 3.20 |
| Ent. Hall | 17'4" x 18'0" | 5.28 x 5.48 |
| Cloak Room | 8'0" x 6'2" | 2.44 x 1.88 |
| Breakfast/Kitchen | 23'0" x 13.2" | 7.01 x 4.01 |
| Utility | 10'4" x 6'7" | 3.15 x 2.01 |
| Garden St/ | | |
| Tack Room | 11'9" x 10'4" | 3.58 x 3.15 |
| Master Bedroom | 13'2" x 13'1" | 4.01 x 3.99 |
| En-Suite | 13'1" x 10'4" | 3.99 x 3.15 |
| Bedroom 2 | 16'0" x 13'9" | 4.88 x 4.20 |
| Bedroom 3 | 14'1" x 10'4" | 4.29 x 3.15 |
| Bedroom 4 | 14'6" x 8'10" | 4.43 x 2.69 |
| Bedroom 5 | 14'0" x 6'6" | 4.26 x 1.98 |
| | | |
| Office Suite | | |
| 1 | 16'8" x 13'1" | 5.08 x 3.98 |
| 2 | 13'1" x 6'6" | 3.98 x 1.83 |
| 3 | 13'1" x 7'3" | 3.98 x 2.21 |
| 4 | 12'0" x 10'4" | 3.67 x 3.15 |

# HOMES WITH OFFICE SPACE

**Ref: W1206**

**200 sq.m.   2152 sq.ft.**
**(exc. garage)**

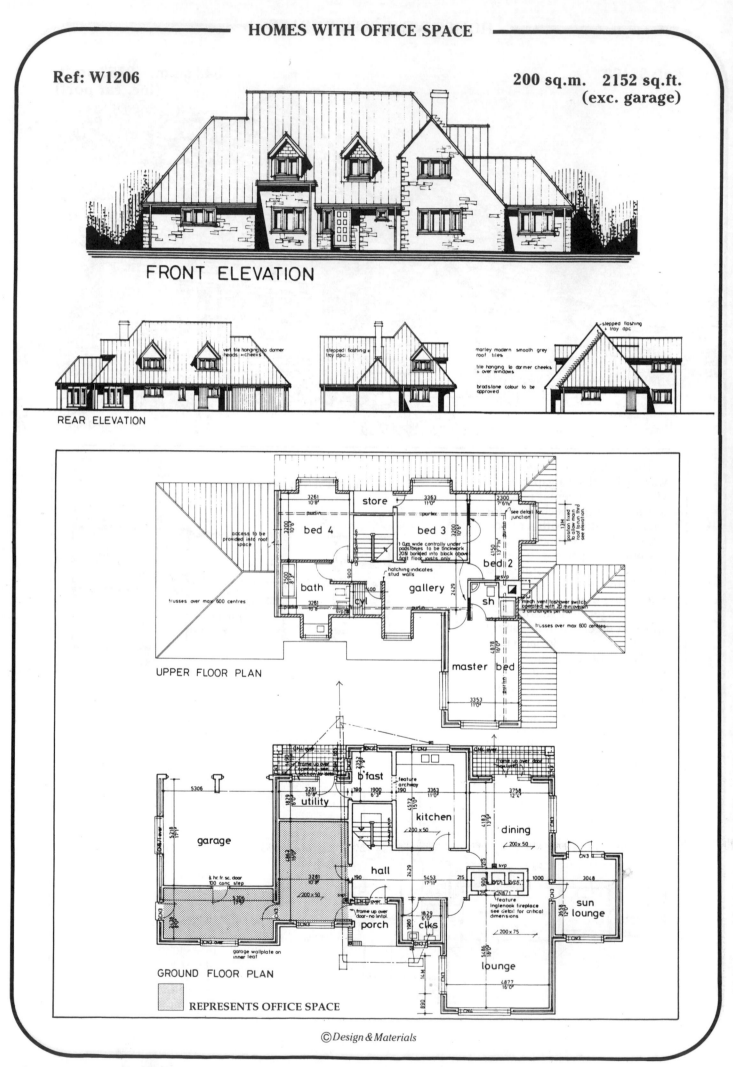

FRONT ELEVATION

REAR ELEVATION

UPPER FLOOR PLAN

GROUND FLOOR PLAN

REPRESENTS OFFICE SPACE

ⒸDesign & Materials

**Ref: P2897**

**285 sq.m.   3067 sq.ft.**

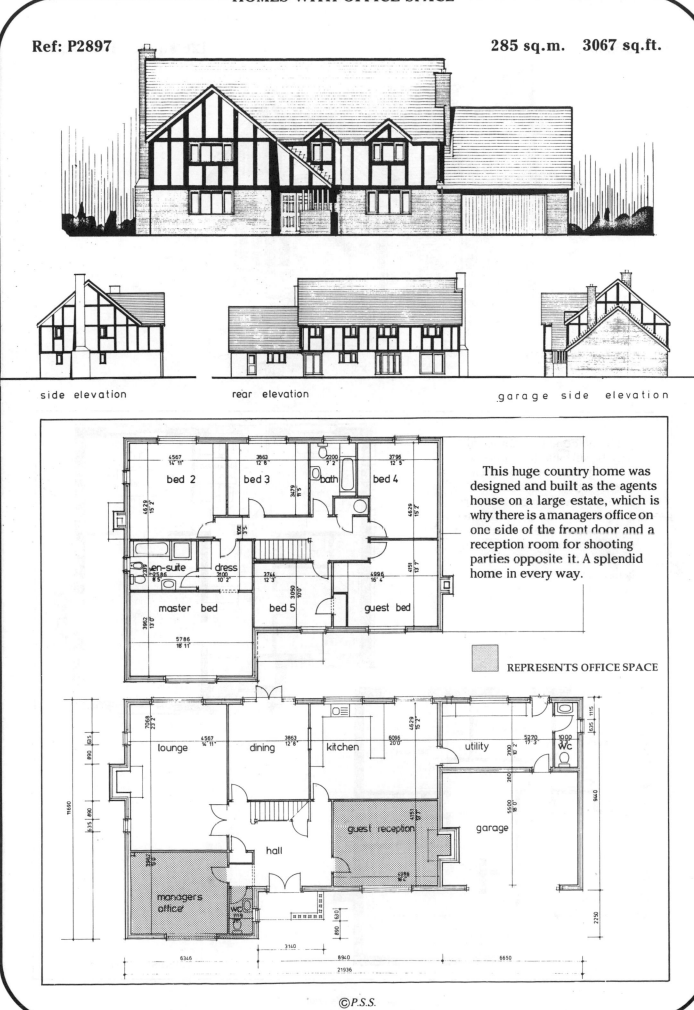

side elevation

rear elevation

garage side elevation

This huge country home was designed and built as the agents house on a large estate, which is why there is a managers office on one side of the front door and a reception room for shooting parties opposite it. A splendid home in every way.

REPRESENTS OFFICE SPACE

©P.S.S.

**Ref: 96265**

**126 sq.m.   1362 sq.ft.**

The office in this home will only be suitable for someone working completely on their own together with the occasional visitor, but there are many who do not ever intend to employ staff. The conventional four bedroom layout has many useful features, including a generous array of built-in cupboards.

REPRESENTS OFFICE SPACE

© *Design & Materials*

**Ref: 96130**

**120 sq.m.    1293 sq.ft.**

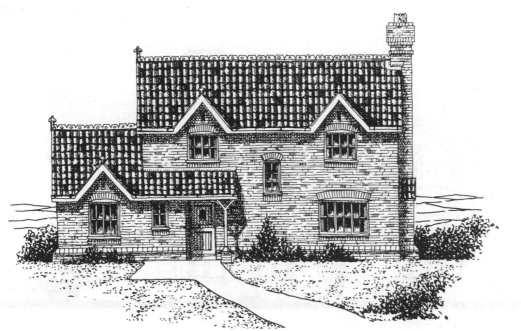

This is a cottage style property for a wide plot, with a simple ground floor layout that has a study with its own cloakroom adjacent to the front door. If a larger study is required, the building can be extended to the left, or the space taken by the utility room can be used to make an office suite.

| Dimensions overall | 43'4" x 23'1" | - 13.21 x 7.02 |
| --- | --- | --- |
| Lounge | 12'6" x 18'0" | - 3.80 x 5.48 |
| Kitchen/Dining | 17'10" x 10'0" | - 5.43 x 3.04 |
| Utility | 10'0" x 7'2" | - 3.04 x 2.18 |
| Office | 10'0" x 10'9" | - 3.04 x 3.27 |
| Master Bedroom | 8'10" x 11'6" | - 2.70 x 3.50 |
| Bedroom 2 (inc WR) | 10'0" x 10'0" | - 3.04 x 3.04 |
| Bedroom 3 | 7'6" x 10'0" | - 2.28 x 3.04 |
| Bedroom 4 | 8'10" x 7'8" | - 2.70 x 2.33 |

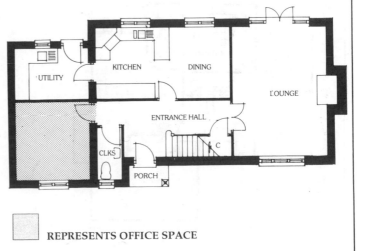

REPRESENTS OFFICE SPACE

*©Design & Materials*

**Ref: PN657**

**261 sq.m.   2810 sq.ft.**
**(exc. conservatory)**

A large four bedroom house with plenty of accommodation for working from home. Office storage space is available by moving the linen cupboard up to the first floor. The staircase that divides at the half landing is a most impressive feature, and the feeling of size and authority is enhanced by the Inglenook fireplaces in the lounge and the unusually shaped dining room.

| Living Room | 7.9 x 4.5 | 25'11" x 14'9" |
|---|---|---|
| Dining Room | 5.8 x 5.8 | 19'0" x 19'0" |
| Utility | 3.5 x 3.2 | 11'6" x 10'6" |
| Kitchen | 6.8 x 4.2 | 22'4" x 13'9" |
| Study | 3.5 x 4.2 | 11'6" x 13'9" |
| Bedroom 1 | 5.8 x 5.3 | 19'0" x 17'5" |
| Bedroom 2 | 4.6 x 4.6 | 15'1" x 15'1" |
| Bedroom 3 | 3.9 x 3.5 | 13'1" x 11'6" |
| Bedroom 4 | 3.4 x 4.3 | 11'2" x 14'1" |

 REPRESENTS OFFICE SPACE

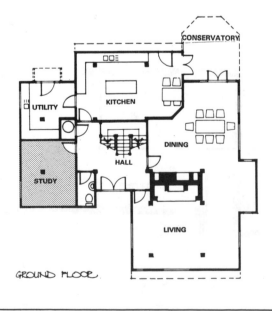

GROUND FLOOR

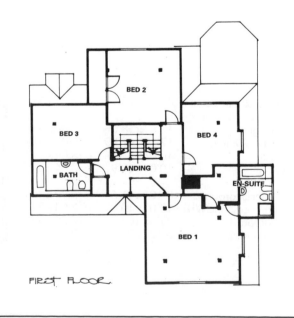

FIRST FLOOR

©Potton

**Ref: W1045**

**239 sq.m.   2572 sq.ft.**

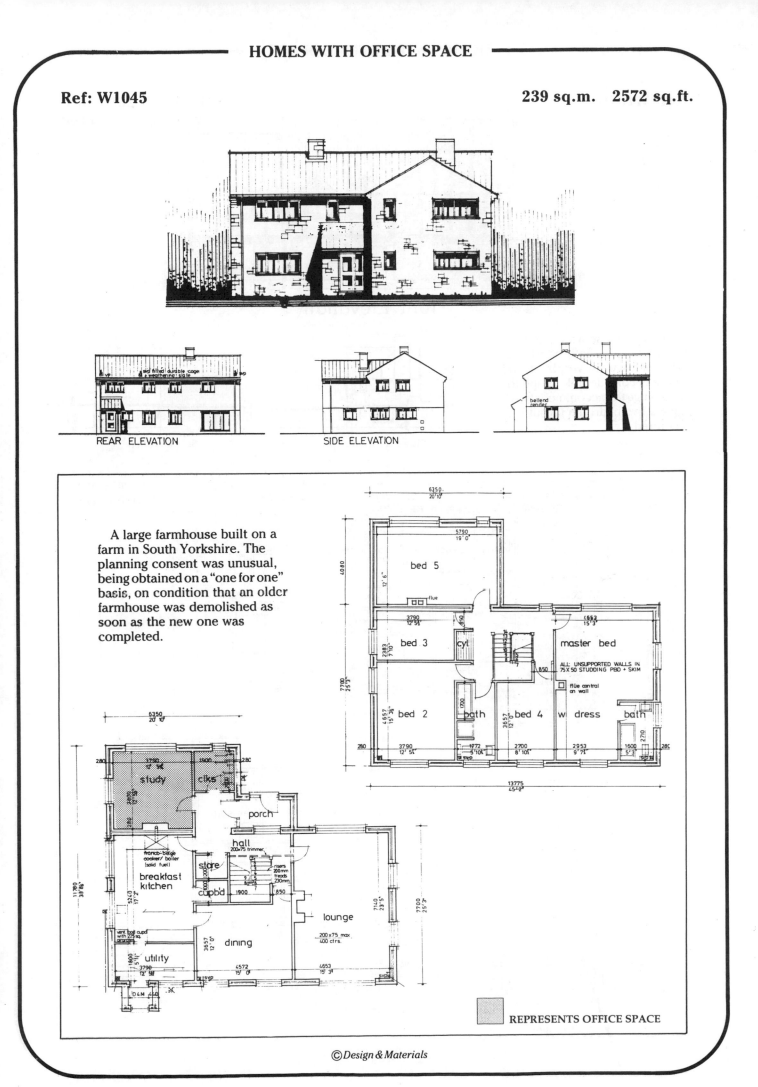

REAR ELEVATION

SIDE ELEVATION

A large farmhouse built on a farm in South Yorkshire. The planning consent was unusual, being obtained on a "one for one" basis, on condition that an older farmhouse was demolished as soon as the new one was completed.

bed 5

bed 3

cyl

master bed

ALL UNSUPPORTED WALLS IN 75 X 50 STUDDING PBD + SKIM

flue central on wall

bed 2

bath

bed 4

w dress

bath

study

cks

porch

hall

franco-belge cooker/ boiler (solid fuel)

store

breakfast kitchen

cupb'd

lounge

dining

utility

REPRESENTS OFFICE SPACE

**Ref: W1376**

**231 sq.m.   2686 sq.ft.**
**(exc. garage)**

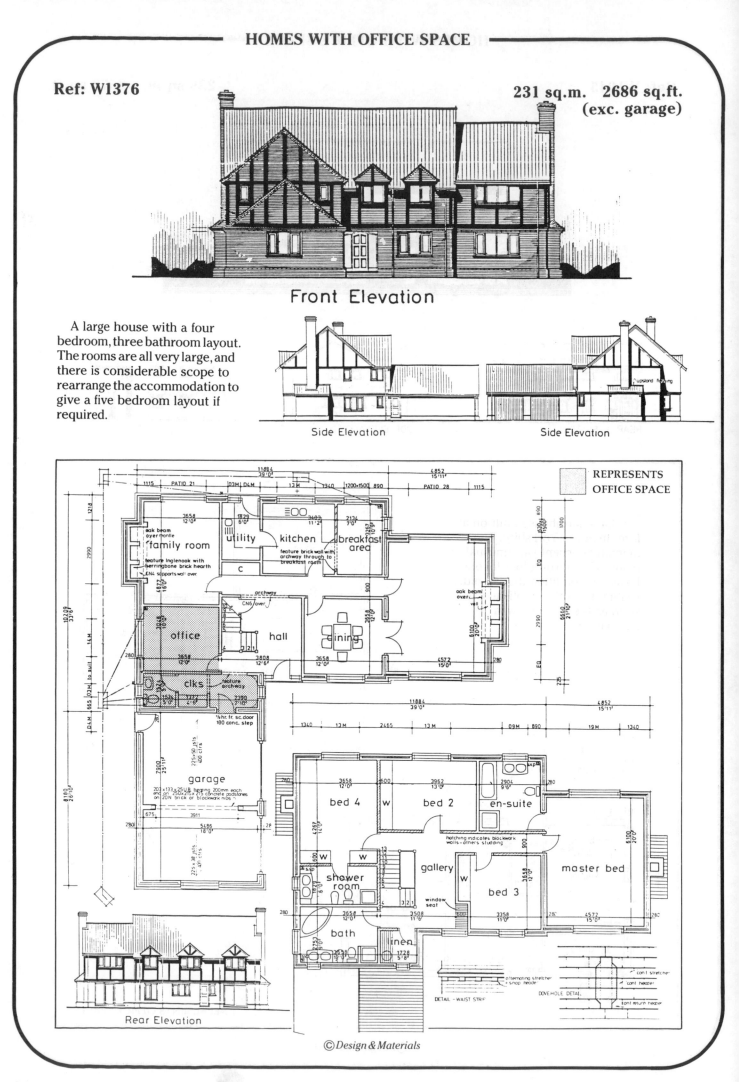

Front Elevation

A large house with a four bedroom, three bathroom layout. The rooms are all very large, and there is considerable scope to rearrange the accommodation to give a five bedroom layout if required.

Side Elevation

Side Elevation

REPRESENTS
OFFICE SPACE

Rear Elevation

© Design & Materials

**Ref: C480**

**2777 sq.ft.
(exc. garage)
258 sq.m.**

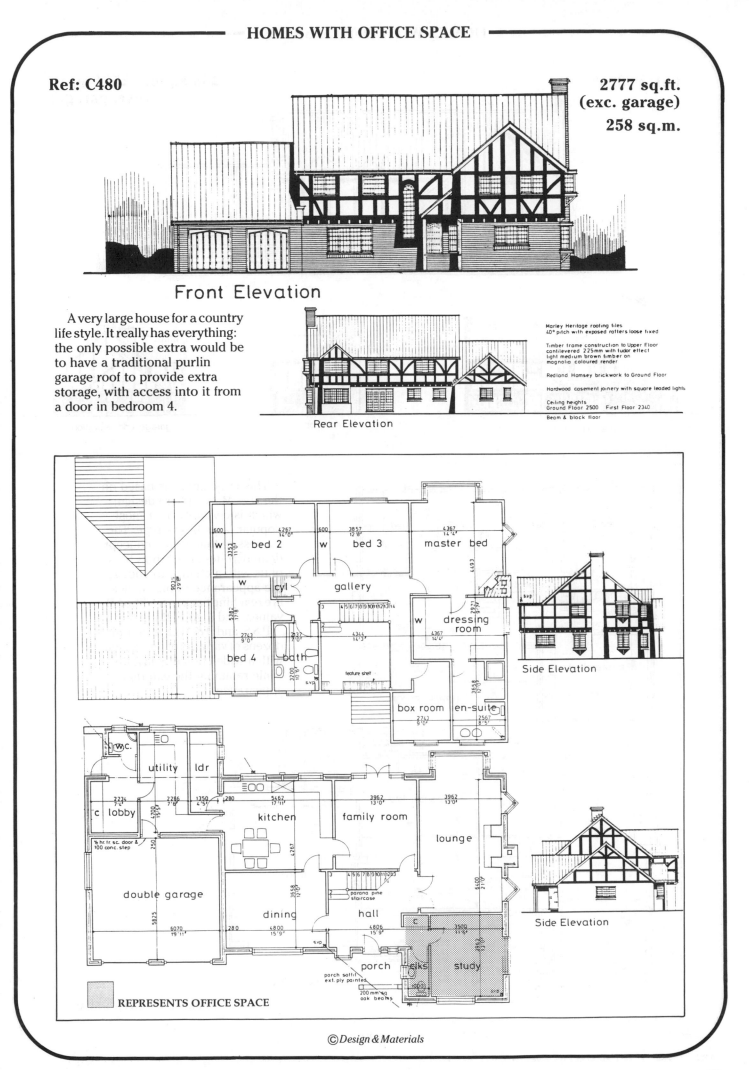

## Front Elevation

A very large house for a country life style. It really has everything: the only possible extra would be to have a traditional purlin garage roof to provide extra storage, with access into it from a door in bedroom 4.

Rear Elevation

Marley Heritage roofing tiles
40° pitch with exposed rafters loose fixed

Timber frame construction to Upper Floor
cantilevered 225mm with tudor effect
light medium brown timber on
magnolia coloured render

Redland Hamsey brickwork to Ground Floor

Hardwood casement joinery with square leaded lights

Ceiling heights
Ground Floor 2500    First Floor 2340

Beam & block floor

Side Elevation

Side Elevation

bed 2
bed 3
master bed
gallery
dressing room
bed 4
bath
en-suite
box room
w.c.
utility   ldr
lobby
kitchen
family room
lounge
double garage
dining
hall
porch
study
clks
cyl
feature shelf
parana pine staircase
½ hr. fr. sc. door & 100 conc. step
svp
porch soffit ext. ply painted
200 mm sq oak beams

**REPRESENTS OFFICE SPACE**

*©Design & Materials*

**Ref: P83265**

**238 sq.m.   2561 sq.ft.**
**(exc. garage)**

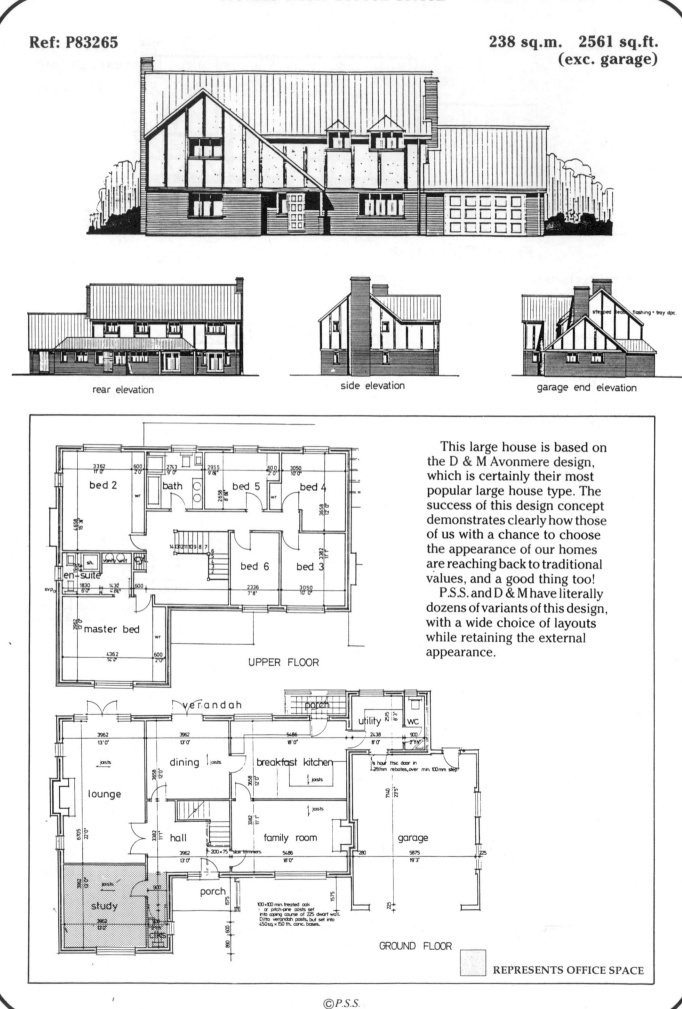

rear elevation

side elevation

garage end elevation

**UPPER FLOOR**

bed 2

bath

bed 5

bed 4

bed 6

bed 3

en-suite

sh. vanity unit

cyl.

master bed

This large house is based on the D & M Avonmere design, which is certainly their most popular large house type. The success of this design concept demonstrates clearly how those of us with a chance to choose the appearance of our homes are reaching back to traditional values, and a good thing too!

P.S.S. and D & M have literally dozens of variants of this design, with a wide choice of layouts while retaining the external appearance.

verandah

porch

utility

WC

dining

breakfast kitchen

½ hour frisc door in 25mm rebates, over min. 100mm step

lounge

hall

family room

garage

porch

study

100 x 100 min. treated oak
or pitch-pine posts set
into coping course of 225 dwarf wall.
Ditto verandah posts, but set into
450sq. x 150 th. conc. bases.

**GROUND FLOOR**

REPRESENTS OFFICE SPACE

©P.S.S.

**Ref: 96151**

**194 sq.m.   2091 sq.ft.**

This house of 2100 square feet has a very practical ground floor layout with four bedrooms and three bathrooms above. The stairs lead into a gallery which has its own window, which is a feature very much to be desired where this can be arranged

The house is shown here with a mock timber framing and herringbone brickwork. These Tudor features can be built very easily using traditional construction.

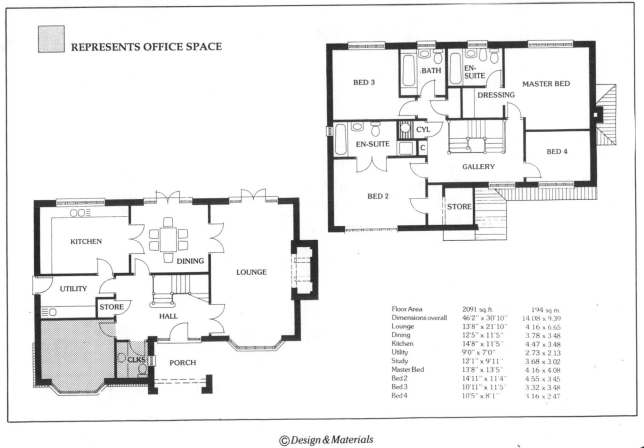

REPRESENTS OFFICE SPACE

BED 3   BATH   EN-SUITE   MASTER BED

DRESSING

EN-SUITE   CYL   C

BED 4

GALLERY

BED 2   STORE

KITCHEN

DINING

LOUNGE

UTILITY

STORE

HALL

CLKS   PORCH

| Floor Area | 2091 sq.ft. | 194 sq.m. |
|---|---|---|
| Dimensions overall | 46'2" x 30'10" | 14.08 x 9.39 |
| Lounge | 13'8" x 21'10" | 4.16 x 6.65 |
| Dining | 12'5" x 11'5" | 3.78 x 3.48 |
| Kitchen | 14'8" x 11'5" | 4.47 x 3.48 |
| Utility | 9'0" x 7'0" | 2.73 x 2.13 |
| Study | 12'1" x 9'11" | 3.68 x 3.02 |
| Master Bed | 13'8" x 13'5" | 4.16 x 4.08 |
| Bed 2 | 14'11" x 11'4" | 4.55 x 3.45 |
| Bed 3 | 10'11" x 11'5" | 3.32 x 3.48 |
| Bed 4 | 10'5" x 8'1" | 3.16 x 2.47 |

**Ref: W1321**

**207 sq.m.   2228 sq.ft.**

REAR ELEVATION

SIDE ELEVATION

SIDE ELEVATION

stepped lead flashing
& tray dpc

Slate roof 24 x 12 x⅜" thick.

ind
& tray dpc

Natural stone
with Stone lintols
( supplied by client)

Hardwood casement joinery

s.v.p fitted durable cage
& weathering slate

bed 2

bath

cyl

gallery

bed 3

bed 4

en-suite   dress

bed 5

master bed

hatching indicates block walls
all othes studding

REPRESENTS OFFICE SPACE

lounge

dining

kitchen

breakfast
area

lobby

w c

fuel
store

utility

st.

hall

family room

garage

office

clks

porch

fireplace dimensions
to suit appliance

sliding
doors

Aga cooker
boiler

fireplace dimensions
to suit appliance

concrete landing

conc. landing

½ hr. fr. sc. door
& 100 conc. step
stack over on conc slab
built in - see detail

door and frame

to septic tank

PATIO 27

*©Design & Materials*

**Ref: 96254**

**172 sq.m. 1847 sq.ft.**
**(exc. garage)**

A four bedroom house with 130 square foot of office space, which is usually considered about the minimum if you intend to employ full time staff.

| Dimensions overall (excl. Garage) | 44'0" x 31'1" | - 13.40 x 9.46 |
|---|---|---|
| Living Room | 12'6" x 19'9" | - 3.81 x 6.01 |
| Dining | 12'6" x 10'0" | - 3.81 x 3.05 |
| Kitchen/Breakfast | 16'0" x 11'9" | - 4.87 x 3.59 |
| Office | 13'3" x 9'8" | - 4.05 x 2.93 |
| Utility | 10'0" x 9'8" | - 3.05 x 2.93 |
| Garage | 18'0" x 17'11" | - 5.48 x 5.46 |
| Master Bedroom | 13'0" x 14'2" | - 3.95 x 4.32 |
| Bedroom 2 | 11'7" x 9'8" | - 3.53 x 2.93 |
| Bedroom 3 | 14'0" x 10'0" | - 4.26 x 3.05 |
| Bedroom 4 | 9'0" x 9'5" | - 2.74 x 2.86 |

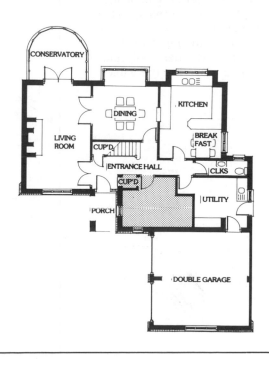

**REPRESENTS OFFICE SPACE**

Ref: C427

113 sq.m.   1200 sq.ft.

FRONT ELEVATION

REAR ELEVATION

SIDE ELEVATION

SIDE ELEVATION

s.v.p. fitted durable cage & weathering slate

stepped lead flashing & tray d.p.c.

1000mm min

Marley Modern Smooth grey tiles

Bradstone Trad. Walling Weathered Ham

Hardwood casement joinery

A house for the country with an office leading off the kitchen. This can easily have an outside door in its side wall if required, and this would suit farmers and others who work from home. Note that the stairs take off from the back of the hall, which is an unusual and rather old fashioned arrangement.

The lounge fireplace is on an inside wall where it can share a flue with a multi-fuel stove in the kitchen. If a stove of this type is not required then it is worth considering whether the fireplace should be moved to the gable wall.

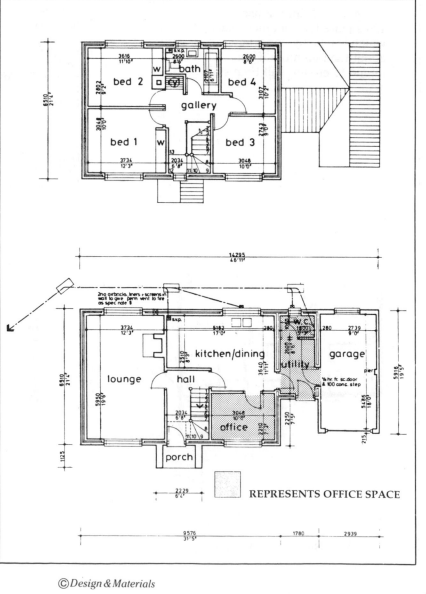

REPRESENTS OFFICE SPACE

**Ref: C309**

**115 sq.m.   1237 sq.ft.**

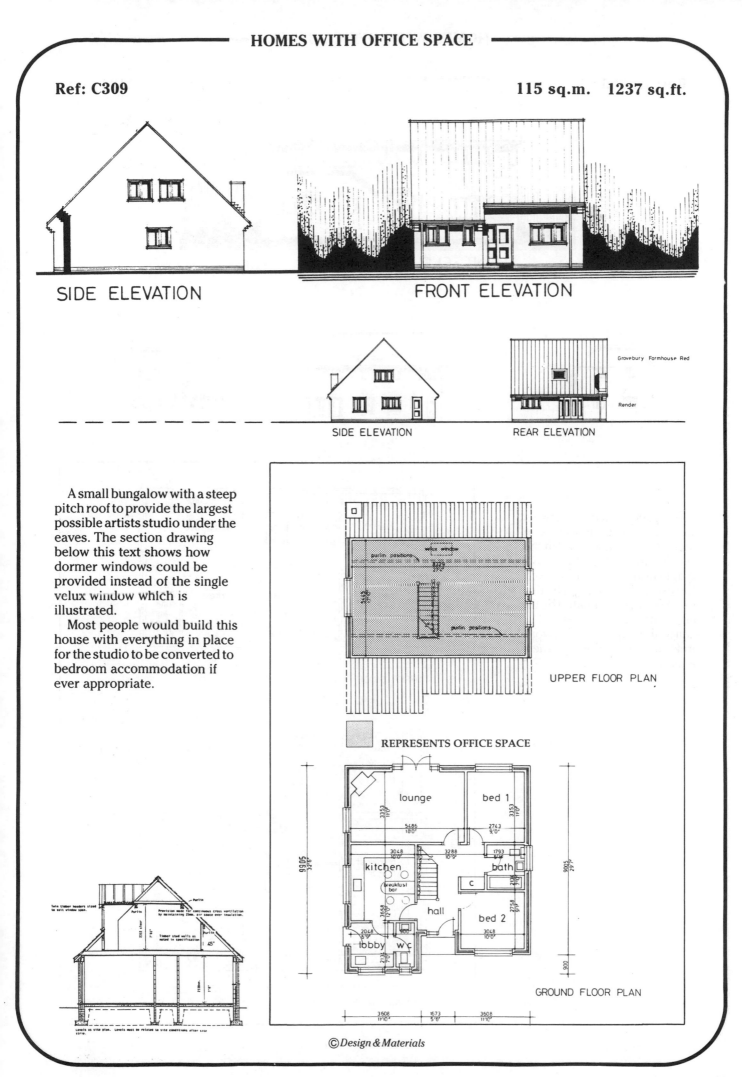

SIDE ELEVATION

FRONT ELEVATION

SIDE ELEVATION

REAR ELEVATION

Grovebury Farmhouse Red

Render

A small bungalow with a steep pitch roof to provide the largest possible artists studio under the eaves. The section drawing below this text shows how dormer windows could be provided instead of the single velux window which is illustrated.

Most people would build this house with everything in place for the studio to be converted to bedroom accommodation if ever appropriate.

UPPER FLOOR PLAN

**REPRESENTS OFFICE SPACE**

lounge

bed 1

kitchen

bath

breakfast bar

c

hall

bed 2

lobby

w c

GROUND FLOOR PLAN

© *Design & Materials*

**59**

**Ref: W1005**

**198 sq.m.   2134 sq.ft.**

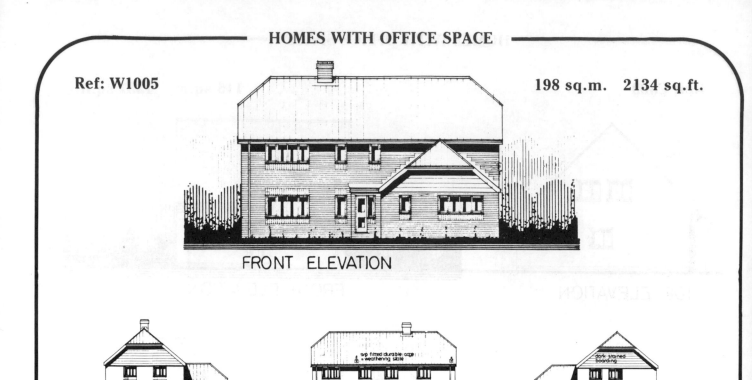

FRONT ELEVATION

An angled front door between two wings of a building gives an interesting entrance, and in this case it enables the office suite to appear quite separate from the rest of the building. The first floor layout is dominated by the large landing with a central stairwell, and personally I would prefer larger windows to the landing.

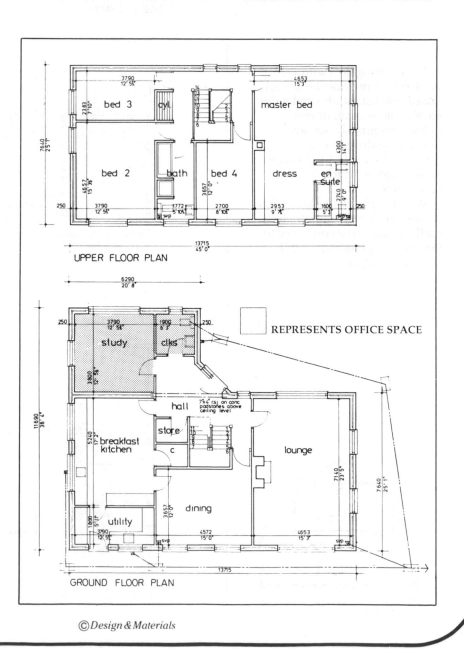

UPPER FLOOR PLAN

REPRESENTS OFFICE SPACE

GROUND FLOOR PLAN

© *Design & Materials*

**Ref: CM178**

**160 sq.m.    1722 sq.ft.**

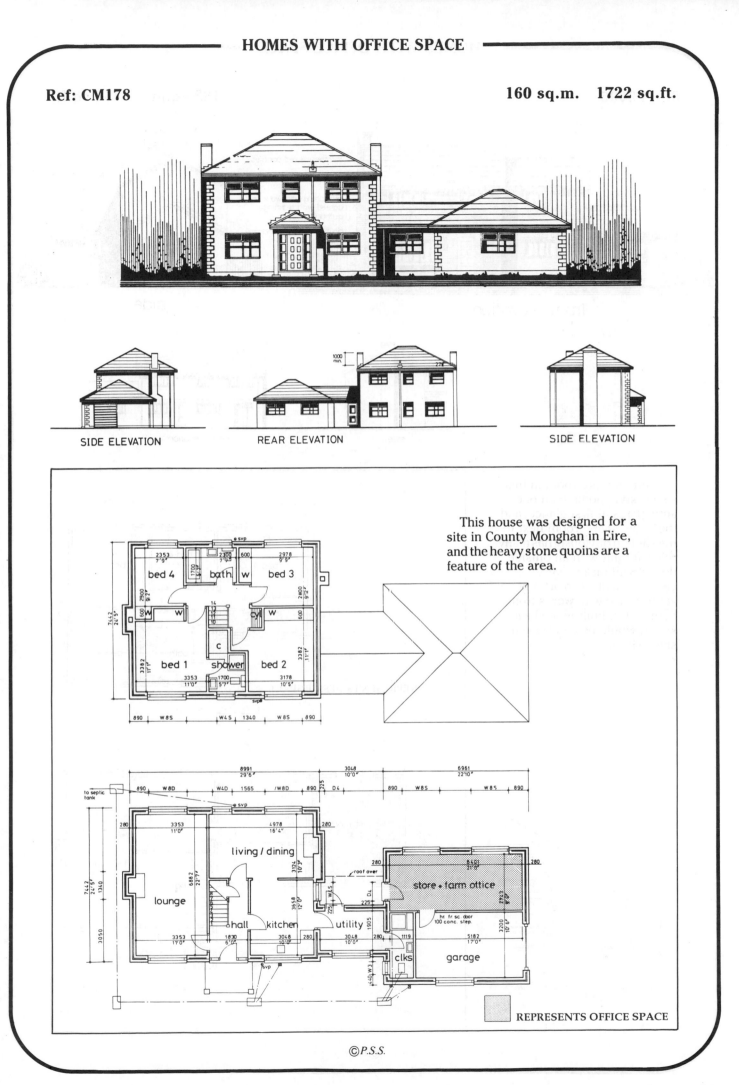

SIDE ELEVATION

REAR ELEVATION

SIDE ELEVATION

This house was designed for a site in County Monghan in Eire, and the heavy stone quoins are a feature of the area.

bed 4    bath    w    bed 3

w    w    cyl    w

c

bed 1    shower    bed 2

living / dining

lounge

store + farm office

hall    kitchen    utility

clks    garage

to septic tank

roof over

REPRESENTS OFFICE SPACE

© P.S.S.

**Ref: P2695**

**163 sq.m.   1754 sq.ft.**

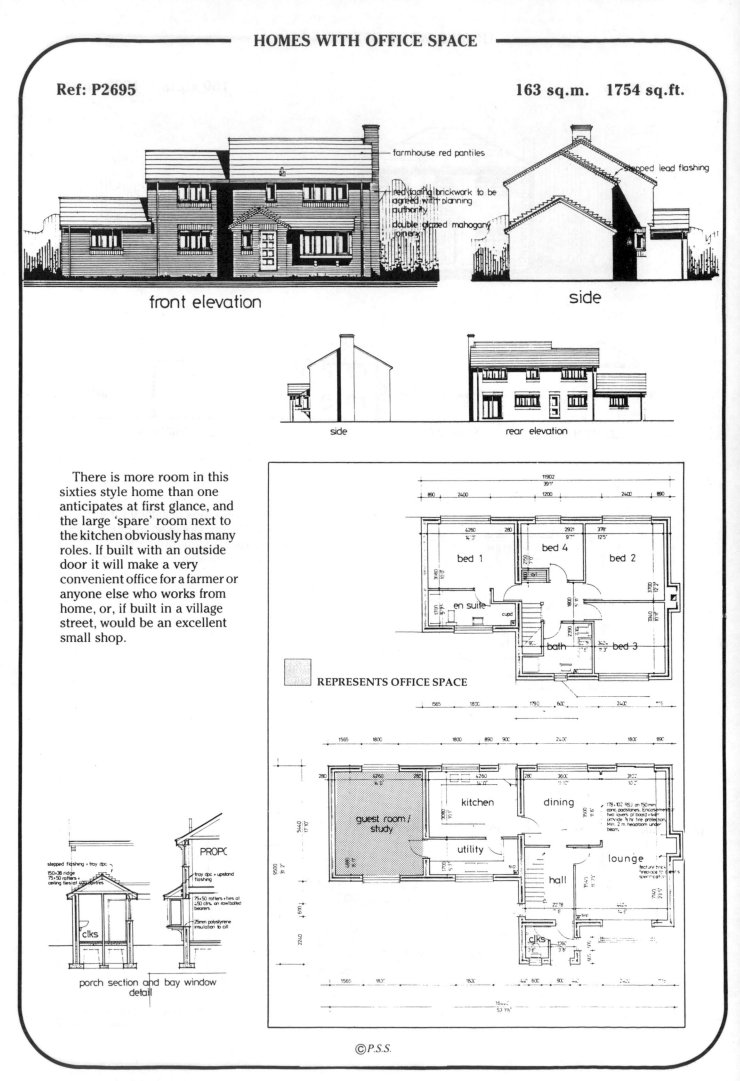

front elevation

side

farmhouse red pantiles

stepped lead flashing

red facing brickwork to be agreed with planning authority

double glazed mahogany joinery

side

rear elevation

There is more room in this sixties style home than one anticipates at first glance, and the large 'spare' room next to the kitchen obviously has many roles. If built with an outside door it will make a very convenient office for a farmer or anyone else who works from home, or, if built in a village street, would be an excellent small shop.

**REPRESENTS OFFICE SPACE**

bed 1

bed 4

bed 2

en suite

cupd

bath

bed 3

guest room / study

kitchen

dining

utility

lounge

hall

clks

stepped flashing + tray dpc
150×38 ridge
75×50 rafters + ceiling ties at 400 centres

PROPO

tray dpc + upstand flashing

75×50 rafters + ties at 450 ctrs. on rawlbolted bearers

25mm polystyrene insulation to cill

178×102 RSJ on 150mm conc. padstones. Encasement of two layers of board + 54th provide ½ hr fire protection. Min. 2 m. headroom under beam.

clks

porch section and bay window detail

©P.S.S.

**Ref: P3064**

**240 sq.m.   2583 sq.ft.**

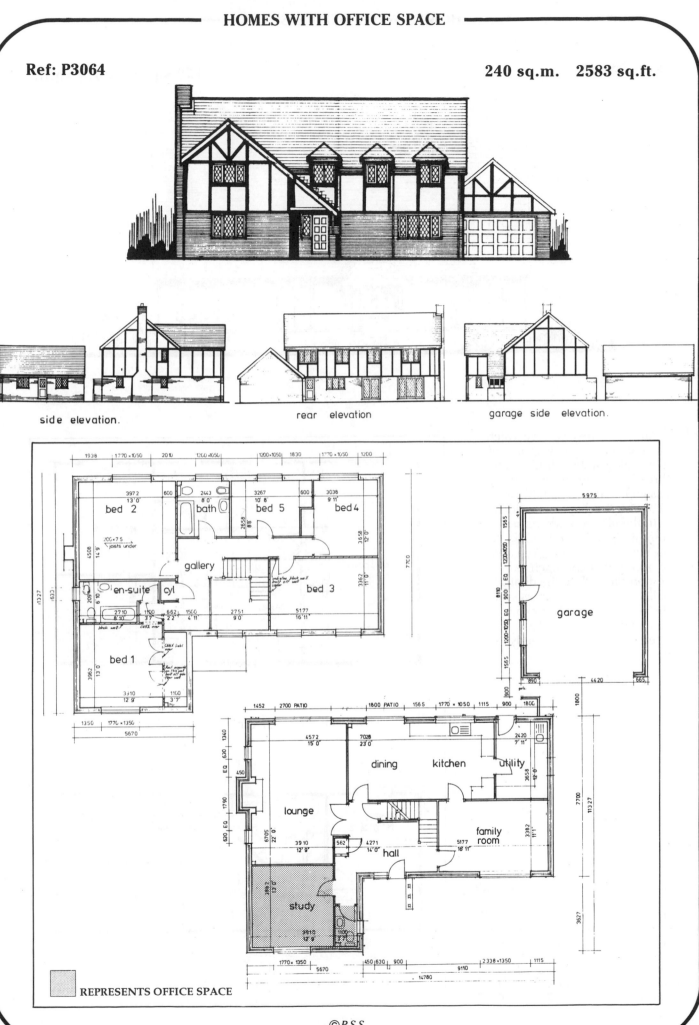

side elevation.

rear elevation

garage side elevation.

REPRESENTS OFFICE SPACE

©P.S.S.

**Ref: PN665**

**150 sq.m.   1614 sq.ft.**

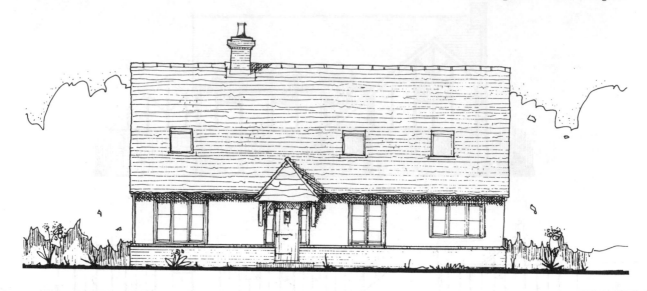

An aisle framed cottage which has the external appearance of a bungalow although there are three bedrooms in the roof. A design like this is usually chosen following negotiations with the planners when they want a 'single storey profile' to the new home, but are prepared to accept this approach as a compromise. Note the dining hall with its island staircase and the very large utility room to suit a family with outdoor interests and lots of muddy boots.

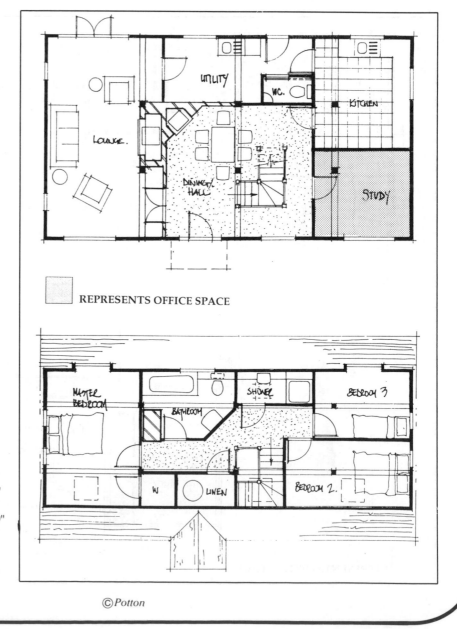

**REPRESENTS OFFICE SPACE**

| Lounge | 4.0 x 7.0 | 13'1" x 23'0" |
|---|---|---|
| Dining/Hall | 5.2 x 4.5 | 17'1" x 14'9" |
| Kitchen | 3.3 x 3.8 | 10'10 x 12'6" |
| Utility | 5.2 x 2.0 | 17'1" x 6'11" |
| Study/office | 3.3 x 3.0 | 10'10" x 9'10" |
| Bedroom 1 | 3.1 x 4.7 | 10'2" x 15'5" |
| Bathroom | 3.0 x 2.2 | 9'10" x 7'3" |
| Bedroom 2 | 4.3 x 2.3 | 14'1" x 7'7" |
| Bedroom 3 | 3.3 x 2.3 | 10'10" x 7'7" |

©*Potton*

**Ref: PN653**

**172 sq.m.   1856 sq.ft.**
**(inc. garage)**

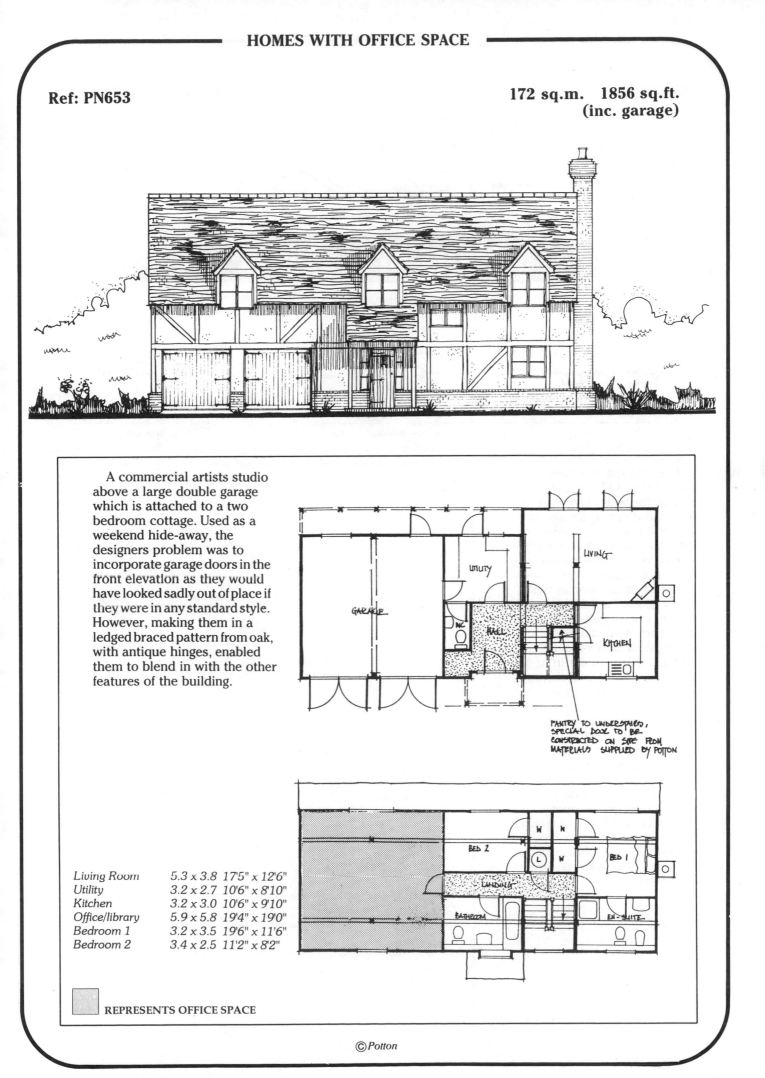

A commercial artists studio above a large double garage which is attached to a two bedroom cottage. Used as a weekend hide-away, the designers problem was to incorporate garage doors in the front elevation as they would have looked sadly out of place if they were in any standard style. However, making them in a ledged braced pattern from oak, with antique hinges, enabled them to blend in with the other features of the building.

| | | |
|---|---|---|
| Living Room | 5.3 x 3.8 | 17'5" x 12'6" |
| Utility | 3.2 x 2.7 | 10'6" x 8'10" |
| Kitchen | 3.2 x 3.0 | 10'6" x 9'10" |
| Office/library | 5.9 x 5.8 | 19'4" x 19'0" |
| Bedroom 1 | 3.2 x 3.5 | 19'6" x 11'6" |
| Bedroom 2 | 3.4 x 2.5 | 11'2" x 8'2" |

REPRESENTS OFFICE SPACE

© Potton

**Ref: P2756**

**163 sq.m.    1755 sq.ft.**

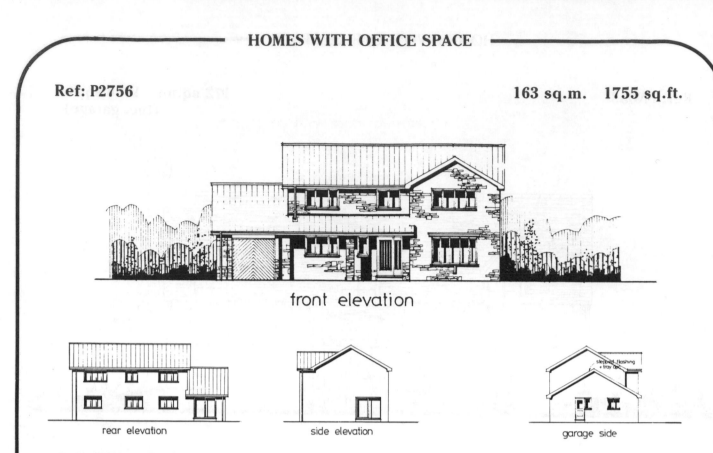

front elevation

rear elevation

side elevation

garage side

The compact hall helps the main rooms to be unusually large in this well laid out family home, and the big lounge with off-set dining area is ideal for entertaining. If a double garage is required the single garage shown can easily be extended.

At just under 70 sq.ft. the study shown on the plan barely qualifies as an office, but with direct access to the front door, adjacent cloakroom facilities and an outlook to the front of the house it meets all the other criteria for working from home.

Although shown here for construction in stone with a stone pillar supporting the front entrance porch, this design will look equally well if built in brick under a pantile roof.

The chevron boarded up-and-over garage door is attractive, and helps to remind us that there are many types of wooden garage doors available today besides the standard ones in pressed steel.

**REPRESENTS OFFICE SPACE**

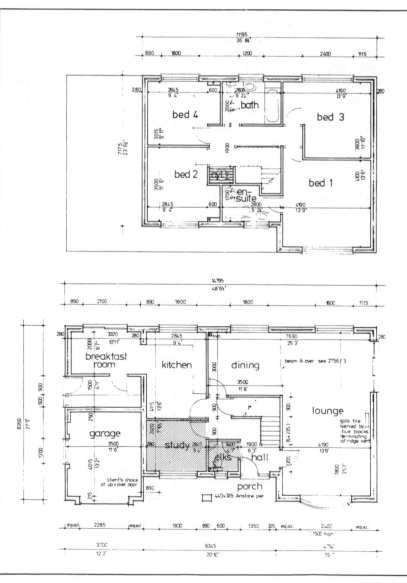

©P.S.S.

**Ref: W1163**

**178 sq.m.    1916 sq.ft.**

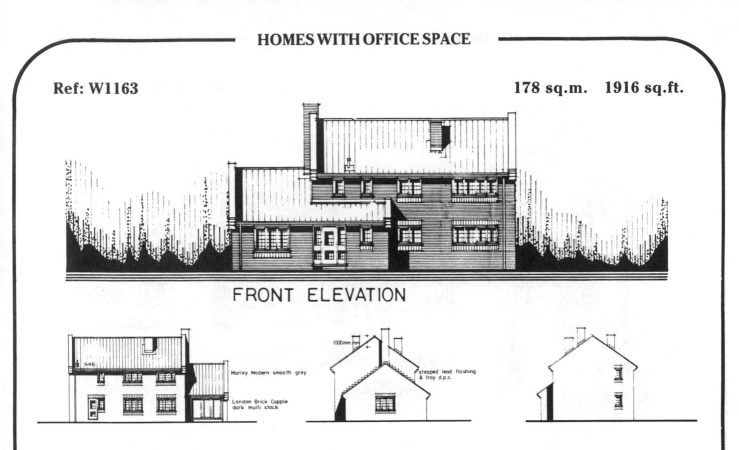

## FRONT ELEVATION

Marley Modern smooth grey

London Brick Capple dark multi stock

1000mm mm.

stepped lead flashing & tray d.p.c.

A house with four fireplaces and a solid fuel Aga cooker — a record for grates to clean out in a new home as far as anyone connected with this book can remember. What a jolly house it must be on a cold day though, with a fire in every downstairs room.

The walls are in a London stock brick, which is irregular in shape and multi-coloured. The use of stone tabling (or coping stones) to the gable walls is unusual above brick walls, and this was a local feature to which the new building conformed.

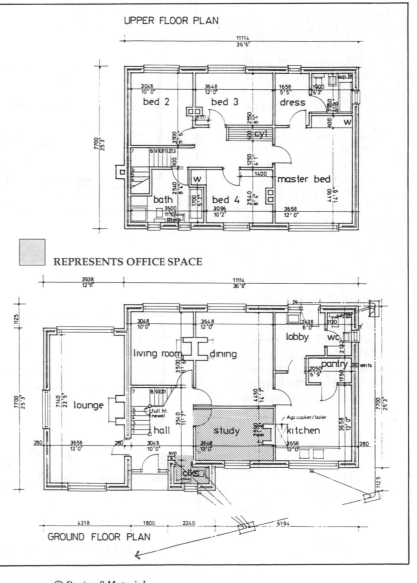

UPPER FLOOR PLAN

bed 2    bed 3    dress

cyl

w

bath    bed 4    master bed

REPRESENTS OFFICE SPACE

living room    dining    lobby    wc

lounge    pantry

full ht. newel

hall    study    kitchen

Aga cooker/boiler

GROUND FLOOR PLAN

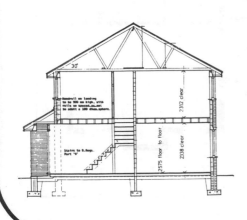

Stairs to B.Regs. Part 'B'

**Ref: 96158**

**254 sq.m.   2739 sq.ft.**

This large family house of over 2700 square feet has the ground floor accommodation arranged with a family room quite separate from the lounge and study. The dining room is integral with the kitchen, but all of this can be rearranged for someone requiring a formal dining room.

A lobby at the back door is a popular feature in rural areas, providing somewhere for wellingtons and for the dogs to sleep! On the first floor all four bedrooms have their own bathrooms, which is an American concept that has recently arrived in this country, and which surely is due to become a standard feature in large houses. More traditional is the window to the gallery above the stairs, which provides light for the hallway below. With the deeply recessed porch the hall would otherwise be rather dark; with the light from above the feature staircase is emphasised

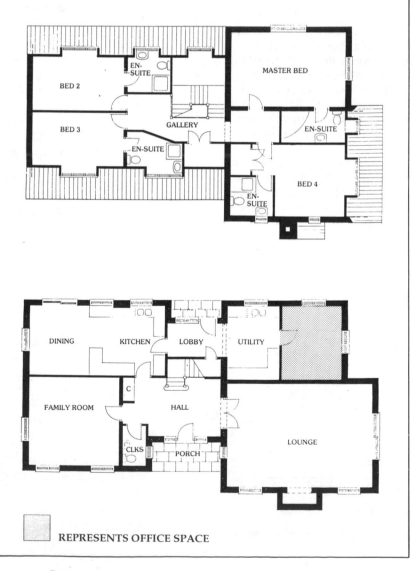

**REPRESENTS OFFICE SPACE**

| Floor Area | 2739 sq.ft. | 254 sq.m. |
|---|---|---|
| Dimensions overall | 59'2" x 32'10" | 18.04 x 10.01 |
| Lounge | 24'5" x 17'6" | 7.44 x 5.33 |
| Family Room | 15'0" x 15'0" | 4.57 x 4.57 |
| Dining Kitchen | 22'7" x 12'0" | 6.89 x 3.65 |
| Utility | 8'11" x 12'11" | 2.72 x 3.93 |
| Office | 10'0" x 12'11" | 3.04 x 3.93 |
| Master Bed | 19'3" x 12'11" | 5.87 x 3.93 |
| Bed 2 | 15'0" x 9'0" | 4.57 x 2.74 |
| Bed 3 | 15'0" x 9'0" | 4.57 x 2.74 |
| Bed 4 | 11'11" x 12'0" | 3.64 x 3.65 |

© Design & Materials

**Ref: 96188**

**266 sq.m.   2859 sq.ft.**
**(inc. garage)**

A large home with a study near the front door. Stairs in the study lead to a space in the roof over the garage that can be fitted out as a studio or in many other ways, or both study and studio would make an office suite.

It is shown here as built in a village in the Vale of York, with traditional stone features, but can easily be adapted for other materials.

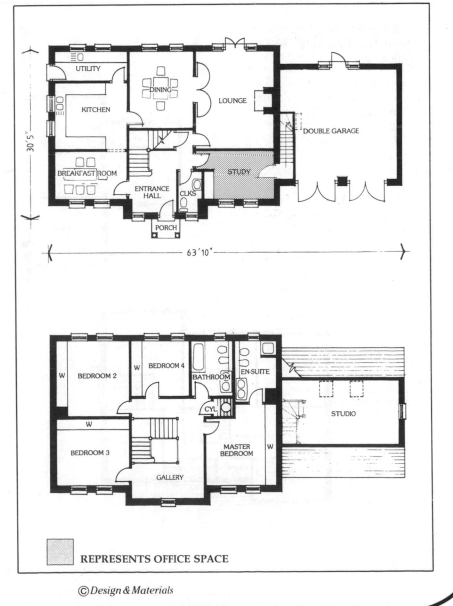

UTILITY

DINING

LOUNGE

KITCHEN

DOUBLE GARAGE

30'5"

BREAKFAST ROOM

STUDY

ENTRANCE HALL

CLKS

PORCH

63'10"

BEDROOM 2   W   BEDROOM 4   BATHROOM   EN-SUITE   STUDIO

W

CYL.

W

BEDROOM 3   MASTER BEDROOM   W

GALLERY

☐ **REPRESENTS OFFICE SPACE**

© *Design & Materials*

**Ref: 96195**

**238 sq.m.    2558 sq.ft.**

An impressive home with a study that provides 130 sq.ft. of office space.

TERRACE

boot room

W.C.

AGA

DINING
12'10" x 12'8"

LOUNGE
14'0" x 17'4"

KITCHEN
12'6" x 18'0"

UTILITY
13'0" x 9'6"

OFFICE
10'0" x 13'0"

HALL

FAMILY ROOM
12'0" x 13'0"

coats

PORCH

CLKS

BEDROOM 2
12'0" x 12'8"

BEDROOM 3
13'0" x 12'8"

MASTER BEDROOM
14'0" x 11'0"

EN-SUITE

BATHROOM

GALLERY

BEDROOM 5
10'0" x 13'0"

BEDROOM 4
13'0" X 9'0"

LINEN

window seat

REPRESENTS OFFICE SPACE

*© Design & Materials*

70

**Ref: 96198**

**186 sq.m.   2000 sq.ft.**

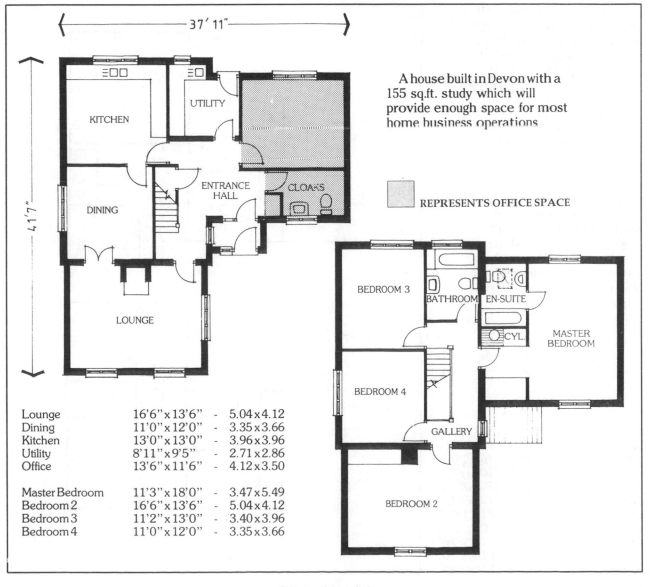

< 37' 11" >

41'7"

KITCHEN

UTILITY

DINING

ENTRANCE
HALL

CLOAKS

LOUNGE

A house built in Devon with a
155 sq.ft. study which will
provide enough space for most
home business operations

REPRESENTS OFFICE SPACE

BEDROOM 3

BATHROOM  EN-SUITE

MASTER
BEDROOM

CYL.

BEDROOM 4

GALLERY

BEDROOM 2

| | | | |
|---|---|---|---|
| Lounge | 16'6" x 13'6" | - | 5.04 x 4.12 |
| Dining | 11'0" x 12'0" | - | 3.35 x 3.66 |
| Kitchen | 13'0" x 13'0" | - | 3.96 x 3.96 |
| Utility | 8'11" x 9'5" | - | 2.71 x 2.86 |
| Office | 13'6" x 11'6" | - | 4.12 x 3.50 |
| | | | |
| Master Bedroom | 11'3" x 18'0" | - | 3.47 x 5.49 |
| Bedroom 2 | 16'6" x 13'6" | - | 5.04 x 4.12 |
| Bedroom 3 | 11'2" x 13'0" | - | 3.40 x 3.96 |
| Bedroom 4 | 11'0" x 12'0" | - | 3.35 x 3.66 |

**Ref: PN660**

**195 sq.m.   2097 sq.ft.**

A house with a study and adjacent cloakroom that are appropriate for someone working from home, although this office accommodation lacks the adjacent storage space that is sometimes very important. As shown here the en suite bathroom to the master bedroom and the individual shower rooms for the other two bedrooms leave the occupant of bedroom 4 with nowhere to wash. This may suit a ten year old son very well indeed, but more seriously, the first floor walls in the Potton aisle framed homes are easily moved, and layouts can be tailored to suit the requirements of individual clients.

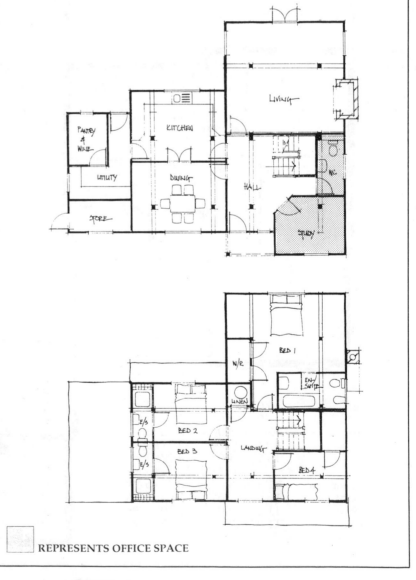

REPRESENTS OFFICE SPACE

| | | |
|---|---|---|
| Living Room | 5.8 x 5.4 | 19'0" x 17'9" |
| Dining Room | 4.6 x 3.4 | 15'11" x 11'2" |
| Kitchen | 3.2 x 4.3 | 10'6 x 14'9" |
| Utility | 3.0 x 2.5 | 9'10" x 8'2" |
| Pantry | 1.9 x 2.5 | 6'3" x 8'2" |
| Store | 3.0 x 1.5 | 9'10" x 4'11" |
| Study/office | 3.3 x 2.8 | 10'10" x 9'2" |
| Bedroom 1 | 5.8 x 3.9 | 19'0" x 12'10" |
| Bedroom 2 | 3.6 x 2.9 | 11'10" x 9'6" |
| Bedroom 3 | 3.6 x 2.9 | 11'10" x 9'6" |
| Bedroom 4 | 3.5 x 2.5 | 11'6" x 8'2" |

© Potton

**Ref: 96125**

**146 sq.m.   1576 sq.ft.**

Turn of the century style house for a narrow plot. This is the new vicarage built in the garden of an 8 room Victorian vicarage which the Church Commissioners decided was too large and too expensive to run, and which was sold. The new building had to match the style of the old one, provide modern living accommodation and have a study where parish business could be transacted and where private meetings could take place.

| Dimensions overall | 30'8" x 38'9" | - | 9.34 x 11.81 |
|---|---|---|---|
| Lounge | 18'0" x 12'6" | - | 5.48 x 3.80 |
| Dining | 10'6" x 12'6" | - | 3.20 x 3.80 |
| Office | 11'9" x 9'0" | - | 3.58 x 2.75 |
| Kitchen | 10'6" x 12'0" | - | 3.20 x 3.65 |
| Utility | 6'11" x 5'3" | - | 2.10 x 1.60 |
| Master Bedroom | 11'4" x 12'6" | - | 3.45 x 3.80 |
| Bedroom 2 | 10'6" x 12'6" | - | 3.20 x 3.80 |
| Bedroom 3 | 10'6" x 11'0" | - | 3.20 x 3.35 |
| Bedroom 4 | 11'4" x 9'0" | - | 3.45 x 2.75 |

**REPRESENTS OFFICE SPACE**

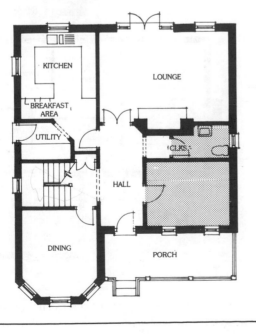

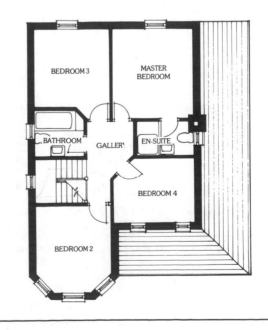

*©Design & Materials*

73

**Ref: 96127**

**134 sq.m.    1446 sq.ft.**

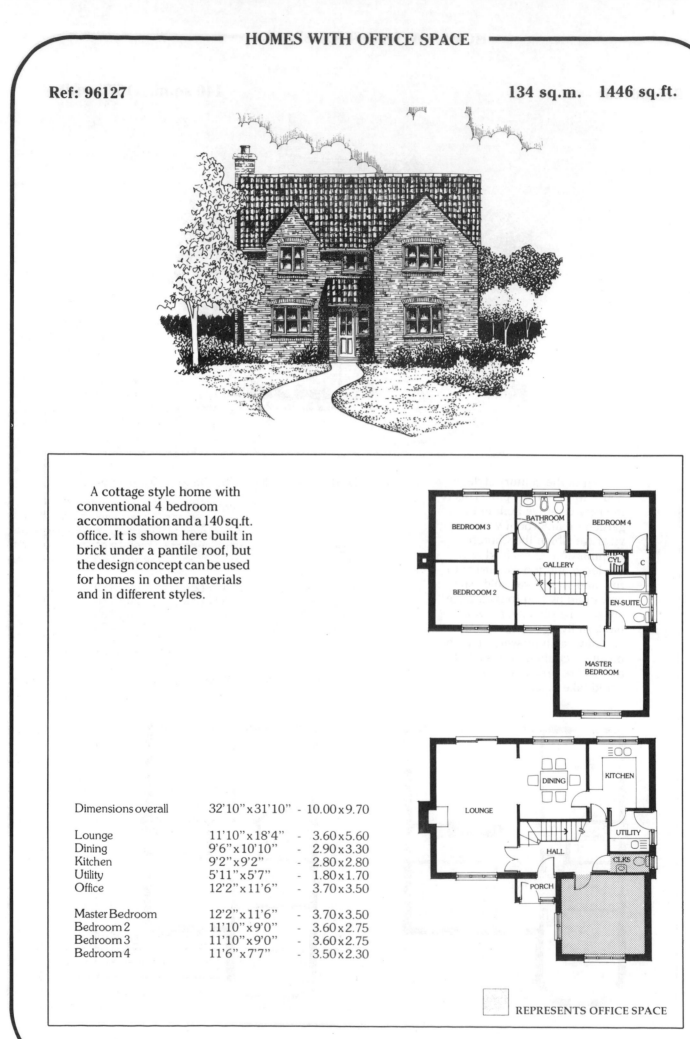

A cottage style home with conventional 4 bedroom accommodation and a 140 sq.ft. office. It is shown here built in brick under a pantile roof, but the design concept can be used for homes in other materials and in different styles.

| Dimensions overall | 32'10" x 31'10" | - | 10.00 x 9.70 |
|---|---|---|---|
| Lounge | 11'10" x 18'4" | - | 3.60 x 5.60 |
| Dining | 9'6" x 10'10" | - | 2.90 x 3.30 |
| Kitchen | 9'2" x 9'2" | - | 2.80 x 2.80 |
| Utility | 5'11" x 5'7" | - | 1.80 x 1.70 |
| Office | 12'2" x 11'6" | - | 3.70 x 3.50 |
| Master Bedroom | 12'2" x 11'6" | - | 3.70 x 3.50 |
| Bedroom 2 | 11'10" x 9'0" | - | 3.60 x 2.75 |
| Bedroom 3 | 11'10" x 9'0" | - | 3.60 x 2.75 |
| Bedroom 4 | 11'6" x 7'7" | - | 3.50 x 2.30 |

REPRESENTS OFFICE SPACE

# Designs with Granny Flats

For many families an advantage of building their own home is the opportunity to provide self contained accommodation for an elderly person, generally known as a granny flat. If this is of interest to you there are three aspects of this to consider.

One is that it is often possible for granny to sell her existing home and put the proceeds towards the cost of accommodation in her childs home in a way that should largely avoid inheritance tax. This is a matter for which the early advice of an accountant or solicitor is essential, and to make it possible it may be necessary that the flat has its own front door or other features. The second consideration is that thought has to be given to the planning situation. A granny flat can be shown on a planning application, or the accommodation can simply be shown as rooms in the house without any special designation. If it is likely that the flat will be used for some other purpose in the future, or will become part of the main house, this may, or may not, require consent for any alterations to facilitate the changes. The option to sell off the flat when it is no longer required may be important.

Both these issues are dealt with at length in *Building Your Own Home,* the companion volume to this book, and they often are crucial to the arrangements made. It is probable that they played their part in decisions made about the designs shown on the following pages, but the actual room layouts and other details were arranged to suit the special situation of the elderly people for which they were built.

Finally, this all depends on what granny wants. Will she value her independence and privacy above all else? If so, she will probably want her own front door, and she may ask that the communicating door between her flat and your house should lead from a hall and not from the living room or kitchen. How important is it going to be that the granny flat should have its own cooking facilities? Need these be any more than one of the mini kitchens which are now available, combining a small cooker, small fridge and sink in one 60 inch kitchen unit? The right decision in these matters can make an enormous difference to the whole arrangement.

There are other decisions to be made as well, many of them concerned with the possibility of granny remaining in the flat when she is very elderly and rather more frail than she is at present. Doors that are three feet wide make life in a wheelchair a great deal easier, and bathroom appliances that suit the elderly are now available and it might be a good idea to install them at this stage. Electric sockets and light switches are more easily used if they are set three feet above the floor, and these and many other matters are dealt with at length in various books on designing for the elderly. The building bookshop attached to the Building Centre at Store Street in London always has a good selection of these, and should be contacted for details of current titles.

If special features of this sort are to be built into the granny flat, it is possible that you will wish to replace them at some time in the future, and consideration should be given to this. For instance, electric socket boxes can be situated at both a high level and in the skirting, and one or the other can be blanked off as appropriate. The tiling around a special bath can be arranged so that the bath can be changed without too much difficulty. Most valuable of all, lintels can be built into walls so that windows or doors can be inserted beneath them at a later date, and you should ensure that partition walls in a granny flat can be readily moved if some rearrangement is ever going to be appropriate.

**Ref: 96209**                    183 sq.m.    1968 sq.ft.

A three bedroom farmhouse with a large granny flat that has its own front entrance. As is usual for a farmhouse there is a utility room and cloakroom at the back door to suit muddy boots and wet dogs!

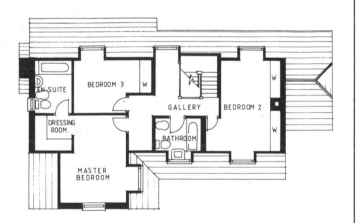

REPRESENTS GRANNY FLAT

| Dimensions overall | 53'4" x 32'6" | - 16.25 x 9.89 |
|---|---|---|
| Lounge | 20'0" x 15'0" | - 6.10 x 4.57 |
| Kitchen | 10'0" x 11'0" | - 3.05 x 3.35 |
| Dining | 12'11" x 12'5" | - 3.94 x 3.79 |
| Granny Lounge | 9'8" x 15'0" | - 2.95 x 4.57 |
| Granny Bed | 10'0" x 8'8" | - 3.05 x 2.64 |
| Granny Bath | 10'0" x 6'0" | - 3.05 x 1.83 |
| Utility | 7'0" x 10'0" | - 2.13 x 3.05 |
| Master Bedroom | 11'6" x 15'0" | - 3.50 x 4.57 |
| Bedroom 2 | 12'11" x 15'4" | - 3.95 x 4.68 |
| Bedroom 3 | 13'5" x 8'10" | - 4.10 x 2.69 |

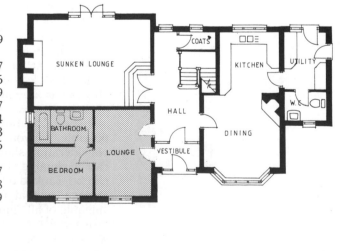

**Ref: 96210**

**153 sq.m.   1650 sq.ft.**

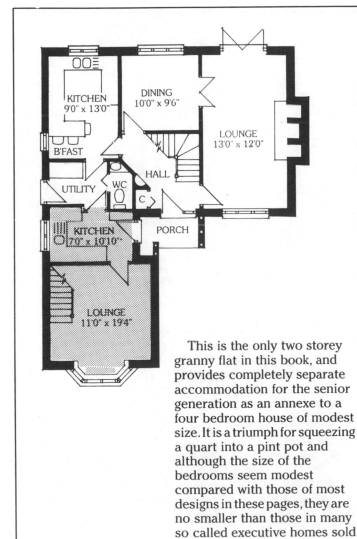

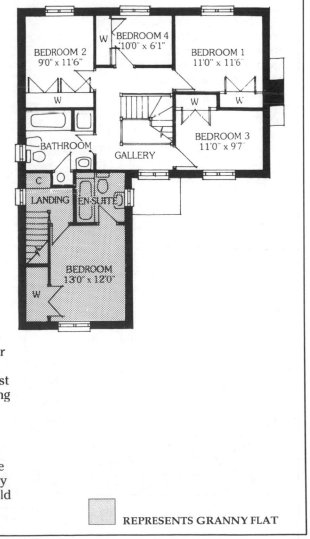

KITCHEN
9'0" x 13'0"

DINING
10'0" x 9'6"

B'FAST

LOUNGE
13'0" x 12'0"

UTILITY

WC

HALL

C

KITCHEN
7'0" x 10'10"

PORCH

LOUNGE
11'0" x 19'4"

BEDROOM 2
9'0" x 11'6"

W

BEDROOM 4
10'0" x 6'1"

BEDROOM 1
11'0" x 11'6"

W

W

W

BATHROOM

GALLERY

BEDROOM 3
11'0" x 9'7"

C

LANDING

EN-SUITE

BEDROOM
13'0" x 12'0"

W

This is the only two storey granny flat in this book, and provides completely separate accommodation for the senior generation as an annexe to a four bedroom house of modest size. It is a triumph for squeezing a quart into a pint pot and although the size of the bedrooms seem modest compared with those of most designs in these pages, they are no smaller than those in many so called executive homes sold by developers.

REPRESENTS GRANNY FLAT

**Ref: C559**

**279 sq.m.   3003 sq.ft.**

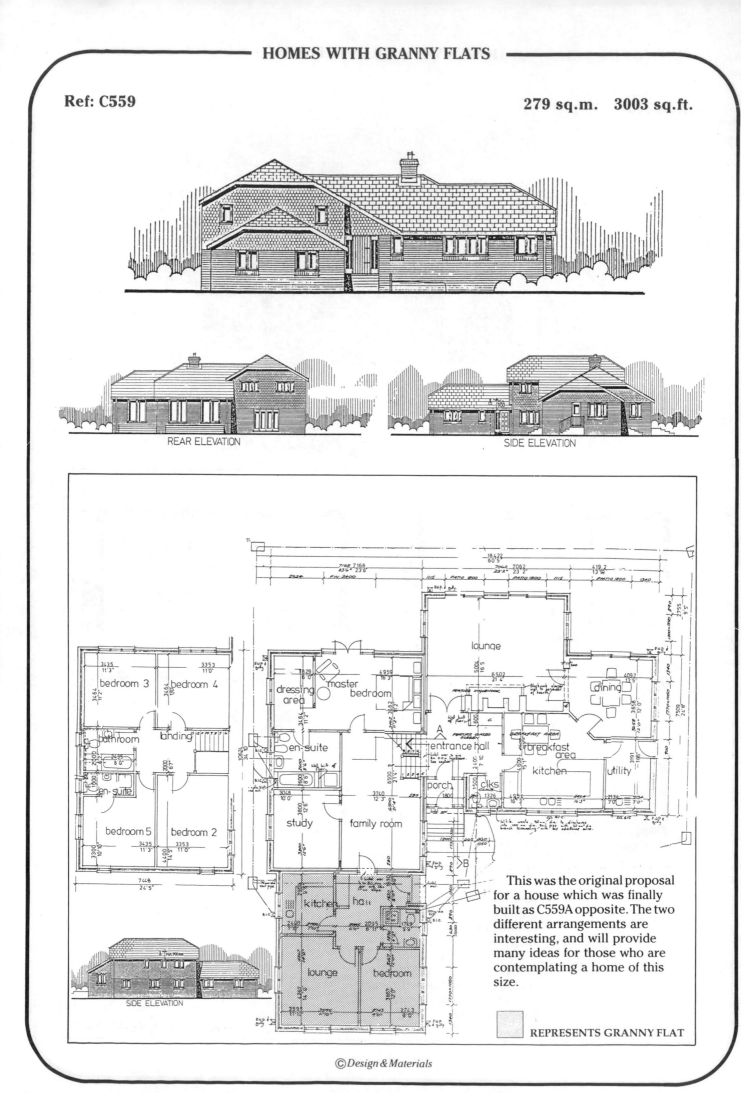

REAR ELEVATION

SIDE ELEVATION

lounge

bedroom 3

bedroom 4

dressing area

master bedroom

dining

bathroom

landing

en-suite

breakfast area

entrance hall

kitchen

utility

en-suite

bedroom 5

bedroom 2

study

family room

porch

clks

kitchen

hall

lounge

bedroom

SIDE ELEVATION

This was the original proposal for a house which was finally built as C559A opposite. The two different arrangements are interesting, and will provide many ideas for those who are contemplating a home of this size.

REPRESENTS GRANNY FLAT

© *Design & Materials*

**Ref: C559A**

**249 sq.m.  2680 sq.ft.**
**(exc. porch)**

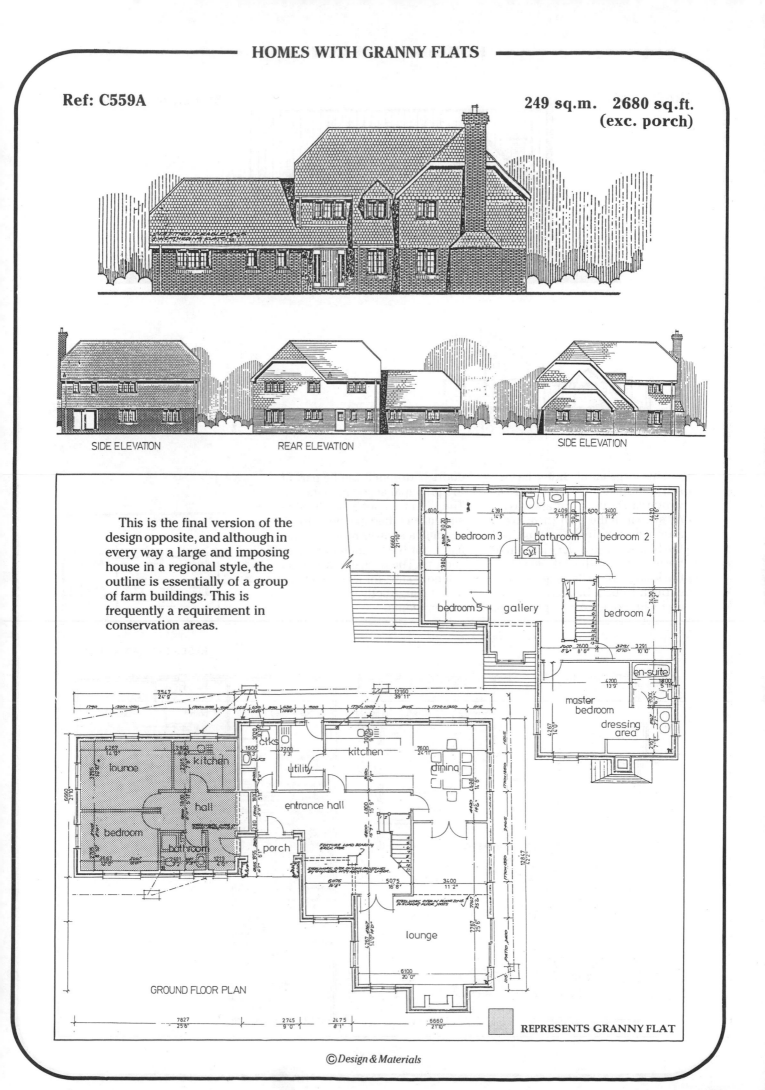

SIDE ELEVATION

REAR ELEVATION

SIDE ELEVATION

This is the final version of the design opposite, and although in every way a large and imposing house in a regional style, the outline is essentially of a group of farm buildings. This is frequently a requirement in conservation areas.

bedroom 3

bathroom

bedroom 2

cyl.

bedroom 5

gallery

bedroom 4

en-suite

master bedroom

dressing area

clks

kitchen

lounge

kitchen

utility

dining

hall

entrance hall

bedroom

bathroom

porch

lounge

GROUND FLOOR PLAN

REPRESENTS GRANNY FLAT

**Ref: P2672**

**390 sq.m.  4198 sq.ft.**

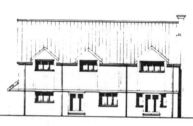

This large family home has a self contained flat over the garage which can be used in many ways. As shewn in the plan there are four bedrooms in the main part of the house, and two very large first floor rooms to the flat. However, the lounge to the flat is quite large enough to be a bed-sitting room, and with some rearrangement of doors bedroom 5 can be part of the principal accommodation. The WC in the lobby to the side entrance is then extended to become a shower room for the flat ... but the permutations are endless! The design concept is a splendid start for a large home which can exactly suit any requirements.

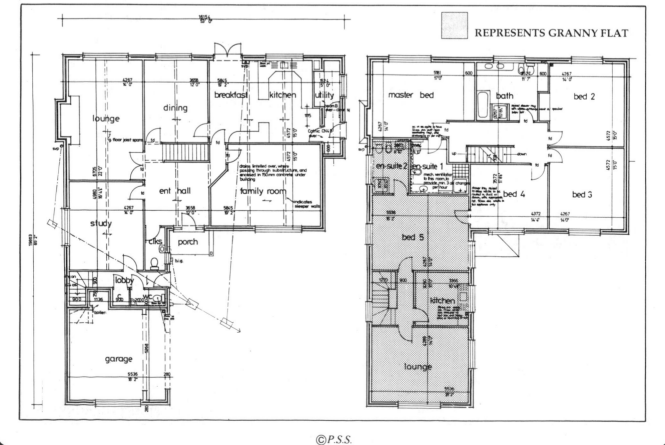

REPRESENTS GRANNY FLAT

**Ref: C530**

**358 sq.m. 3853 sq.ft.**
**(inc. garage)**

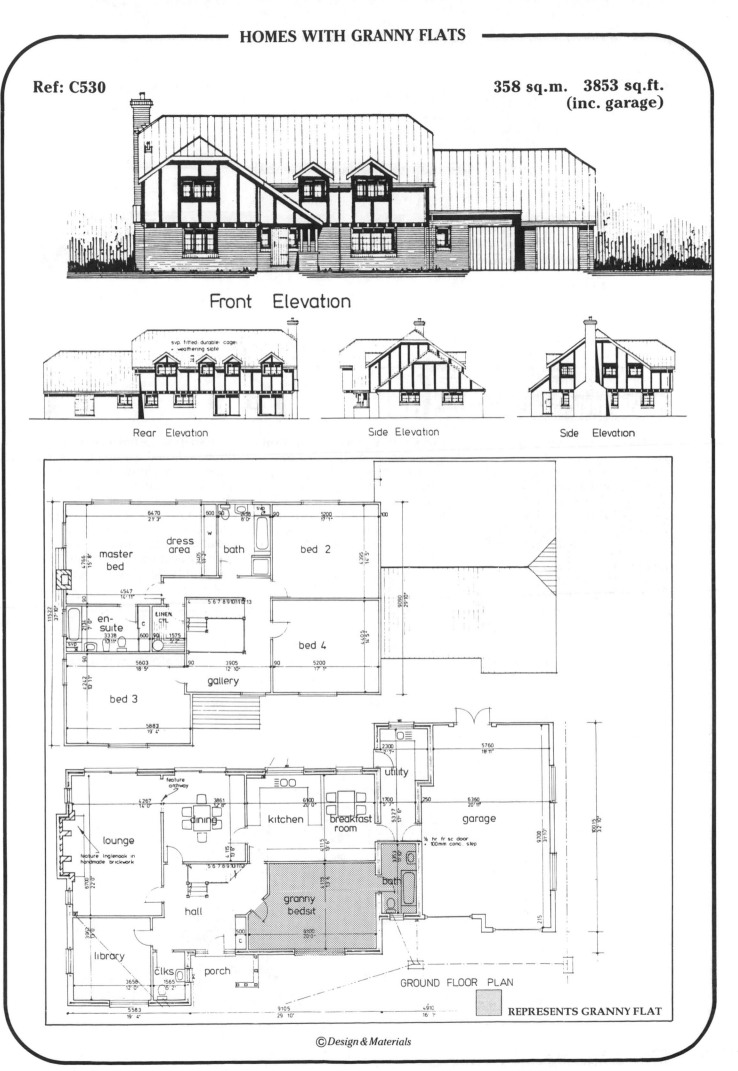

Front Elevation

Rear Elevation

Side Elevation

Side Elevation

svp. fitted: durable: cage: + weathering slate

master bed

dress area

bath

bed 2

en-suite

LINEN CYL

bed 4

bed 3

gallery

feature archway

dining

kitchen

breakfast room

utility

garage

lounge

feature inglenook in handmade brickwork

hall

granny bedsit

bath

library

clks

porch

½ hr fr sc door + 100mm conc. step

GROUND FLOOR PLAN

REPRESENTS GRANNY FLAT

© Design & Materials

**Ref: W983**

**289 sq.m.    3110 sq.ft.**

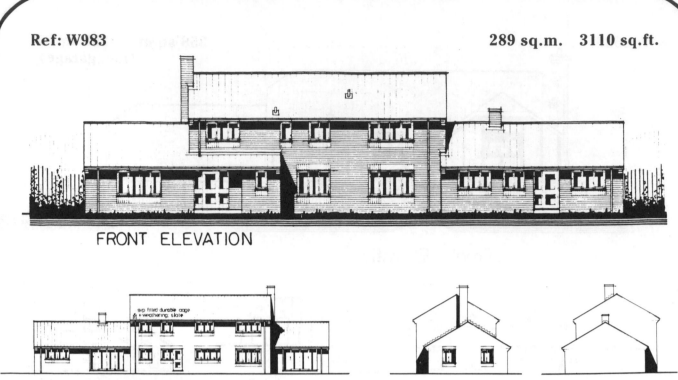

FRONT ELEVATION

This very large house has a self contained granny flat as one wing, and at nearly a hundred feet long is a well balanced and most impressive home. The granny flat is completely self contained with two bedrooms, its own kitchen, and, what is most important with a granny flat, its own front door. The connecting door into the main house is through a two skin cavity wall, so there is excellent sound insulation between the two parts of the building.

Sound insulation has also been a major consideration in planning the rest of the building, with all the walls between bedrooms lining up with the walls between rooms below: this means that the first floor walls can be in 4" solid blockwork, giving 40db sound reduction.

The big lounge has windows in three walls and the fireplace and other features in the fourth. This gives a marvellously light and airy room, but careful consideration has to be given to whether there is room left for radiators and furniture that has to stand against walls. Generally speaking, the larger the room the easier this is.

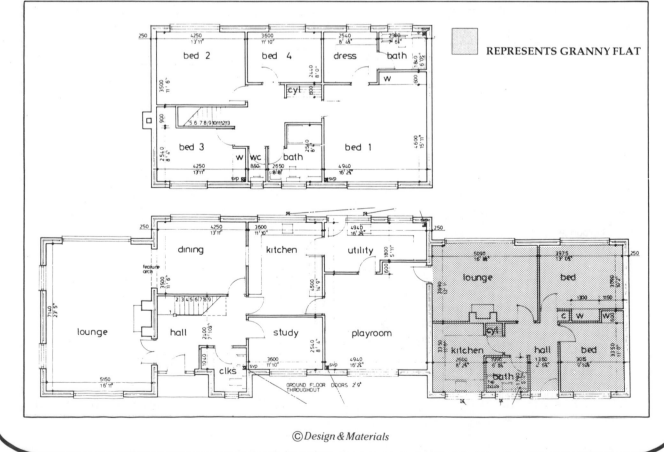

REPRESENTS GRANNY FLAT

**Ref: S574**

**207 sq.m.   2228 sq.ft.**

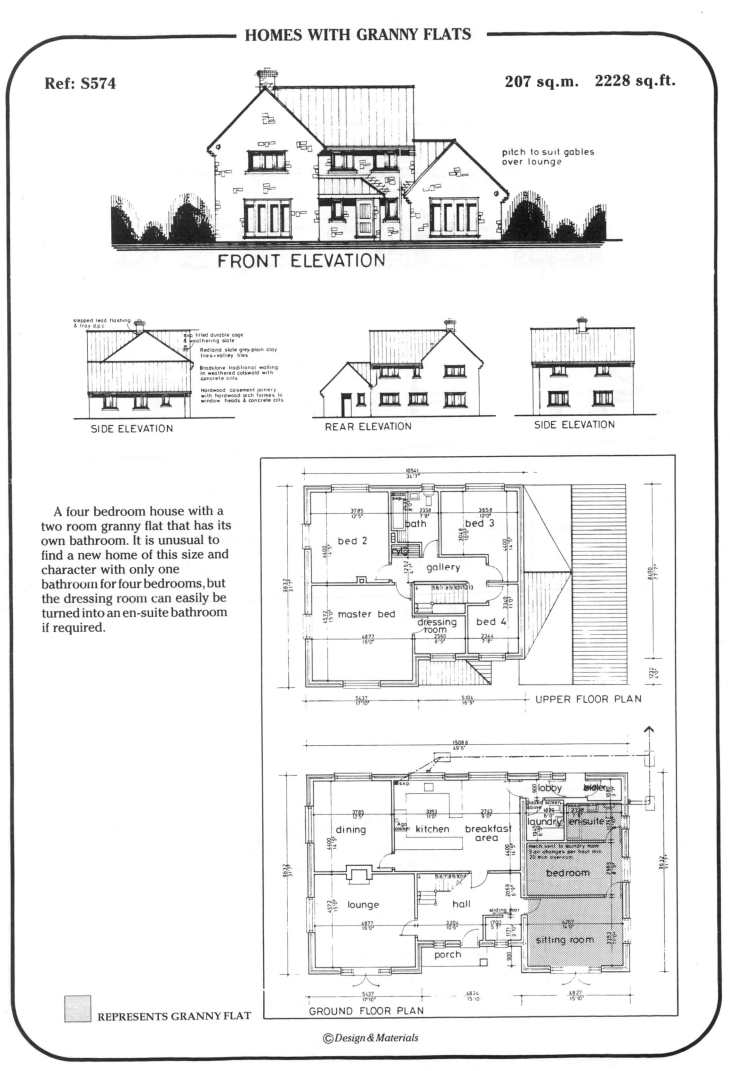

pitch to suit gables
over lounge

FRONT ELEVATION

slepped lead flashing
& tray d.p.c.

s.v.p. fitted durable cage
& weathering slate

Redland slate grey-plain clay
tiles • valley tiles

Bradstone traditional walling
in weathered colswold with
concrete cills

Hardwood casement joinery
with hardwood arch formes to
window heads & concrete cills

SIDE ELEVATION

REAR ELEVATION

SIDE ELEVATION

A four bedroom house with a
two room granny flat that has its
own bathroom. It is unusual to
find a new home of this size and
character with only one
bathroom for four bedrooms, but
the dressing room can easily be
turned into an en-suite bathroom
if required.

bed 2  bath  bed 3

gallery

master bed

dressing
room  bed 4

UPPER FLOOR PLAN

dining  kitchen  breakfast
area

lobby

glazed screen
above  laundry  en-suite

lounge  hall  bedroom

porch  sitting room

GROUND FLOOR PLAN

REPRESENTS GRANNY FLAT

© Design & Materials

83

**Ref: S468-3**

**205 sq.m.   2206 sq.ft.**

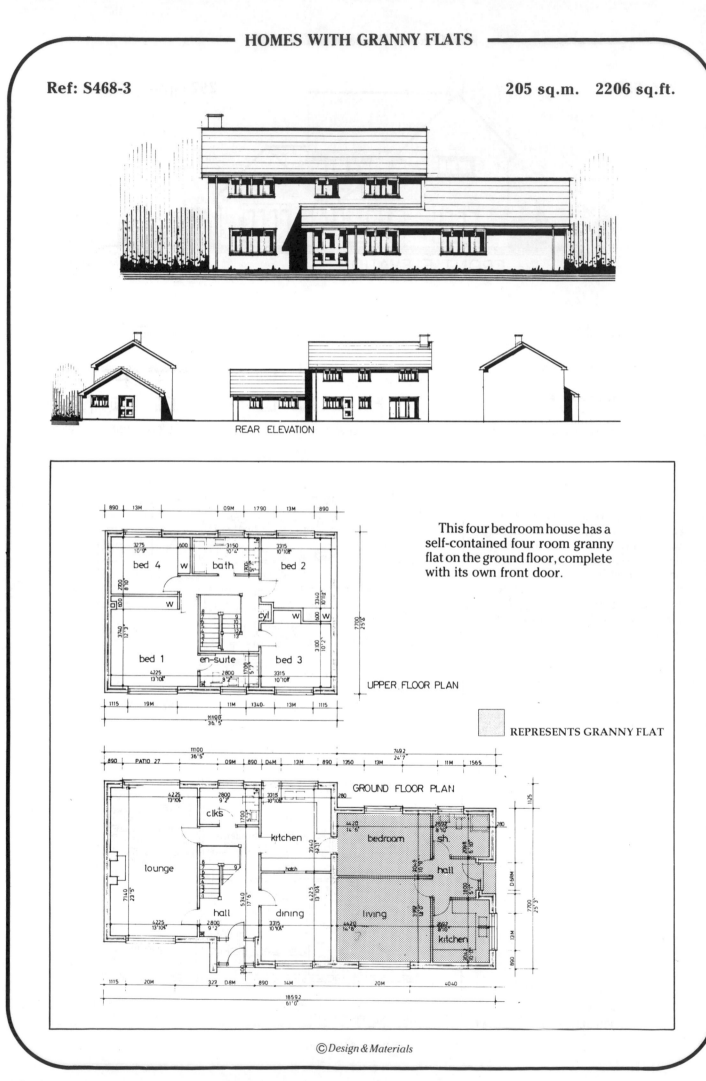

REAR ELEVATION

This four bedroom house has a self-contained four room granny flat on the ground floor, complete with its own front door.

UPPER FLOOR PLAN

REPRESENTS GRANNY FLAT

GROUND FLOOR PLAN

bed 4   bath   bed 2

bed 1   en-suite   bed 3

cyl

clks   kitchen   bedroom   sh

lounge   hall   hall

hall   dining   living   kitchen

© *Design & Materials*

**Ref: W1171**

**250 sq.m.   2691 sq.ft.**

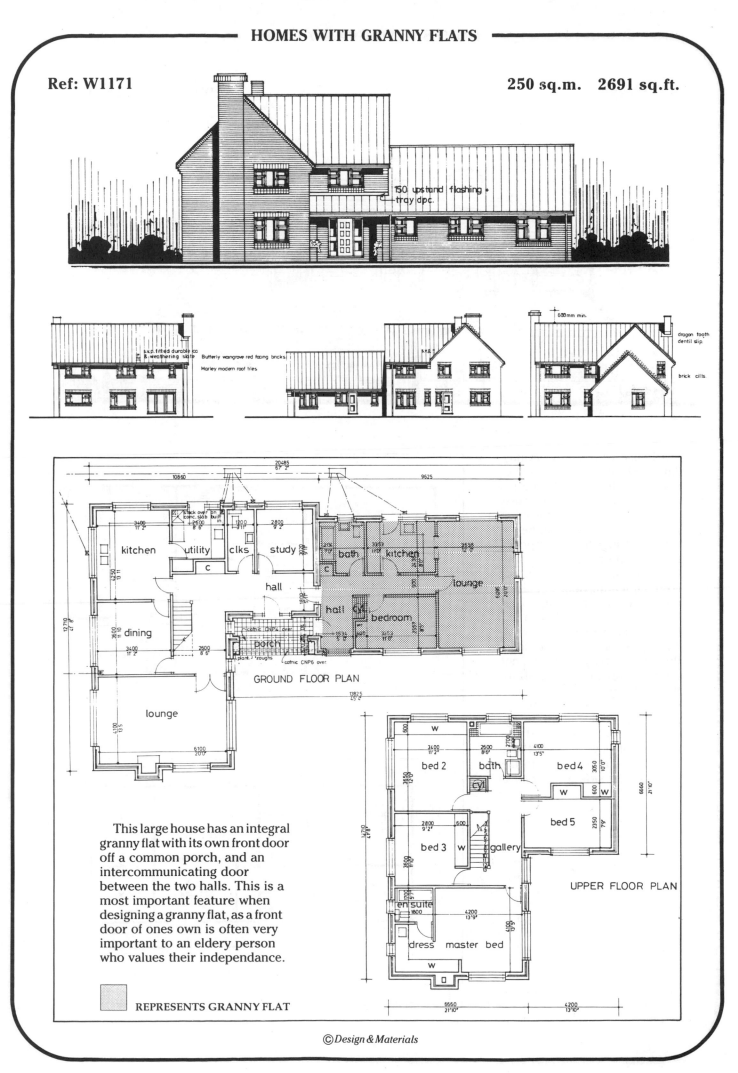

GROUND FLOOR PLAN

UPPER FLOOR PLAN

This large house has an integral granny flat with its own front door off a common porch, and an intercommunicating door between the two halls. This is a most important feature when designing a granny flat, as a front door of ones own is often very important to an eldery person who values their independance.

REPRESENTS GRANNY FLAT

ⓒ *Design & Materials*

**Ref: PN655**                                        **199 sq.m.   2145 sq.ft.**

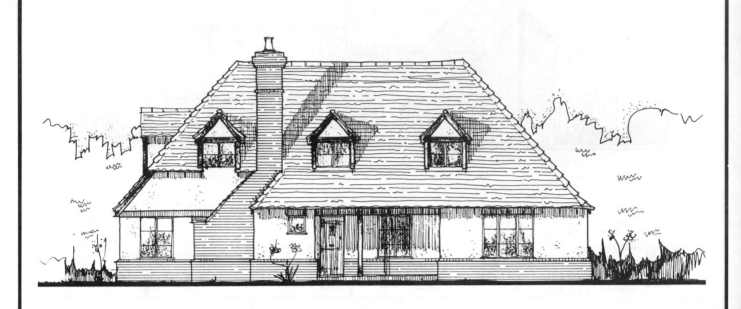

A house with a large granny flat which has its own outside door as well as direct access into the family part of the house. This establishes that it is all a single dwelling, and can be treated as such for tax purposes. Because the granny flat has an external door, if there was not a communicating door it could be regarded as two dwellings. This is a major consideration, and if it presents problems the whole concept should be discussed at the design study stage and not after the drawings have gone to the planners.

The roof void above the granny flat is shown as a storage area, but could be utilised in a number of ways. Most of them would require a further dormer in either the side or the rear of the roof.

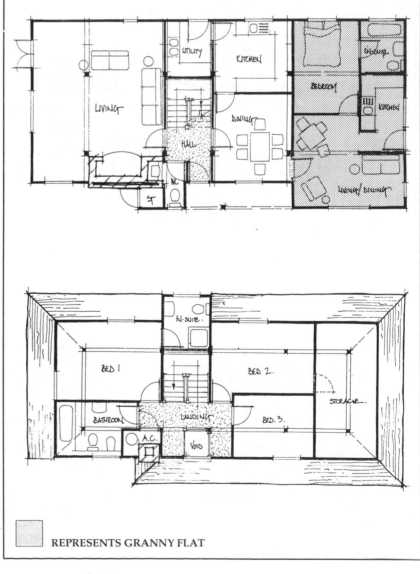

REPRESENTS GRANNY FLAT

| Living | 5.6 x 6.9 | 18'4" x 22'8" |
|---|---|---|
| Kitchen | 3.4 x 3.1 | 11'2" x 10'2" |
| Utility | 2.0 x 2.4 | 6'7" x 7'10" |
| Dining | 3.4 x 3.7 | 11'2" x 12'2" |
| Bedroom 1 | 4.5 x 3.3 | 14'9" x 10'10" |
| Bedroom 2 | 4.4 x 3.0 | 14'5" x 9'10" |
| Bedroom 3 | 3.4 x 2.7 | 11'2" x 8'10" |
| | | |
| *Granny suite* | | |
| Living/Dining | 4.7 x 3.2 | 15'5" x 10'6" |
| Bedroom | 2.8 x 4.0 | 9'2" x 13'1" |
| Kitchen | 1.9 x 3.3 | 6'3" x 10'10" |

© *Potton*

**Ref: PN659**

**225 sq.m.  2425 sq.ft.**

This modification to a standard Potton Gamlingay design has a large ground floor bedsit room with a generous en suite bathroom for an elderly person. The extension which houses the bathroom is under a lean to roof, appropriate to the style of the building as a whole, and the inset section drawing shows the implications of this for headroom.

The plan shows two large bedroom suites and a study on the first floor, but if required these can be arranged to provide four more modest bedrooms.

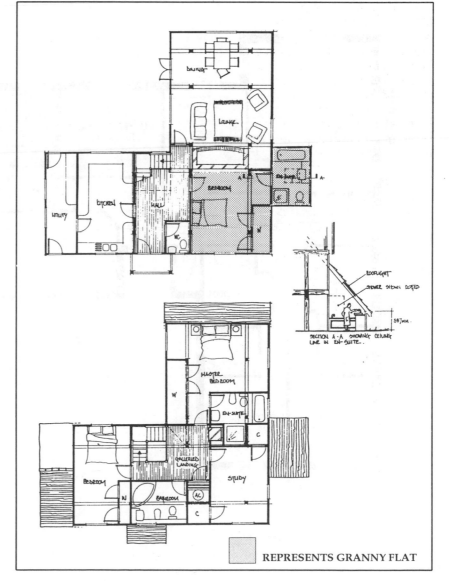

| | | |
|---|---|---|
| *Lounge/Dining* | 5.8 x 7.5 | 19'0" x 24'7" |
| *Kitchen* | 3.3 x 5.8 | 10'10" x 19'0" |
| *Utility* | 1.8 x 5.8 | 5'8" x 19'0" |
| *Master Bedroom* | 3.8 x 4.0 | 19'0" x 13'1" |
| *Bedroom 2* | 2.9 x 5.8 | 9'6" x 19'0" |
| *Study/Bedroom 3* | 3.2 x 4.5 | 10'6" x 14'9" |
| | | |
| *Granny suite* | | |
| *Bedroom* | 4.0 x 4.9 | 13'1" x 16'1" |

REPRESENTS GRANNY FLAT

©*Potton*

87

**Ref: 96202**

**177 sq.m.    1900 sq.ft.**

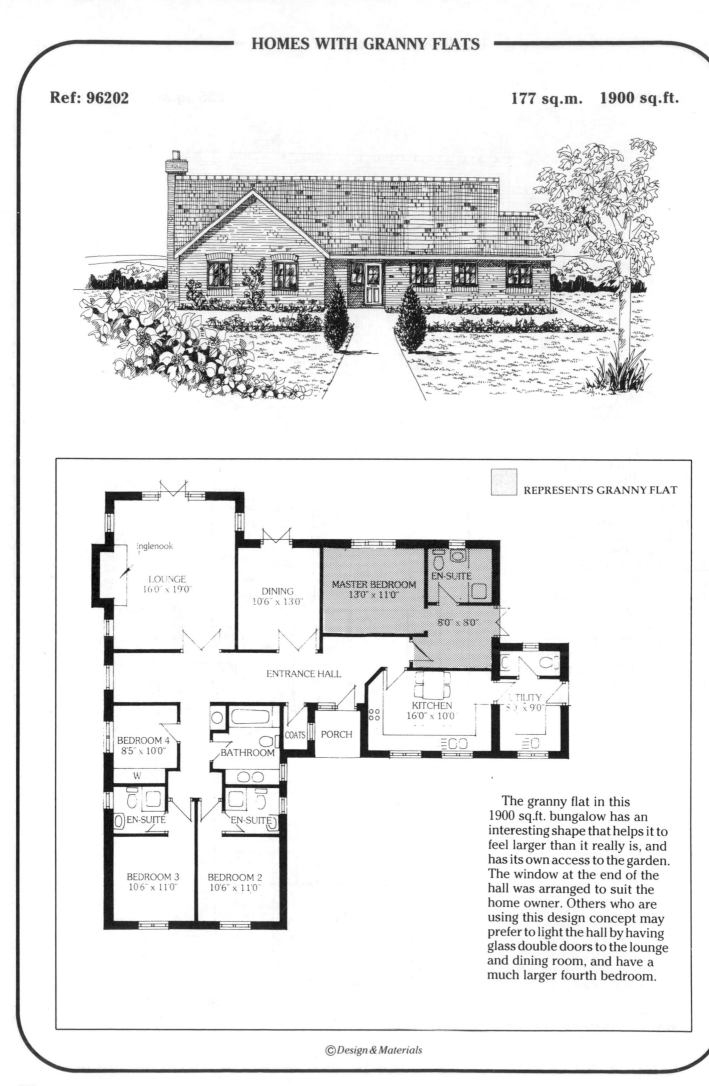

REPRESENTS GRANNY FLAT

inglenook

LOUNGE
16'0" x 19'0"

DINING
10'6" x 13'0"

MASTER BEDROOM
13'0" x 11'0"

EN-SUITE

8'0" x 8'0"

ENTRANCE HALL

UTILITY
8'0" x 9'0"

KITCHEN
16'0" x 10'0"

BEDROOM 4
8'5" x 10'0"

W

BATHROOM

COATS

PORCH

EN-SUITE

EN-SUITE

BEDROOM 3
10'6" x 11'0"

BEDROOM 2
10'6" x 11'0"

The granny flat in this
1900 sq.ft. bungalow has an
interesting shape that helps it to
feel larger than it really is, and
has its own access to the garden.
The window at the end of the
hall was arranged to suit the
home owner. Others who are
using this design concept may
prefer to light the hall by having
glass double doors to the lounge
and dining room, and have a
much larger fourth bedroom.

**Ref: 96206**

**135 sq.m.    1450 sq.ft.**

The granny flat in this 1450 sq.ft. home occupies a lot of space on the ground floor, but can be easily converted into a master bedroom suite as shown by the inset sketch. The two bedrooms on the first floor are small, but enjoy a large bathroom.

The dining hall is the key to getting so much accommodation in the limited space available, and if the idea of the front door being in the dining room seems strange, remember a small external porch can be added.

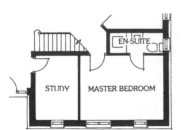

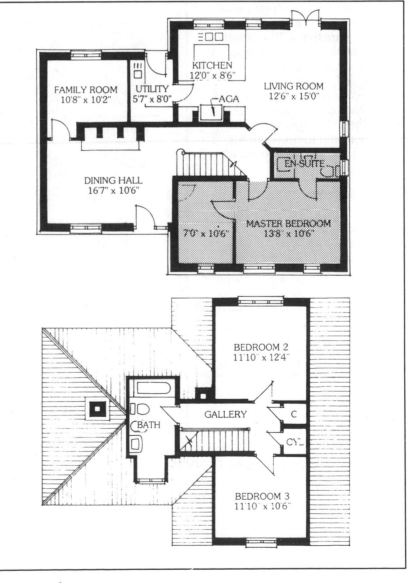

☐ **REPRESENTS GRANNY FLAT**

© *Design & Materials*

**Ref: 96111**

**146 sq.m.    1572 sq.ft.**

This is a village street home, and a text book example of a design genre that will be greeted enthusiastically by any planning officer. Or should be.

The self contained accommodation on the ground floor has the bedroom larger than the living room, but the wall between them is not load bearing and can be moved as required.

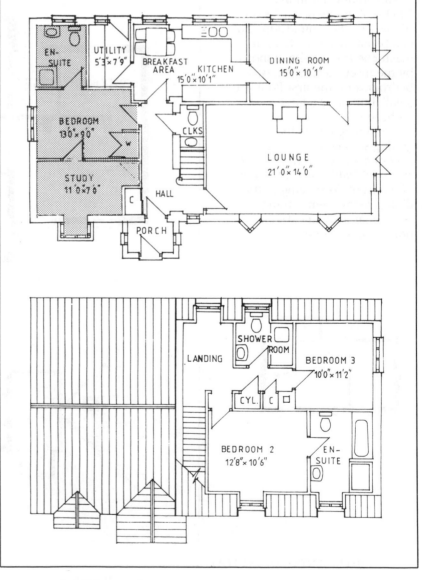

REPRESENTS GRANNY FLAT

© Design & Materials

**Ref: 96109**

**221 sq.m.   2378 sq.ft.**

This home has a granny wing rather than a granny flat! It was built with the family accommodation on two floors at the right of the plan, with generous separate accommodation with larger rooms for granny to the left. There is provision for further first floor bedrooms in the roof at a future date, with space left for a prestige staircase.

An unkind planning officer might well view this as two properties, and the way in which the submission drawings are labelled up require careful consideration.

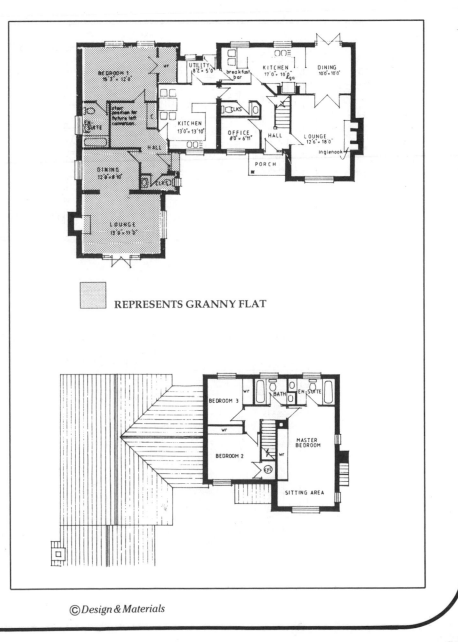

REPRESENTS GRANNY FLAT

**Ref: P2586**

**186 sq.m.   2002 sq.ft.**

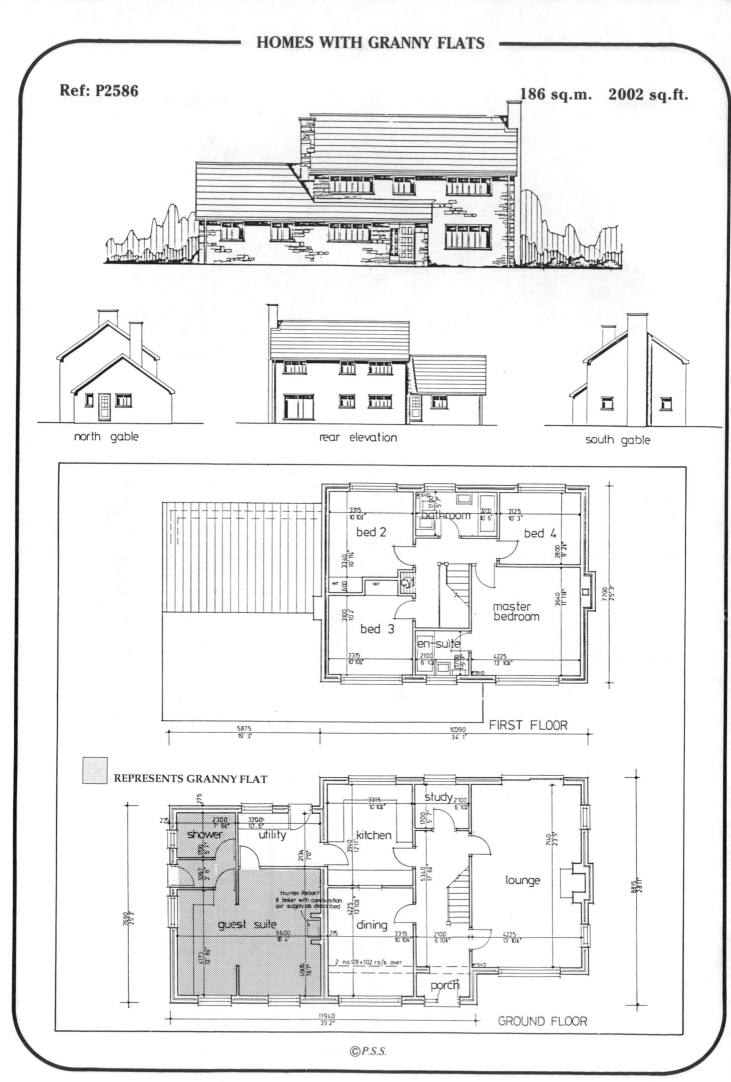

north gable

rear elevation

south gable

REPRESENTS GRANNY FLAT

bed 2

bathroom

bed 4

wr

wr

cyl

master bedroom

bed 3

en-suite

FIRST FLOOR

shower

utility

study

kitchen

guest suite

Hunter Herald
8 boiler with combustion
air supply as described

lounge

dining

2 no 178 x 102 rsj's over

porch

GROUND FLOOR

©P.S.S.

92

**Ref: 96257**

**307 sq.m.    3300 sq.ft.**

A large house with five generous bedrooms on the first floor and a bedroom/bathroom suite for an elderly parent below. The space by the landing window on the first floor will enable a stairway to be installed to an attic room if this is ever required.

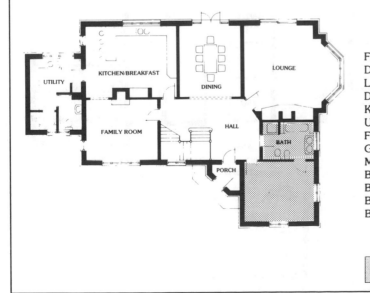

| | | |
|---|---|---|
| Floor Area | 3300 sq.ft. | 307 sq.m. |
| Dimensions overall | 62'0" x 43'6" | 18.89 x 13.24 |
| Lounge | 15'0" x 20'0" | 4.57 x 6.10 |
| Dining | 13'0" x 15'0" | 3.96 x 4.57 |
| Kitchen/Breakfast | 19'0" x 15'0" | 5.80 x 4.57 |
| Utility | 11'0" x 11'0" | 3.35 x 3.35 |
| Family Room | 15'0" x 13'0" | 4.57 x 3.96 |
| Gym/Study | 15'0" x 13'0" | 4.57 x 3.96 |
| Master Bed | 12'8" x 15'0" | 3.87 x 4.57 |
| Bed 2 | 15'0" x 20'0" | 4.57 x 6.10 |
| Bed 3 | 15'0" x 13'0" | 4.57 x 3.96 |
| Bed 4 | 15'0" x 13'0" | 4.57 x 3.96 |
| Bed 5 | 13'0" x 13'0" | 3.96 x 3.96 |

REPRESENTS GRANNY FLAT

**Ref: 96252**

**222 sq.m.   2387 sq.ft.**
**(exc. garage)**

A big house with three large family bedrooms upstairs, and granny's bedroom suite downstairs. The hall is lit by a small window at the half landing and another in a dormer at the head of the stairs, but glazed double doors to the dining room may also be appropriate: all will depend on how light in feel your decor is.

| | | | |
|---|---|---|---|
| Garage | 309 sq. ft. | - | 29 sq. mtrs. |
| Dimensions overall | 43'5" x 58'10" | - | 13.24 x 17.93 |
| | | | |
| Lounge | 15'9" x 19'1" | - | 4.80 x 5.82 |
| Dining | 13'1" x 15'4" | - | 4.00 x 4.67 |
| Kitchen/Breakfast | 11'6" x 15'4" | - | 3.50 x 4.67 |
| Utility | 7'4" x 8'3" | - | 2.23 x 2.52 |
| Study | 11'6" x 8'11" | - | 3.50 x 2.71 |
| Guest Bedroom | 15'9" x 13'10" | - | 4.80 x 4.23 |
| | | | |
| Master Bedroom (incl. W.R.) | 15'9" x 16'5" | - | 4.80 x 5.00 |
| Bedroom 2 (incl. W.R.) | 13'1" x 10'9" | - | 4.00 x 3.27 |
| Bedroom 3 (incl. W.R.) | 11'6" x 10'9" | - | 3.50 x 3.27 |

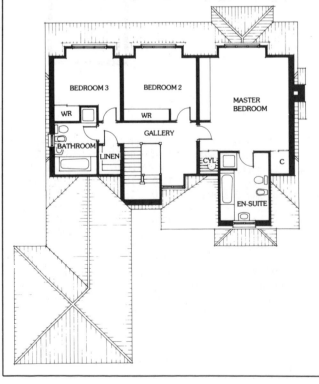

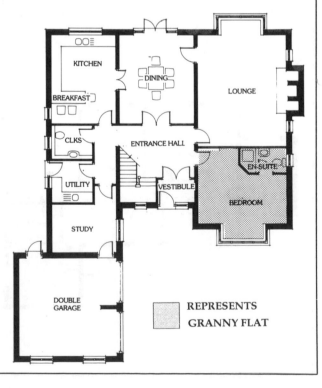

REPRESENTS
GRANNY FLAT

# Designs for Homes for Sloping Sites

The main text chapter about building on sloping sites starts at page 20 and explains how there are four basic approaches: to build into the slope, to build above the slope, to cut and fill, and to design a home with changes of floor level that follow the slope. The first three of these techniques enable any house or bungalow design for a level site to be built on a slope, and the designs on the following pages are those which use the 'follow the slope' approach.

Designing a home of this sort has to start with a survey of the existing ground levels, for you will be lucky indeed if the gradients permit an entrance at ground level, six steps down to bedrooms and seven up to the living accommodation as shown in a specific design on the following pages. Usually either the design or the ground levels will have to be adjusted. There is an individual solution to the challenge of building on any particular slope, and the designs on the pages that follow show a selection of real solutions to real challenges.

**Ref: 96154**

**204 sq.m.  2194 sq.ft.**
**(inc. garage and balconies)**

A home on three levels with a garage below for a slope across the site. Compare with the design 96153 opposite which is for a slope which falls away from the front of the plot.

The stairs from the garage to the utility room are a useful feature, and the large family room could be used as a home office.

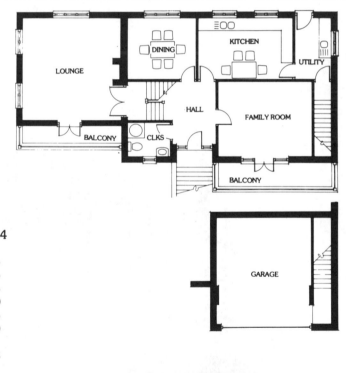

| Dimensions overall | 52'0" x 29'0" | - | 15.84 x 8.84 |
|---|---|---|---|
| Lounge | 16'0" x 16'7" | - | 4.88 x 5.05 |
| Dining | 11'3" x 10'0" | - | 3.43 x 3.05 |
| Kitchen/Breakfast | 15'4" x 10'0" | - | 4.66 x 3.05 |
| Family Room | 15'3" x 12'2" | - | 4.64 x 3.70 |
| Utility | 6'0" x 10'0" | - | 1.83 x 3.05 |
| Cloaks | 6'11" x 5'7" | - | 2.12 x 1.70 |
| Garage | 15'3" x 17'0" | - | 4.64 x 5.18 |
| Master Bedroom | 13'4" x 12'2" | - | 4.06 x 3.70 |
| En-Suite | 6'0" x 10'0" | - | 1.83 x 3.05 |
| Bedroom 2 | 13'4" x 10'0" | - | 4.06 x 3.05 |
| Bedroom 3 | 11'3" x 10'0" | - | 3.43 x 3.05 |
| Bedroom 4 | 9'0" x 8'10" | - | 2.74 x 2.70 |
| Bathroom | 10'3" x 5'7" | - | 3.12 x 1.70 |

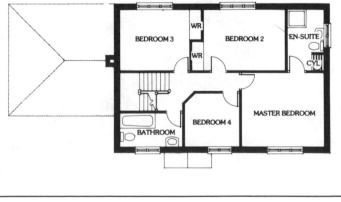

© *Design & Materials*

96

**Ref: 96153**

**140 sq.m.    1504 sq.ft.**

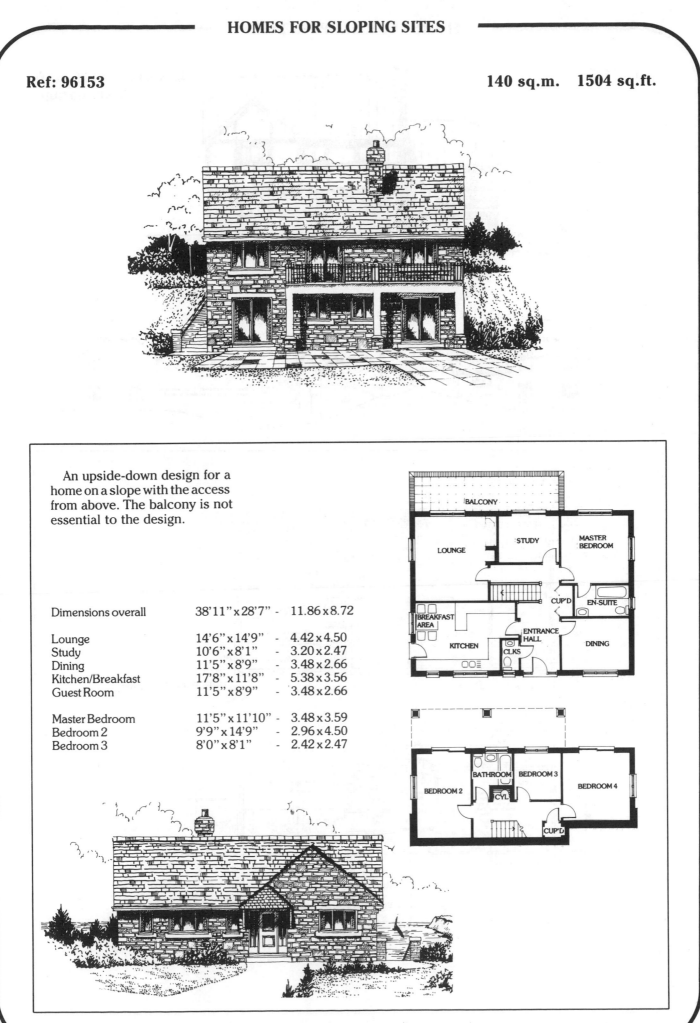

An upside-down design for a home on a slope with the access from above. The balcony is not essential to the design.

| | | |
|---|---|---|
| Dimensions overall | 38'11" x 28'7" | - 11.86 x 8.72 |
| Lounge | 14'6" x 14'9" | - 4.42 x 4.50 |
| Study | 10'6" x 8'1" | - 3.20 x 2.47 |
| Dining | 11'5" x 8'9" | - 3.48 x 2.66 |
| Kitchen/Breakfast | 17'8" x 11'8" | - 5.38 x 3.56 |
| Guest Room | 11'5" x 8'9" | - 3.48 x 2.66 |
| Master Bedroom | 11'5" x 11'10" | - 3.48 x 3.59 |
| Bedroom 2 | 9'9" x 14'9" | - 2.96 x 4.50 |
| Bedroom 3 | 8'0" x 8'1" | - 2.42 x 2.47 |

# HOMES FOR SLOPING SITES

**Ref: C425**

**165 sq.m.   1776 sq.ft.**
**(exc. garage)**

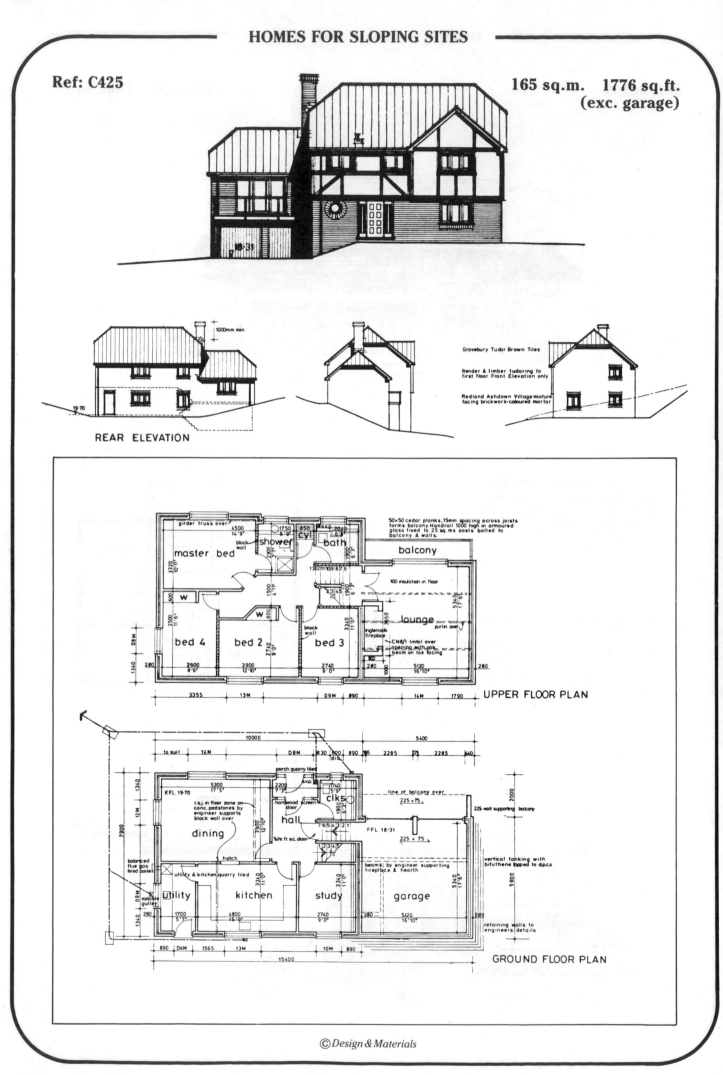

REAR ELEVATION

Grovebury Tudor Brown Tiles

Render & timber tudoring to
first floor Front Elevation only

Redland Ashdown Village mixture
facing brickwork-coloured mortar

UPPER FLOOR PLAN

GROUND FLOOR PLAN

*© Design & Materials*

**Ref: S536**

**140 sq.m. 1506 sq.ft.**
**(exc. garage)**

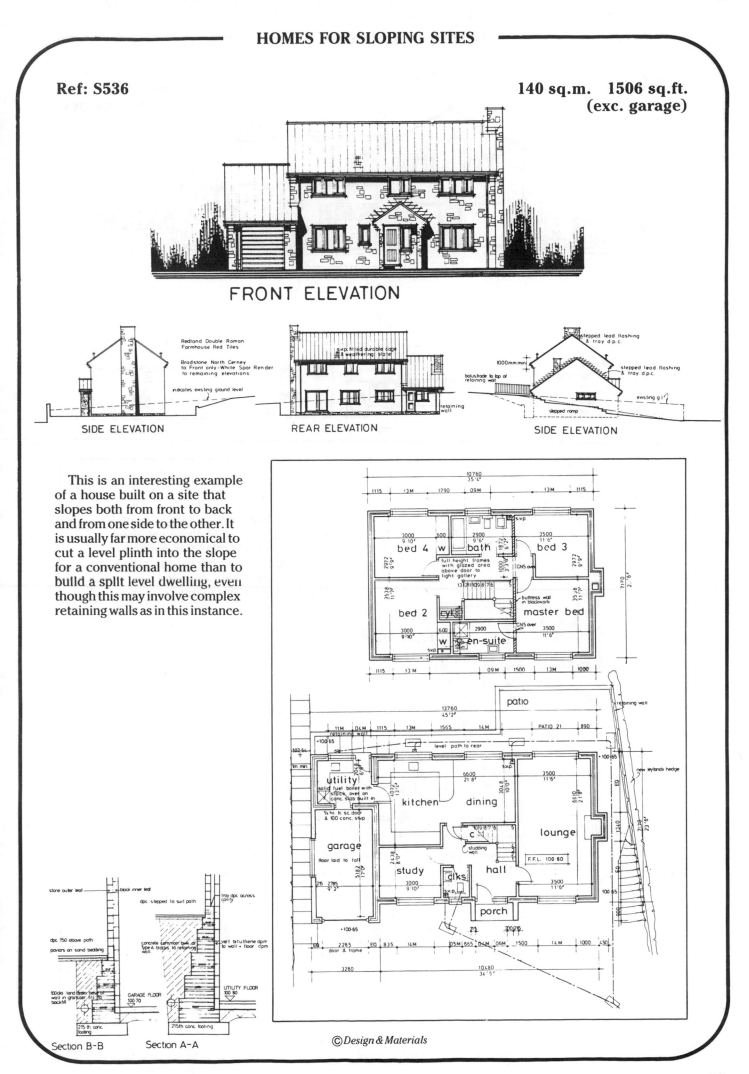

FRONT ELEVATION

SIDE ELEVATION

Redland Double Roman
Farmhouse Red Tiles

Bradstone North Cerney
to Front only - White Spar Render
to remaining elevations

indicates existing ground level

REAR ELEVATION

s.v.p. fitted durable cage
weathering slate

retaining wall

SIDE ELEVATION

stepped lead flashing
& tray d.p.c.

1000mm min

stepped lead flashing
& tray d.p.c.

balustrade to top of
retaining wall

existing gl

stepped ramp

This is an interesting example of a house built on a site that slopes both from front to back and from one side to the other. It is usually far more economical to cut a level plinth into the slope for a conventional home than to build a split level dwelling, even though this may involve complex retaining walls as in this instance.

bed 4   bath   bed 3

full height frames
with glazed area
above door to
light gallery

buttress wall
in blockwork

bed 2   cyl   master bed

en-suite

patio

retaining wall

level path to rear

utility

solid fuel boiler with
stack over on
conc. slab built in

½ hr. fr. sc. door
& 100 conc. step

kitchen   dining

lounge

F.F.L. 100 80

studding
wall

garage

floor laid to fall

study   hall

cloaks

porch

new leylandii hedge

Section B-B

stone outer leaf
block inner leaf

dpc stepped to suit path

tray dpc across
cavity

dpc 150 above path

pavors on sand bedding

concrete common brick or
Type A blocks to retaining
wall

vert bituthene dpm
to wall + floor dpm

100 dia. land drain behind
wall in granular fill to
backfill

GARAGE FLOOR
100 70

UTILITY FLOOR
100 80

215 th conc. footing

215th conc. footing

Section A-A

**Ref: W985**

**192 sq.m.   2066 sq.ft.**
**(inc. garage)**

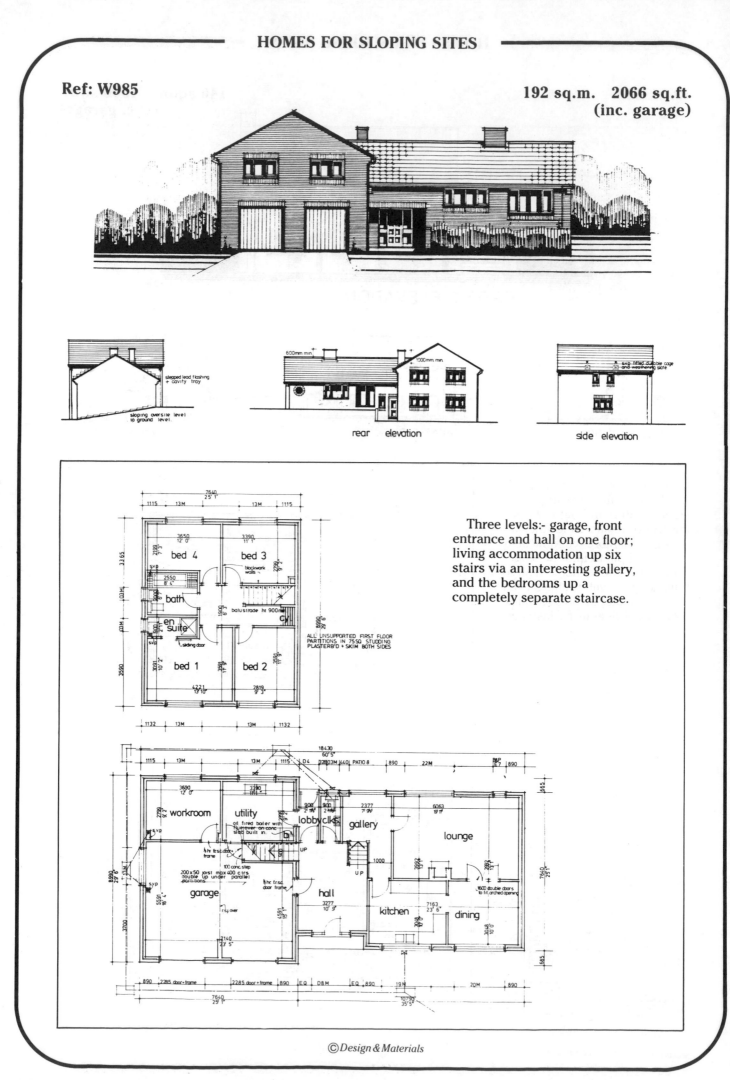

rear   elevation

side   elevation

Three levels:- garage, front
entrance and hall on one floor;
living accommodation up six
stairs via an interesting gallery,
and the bedrooms up a
completely separate staircase.

bed 4

bed 3

bath

en suite

bed 1

bed 2

ALL UNSUPPORTED FIRST FLOOR
PARTITIONS IN 75SQ STUDDING
PLASTERB'D + SKIM BOTH SIDES

workroom

utility

lobby

gallery

lounge

garage

hall

kitchen

dining

© *Design & Materials*

**Ref: W1294**

**150 sq.m. 1614 sq.ft.**
**(exc. garage)**

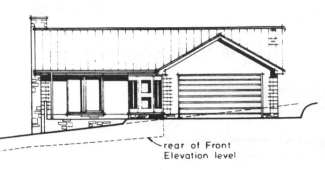

## FRONT ELEVATION

rear of Front
Elevation level

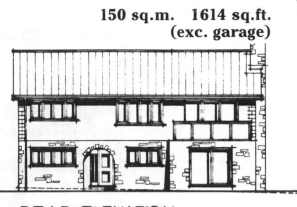

## REAR ELEVATION

Marley Modern grey roof tiles

render with
Bradstone quoins

existing garden level        drain

### SIDE ELEVATION

banking

### SIDE ELEVATION

This "upside-down" house for a sloping site has the garage, entrance and living accommodation on the upper floor with three bedrooms and two bathrooms below. If everything else suits, then this arrangement has many advantages, particularly if there are good views to be enjoyed from the lounge window. The disadvantage is that the front door is the only way out into the back garden, although in this case there is a balcony outside the patio windows in the lounge.

This sort of home is usually fairly expensive to build, but can be expected to have a high re-sale value. The plans are for it to be built on a massive stone plinth, with the superstructure in rendered blockwork with stone features. This sort of design always looks well in stone and render, but if built in brick it can be made to look just as attractive by building planting boxes against the exposed plinth brickwork.

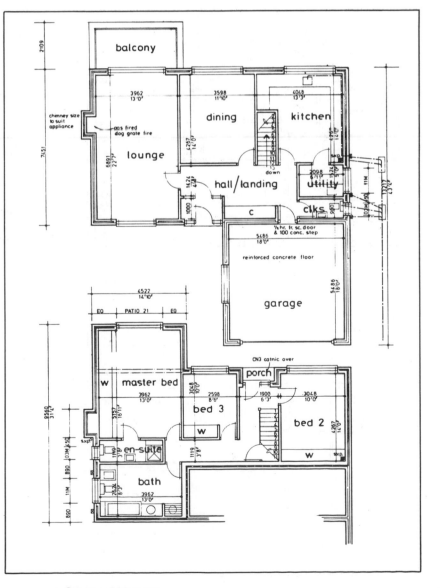

**Ref: W1063**

**170 sq.m.   1829 sq.ft.**
**(exc. garage)**

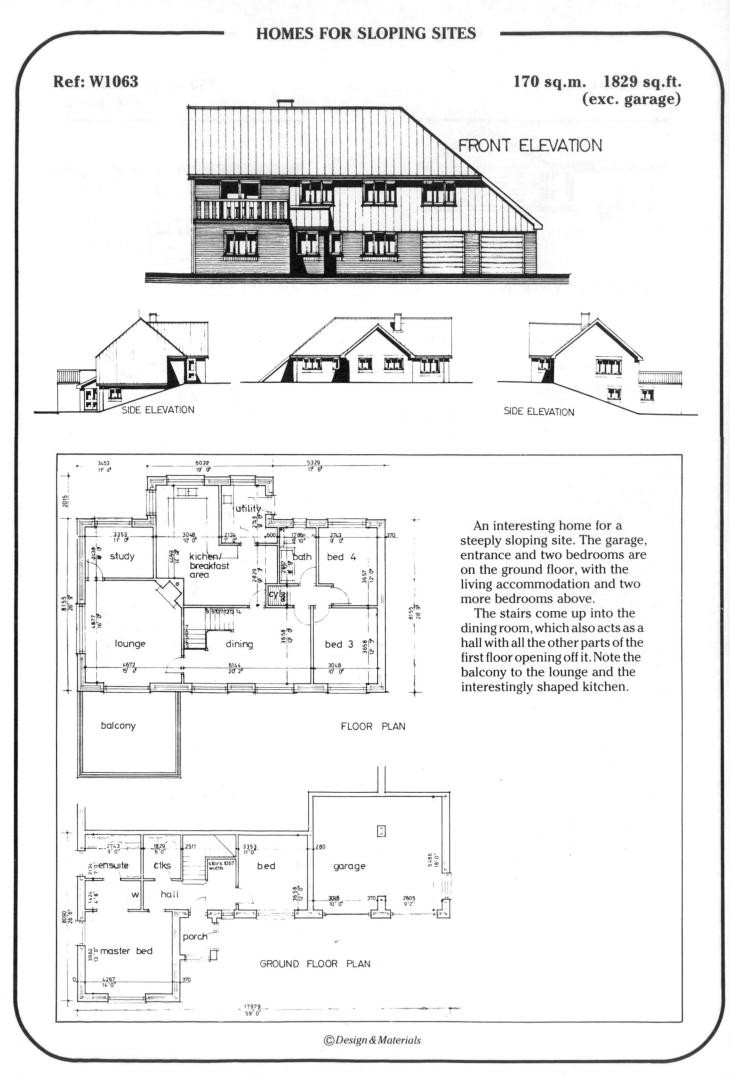

FRONT ELEVATION

SIDE ELEVATION

SIDE ELEVATION

An interesting home for a steeply sloping site. The garage, entrance and two bedrooms are on the ground floor, with the living accommodation and two more bedrooms above.

The stairs come up into the dining room, which also acts as a hall with all the other parts of the first floor opening off it. Note the balcony to the lounge and the interestingly shaped kitchen.

FLOOR PLAN

GROUND FLOOR PLAN

**Ref: P2780**

**173 sq.m.    1862 sq.ft.**
**(exc. garage)**

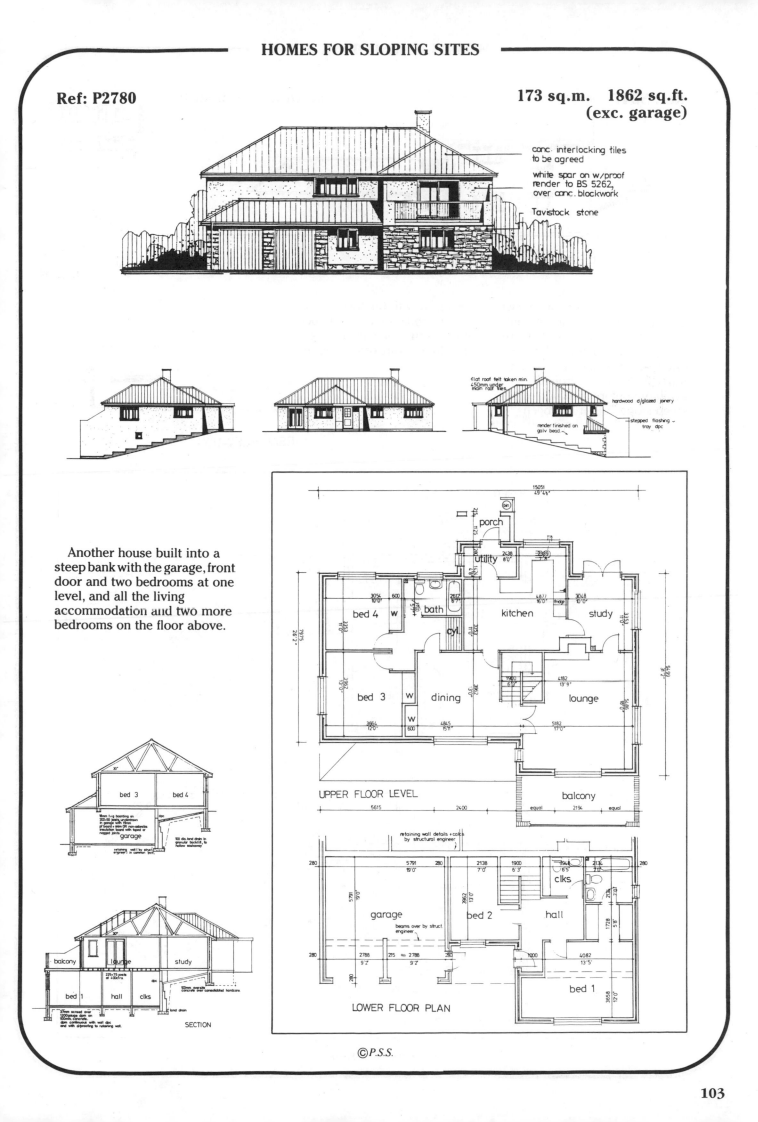

conc. interlocking tiles
to be agreed

white spar on w/proof
render to BS 5262,
over conc. blockwork

Tavistock stone

flat roof felt taken min.
450mm under
main roof tiles

hardwood d/glazed joinery

stepped flashing
tray dpc

render finished on
galv bead

Another house built into a steep bank with the garage, front door and two bedrooms at one level, and all the living accommodation and two more bedrooms on the floor above.

bed 3    bed 4

garage

18mm t+g boarding on
200×50 joists, underdrawn
in garage with 15mm
pl'board + skim or non-asbestos
insulation board with taped or
ragged joints

100 dia. land drain in
granular backfill, to
hollow soakaway

retaining wall by struct.
engineer in common bwk.

bed 4    w    bath    cyl.    kitchen    study

bed 3    w    dining    lounge

w

UPPER FLOOR LEVEL

porch

utility

balcony

retaining wall details + calcs
by structural engineer.

garage    bed 2    hall    clks

beams over by struct.
engineer

bed 1

LOWER FLOOR PLAN

balcony    lounge    study

bed 1    hall    clks

225×75 joists
at 400crs.

100mm oversite
concrete over consolidated hardcore.

37mm screed over
1200gauge dpm on
100mm concrete,
dpm continuous with wall dpc
and with dproofing to retaining wall.

land drain

SECTION

©P.S.S.

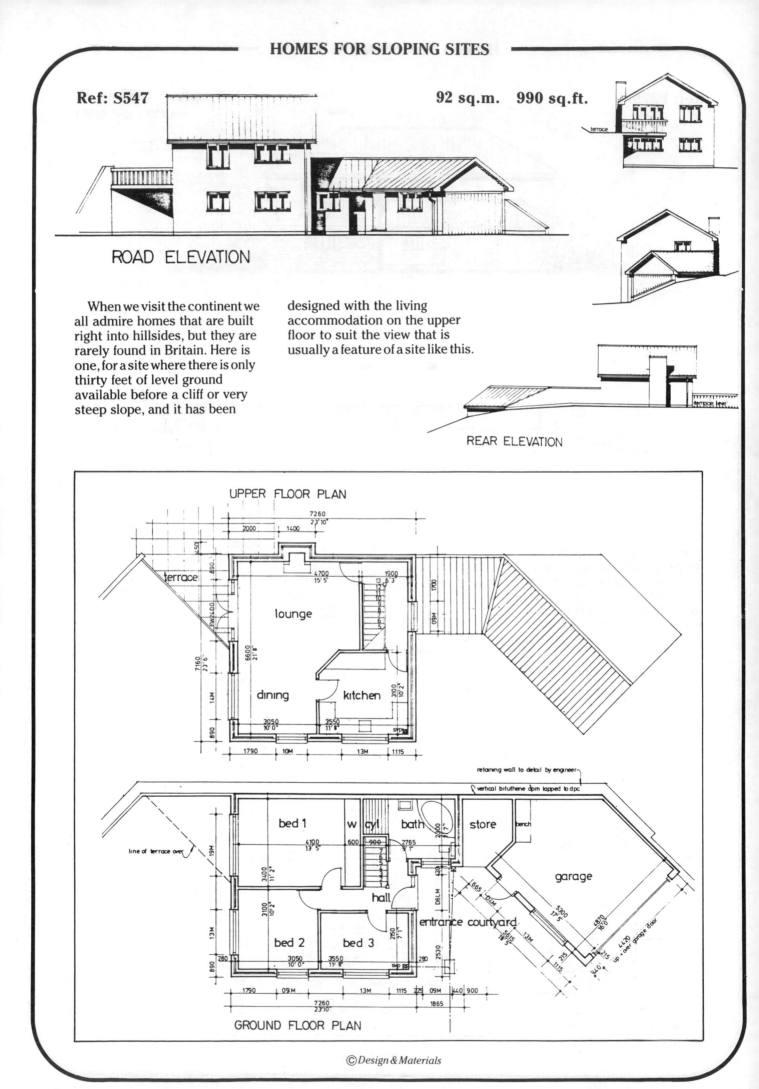

**Ref: S547**

**92 sq.m.   990 sq.ft.**

## ROAD ELEVATION

When we visit the continent we all admire homes that are built right into hillsides, but they are rarely found in Britain. Here is one, for a site where there is only thirty feet of level ground available before a cliff or very steep slope, and it has been designed with the living accommodation on the upper floor to suit the view that is usually a feature of a site like this.

## REAR ELEVATION

### UPPER FLOOR PLAN

terrace

lounge

dining        kitchen

### GROUND FLOOR PLAN

bed 1    w cyl    bath    store

hall

entrance courtyard

garage

line of terrace over

bed 2    bed 3

retaining wall to detail by engineer

vertical bituthene dpm lapped to dpc

© *Design & Materials*

# HOMES FOR SLOPING SITES

**Ref: W906**

**136 sq.m.   1463 sq.ft.**

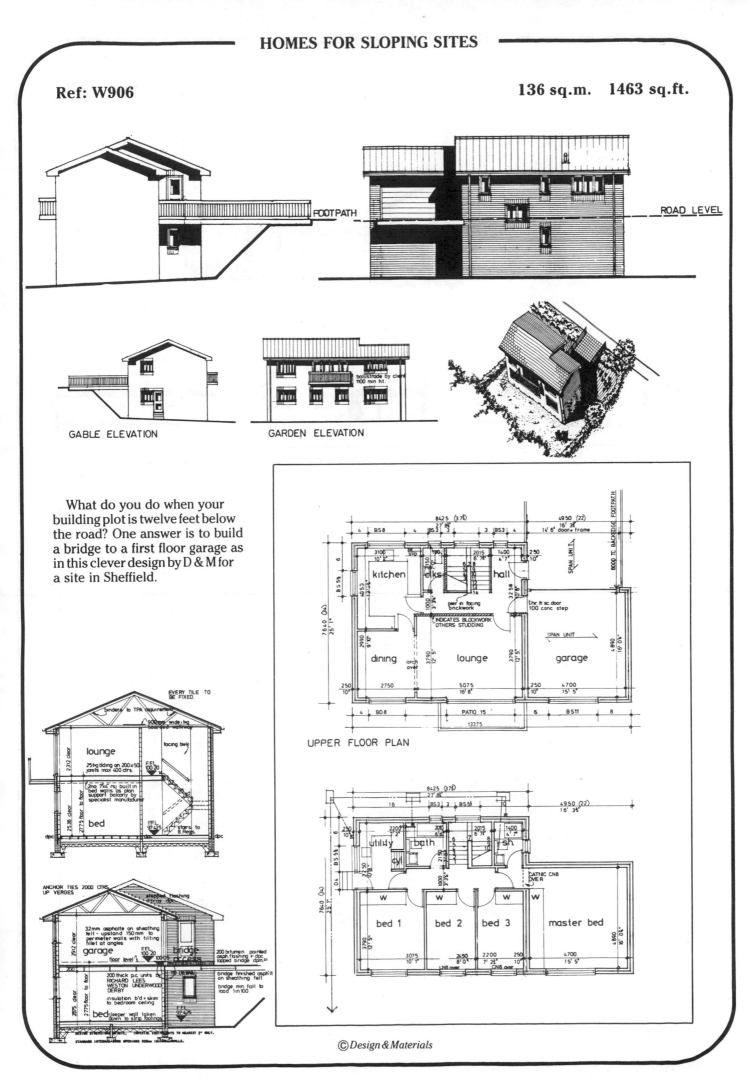

FOOTPATH

ROAD LEVEL

GABLE ELEVATION

GARDEN ELEVATION

balustrade by client
1100 min ht.

What do you do when your building plot is twelve feet below the road? One answer is to build a bridge to a first floor garage as in this clever design by D & M for a site in Sheffield.

UPPER FLOOR PLAN

kitchen    cloaks    hall

dining     lounge    garage

utility    bath    sh.

cyl

bed 1    bed 2    bed 3    master bed

EVERY TILE TO BE FIXED.

lounge

bed

garage    bridge

bed

**Ref: S483**

**138 sq.m.    1485 sq.ft.**

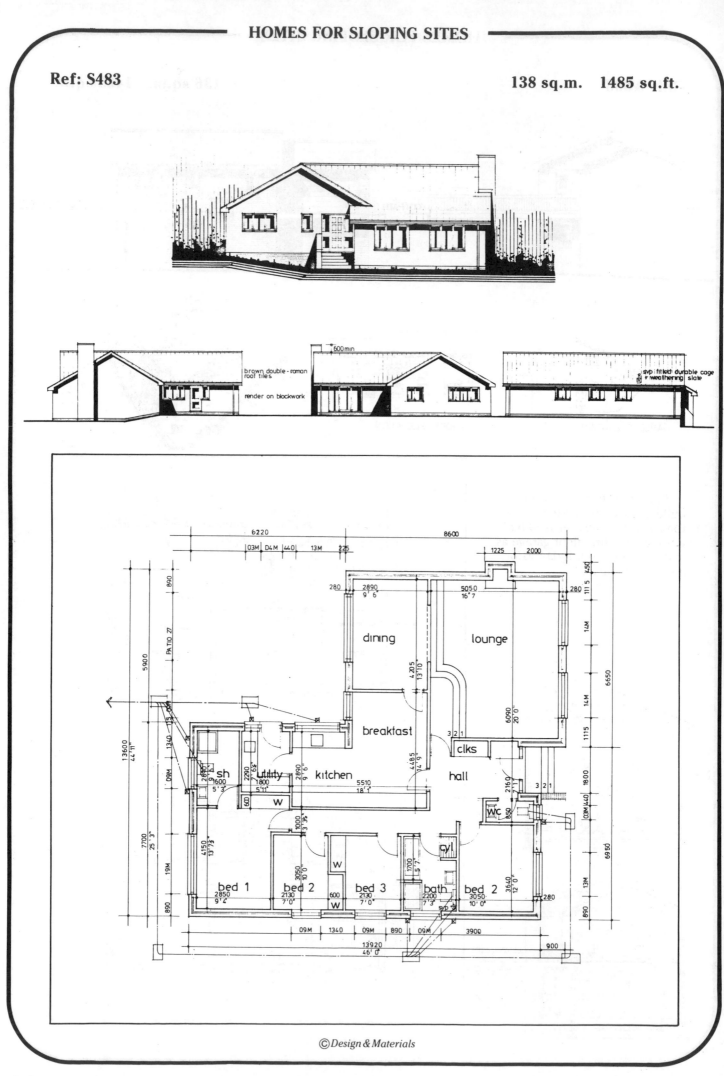

brown double - roman
roof tiles

render on blockwork

600 min

svp fitted durable cage
r weathering slate

**Ref: P2554**

**115 sq.m. 1237 sq.ft.**
**(exc. garage and store)**

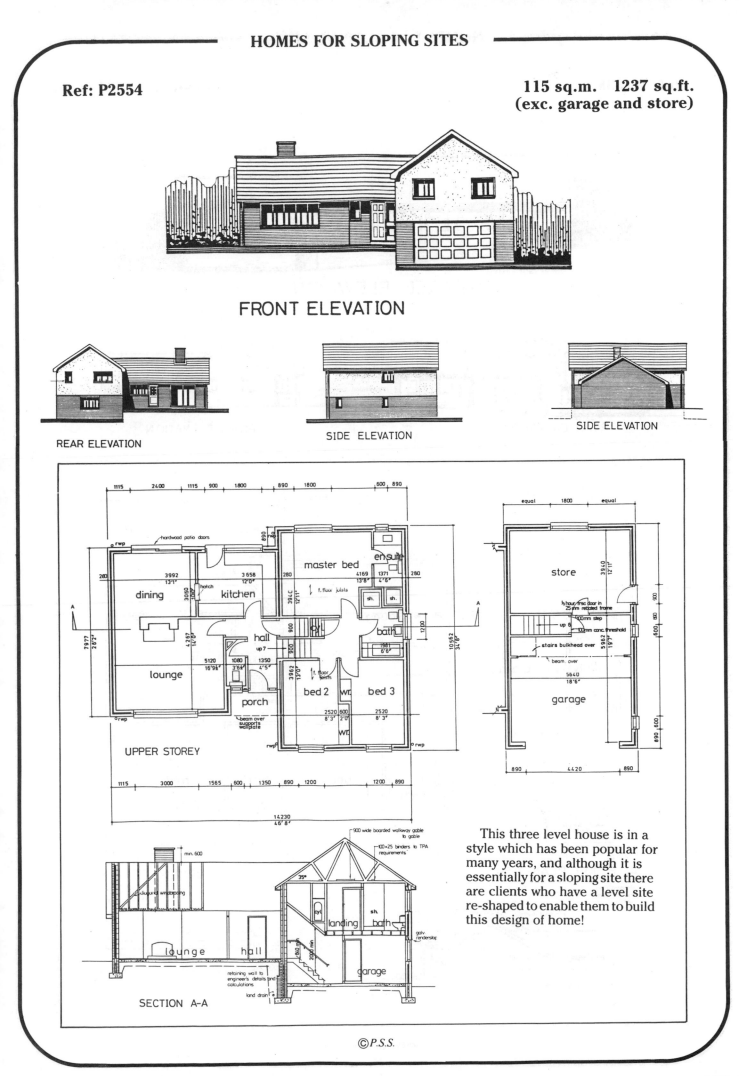

FRONT ELEVATION

REAR ELEVATION

SIDE ELEVATION

SIDE ELEVATION

UPPER STOREY

SECTION A-A

This three level house is in a style which has been popular for many years, and although it is essentially for a sloping site there are clients who have a level site re-shaped to enable them to build this design of home!

©P.S.S.

# HOMES FOR SLOPING SITES

**Ref: W1338**

**146 sq.m.  1571 sq.ft.**

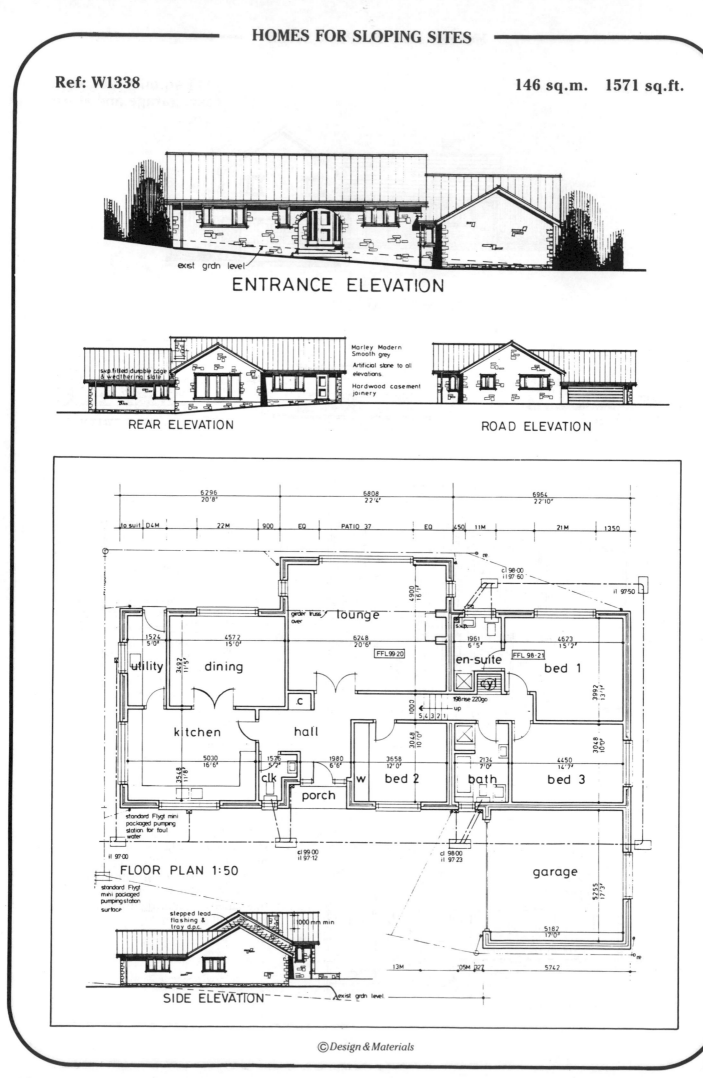

exist grdn level

## ENTRANCE ELEVATION

Marley Modern
Smooth grey

Artificial stone to all
elevations.

Hardwood casement
joinery

## REAR ELEVATION

## ROAD ELEVATION

FLOOR PLAN 1:50

SIDE ELEVATION

**Ref: W1076**

**109 sq.m.   1173 sq.ft.**

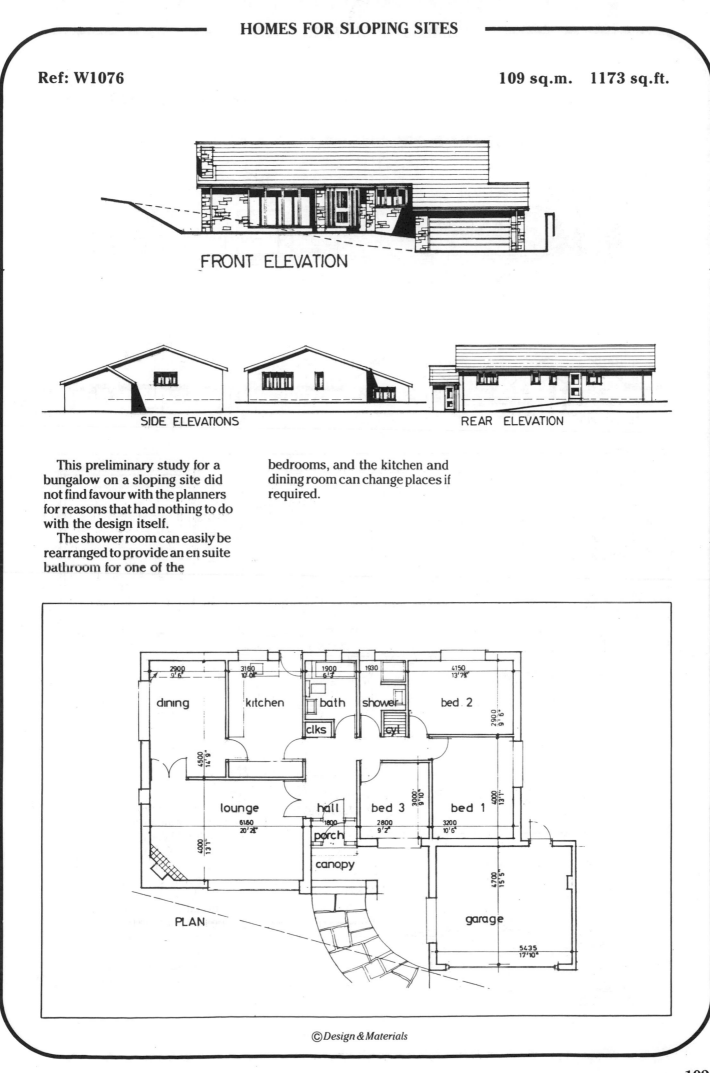

FRONT ELEVATION

SIDE ELEVATIONS

REAR ELEVATION

This preliminary study for a bungalow on a sloping site did not find favour with the planners for reasons that had nothing to do with the design itself.

The shower room can easily be rearranged to provide an en suite bathroom for one of the bedrooms, and the kitchen and dining room can change places if required.

PLAN

**Ref: W1181**

**163 sq.m.   1745 sq.ft.**
**(exc. garage and basement)**

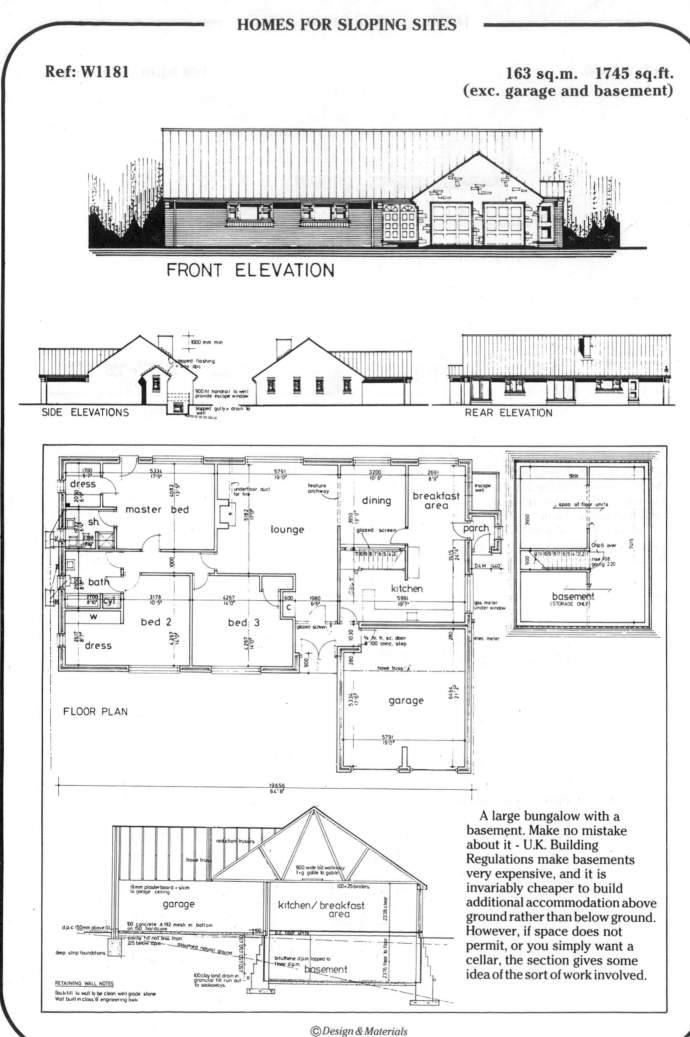

FRONT ELEVATION

SIDE ELEVATIONS

REAR ELEVATION

FLOOR PLAN

A large bungalow with a basement. Make no mistake about it - U.K. Building Regulations make basements very expensive, and it is invariably cheaper to build additional accommodation above ground rather than below ground. However, if space does not permit, or you simply want a cellar, the section gives some idea of the sort of work involved.

© *Design & Materials*

**Ref: S538**

**182 sq.m.    1959 sq.ft.**

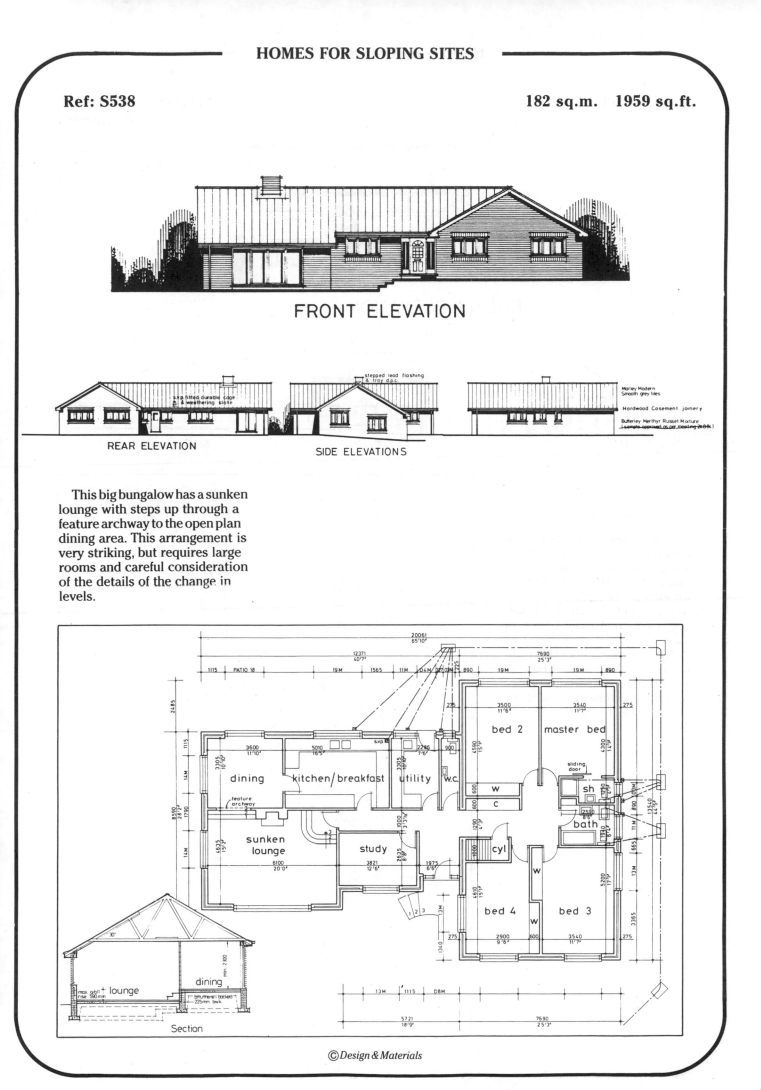

## FRONT ELEVATION

REAR ELEVATION

SIDE ELEVATIONS

This big bungalow has a sunken lounge with steps up through a feature archway to the open plan dining area. This arrangement is very striking, but requires large rooms and careful consideration of the details of the change in levels.

**Ref: W1212**

**133 sq.m.  1431 sq.ft.**
**(exc. garage)**

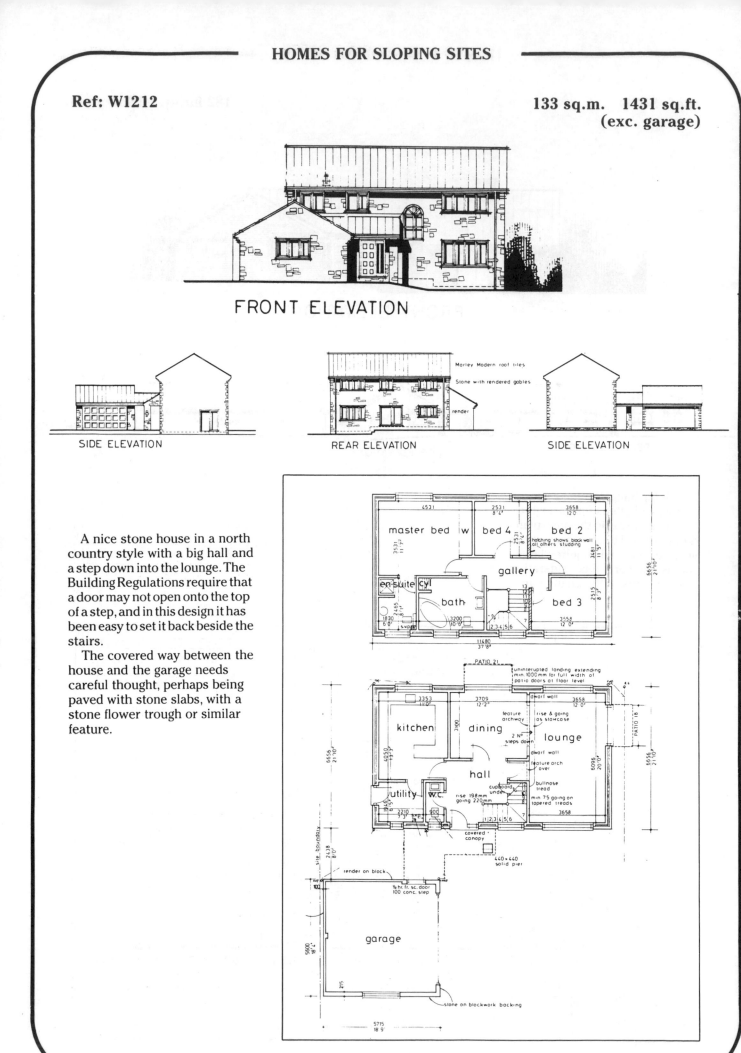

FRONT ELEVATION

SIDE ELEVATION

REAR ELEVATION

SIDE ELEVATION

Marley Modern roof tiles

Stone with rendered gables

render

A nice stone house in a north country style with a big hall and a step down into the lounge. The Building Regulations require that a door may not open onto the top of a step, and in this design it has been easy to set it back beside the stairs.

The covered way between the house and the garage needs careful thought, perhaps being paved with stone slabs, with a stone flower trough or similar feature.

© Design & Materials

**Ref: W1325**

**164 sq.m. 1765 sq.ft.**
**(exc. garage)**

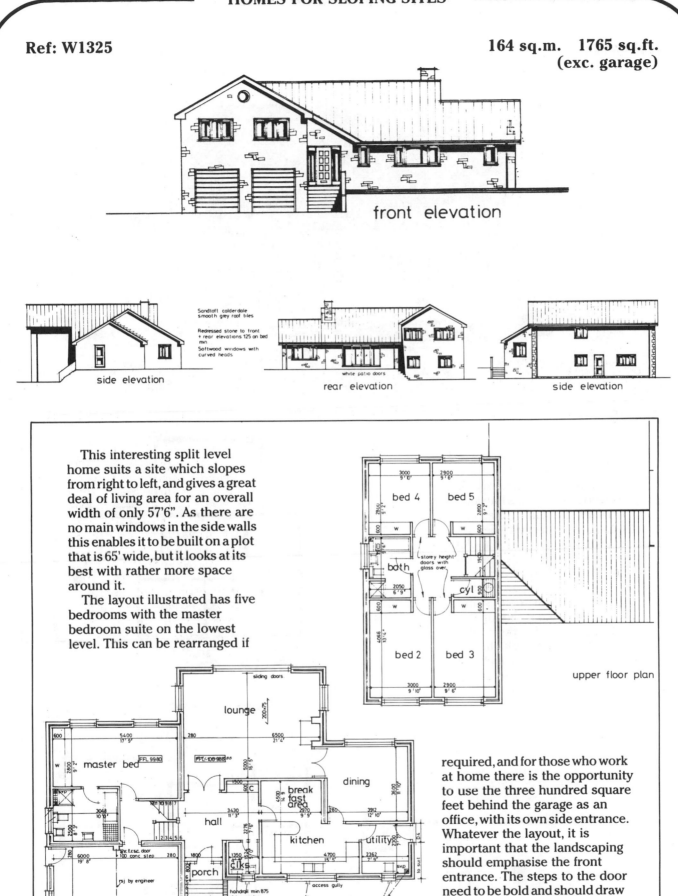

front elevation

side elevation

Sandtoft calderdale
smooth grey roof tiles

Redressed stone to front
+ rear elevations 125 on bed
min

Softwood windows with
curved heads

white patio doors

rear elevation

side elevation

This interesting split level home suits a site which slopes from right to left, and gives a great deal of living area for an overall width of only 57'6". As there are no main windows in the side walls this enables it to be built on a plot that is 65' wide, but it looks at its best with rather more space around it.

The layout illustrated has five bedrooms with the master bedroom suite on the lowest level. This can be rearranged if

bed 4

bed 5

bath

cyl

bed 2

bed 3

upper floor plan

required, and for those who work at home there is the opportunity to use the three hundred square feet behind the garage as an office, with its own side entrance. Whatever the layout, it is important that the landscaping should emphasise the front entrance. The steps to the door need to be bold and should draw attention to themselves, and the layout of the garden at the front should be designed with this as the main objective.

lounge

master bed

dining

break fast area

hall

kitchen

utility

porch

garage

ground floor plan

**Ref: 96155**

**394 sq.m.   4238 sq.ft.**

A huge home to suit a one-in-five slope on a large site. As with most designs for sloping sites which are illustrated in this book, it is unlikely to be appropriate to a specific plot anywhere else but it is a good source of design idea.

There are two parts to the ground floor: the open plan area, and the conventional lounge and dining room. To move from one area to the other involves passing through two doors and the hall: no doubt a valuable feature when some family members value peace and quiet more than others.

BEDROOM 2
20'10" x 14'1"

EN-SUITE    C    BATHROOM    EN-SUITE

GALLERY    WR    WR

MASTER BEDROOM
12'8" x 15'0"    WR    BEDROOM 3
12'6" x 10'9"    BEDROOM 4/ GUEST SUITE
16'0" x 16'3" (max)

WR

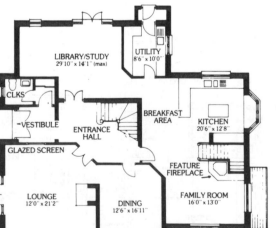

LIBRARY/STUDY
29'10" x 14'1" (max)    UTILITY
8'6" x 10'0"

CLKS

VESTIBULE    BREAKFAST AREA    KITCHEN
20'6" x 12'8"

ENTRANCE HALL

GLAZED SCREEN    FEATURE FIREPLACE

TRIPLE GARAGE
31'1" x 21'2" (max)    PHYSIO ROOM
16'0" x 16'4" (max)    LOUNGE
12'0" x 21'2"    DINING
12'6" x 16'11"    FAMILY ROOM
16'0" x 13'0"

# HOMES FOR SLOPING SITES

**Ref: S540**

**192 sq.m.   2006 sq.ft.**
**(exc. garage and workshop)**

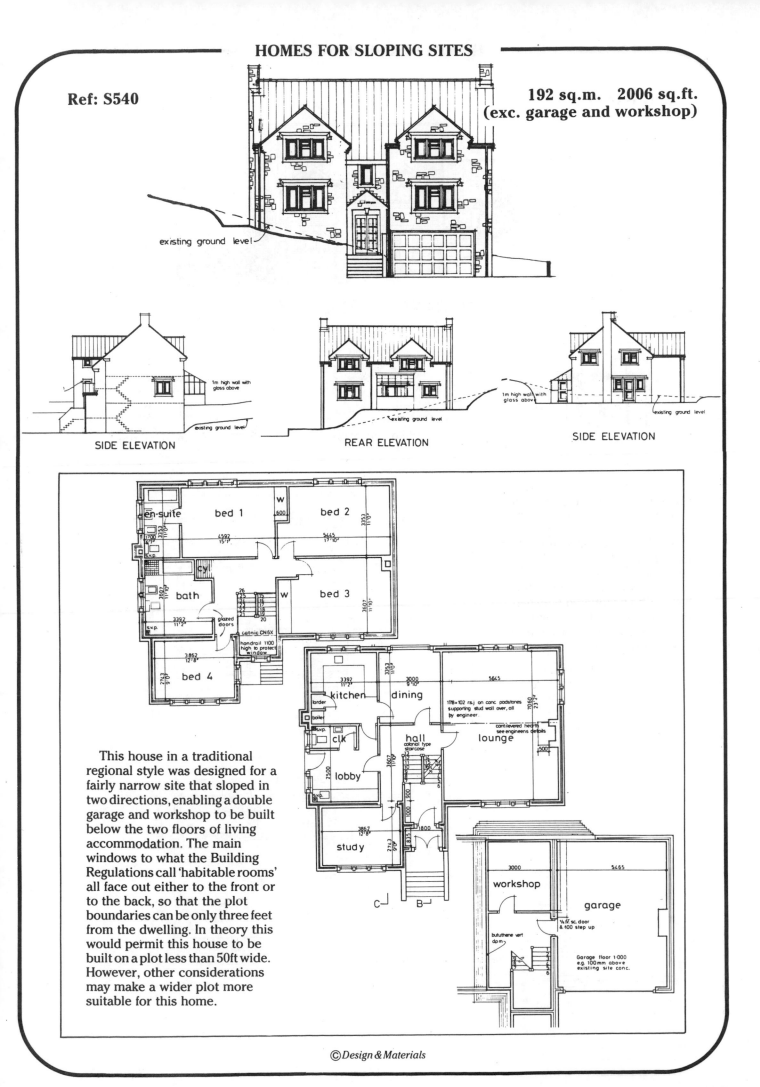

existing ground level

SIDE ELEVATION

REAR ELEVATION

SIDE ELEVATION

This house in a traditional regional style was designed for a fairly narrow site that sloped in two directions, enabling a double garage and workshop to be built below the two floors of living accommodation. The main windows to what the Building Regulations call 'habitable rooms' all face out either to the front or to the back, so that the plot boundaries can be only three feet from the dwelling. In theory this would permit this house to be built on a plot less than 50ft wide. However, other considerations may make a wider plot more suitable for this home.

**Ref: W1125**

**121 sq.m.   1302 sq.ft.**

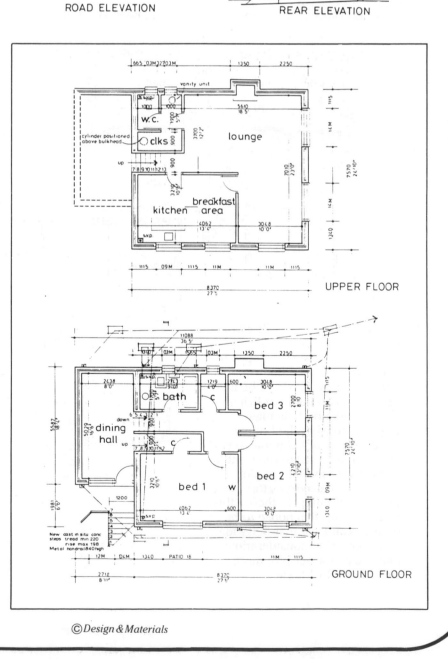

path level

## ENTRANCE   ELEVATION

SIDE ELEVATION

stepped lead flashing
& tray d.p.c.

ROAD ELEVATION

path level

REAR ELEVATION

Another house with the living accommodation on the first floor and the bedrooms below. In this instance there is a dining hall at a level half way between the two main floors of the home. This suits the sloping site very well, but it does mean that five steps have to be negotiated between the kitchen and the dining table.

Lots of cupboard space in this interesting house.

vanity unit

w.c.

cylinder positioned
above bulkhead

clks

lounge

up

kitchen

breakfast
area

**UPPER FLOOR**

bath

c

bed 3

dining
hall

up

down

c

bed 1

w

bed 2

New cast in situ conc
steps tread min 220
rise max 198
Metal handrail 840 high

PATIO

**GROUND FLOOR**

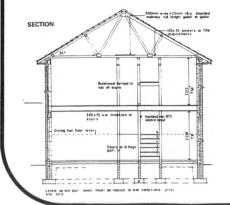

**SECTION**

900mm wide x 25mm t&g  boarded
walkway full length gable to gable

100x25 binders to T.R.A
requirements

Bulkhead formed to
top of stairs

200x75 s.w. trimmers to
stairs

handrail min 875
above tread

Dining hall floor level

Stairs to B Regs
part I

Levels as site plan  levels must be related to site conditions  after
site strip

*©Design & Materials*

**Ref: 96116**

**217 sq.m.    2336 sq.ft.**

A house of 2336 sq. ft. which has a large study with adjacent cloakroom and easy access to the front door, suiting the requirements of someone who works from home. The garage which is situated under the building to take advantage of the slope gives the property an uncompromisingly urban look, and it will be most at home on an infil site in a street of Victorian or Edwardian homes.

Note how the railings to the balcony leading from the lounge are balanced by a similar run of railings to the right of the front door. This balustrading will be a key feature in the appearance of the home and should be chosen with great care. The garage door design will also require careful consideration.

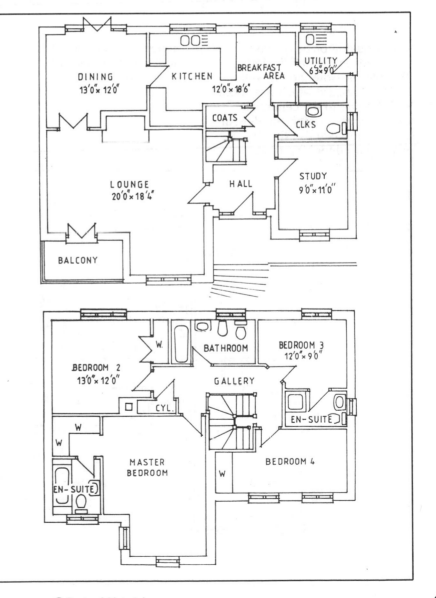

© Design & Materials

**Ref: S328**

**134 sq.m.   1442 sq.ft.**

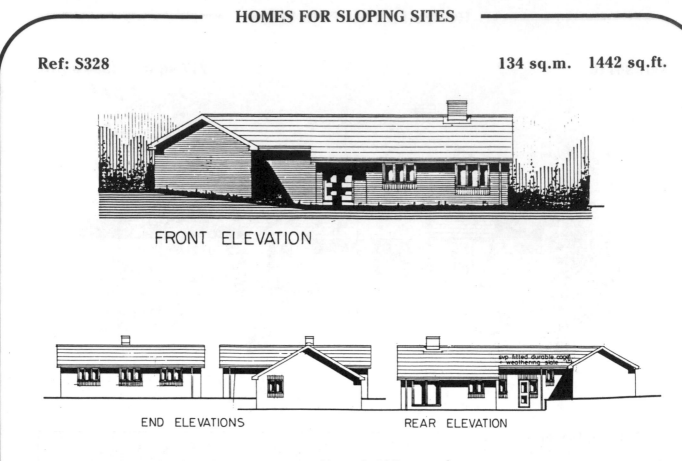

FRONT ELEVATION

END ELEVATIONS          REAR ELEVATION

A bungalow on two levels with five steps in the hall linking the two halves. Note the big walk-in airing cupboard which has room for shelving to the ceiling all around the hot water cylinder. An airing cupboard like this is usually used for long term storage of household linen, and so it saves storage space elsewhere.

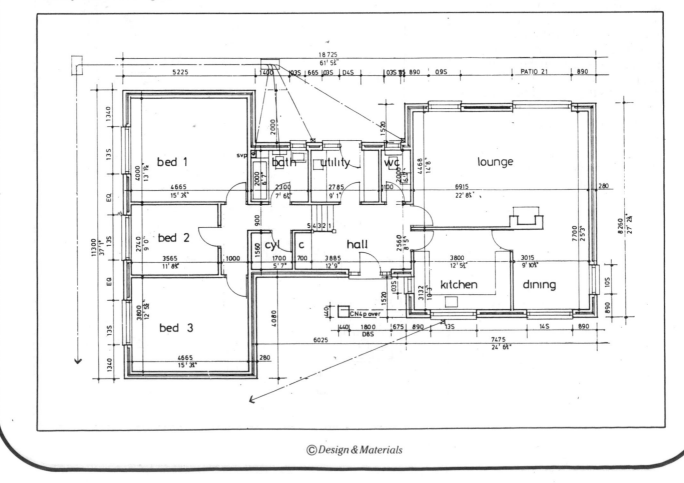

© Design & Materials

**Ref: W1311**

**162 sq.m.   1743 sq.ft.
(exc. garage)**

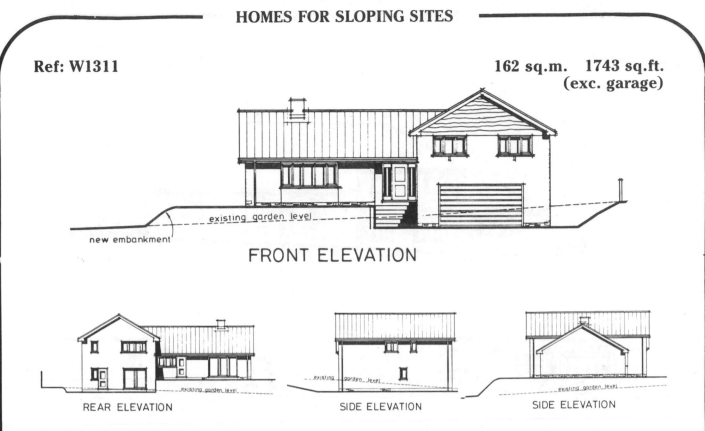

FRONT ELEVATION

*existing garden level*

*new embankment*

REAR ELEVATION

SIDE ELEVATION

SIDE ELEVATION

A split level home is a very popular way of building on a site which slopes from one side to the other, and this interesting house with the rooms on three different levels is one of the most effective ways of arranging a split level layout. Within the general arrangement the different rooms can be changed around to suit family needs, and because there are only six steps between any two levels it has much of the feel of a bungalow, which is popular with the elderly.

The study and utility room shewn in this layout can be rearranged to make another bedroom suite, and this is a convenient way of providing a granny flat.

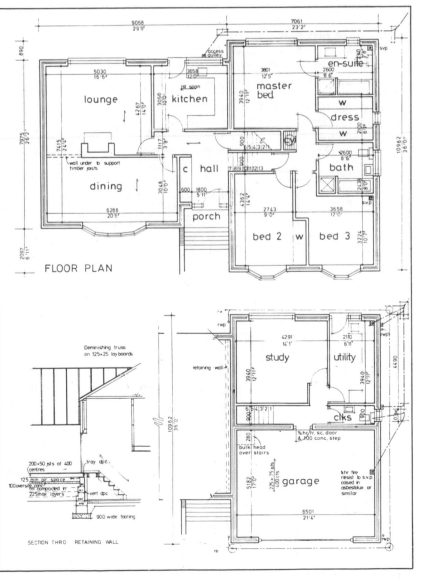

FLOOR PLAN

SECTION THRO RETAINING WALL

**Ref: W1081**

**232 sq.m.    2497 sq.ft.**

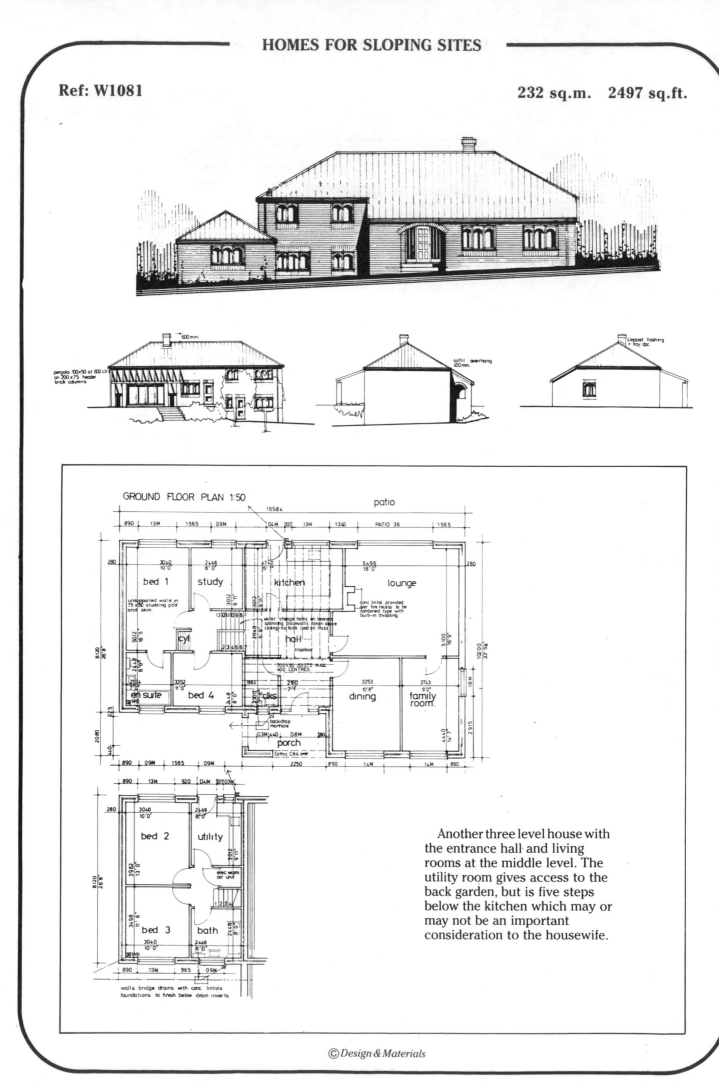

Another three level house with the entrance hall and living rooms at the middle level. The utility room gives access to the back garden, but is five steps below the kitchen which may or may not be an important consideration to the housewife.

**Ref: W1312A**

**147 sq.m.    1582 sq.ft.**

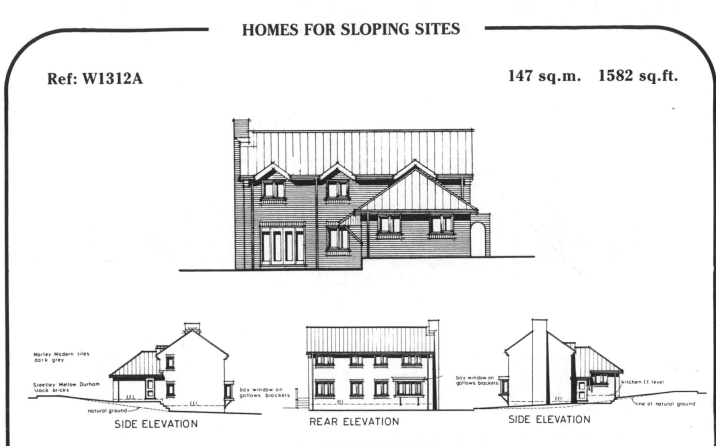

Marley Modern tiles
dark grey

Steetley Mellow Durham
stock bricks

natural ground

bay window on
gallows brackets

SIDE ELEVATION

REAR ELEVATION

bay window on
gallows brackets

kitchen f.f level

line of natural ground

SIDE ELEVATION

A house for a plot that falls away from the road, and where the overall depth to the main building had to be less than 20 feet. The french windows to the lounge which face the road were shielded from the road by a high boundary wall, but if this had not been the case it is likely that this feature would have attracted adverse comment from planners. Note the steps up into the kitchen to make use of the slope.

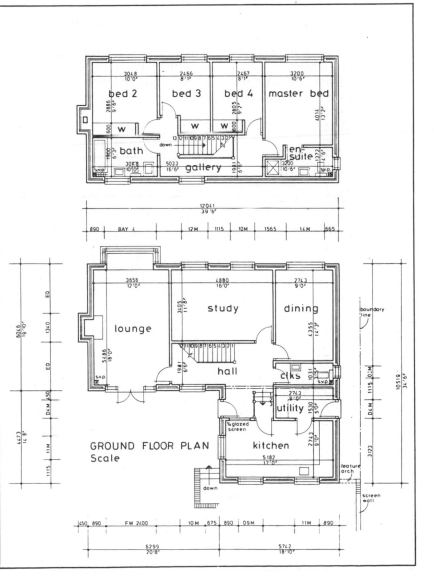

bed 2
bed 3
bed 4
master bed

bath
gallery
en-suite

GROUND FLOOR PLAN
Scale

lounge
study
dining
hall
clks
utility
kitchen

boundary line

½ glazed screen

feature arch

screen wall

**Ref: W1234**

**129 sq.m.   1388 sq.ft.**

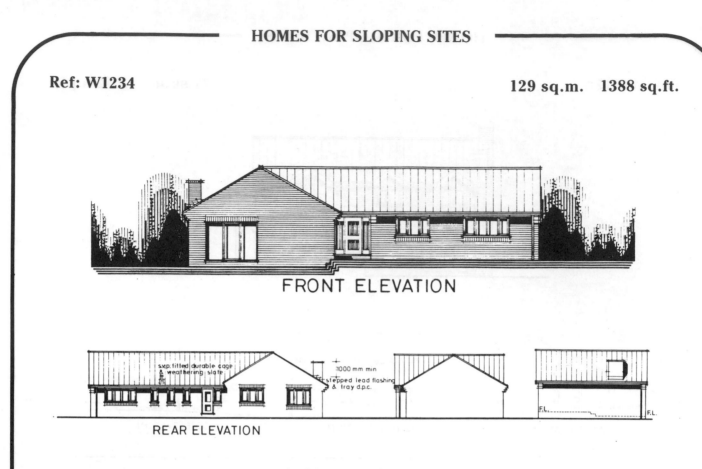

FRONT ELEVATION

REAR ELEVATION

This bungalow with its attractive sunken lounge was originally designed for a site in Leicestershire where the views were to the front and back, so there are no side windows. The inset detail shews what is involved in dropping a floor level as in this case, and this is something that can only be arranged at the very start of the project, and cannot be dealt with as an afterthought.

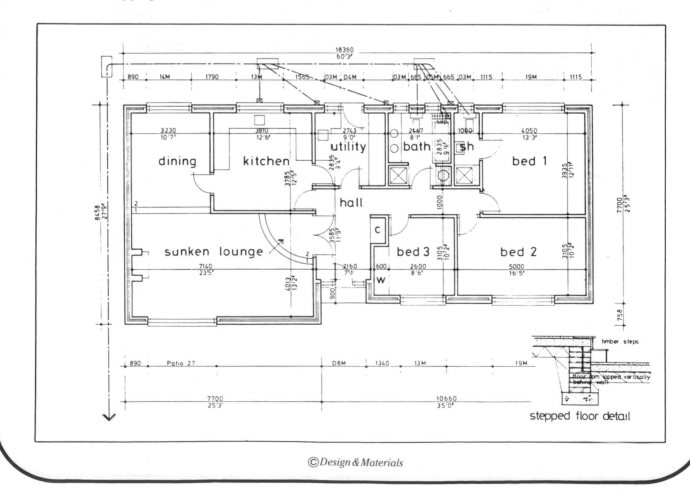

stepped floor detail

**Ref: W1351**

**106 sq.m.   1141 sq.ft.**

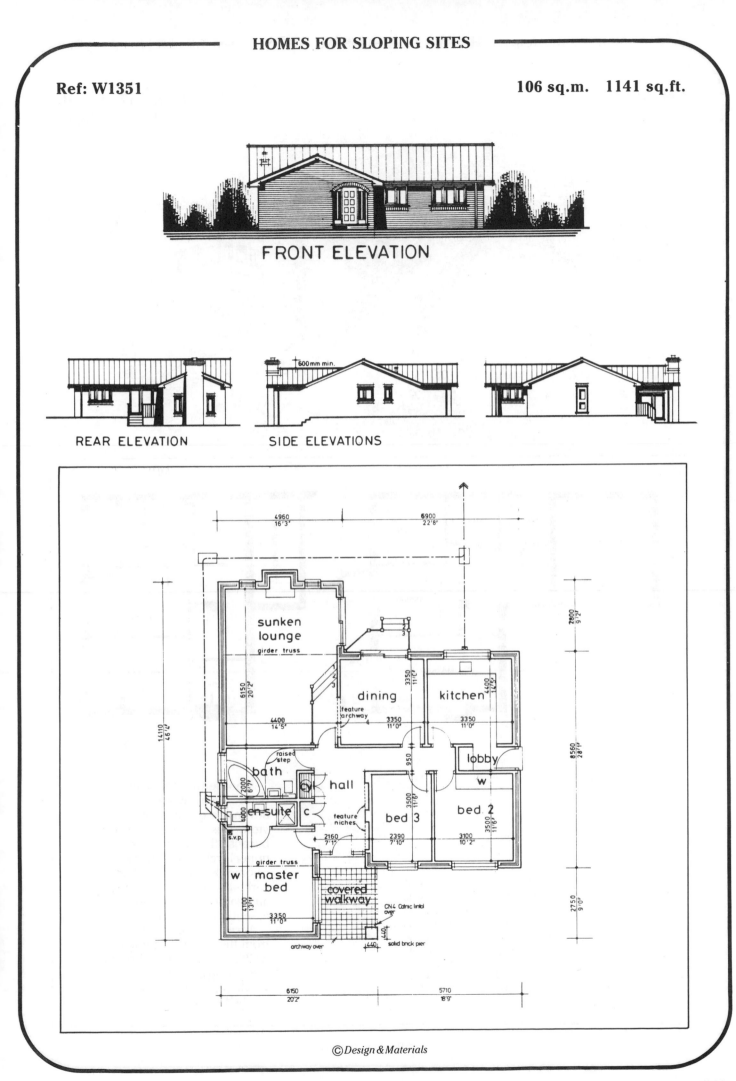

FRONT ELEVATION

REAR ELEVATION

SIDE ELEVATIONS

**Ref: 96137**

**160 sq.m.   1710 sq.ft.**
**(exc. garage)**

| | | |
|---|---|---|
| Dimensions overall | 37'10" x 54'9" | 11.52 x 16.69 |
| Lounge | 12'0" x 21'0" | 3.65 x 6.40 |
| Dining | 12'0" x 11'0" | 3.65 x 3.35 |
| Kitchen | 11'0" x 12'0" | 3.35 x 3.65 |
| Study | 7'9" x 8'8" | 2.35 x 2.64 |
| Utility | 7'9" x 8'0" | 2.35 x 2.43 |
| Master Bed | 12'0" x 17'0" | 3.65 x 5.18 |
| Bed 2 | 12'0" x 17'0" | 3.65 x 5.18 |
| Bed 3 | 11'0" x 9'0" | 3.35 x 2.74 |
| Bed 4 | 11'0" x 8'8" | 3.35 x 2.64 |

A house with the bedrooms below the living area to take advantage of a magnificent view. This also made sense because the access was at the upper level. Lots of character in a home like this, remember that carefully designed landscaping and garden features are essential in this sort of situation.

Access to the dining room from the lounge is gained by walking round the hall or along the balcony. Or perhaps you would prefer a doorway linking the two rooms.

# *Extendable Homes*

Building your own home provides you with the opportunity to have a house or bungalow that can be extended at a later date, and this is an opportunity which is often overlooked. You can extend a house at ground level, by building out from the existing structure, or by putting rooms into a roof void. Both approaches are more easily arranged if the extension has been considered at project planning stage. However, this will depend to a large extent on the planning acts. You have alternatives.

If you wish you can apply for planning consent for the building in its ultimate state, with your plans showing the home after you have extended the first interim version. This is quite normal, and building only the first stage and living in it for some years before giving it the final shape is unlikely to attract adverse comment if stage one looks complete and is not an eyesore. This possibility is something to be discussed with the expert who is handling your planning application.

The alternative is to obtain planning consent for the original structure and then either obtain a subsequent planning consent to extend it when you wish to do so, or else to use the Permitted Development provisions of the Planning Acts which may sanction the extensions that you have in mind. There are a lot of planning rules about extensions, and excellent informative booklets about them are available at town halls. Even if you have only the vaguest interest in possibly extending your home in the future, or in building it so that it can be extended if required just to enhance its value, these booklets are essential reading.

If you want to be able to put rooms in the roof in the future you must

* construct the roof with purlins or attic trusses
* upgrade the floor/ceiling joists to suit your ambitions
* leave space in your room layout for the future stairway
* provide for the extension when designing and installing the heating and electrical installation
* and consider how you will provide a statutory level of insulation to the new rooms

You do not have to understand all of this, merely remember to discuss these matters with whoever is drawing your plans.

If you wish to provide for an extension that will need its own foundations it is well worth considering building them at the same time as those for stage one of the building. Once they are in place they can be covered up or used as a base for a patio, and when you build on them at a later date there will be no risk of differential movement between the two parts of the building. Similarly there are many advantages in installing both foul and surface water drains in advance of the time that they will be required. Landscaping, and particularly tree planting should be arranged with an eye on the long term future.

Other details are cheap to arrange and will make the second stage of the building work a good deal easier. Lintels can be built into walls to suit future openings, provision made for the extension when arranging piping for plumbing and central heating, and appropriately sized boilers and fuse boards installed for the future. If unusual materials are to be used, such as reclaimed tiles, a special type of window or a particular style of parquet flooring, you may decide to buy the materials for the extension in advance and store them away ready for their eventual use.

At least half of the designs in this book can be modified for future extensions: the designs in this particular section were drawn with the specific intention of being extended in the future.

**Ref: 96222**

**110 sq.m.   1185 sq.ft.**

A bungalow with potential for two bedrooms and a bathroom in the roof with 1100 sq.ft. of conventional three bedroom accommodation on the ground floor. The first floor is shown to be reached with a spiral staircase in a corner of the lounge, but various alternatives to this are available.

| Dimensions overall | 50'8" x 26'1" | 15.44 x 7.96 |
|---|---|---|
| Lounge | 19'11" x 12'0" | 6.07 x 3.65 |
| Kitchen/Dining | 19'11" x 12'0" | 6.07 x 3.65 |
| Bed 1 | 15'0" x 12'0" | 4.57 x 3.65 |
| Bed 2 | 12'0" x 12'0" | 3.65 x 3.65 |
| Bed 3 | 12'0" x 8'8" | 3.65 x 2.65 |

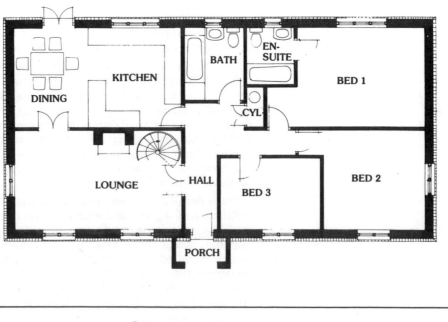

**Ref: 96170**

**197 sq.m.    2122 sq.ft.**

Space for a room in the roof is usually a requirement for a bungalow, but it is perfectly practicable to design a two storey house with provision for a third floor to be built at a later date.

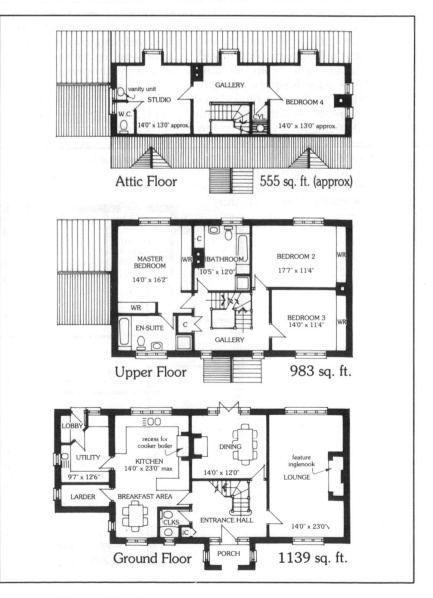

**Attic Floor**

vanity unit
STUDIO
W.C.
14'0" x 13'0" approx.
GALLERY
CYL
BEDROOM 4
14'0" x 13'0" approx.

**Attic Floor**            **555 sq. ft. (approx)**

MASTER BEDROOM
14'0" x 16'2"
WR
EN-SUITE
C
BATHROOM
10'5" x 12'0"
GALLERY
BEDROOM 2
17'7" x 11'4"
WR
BEDROOM 3
14'0" x 11'4"
WR

**Upper Floor**            **983 sq. ft.**

LOBBY
UTILITY
9'7" x 12'6"
LARDER
recess for cooker boiler
KITCHEN
14'0" x 23'0" max
BREAKFAST AREA
CLKS
C
DINING
14'0" x 12'0"
ENTRANCE HALL
PORCH
feature inglenook
LOUNGE
14'0" x 23'0"

**Ground Floor**          **1139 sq. ft.**

**Ref: 96122**

**171 sq.m.    1842 sq.ft.**

A large bungalow for a large or secluded site where views from the lounge can be enjoyed from a floor to ceiling window. This window is emphasised as a feature by the matching glazed screen between the lounge and hall, giving a very open feel to the principal room. There is a door to the corridor from the hall which leads to the bedrooms, providing a measure of security. This is a feature which is becoming very popular in large bungalows where all the bedrooms are grouped at one end of the property.

The design provides room for a future stairway to the roof void, where there is room for three further bedrooms and two bathrooms, making this potentially a very large home.

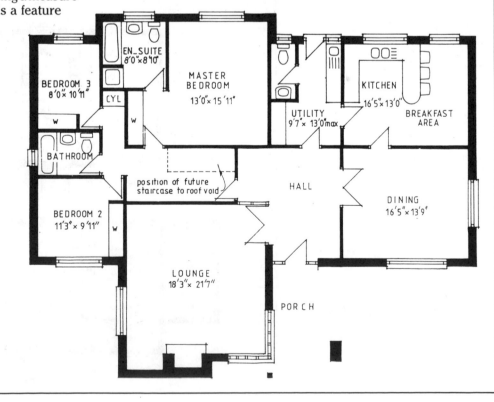

**Ref: 96131**

**116 sq.m.  1255 sq.ft.**

There are a lot of interesting features to this bungalow, among them the garage/car port arrangement which has its roofline broken by an Oxford cupola with a weathervane, the porch to the front door, and the brick features in the rendered walls. Internally the layout had to meet a requirement for rooms in the roof at a later date, and the large hall is designed for the stairway that will be installed in due course.

The open plan lounge/dining area/kitchen is now unusual, although many homes were built like this in the 60's. Most of them subsequently had walls built to provide separate rooms, so if you like open plan living it is important to consider how easily division walls could be built if your ideas change, or if you sell the home to a family which prefers smaller rooms.

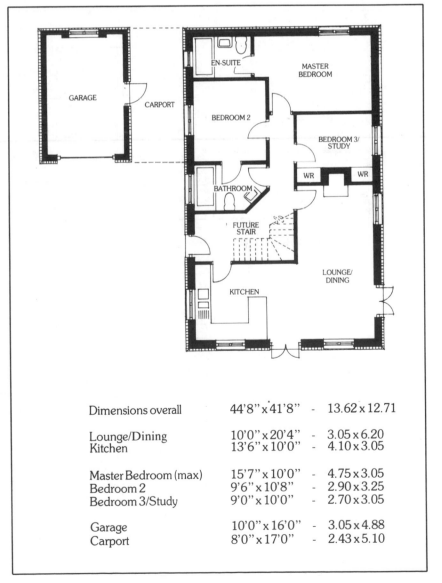

| | | |
|---|---|---|
| Dimensions overall | 44'8" x 41'8" | - 13.62 x 12.71 |
| Lounge/Dining | 10'0" x 20'4" | - 3.05 x 6.20 |
| Kitchen | 13'6" x 10'0" | - 4.10 x 3.05 |
| Master Bedroom (max) | 15'7" x 10'0" | - 4.75 x 3.05 |
| Bedroom 2 | 9'6" x 10'8" | - 2.90 x 3.25 |
| Bedroom 3/Study | 9'0" x 10'0" | - 2.70 x 3.05 |
| Garage | 10'0" x 16'0" | - 3.05 x 4.88 |
| Carport | 8'0" x 17'0" | - 2.43 x 5.10 |

# EXTENDABLE HOMES

**Ref: C406-8**

**111 sq.m.   1194 sq.ft.**
**(exc. garage)**

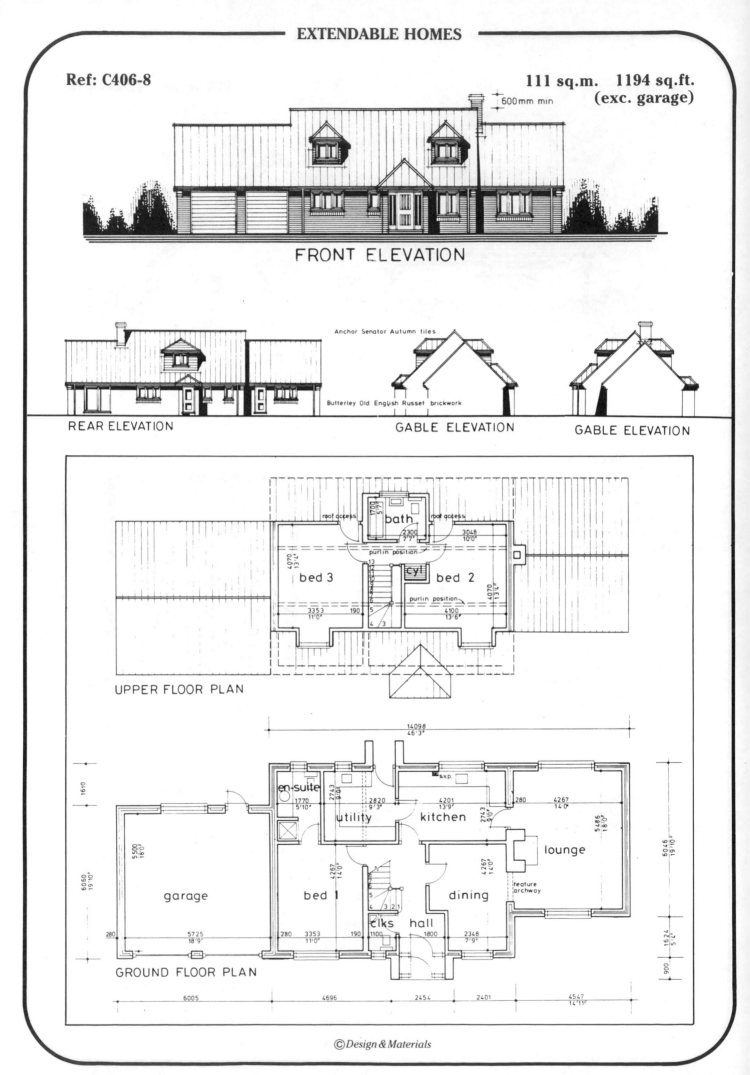

FRONT ELEVATION

600mm min

REAR ELEVATION

Anchor Senator Autumn tiles

GABLE ELEVATION

Butterley Old English Russet brickwork

GABLE ELEVATION

UPPER FLOOR PLAN

roof access
bath
roof access
1700 5'7"
2300 7'7"
3048 10'0"
purlin position
4070 13'4"
bed 3
13
12
11
10
9
8
7
cyl
bed 2
4070 13'4"
3353 11'0"
190
6
5
4   3
purlin position
4100 13'6"

GROUND FLOOR PLAN

14098 46'3"
1610
en-suite
1770 5'10"
2743 9'0"
utility
2820 9'3"
s.v.p.
4201 13'9"
280
4267 14'0"
2743 9'0"
kitchen
5500 18'0"
5486 18'0"
6060 19'10"
garage
bed 1
4267 14'0"
4267 14'0"
lounge
6046 19'10"
clks
hall
feature archway
280
5725 18'9"
280
3353 11'0"
190
1100
1800
2348 7'9"
dining
1624 5'4"
900
6005
4696
2454
2401
4547 14'11"

**Ref: W883**

**175 sq.m.   1883 sq.ft.**
**(inc. garage)**

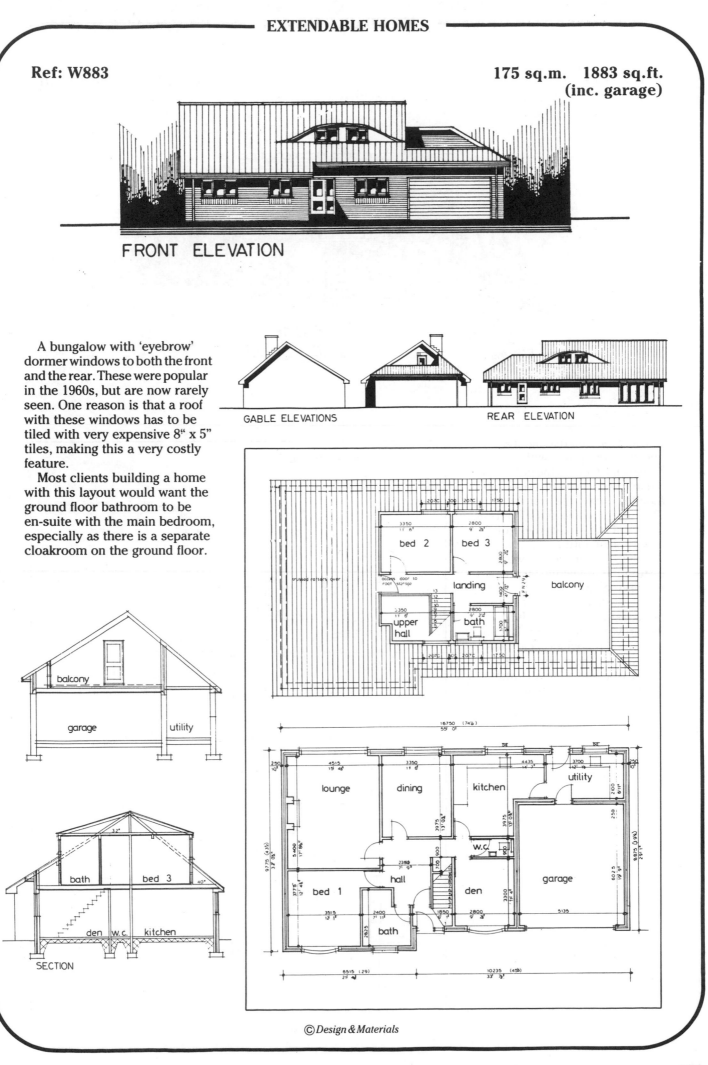

FRONT ELEVATION

A bungalow with 'eyebrow' dormer windows to both the front and the rear. These were popular in the 1960s, but are now rarely seen. One reason is that a roof with these windows has to be tiled with very expensive 8" x 5" tiles, making this a very costly feature.

Most clients building a home with this layout would want the ground floor bathroom to be en-suite with the main bedroom, especially as there is a separate cloakroom on the ground floor.

GABLE ELEVATIONS

REAR ELEVATION

SECTION

© *Design & Materials*

**Ref: 96114**

**177 sq.m.    1910 sq.ft.**

This is an interesting one bedroom bungalow with an Edwardian feel and the potential to have two more bedrooms and a bathroom on the first floor. The design would suit a 40 ft. plot, and the arrangement of gable end or dormer windows to the bedrooms in the roof would be to suit the view and planning requirements.

The large bay window to the breakfast area makes this design very appropriate for a site where this window can face the east for the morning sun, and it will give a great deal of character to the kitchen.

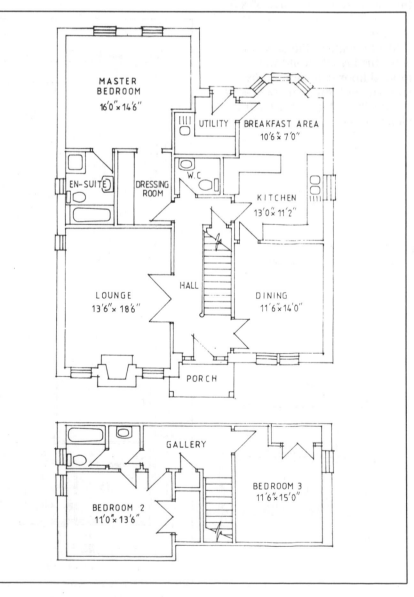

**Ref: 95105**

**133 sq.m.  1430 sq.ft.**
**(with upper floor)**

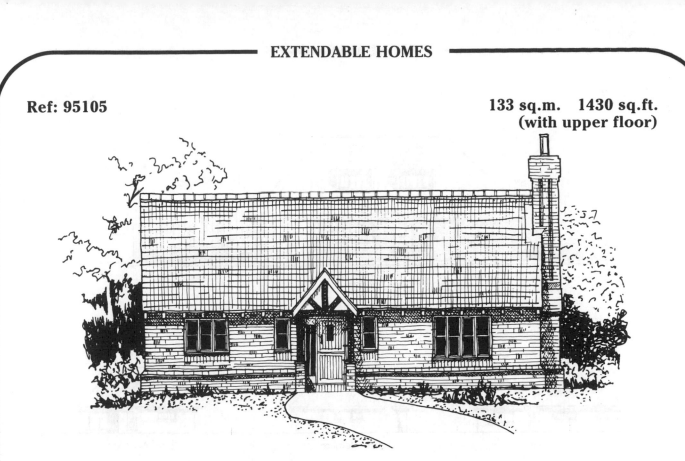

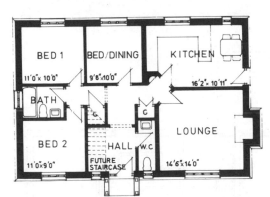

GROUND FLOOR PLAN 950 sq. ft.

BED 1
11'0" x 10'0"

BED/DINING
9'8" x 10'0"

KITCHEN
16'2" x 10'11"

BATH

BED 2
11'0" x 9'0"

HALL   W.C

FUTURE
STAIRCASE

LOUNGE
14'6" x 14'0"

UPPER FLOOR CONVERSION 480 sq. ft.

BED 4
12'9" x 13'9"

GALLERY   linen

BED 3
14'6" x 13'9"

BATH

CONVERSION WITH DORMER WINDOWS

Only the ground floor of this attractive cottage was built when the owners moved in, but there is room for two more bedrooms and a bathroom in the roof, and the heating piping, plumbing runs and the electricity wiring for this extension has already been installed. Without the first floor it is only 950 sq.ft., and it can be built on a 45 ft. frontage.

The illustrations show the building before and after the extension, with dormer windows for the new bedrooms. If appropriate these can be in the gable end walls, with only a bathroom window in the tiled roof. This is something that will probably be of interest to the planners, and in some situations they may not want any windows in the front of the roof at all. Fortunately the Building Regulations will permit an extractor fan ventilation system for the first floor bathroom, and no window at all.

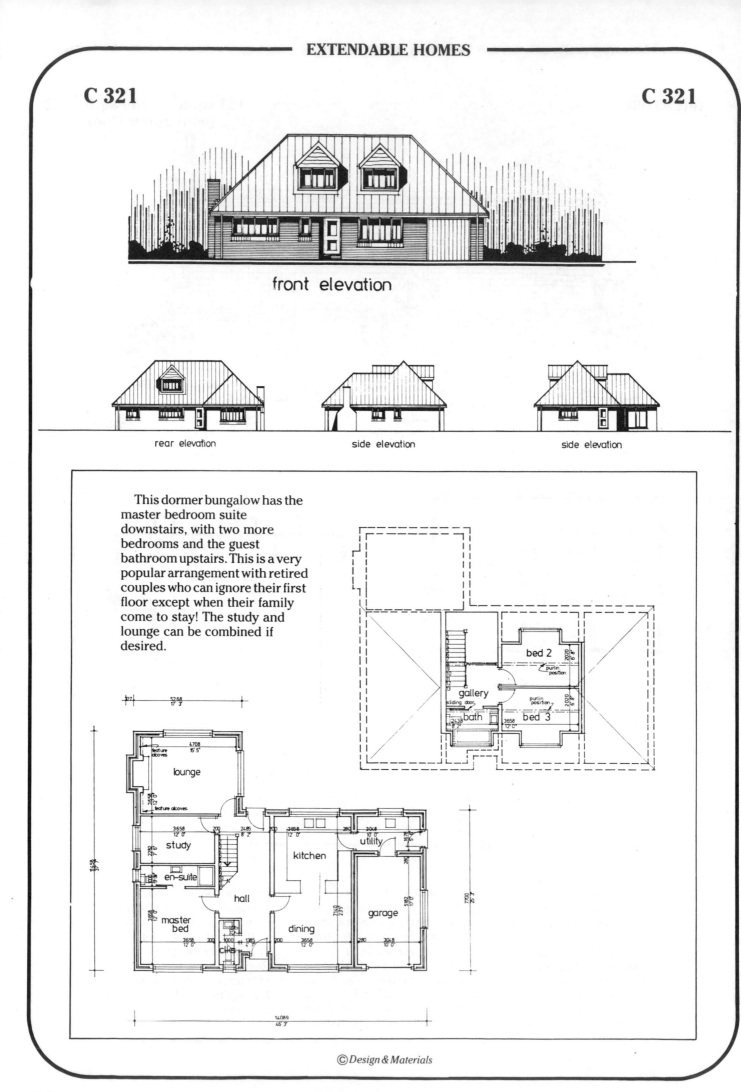

front elevation

rear elevation            side elevation            side elevation

This dormer bungalow has the master bedroom suite downstairs, with two more bedrooms and the guest bathroom upstairs. This is a very popular arrangement with retired couples who can ignore their first floor except when their family come to stay! The study and lounge can be combined if desired.

gallery

bed 2

purlin position

sliding door

bath

purlin position

bed 3
3658
12' 0"

lounge

4708
15' 5"

feature alcoves

feature alcoves

study

3658
12' 0"

kitchen

3658
12' 0"

utility

3048
10' 0"

en-suite

hall

master bed
3658
12' 0"

clks

dining
3658
12' 0"

garage
3048
10' 0"

52.68
17' 3"

16089
46' 3"

**Ref: W1009**

**118 sq.m.   1270 sq.ft.**

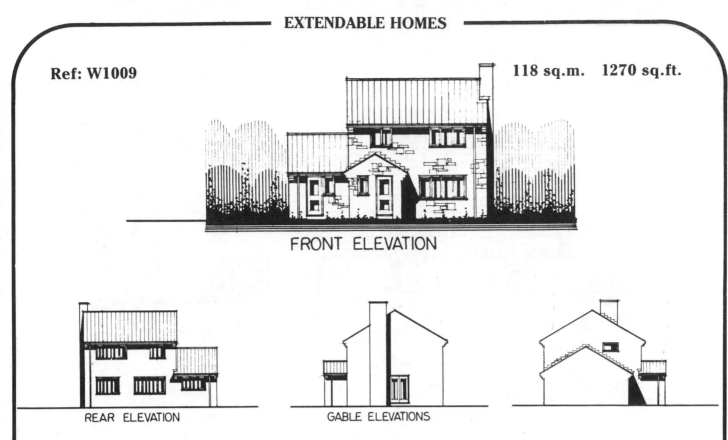

FRONT ELEVATION

REAR ELEVATION

GABLE ELEVATIONS

The key to the design concept for this house is to be found in the note at the head of the stairs: — "build in lintol for opening to future extension". Besides this, the ceiling joists to the kitchen and utility room are big enough to act as floor joists, so that two more bedrooms can be built above the single storey part of the house when required. An extension like this is easily arranged at the design stage, and the extra cost of providing for it all is very little. For instance, using 8" x 2" timber for the ceiling instead of 5" x 2" costs very little extra, and will save taking the whole ceiling down when the new rooms are to be built above. This forethought can also extend to the planning consent, which can show that the home is to be built in two stages if this can be negotiated at the planning office, avoiding having to make another application when the extension is required.

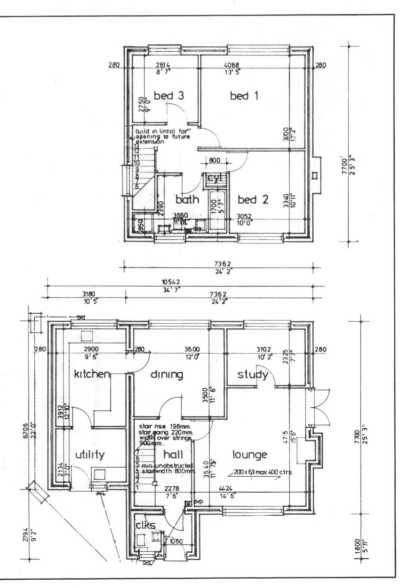

**Ref: 96217**

**103 sq.m.    1113 sq.ft.**

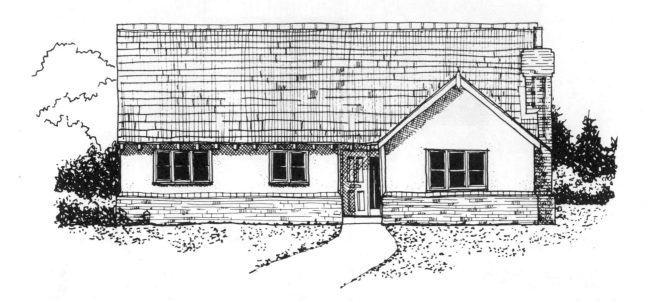

Most bungalows which are designed with an eye to using a space in the roof at a later date have to be built with a large entrance hall where the stairs can be installed when they are required. In this design a different approach has been taken, and there is a large store or linen cupboard for the future staircase.

517 sq. ft.

UPPER FLOOR CONVERSION

1113 sq. ft.

GROUND FLOOR PLAN

**Ref: 96218**

**102 sq.m.   1100 sq.ft.**

A bungalow designed for use to be made of the space in the roof at a later date, with room in the hallway for the staircase. These arrangements are often made by someone building the home who has no need for the extra space themselves, but who is concerned to maximise the value of the property. The potential for the two extra rooms with their own bathroom certainly does this.

CONVERSION WITH VELUX WINDOWS

CONVERSION WITH DORMER WINDOWS
SHOWING ALL BRICK AND ALTERNATIVE BAY DETAIL

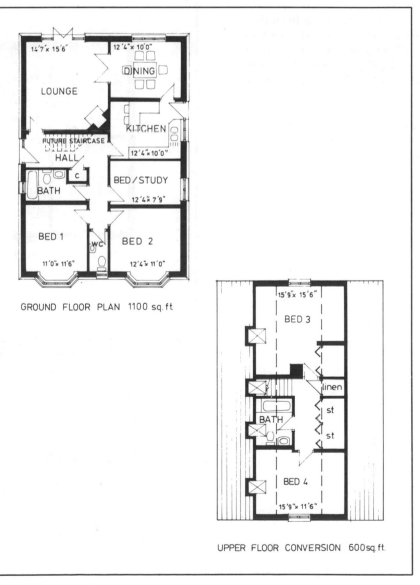

14'7" x 15'6"

12'4" x 10'0"

DINING

LOUNGE

KITCHEN

FUTURE STAIRCASE

HALL

12'4" x 10'0"

c

BATH

BED / STUDY

12'4" x 7'9"

BED 1

WC

BED 2

11'0" x 11'6"

12'4" x 11'0"

GROUND FLOOR PLAN 1100 sq.ft.

15'9" x 15'6"

BED 3

linen

st

BATH

st

BED 4

15'9" x 11'6"

UPPER FLOOR CONVERSION 600 sq.ft.

**Ref: 96199**

**79 sq.m.    850 sq.ft.**

A small bungalow from the Welsh borders which was built with the intention of providing two additional rooms in the roof at a later date.

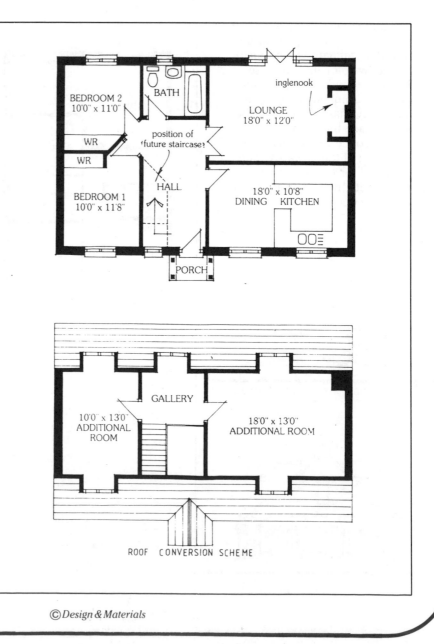

BEDROOM 2
10'0" x 11'0"

BATH

inglenook

LOUNGE
18'0" x 12'0"

WR

position of 'future staircase'

WR

BEDROOM 1
10'0" x 11'8"

HALL

18'0" x 10'8"
DINING    KITCHEN

PORCH

GALLERY

10'0" x 13'0"
ADDITIONAL ROOM

18'0" x 13'0"
ADDITIONAL ROOM

ROOF  CONVERSION  SCHEME

# Homes for Narrow Sites

There are two aspects of building on a narrow site which require careful consideration – how you achieve your ambitions within the constraints of the building regulations, and how you ensure that the building does not look cramped between the boundaries. This may not be easily achieved, and a narrow site is a challenge to a designer. If this is your problem, ask any designer who may work for you to take you to see homes which he has designed for similar difficult sites.

The building regulations require that there is a zone of open space outside the principal window to all principal rooms, and this usually means that such windows, french windows and sometimes even doors, have to be 12ft. from a boundary. Principal rooms are drawing rooms, dining rooms and bedrooms: principal windows are the largest windows in each room. The actual details of the rules are complex, and your designer should offer to discuss them with you in detail. A general understanding of this will enable you to appreciate why some of the designs on the following pages are laid out as they are.

However cramped your site may be, always try to avoid building right up to a boundary, even if there are no openings in the wall which will face the boundary. A metre wide path around a dwelling enables the property owner to control what is happening to his foundations, to enjoy access for maintenance, and to be able to erect scaffolding if ever necessary.

As far as appearance is concerned, a building which fills a narrow site will look large if it has a steep pitch roof of 50% or above, or if it is in a ranch style with a low pitch roof of 20% or 22.5% with a wide overhang at the eaves. 'Standard' pitches of 30% or 35% do not seem to suit cramped plots, and tend to make the buildings concerned look small. Also avoid central windows where there is a single gable elevation to the road, and generally try to add properly balanced features, such as a projecting porch if the entrance faces the road. A circular or lancet window to light the loft behind a gable will often help.

Perhaps most important of all is well thought out landscaping, and in urban areas this can include special features like raised flower beds, large areas of paving or a tree of a species that will not dwarf the building – a dwarf willow or a flowering almond, and not a Leylandii!

**Ref: 96139**

**176 sq.m.   1897 sq.ft.**

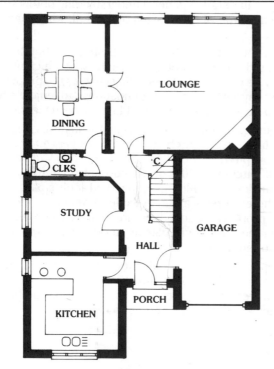

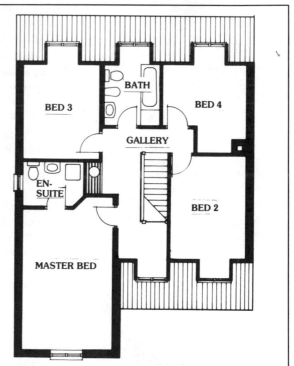

A 4 bedroomed house with integral garage that can be built on sites down to only 35 ft. wide.

As built there was no room for an external kitchen door, but as the kitchen is adjacent to the front door this was acceptable to the family concerned.

The corner fireplace and the glazed double doors between the lounge and dining room give a lot of character to the living area.

| Dimensions overall | 30'5" x 42'9" | 9.27 x 13.03 |
|---|---|---|
| Lounge | 18'6" x 16'0" | 5.62 x 4.87 |
| Dining | 9'6" x 16'0" | 2.90 x 4.87 |
| Kitchen | 11'10" x 12'0" | 3.60 x 3.65 |
| Study | 11'10" x 9'0" | 3.60 x 2.74 |
| Master Bed | 11'10" x 17'9" | 3.60 x 5.30 |
| Bed 2 | 9'7" x 12'11" | 2.92 x 3.94 |
| Bed 3 | 9'6" x 12'0" | 2.90 x 3.65 |
| Bed 4 | 11'2" x 11'0" | 3.39 x 3.35 |

**Ref: 96126**

**168 sq.m.    1808 sq.ft.**

A house for an infill plot which was only 39 ft. wide. It has an interesting layout made possible by the half landing stairway, with the rooms arranged to take advantage of an attractive view over the back garden.

| Dimensions overall | 34'7" x 37'9" | - | 10.55 x 11.50 |
|---|---|---|---|
| Lounge | 13'6" x 20'0" | - | 4.12 x 6.10 |
| Dining | 10'0" x 13'0" | - | 3.05 x 3.96 |
| Kitchen/Breakfast | 10'0" x 15'0" | - | 3.05 x 4.57 |
| Study | 8'0" x 9'0" | - | 2.44 x 2.74 |
| Utility | 8'0" x 6'1" | - | 2.44 x 1.85 |
| Master Bedroom (incl. W.R.) | 13'6" x 13'7" | - | 4.12 x 4.14 |
| Bedroom 2 | 13'6" x 9'0" | - | 4.12 x 2.74 |
| Bedroom 3 | 10'0" x 11'2" | - | 3.05 x 3.40 |
| Bathroom | 10'0" x 8'0" | - | 3.05 x 2.44 |
| En-Suite | 6'7" x 6'1" | - | 2.02 x 1.86 |

**Ref: 96180**

**139 sq.m.    1500 sq.ft.**

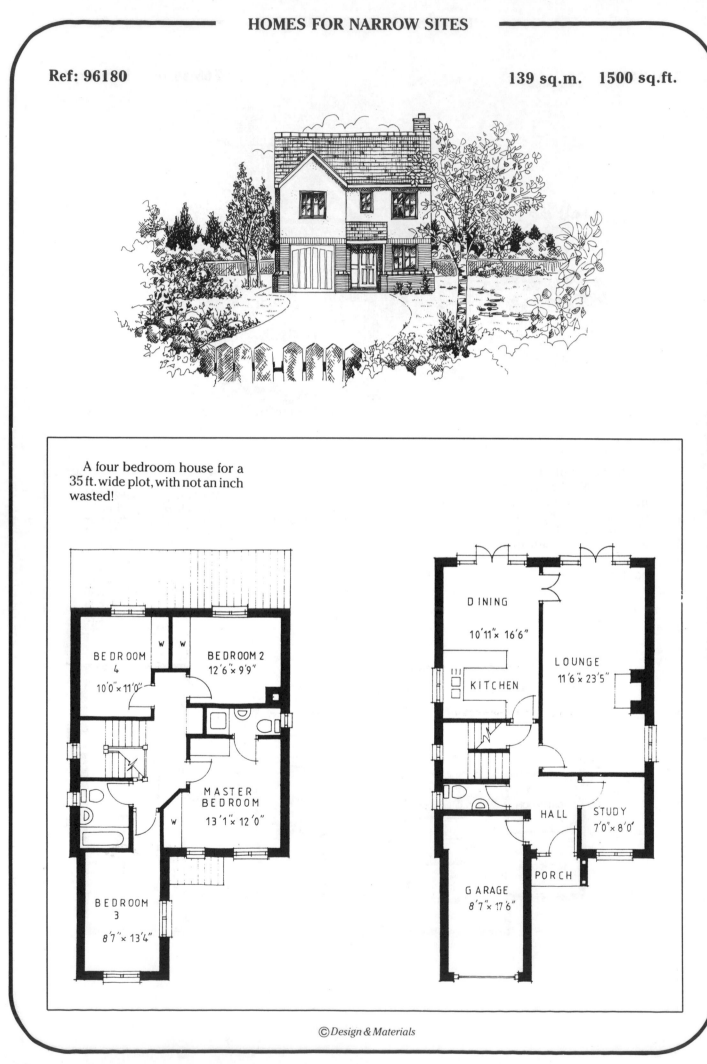

A four bedroom house for a 35 ft. wide plot, with not an inch wasted!

BEDROOM 4
10'0" × 11'0"

W   W

BEDROOM 2
12'6" × 9'9"

MASTER BEDROOM
13'1" × 12'0"

W

BEDROOM 3
8'7" × 13'4"

DINING
10'11" × 16'6"

LOUNGE
11'6" × 23'5"

KITCHEN

HALL

STUDY
7'0" × 8'0"

PORCH

GARAGE
8'7" × 17'6"

**Ref: 96181**

**108 sq.m.   1162 sq.ft.**

A typical design for a low budget home on a narrow plot with two alternative first floor layouts.

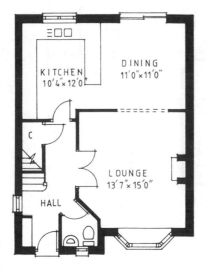

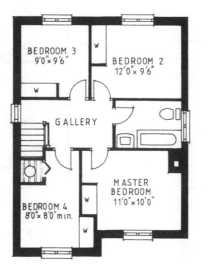

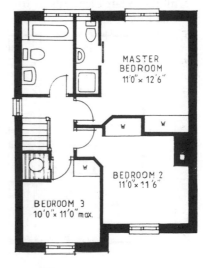

GROUND FLOOR PLAN

UPPER FLOOR PLAN (4 BED)

UPPER FLOOR PLAN (3 BED)

**Ref: PN654**

**150 sq.m.   1620 sq.ft.**
**(inc. garage)**

Drawing up plans for an aisle frame home with an integral garage on a narrow plot is a design challenge, particularly if it is being built in a conservation area. This house has met the challenge successfully, with the garage door forward of the main building under its own roof, and with the door itself in stained timber to be in character with all the other elements in the building.

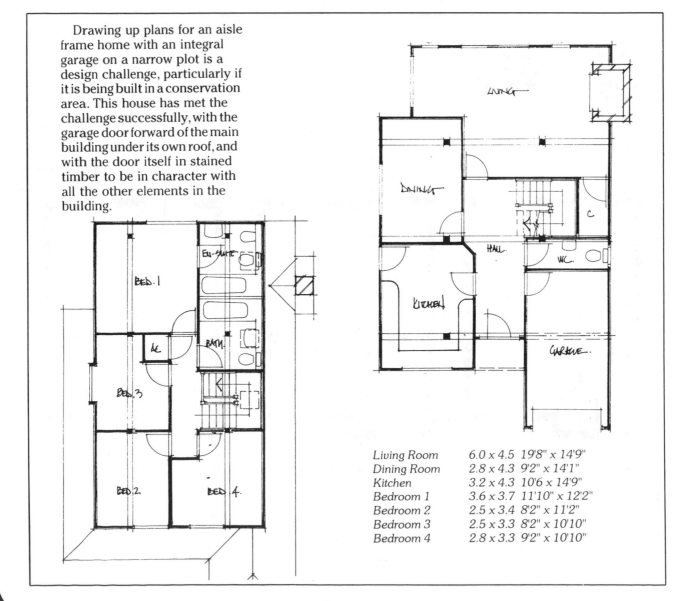

| | | |
|---|---|---|
| Living Room | 6.0 x 4.5 | 19'8" x 14'9" |
| Dining Room | 2.8 x 4.3 | 9'2" x 14'1" |
| Kitchen | 3.2 x 4.3 | 10'6 x 14'9" |
| Bedroom 1 | 3.6 x 3.7 | 11'10" x 12'2" |
| Bedroom 2 | 2.5 x 3.4 | 8'2" x 11'2" |
| Bedroom 3 | 2.5 x 3.3 | 8'2" x 10'10" |
| Bedroom 4 | 2.8 x 3.3 | 9'2" x 10'10" |

©Potton

**Ref: W819**

**145 sq.m.    1560 sq.ft.**
**(inc. garage)**

FRONT ELEVATION

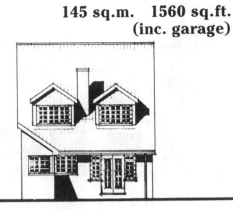

REAR ELEVATION

GABLE ELEVATION

This house was built in South Yorkshire on a very narrow plot. There was a lot of argument with the planners about it, but both sides of the building were masked by other structures, and consent was eventually obtained. Four bedrooms on a site only 28ft wide!

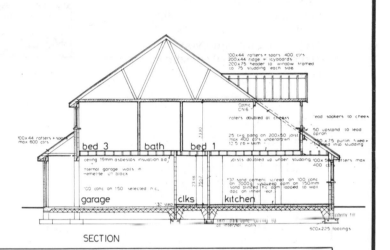

SECTION

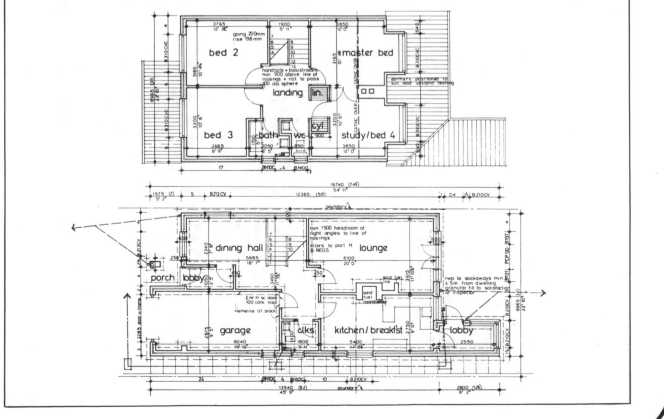

**Ref: S570**

**143 sq.m.   1539 sq.ft.**

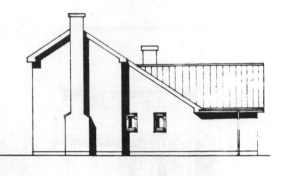

## front elevation

A home with the appearance of a bungalow from one side, but uncompromisingly two storeys at the other. This arrangement is very useful where outline planning consent for a dwelling on a narrow plot is for a "single storey structure", and you want to negotiate for detail consent for a house!

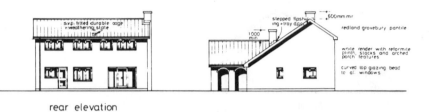

rear elevation

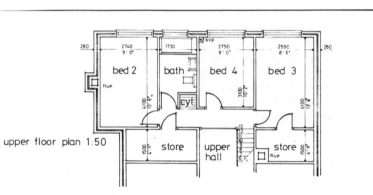

upper floor plan 1:50

Section 1:50

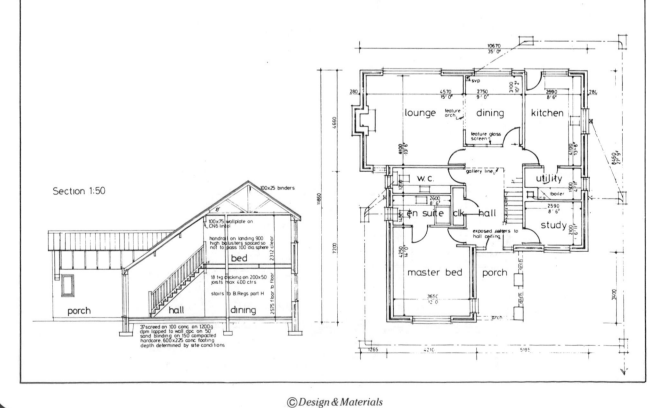

**Ref: W928**

**98 sq.m.   1054 sq.ft.**

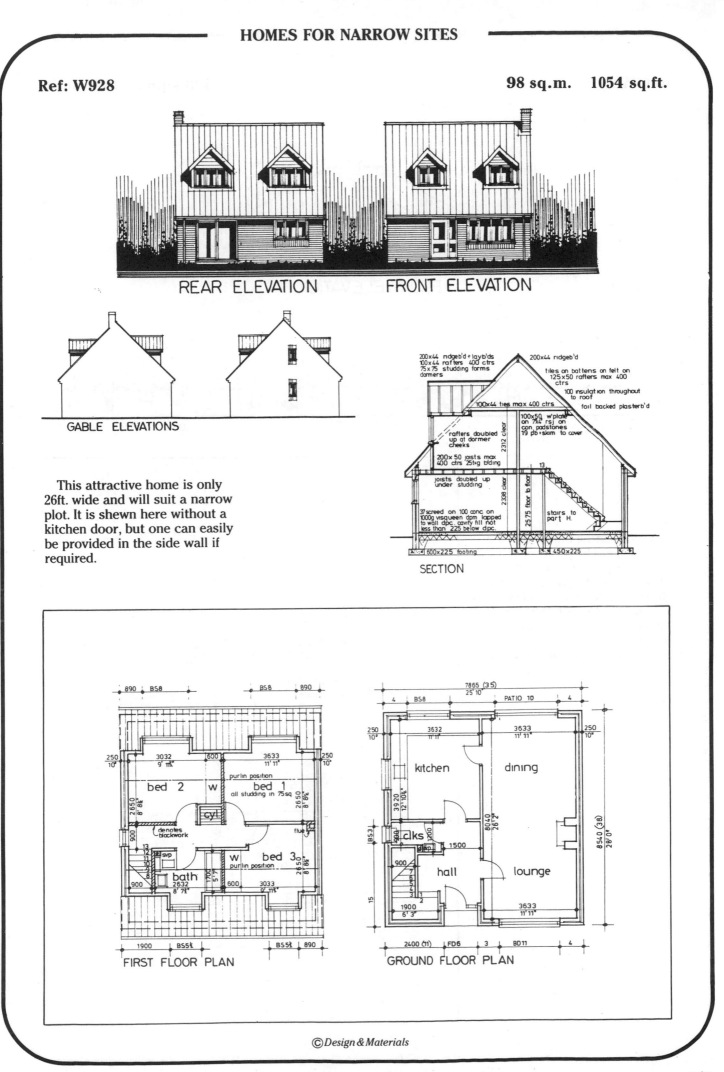

REAR ELEVATION   FRONT ELEVATION

GABLE ELEVATIONS

This attractive home is only 26ft. wide and will suit a narrow plot. It is shewn here without a kitchen door, but one can easily be provided in the side wall if required.

SECTION

FIRST FLOOR PLAN

GROUND FLOOR PLAN

**Ref: W1547**

**128 sq.m.    1377 sq.ft.**

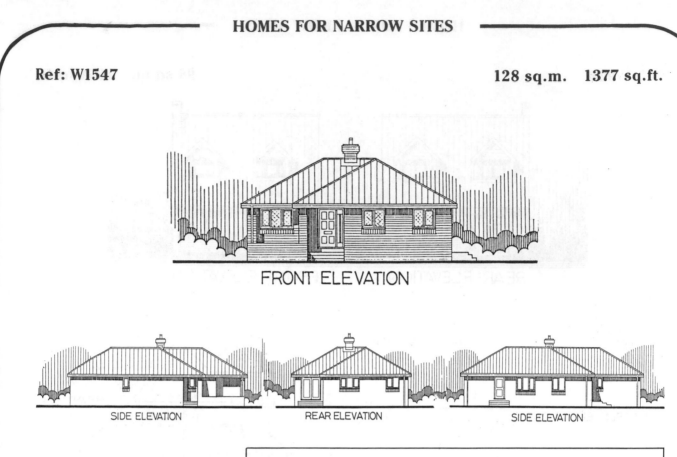

FRONT ELEVATION

SIDE ELEVATION        REAR ELEVATION        SIDE ELEVATION

An interesting bungalow for a narrow site. The position of the corner fireplace enables the chimney to be taken out through the roof ridge, which is always the preferred way of doing this. A kitchen on the front elevation is a feature asked for by many housewives, and here there are two windows to add to the balance of the look of the property.

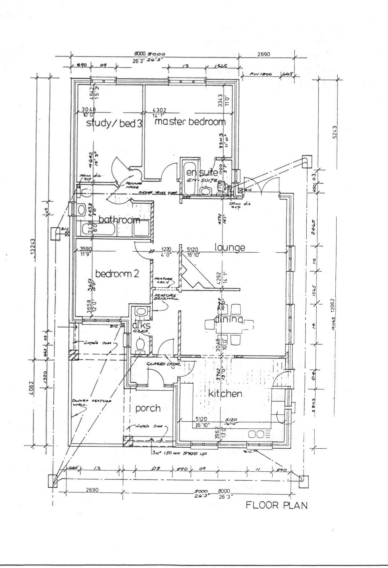

FLOOR PLAN

**Ref: P2785**

**98 sq.m. 1054 sq.ft.**

front elevation 1·10

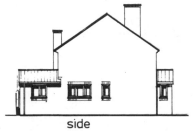

side

side elevation

rear

A straightforward conventional three bedroom house to fit on a narrow plot. Designs like this are so popular because they are convenient, cost-effective to build, and always a good re-sale proposition. If you have a plot for which the conventional design would be something like this, beware seeking a design that is 'different' without giving it all very careful consideration.

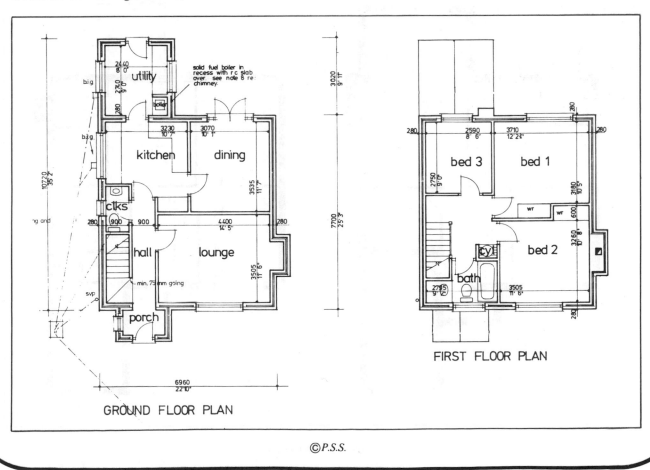

GROUND FLOOR PLAN

FIRST FLOOR PLAN

©P.S.S.

**Ref: 96118**

**171 sq.m.   1840 sq.ft.**

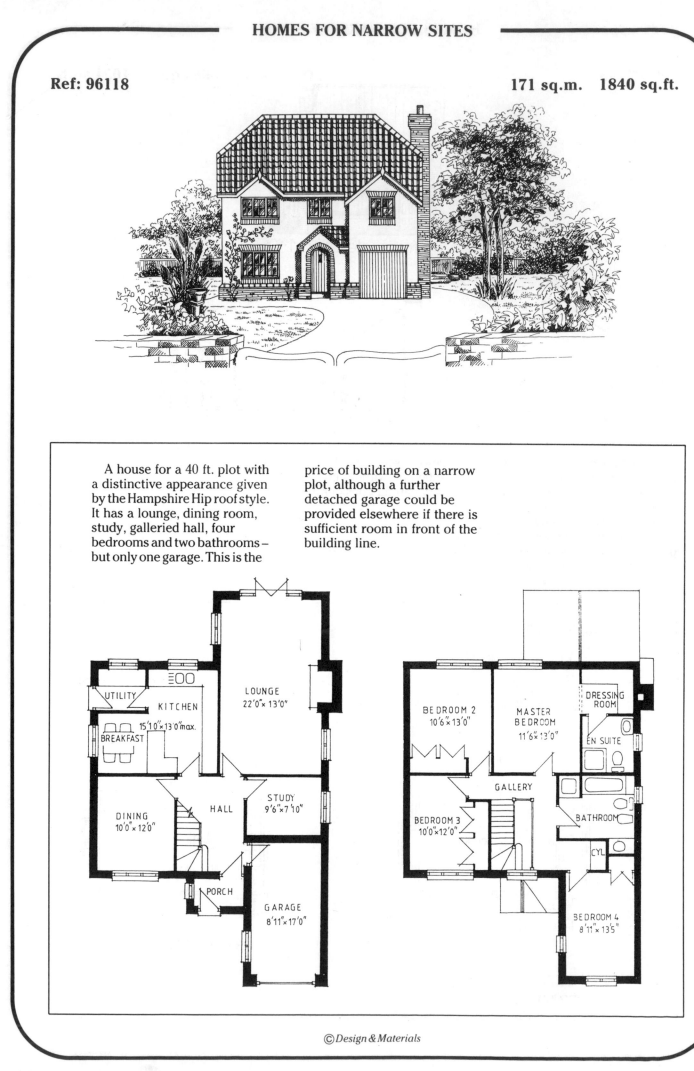

A house for a 40 ft. plot with a distinctive appearance given by the Hampshire Hip roof style. It has a lounge, dining room, study, galleried hall, four bedrooms and two bathrooms – but only one garage. This is the price of building on a narrow plot, although a further detached garage could be provided elsewhere if there is sufficient room in front of the building line.

UTILITY

KITCHEN
15'10" × 13'0" max.

BREAKFAST

LOUNGE
22'0" × 13'0"

DINING
10'0" × 12'0"

HALL

STUDY
9'6" × 7'10"

PORCH

GARAGE
8'11" × 17'0"

BEDROOM 2
10'6" × 13'0"

MASTER BEDROOM
11'6" × 13'0"

DRESSING ROOM

EN SUITE

GALLERY

BEDROOM 3
10'0" × 12'0"

BATHROOM

CYL

BEDROOM 4
8'11" × 13'5"

© *Design & Materials*

**Ref: 96115**

**181 sq.m.   1950 sq.ft.**

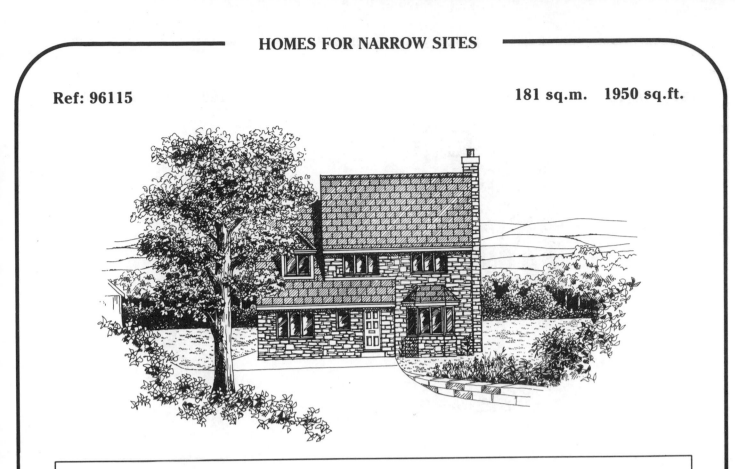

A house for a 40 ft. plot where the best views are over the back garden. The kitchen door is at the back of the property, leading into the utility room. This arrangement would suit young children who play in the garden, but may be inconvenient for others. However, some re-arrangement of the French window to the breakfast area can take care of this.

Note the large en suite bathroom to the master bedroom, and the more modest family bathroom. As discussed elsewhere in this book, this follows a growing fashion.

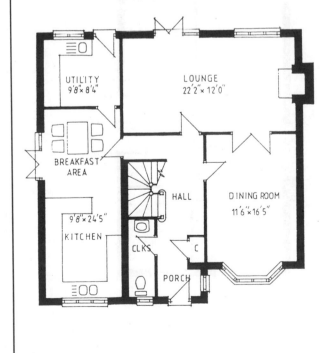

UTILITY
9'8" x 8'4"

LOUNGE
22'2" x 12'0"

BREAKFAST AREA

9'8" x 24'5"

KITCHEN

HALL

DINING ROOM
11'6" x 16'5"

CLKS

C

PORCH

MASTER BEDROOM
12'3" x 18'0"

BEDROOM 4
10'4" x 2'0"

BEDROOM 2
9'0" x 15'10"

CYL

EN-SUITE

BATHROOM

BEDROOM 3
11'6" x 12'7"

**Ref: 96113**

**160 sq.m.    1720 sq.ft.**

One of the few designs in this book with a walk-in larder. This is a feature which is often requested at an architects first briefing, but it is usually difficult to arrange and gets ruled out. If as here it suits the overall design concept, considerations can be given to building it with an insulated floor and walls, installing a small chiller unit, and doing away with the fridge.

The position of the garage door adjacent to the front door is unusual and care must be taken that they compliment each other in appearance.

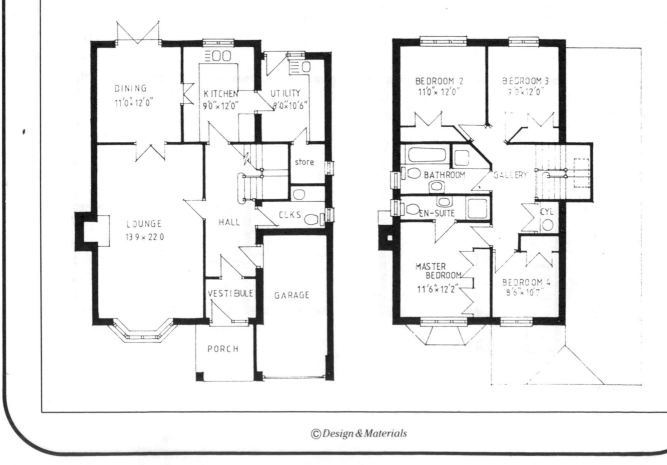

DINING 11'0" x 12'0"

KITCHEN 9'0" x 12'0"

UTILITY 8'0" x 10'6"

store

LOUNGE 13'9" x 22'0"

HALL

CLKS

VESTIBULE

GARAGE

PORCH

BEDROOM 2 11'0" x 12'0"

BEDROOM 3 9'0" x 12'0"

BATHROOM

GALLERY

EN-SUITE

CYL

MASTER BEDROOM 11'6" x 12'2"

BEDROOM 4 9'6" x 10'7"

**Ref: 96211**

**161 sq.m.    1730 sq.ft.**

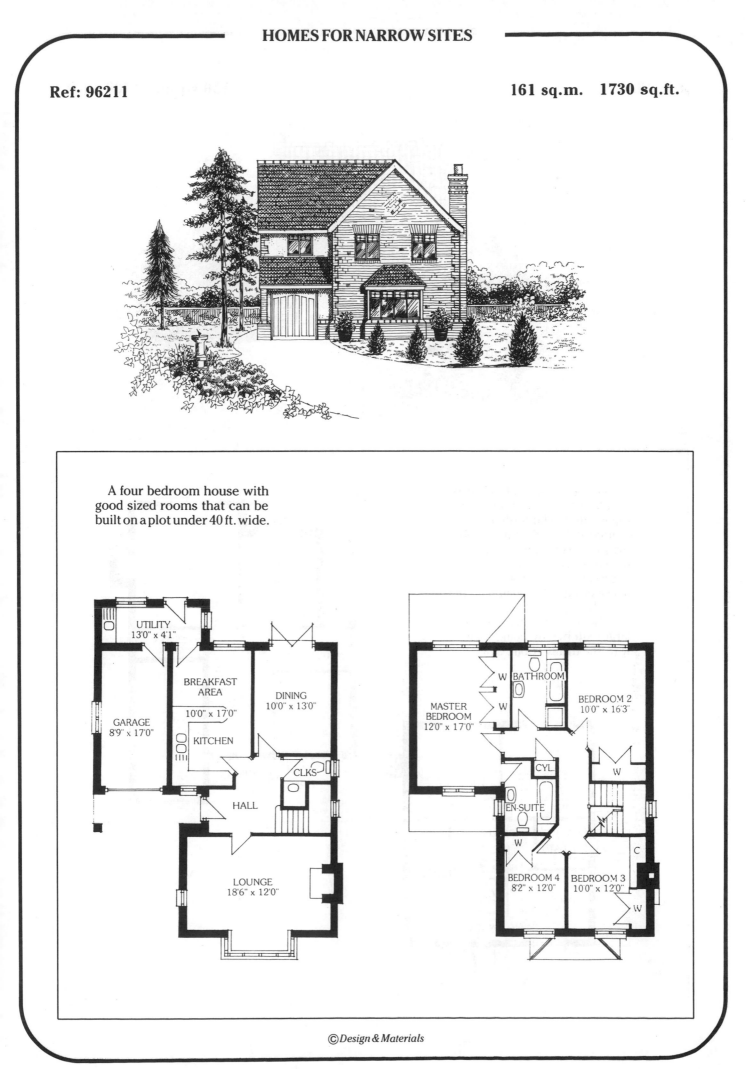

A four bedroom house with good sized rooms that can be built on a plot under 40 ft. wide.

UTILITY
13'0" x 4'1"

BREAKFAST
AREA
10'0" x 17'0"

DINING
10'0" x 13'0"

GARAGE
8'9" x 17'0"

KITCHEN

CLKS

HALL

LOUNGE
18'6" x 12'0"

MASTER
BEDROOM
12'0" x 17'0"

W

BATHROOM

W

BEDROOM 2
10'0" x 16'3"

CYL.

W

EN-SUITE

W

BEDROOM 4
8'2" x 12'0"

BEDROOM 3
10'0" x 12'0"

C

W

**Ref: 96208**

**130 sq.m.    1400 sq.ft.**

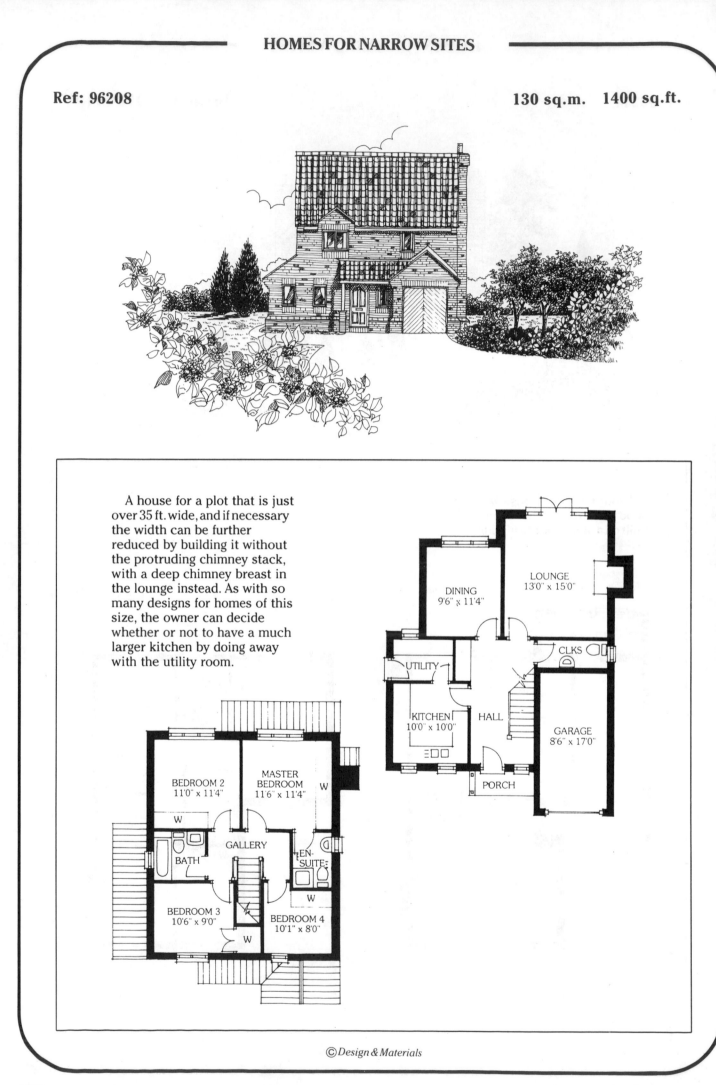

A house for a plot that is just over 35 ft. wide, and if necessary the width can be further reduced by building it without the protruding chimney stack, with a deep chimney breast in the lounge instead. As with so many designs for homes of this size, the owner can decide whether or not to have a much larger kitchen by doing away with the utility room.

DINING
9'6" x 11'4"

LOUNGE
13'0" x 15'0"

UTILITY

CLKS

KITCHEN
10'0" x 10'0"

HALL

GARAGE
8'6" x 17'0"

PORCH

BEDROOM 2
11'0" x 11'4"

MASTER
BEDROOM
11'6" x 11'4"

W

W

GALLERY

EN-SUITE

BATH

BEDROOM 3
10'6" x 9'0"

BEDROOM 4
10'1" x 8'0"

W

**Ref: C347**

**120 sq.m.   1291 sq.ft.**

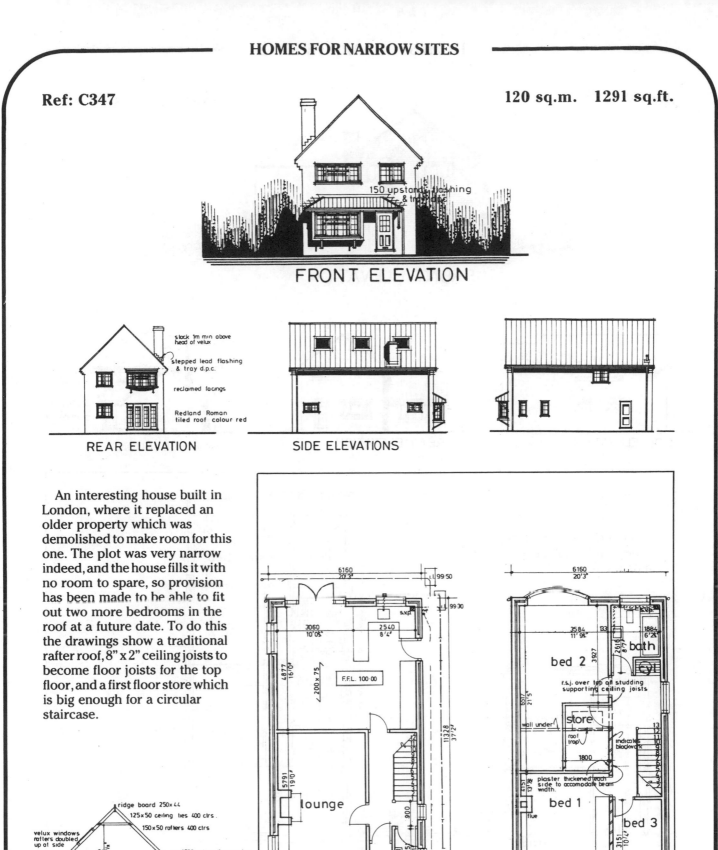

150 upstands flashing & tray d.p.c.

FRONT ELEVATION

slock 1m min above head of velux

stepped lead flashing & tray d.p.c.

reclamed facings

Redland Roman tiled roof colour red

REAR ELEVATION          SIDE ELEVATIONS

An interesting house built in London, where it replaced an older property which was demolished to make room for this one. The plot was very narrow indeed, and the house fills it with no room to spare, so provision has been made to be able to fit out two more bedrooms in the roof at a future date. To do this the drawings show a traditional rafter roof, 8" x 2" ceiling joists to become floor joists for the top floor, and a first floor store which is big enough for a circular staircase.

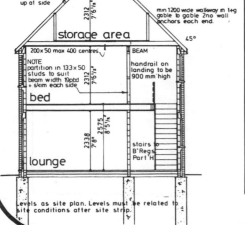

ridge board 250x44

velux windows rafters doubled up at side

125x50 ceiling ties 400 ctrs.

150x50 rafters 400 ctrs

2312 7'6¼"

storage area

45°

200x50 max 400 centres

min 1200 wide walkway in t+g gable to gable 2no wall anchors each end.

NOTE partition in 133x50 studs to suit beam width 19pbd + skim each side

BEAM

handrail on landing to be 900 mm high

2312 7'6¼"

bed

2338 7'8"

2575 8'5¼"

stairs B'Regs Part H

lounge

Levels as site plan. Levels must be related to site conditions after site strip.

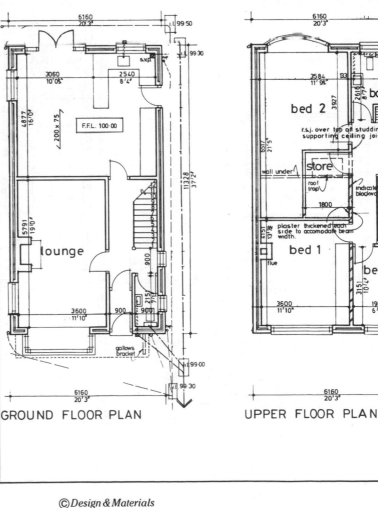

6160 20'3"

99·50

99·30

3060 10'05"

2540 8'4"

s.v.p.

4877 16'0"

200 x 75

F.F.L. 100·00

11328 37'2"

5791 19'0"

lounge

900

215 7'½

3600 11'10"

900

900

gallows bracket

99·00

99·30

6160 20'3"

GROUND FLOOR PLAN

6160 20'3"

3584 11'9¾"

133

1884 6'2½"

bath

2616 8'7"

bed 2

3927

cyl

r.s.j. over top of studding supporting ceiling joists

6517 21'5"

wall under

store

roof trap

indicates blockwork

1800

plaster thickened each side to accomodate beam width.

4151 13'7½"

flue

bed 1

bed 3

3151 10'4"

3600 11'10"

1900 6'3"

UPPER FLOOR PLAN

**Ref: W1220**

**193 sq.m.   2077 sq.ft.**

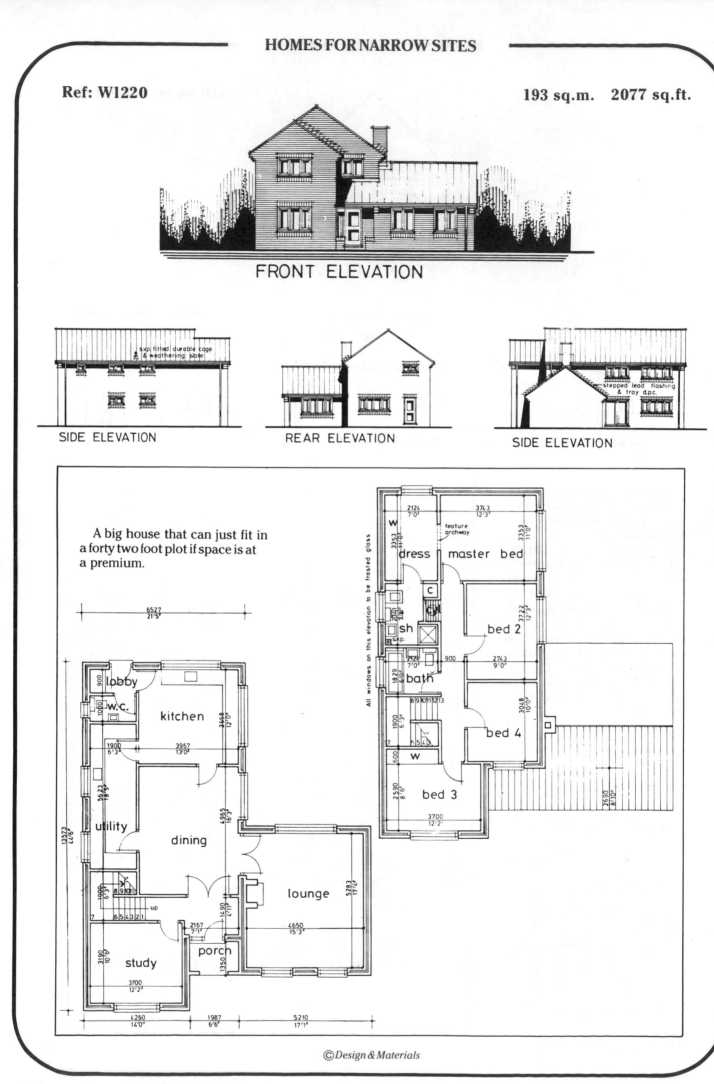

FRONT ELEVATION

SIDE ELEVATION

REAR ELEVATION

SIDE ELEVATION

A big house that can just fit in a forty two foot plot if space is at a premium.

© Design & Materials

**Ref: W1179**

**130 sq.m.   1399 sq.ft.**

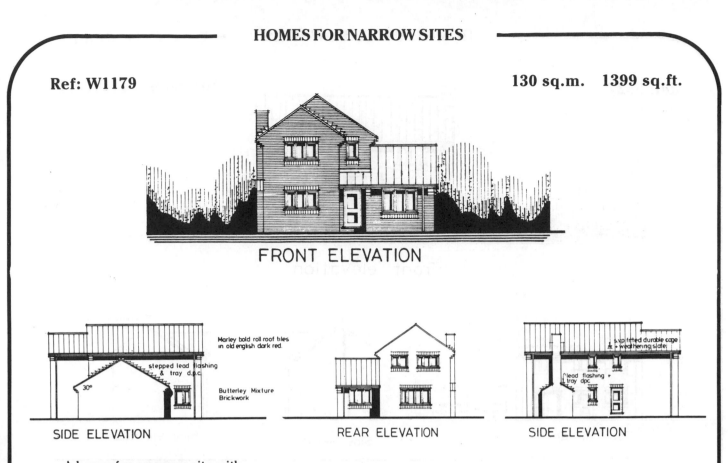

FRONT ELEVATION

SIDE ELEVATION

Marley bold roll roof tiles in old english dark red.

stepped lead flashing & tray d.p.c.

30°

Butterley Mixture Brickwork

REAR ELEVATION

SIDE ELEVATION

exp fitted durable edge & weathering slate

lead flashing + tray dpc

A house for a narrow site with an interesting arrangement of the rooms. The inglenook fireplace was designed to suit the client of D & M Ltd who built this house, and of course it can be replaced with a fireplace that will be flush with the wall, giving a lot more room in the lounge.

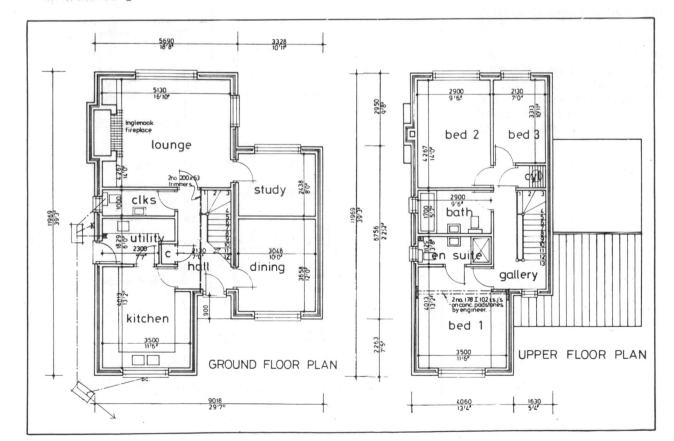

GROUND FLOOR PLAN

UPPER FLOOR PLAN

**Ref: S527**

**104 sq.m.   1119 sq.ft.**

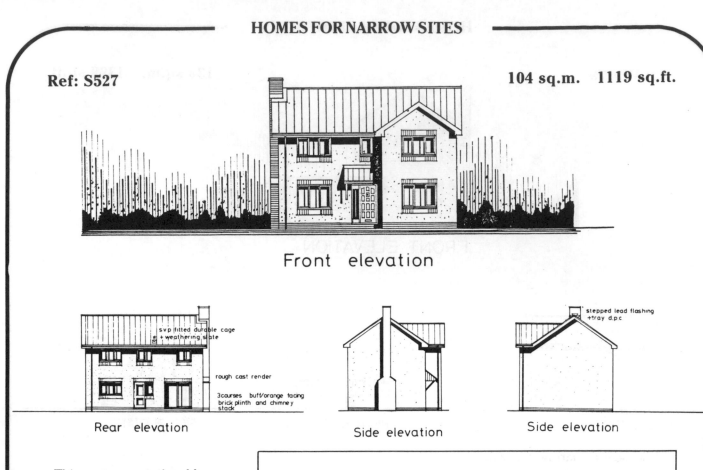

Front elevation

Rear elevation

Side elevation

Side elevation

*svp fitted durable cage + weathering slate*

*rough cast render*

*3 courses buff/orange facing brick plinth and chimney stack*

*stepped lead flashing + tray d.p.c*

This neat, conventional house is economical to build and is very compactly laid out. It is illustrated here with a rough cast rendered finish on a brick plinth, with a brick chimney and brick soldier courses above and below the windows. Contrasting render and brickwork like this is always very effective, but it is important that the junction of the two materials should be crisp and clean cut. One of the best ways of doing this is to use proprietory render stop laths at the horizontal joints, and it is important to discuss this with whoever is doing the rendering.

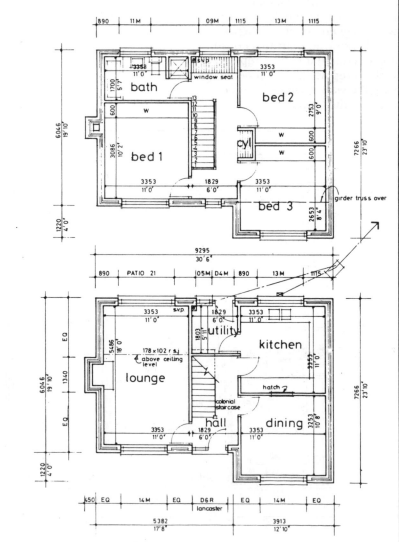

**Ref: P2500**

**128 sq.m.   1377 sq.ft.**

front elevation 1·100

side elevation

rear elevation 1·100

side elevation

A compact house designed for a site near Southampton where it had to match the general style of adjacent 1930s properties. The rendered walling to the first floor rises from a sloping brick-on-edge string course in true period fashion, instead of using the galvanised render-stop that is now more usually used.

The dining room is linked with the kitchen through a feature arch, but could easily be built as a separate room with a door into the hall.

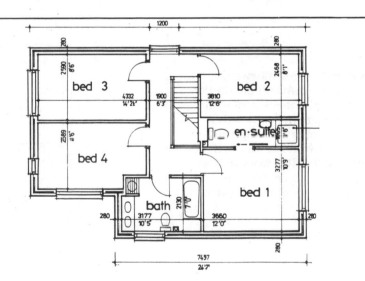

bed 3

bed 2

en·suite

bed 4

bath

bed 1

UPPER FLOOR PLAN

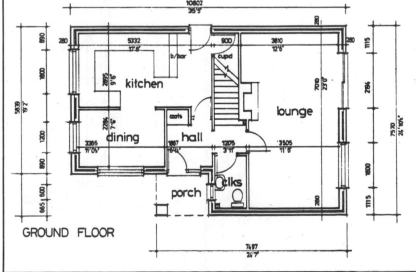

kitchen

b/bar

cupd

dining

coats

hall

lounge

clks

porch

GROUND FLOOR

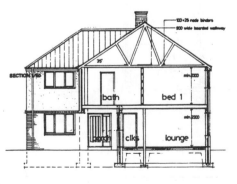

bath

bed 1

clks

lounge

SECTION 1·50

100×25 nade binders
800 wide boarded walkway

©P.S.S.

**Ref: W1244**

**131 sq.m.    1410 sq.ft.**

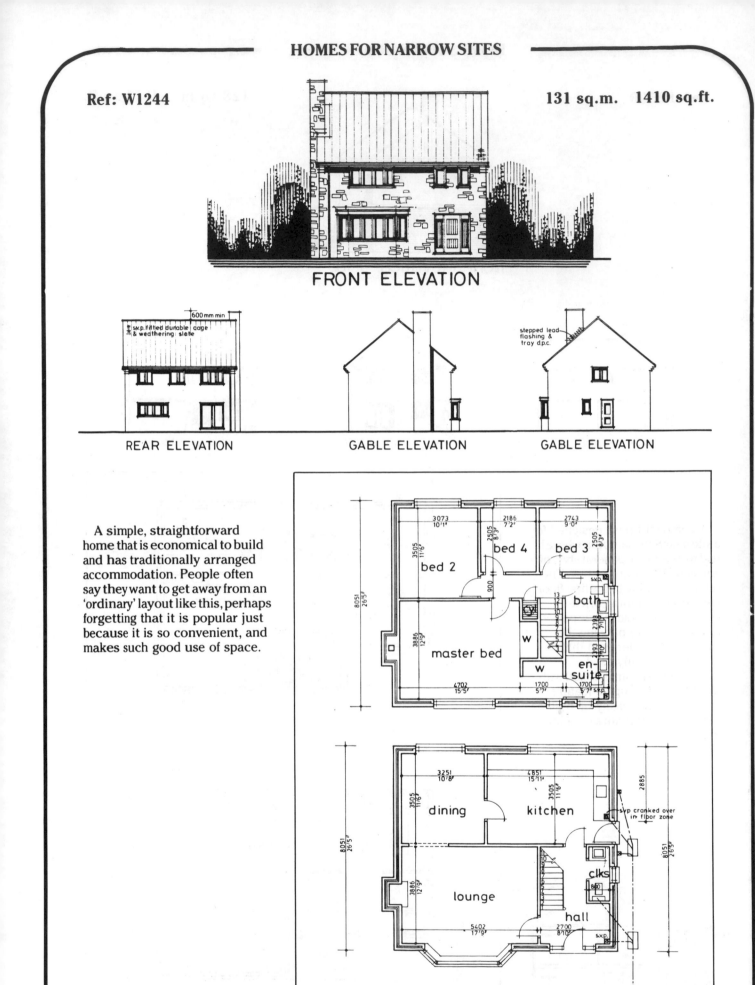

## FRONT ELEVATION

### REAR ELEVATION

600 mm min

s.v.p. fitted durable cage & weathering slate

### GABLE ELEVATION

### GABLE ELEVATION

stepped lead flashing & tray d.p.c.

A simple, straightforward home that is economical to build and has traditionally arranged accommodation. People often say they want to get away from an 'ordinary' layout like this, perhaps forgetting that it is popular just because it is so convenient, and makes such good use of space.

bed 2
bed 4
bed 3
bath
master bed
en-suite
w
w

dining
kitchen
lounge
hall
clks

svp cranked over in floor zone

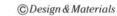

**Ref: W1288**

**127 sq.m.   1347 sq.ft.**
**(inc. garage)**

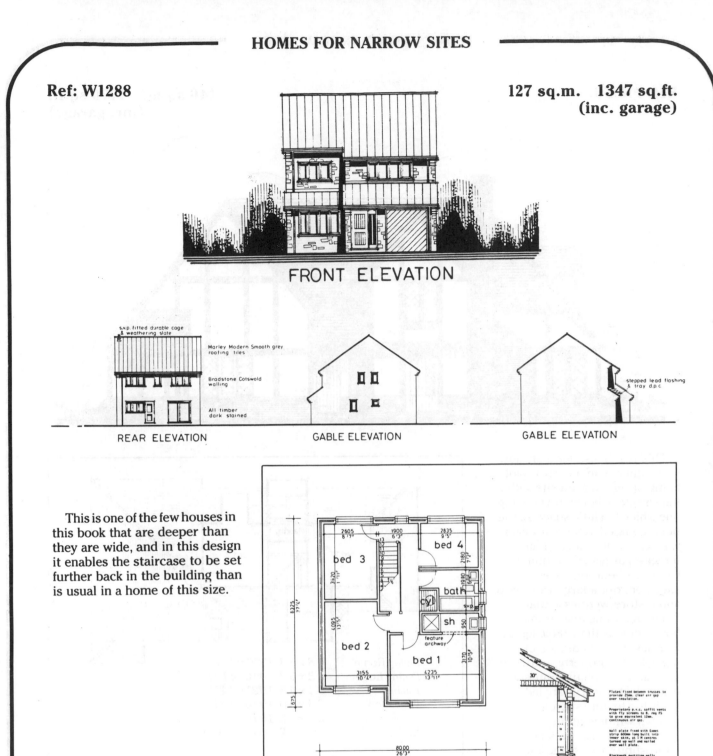

FRONT ELEVATION

s.w.p. fitted durable cage
& weathering slate

Marley Modern Smooth grey
roofing tiles

Bradstone Cotswold
walling

All timber
dark stained

REAR ELEVATION

GABLE ELEVATION

stepped lead flashing
& tray d.p.c.

GABLE ELEVATION

This is one of the few houses in
this book that are deeper than
they are wide, and in this design
it enables the staircase to be set
further back in the building than
is usual in a home of this size.

**Ref: PN658**

146 sq.m.   1770 sq.ft.
(inc. garage)

This is a house for a shallow plot rather than a narrow plot, being designed for a site with a long frontage but with a building line which left little space for the building itself. Access for cars was from one side, and an integral garage was required. Only two bedrooms were specified, but a large workshop and a store were essential.

The resulting aisle frame house of less than 1800 square feet has the appearance of a much larger property, and there are many interesting interior design features. The angled hall leads to a feature staircase with its own window at the half landing, and this gives an interesting shape to the kitchen. In the lounge the Inglenook fireplace is positioned to share a feature chimney stack with the flue from the Aga cooker, while on the first floor each bedroom has its own large bathroom. The second of these bathrooms is shown notionally, as the actual layout depended on the outcome of negotiations with the planning authority for a Velux light in the roof.

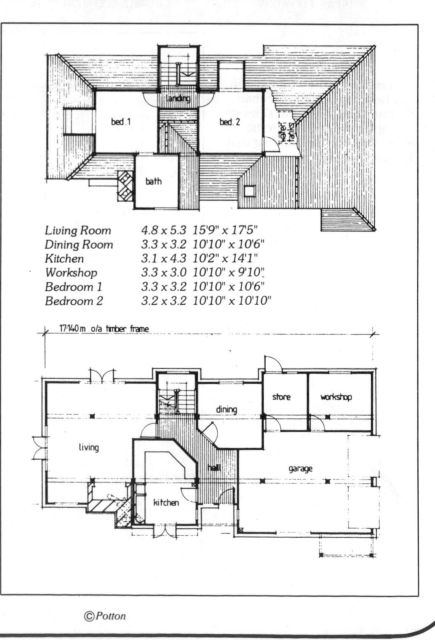

| | | |
|---|---|---|
| *Living Room* | *4.8 x 5.3* | *15'9" x 17'5"* |
| *Dining Room* | *3.3 x 3.2* | *10'10" x 10'6"* |
| *Kitchen* | *3.1 x 4.3* | *10'2" x 14'1"* |
| *Workshop* | *3.3 x 3.0* | *10'10" x 9'10"* |
| *Bedroom 1* | *3.3 x 3.2* | *10'10" x 10'6"* |
| *Bedroom 2* | *3.2 x 3.2* | *10'10" x 10'10"* |

©Potton

162

**Ref: PN664**

**157 sq.m.   1688 sq.ft.**

*WEST ELEVATION*          *EAST ELEVATION*

This timber frame bungalow was designed by Potton Limited for a very narrow site, and was constructed using timber wall panels, and not the company's better known aisle frame system. The clients required a few large rooms with a potential ground floor bedroom for use if the stairs become a problem in the future and this is shown on the plan as a Study/Bedroom.

There is direct access from the garage to the hall, shown here with a sliding door to suit a Volvo estate car which takes up all the room in the garage. A smaller car would permit a swung door opening into the garage. The kitchen/dining room arrangement was also drawn to suit the clients.

| Living Room | 4.6 x 6.4 | 15'1" x 21'0" |
| Kitchen/Dining | 5.7 x 2.7 | 18'8" x 8'10" |
| Study/Bedroom | 3.5 x 2.7 | 11'6" x 8'10" |
| Garage | 5.5 x 2.5 | 18'1" x 8'2" |
| Bedroom 1 | 4.9 x 4.4 | 16'1" x 14'5" |
| Spare Room | 3.9 x 4.4 | 13'1" x 14'5" |

**Ref: 96215**

**116 sq.m.   1250 sq.ft.**

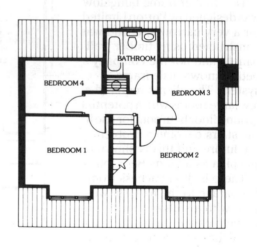

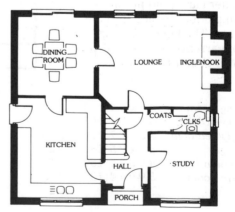

The story of this home is a good example of the realities of choosing a house design. It started with a small plot where the client wanted four bedrooms on the first floor, and could afford 1200 sq.ft. The planners wanted a bungalow. After a lot of talk it was conceded that dormer windows would be acceptable in a steep pitch roof. Four bedrooms required 20 feet of depth to the first floor, so the minimum overall depth of the property had to be 28'3". That led to this cost effective layout and everyone was happy!

| | | | |
|---|---|---|---|
| Lounge | 16'1" x 13'0" | - | 4.90 x 3.97 |
| Dining | 11'0" x 11'4" | - | 3.35 x 3.46 |
| Kitchen | 11'11" x 14'8" | - | 3.63 x 4.48 |
| Study | 8'8" x 9'5" | - | 2.63 x 2.87 |
| | | | |
| Bedroom 1 | 11'11" x 10'1" | - | 3.63 x 3.08 |
| Bedroom 2 | 11'11" x 8'1" | - | 3.63 x 2.46 |
| Bedroom 3 | 8'6" x 9'8" | - | 2.60 x 2.94 |
| Bedroom 4 | 11'0" x 7'7" | - | 3.35 x 2.32 |

**Ref: 96212**

**135 sq.m.    1450 sq.ft.**

A simple and cost effective design for a four bedroom house with the main views to the rear.

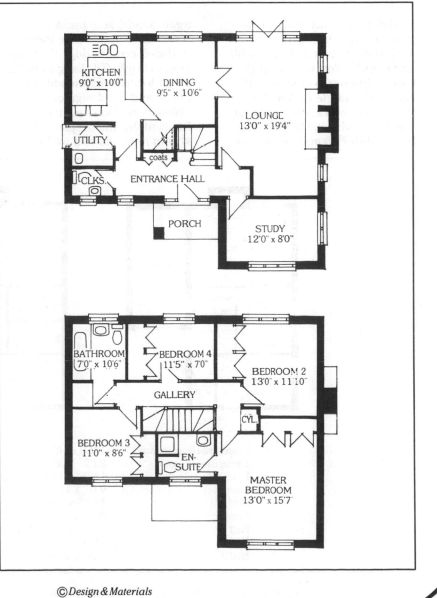

**Ref: 96138**

**135 sq.m.   1460 sq.ft.**
**(inc. garage)**

This house was designed to meet a requirement for a Victorian style town house with three bedrooms, each with its own bathroom, a lounge to the rear and a single garage. It is illustrated with many Victorian features and suitable Victorian materials for them are now once again available in builders merchants. In this case these included crested ridge tiles and special bricks. Tile hanging to the small dormer window adds to the effect, and the design of the chimney is also important. Incidentally, the fireplace is shown in the garden wall of the lounge but it can easily be moved into any of the other walls if required.

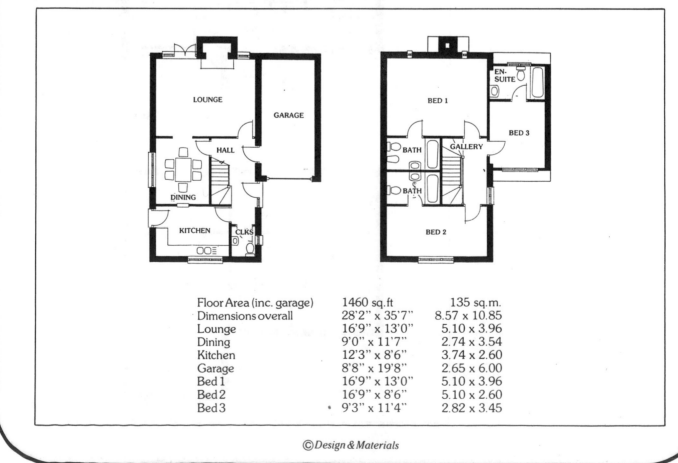

| | | |
|---|---|---|
| Floor Area (inc. garage) | 1460 sq.ft | 135 sq.m. |
| Dimensions overall | 28'2" x 35'7" | 8.57 x 10.85 |
| Lounge | 16'9" x 13'0" | 5.10 x 3.96 |
| Dining | 9'0" x 11'7" | 2.74 x 3.54 |
| Kitchen | 12'3" x 8'6" | 3.74 x 2.60 |
| Garage | 8'8" x 19'8" | 2.65 x 6.00 |
| Bed 1 | 16'9" x 13'0" | 5.10 x 3.96 |
| Bed 2 | 16'9" x 8'6" | 5.10 x 2.60 |
| Bed 3 | 9'3" x 11'4" | 2.82 x 3.45 |

**Ref: C451**

**130 sq.m.   1399 sq.ft.**
**(exc. garage)**

FRONT ELEVATION

morley mendip brown tiles

ibstock sevenooks multi-stock facings

h.w. joinery with arch top beads + leaded lights

dpc 150 above g.l.

REAR ELEVATION

A compact house, with the main building nearly square, but which looks larger and more complex because of the careful arrangement on the site of the garage and back porch. A cost effective house to build.

This is another design with a projecting front porch that is supported by a timber post: as always this support should be really massive.

The lounge is interesting, with the angled door facing the corner fireplace making it an unusual and attractive room, although not an easy one to furnish.

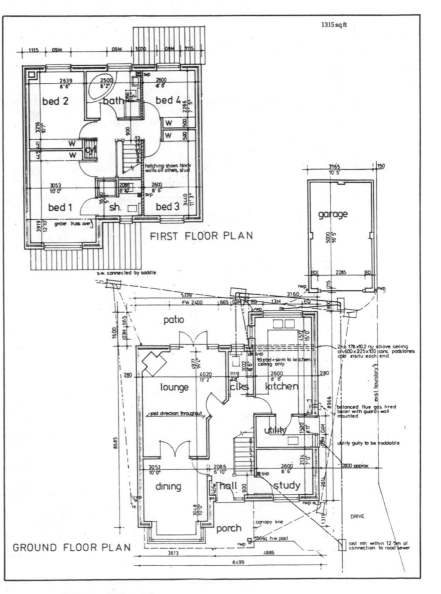

1315 sq ft

FIRST FLOOR PLAN

GROUND FLOOR PLAN

**Ref: P2634**

**104 sq.m.   1119 sq.ft.**

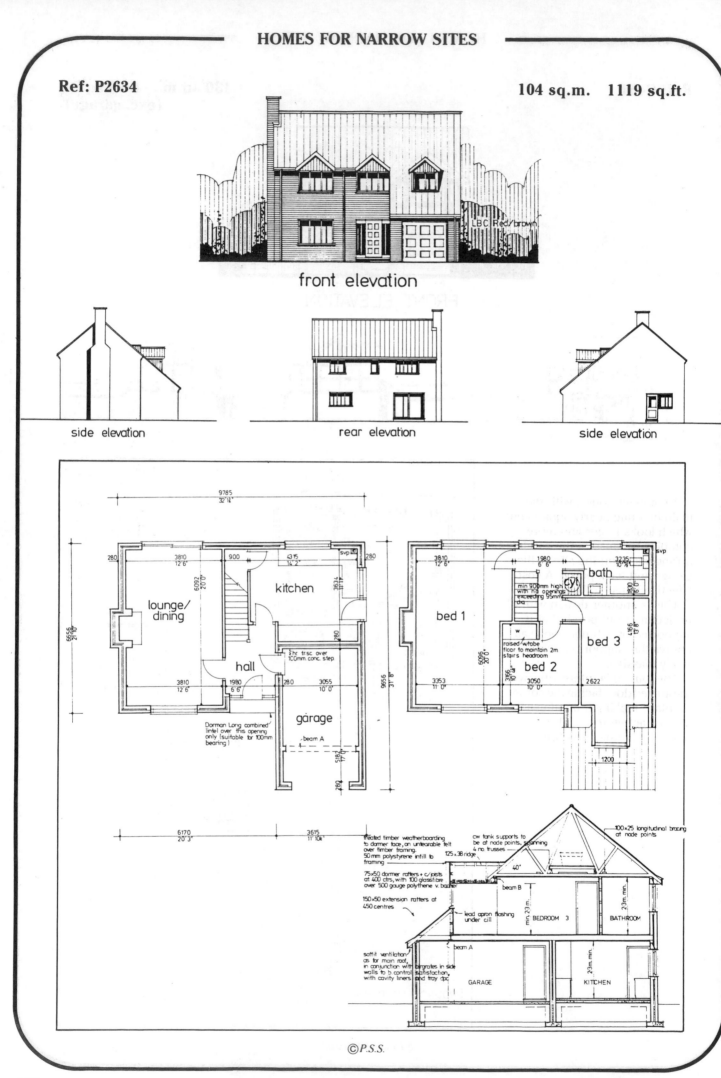

LBC Red/brown

front elevation

side elevation

rear elevation

side elevation

lounge/dining

kitchen

hall

garage

bed 1

bath

bed 2

bed 3

©P.S.S.

**Ref: C415**

**130 sq.m.   1410 sq.ft.**
**(exc. garage)**

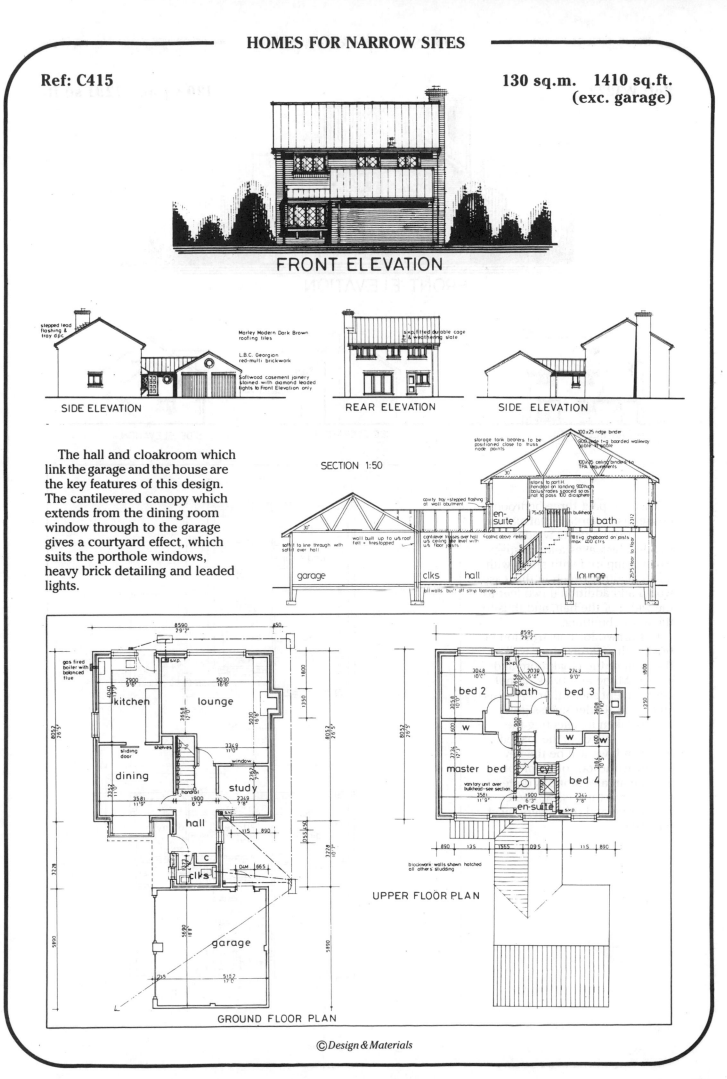

FRONT ELEVATION

SIDE ELEVATION

REAR ELEVATION

SIDE ELEVATION

stepped lead flashing & tray dpc

Marley Modern Dark Brown roofing tiles

L.B.C. Georgian red-multi brickwork

Softwood casement joinery stained with diamond leaded lights to Front Elevation only

s.v.p. fitted durable cage & weathering slate

The hall and cloakroom which link the garage and the house are the key features of this design. The cantilevered canopy which extends from the dining room window through to the garage gives a courtyard effect, which suits the porthole windows, heavy brick detailing and leaded lights.

SECTION 1:50

garage     clks   hall            lounge

GROUND FLOOR PLAN

kitchen   lounge
dining    study
hall
clks
C
garage

gas fired boiler with balanced flue

UPPER FLOOR PLAN

bed 2   bath   bed 3
master bed   cy   bed 4
en-suite

blockwork walls shown hatched all others studding

**Ref: W1222**

**120 sq.m.    1291 sq.ft.**

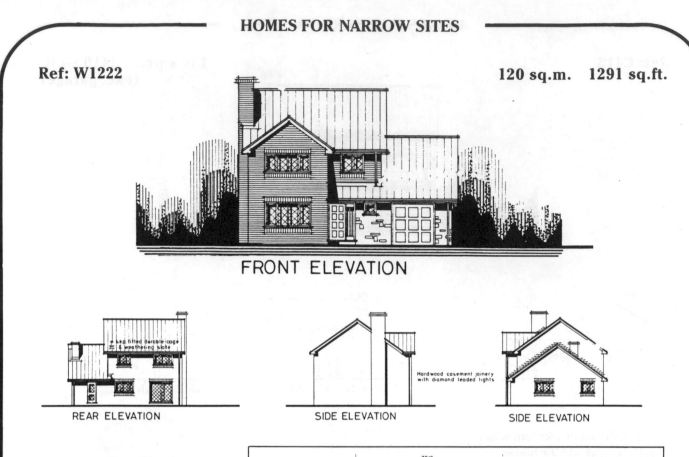

FRONT ELEVATION

REAR ELEVATION

SIDE ELEVATION

SIDE ELEVATION

This compact three bedroom house has a staircase that makes a 180° turn by using winder treads. This saves a lot of space when compared with stairs with a half landing, which in this case would add additional two feet to the width of the hall, and thus to the whole building.

It is drawn for construction in brick with a feature stone wall to the front of the cloakroom and garage. Stone and brick do not complement each other as well as stone and render unless great care is taken in selecting the bricks. In this case the leaded light windows will be the key feature to the look of the property, and the area of stone is quite small. Nevertheless, the choice of both stone and brick were most important.

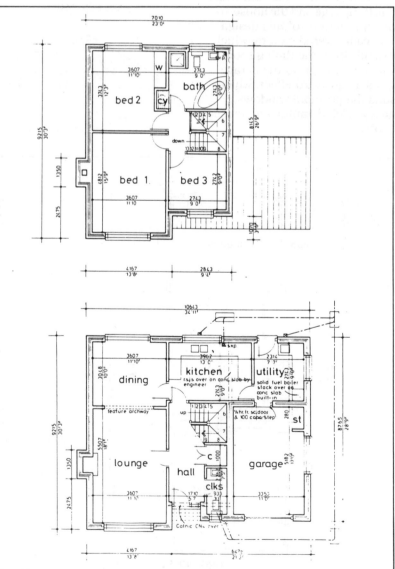

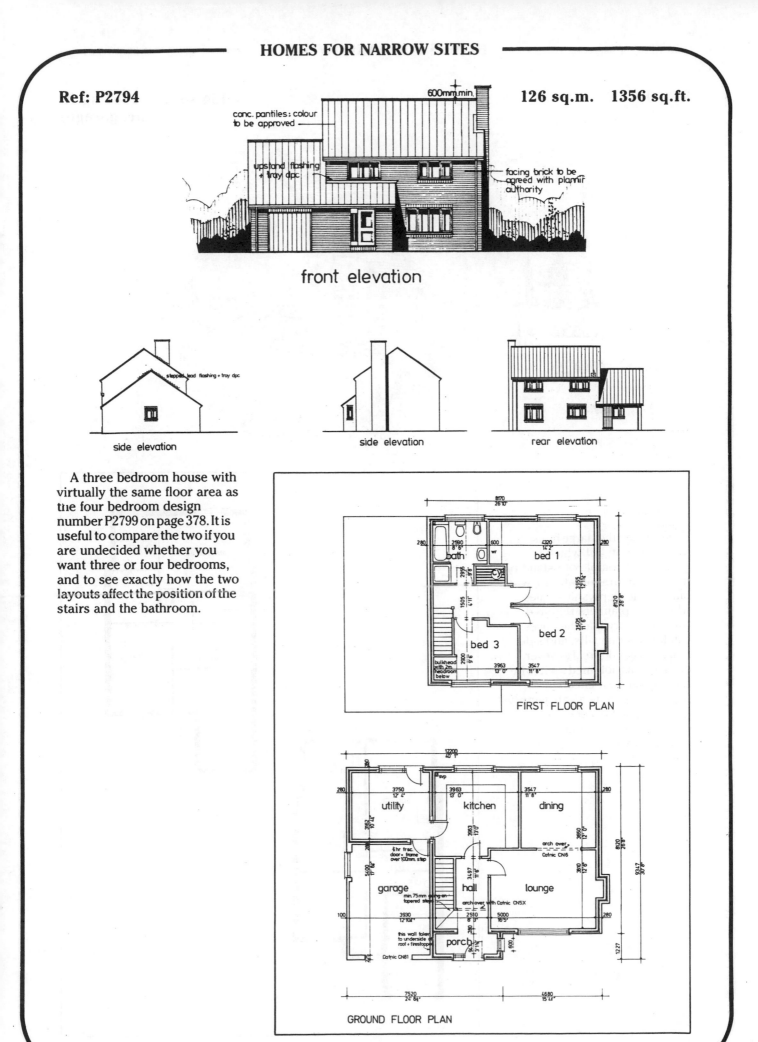

**Ref: P2794**

126 sq.m.   1356 sq.ft.

conc. pantiles: colour to be approved

600mm min.

upstand flashing + tray dpc

facing brick to be agreed with planning authority

front elevation

stepped lead flashing + tray dpc

side elevation

side elevation

rear elevation

A three bedroom house with virtually the same floor area as the four bedroom design number P2799 on page 378. It is useful to compare the two if you are undecided whether you want three or four bedrooms, and to see exactly how the two layouts affect the position of the stairs and the bathroom.

bath

bed 1

bed 3

bed 2

bulkhead with 2m headroom below

FIRST FLOOR PLAN

utility

kitchen

dining

arch over Catnic CN6

½ hr frsc. door + frame over 100mm step

garage

min 75mm diming on tapered steps

hall

lounge

arch over with Catnic CN5X

this wall taken to underside of roof + firestopped

porch

Catnic CN81

GROUND FLOOR PLAN

**Ref: 96175**

**154 sq.m.   1667 sq.ft.**
**(inc. garage)**

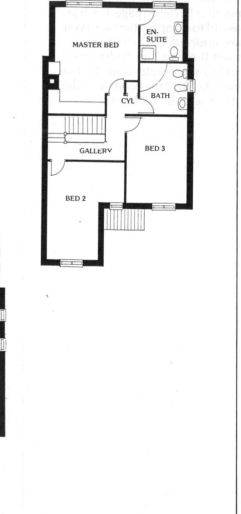

This is another large house for a narrow plot, but which is sufficiently complex to stand on its own in a rural situation. It was built in the Derbyshire Dales, where the planners required traditional brick arches over windows, stone sills, and side hung garage doors. However, consent was obtained for it to be built under cost effective pantiles, effecting a satisfactory compromise between cost effective construction and regional styling.

| Floor Area (inc. garage) | 1667 sq.ft. | 154 sq.m. |
|---|---|---|
| Dimensions overall | 25'5" x 44'5" | 7.74 x 13.55 |
| Lounge | 11'8" x 18'1" | 3.55 x 5.52 |
| Dining | 10'6" x 10'10" | 3.19 x 3.31 |
| Kitchen | 9'5" x 14'10" | 2.86 x 4.52 |
| Utility | 6'4" x 6'3" | 1.93 x 1.90 |
| Garage | 8'7" x 16'8" | 2.60 x 5.09 |
| Bed 1 | 14'9" x 18'1" | 4.50 x 5.52 |
| Bed 2 (max) | 12'9" x 17'3" | 3.88 x 5.26 |
| Bed 3 | 10'6" x 14'2" | 3.20 x 4.31 |

# Designs for Houses over 2500 sq. ft.

A house of this size will normally be designed to the specific requirements of the family that commissions it, and the examples that follow should be a source of design ideas for consideration rather than homes that can be imitated.

Most large houses in this country were built in the 19th century when they were expected to provide accommodation on a fixed scale appropriate to their size: perhaps a drawing room, dining room, breakfast room, library, ladies drawing room, billiard room etc., with a huge range of domestic accommodation beyond the green baize door. The same space is now used much more flexibly to reflect the interests and life style of the owner. Room sizes and the way in which they relate to each other might be designed to suit lavish entertaining, or a concern to display a collection of art to best advantage, or to reflect the owners taste in fashionable interior decor. Some of the houses on the pages that follow have a swimming pool as a key feature, others a large impressive entrance hall, and many have double inter connecting doors between principal rooms to enhance the scale of everything.

If you can afford a home of this size the difficult first steps are to identify the style and feel which you want for the building, to find the right person to design it, and to convey to him or her exactly what you want. A scrap book of illustrations or photographs of other properties is a very good start with this, and can be marked with the comments of all the family. For instance you may prefer the doors from the hall to the drawing room to be set in a 10" wall, which is always impressive. Take a photo of doors like this which you like. Are they set in the centre of the reveal, or on the hall side, or on the other side? They will merit door handles that are very carefully chosen, and the pattern of door furniture will usually be used throughout the house. Door handles are parts of the house that you actually *touch* more than any other: choose them with care. But is their style appropriate to the style of the skirtings and architraves that you admire? Your architect or designer should discuss all this with you, but will do so more effectively if you have sorted out and listed all your own likes and dislikes.

Finally, before looking at the real homes in this category on the following pages, remember that the larger the house, the more time and money should be spent on landscaping and garden features, from drives to terraces, and paved garden walks to tree planting. All should be part of a master plan to build a home that will reflect your taste and your standing.

**Ref: 96260**

**266 sq.m.    2862 sq.ft.**

An imposing double staircase leading to an imposing gallery is a key feature of this house, which has a simple layout with large rooms.

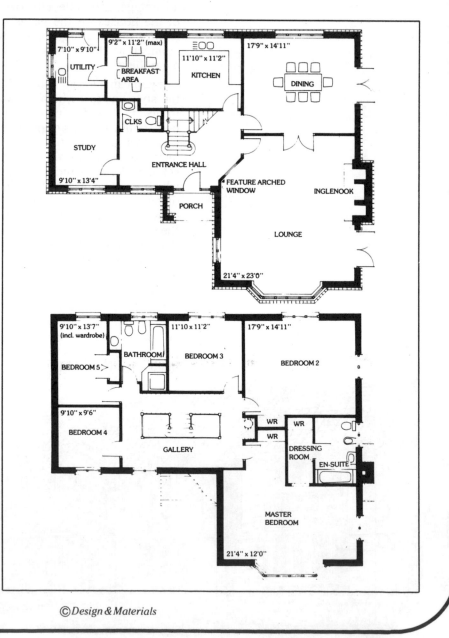

UTILITY 7'10" x 9'10"

BREAKFAST AREA 9'2" x 11'2" (max)

KITCHEN 11'10" x 11'2"

DINING 17'9" x 14'11"

CLKS

STUDY 9'10" x 13'4"

ENTRANCE HALL

FEATURE ARCHED WINDOW

PORCH

INGLENOOK

LOUNGE 21'4" x 23'0"

BEDROOM 5 9'10" x 13'7" (incl. wardrobe)

BATHROOM

BEDROOM 3 11'10 x 11'2"

BEDROOM 2 17'9" x 14'11"

BEDROOM 4 9'10" x 9'6"

GALLERY

WR
WR
WR

DRESSING ROOM

EN-SUITE

MASTER BEDROOM 21'4" x 12'0"

© Design & Materials

**Ref: 96150**

**246 sq.m.   2650 sq.ft.**

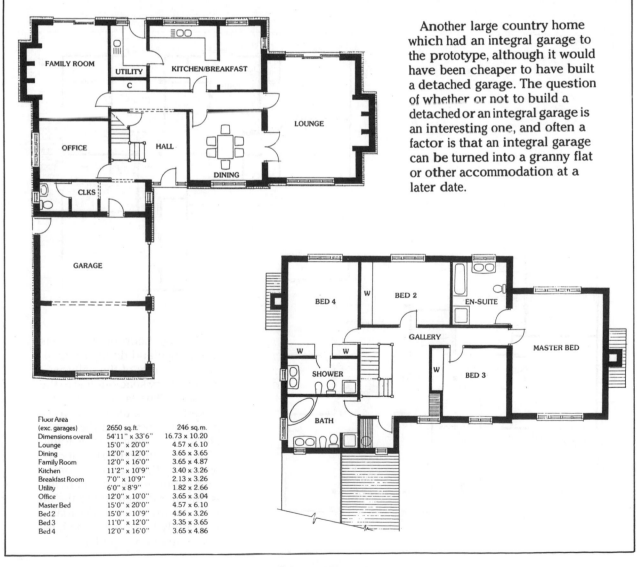

Another large country home which had an integral garage to the prototype, although it would have been cheaper to have built a detached garage. The question of whether or not to build a detached or an integral garage is an interesting one, and often a factor is that an integral garage can be turned into a granny flat or other accommodation at a later date.

| Floor Area | | |
|---|---|---|
| (exc. garages) | 2650 sq.ft. | 246 sq.m. |
| Dimensions overall | 54'11" x 33'6" | 16.73 x 10.20 |
| Lounge | 15'0" x 20'0" | 4.57 x 6.10 |
| Dining | 12'0" x 12'0" | 3.65 x 3.65 |
| Family Room | 12'0" x 16'0" | 3.65 x 4.87 |
| Kitchen | 11'2" x 10'9" | 3.40 x 3.26 |
| Breakfast Room | 7'0" x 10'9" | 2.13 x 3.26 |
| Utility | 6'0" x 8'9" | 1.82 x 2.66 |
| Office | 12'0" x 10'0" | 3.65 x 3.04 |
| Master Bed | 15'0" x 20'0" | 4.57 x 6.10 |
| Bed 2 | 15'0" x 10'9" | 4.56 x 3.26 |
| Bed 3 | 11'0" x 12'0" | 3.35 x 3.65 |
| Bed 4 | 12'0" x 16'0" | 3.65 x 4.86 |

**Ref: PN679**

**261 sq.m.   2801 sq.ft.**

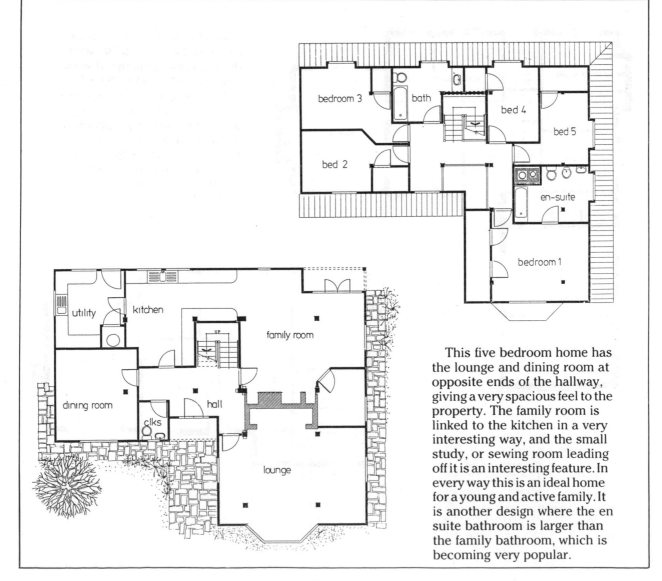

This five bedroom home has the lounge and dining room at opposite ends of the hallway, giving a very spacious feel to the property. The family room is linked to the kitchen in a very interesting way, and the small study, or sewing room leading off it is an interesting feature. In every way this is an ideal home for a young and active family. It is another design where the en suite bathroom is larger than the family bathroom, which is becoming very popular.

© *Potton*

**Ref: PN683**

**242 sq.m.    2600 sq.ft.**

This generously proportioned five bedroomed aisle frame house has interesting features, including the long first floor gallery overlooking the entrance hall. The hall itself is generously proportioned and virtually a room in its own right. As is becoming very common with larger houses today, the bathroom which is en suite to the master bedroom is very fully equipped, and is larger than the family bathroom. This reflects consideration of who paid for the house anyway! The huge Inglenook fireplace in the lounge backs onto another fireplace in the dining room with which it shares a common chimney, and the chimney breast in the dining room has two alcoves which lend themselves to a variety of uses.

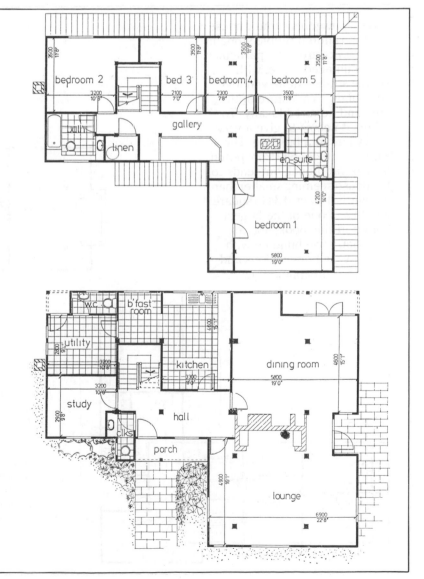

©Potton

**Ref: PN665**

**320 sq.m.   3445 sq.ft.**

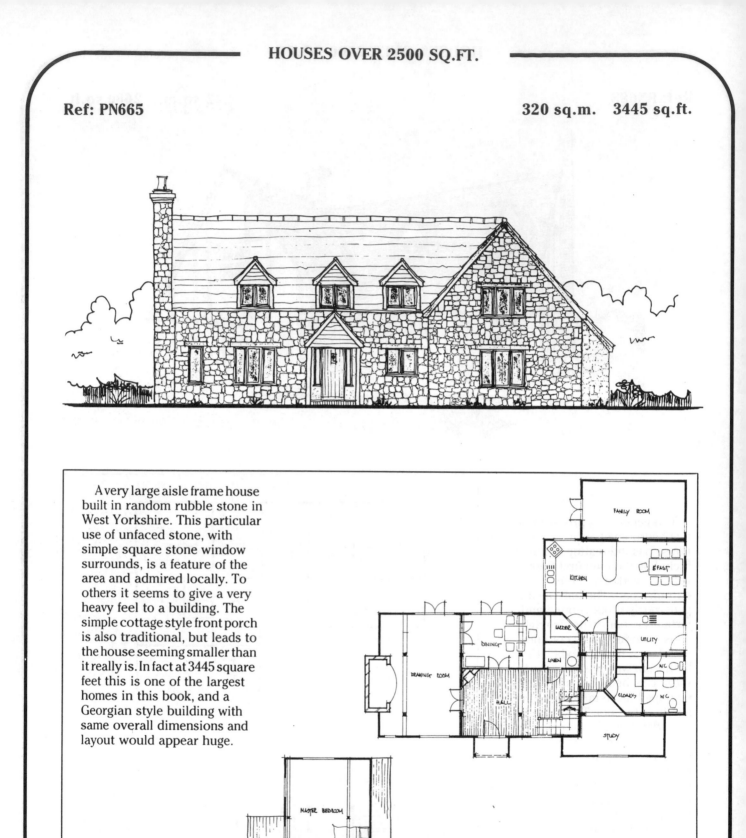

A very large aisle frame house built in random rubble stone in West Yorkshire. This particular use of unfaced stone, with simple square stone window surrounds, is a feature of the area and admired locally. To others it seems to give a very heavy feel to a building. The simple cottage style front porch is also traditional, but leads to the house seeming smaller than it really is. In fact at 3445 square feet this is one of the largest homes in this book, and a Georgian style building with same overall dimensions and layout would appear huge.

| Drawing Room | 4.7 x 6.9 | 15'5" x 22'8" |
|---|---|---|
| Dining | 4.6 x 3.0 | 15'1" x 9'10" |
| Family Room | 5.8 x 3.3 | 19'0" x 10'10" |
| Kitchen | 7.9 x 4.5 | 25'11" x 14'9" |
| Utility | 3.8 x 2.5 | 12'6" x 8'2" |
| Study | 5.7 x 2.3 | 18'8" x 7'7" |
| Master Bedroom | 4.7 x 5.7 | 15'5" x 18'8" |
| Guest Bedroom | 4.7 x 3.2 | 15'5" x 10'6" |
| Bedroom 3 | 3.8 x 2.8 | 12'6" x 9'2" |
| Bedroom 4 | 3.8 x 2.8 | 11'6" x 9'2" |
| Bedroom 5 | 3.3 x 2.1 | 10'10" x 6'11" |

© Potton

**Ref: PN663**

**469 sq.m.   5050 sq.ft.**
**(inc. pool)**

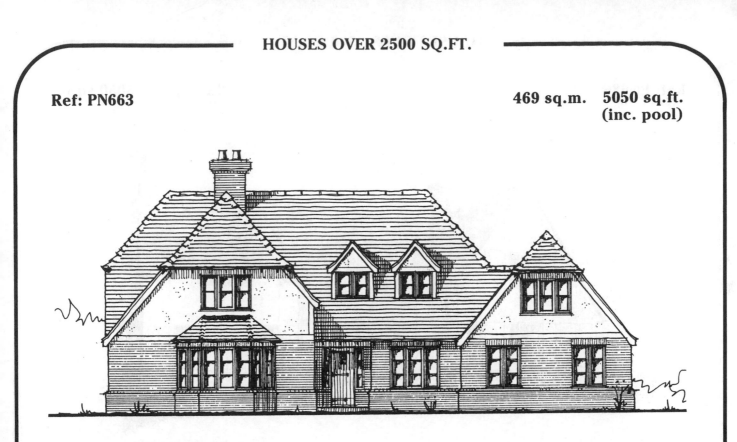

Nearly half of the area of this house is taken up by leisure space – an indoor swimming pool, a hobbies room and rooms above the leisure area for a studio – and all of this has been cleverly incorporated into a building which is one coherant whole, and makes a most impressive home.

| | | |
|---|---|---|
| Living Room | 7.0 x 5.0 | 25'3" x 16'5" |
| Dining Room | 4.5 x 4.7 | 14'9" x 15'5" |
| Family Room | 3.0 x 2.2 | 9'10" x 7'3" |
| Kitchen | 5.7 x 6.0 | 18'8" x 19'8" |
| Utility | 3.0 x 4.5 | 9'10" x 14'9" |
| Hobbies | 4.2 x 4.5 | 13'9" x 14'9" |
| Garden Store | 2.8 x 2.7 | 9'2" x 8'10" |
| Changing Area | 3.0 x 2.0 | 9'10" x 7'3" |
| Pool | 6.6 x 12 | 21'8" x 40'0" |
| Master Bedroom | 4.6 x 4.2 | 15'1" x 13'9" |
| Bedroom 2 | 4.5 x 5.5 | 14'9" x 18'1" |
| Bedroom 3 | 3.0 x 3.5 | 9'0" x 11'6" |
| Bedroom 4 | 3.3 x 3.0 | 10'10" x 9'0" |
| Study | 4.0 x 5.4 | 13'1" x 17'9" |

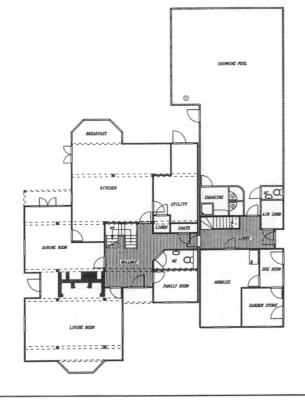

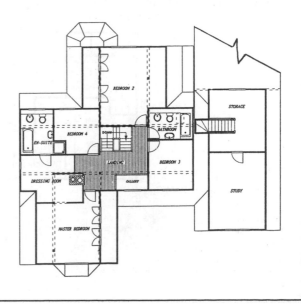

**Ref: PN686**

**283 sq.m.   3050 sq.ft.**

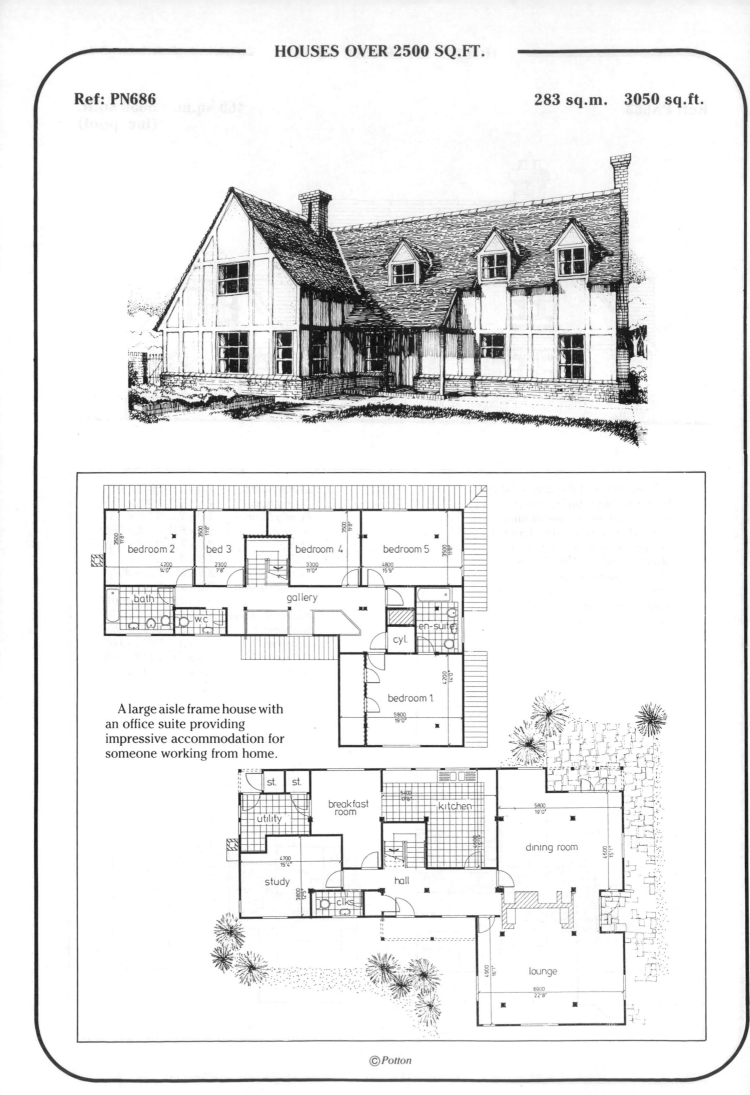

A large aisle frame house with an office suite providing impressive accommodation for someone working from home.

© Potton

**Ref: PN689**

**359 sq.m.    3870 sq.ft.**

This stately home has the feeling of a traditional 'E' shape Elizabethan manor house. There are no fewer than four fireplaces which serve the lounge, the dining room, the morning room and the study. The boiler has its own separate chimney, providing the forest of chimney stacks which is so typical of period houses of this size.

The arrangement illustrated provides six bedrooms, three of which are generous doubles, and three bathrooms.

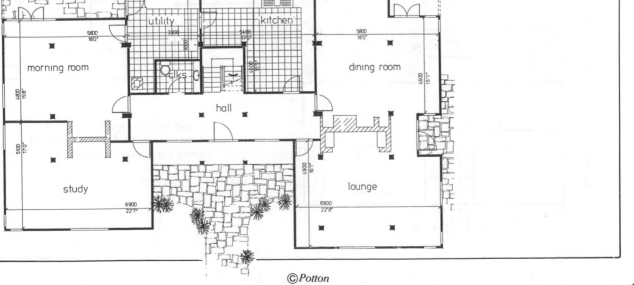

©*Potton*

**Ref: PN687**

**226 sq.m.    2865 sq.ft.**

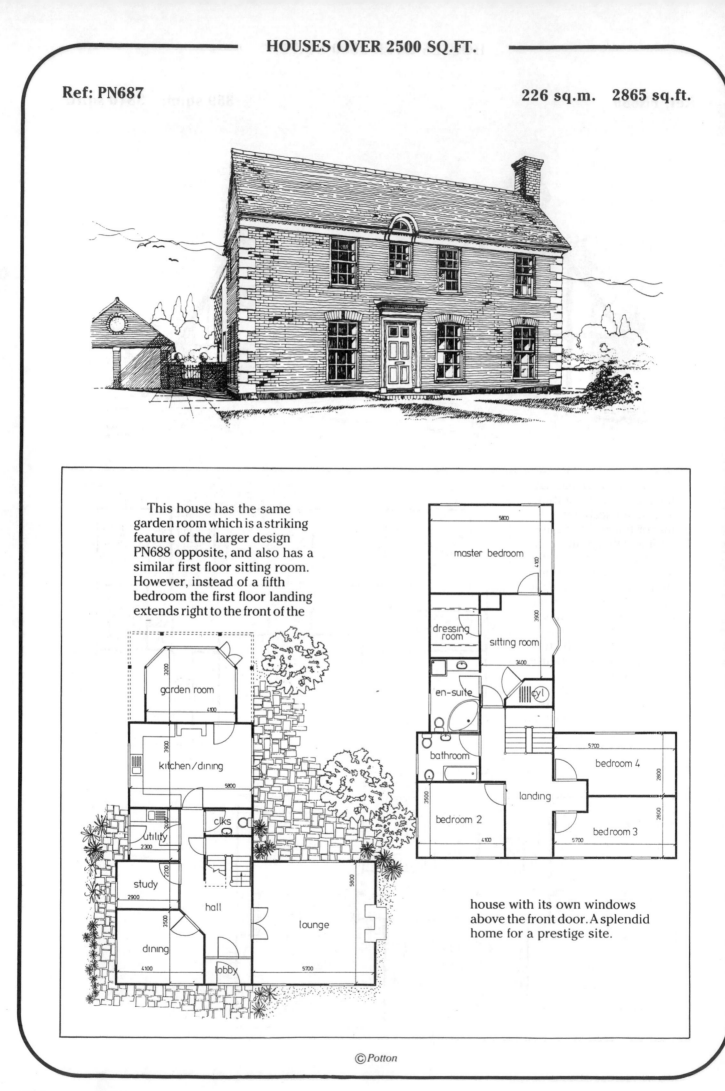

This house has the same garden room which is a striking feature of the larger design PN688 opposite, and also has a similar first floor sitting room. However, instead of a fifth bedroom the first floor landing extends right to the front of the house with its own windows above the front door. A splendid home for a prestige site.

© *Potton*

**Ref: PN688**

**286 sq.m.   3075 sq.ft.**

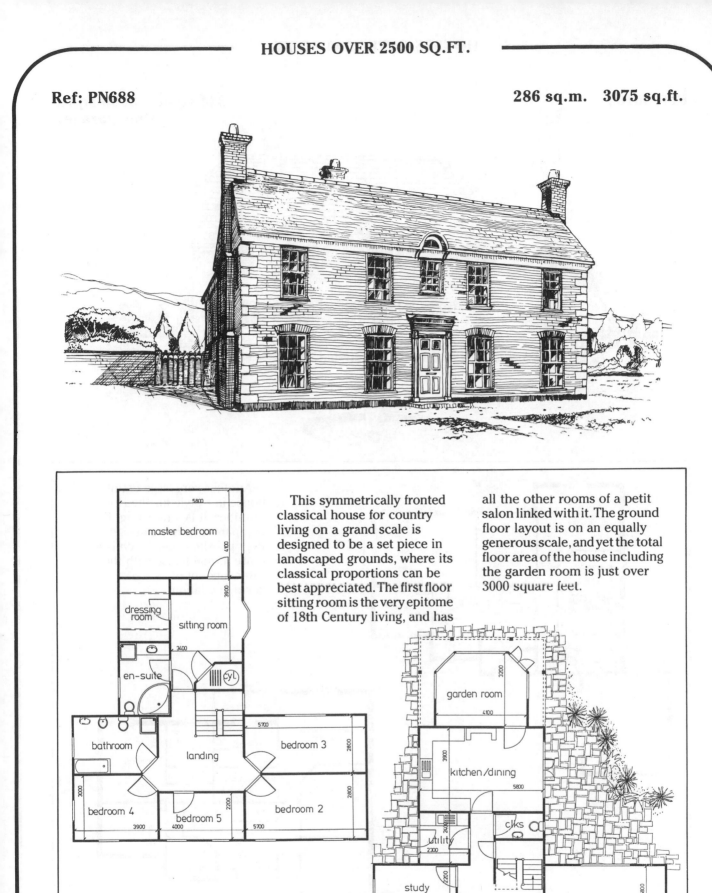

This symmetrically fronted classical house for country living on a grand scale is designed to be a set piece in landscaped grounds, where its classical proportions can be best appreciated. The first floor sitting room is the very epitome of 18th Century living, and has all the other rooms of a petit salon linked with it. The ground floor layout is on an equally generous scale, and yet the total floor area of the house including the garden room is just over 3000 square feet.

©Potton

**Ref: 96185**

**344 sq.m.  3700 sq.ft.
(inc. garage)**

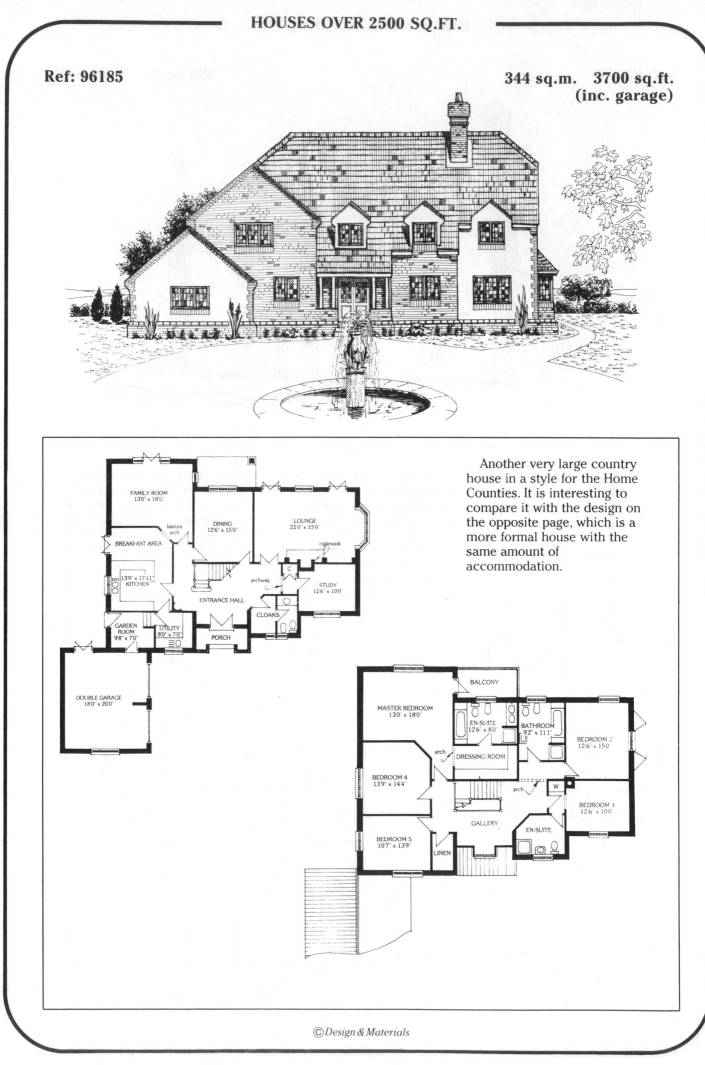

Another very large country house in a style for the Home Counties. It is interesting to compare it with the design on the opposite page, which is a more formal house with the same amount of accommodation.

FAMILY ROOM
13'0" x 18'0"

DINING
12'6" x 15'0"

LOUNGE
22'0" x 15'0"

feature arch

BREAKFAST AREA

inglenook

KITCHEN
13'9" x 17'11"

archway

C

STUDY
12'6" x 10'0"

ENTRANCE HALL

GARDEN ROOM
9'8" x 7'0"

UTILITY
8'0" x 7'0"

PORCH

CLOAKS

DOUBLE GARAGE
18'0" x 20'0"

BALCONY

MASTER BEDROOM
13'0" x 18'0"

EN-SUITE
12'6" x 8'0"

BATHROOM
9'2" x 11'1"

BEDROOM 2
12'6" x 15'0"

BEDROOM 4
13'9" x 14'4"

arch

DRESSING ROOM

BEDROOM 3
12'6" x 10'0"

W

arch

GALLERY

EN-SUITE

BEDROOM 5
10'7" x 13'9"

LINEN

EN-SUITE

**Ref: 96184**

**342 sq.m.    3680 sq.ft.**

A large country home for a site in Surrey, with five bedrooms, each with an en suite bathroom. The very large gallery at the head of the stairs can be reduced in size to give a larger master bedroom if required, reducing the size of the walk-in linen cupboard accordingly.

**Ref: 96250**

**237 sq.m.    2562 sq.ft.**

A house with a snooker room, built for an amateur player and not a professional. However, the snooker room is adaptable and because it has its own w.c. it would make a good office or be the basis of a granny flat. The three very large bedrooms are not so adaptable and would be difficult to sub divide to suit another owner, so this will always be a home for a family with special ground floor requirements who want three large bedrooms only.

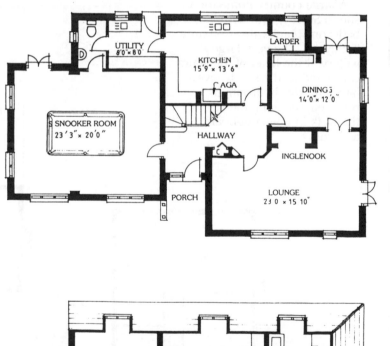

© *Design & Materials*

**Ref: 96194**

**437 sq.m.   4700 sq.ft.**

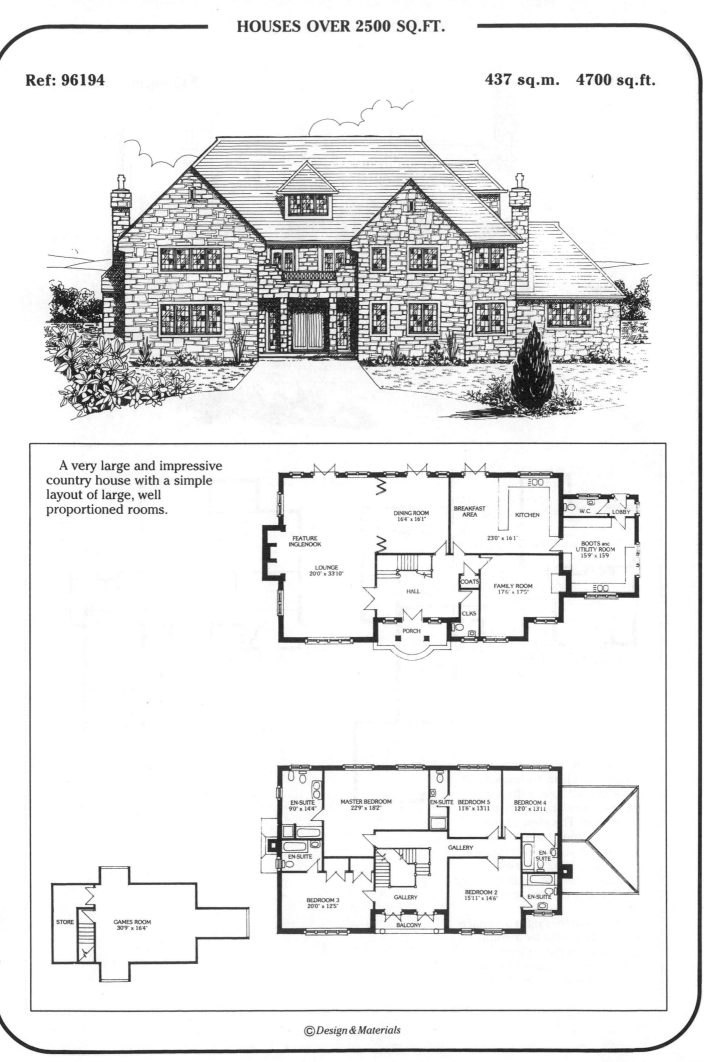

A very large and impressive country house with a simple layout of large, well proportioned rooms.

DINING ROOM
16'4" x 16'1"

BREAKFAST AREA

KITCHEN
23'0" x 16'1"

W.C.

LOBBY

FEATURE INGLENOOK

LOUNGE
20'0" x 33'10"

COATS

FAMILY ROOM
17'6" x 17'5"

BOOTS and UTILITY ROOM
15'9" x 15'9

HALL

CLKS

PORCH

EN-SUITE
9'0" x 14'4"

MASTER BEDROOM
22'9" x 18'2"

EN-SUITE

BEDROOM 5
11'6" x 13'11

BEDROOM 4
12'0" x 13'11

EN-SUITE

GALLERY

EN-SUITE

BEDROOM 3
20'0" x 12'5"

GALLERY

BEDROOM 2
15'11" x 14'6"

EN-SUITE

BALCONY

STORE

GAMES ROOM
30'9" x 16'4"

**Ref: 96166**

**545 sq.m.   5865 sq.ft.**

A huge modern home with many American features, built on a level site but with changes of floor level internally to add character. The view of the sunken dining room which greets the visitor entering the front door is a typically American device, as is the very large and well equipped guest suite.

Access to the huge roof space can be provided by a spiral staircase on the gallery, providing many options for even more accommodation.

**Ref: 96187**

**323 sq.m.    3476 sq.ft.**

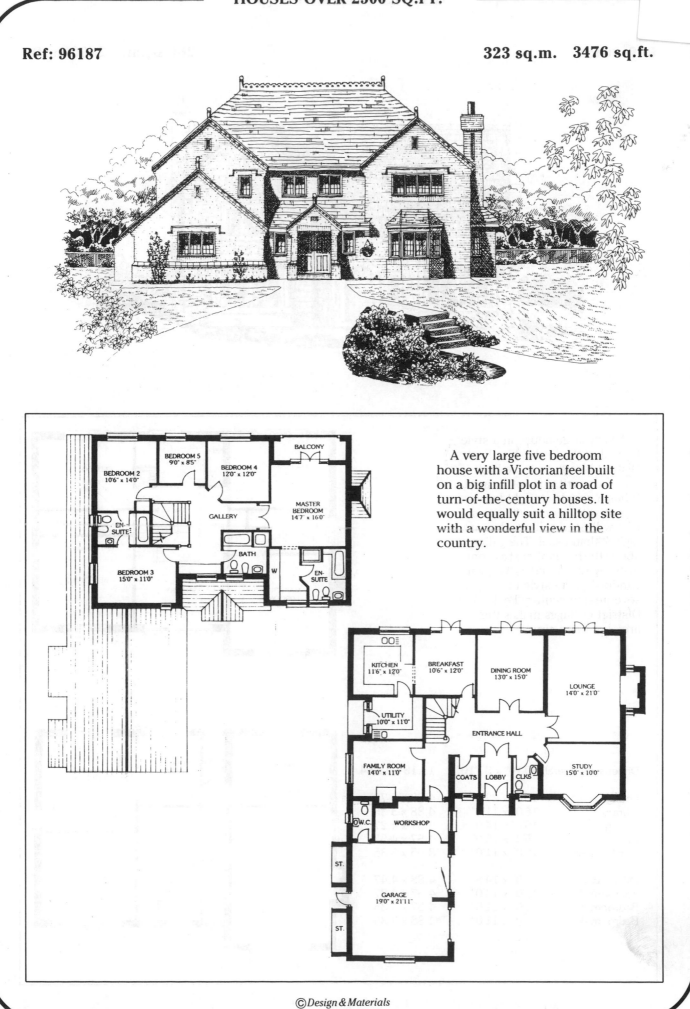

A very large five bedroom house with a Victorian feel built on a big infill plot in a road of turn-of-the-century houses. It would equally suit a hilltop site with a wonderful view in the country.

BEDROOM 2
10'6" x 14'0"

BEDROOM 5
9'0" x 8'5"

BEDROOM 4
12'0" x 12'0"

BALCONY

MASTER BEDROOM
14'7" x 16'0"

GALLERY

EN-SUITE

BATH

W

EN-SUITE

BEDROOM 3
15'0" x 11'0"

KITCHEN
11'6" x 12'0"

BREAKFAST
10'6" x 12'0"

DINING ROOM
13'0" x 15'0"

LOUNGE
14'0" x 21'0"

UTILITY
10'0" x 11'0"

ENTRANCE HALL

FAMILY ROOM
14'0" x 11'0"

COATS

LOBBY

CLKS

STUDY
15'0" x 10'0"

W.C.

WORKSHOP

ST.

GARAGE
19'0" x 21'11"

ST.

© *Design & Materials*

**Ref: 96159**

**260 sq.m.    2800 sq.ft.**

A very large house in a style typical of the Derbyshire Peak District, designed to be built in the coarse grit stone of the area. It has a simple straight forward layout with very large rooms that will need ceilings that are higher than usual. The gallery above the hall is almost a room in its own right, and its 'Weavers window' in the style of seventeenth century Peak District cottages makes this area light and airy.

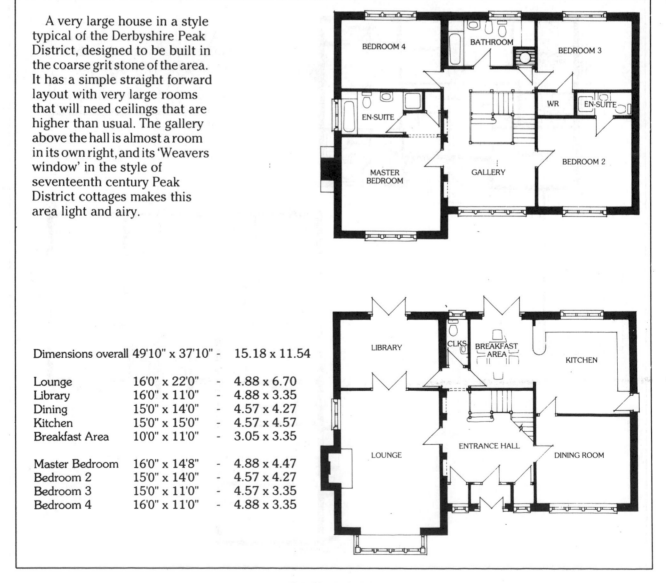

| | | |
|---|---|---|
| Dimensions overall 49'10" x 37'10" | - | 15.18 x 11.54 |
| Lounge | 16'0" x 22'0" | - 4.88 x 6.70 |
| Library | 16'0" x 11'0" | - 4.88 x 3.35 |
| Dining | 15'0" x 14'0" | - 4.57 x 4.27 |
| Kitchen | 15'0" x 15'0" | - 4.57 x 4.57 |
| Breakfast Area | 10'0" x 11'0" | - 3.05 x 3.35 |
| Master Bedroom | 16'0" x 14'8" | - 4.88 x 4.47 |
| Bedroom 2 | 15'0" x 14'0" | - 4.57 x 4.27 |
| Bedroom 3 | 15'0" x 11'0" | - 4.57 x 3.35 |
| Bedroom 4 | 16'0" x 11'0" | - 4.88 x 3.35 |

**Ref: 96179**

**234 sq.m.    2523 sq.ft.**

| Floor Area | | |
|---|---|---|
| (exc. garage/utility) | 2523 sq.ft. | 234 sq.m. |
| Dimensions overall | 47'6" x 36'6" | 14.46 x 11.11 |
| Lounge | 15'0" x 22'4" | 4.57 x 6.81 |
| Dining | 12'0" x 11'0" | 3.65 x 3.35 |
| Family Room | 18'0" x 15'0" | 5.48 x 4.57 |
| Kitchen/Breakfast | 18'0" x 12'0" | 5.48 x 3.65 |
| Study | 11'9" x 7'0" | 3.58 x 2.13 |
| Master Bed | 18'0" x 12'0" | 5.48 x 3.65 |
| Bed 2 | 15'0" x 11'0" | 4.57 x 3.36 |
| Bed 3 | 15'0" x 11'0" | 4.57 x 3.35 |
| Bed 4 | 10'0" x 15'0" | 3.04 x 4.57 |
| Bed 5 | 9'8" x 11'9" | 2.93 x 3.57 |

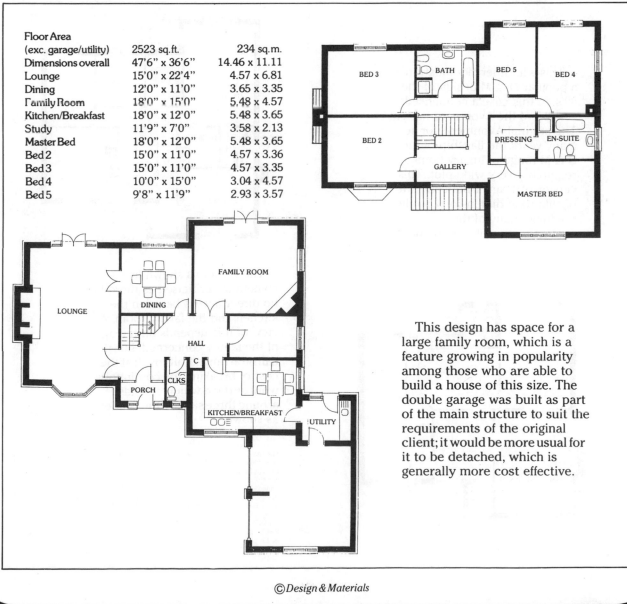

This design has space for a large family room, which is a feature growing in popularity among those who are able to build a house of this size. The double garage was built as part of the main structure to suit the requirements of the original client; it would be more usual for it to be detached, which is generally more cost effective.

*©Design & Materials*

**Ref: 96165**

**193 sq.m.    2079 sq.ft.**

This is another modification of a popular D & M design of the 80's, in this case a condensed version of the Avonmere design. The original Avonmere, for so many years the flagship of the D & M range of luxury homes, required a very wide plot. This version of it can be built on a site of suburban dimensions, while retaining many of the characteristics of the original.

The layout as shown is sometimes criticised as there is no direct access between the kitchen and the family room. A view of this depends on the age of the family concerned, but it can be arranged, although at the cost of breaking the continuous work surface which extends around three sides of the kitchen as shown.

| Floor Area | 2079 sq.ft. | 193 sq.m. |
|---|---|---|
| Dimensions overall | 37'2" x 37'4" | 11.32 x 11.37 |
| Drawing Room | 13'0" x 18'0" | 3.96 x 5.48 |
| Family Room | 12'0" x 14'0" | 3.65 x 4.26 |
| Dining | 12'0" x 17'2" | 3.65 x 5.23 |
| Study | 7'0" x 10'0" | 2.13 x 3.04 |
| Kitchen (max) | 12'8" x 12'0" | 4.76 x 3.65 |
| Utility | 5'3" x 6'10" | 1.60 x 2.07 |
| Master Bed | 12'0" x 17'2" | 3.65 x 5.23 |
| Bed 2 | 13'0" x 11'0" | 3.96 x 3.35 |
| Bed 3 | 10'0" x 13'0" | 3.05 x 3.65 |
| Bed 4 | 8'1" x 12'0" | 2.46 x 3.65 |
| Bed 5 | 8'0" x 8'9" | 2.43 x 2.65 |

**Ref: 96176**

**241 sq.m.    2595 sq.ft.**

This large family house of over 2500 square feet has a fashionable raised plinth to window sill level. Above the eaves a bell moulding marks the start of the rendered finish to the first storey, while above there are three separate levels to the eaves, achieved by having dormer windows to one wing. In this way a large house, which a few years ago would have been an uncompromising functional block, is given the complex shape and appeal of a period farmhouse.

The first floor layout illustrated here has a very large games room on the first floor. Most families would probably prefer a four or five bedroom layout, and if the games room becomes the master bedroom suite it can be of very generous proportions.

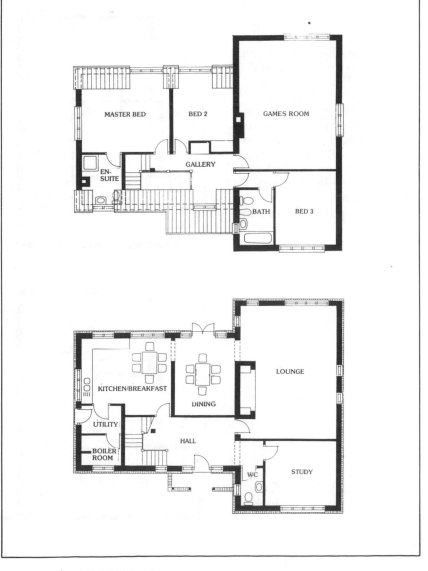

| Floor Area | 2595 sq.ft. | 241 sq.m. |
|---|---|---|
| Dimensions overall | 47'7" x 38'6" | 14.50 x 11.73 |
| Lounge | 17'2" x 24'0" | 5.24 x 7.31 |
| Dining | 10'7" x 14'0" | 3.23 x 4.26 |
| Kitchen/Breakfast | 16'4" x 14'0" | 4.98 x 4.26 |
| Utility | 7'3" x 5'0" | 2.21 x 1.52 |
| Study | 12'10" x 12'0" | 3.92 x 3.65 |
| Master Bedroom | 16'4" x 14'0" | 4.98 x 4.26 |
| Bedroom 2 | 10'7" x 14'0" | 3.23 x 4.26 |
| Bedroom 3 | 10'7" x 13'4" | 3.24 x 4.05 |
| Games Room | 17'2" x 23'0" | 5.24 x 7.01 |

**Ref: 96160**

**244 sq.m.    2627 sq.ft.**

A large house designed for a professional athlete who had wide business interests which he managed from home. The home was designed on three levels to suit a sloping site.

The front door leads to a hall with a study/gym/sauna suite on one side, and a guest suite on the other. One flight of the stairs leads down to a lounge, dining room and kitchen area with access to a terrace, and the other goes up to the bedrooms.

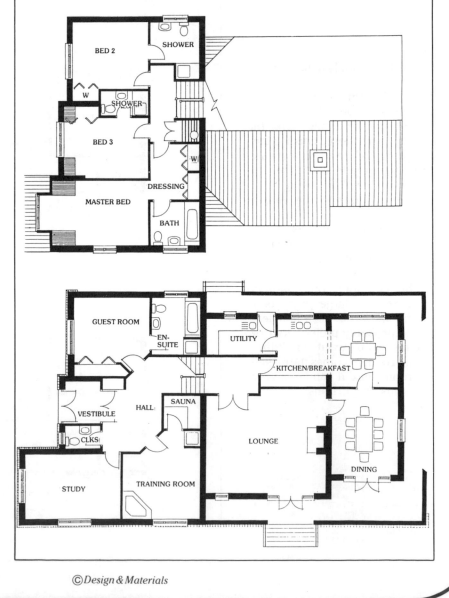

| Floor Area | 2627 sq.ft. | 244 sq.m. |
|---|---|---|
| Dimensions overall | 39'6" x 64'3" | 12.03 x 19.57 |
| Lounge | 20'0" x 17'7" | 6.10 x 5.36 |
| Dining | 11'0" x 14'6" | 3.35 x 4.42 |
| Kitchen | 8'2" x 11'6" | 2.50 x 3.50 |
| Utility | 11'6" x 6'0" | 3.50 x 1.83 |
| Breakfast Room | 11'0" x 11'6" | 3.35 x 3.50 |
| Study | 16'2" x 11'0" | 4.93 x 3.35 |
| Training Room (max) | 13'0" x 15'0" | 3.96 x 4.57 |
| Guest Room | 12'11" x 13'6" | 3.94 x 4.10 |
| Master Bed | 16'5" x 11'0" | 5.00 x 3.35 |
| Bed 2 | 12'11" x 11'6" | 3.94 x 3.50 |
| Bed 3 | 14'5" x 9'5" | 4.39 x 2.86 |

**Ref: 96251**

**246 sq.m.   2650 sq.ft.**
**(inc. garage)**

A house in the country designed to look like neighbouring farm buildings, even to the barn door look of the garage doors.

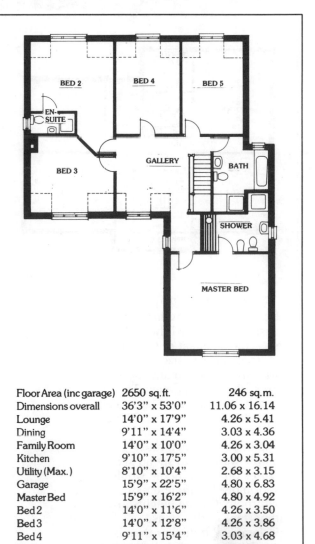

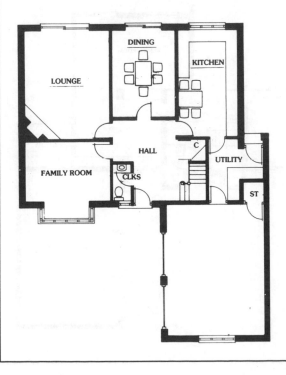

| Floor Area (inc garage) | 2650 sq.ft. | 246 sq.m. |
|---|---|---|
| Dimensions overall | 36'3" x 53'0" | 11.06 x 16.14 |
| Lounge | 14'0" x 17'9" | 4.26 x 5.41 |
| Dining | 9'11" x 14'4" | 3.03 x 4.36 |
| Family Room | 14'0" x 10'0" | 4.26 x 3.04 |
| Kitchen | 9'10" x 17'5" | 3.00 x 5.31 |
| Utility (Max.) | 8'10" x 10'4" | 2.68 x 3.15 |
| Garage | 15'9" x 22'5" | 4.80 x 6.83 |
| Master Bed | 15'9" x 16'2" | 4.80 x 4.92 |
| Bed 2 | 14'0" x 11'6" | 4.26 x 3.50 |
| Bed 3 | 14'0" x 12'8" | 4.26 x 3.86 |
| Bed 4 | 9'11" x 15'4" | 3.03 x 4.68 |
| Bed 5 | 9'10" x 15'4" | 3.00 x 4.68 |

**Ref: 96145**

307 sq.m.  3312 sq.ft.
(exc. garage)

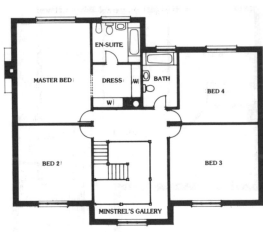

| Dimensions overall | | |
|---|---|---|
| inc. Garage | 61'1" x 58'9" | 18.61 x 17.90 |
| Lounge | 25'0" x 20'0" | 7.62 x 6.09 |
| Family Room | 22'8" x 14'0" | 6.92 x 4.26 |
| Dining | 14'8" x 15'0" | 4.48 x 4.57 |
| Kitchen | 17'8" x 15'4" | 5.39 x 4.67 |
| Utility | 10'0" x 8'0" | 3.04 x 2.43 |
| Master Bedroom | 15'0" x 20'0" | 4.57 x 6.09 |
| Bedroom 2 | 15'0" x 15'0" | 4.57 x 4.57 |
| Bedroom 3 | 18'0" x 15'0" | 5.48 x 4.57 |
| Bedroom 4 | 15'8" x 14'0" | 4.76 x 4.26 |

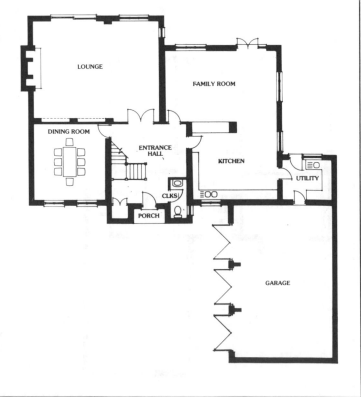

A large house with rooms that are the size of rooms in a middle class home of the Edwardian era – the smallest of the four bedrooms is the size of the drawing room in many modern 'executive style homes'. The huge hall has a feature staircase, but otherwise there is nothing unusual in the layout or amenities, although most people wanting to spend six figures on a new home would want more than one en-suite bathroom. Ceiling heights are important in this house – preferably 2 ft. higher than is usual these days, in spite of what this will do to heating costs.

**Ref: 96162**

**311 sq.m.   3353 sq.ft.**

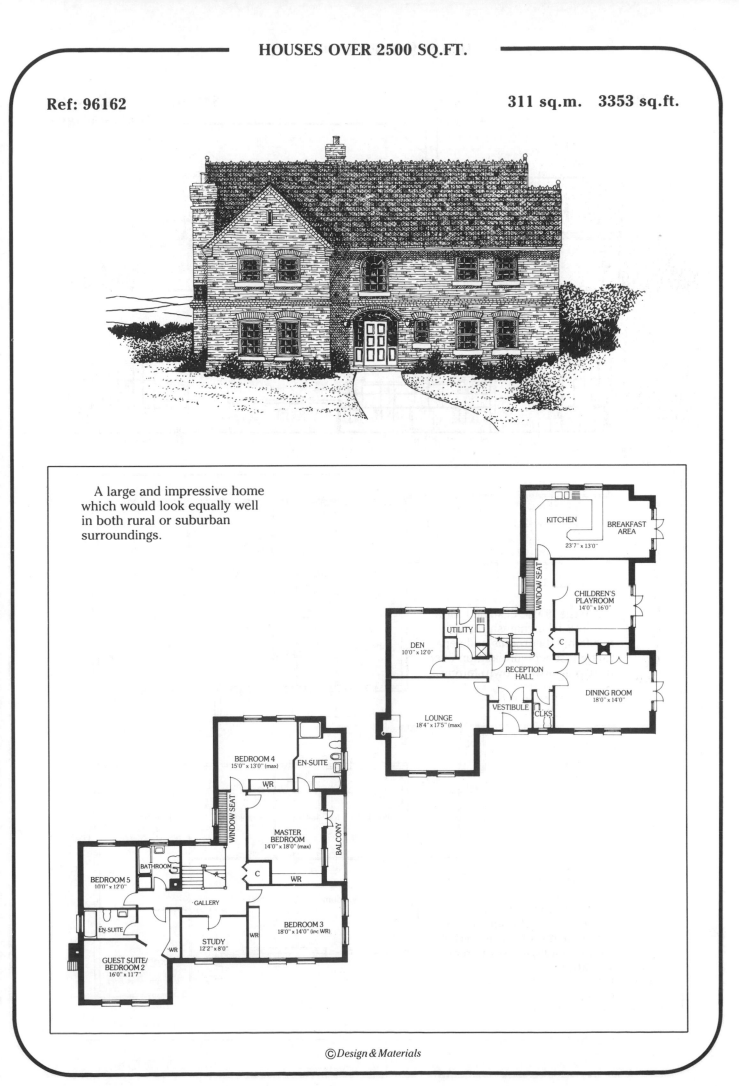

A large and impressive home which would look equally well in both rural or suburban surroundings.

KITCHEN
23'7" x 13'0"

BREAKFAST AREA

WINDOW SEAT

UTILITY

CHILDREN'S PLAYROOM
14'0" x 16'0"

DEN
10'0" x 12'0"

C

RECEPTION HALL

DINING ROOM
18'0" x 14'0"

LOUNGE
18'4" x 17'5" (max)

VESTIBULE

CLKS

BEDROOM 4
15'0" x 13'0" (max)

EN-SUITE

WR

WINDOW SEAT

MASTER BEDROOM
14'0" x 18'0" (max)

BALCONY

BATHROOM

BEDROOM 5
10'0" x 12'0"

C

WR

GALLERY

EN-SUITE

WR

BEDROOM 3
18'0" x 14'0" (inc WR)

STUDY
12'2" x 8'0"

WR

GUEST SUITE/ BEDROOM 2
16'0" x 11'7"

*© Design & Materials*

**Ref: P3031**

**343 sq.m.   3692 sq.ft.**
**(exc. garage)**

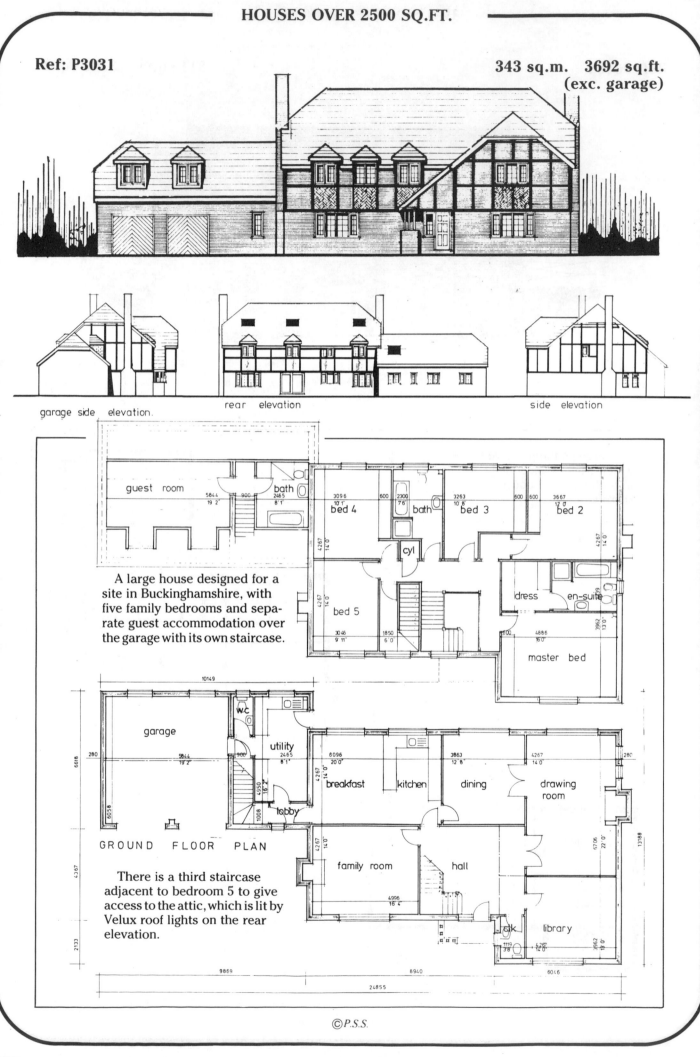

garage side elevation.

rear elevation

side elevation

guest room

bath

5844
19 2

900

2465
8 1

3096
10 1

600

2300
7 6

bath

3263
10 8

600 600

3667
12 0

bed 4

bed 3

bed 2

4267
14 0

cyl

4267
14 0

4267
14 0

bed 5

dress

en-suite

3962
13 0

3046
9 11

1850
6 0

600

4886
16 0

master bed

A large house designed for a
site in Buckinghamshire, with
five family bedrooms and separate guest accommodation over
the garage with its own staircase.

10149

wc

garage

utility
2465
8 1

280

5844
19 2

900

6058

4950
16 2

4267
14 0

6096
20 0

breakfast

kitchen

3863
12 8

dining

4267
14 0

drawing
room

280

6618

1008

lobby

GROUND FLOOR PLAN

4267
14 0

family room

hall

6706
22 0

13188

4367

There is a third staircase
adjacent to bedroom 5 to give
access to the attic, which is lit by
Velux roof lights on the rear
elevation.

4996
16 4

clk

library

2133

1119
7 6

4267
14 0

3962
13 0

9869

8940

6046

24855

©P.S.S.

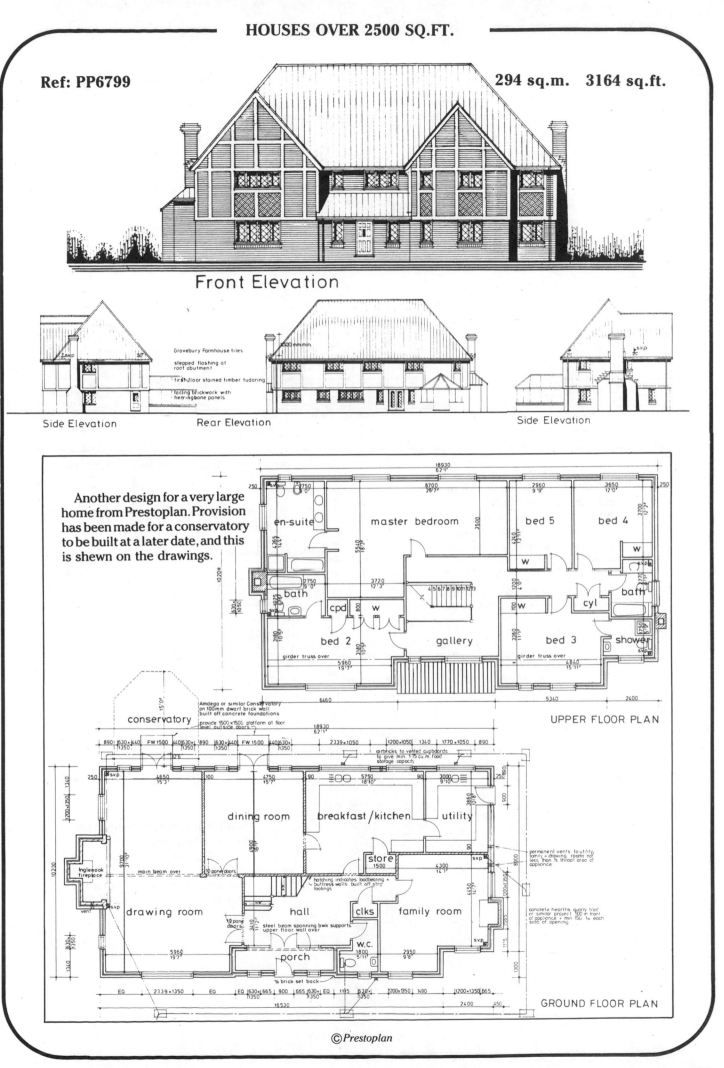

**Ref: PP6799**

**294 sq.m.   3164 sq.ft.**

Front Elevation

Side Elevation

Rear Elevation

Grovebury Farmhouse tiles

stepped flashing at roof abutment

first floor stained timber tudoring

facing brickwork with herringbone panels

Side Elevation

Another design for a very large home from Prestoplan. Provision has been made for a conservatory to be built at a later date, and this is shewn on the drawings.

en-suite

master bedroom

bed 5

bed 4

w

w

bath

cpd

w

gallery

w

cyl

bath

bed 2

bed 3

shower

girder truss over

girder truss over

UPPER FLOOR PLAN

conservatory

Amdega or similar Conservatory on 100mm dwarf brick wall built off concrete foundations

provide 1500 x1500 platform at floor level outside doors

airbricks to vented cupboards to give min. 1.75 cu.m food storage capacity

dining room

breakfast/kitchen

utility

Inglenook fireplace

mbin beam over

store
1500

permanent vents to utility, family + drawing rooms not less than ½ throat area of appliance

concrete hearths quarry tiled or similar project 500 in front of appliance + min 150 to each side of opening.

drawing room

hall

clks

family room

vent

10 pane doors

steel beam spanning bwk supports upper floor wall over

hatching indicates loadbearing + buttress walls built off strip footings

W.C.

porch

¼ brick set back

GROUND FLOOR PLAN

**Ref: C626A**

**235 sq.m.    2529 sq.ft.**

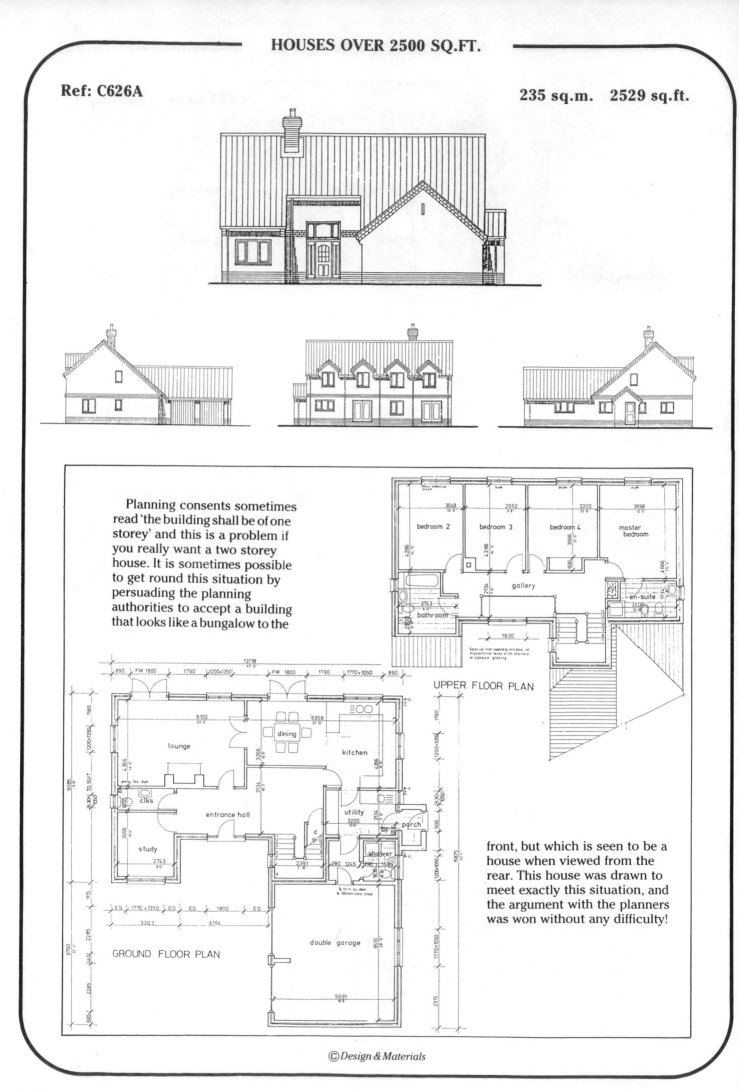

Planning consents sometimes read 'the building shall be of one storey' and this is a problem if you really want a two storey house. It is sometimes possible to get round this situation by persuading the planning authorities to accept a building that looks like a bungalow to the

UPPER FLOOR PLAN

bedroom 2

bedroom 3

bedroom 4

master bedroom

gallery

bathroom

en-suite

GROUND FLOOR PLAN

lounge

dining

kitchen

clks

entrance hall

utility

porch

study

shower

double garage

front, but which is seen to be a house when viewed from the rear. This house was drawn to meet exactly this situation, and the argument with the planners was won without any difficulty!

**Ref: PP6519**

**269 sq.m.   2895 sq.ft.**
**(exc. garage)**

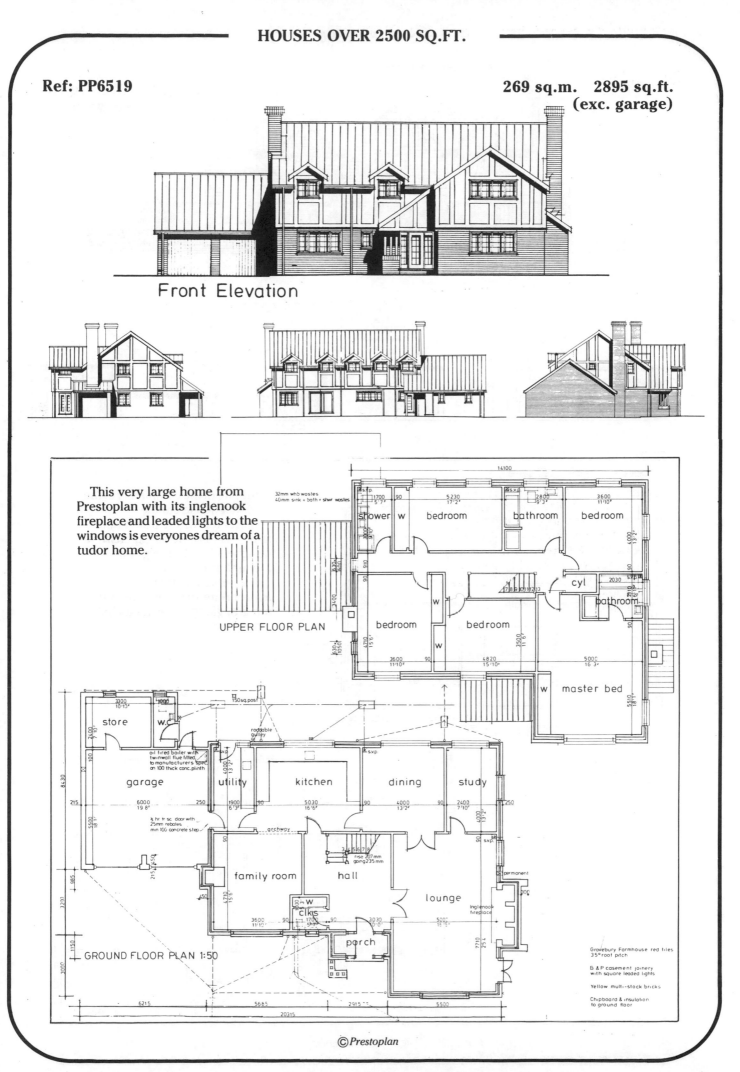

Front Elevation

This very large home from Prestoplan with its inglenook fireplace and leaded lights to the windows is everyones dream of a tudor home.

UPPER FLOOR PLAN

GROUND FLOOR PLAN 1:50

Grovebury Farmhouse red tiles
35° roof pitch

B & P casement joinery
with square leaded lights

Yellow multi-stock bricks

Chipboard & insulation
to ground floor

© Prestoplan

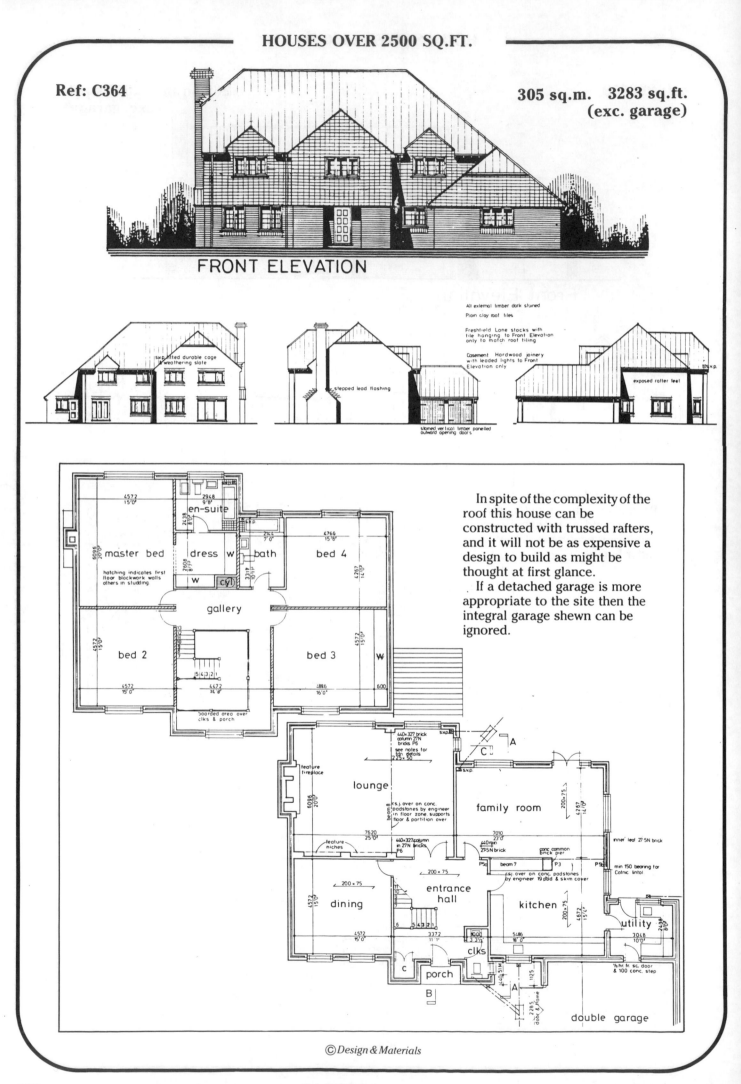

**Ref: C364**

**305 sq.m.   3283 sq.ft.**
**(exc. garage)**

## FRONT ELEVATION

All external timber dark stained

Plain clay roof tiles

Freshfield Lane stocks with tile hanging to Front Elevation only to match roof tiling

Casement Hardwood joinery with leaded lights to Front Elevation only

s.v.p. fitted durable cage & weathering slate

stepped lead flashing

exposed rafter feet

stained vertical timber panelled outward opening doors

In spite of the complexity of the roof this house can be constructed with trussed rafters, and it will not be as expensive a design to build as might be thought at first glance.

If a detached garage is more appropriate to the site then the integral garage shewn can be ignored.

master bed

hatching indicates first floor blockwork walls others in studding.

en-suite

dress

bath

bed 4

gallery

bed 2

bed 3

boarded area over clks & porch

lounge

feature fireplace

feature niches

family room

dining

entrance hall

kitchen

utility

clks

porch

double garage

**Ref: C498**

**284 sq.m.   3057 sq.ft.**

A large country home where the principle part of the roof has a very wide span, resulting in the roof ridge being particularly high. This would have led to it dominating any adjacent properties but in fact it was built in an isolated position. The Inglenook fireplace is in a lounge that is large enough to show it to the best advantage, and everything else is on the same generous scale.

rear elevation

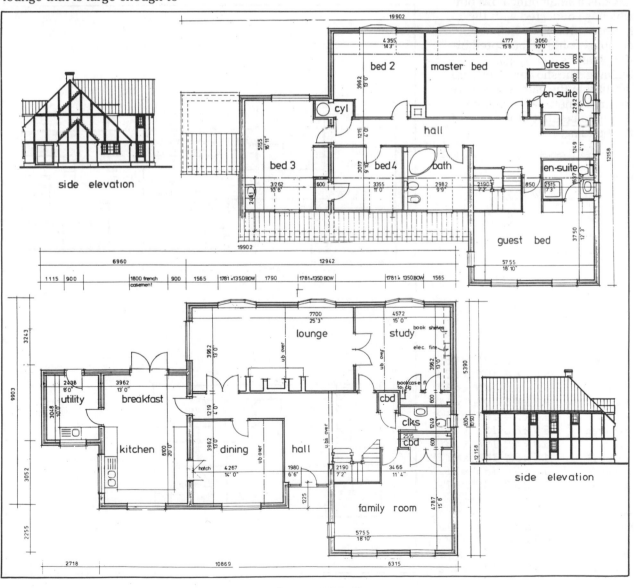

side elevation

side elevation

© Design & Materials

**Ref: PN664**

**451 sq.m.   4857 sq.ft.**

This very large country house has a granny annexe which is as large as a small bungalow, but which is connected with the house so that the whole complex could be accepted by the planners as a single building. The shower, sauna and jaccuzzi in the games room are to serve a new swimming pool that is to be built at the rear of the building.

| | | |
|---|---|---|
| Living Room | 6.9 x 5.0 | 22'8" x 16'5" |
| Dining Room | 5.8 x 6.8 | 19'0" x 22'4" |
| Kitchen | 4.5 x 8.0 | 14'9" x 25'7" |
| Utility | 3.3 x 4.5 | 10'10" x 14'9" |
| Sauna area | 5.8 x 3.4 | 19'0" x 11'2" |
| Games area | 5.5 x 8.6 | 18'1" x 28'4" |
| Bedroom 1 | 5.8 x 4.2 | 19'0" x 13'9" |
| Bedroom 2 | 4.5 x 3.4 | 14'9" x 11'22 |
| Bedroom 3 | 5.7 x 3.4 | 18'8" x 11'2" |
| Bedroom 4 | 4.5 x 3.2 | 14'9" x 11'22 |
| | | |
| *Annexe* | | |
| Living Room | 6.9 x 3.4 | 22'8" x 11'2" |
| Kitchen/Dining | 5.5 x 3.8 | 18'1" x 12'6" |
| Bedroom 1 | 3.6 x 3.7 | 11'10" x 12'2" |
| Bedroom 2 | 3.1 x 3.7 | 10'2" x 12'2" |

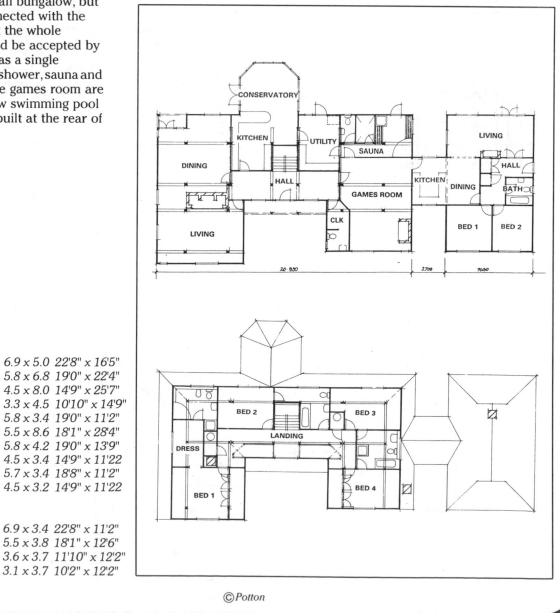

©Potton

**Ref: 96163**

**612 sq.m.   6580 sq.ft.**

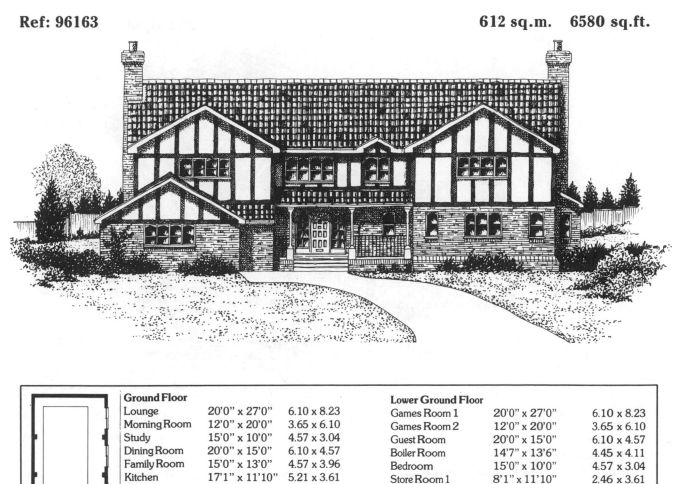

| Ground Floor | | |
|---|---|---|
| Lounge | 20'0" x 27'0" | 6.10 x 8.23 |
| Morning Room | 12'0" x 20'0" | 3.65 x 6.10 |
| Study | 15'0" x 10'0" | 4.57 x 3.04 |
| Dining Room | 20'0" x 15'0" | 6.10 x 4.57 |
| Family Room | 15'0" x 13'0" | 4.57 x 3.96 |
| Kitchen | 17'1" x 11'10" | 5.21 x 3.61 |
| Utility | 11'0" x 10'2" | 3.35 x 3.11 |

| Lower Ground Floor | | |
|---|---|---|
| Games Room 1 | 20'0" x 27'0" | 6.10 x 8.23 |
| Games Room 2 | 12'0" x 20'0" | 3.65 x 6.10 |
| Guest Room | 20'0" x 15'0" | 6.10 x 4.57 |
| Boiler Room | 14'7" x 13'6" | 4.45 x 4.11 |
| Bedroom | 15'0" x 10'0" | 4.57 x 3.04 |
| Store Room 1 | 8'1" x 11'10" | 2.46 x 3.61 |
| Store Room 2 | 8'8" x 10'1" | 2.64 x 3.07 |

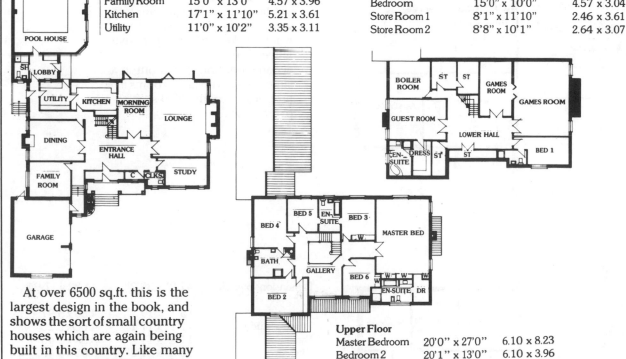

| Upper Floor | | |
|---|---|---|
| Master Bedroom | 20'0" x 27'0" | 6.10 x 8.23 |
| Bedroom 2 | 20'1" x 13'0" | 6.10 x 3.96 |
| Bedroom 3 | 12'4" x 15'0" | 3.74 x 4.57 |
| Bedroom 4 | 11'10" x 17'9" | 3.60 x 5.41 |
| Bedroom 5 | 11'6" x 12'0" | 3.50 x 3.65 |
| Bedroom 6 | 12'0" x 13'9" | 3.65 x 4.20 |

At over 6500 sq.ft. this is the largest design in the book, and shows the sort of small country houses which are again being built in this country. Like many of them it reaches back to the Edwardian era for many aspects of the design. Note the treatment of the garage end wall so that from many angles the garage appears to be part of the main house, enhancing its proportions and its prestige.

The largest single element in the design is the splendid indoor swimming pool, which is built with a cathedral ceiling. Unusually there is not a changing room for guests, nor are there the sauna or exercise rooms which are usually built with a pool.

**Ref: 96161**

**242 sq.m.    2607 sq.ft.**

A house in an Edwardian style with a study 15 ft. x 17 ft. that would make a most impressive office. The living accommodation is laid out in a simple way, with large rooms in proportion to the 2600 sq.ft. overall size.

| Dimensions overall | 47'0" x 39'2" | - | 14.32 x 11.94 |
|---|---|---|---|
| Lounge | 15'1" x 19'7" | - | 4.60 x 5.97 |
| Library/Study | 15'1" x 17'1" | - | 4.60 x 5.20 |
| Dining | 11'8" x 11'2" | - | 3.55 x 3.40 |
| Kitchen | 12'8" x 11'2" | - | 3.85 x 3.40 |
| Utility | 4'9" x 11'2" | - | 1.45 x 3.40 |
| Family Room | 11'10" x 13'1" | - | 3.61 x 4.00 |
| Master Bedroom | 15'1" x 18'6" | - | 4.60 x 5.63 |
| Bedroom 2 | 15'1" x 12'0" | - | 4.60 x 3.65 |
| Bedroom 3 | 11'10" x 13'1" | - | 3.61 x 4.00 |
| Bedroom 4 | 11'8" x 11'2" | - | 3.55 x 3.40 |
| Bedroom 5 | 9'0" x 11'2" | - | 2.74 x 3.40 |

**Ref: 96261**

**280 sq.m.    3014 sq.ft.**

There was plenty of room in this large house for both a waiting room/office and a consulting room for the psychiatric consultant who built it to meet his own specific requirements.

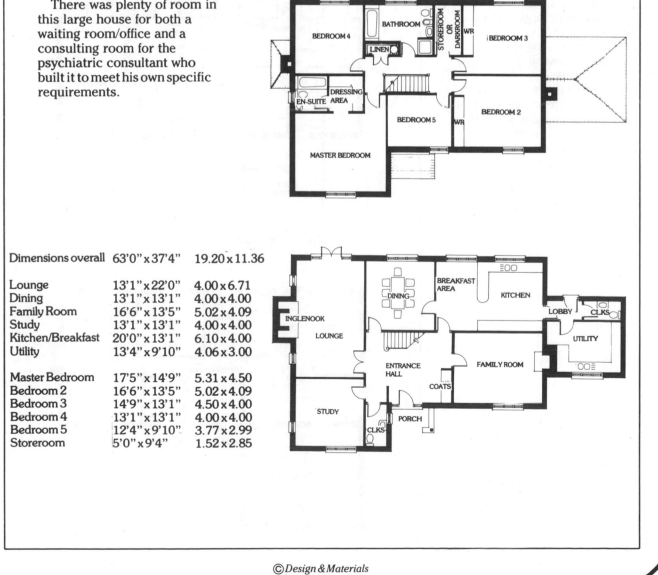

| Dimensions overall | 63'0" x 37'4" | 19.20 x 11.36 |
|---|---|---|
| Lounge | 13'1" x 22'0" | 4.00 x 6.71 |
| Dining | 13'1" x 13'1" | 4.00 x 4.00 |
| Family Room | 16'6" x 13'5" | 5.02 x 4.09 |
| Study | 13'1" x 13'1" | 4.00 x 4.00 |
| Kitchen/Breakfast | 20'0" x 13'1" | 6.10 x 4.00 |
| Utility | 13'4" x 9'10" | 4.06 x 3.00 |
| | | |
| Master Bedroom | 17'5" x 14'9" | 5.31 x 4.50 |
| Bedroom 2 | 16'6" x 13'5" | 5.02 x 4.09 |
| Bedroom 3 | 14'9" x 13'1" | 4.50 x 4.00 |
| Bedroom 4 | 13'1" x 13'1" | 4.00 x 4.00 |
| Bedroom 5 | 12'4" x 9'10" | 3.77 x 2.99 |
| Storeroom | 5'0" x 9'4" | 1.52 x 2.85 |

**Ref: 96263**

**246 sq.m.    2646 sq.ft.**
**(inc. garage)**

There are two unusual features of this impressive home: the very large master bedroom suite with a big dressing room, and the workshop between the garage and the kitchen for someone with a lot of practical interests. As often in large homes with first floor dormer windows, the first floor gallery has room for furniture and provides many interesting opportunities.

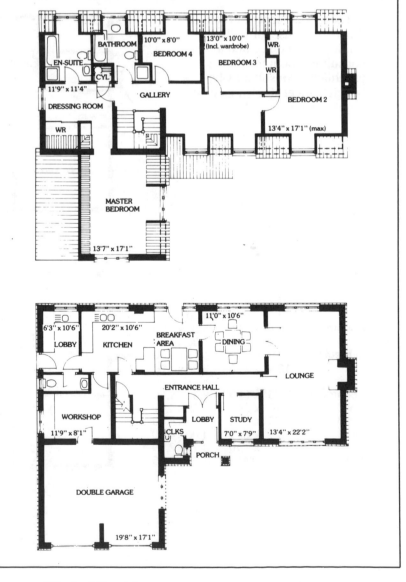

EN-SUITE
11'9" x 11'4"
DRESSING ROOM
WR
BATHROOM
10'0" x 8'0"
BEDROOM 4
CYL
GALLERY
13'0" x 10'0" (incl. wardrobe)
BEDROOM 3
WR
WR
BEDROOM 2
13'4" x 17'1" (max)
MASTER BEDROOM
13'7" x 17'1"

LOBBY
6'3" x 10'6"
KITCHEN
20'2" x 10'6"
BREAKFAST AREA
11'0" x 10'6"
DINING
LOUNGE
ENTRANCE HALL
WORKSHOP
11'9" x 8'1"
CLKS
LOBBY
7'0" x 7'9"
STUDY
13'4" x 22'2"
PORCH
DOUBLE GARAGE
19'8" x 17'1"

© Design & Materials

# *Designs for Houses 2001 to 2500 sq. ft.*

Houses between 2001 sq. ft. and 2500 sq. ft. provide the home builder with an opportunity to have design features that are difficult to arrange in smaller properties. Large rooms permit higher ceilings, which facilitate changes of level within a room, such as a raised or lowered dining area or study. Two storey cathedral·ceilings can provide an opportunity for striking internal decor. Almost any feature which you have always admired becomes possible without looking cramped or contrived.

Large halls can have striking feature staircases which provide a feel of country house living at a modest cost: remember a really superb staircase will probably cost less than your kitchen units did, and will be seen by all your visitors, not just by the ones who help with the washing up! On the upper floor houses of this size can have an en suite bathroom to every bedroom, which is already popular for large homes in the USA and parts of Europe.

**Ref: 96177**

**204 sq.m.   2194 sq.ft.**

A long shallow design for a country house. It was originally conceived to meet the planners design requirements for a house in the Lincolnshire Wolds, and has since been built in many other parts of the country. At under 2200 sq.ft. it looks far larger than it really is, and has also proved very cost effective to build.

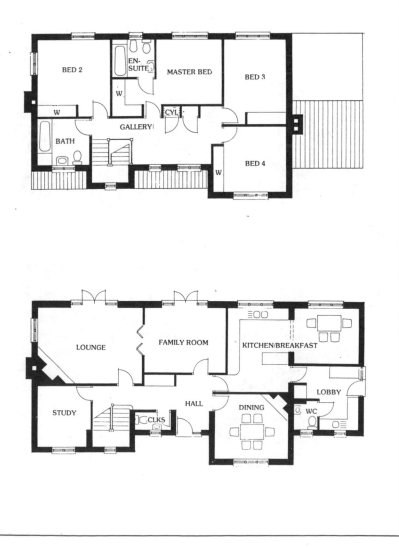

| | | |
|---|---|---|
| Floor Area | 2194 sq.ft. | 204 sq.m. |
| Dimensions overall | 56'5" x 25'10" | 17.18 x 7.86 |
| Lounge | 17'6" x 13'0" | 5.33 x 3.96 |
| Family Room | 14'0" x 11'0" | 4.26 x 3.35 |
| Study | 9'0" x 10'8" | 2.74 x 3.25 |
| Dining | 12'6" x 11'8" | 3.81 x 3.55 |
| Kitchen | 10'6" x 14'3" | 3.21 x 4.35 |
| Breakfast Room | 11'0" x 9'8" | 3.35 x 2.95 |
| Lobby/Utility | 11'0" x 11'0" | 3.35 x 3.35 |
| Master Bed | 11'8" x 11'0" | 3.55 x 3.35 |
| Bed 2 | 12'6" x 13'0" | 3.81 x 3.96 |
| Bed 3 | 10'6" x 14'3" | 3.21 x 4.35 |
| Bed 4 | 12'6" x 11'8" | 3.81 x 3.55 |

**Ref: 96262**

**224 sq.m.   2409 sq.ft.**

A large house in a turn of the century style which has rooms for both a library and a music room on the ground floor. There are five large bedrooms off the first floor gallery, which is itself big enough to be furnished and used in any of a hundred different ways.

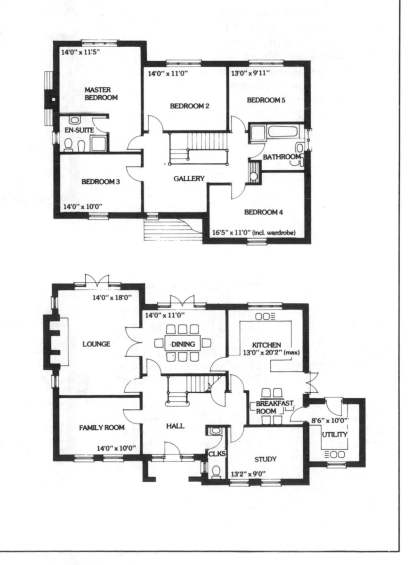

MASTER BEDROOM
14'0" x 11'5"

BEDROOM 2
14'0" x 11'0"

BEDROOM 5
13'0" x 9'11"

EN-SUITE

BATHROOM

BEDROOM 3
14'0" x 10'0"

GALLERY

BEDROOM 4
16'5" x 11'0" (incl. wardrobe)

LOUNGE
14'0" x 18'0"

DINING
14'0" x 11'0"

KITCHEN
13'0" x 20'2" (max)

BREAKFAST ROOM

FAMILY ROOM
14'0" x 10'0"

HALL

CLKS

STUDY
13'2" x 9'0"

UTILITY
8'6" x 10'0"

**Ref: 96253**

**192 sq.m.   2071 sq.ft.**

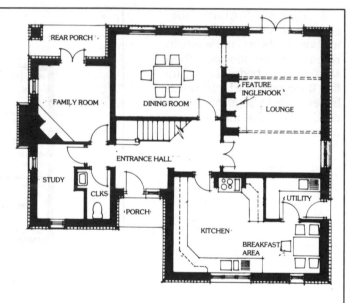

At 2071 square feet this is one of the larger houses in this category, and provides generous ground floor accommodation and four bedrooms with dormer windows in the roof.

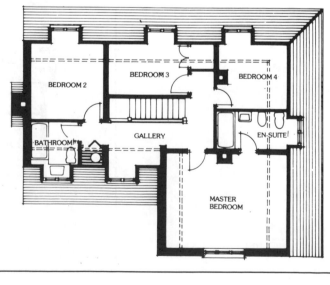

| Dimensions overall | 42'7" x 35'7" | 12.97 x 10.84 |
|---|---|---|
| Lounge | 14'0" x 18'9" | 4.26 x 5.72 |
| Dining | 15'0" x 11'5" | 4.57 x 3.47 |
| Family Room | 10'6" x 11'0" | 3.20 x 3.35 |
| Study | 6'11" x 10'6" | 2.10 x 3.20 |
| Breakfast/Kitchen (max) | 21'10" x 14'0" | 6.65 x 4.26 |
| Utility | 7'10" x 5'11" | 2.40 x 1.80 |
| Master Bedroom | 17'5" x 14'0" | 5.31 x 4.26 |
| Bedroom 2 | 10'6" x 11'0" | 3.20 x 3.35 |
| Bedroom 3 (incl. W.R.) | 15'0" x 7'0" | 4.57 x 2.13 |
| Bedroom 4 | 9'7" x 8'10" | 2.92 x 2.68 |

**Ref: 96123**

**200 sq.m.    2156 sq.ft.**

A three bedroom home in the Cotswold style with an impressive study, library or office. The overall area is 2156 sq. ft., and having only three bedrooms in a house of this size permits large rooms and a galleried hall with a wide central staircase which divides at a quarter landing. What a staircase to come down in evening dress to meet your partner waiting below – it is featured in every Hollywood movie of the 30's!

Cotswold style homes like this need very careful attention to the design of the stonework at the eaves and around windows and doors. These stone features are called 'dressings', and while they are relatively expensive they are all worth it. The companion volume to this book called Home Plans deals with this in detail.

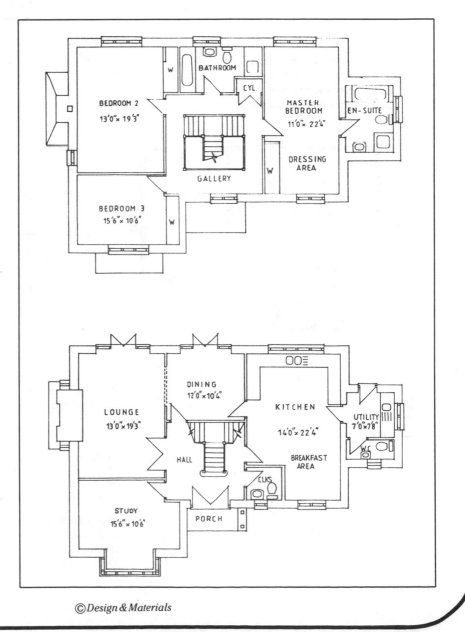

213

**Ref: 96132**

**192 sq.m.    2067 sq.ft.**
**(inc. garage)**

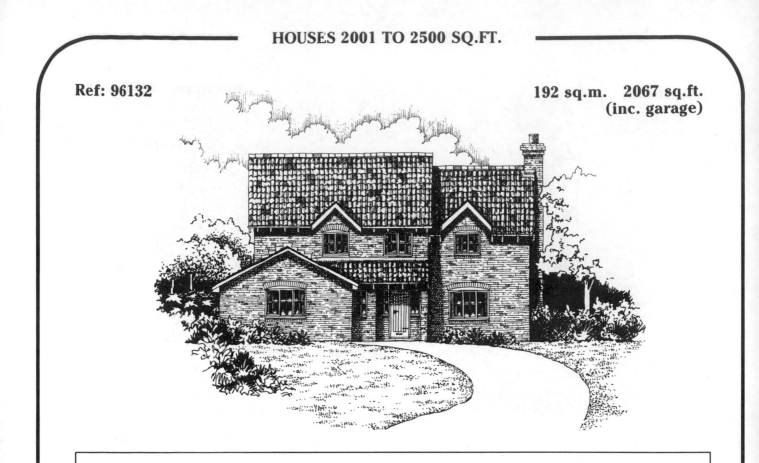

A 4 bedroomed home in a cottage style with a garage that has space for a workshop and bench for the car enthusiast.

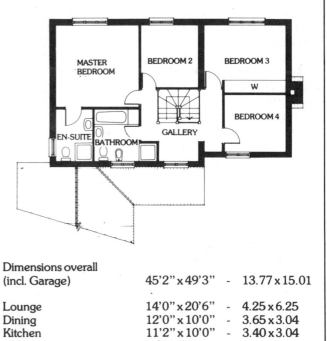

Dimensions overall
(incl. Garage)                    45'2" x 49'3"   -   13.77 x 15.01

| | | |
|---|---|---|
| Lounge | 14'0" x 20'6" | - 4.25 x 6.25 |
| Dining | 12'0" x 10'0" | - 3.65 x 3.04 |
| Kitchen | 11'2" x 10'0" | - 3.40 x 3.04 |
| Utility | 9'2" x 8'5" | - 2.80 x 2.55 |
| Study | 9'10" x 9'0" | - 3.00 x 2.75 |
| Garage (max) | 18'0" x 24'9" | - 5.48 x 7.53 |
| Master Bedroom | 13'9" x 13'3" | - 4.20 x 4.04 |
| Bedroom 2 | 9'4" x 10'0" | - 2.85 x 3.04 |
| Bedroom 3 (incl. W.R.) | 14'0" x 10'0" | - 4.25 x 3.05 |
| Bedroom 4 | 10'4" x 10'2" | - 3.15 x 3.10 |

© Design & Materials

**Ref: 96196**

**192 sq.m.   2069 sq.ft.**

A family house with a very
large master bedroom suite.
This home was designed for an
infill site in a Scottish town but
would look equally well in the
depths of the country.

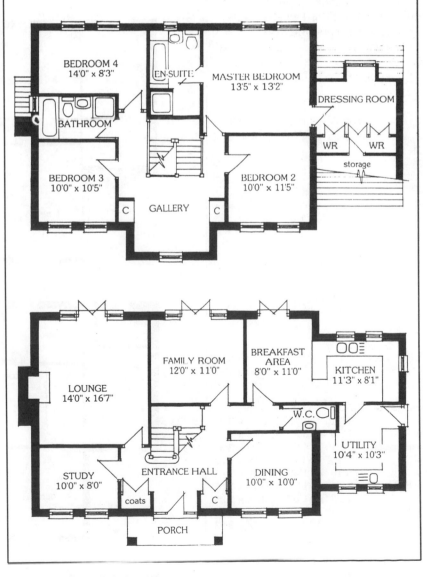

**Ref: 96144**

**226 sq.m.    2434 sq.ft.**

A large house designed for a site in a suburb of Oxford where it was built in natural stone with a stone slate roof.

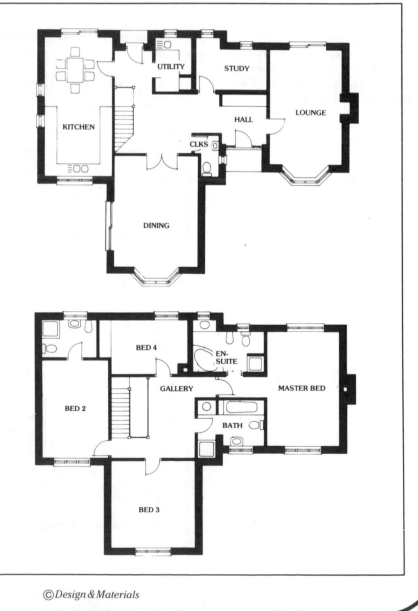

| | | |
|---|---|---|
| Dimensions overall | 50'0" x 39'9" | 15.24 x 12.10 |
| Lounge | 18'10" x 11'8" | 5.74 x 3.55 |
| Dining | 18'0" x 13'6" | 5.48 x 4.11 |
| Kitchen/Breakfast | 22'10" x 11'0" | 6.96 x 3.35 |
| Utility | 8'10" x 6'0" | 2.69 x 1.83 |
| Study | 6'10" x 11'4" | 2.08 x 3.45 |
| Master Bed | 18'10" x 11'8' | 5.74 x 3.55 |
| Bed 2 | 16'3" x 11'0" | 4.96 x 3.35 |
| Bed 3 | 16'4" x 13'6" | 5.00 x 4.11 |
| Bed 4 | 9'1" x 12'7" | 2.78 x 3.83 |

**Ref: 96121**

**193 sq.m.   2076 sq.ft.**

A five bedroom house in a style that is common in Essex and Suffolk, with a jettied window and steep gables. Although the rooms are modestly sized, the house has plenty of interesting features in its 2070 sq. ft.

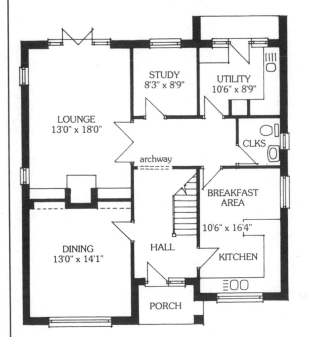

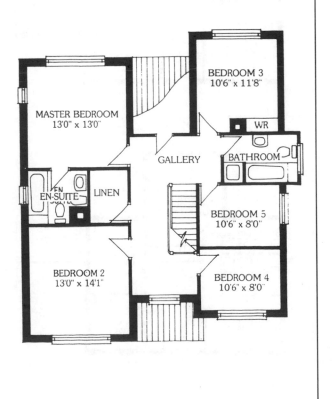

**Ref: 96192**

**194 sq.m.    2084 sq.ft.**

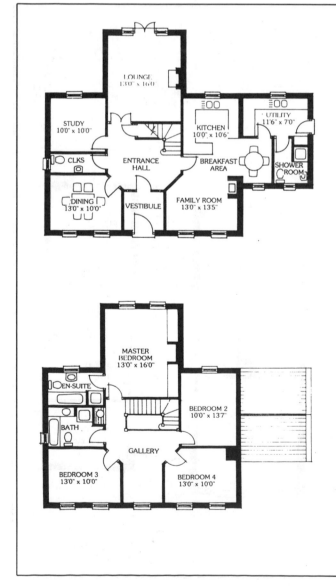

A house which was built behind a low wall in the High Street of a West Midlands village for a veterinary surgeon. It has a shower room at the side door for cleaning up after farm visits, and a traditional vestibule for wet coats and umbrellas at the front door.

©*Design & Materials*

**Ref: 96112**

**193 sq.m.    2074 sq.ft.**

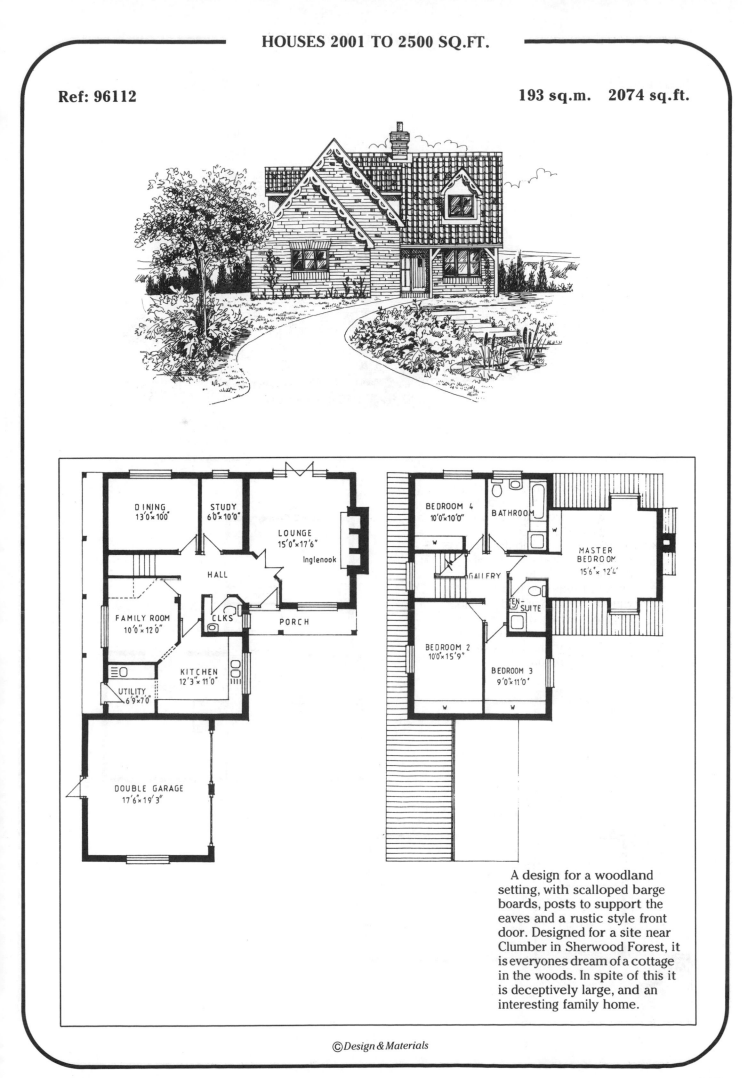

DINING
13'0"×10'0"

STUDY
6'0"×10'0"

LOUNGE
15'0"×17'6"

Inglenook

HALL

FAMILY ROOM
10'0"×12'0"

CLKS

PORCH

KITCHEN
12'3"×11'0"

UTILITY
6'9"×7'0"

DOUBLE GARAGE
17'6"×19'3"

BEDROOM 4
10'0"×10'0"

BATHROOM

MASTER BEDROOM
15'6"×12'4"

GALLERY

EN-SUITE

BEDROOM 2
10'0"×15'9"

BEDROOM 3
9'0"×11'0"

A design for a woodland setting, with scalloped barge boards, posts to support the eaves and a rustic style front door. Designed for a site near Clumber in Sherwood Forest, it is everyones dream of a cottage in the woods. In spite of this it is deceptively large, and an interesting family home.

**Ref: PN685**

**226 sq.m.   2435 sq.ft.**

The Brandham design in the Potton Rectory range has four bedroom accommodation with particularly generously sized rooms. The hall and drawing room are linked with double doors, and usually these are glazed. The stairs are lit by a window on the half landing, and the stairwell needs a carefully chosen chandelier to give it the style appropriate to this well proportioned home.

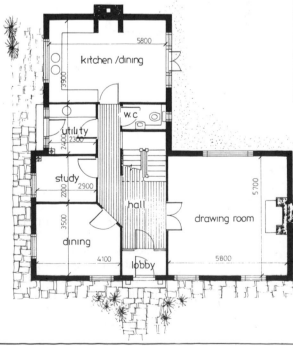

© *Potton*

**Ref: 96173**

**203 sq.m.   2183 sq.ft.**
**(inc. garage)**

A house with many Edwardian features which was built in a garden plot in a northern town where it had to match adjacent properties.

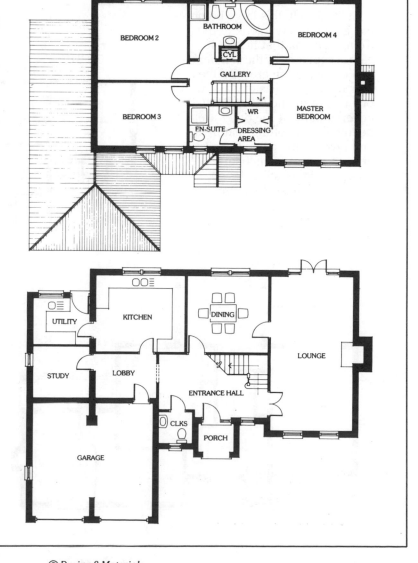

| | |
|---|---|
| Dimensions overall | 51'2" x 38'2" |
| | |
| Lounge | 12'6" x 23'6" |
| Dining | 12'6" x 11'6" |
| Kitchen | 14'0" x 11'6" |
| Utility | 8'9" x 6'7" |
| Study | 8'9" x 8'0" |
| Garage | 18'8" x 17'0" |
| | |
| Master Bedroom | 12'6" x 14'11" |
| Bedroom 2 | 14'0" x 11'6" |
| Bedroom 3 | 14'0" x 9'6" |
| Bedroom 4 | 12'6" x 8'3" |

*© Design & Materials*

**Ref: 96135**

**192 sq.m.   2085 sq.ft.**
**(exc. conservatory)**

At 2085 sq.ft. this large home has a cottage style look to the front elevation that helped it gain acceptance by the planners in a conservation area. To the rear the large areas of glass at one end of the house and the covered patio at the other are definitely not cottage features, and provide the amenity and atmosphere of a much larger home. An interesting design, with many unusual features.

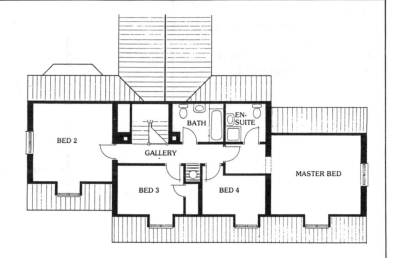

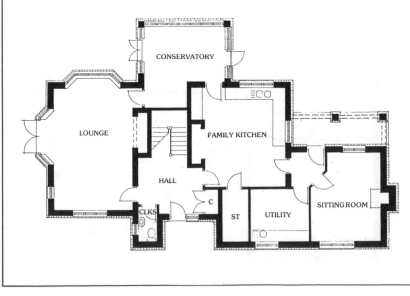

| Floor Area | | |
|---|---|---|
| (exc. conservatory) | 2085 sq.ft. | 193 sq.m. |
| Dimensions overall | 58'4" x 28'2" | 17.78 x 8.57 |
| Lounge | 14'0" x 21'0" | 4.26 x 6.40 |
| Family Kitchen | 16'0" x 17'0" | 4.87 x 5.18 |
| Sitting Room | 12'0" x 15'4" | 3.65 x 4.67 |
| Utility | 10'3" x 9'0" | 3.12 x 2.74 |
| Master Bed | 15'8" x 13'3" | 4.76 x 4.05 |
| Bed 2 | 14'0" x 13'3" | 4.26 x 4.05 |
| Bed 3 | 11'1" x 8'5" | 3.37 x 2.57 |
| Bed 4 | 10'10" x 6'7" | 3.29 x 2.00 |

© *Design & Materials*

**Ref: PN684**

**215 sq.m.   2310 sq.ft.**

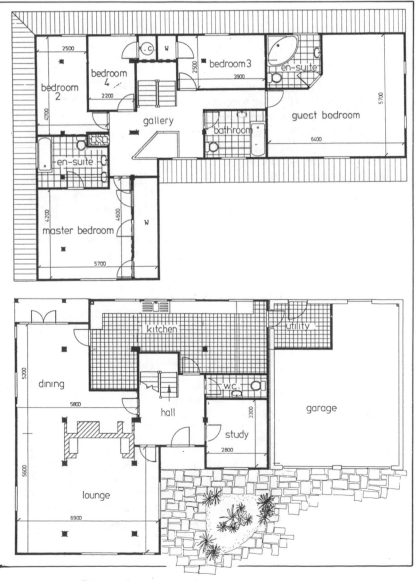

An aisle frame house with particularly large rooms for its overall size. A modest office suite is incorporated.

©*Potton*

**Ref: S409**

**195 sq.m.   2099 sq.ft.**

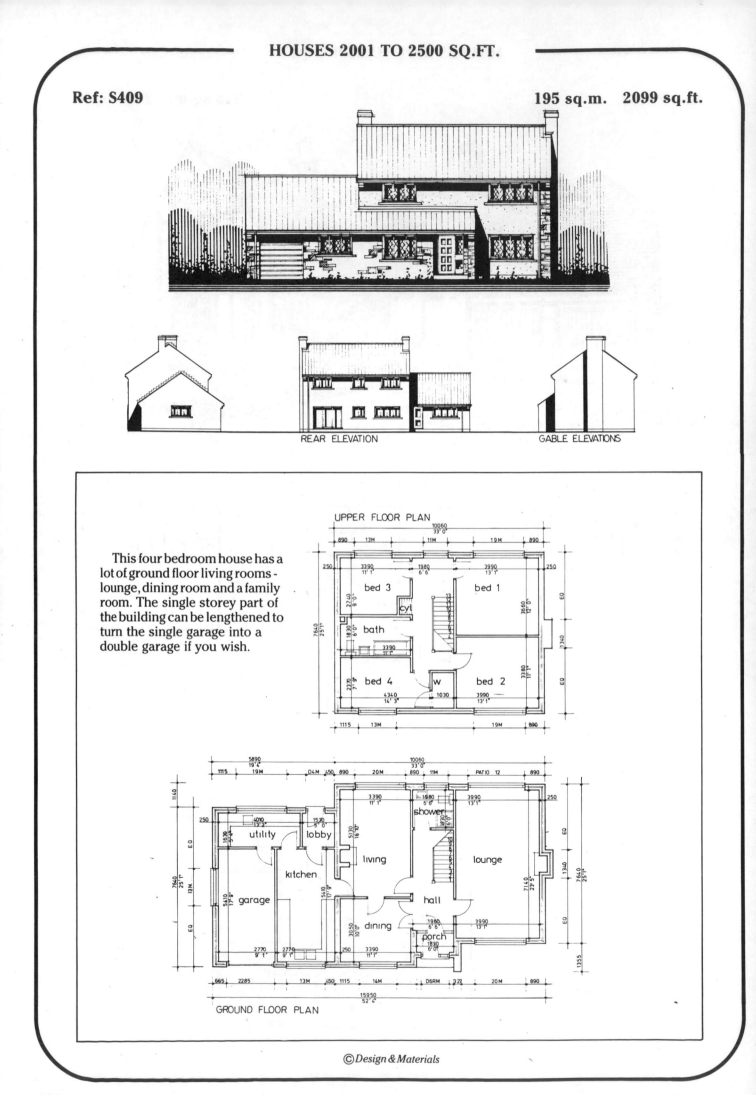

REAR ELEVATION

GABLE ELEVATIONS

UPPER FLOOR PLAN

bed 3

cyl

bath

bed 4

w

bed 1

bed 2

This four bedroom house has a lot of ground floor living rooms - lounge, dining room and a family room. The single storey part of the building can be lengthened to turn the single garage into a double garage if you wish.

utility

lobby

kitchen

garage

living

shower

lounge

hall

dining

porch

GROUND FLOOR PLAN

**Ref: P2718**

**189 sq.m.   2034 sq.ft.**

blue slate

coursed natural gritstone

timber or timberclad garage doors

front elevation

rear elevation

garage side

side elevation

A straightforward house built in stone under a slate roof. The enclosed front porch will tend to make the hall rather dark, even with glazed doors. This can be helped by providing a window in the side wall of the porch, and perhaps double doors between the porch and the hall itself.

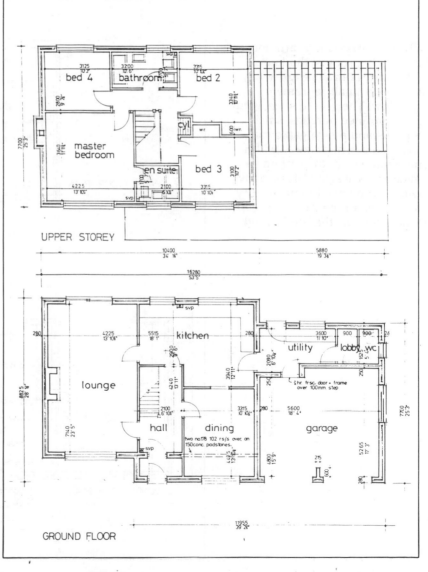

UPPER STOREY

bed 4

bathroom

bed 2

master bedroom

cyl

en suite

bed 3

GROUND FLOOR

lounge

kitchen

utility

lobby wc

hall

dining

garage

©P.S.S.

**Ref: W1064**

188 sq.m.   2023 sq.ft.

GABLE ELEVATIONS

stepped flashing + tray dpc

stepped flashing + tray dpc

This north country farmhouse has very big rooms: the lounge and dining room alone are nearly as big as a small retirement bungalow. The severe style, with small entrance porches, small windows and a high gable roof looks severe when viewed with a suburban eye. In the setting for which it was designed it is exactly right — you have to imagine dry stone walls to the garden, sheep in the fields, and the fells beyond.

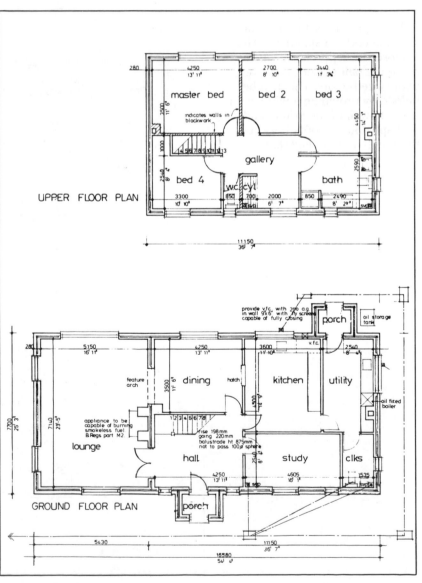

UPPER FLOOR PLAN

master bed

bed 2

bed 3

indicates walls in blockwork

gallery

bed 4

wc cyl

bath

GROUND FLOOR PLAN

feature arch

dining

kitchen

utility

porch

oil storage tank

v.f.c.

provide v.f.c. with 200 a.g. in wall 9½"6" with fly screen capable of fully closing

oil fired boiler

appliance to be capable of burning smokeless fuel B.Regs part M2

rise 198mm going 220mm balustrade ht 875mm not to pass 100ø sphere

lounge

hall

study

clks

porch

**Ref: C382**

**2019 sq.ft.**

**196 sq.m.**

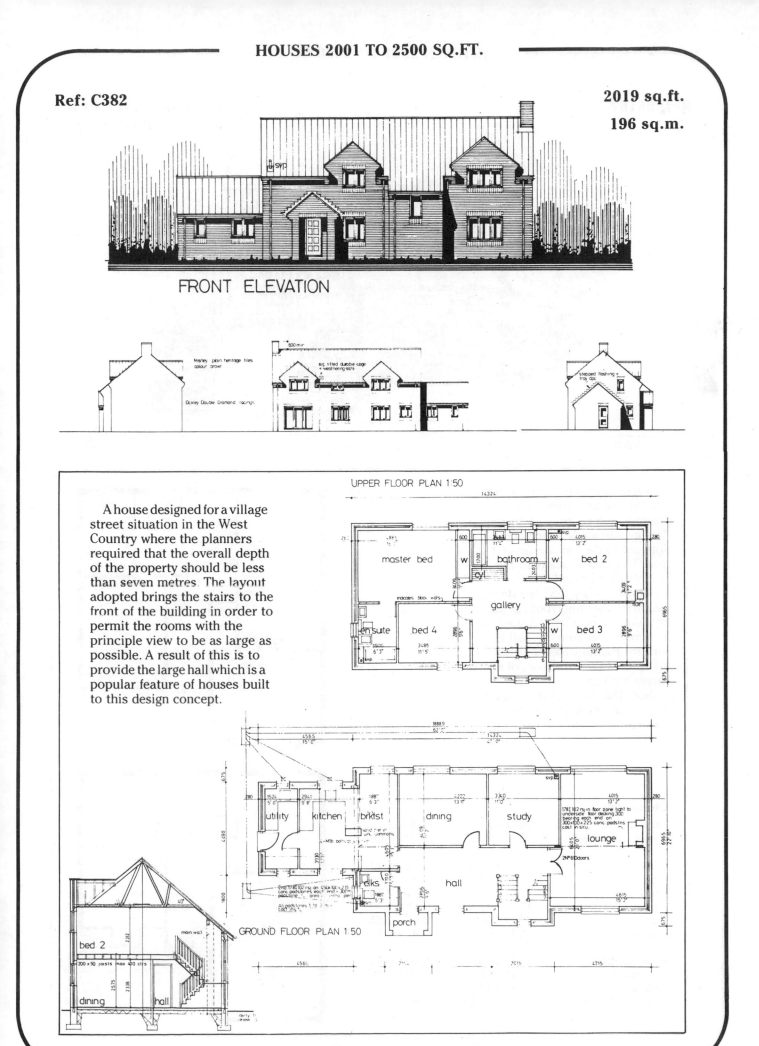

FRONT ELEVATION

UPPER FLOOR PLAN 1:50

A house designed for a village street situation in the West Country where the planners required that the overall depth of the property should be less than seven metres. The layout adopted brings the stairs to the front of the building in order to permit the rooms with the principle view to be as large as possible. A result of this is to provide the large hall which is a popular feature of houses built to this design concept.

master bed

bathroom

bed 2

cyl

gallery

en suite

bed 4

bed 3

utility

kitchen

brkfst

dining

study

lounge

cks

hall

porch

GROUND FLOOR PLAN 1:50

bed 2

dining

hall

main wall

© Design & Materials

**Ref: 96167**

**226 sq.m.   2427 sq.ft.**
**(inc. garage)**

A four bedroom home with rooms that are larger than average and an archway to the lounge and study which adds interest to the hall. Because it was designed for a site in the country the ground floor cloakroom is by the back door, requiring the utility room as the mandatory 'ventilated lobby'. If it were moved into the hall to suit an urban site then the utility room could become part of a larger kitchen.

Note that the garage is much wider than usual, with room for storage alongside the car.

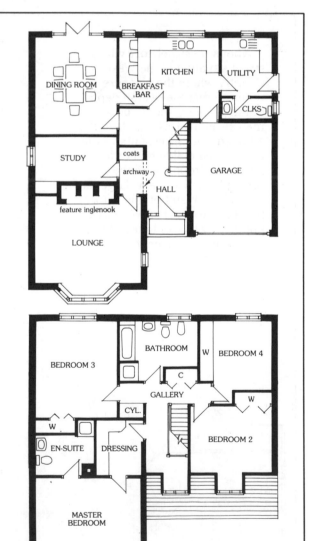

## Dimensions

| | | | |
|---|---|---|---|
| Floor Area (inc garage) | 2427 sq. ft. | - | 226 sq. mtrs. |
| Dimensions overall | 39'5" x 42'3" | - | 12.00 x 12.87 |
| | | | |
| Lounge | 16'7" x 13'6" | - | 5.06 x 4.12 |
| Dining | 12'8" x 15'3" | - | 3.86 x 4.66 |
| Study | 12'8" x 9'0" | - | 3.86 x 2.74 |
| Kitchen | 16'3" x 12'11" | - | 4.95 x 3.93 |
| Utility | 8'0" x 9'3" | - | 2.44 x 2.83 |
| Garage | 12'10" x 17'0" | - | 3.91 x 5.18 |
| | | | |
| Master Bedroom | 16'7" x 13'6" | - | 5.06 x 4.12 |
| Bedroom 2 inc wr | 13'1" x 13'4" | - | 4.00 x 4.06 |
| Bedroom 3 inc wr | 12'8" x 17'7" | - | 3.86 x 5.36 |
| Bedroom 4 inc wr | 11'6" x 10'11" | - | 3.50 x 3.33 |

**Ref: P3010**

**190 sq.m.    2045 sq.ft.**
**(exc. garage)**

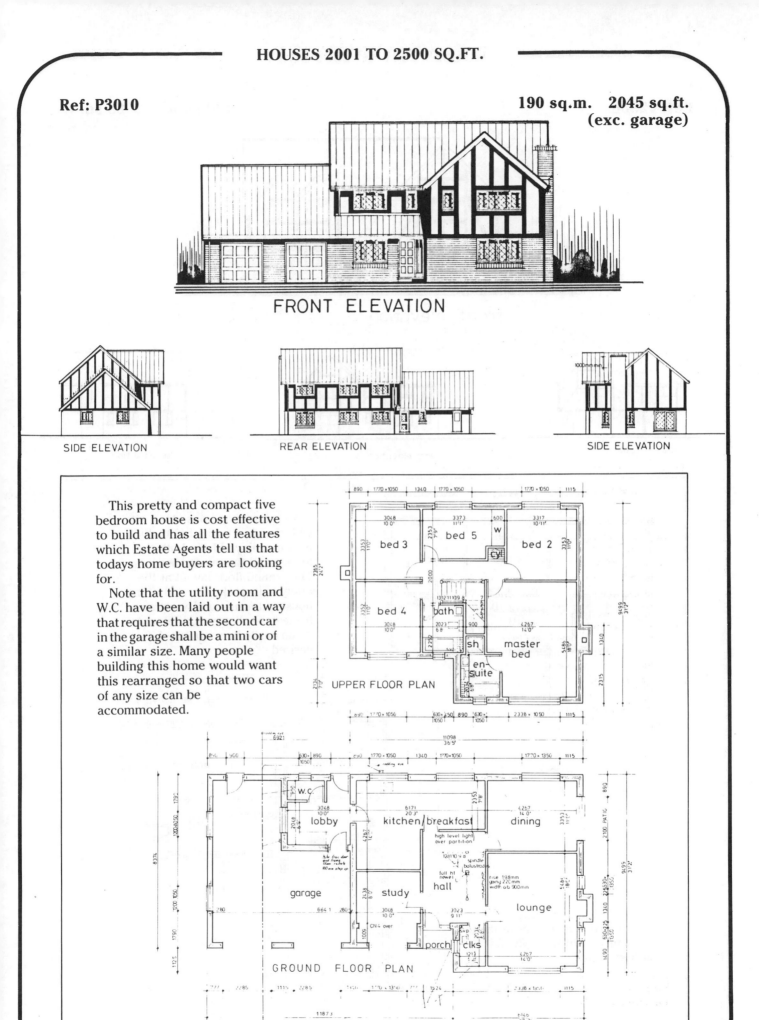

FRONT ELEVATION

SIDE ELEVATION

REAR ELEVATION

SIDE ELEVATION

This pretty and compact five bedroom house is cost effective to build and has all the features which Estate Agents tell us that todays home buyers are looking for.

Note that the utility room and W.C. have been laid out in a way that requires that the second car in the garage shall be a mini or of a similar size. Many people building this home would want this rearranged so that two cars of any size can be accommodated.

UPPER FLOOR PLAN

bed 3

bed 5

bed 2

bed 4

bath

master bed

en-suite

sh

GROUND FLOOR PLAN

W.C.

lobby

kitchen/breakfast

dining

garage

study

hall

lounge

porch

clks

**Ref: P2900**

**194 sq.m.   2088 sq.ft.**

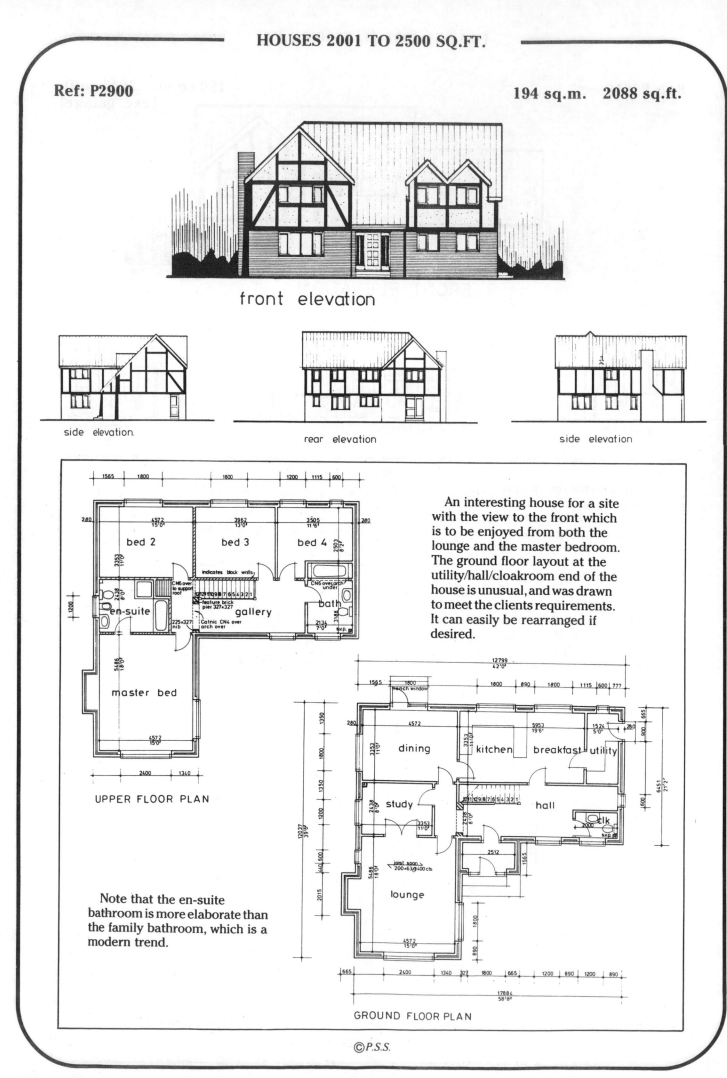

front elevation

side elevation

rear elevation

side elevation

An interesting house for a site with the view to the front which is to be enjoyed from both the lounge and the master bedroom. The ground floor layout at the utility/hall/cloakroom end of the house is unusual, and was drawn to meet the clients requirements. It can easily be rearranged if desired.

UPPER FLOOR PLAN

Note that the en-suite bathroom is more elaborate than the family bathroom, which is a modern trend.

GROUND FLOOR PLAN

©P.S.S.

**Ref: C465**

**190 sq.m. 2045 sq.ft.**

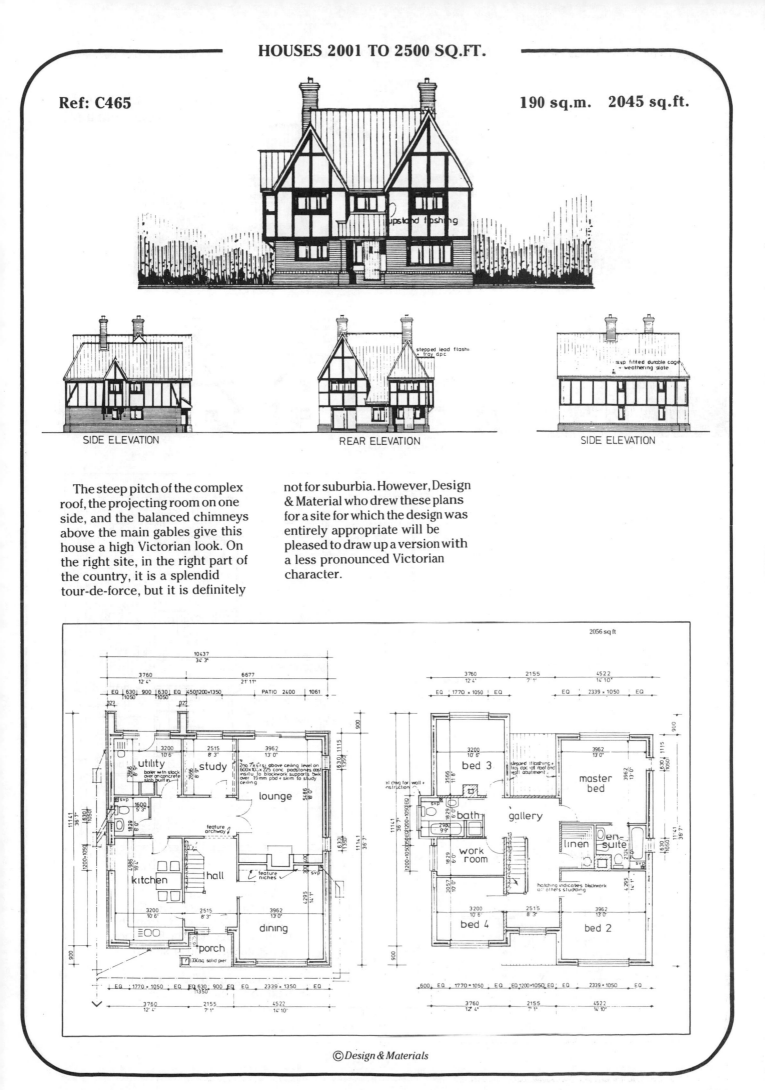

SIDE ELEVATION

REAR ELEVATION

SIDE ELEVATION

The steep pitch of the complex roof, the projecting room on one side, and the balanced chimneys above the main gables give this house a high Victorian look. On the right site, in the right part of the country, it is a splendid tour-de-force, but it is definitely not for suburbia. However, Design & Material who drew these plans for a site for which the design was entirely appropriate will be pleased to draw up a version with a less pronounced Victorian character.

*© Design & Materials*

# HOUSES 2001 TO 2500 SQ.FT.

**Ref: S305**

**191 sq.m.   2055 sq.ft.**
**(exc. garage)**

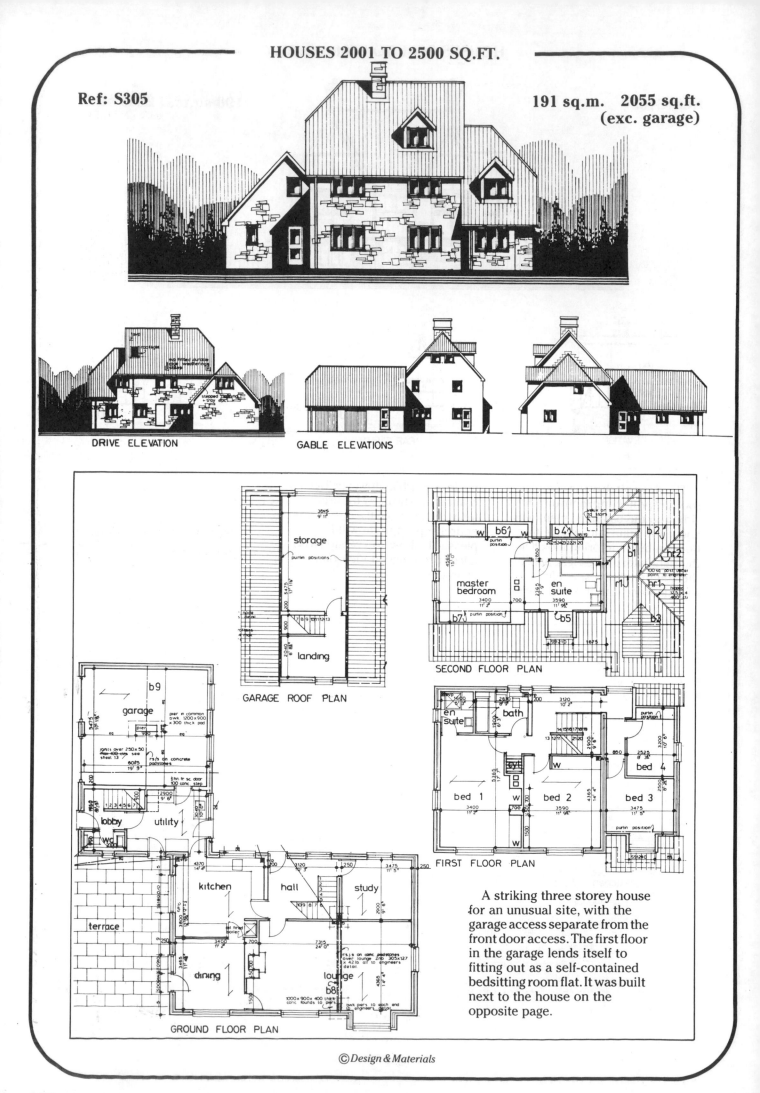

DRIVE ELEVATION

GABLE ELEVATIONS

GARAGE ROOF PLAN

storage

landing

SECOND FLOOR PLAN

master bedroom

en suite

FIRST FLOOR PLAN

en suite

bath

bed 1

bed 2

bed 3

bed 4

garage

lobby

utility

wc

kitchen

hall

study

terrace

dining

lounge

GROUND FLOOR PLAN

A striking three storey house for an unusual site, with the garage access separate from the front door access. The first floor in the garage lends itself to fitting out as a self-contained bedsitting room flat. It was built next to the house on the opposite page.

# HOUSES 2001 TO 2500 SQ.FT.

**Ref: S304C**

**193 sq.m.   2077 sq.ft.**
**(exc. garage)**

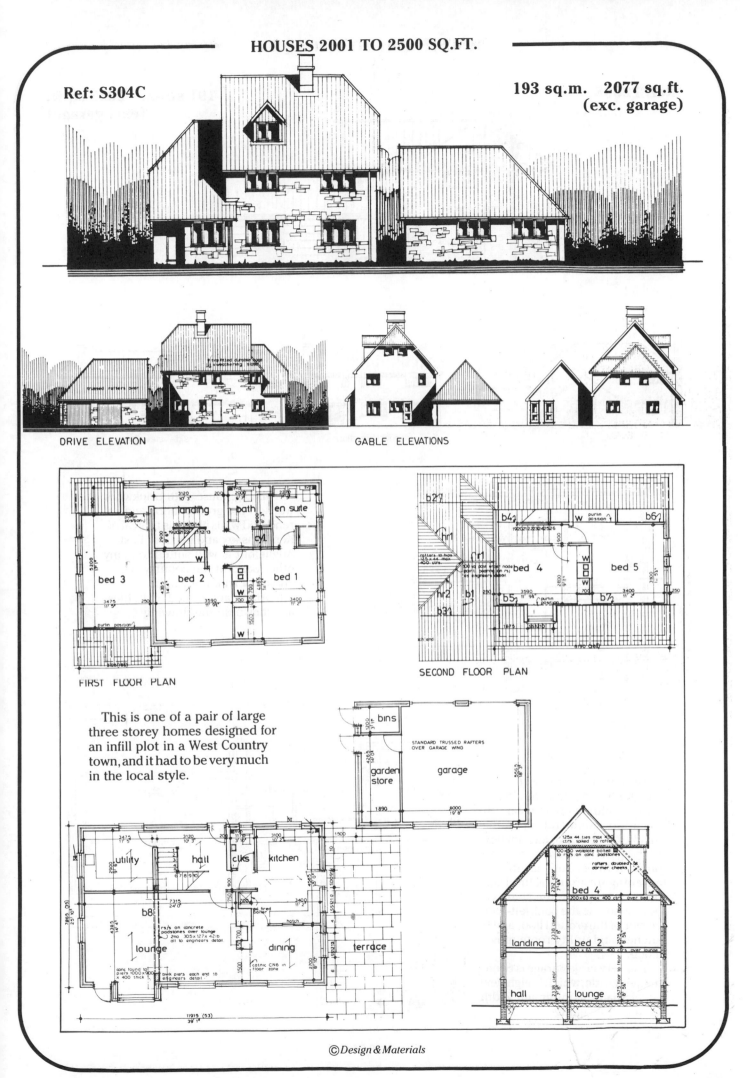

DRIVE ELEVATION

GABLE ELEVATIONS

FIRST FLOOR PLAN

SECOND FLOOR PLAN

This is one of a pair of large three storey homes designed for an infill plot in a West Country town, and it had to be very much in the local style.

**Ref: P2608**

**191 sq.m.   2055 sq.ft.**
**(exc. garage)**

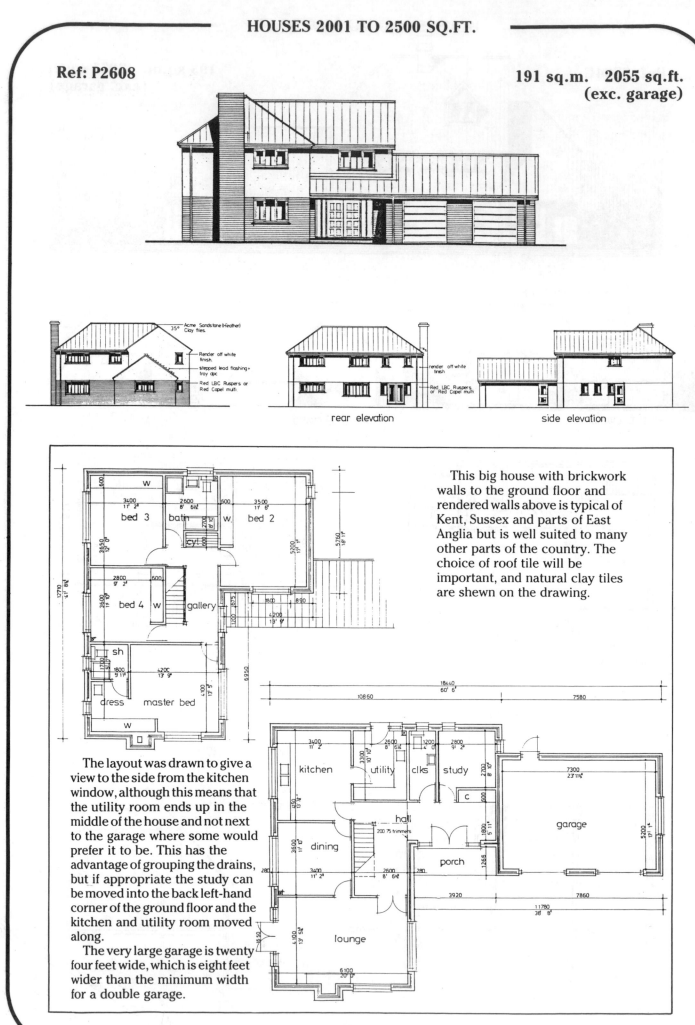

rear elevation

side elevation

This big house with brickwork walls to the ground floor and rendered walls above is typical of Kent, Sussex and parts of East Anglia but is well suited to many other parts of the country. The choice of roof tile will be important, and natural clay tiles are shewn on the drawing.

The layout was drawn to give a view to the side from the kitchen window, although this means that the utility room ends up in the middle of the house and not next to the garage where some would prefer it to be. This has the advantage of grouping the drains, but if appropriate the study can be moved into the back left-hand corner of the ground floor and the kitchen and utility room moved along.

The very large garage is twenty four feet wide, which is eight feet wider than the minimum width for a double garage.

© P.S.S.

**Ref: P2615**

**192 sq.m. 2066 sq.ft.**
**(exc. garage)**

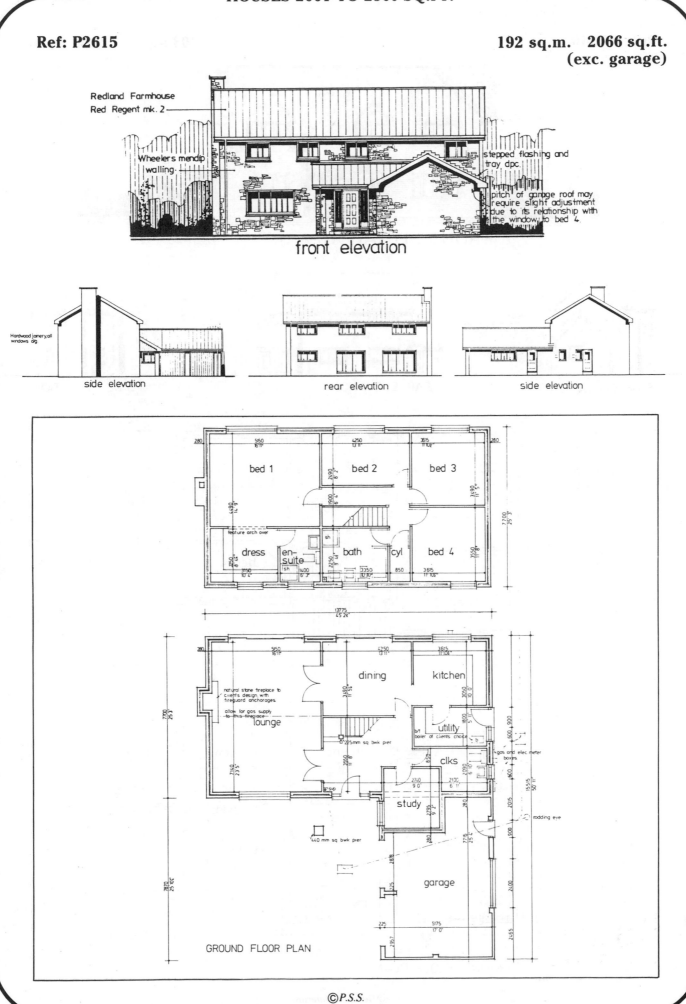

Redland Farmhouse
Red Regent mk. 2

Wheeler's mendip
walling.

stepped flashing and
tray dpc.

pitch of garage roof may
require slight adjustment
due to its relationship with
the window to bed 4.

front elevation

Hardwood joinery, all
windows d/g

side elevation

rear elevation

side elevation

bed 1

bed 2

bed 3

bed 4

feature arch over

dress

en-suite

bath

cyl

natural stone fireplace to
clients design, with
fireguard anchorages.

allow for gas supply
to this fireplace

dining

kitchen

lounge

utility

boiler of clients choice

225mm sq bwk pier

clks

gas and elec meter
boxes

study

440 mm sq bwk pier

rodding eye

garage

GROUND FLOOR PLAN

**Ref: W1346**

**203 sq.m.   2185 sq.ft.**

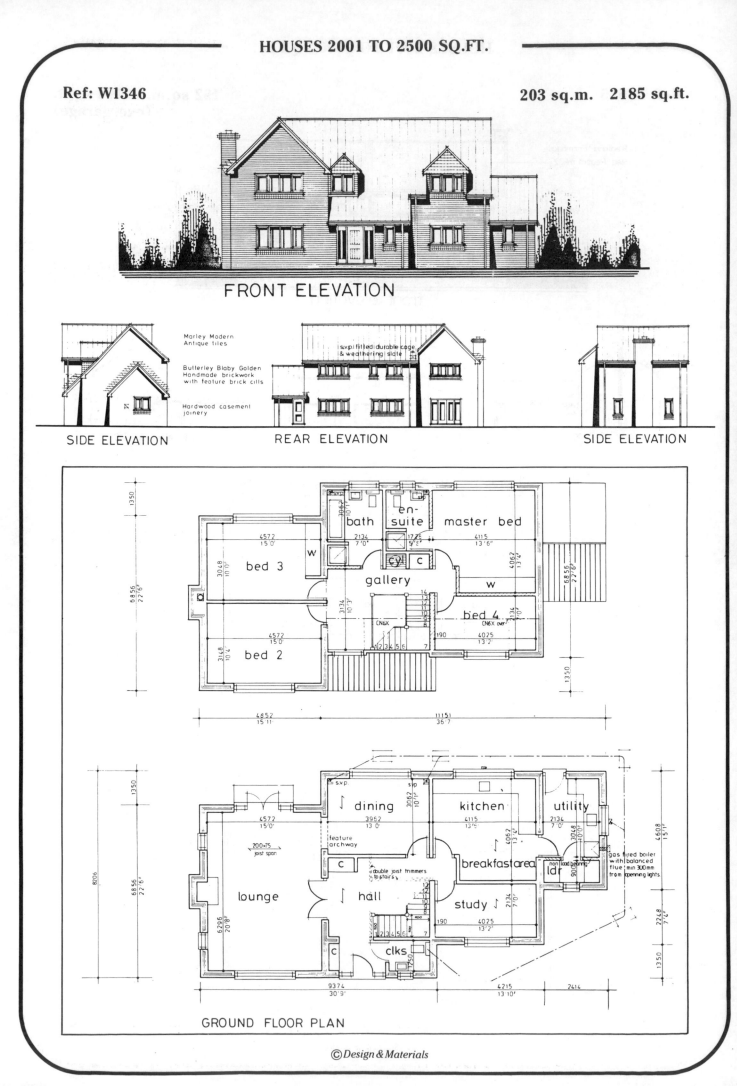

FRONT ELEVATION

Marley Modern
Antique tiles

Butterley Blaby Golden
Handmade brickwork
with feature brick cills

Hardwood casement
joinery

s.v.p. fitted durable cage
& weathering slate

SIDE ELEVATION

REAR ELEVATION

SIDE ELEVATION

bath

en-suite

master bed

bed 3

gallery

bed 4

bed 2

dining

kitchen

utility

lounge

hall

breakfast area

study

clks

feature archway

gas fired boiler
with balanced
flue min 300mm
from opening lights.

200×75
joist span

double joist trimmers
to stairs

GROUND FLOOR PLAN

© *Design & Materials*

**Ref: W1160**

**205 sq.m.  2206 sq.ft.**
**(exc. garage)**

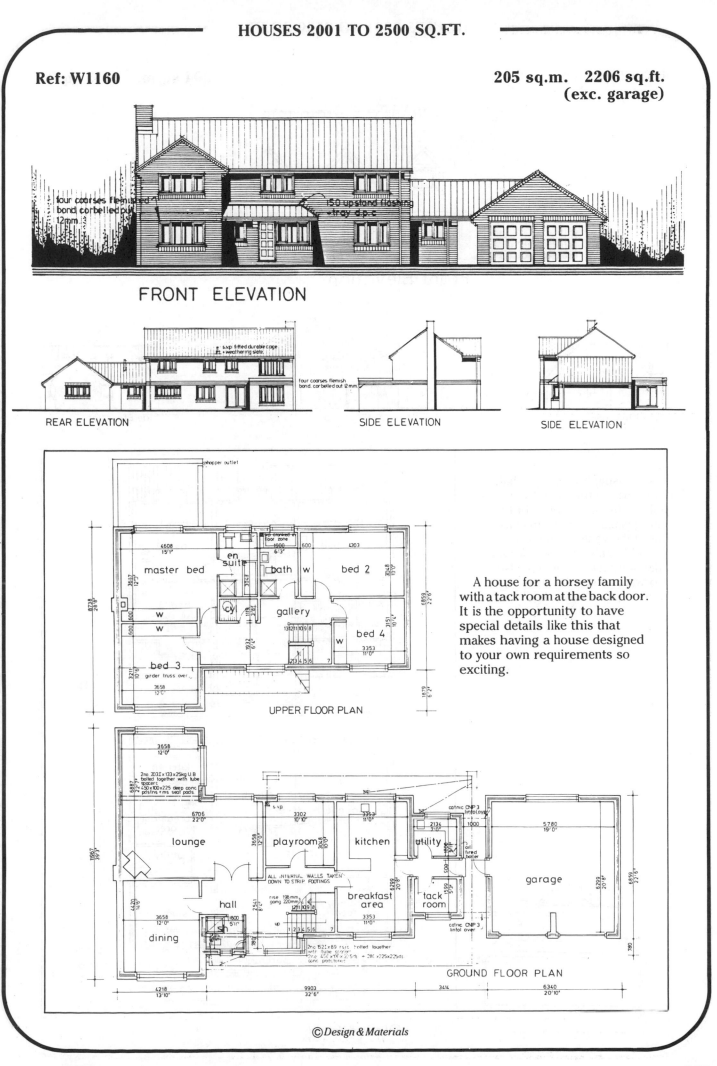

FRONT ELEVATION

four coarses flemish bond corbelled out 12mm

150 upstand flashing tray d.p.c

REAR ELEVATION

s.v.p. fitted durable cage + weathering slate.

four coarses flemish bond. corbelled out 12 mm.

SIDE ELEVATION

SIDE ELEVATION

chopper outlet

master bed

en suite

bath

bed 2

gallery

bed 4

bed 3

girder truss over

UPPER FLOOR PLAN

A house for a horsey family with a tack room at the back door. It is the opportunity to have special details like this that makes having a house designed to your own requirements so exciting.

lounge

playroom

kitchen

utility

oil fired boiler

garage

hall

breakfast area

tack room

dining

up

ALL INTERNAL WALLS TAKEN DOWN TO STRIP FOOTINGS

rise 198mm going 220mm

GROUND FLOOR PLAN

© Design & Materials

**Ref: C513**

**204 sq.m.   2195 sq.ft.**

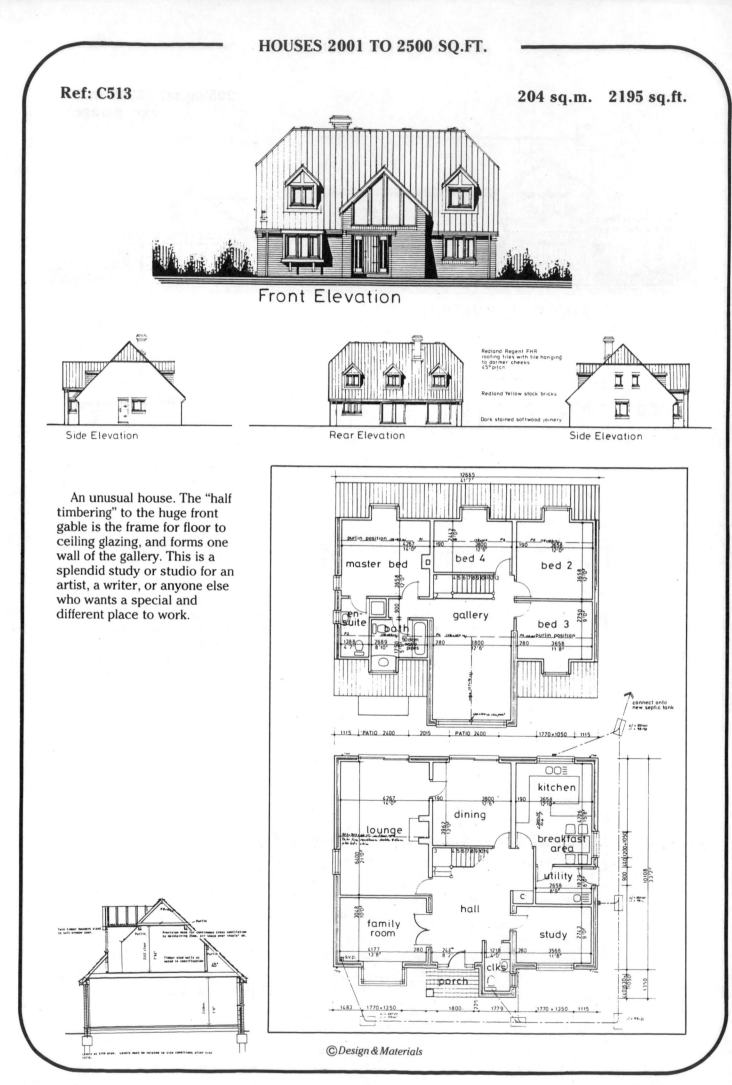

Front Elevation

Side Elevation

Rear Elevation

Redland Regent FHR
roofing tiles with tile hanging
to dormer cheeks
45° pitch

Redland Yellow stock bricks

Dark stained softwood joinery

Side Elevation

An unusual house. The "half timbering" to the huge front gable is the frame for floor to ceiling glazing, and forms one wall of the gallery. This is a splendid study or studio for an artist, a writer, or anyone else who wants a special and different place to work.

© *Design & Materials*

**Ref: P2861**

**203 sq.m.   2185 sq.ft.**

front elevation

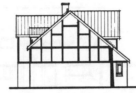

rear elevation          side elevation          side elevation.

A house with a playroom that is as far away from the study as possible, which many parents will envy. It is unusual for a house of this size to have only one bathroom, but the five bedroom accommodation can easily be rearranged to provide additional facilities.

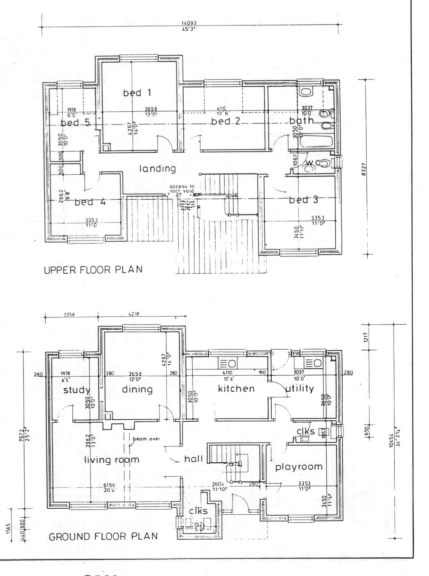

UPPER FLOOR PLAN

GROUND FLOOR PLAN

©P.S.S.

**Ref: C367**

**203 sq.m.   2185 sq.ft.**
**(exc. garage)**

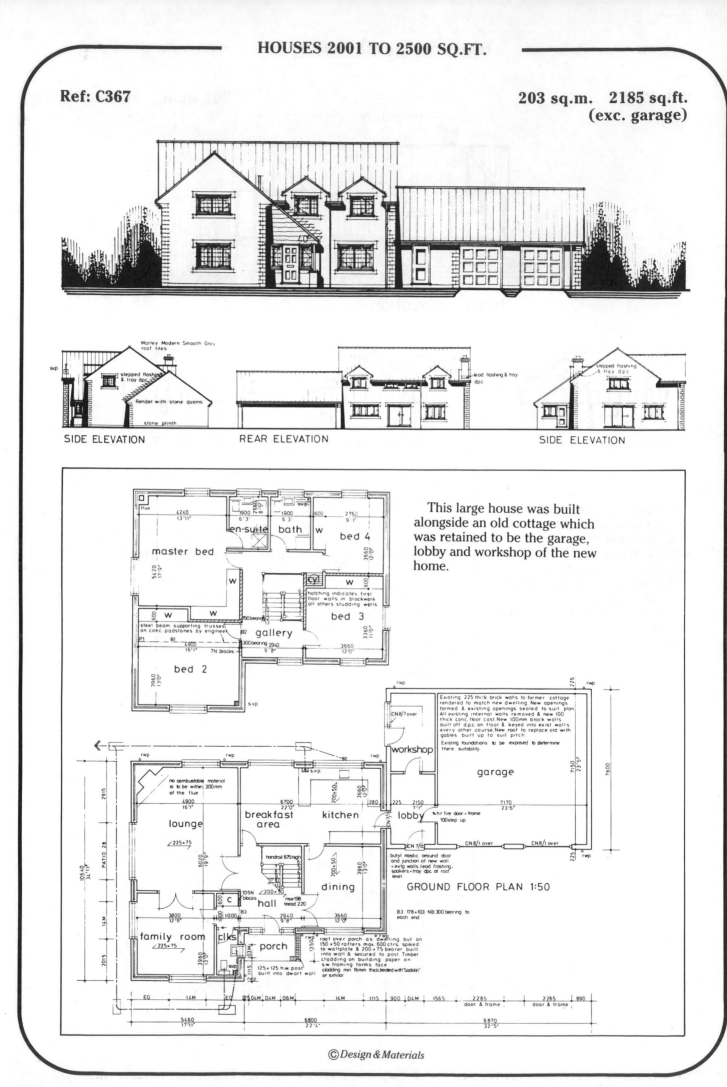

SIDE ELEVATION

Marley Modern Smooth Grey roof tiles

svp

stepped flashing & tray dpc.

Render with stone quoins

stone plinth

REAR ELEVATION

lead flashing & tray dpc

SIDE ELEVATION

stepped flashing & tray dpc

This large house was built alongside an old cottage which was retained to be the garage, lobby and workshop of the new home.

flue

en-suite    bath    w    bed 4

master bed

hatching indicates first floor walls in blockwork all others studding walls

cyl    w

steel beam supporting trusses on conc. padstones by engineer

bed 3

gallery

bed 2

no combustable material is to be within 300mm of the flue

lounge    breakfast area    kitchen    lobby    garage

workshop

Existing 225 thick brick walls to former cottage rendered to match new dwelling. New openings formed & existing openings sealed to suit plan. All existing internal walls removed & new 100 thick conc. floor cast. New 100mm block walls built off d.p.c. on floor & keyed into exist. walls every other course. New roof to replace old with gables built up to suit pitch. Existing foundations to be exposed to determine there suitability

½ hr fire door + frame 100 step up

handrail 875 high

105N blocks

dining

butyl mastic around door and junction of new wall + extg walls. lead flashing, soakers & tray dpc at roof level

**GROUND FLOOR PLAN 1:50**

B3  178×103 NB 300 bearing to each end

rse198 tread 220

hall

family room    clks    porch

125×125 h.w. post built into dwarf wall

roof over porch as dwelling but on 150×50 rafters max. 600 ctrs. spiked to wallplate & 200×75 bearer built into wall & secured to post. Timber cladding on building paper on sw framing forms face cladding min 16mm thick treated with 'Sadolin' or similar

**Ref: S525**

198 sq.m.   2131 sq.ft.
(inc. garage)

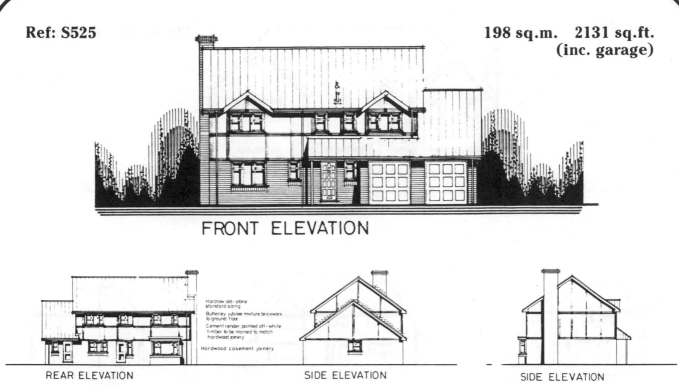

FRONT ELEVATION

REAR ELEVATION

Hardrow old-stone
standard sizing

Butterley jubilee mixture brickwork
to ground floor

Cement render pointed off-white
timber to be stained to match
hardwood joinery

Hardwood casement joinery

SIDE ELEVATION

SIDE ELEVATION

A tudor style house. The notes on the drawing shew how much thought was given to the materials. The bricks are Butterley Jubilee Mixture from South Yorkshire, and are a mottled colour like the soft clamp-fired bricks used in Tudor times, although in fact they are very hard semi-engineering bricks. The render is off-white, and the timber framing is to be stained to match the hardwood joinery. The roof tiles are Hardrow slates, which look like old stone slates, and which can be laid in diminishing courses with larger slates at the bottom and smaller ones above. All of this will have been debated at length with the planners.

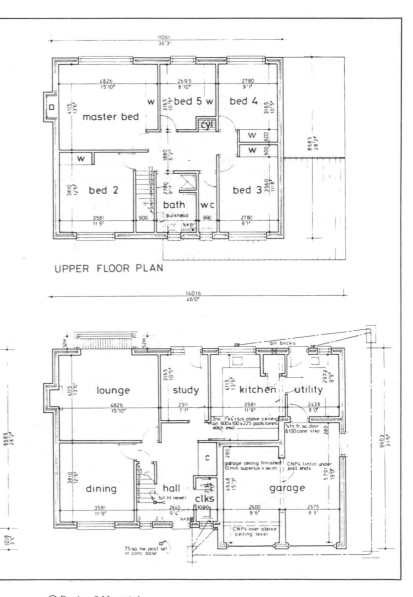

UPPER FLOOR PLAN

**Ref: P2713**

**220 sq.m.    2368 sq.ft.**

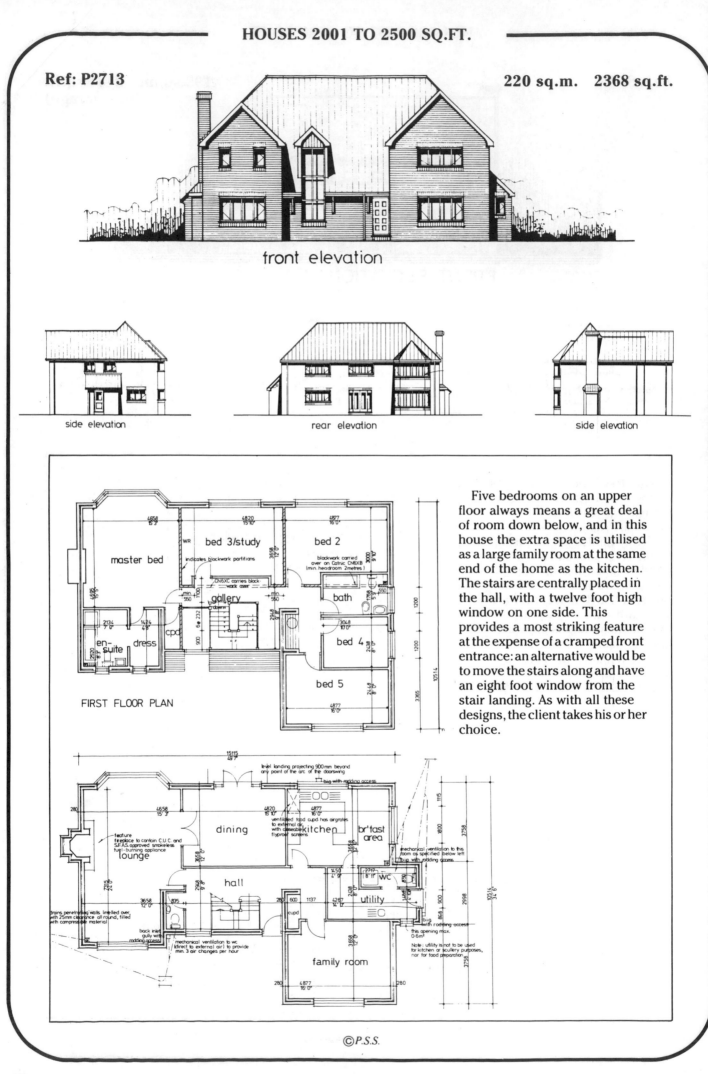

front elevation

side elevation

rear elevation

side elevation

FIRST FLOOR PLAN

master bed

bed 3/study

bed 2

gallery

bath

en-suite

dress

cpd

bed 4

bed 5

Five bedrooms on an upper floor always means a great deal of room down below, and in this house the extra space is utilised as a large family room at the same end of the home as the kitchen. The stairs are centrally placed in the hall, with a twelve foot high window on one side. This provides a most striking feature at the expense of a cramped front entrance: an alternative would be to move the stairs along and have an eight foot window from the stair landing. As with all these designs, the client takes his or her choice.

lounge

dining

kitchen

br'fast area

hall

wc

utility

family room

**Ref: W1395**

**231 sq.m.    2486 sq.ft.**

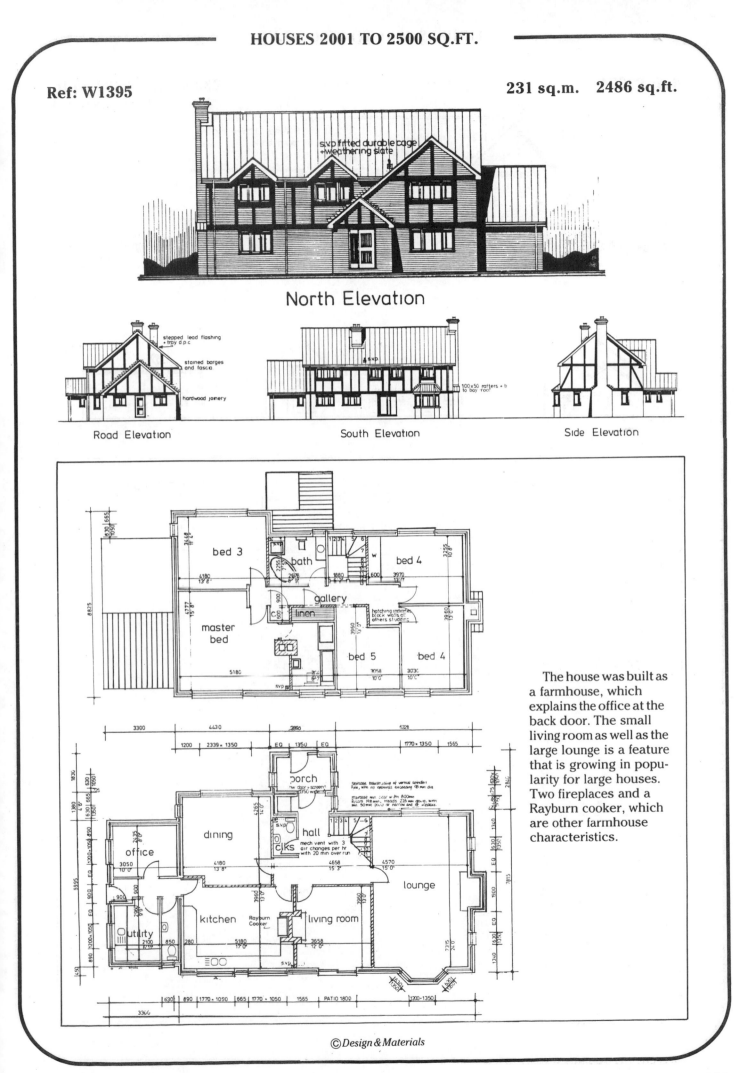

North Elevation

Road Elevation

South Elevation

Side Elevation

The house was built as a farmhouse, which explains the office at the back door. The small living room as well as the large lounge is a feature that is growing in popularity for large houses. Two fireplaces and a Rayburn cooker, which are other farmhouse characteristics.

*© Design & Materials*

**Ref: P2574**

**232 sq.m.    2497 sq.ft.**
**(exc. garage)**

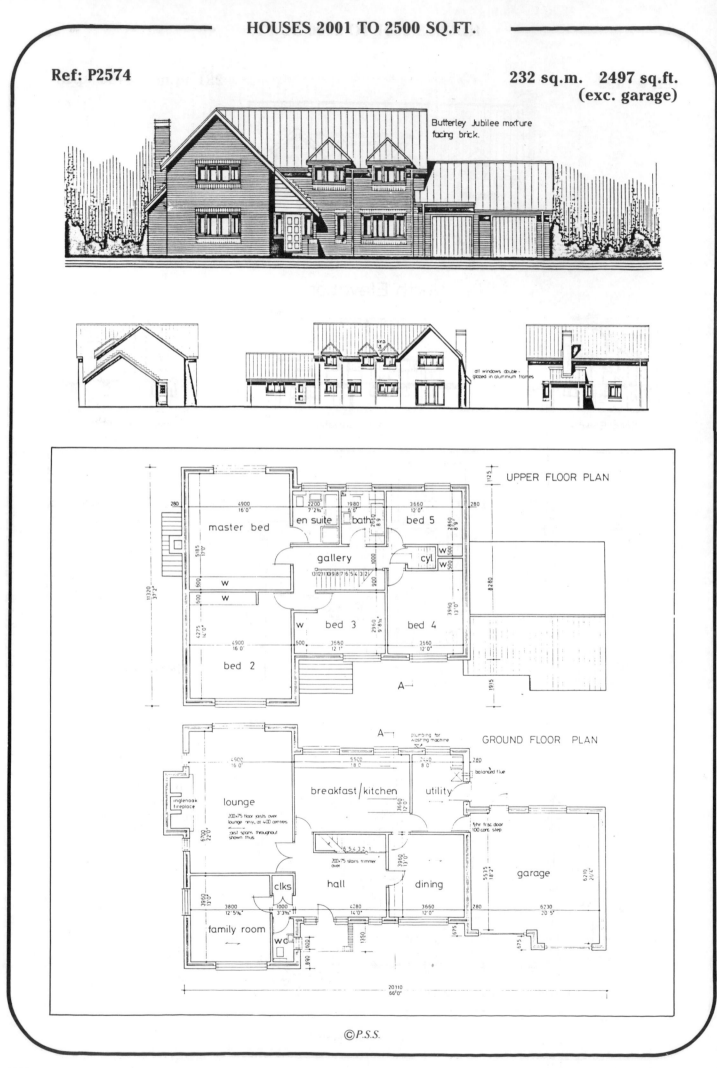

Butterley Jubilee mixture
facing brick.

all windows double -
glazed in aluminium frames

UPPER FLOOR PLAN

master bed

en suite    bath    bed 5

gallery    cyl

w
w

bed 3    bed 4

bed 2

A →

GROUND FLOOR PLAN

plumbing for
washing machine

balanced flue

breakfast/kitchen    utility

lounge

inglenook
fireplace

200×75 floor joists over
lounge only, at 400 centres

cast spars throughout
shown thus

200×75 stairs trimmer
over

clks    hall    dining    garage

family room

w c

**Ref: W1216**

**2368 sq.ft.**
**220 sq.m.**

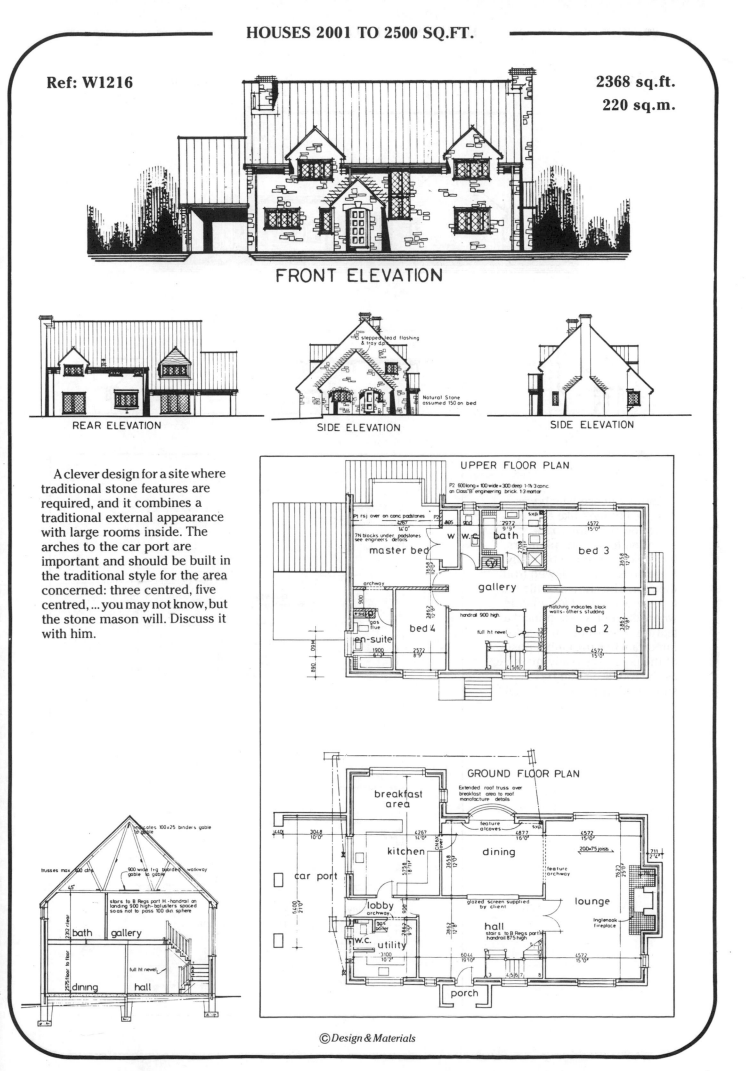

FRONT ELEVATION

REAR ELEVATION

SIDE ELEVATION

SIDE ELEVATION

A clever design for a site where traditional stone features are required, and it combines a traditional external appearance with large rooms inside. The arches to the car port are important and should be built in the traditional style for the area concerned: three centred, five centred, ... you may not know, but the stone mason will. Discuss it with him.

UPPER FLOOR PLAN

GROUND FLOOR PLAN

© Design & Materials

**Ref: W1026**

**203 sq.m.   2185 sq.ft.**

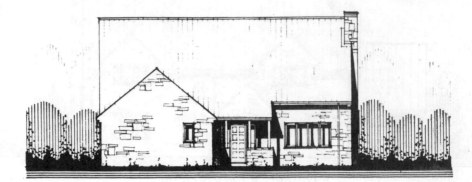

Another house which was designed to look like a bungalow from the road elevation to suit the planners, but which is seen to be really a large house when viewed from the rear. The choice of tile has to be exactly right for a home where the roof is as dominant a feature as it is here. It is also important that the timber posts of the porch are really massive, as the roof seems to be supported by them – although this is really an illusion.

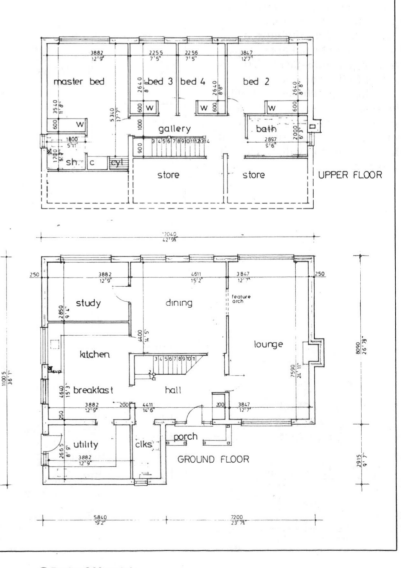

*© Design & Materials*

**Ref: W1135**

**219 sq.m.   2357 sq.ft.**

FRONT            REAR

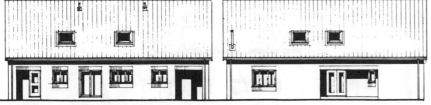

SIDE ELEVATIONS

A design with many unusual features, including the Swedish style balcony to the master bedroom, a gallery over the dining area, and much else. Study the plans - they are full of ideas.

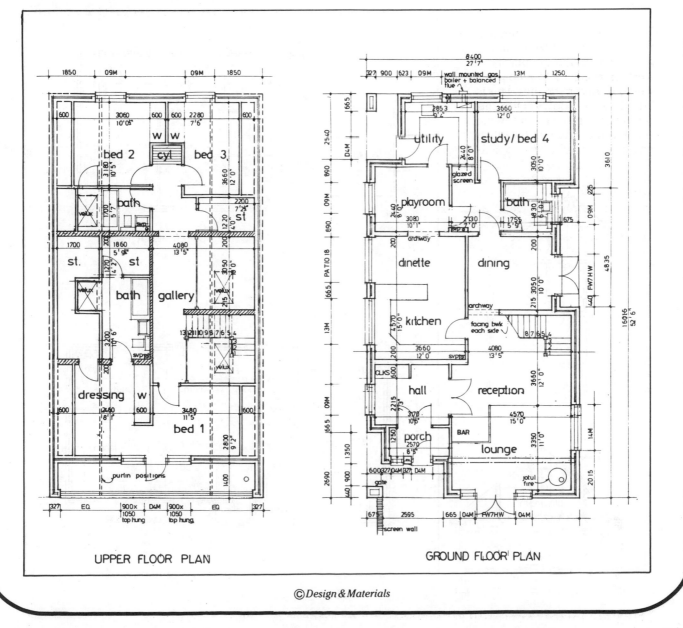

UPPER FLOOR PLAN            GROUND FLOOR PLAN

© *Design & Materials*

**Ref: P2806**

**198 sq.m.    2131 sq.ft.**

front elevation

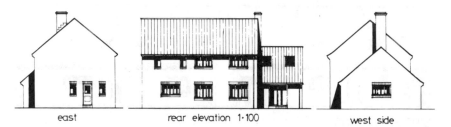

east

rear elevation 1·100

west side

A house with a cost-effective trussed rafter roof to the main two storey part and a purlin roof over the lounge with a childrens play room under the tiles. This is lit by Velux windows set in the sloping ceiling, but a window can be set in the gable end wall if required.

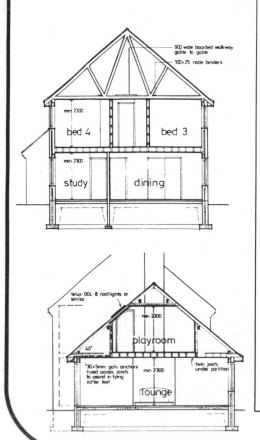

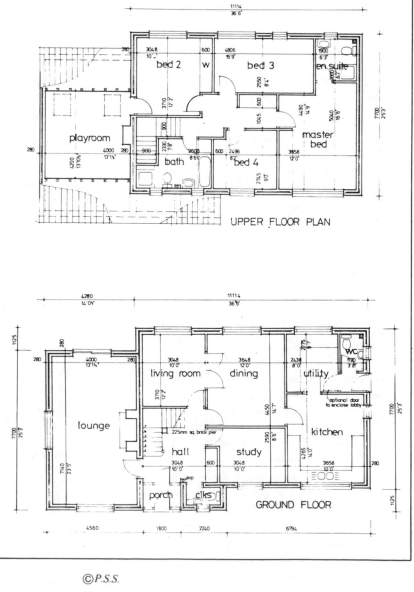

UPPER FLOOR PLAN

GROUND FLOOR

©P.S.S.

**Ref: P2753**

**208 sq.m.  2238 sq.ft.**
**(exc. garage)**

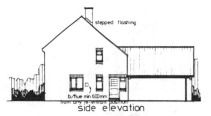

side elevation

rear elevation

side elevation

An interesting house with a large hall and equally large landing that helps to make it feel even bigger than it actually is. Note the side window to the half landing of the stairs. To be of full height it had to be in the side wall, as there is insufficient clearance for it below the roof at the front. A shallower window in the front wall would have looked out of place in this building which has such a strong vertical emphasis in the joinery.

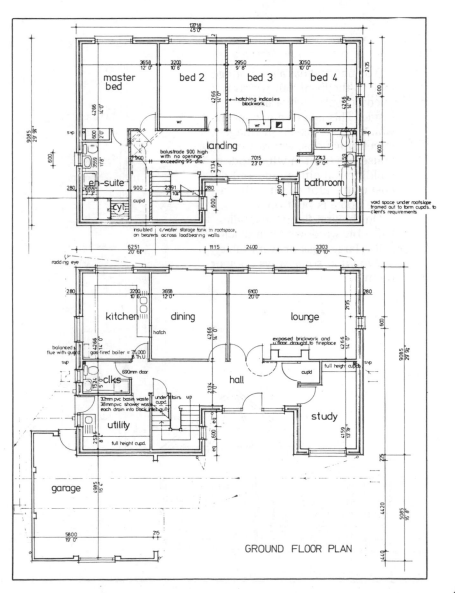

GROUND FLOOR PLAN

©P.S.S.

**Ref: P3013**

**188 sq.m.    2023 sq.ft.**

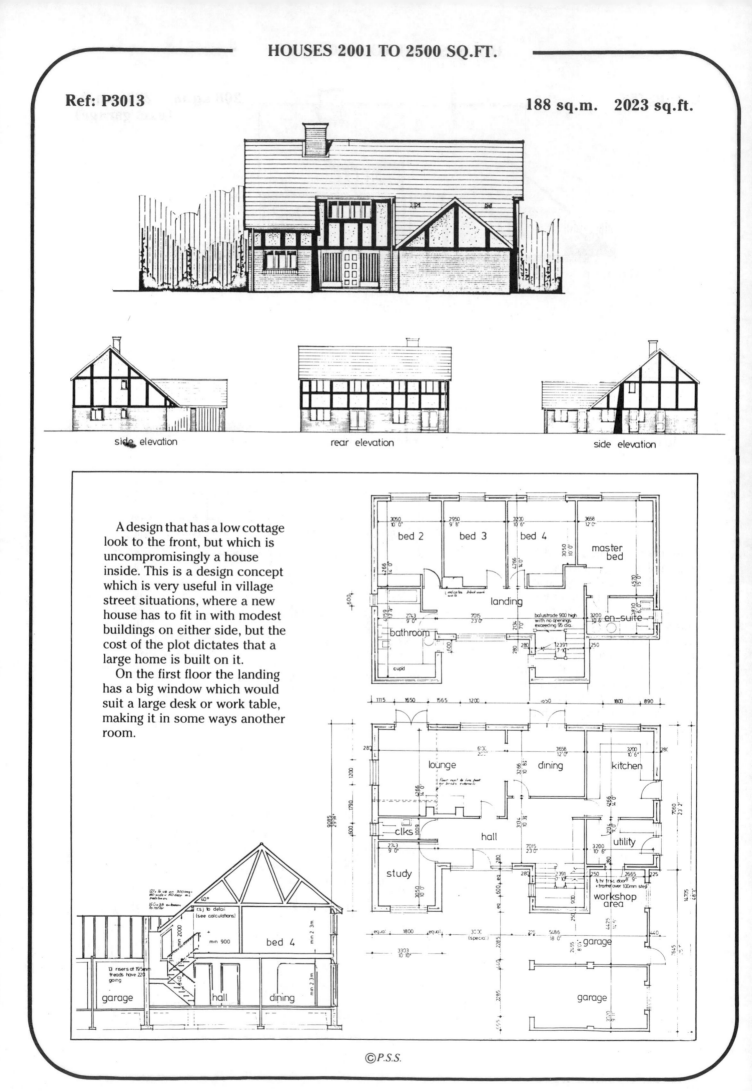

side elevation

rear elevation

side elevation

A design that has a low cottage look to the front, but which is uncompromisingly a house inside. This is a design concept which is very useful in village street situations, where a new house has to fit in with modest buildings on either side, but the cost of the plot dictates that a large home is built on it.

On the first floor the landing has a big window which would suit a large desk or work table, making it in some ways another room.

©P.S.S.

**Ref: C543**

**217 sq.m.    2335 sq.ft.**

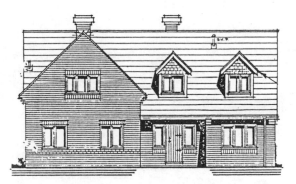

This is really an example of a large house disguised as a cottage, which is sometimes necessary in order to get planning consent to build in a rural situation. By keeping the eaves level well below the sills to the first floor windows on all the elevations, and by keeping all continuous lengths of walling to a minimum, the overall effect is well suited to a village street site or other situation where a more imposing structure would not be acceptable. Two chimneys are required, for the inglenook fireplace and the AGA cooker, and with careful attention paid to the brick detailing the chimney stacks will add to the character of the property.

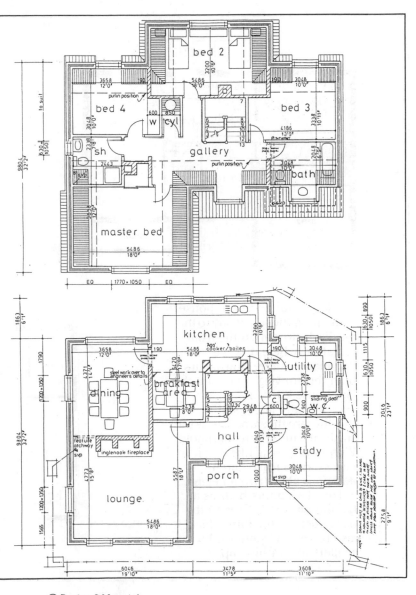

*© Design & Materials*

**Ref: 96164**

**618 sq.m.    2345 sq.ft.**

| | | |
|---|---|---|
| Floor Area | 2345 sq.ft. | 218 sq.m. |
| Dimensions overall | 46'3" x 37'9" | 14.09 x 11.49 |
| Drawing Room | 14'9" x 22'11" | 4.49 x 6.99 |
| Farmhouse Kitchen | 16'0" x 20'0" | 4.87 x 6.10 |
| Dining | 13'0" x 12'0" | 3.96 x 3.65 |
| Office | 7'0" x 10'7" | 2.13 x 3.23 |
| Master Bed | 14'9" x 22'11" | 4.49 x 6.99 |
| Bed 2 | 16'0" x 13'0" | 4.87 x 3.96 |
| Bed 3 | 15'7" x 10'7" | 4.74 x 3.23 |
| Bed 4 | 8'2" x 12'0" | 2.49 x 3.65 |

A large four bedroom house with a prominent balcony to the master bedroom on the front elevation, where it is the dominant feature. Downstairs both the drawing room and the farmhouse kitchen are exceptionally large, and together are the same size as the smallest bungalow in this book! With large rooms like this it is necessary to make careful decisions about room heights.

This design was built as a farmhouse with access to the back door via the farm office. It also has an old fashioned scullery for washing up.

# Designs for Houses 1751 to 2000 sq. ft.

The houses between 1751 and 2000 sq. ft. that are illustrated on the pages that follow demonstrate the choice available between having a few large rooms or rather more smaller rooms. At first thought the former often appears more attractive, providing an opportunity for 25 ft. drawing rooms and dining rooms for tables that seat eight or ten, but the realities of every day family living often make it more practicable to provide a study *and* a family room, or, if living in the country, a utility room for muddy boots and wet dogs at the back. The right decision depends on a careful appraisal of one's present and future living requirements.

Among the plans on the following pages you will find two design features that are growing in popularity – the dining hall, and the small snug or family room. Both are American ideas.

The dining hall, usually with a porch to the front door, provides an impressive entrance to the house and is usually enhanced by a feature staircase. It provides a much larger dining area than would have otherwise been possible, and is a design feature which is bound to become more fashionable. Indeed, a few speculative developers are now using the idea.

A snug is a small room with room only for armchairs and a TV where the householders can spend their evenings when they are alone, or when they want to get away from a noisy family. In American design it is also called a den. For some this feature is very important indeed.

**Ref: 96172**

**168 sq.m.    1803 sq.ft.**

This cottage style home has really big rooms, and is larger than many of the more formal looking large houses in this book. The study would make a home office, and perhaps this design really belongs in the category of homes with office space.

| Dimensions overall | 36'5" x 37'5" | - | 11102 x 11420 |
|---|---|---|---|
| Lounge | 15'0" x 20'0" | - | 4.57 x 6.10 |
| Dining Room | 17'0" x 10'0" | - | 5.18 x 3.04 |
| Kitchen | 17'0" x 8'6" | - | 5.18 x 2.60 |
| Study | 10'6" x 11'6" | - | 3.20 x 3.50 |
| Master Bedroom | 15'0" x 11'2" | - | 4.57 x 3.40 |
| Bedroom 2 | 17'0" x 10'0" | - | 5.18 x 3.04 |
| Bedroom 3 | 17'0" x 8'6" | - | 5.18 x 2.60 |
| Bedroom 4 | 10'6" x 7'6" | - | 3.20 x 2.28 |

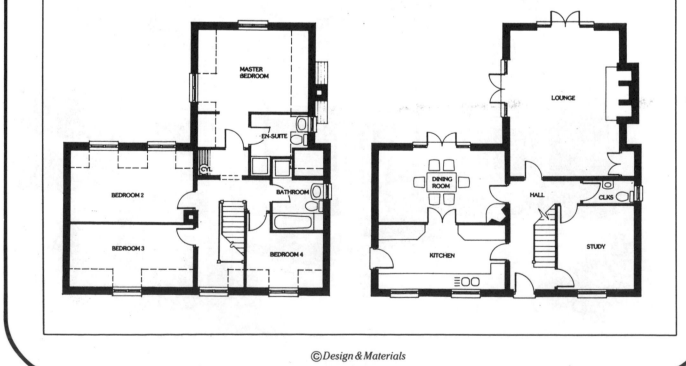

**Ref: 96152**

**173 sq.m.   1858 sq.ft.**

This Edwardian style suburban home can be built with or without the integral garage.

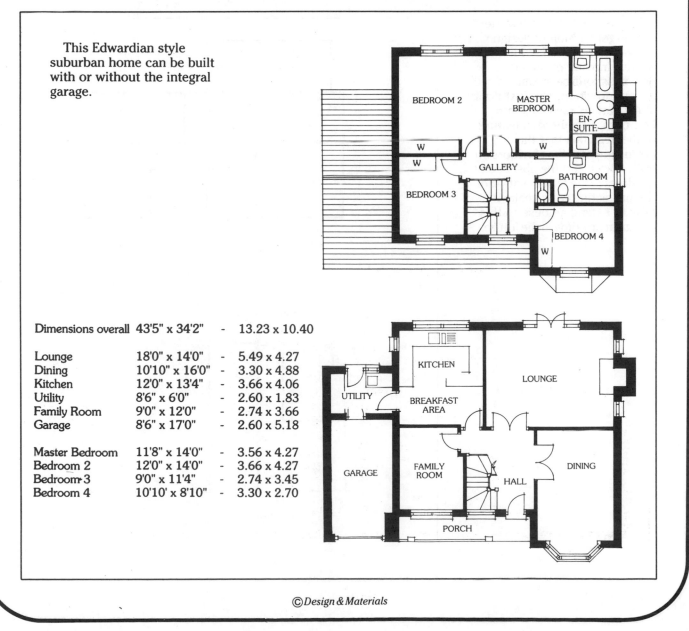

| Dimensions overall | 43'5" x 34'2" | - | 13.23 x 10.40 |
|---|---|---|---|
| Lounge | 18'0" x 14'0" | - | 5.49 x 4.27 |
| Dining | 10'10" x 16'0" | - | 3.30 x 4.88 |
| Kitchen | 12'0" x 13'4" | - | 3.66 x 4.06 |
| Utility | 8'6" x 6'0" | - | 2.60 x 1.83 |
| Family Room | 9'0" x 12'0" | - | 2.74 x 3.66 |
| Garage | 8'6" x 17'0" | - | 2.60 x 5.18 |
| Master Bedroom | 11'8" x 14'0" | - | 3.56 x 4.27 |
| Bedroom 2 | 12'0" x 14'0" | - | 3.66 x 4.27 |
| Bedroom 3 | 9'0" x 11'4" | - | 2.74 x 3.45 |
| Bedroom 4 | 10'10' x 8'10" | - | 3.30 x 2.70 |

**Ref: PN676**

**178 sq.m.   1920 sq.ft.**

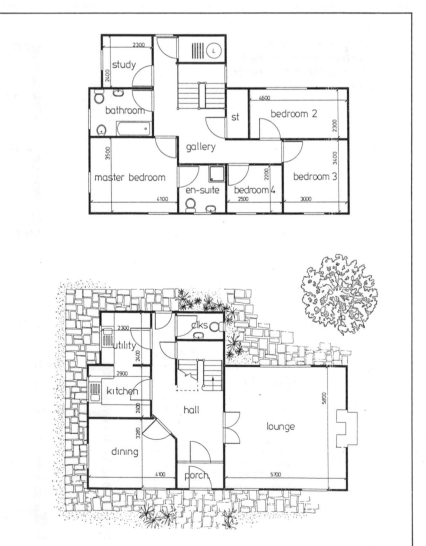

This house of 1900 square feet is a larger version of design PN674, on page 307, with a bigger drawing room and generous four bedroom accommodation. The first floor study can be used as a fifth bedroom if required. A feature of the design is that the arrangement of the corridors on both floors, and the absence of windows in the rear elevation of the projecting wing, make it easy to extend a house to this design at any time in the future.

© Potton

**Ref: PN678**

**163 sq.m.   1750 sq.ft.**

An example of an aisle frame house with a dining hall of the sort which many predict will become a common design feature now that doors that are 100% draught proof are readily available. The projecting dormer jettied out over the front door is a feature typical of East Anglia.

A corresponding dormer to the rear elevation permits a private bathroom to the master bedroom suite. Note how the chimney to the Inglenook fireplace is used to warm the first floor airing cupboard.

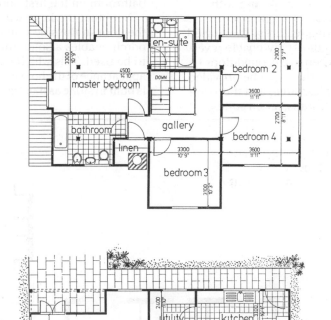

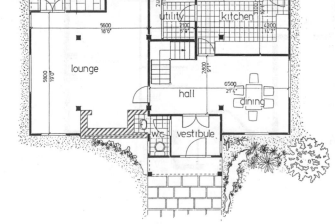

© *Potton*

**Ref: 96171**

**172 sq.m.   1861 sq.ft.
(inc. garage)**

The Penarth house was designed for a site in South Wales, and has a number of interesting features. The angled walls to the study enable a very comprehensive ground floor accommodation to be provided in a modest area, and there are five bedrooms, an en suite bathroom and a large family bathroom on the first floor.

Note that the large window to the floor in the side wall of the porch enables a solid front door to be used. This which suits the appearance of the house when it is built in stone as illustrated, and gives plenty of light for the porch and the hall.

| Floor Area (inc. garage) | 1861 sq.ft. | 172 sq m |
|---|---|---|
| Dimensions overall | 45'9" x 29'10" | 13.94 x 9.10 |
| Lounge | 12'0" x 22'0" | 3.65 x 6.70 |
| Sitting Room | 10'8" x 11'0" | 3.25 x 3.35 |
| Kitchen Dining | 10'8" x 22'0" | 3.25 x 6.70 |
| Utility | 9'0" x 5'7" | 2.74 x 1.70 |
| Study | 8'0" x 9'0" | 2.43 x 2.74 |
| Garage | 9'0" x 17'0" | 2.74 x 5.19 |
| Master Bed | 12'0" x 10'8" | 3.65 x 3.24 |
| Bed 2 | 12'0" x 9'0" | 3.65 x 2.75 |
| Bed 3 | 10'8" x 9'2" | 3.25 x 2.80 |
| Bed 4 | 10'8" x 9'2" | 3.25 x 2.80 |
| Bed 5 | 10'8" x 7'9" | 3.25 x 2.35 |

© Design & Materials

**Ref: 96169**

**167 sq.m.    1800 sq.ft.**

The Hatfield design house is shown here with a rendered finish above brickwork and a projecting timber clad bay on the front elevation, which is very much the traditional style in Essex where the prototype was built.

The kitchen layout is illustrated with a separate utility room, although this can be dispensed with if required, and perhaps an external porch built at the kitchen door. The master bedroom is shown with separate doors to the dressing room and

to the en suite bathroom. This was to suit the clients for whom the original house was designed. A more usual arrangement would be to have the bathroom leading off the dressing room.

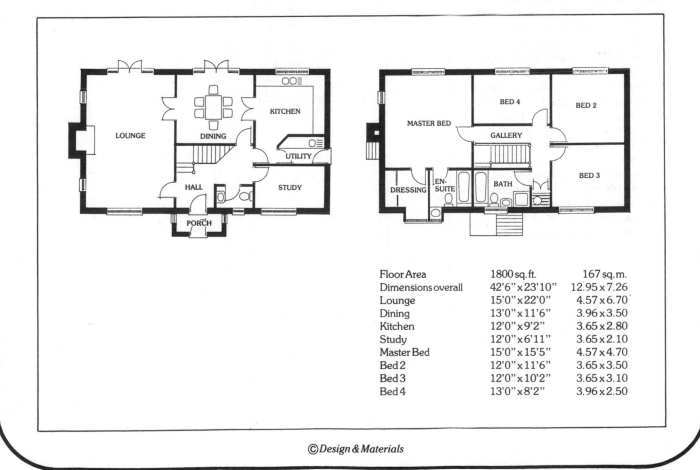

| Floor Area | 1800 sq.ft. | 167 sq.m. |
|---|---|---|
| Dimensions overall | 42'6" x 23'10" | 12.95 x 7.26 |
| Lounge | 15'0" x 22'0" | 4.57 x 6.70 |
| Dining | 13'0" x 11'6" | 3.96 x 3.50 |
| Kitchen | 12'0" x 9'2" | 3.65 x 2.80 |
| Study | 12'0" x 6'11" | 3.65 x 2.10 |
| Master Bed | 15'0" x 15'5" | 4.57 x 4.70 |
| Bed 2 | 12'0" x 11'6" | 3.65 x 3.50 |
| Bed 3 | 12'0" x 10'2" | 3.65 x 3.10 |
| Bed 4 | 13'0" x 8'2" | 3.96 x 2.50 |

**Ref: P3022**

**176 sq.m.    1894 sq.ft.**

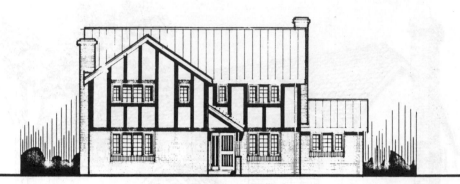

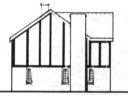

side elevation

rear elevation

side elevation

A house designed to a clients very precise brief for a site in Gwent.

Note the projecting porch to the front door: this will be a key feature and will be much more obvious than would appear from the drawings. The four wooden posts supporting the roof should be really massive, possibly with chamfered corners, and the detailing of the dwarf wall that supports them is most important. Any feature that appears to support part of the roof of the house – whether it does or not – has to be absolutely right. Often the best way of making sure it is right and in the correct regional style is to discuss it in detail with the bricklayer and carpenter.

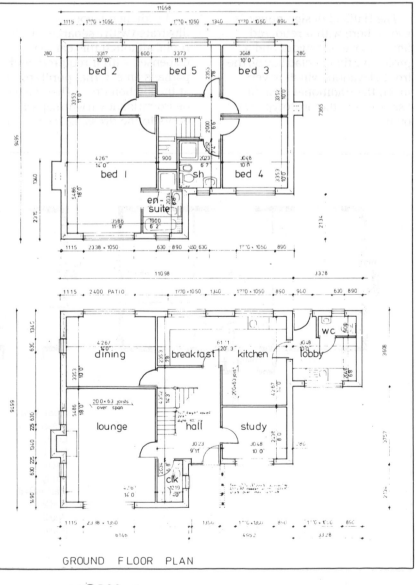

GROUND FLOOR PLAN

© P.S.S.

**Ref: S493**

**178 sq.m.    1916 sq.ft.**
**(inc. garage)**

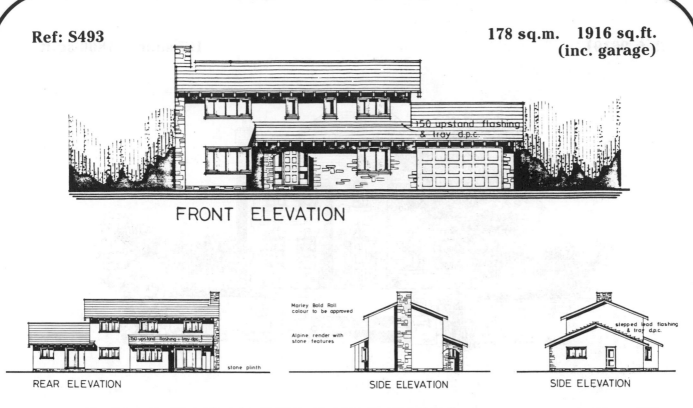

FRONT ELEVATION

150 upstand flashing & tray d.p.c.

REAR ELEVATION

150 upstand flashing + tray dpc.

stone plinth

Marley Bold Roll colour to be approved

Alpine render with stone features

SIDE ELEVATION

stepped lead flashing & tray d.p.c.

SIDE ELEVATION

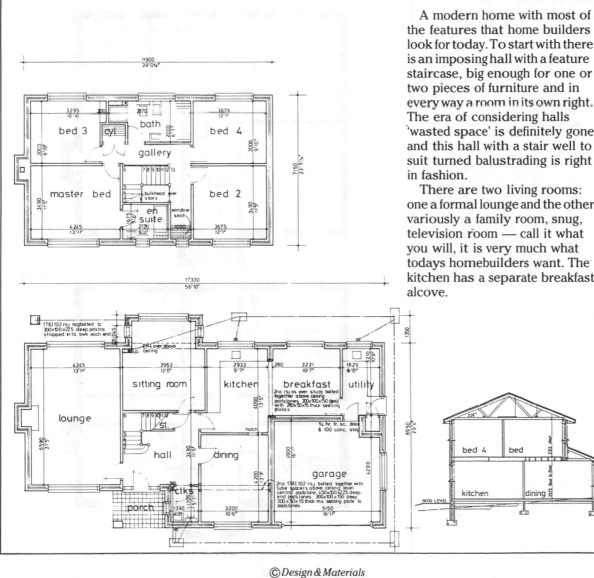

A modern home with most of the features that home builders look for today. To start with there is an imposing hall with a feature staircase, big enough for one or two pieces of furniture and in every way a room in its own right. The era of considering halls 'wasted space' is definitely gone, and this hall with a stair well to suit turned balustrading is right in fashion.

There are two living rooms: one a formal lounge and the other variously a family room, snug, television room — call it what you will, it is very much what todays homebuilders want. The kitchen has a separate breakfast alcove.

**Ref: 96191**

**167 sq.m.    1800 sq.ft.**

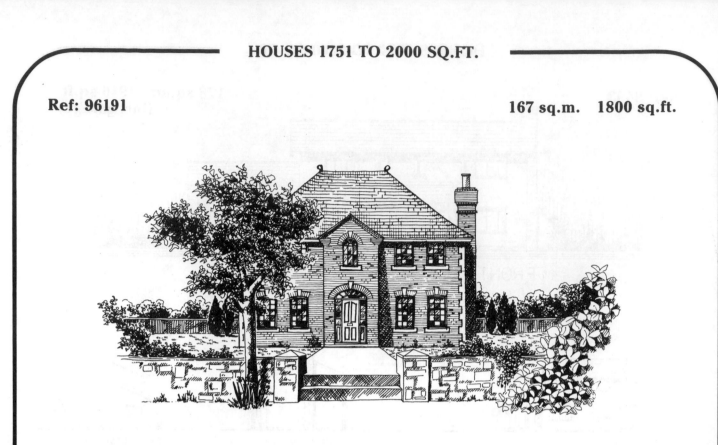

A house for today in the Georgian style.

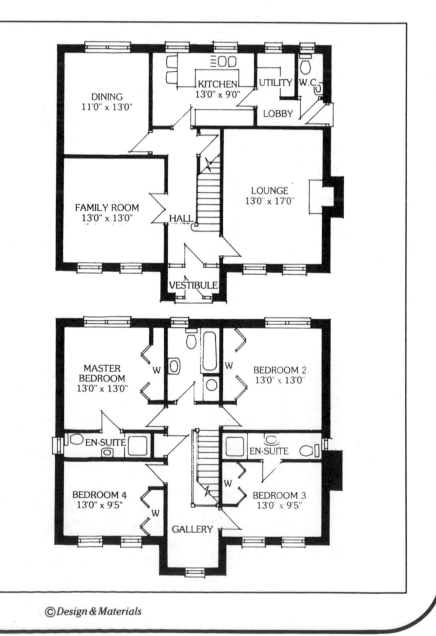

**Ref: 96146**

**175 sq.m.    1888 sq.ft.**

It is unlikely that many other people in Britain will want to build this American style home exactly as it is shown here. The owners had lived in the USA, and wanted a Colonial style house. Look at the interesting ground floor layout which can be adapted for more conventional buildings. The angled wall in the hall give corner doors to the study and kitchen, and the kitchen/breakfast room arrangement has eight different wall surfaces. All of this helps to make it a strikingly different home, although it is all very logical and makes excellent use of space.

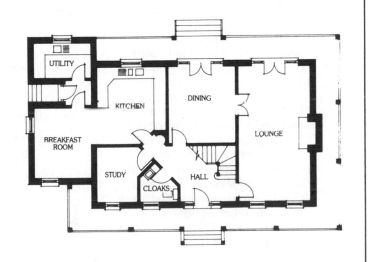

| | | | |
|---|---|---|---|
| Dimensions overall | 52'4" x 32'7" | - | 15.95 x 9.92 |
| Lounge | 12'0" x 22'10" | - | 3.65 x 6.96 |
| Dining | 11'6" x 13'0" | - | 3.50 x 3.96 |
| Kitchen | 12'0" x 13'0" | - | 3.65 x 3.96 |
| Breakfast Room | 9'6" x 12'0" | - | 2.90 x 3.65 |
| Study | 7'0" x 9'6" | - | 2.13 x 2.90 |
| Utility | 9'6" x 6'1" | - | 2.90 x 1.84 |
| Master Bedroom | 12'0" x 13'0" | - | 3.65 x 3.96 |
| Bedroom 2 | 12'0" x 13'0" | - | 3.65 x 3.96 |
| Bedroom 3 | 12'0" x 9'6" | - | 3.65 x 2.90 |
| Bedroom 4 | 12'0" x 9'6" | - | 3.65 x 2.90 |

**Ref: PN682**

**181 sq.m.    1950 sq.ft.**

The Grandsden four bedroomed home has become the best known of all the Potton Heritage designs since it first caused a stir at the Ideal Homes Exhibition in 1981. Since then many hundreds have been built. The version illustrated is the original, but a number of variants of the design concept have been developed to meet special requirements. Together with a number of other aisle frame homes the Grandsden can be inspected at the Potton

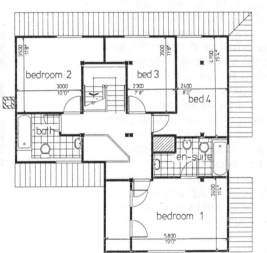

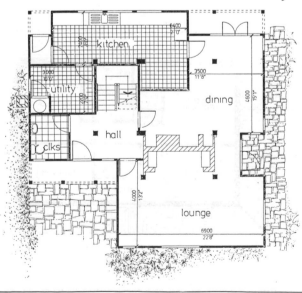

showhouse complex within ten minutes drive of the A1 in Bedfordshire, and in fact was the original house to be constructed there.

**Ref: PN680**

**164 sq.m.    1770 sq.ft.**

When is a cottage so large that it should be classified as a house? It is all about the feel of the property and how easily it would fit into a village street. At 1770 square feet this aisle framed house has a character and atmosphere that qualifies it as a cottage although it is larger than many more pretentious properties.

The traditional 'rooms in the roof' cottage arrangement requires that the first floor gallery is lit by having glazed lights over the bedroom doors, and the bathroom will require mechanical ventilation unless the site lends itself to Velux roof lights in the bathroom and above the stairs.

The kitchen is very generously proportioned for a home of this size, and is well suited to fitting out in the fashionable 'farmhouse kitchen' style.

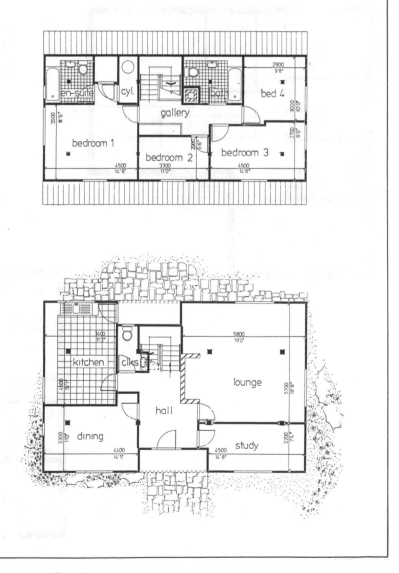

© Potton

**Ref: 96190**

**168 sq.m.   1808 sq.ft.**

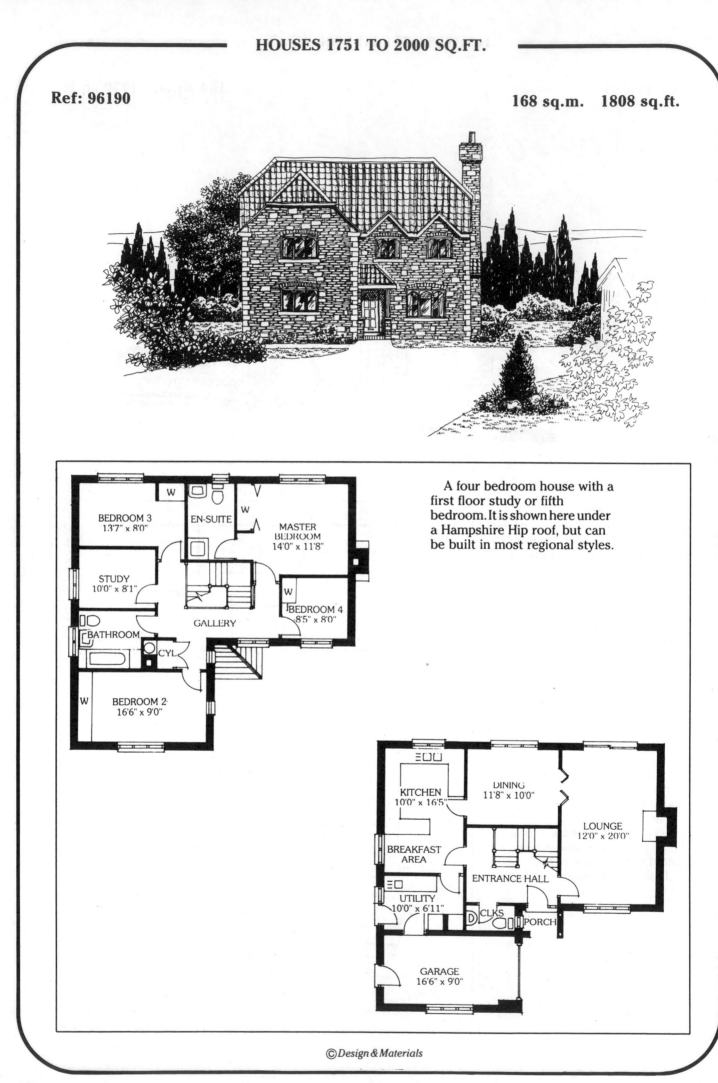

A four bedroom house with a first floor study or fifth bedroom. It is shown here under a Hampshire Hip roof, but can be built in most regional styles.

BEDROOM 3
13'7" x 8'0"

EN-SUITE

MASTER BEDROOM
14'0" x 11'8"

STUDY
10'0" x 8'1"

BEDROOM 4
8'5" x 8'0"

GALLERY

BATHROOM

CYL

BEDROOM 2
16'6" x 9'0"

KITCHEN
10'0" x 16'5"

DINING
11'8" x 10'0"

LOUNGE
12'0" x 20'0"

BREAKFAST AREA

ENTRANCE HALL

UTILITY
10'0" x 6'11"

CLKS

PORCH

GARAGE
16'6" x 9'0"

**Ref: 96213**

**181 sq.m.    1952 sq.ft.**

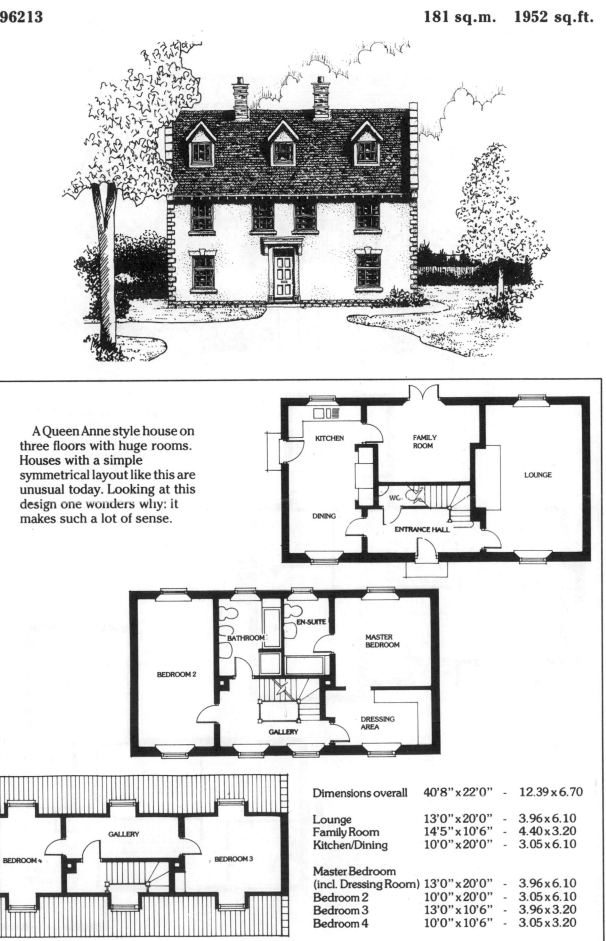

A Queen Anne style house on three floors with huge rooms. Houses with a simple symmetrical layout like this are unusual today. Looking at this design one wonders why: it makes such a lot of sense.

| Dimensions overall | 40'8" x 22'0" | - | 12.39 x 6.70 |
|---|---|---|---|
| Lounge | 13'0" x 20'0" | - | 3.96 x 6.10 |
| Family Room | 14'5" x 10'6" | - | 4.40 x 3.20 |
| Kitchen/Dining | 10'0" x 20'0" | - | 3.05 x 6.10 |
| Master Bedroom (incl. Dressing Room) | 13'0" x 20'0" | - | 3.96 x 6.10 |
| Bedroom 2 | 10'0" x 20'0" | - | 3.05 x 6.10 |
| Bedroom 3 | 13'0" x 10'6" | - | 3.96 x 3.20 |
| Bedroom 4 | 10'0" x 10'6" | - | 3.05 x 3.20 |

*©Design & Materials*

**Ref: 96197**

**179 sq.m.    1930 sq.ft.**

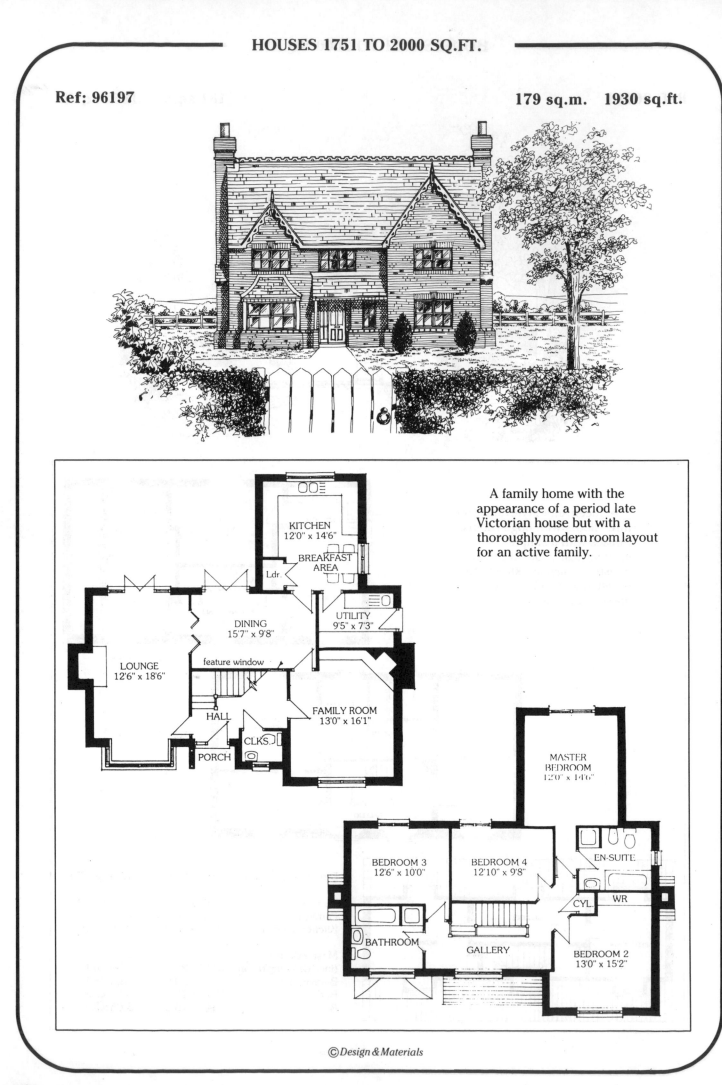

A family home with the appearance of a period late Victorian house but with a thoroughly modern room layout for an active family.

KITCHEN
12'0" x 14'6"

BREAKFAST AREA

Ldr.

DINING
15'7" x 9'8"

UTILITY
9'5" x 7'3"

LOUNGE
12'6" x 18'6"

feature window

HALL

FAMILY ROOM
13'0" x 16'1"

CLKS.

PORCH

MASTER BEDROOM
12'0" x 14'6"

BEDROOM 3
12'6" x 10'0"

BEDROOM 4
12'10" x 9'8"

EN-SUITE

CYL.

WR

BATHROOM

GALLERY

BEDROOM 2
13'0" x 15'2"

© *Design & Materials*

**Ref: 96124**

**176 sq.m.    1894 sq.ft.**

A conventional four bedroom house with an Inglenook fireplace. Shown here in brick under a plain tile roof with an ornamental ridge, it can happily adapt to a wide range of materials to suit planners requirements in different parts of the country, although it will always look best on a brick plinth. The front door is in the angle of the two wings, and requires careful detailing to the porch to make it a focal point on the front elevation.

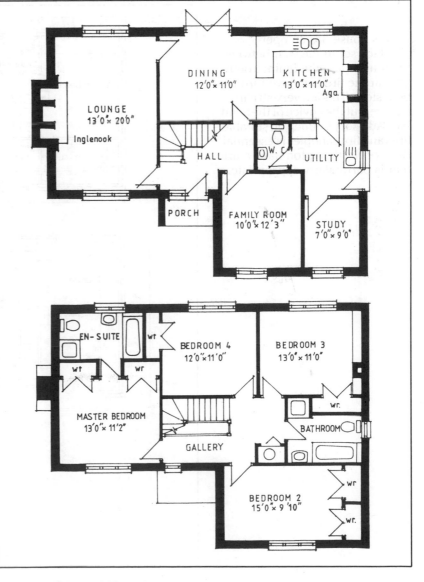

**Ref: P2543**

**164 sq.m.   1765 sq.ft.**
**(exc. garage)**

front elevation (south)

rear elevation      side elevation      side elevation

This house has an open fireplace set in the wall between the lounge and the dining room, so that the fire is enjoyed from both sides. This is a very striking feature, but the advice of the Solid Fuel Advisory Council on suitable fires and fire canopies is essential. Bells of Northampton have a fire that is particularly appropriate.

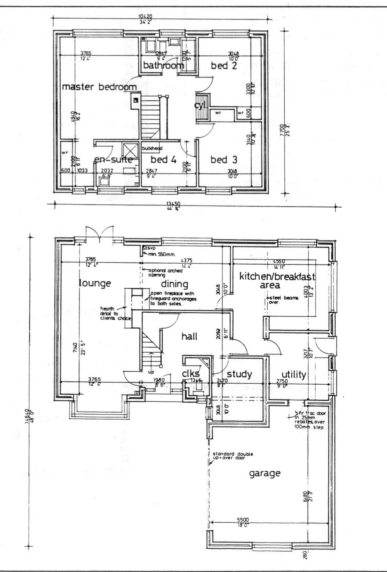

**Ref: W1268**

**171 sq.m.   1840 sq.ft.**
**(exc. garage)**

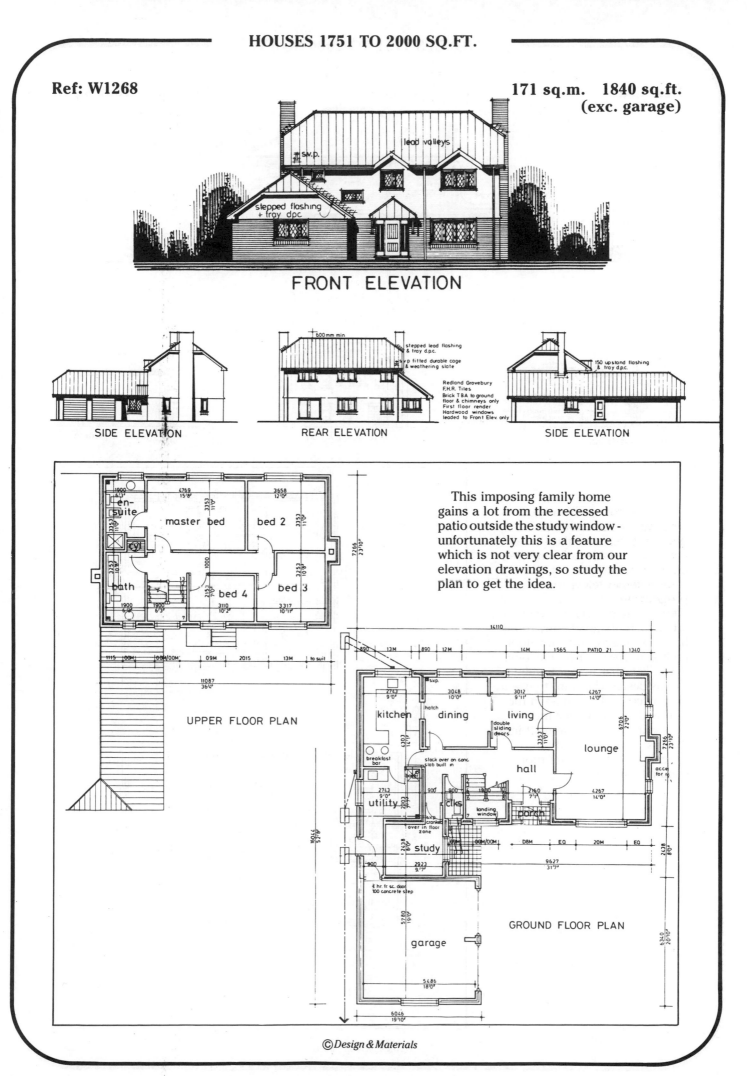

FRONT ELEVATION

lead valleys

s.v.p.

stepped flashing
+ tray dpc

SIDE ELEVATION

REAR ELEVATION

600 mm min

stepped lead flashing
& tray d.p.c.
v.p fitted durable cage
& weathering slate

Redland Grovebury
F.H.R. Tiles
Brick TBA to ground
floor & chimneys only
First floor render
Hardwood windows
leaded to Front Elev. only

SIDE ELEVATION

150 upstand flashing
& tray d.p.c.

UPPER FLOOR PLAN

en-suite

master bed

bed 2

bath

bed 4

bed 3

This imposing family home
gains a lot from the recessed
patio outside the study window -
unfortunately this is a feature
which is not very clear from our
elevation drawings, so study the
plan to get the idea.

GROUND FLOOR PLAN

kitchen

dining

living

lounge

hall

breakfast bar

double
sliding
doors

utility

clks

porch

study

landing window

garage

**Ref: C397**

**170 sq.m.   1829 sq.ft.**

stepped lead flashing
+ tray d.p.c

tray dpc to parapet
walls

FRONT ELEVATION

Marley mendip roof tiles
colour smooth brown

L.B.C. georgian red-multi
brickwork

Boulton + Paul doublehung
sash windows  all bar

Fibreglass portico + columns
to clients supply

gable elevation

skp fitted durable cdge
+ weathering slab

rear elevation

gable elevation

A family room which is quite separate from the lounge is becoming very popular these days, and must be a boon when different generations of a family want different television programmes.

Note that the flat roof over the kitchen, utility and family room has no access from the first floor, and cannot be used as a balcony. If it is likely that anyone building to this design will want to use it as a balcony at any time in the future, then a lintel for the necessary door can be built into the first floor wall, and the specification for the flat roof should be up-rated.

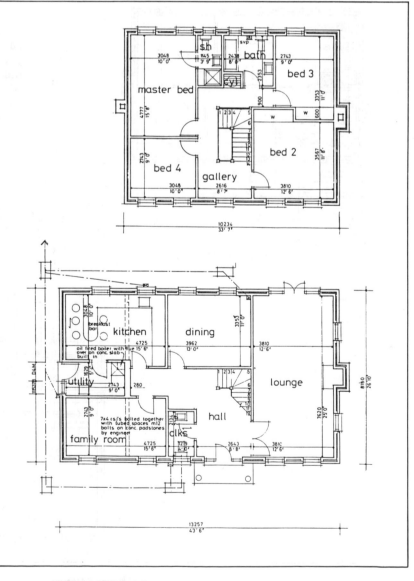

**Ref: S512**

**175 sq.m.    1883 sq.ft.**

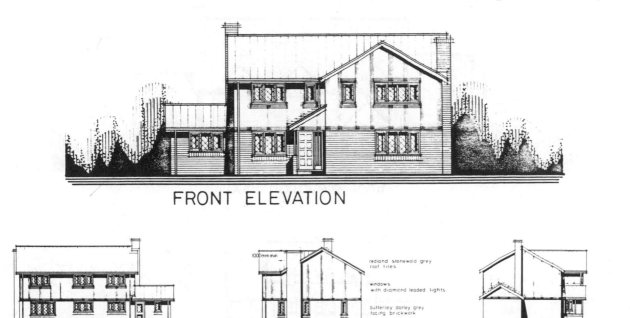

FRONT ELEVATION

REAR ELEVATION          SIDE ELEVATION          SIDE ELEVATION

redland stonewold grey
roof tiles

windows
with diamond leaded lights

butterley darley grey
facing brickwork

1000mm min

A very pretty, very well laid out house in a style that is currently enormously popular. In only 1900 sq.ft. it has just about every feature for a dream home: five bedrooms, huge kitchen with breakfast alcove, impressive study, luxury bathroom to the master suite and a sensible "dirty boots" lobby at the back door. The deeply recessed porch and feature stairs in the large hall give this home a really prestigous feel.

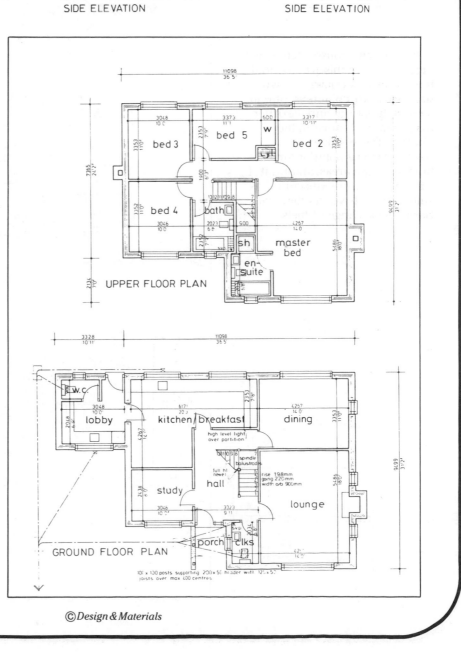

UPPER FLOOR PLAN

GROUND FLOOR PLAN

**Ref: P2733**

**167 sq.m.   1797 sq.ft.**

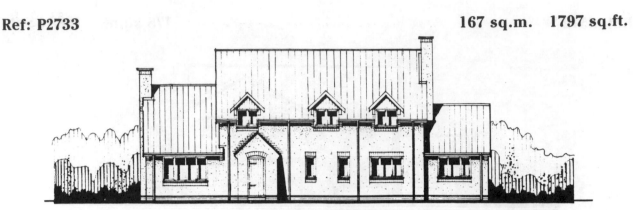

front elevation 1·100

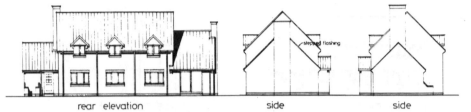

rear elevation                    side                    side

With its farmhouse kitchen and big utility room this is a splendid house for the country, shewn here with two chimneys, one for a fire in the lounge and the other for a solid fuel stove in the kitchen. These stoves are becoming very popular for big homes in rural areas, and most of them are properly described as "multi-fuel" stoves as they can burn a wide range of fuels.

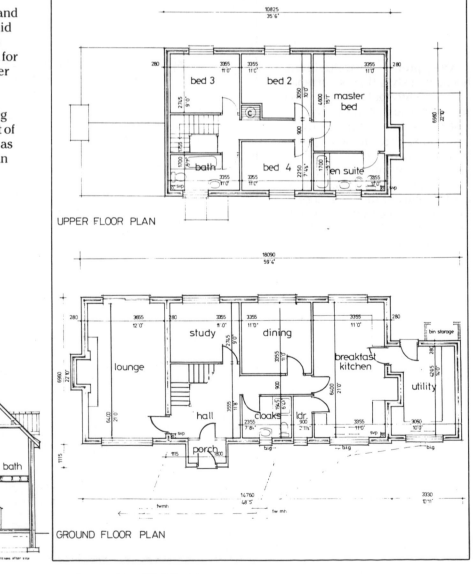

UPPER FLOOR PLAN

GROUND FLOOR PLAN

SECTION

©P.S.S.

**Ref: W1193**

172 sq.m.    1851 sq.ft.
(exc. garage)

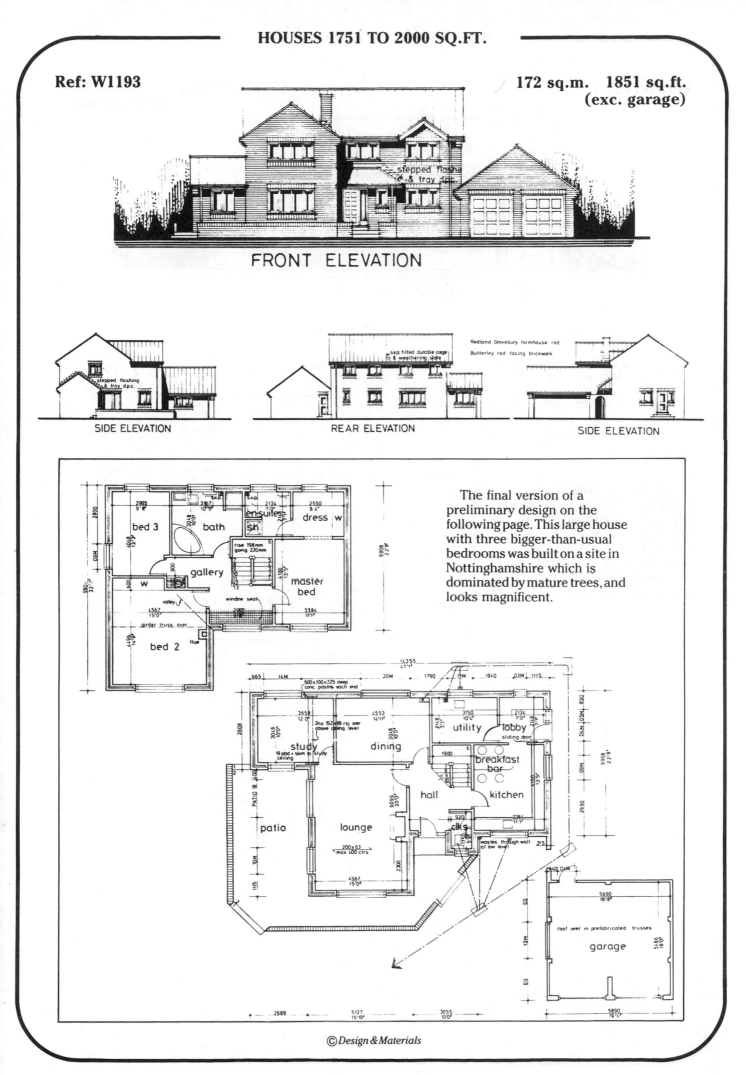

FRONT ELEVATION

SIDE ELEVATION

REAR ELEVATION

SIDE ELEVATION

The final version of a preliminary design on the following page. This large house with three bigger-than-usual bedrooms was built on a site in Nottinghamshire which is dominated by mature trees, and looks magnificent.

**Ref: W1193A**

**172 sq.m.   1951 sq.ft.**
**(exc. garage)**

FRONT ELEVATION

REAR ELEVATION

SIDE ELEVATION

SIDE ELEVATION

This was the original proposal for the design number W1193 which appears on the previous page, and by comparing the two you can see how the design developed from this relatively simple builting into a more complex structure.

GROUND FLOOR PLAN

© Design & Materials

**Ref: W938**

**177 sq.m.    1905 sq.ft.**

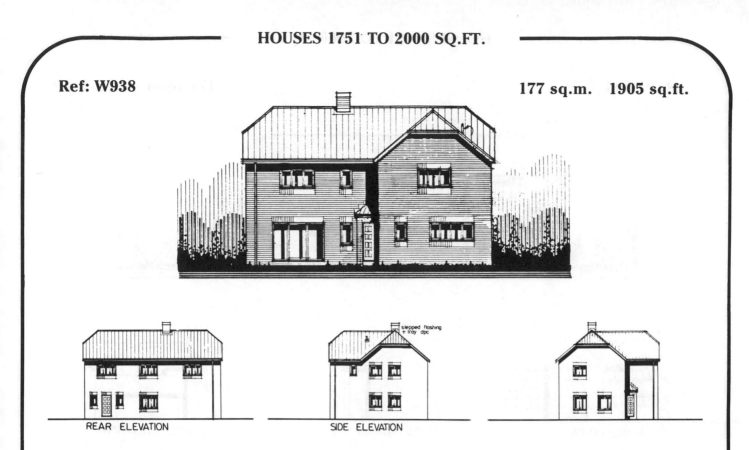

REAR ELEVATION

SIDE ELEVATION

A front door set across the angle between two wings of a house looks far more striking than it appears in these 'architects elevations' drawings. It adds an extra dimension to the hall, and in this case helps to set off a feature staircase. This design concept has been used in many different guises by D & M over the years, and is particularly effective with the half-hip roof shewn here.

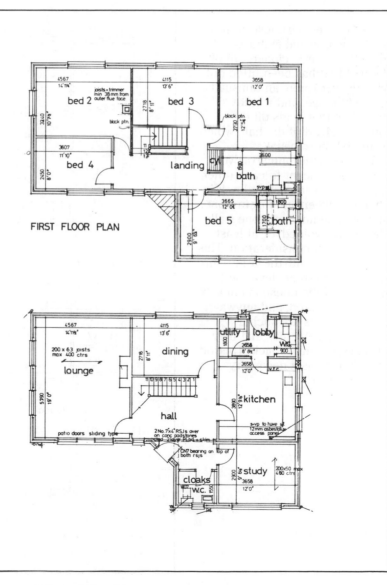

FIRST FLOOR PLAN

**Ref: S511**

**178 sq.m.   1916 sq.ft.**

REAR ELEVATION                    SIDE ELEVATION                    SIDE ELEVATION

This interesting house in stone has some unusual features, including a large cloakroom off the hall that has been fitted out as a shower room, an unusually shaped lounge, and a study/playroom that leads off the lounge instead of the hall, which would be more usual.

The use in the lounge of two 4' windows adjacent to each other instead of one larger window is in character when building in stone, and big openings in stone walls should be avoided, or at least given careful consideration. This rule is broken with the large patio window in the rear elevation, but this side of the house is unlikely to be overlooked, and anyway patio windows are such a tremendous amenity that they are accepted in the back of period style homes as a necessary anachronism.

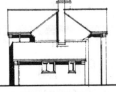

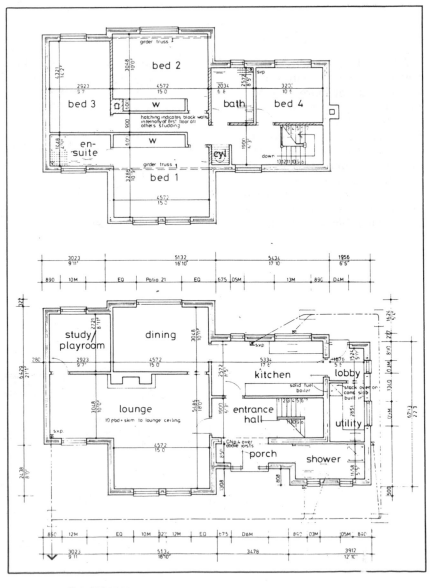

© *Design & Materials*

**Ref: P2613**

**165 sq.m.   1776 sq.ft.**
**(inc. garage)**

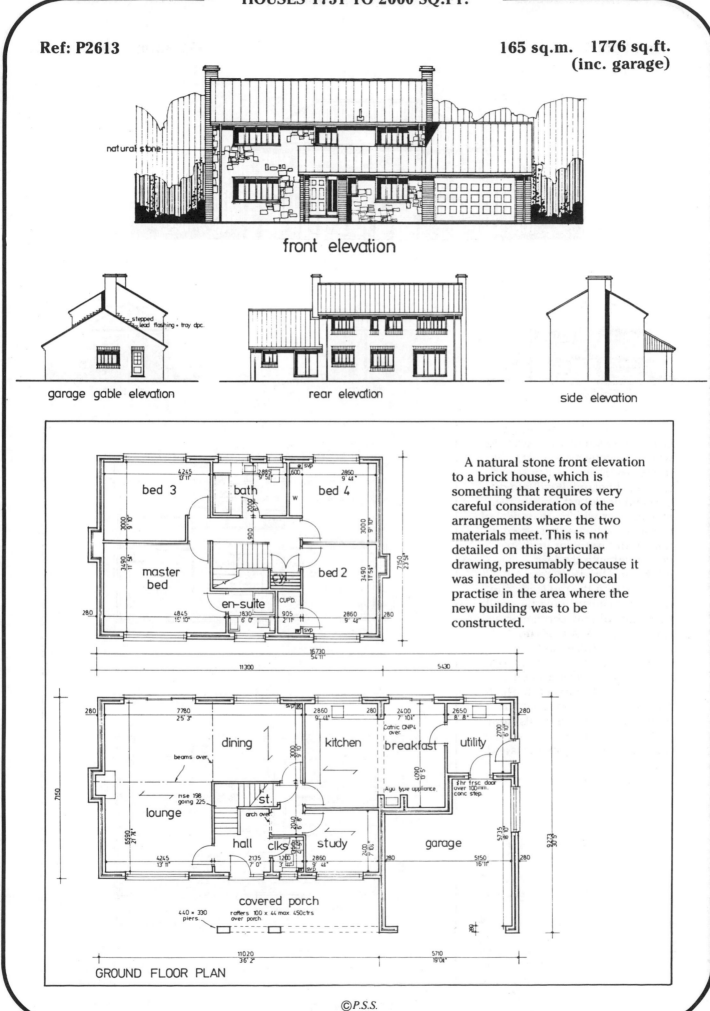

natural stone

front elevation

stepped lead flashing + tray dpc.

garage gable elevation

rear elevation

side elevation

bed 3    bath    4245 / 13'11"    2885 / 9'5⅝"    600    2860 / 9'4⅝"    svp    bed 4

3000 / 9'10"

master bed    3490 / 11'5⅜"    cyl    bed 2    3490 / 11'5⅜"    7150 / 23'5⅜"    3000 / 9'10"

280    4845 / 15'10"    en-suite    1830 / 6'0"    CUPD.    905 / 2'11"    2860 / 9'4⅝"    280    svp

16730 / 54'11"

11300    5430

A natural stone front elevation to a brick house, which is something that requires very careful consideration of the arrangements where the two materials meet. This is not detailed on this particular drawing, presumably because it was intended to follow local practise in the area where the new building was to be constructed.

280    7780 / 25'3"    svp    2860 / 9'4⅝"    280    2400 / 7'10½"    2650 / 8'8"    280

dining    kitchen    breakfast    utility    2700 / 8'10"

Catnic CN9P4 over.

beams over    3000 / 9'10"    4.090 / 13'5"    5735 / 8'10"

rise 198 going 225    st.    Aga type appliance    1hr frsc door over 100mm conc. step.    7150

lounge    5590 / 21'7⅜"    arch over    2040 / 6'9"    9273 / 30'5"

hall    clks    study    garage    2400 / 7'0½"

4245 / 13'11"    2135 / 7'0"    1200 / 3'11"    2860 / 9'4⅝"    280    5150 / 16'11"    280    5735 / 8'10"

svp

covered porch

440 x 330 piers.    rafters 100 x 44 max 450ctrs over porch.

11020 / 36'2"    5710 / 19'0⅜"

**GROUND FLOOR PLAN**

©P.S.S.

279

**Ref: P2595**

**172 sq.m.    1851 sq.ft.**

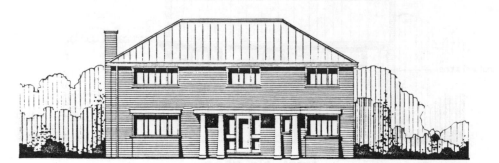

rear elevation

elevation

side elevation

This pleasant home with its Georgian style entrance will fit in well in the suburbs of most large towns, and in some villages in the South of England. It will almost certainly look best built in the stock bricks which are typical of the south, which are mottled in colour and irregular in shape compared with the less interesting bricks from brickyards in the midlands and north. The tiles should be small plain tiles or clay pantiles in a colour chosen carefully to complement the bricks

As the entrance is such a key feature of this design when viewed from the outside, the hall deserves to be given a similar emphasis inside, and calls for a prestige staircase with great care taken in the choice of newels and balustrading.

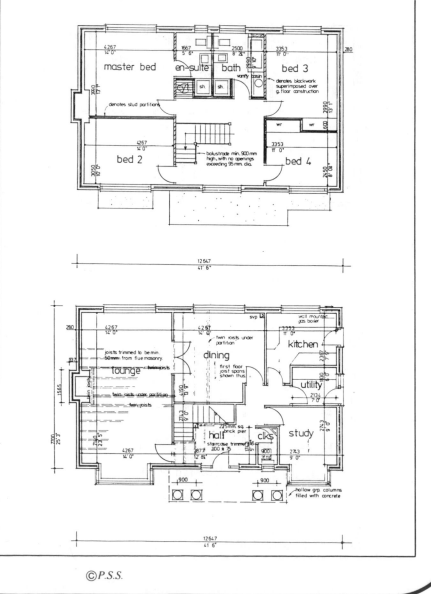

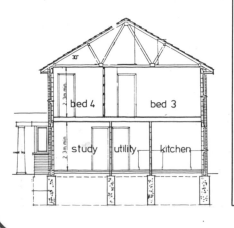

**Ref: P2764**

**176 sq.m.   1894 sq.ft.**
**(exc. garage)**

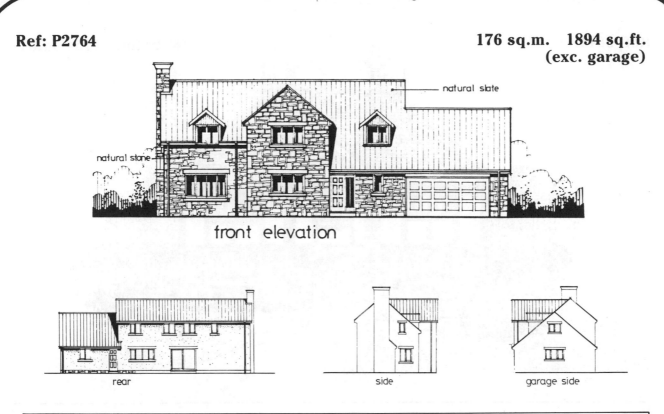

front elevation

rear

side

garage side

This imposing home is in a style that is best suited to the West or North of the country, and should incorporate the regional stone features appropriate to the county where it is to be built.

Note the playroom over the garage: this can be fitted out as another bedroom with its own bathroom at a later date if required.

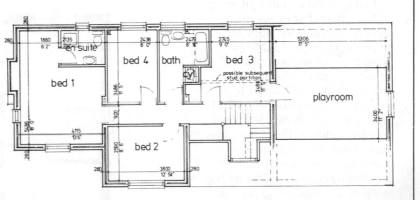

FIRST FLOOR PLAN

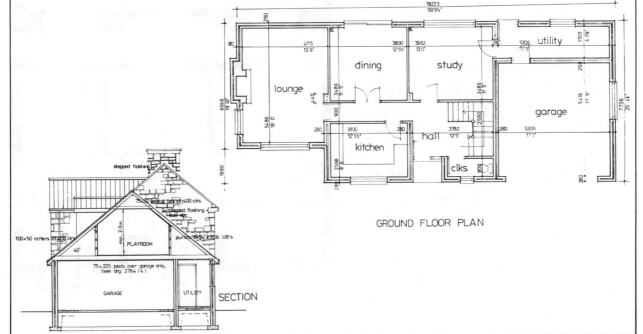

GROUND FLOOR PLAN

SECTION

©P.S.S.

**Ref: 96149**

**163 sq.m.    1754 sq.ft.**

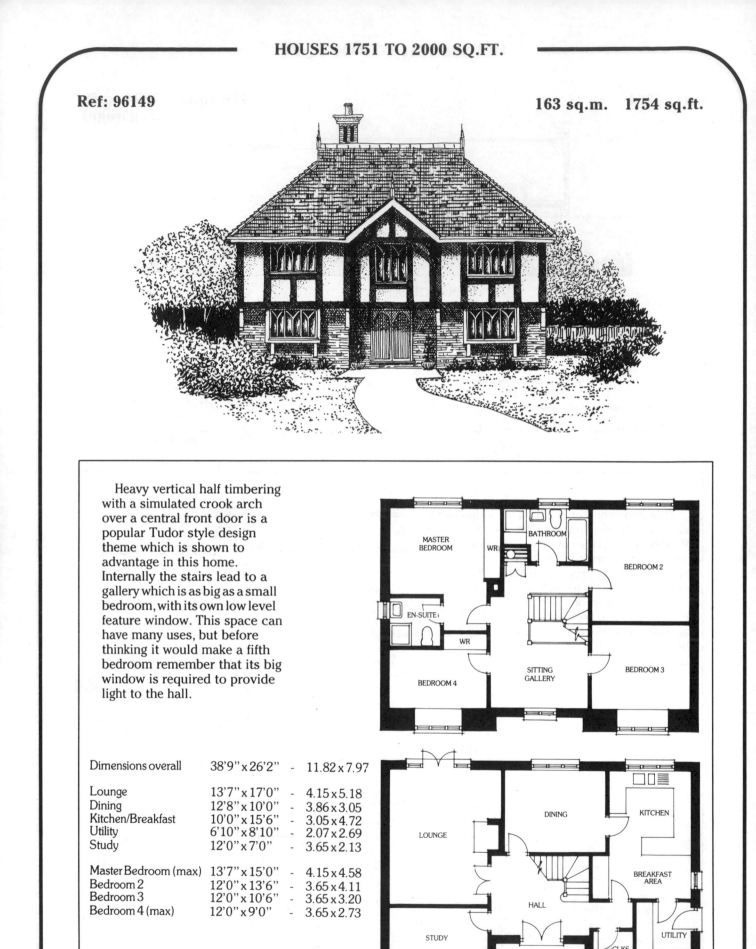

Heavy vertical half timbering with a simulated crook arch over a central front door is a popular Tudor style design theme which is shown to advantage in this home. Internally the stairs lead to a gallery which is as big as a small bedroom, with its own low level feature window. This space can have many uses, but before thinking it would make a fifth bedroom remember that its big window is required to provide light to the hall.

| | | | |
|---|---|---|---|
| Dimensions overall | 38'9" x 26'2" | - | 11.82 x 7.97 |
| Lounge | 13'7" x 17'0" | - | 4.15 x 5.18 |
| Dining | 12'8" x 10'0" | - | 3.86 x 3.05 |
| Kitchen/Breakfast | 10'0" x 15'6" | - | 3.05 x 4.72 |
| Utility | 6'10" x 8'10" | - | 2.07 x 2.69 |
| Study | 12'0" x 7'0" | - | 3.65 x 2.13 |
| Master Bedroom (max) | 13'7" x 15'0" | - | 4.15 x 4.58 |
| Bedroom 2 | 12'0" x 13'6" | - | 3.65 x 4.11 |
| Bedroom 3 | 12'0" x 10'6" | - | 3.65 x 3.20 |
| Bedroom 4 (max) | 12'0" x 9'0" | - | 3.65 x 2.73 |

*©Design & Materials*

**Ref: 96264**

**165 sq.m.    1782 sq.ft.**

The low eaves line at the front of this interesting home will enable it to be accepted in village street situations where the planners are concerned that existing buildings will not be dominated by a new one. In fact this is a generously proportioned four bedroom home of above average size, with a conventional rear appearance.

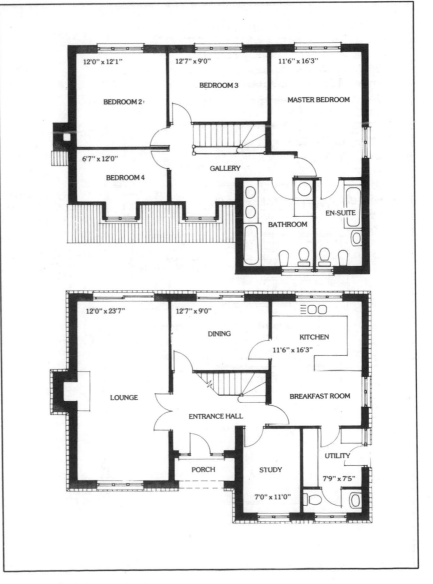

**Ref: W1409**

**170 sq.m.   1829 sq.ft.**
**(exc. garage)**

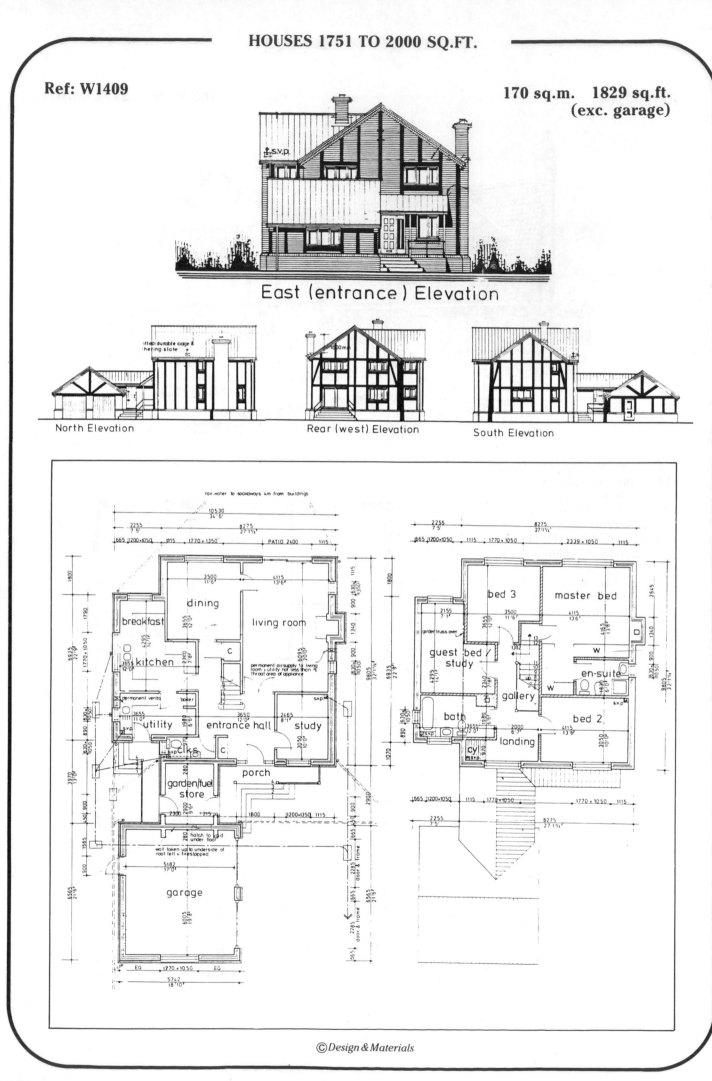

East (entrance) Elevation

North Elevation

Rear (west) Elevation

South Elevation

**Ref: C417**

**173 sq.m.   1862 sq.ft.**

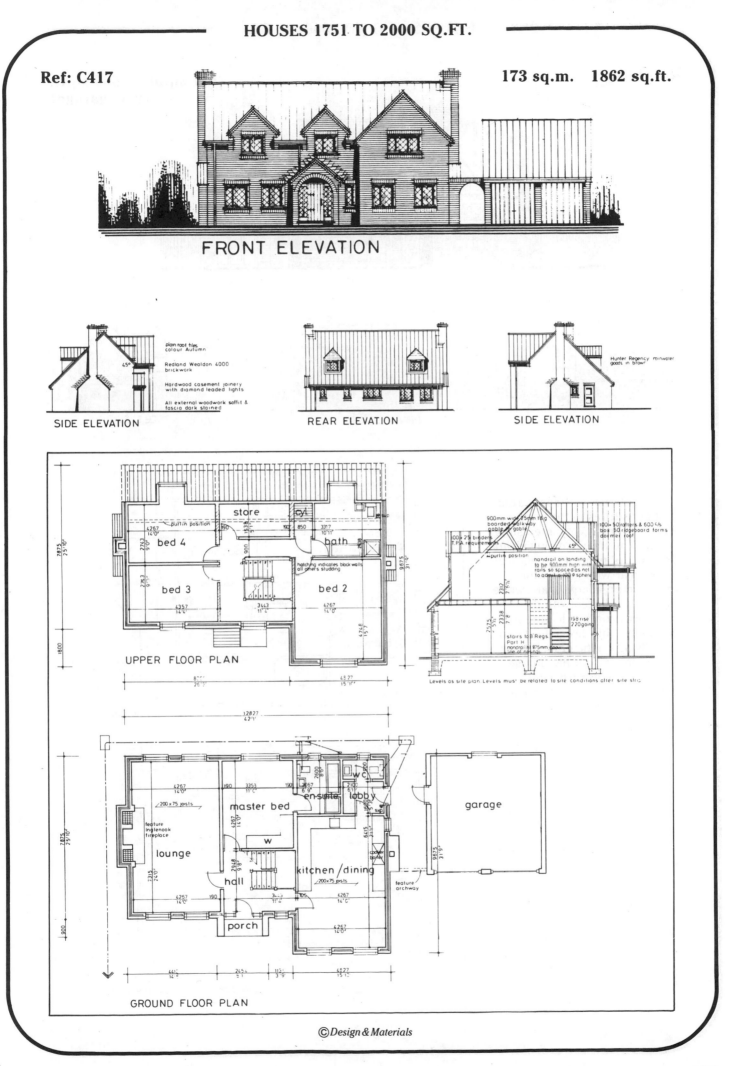

FRONT ELEVATION

plain roof tiles
colour Autumn

Redland Wealdon 4000
brickwork

Hardwood casement joinery
with diamond leaded lights

All external woodwork soffit &
fascia dark stained

SIDE ELEVATION

REAR ELEVATION

Hunter Regency rainwater
goods in brown

SIDE ELEVATION

UPPER FLOOR PLAN

store     cyl

bed 4

bath

bed 3

bed 2

hatching indicates block walls
all others studding

900mm wide 25mm t&g
boarded walkway
gable to gable
P.A. requirements

100 x 25 binders

purlin position

handrail on landing
to be 900mm high with
rails so spaced as not
to admit a 100 Ø sphere

100 x 50 rafters & 600 c/s
bias 50 ridgeboard forms
dormer roof

198 rise
270 going

stairs to B.Regs
Part H
handrail 875mm
line of nosing

Levels as site plan. Levels must be related to site conditions after site strip.

GROUND FLOOR PLAN

lounge

feature
inglenook
fireplace

master bed

ens-suite   lobby

w

hall

kitchen / dining

200 x 75 joists

200 x 75 posts

feature
archway

w.c.

garage

porch

**Ref: C578**

**177 sq.m. 1905 sq.ft.**
**(exc. garage)**

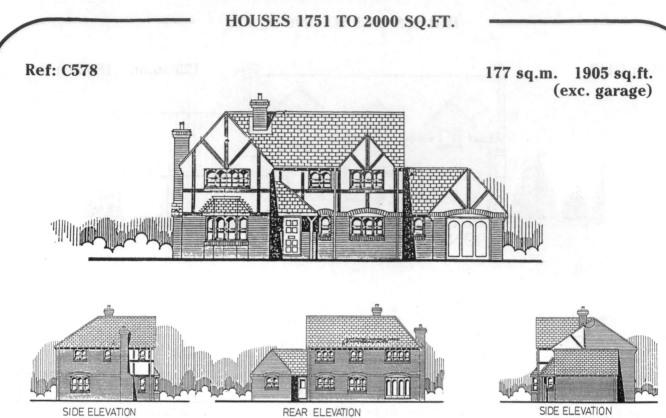

SIDE ELEVATION        REAR ELEVATION        SIDE ELEVATION

A large house with applied half timber features to the front elevation and a very interesting layout. The lounge/dining room/drawing room arrangement will be popular with those who entertain on a large scale, while the kitchen linked with the breakfast room by a feature arch completes this design for open-plan living on the ground floor.

The upper floor has a large gallery lit by its own window, giving a very spacious feel to the whole property.

UPPER FLOOR PLAN

master bedroom
bathroom
bedroom 3
en-suite
bedroom 4
bedroom 2
gallery

GROUND FLOOR PLAN

lounge
dining
kitchen
rear porch
utility
garage
hall
drawing room
breakfast room
cloaks
porch

**Ref: C393**

**166 sq.m.    1786 sq.ft.**

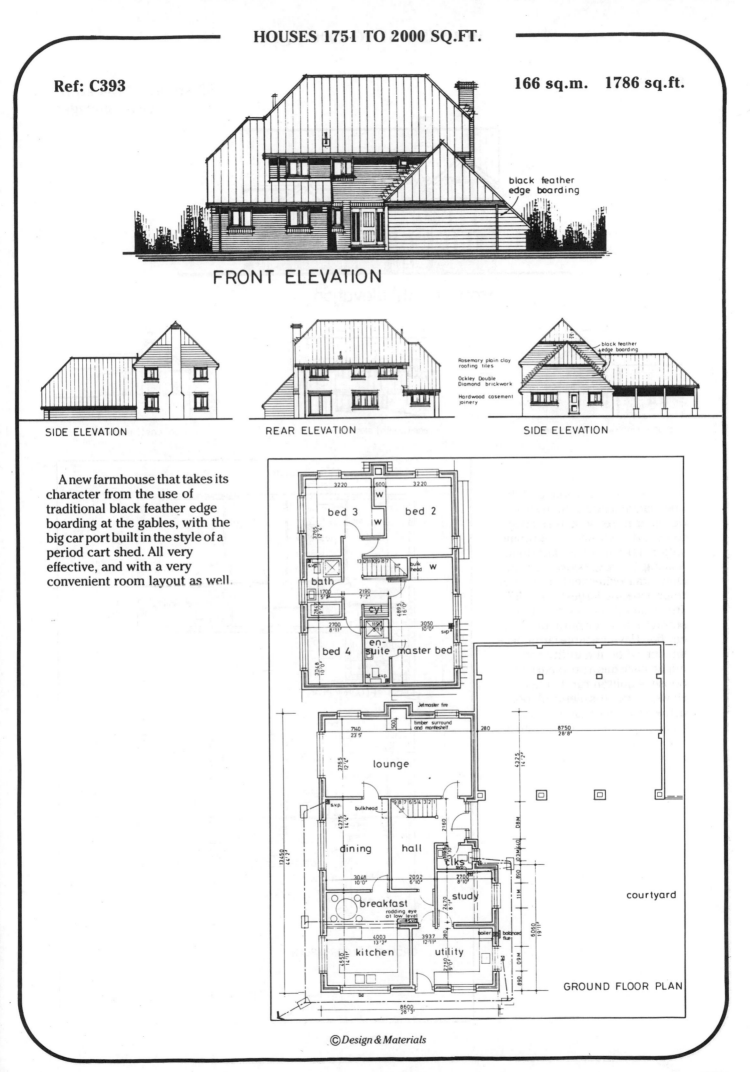

black feather
edge boarding

FRONT ELEVATION

SIDE ELEVATION

REAR ELEVATION

Rosemary plain clay
roofing tiles

Ockley Double
Diamond brickwork

Hardwood casement
joinery

black feather
edge boarding

SIDE ELEVATION

A new farmhouse that takes its character from the use of traditional black feather edge boarding at the gables, with the big car port built in the style of a period cart shed. All very effective, and with a very convenient room layout as well.

bed 3

bed 2

bath

bed 4

en-suite

master bed

cyl

lounge

dining

hall

clks

breakfast

study

kitchen

utility

courtyard

GROUND FLOOR PLAN

**Ref: P2976**

163 sq.m. 1754 sq.ft.
(exc. garage)

front (north) elevation

garage side (west) elevation

rear (south) elevation

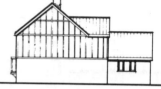

side (east) elevation

The second bedroom and the huge family bathroom in this design can easily be rearranged to provide two single bedrooms with a more modest bathroom, making this a five bedroom home. Downstairs the clients brief was to provide the largest possible study, and this has restricted storage space for outdoor clothes. Having a large farmhouse kitchen without a utility room might make this a problem if this house is built in rural areas. However, there is plenty of room in the twenty foot garage, and the basic plan can accommodate all sorts of alterations to suit individual requirements.

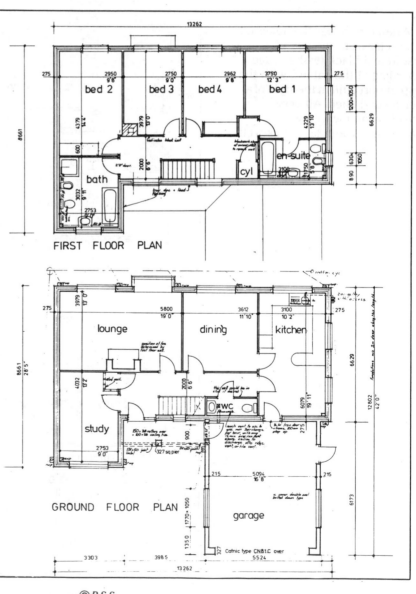

FIRST FLOOR PLAN

GROUND FLOOR PLAN

**Ref: P2629**

**166 sq.m.   1786 sq.ft.**
**(inc. garage)**

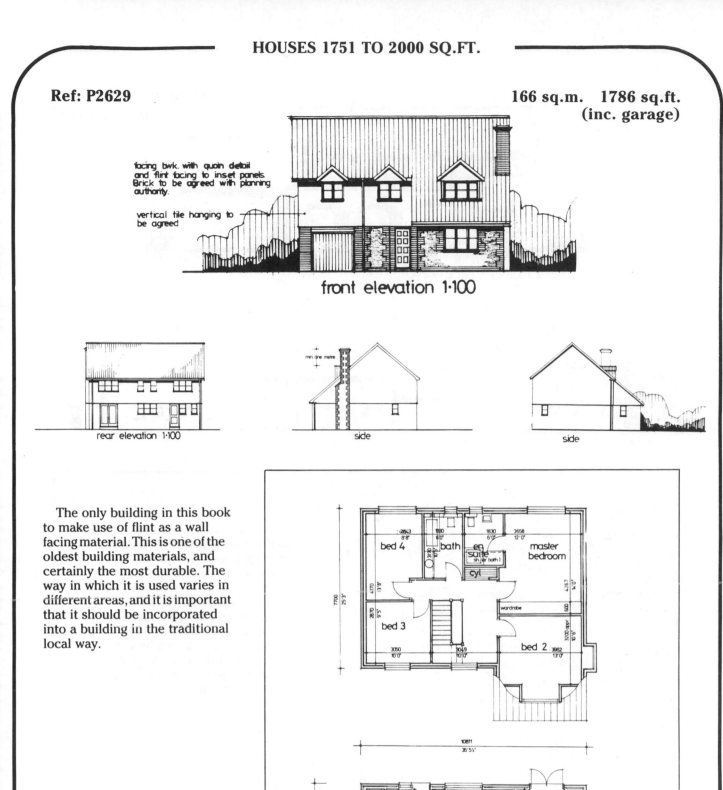

facing bwk. with quoin detail
and flint facing to inset panels.
Brick to be agreed with planning
authority.

vertical tile hanging to
be agreed

front elevation 1·100

rear elevation 1·100

side

side

The only building in this book
to make use of flint as a wall
facing material. This is one of the
oldest building materials, and
certainly the most durable. The
way in which it is used varies in
different areas, and it is important
that it should be incorporated
into a building in the traditional
local way.

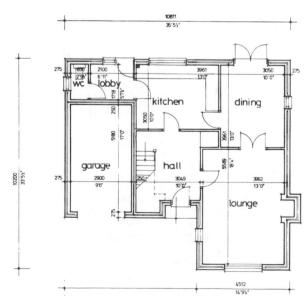

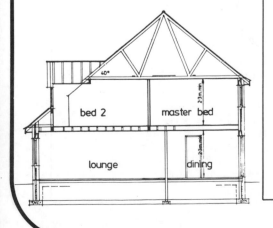

©P.S.S.

**Ref: W944**

**181 sq.m. 1948 sq.ft.**
**(exc. garage)**

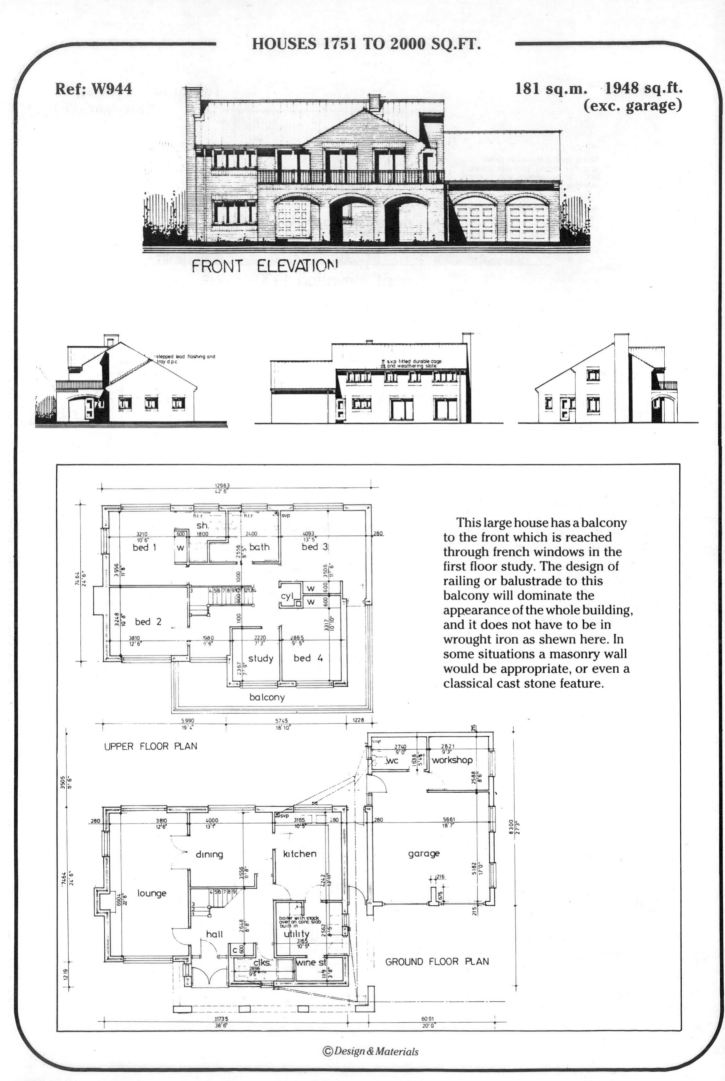

FRONT ELEVATION

This large house has a balcony to the front which is reached through french windows in the first floor study. The design of railing or balustrade to this balcony will dominate the appearance of the whole building, and it does not have to be in wrought iron as shewn here. In some situations a masonry wall would be appropriate, or even a classical cast stone feature.

UPPER FLOOR PLAN

GROUND FLOOR PLAN

© Design & Materials

**Ref: C518**

**173 sq.m.   1862 sq.ft.**
**(inc. garage)**

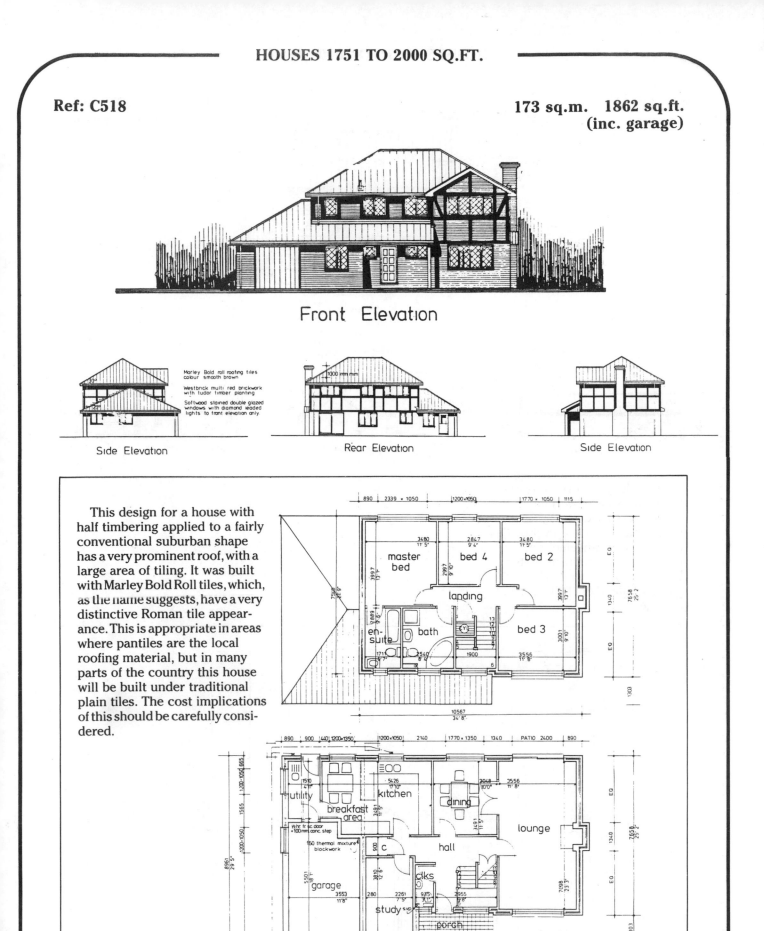

Front Elevation

Marley Bold roll roofing tiles
colour smooth brown

Westbrick multi red brickwork
with tudor timber planting

Softwood stained double glazed
windows with diamond leaded
lights to front elevation only

Side Elevation

Rear Elevation

Side Elevation

This design for a house with half timbering applied to a fairly conventional suburban shape has a very prominent roof, with a large area of tiling. It was built with Marley Bold Roll tiles, which, as the name suggests, have a very distinctive Roman tile appearance. This is appropriate in areas where pantiles are the local roofing material, but in many parts of the country this house will be built under traditional plain tiles. The cost implications of this should be carefully considered.

master bed

bed 4

bed 2

landing

en-suite

bath

bed 3

utility

breakfast area

kitchen

dining

lounge

garage

c

hall

clks

study

porch

supporting pillar

**Ref: W1322**

**174 sq.m.   1872 sq.ft.**
**(inc. garage)**

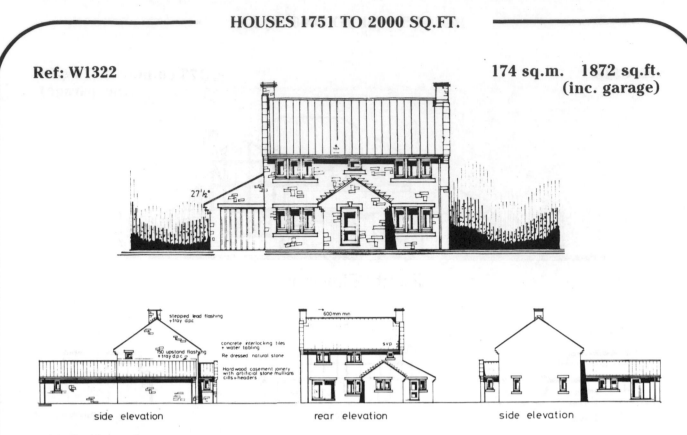

27'½°

stepped lead flashing
+ tray d.p.c

150 upstand flashing
+ tray d.p.c

600 mm min

svp

concrete interlocking tiles
+ water tabling

Re dressed natural stone

Hardwood casement joinery
with artificial stone mullions
cills + headers

side elevation        rear elevation        side elevation

A plan drawn for a cottage on a small infill plot in a picture book Yorkshire village, working to the clients very specific requirements. It not only provides exactly the arrangement of rooms to suit their living pattern, but also from outside has all the feel and character of the adjacent cottages.

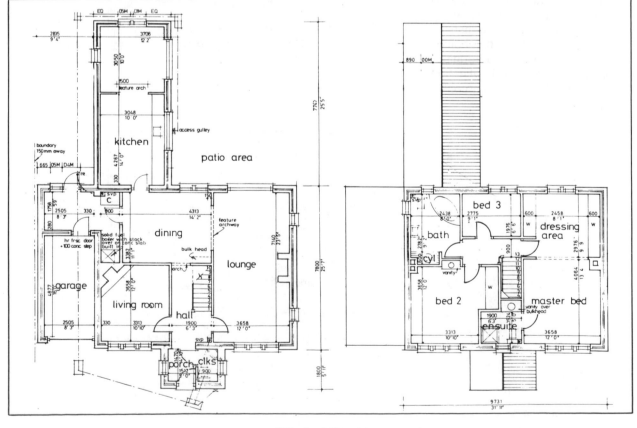

# HOUSES 1751 TO 2000 SQ.FT.

**Ref: C334**

**167 sq.m.   1797 sq.ft.**

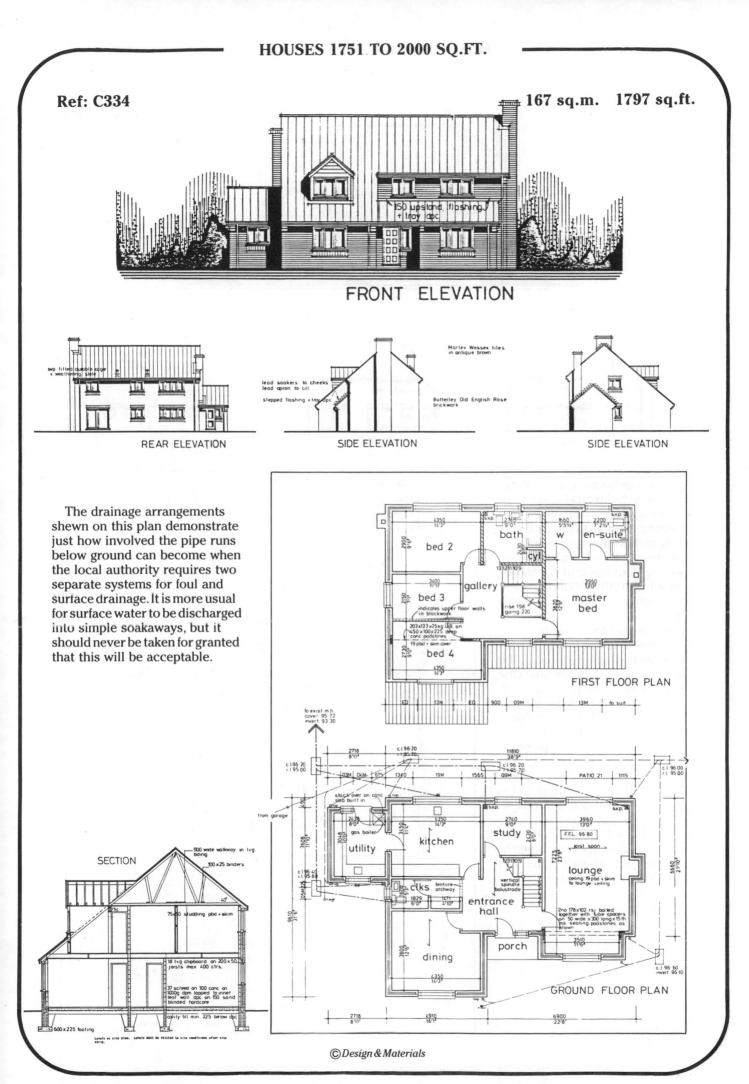

150 upstand, flashing + tray dpc

FRONT ELEVATION

swp fitted durable edge + weathering slate

REAR ELEVATION

Marley Wessex tiles in antique brown

lead soakers to cheeks
lead apron to cill

stepped flashing + tray dpc

Butterley Old English Rose brickwork

SIDE ELEVATION

SIDE ELEVATION

The drainage arrangements shewn on this plan demonstrate just how involved the pipe runs below ground can become when the local authority requires two separate systems for foul and surface drainage. It is more usual for surface water to be discharged into simple soakaways, but it should never be taken for granted that this will be acceptable.

FIRST FLOOR PLAN

bed 2

bath    w    en-suite

cyl

bed 3    gallery    master bed

indicates upper floor walls in blockwork

rise 198
going 220

203x133 x25kg UB on 450 x 100 x 225 deep conc padstones
19 pbd + skim cover

bed 4

SECTION

900 wide walkway in t+g bding

100 x 25 binders

75x50 studding pbd + skrm

18 t+g chipboard on 200 x 50 joists max 400 ctrs.

37 screed on 100 conc on 1000g dpm lapped to inner leaf wall dpc on 150 sand blinded hardcore

600 x 225 footing

cavity fill min 225 below dpc

Levels as site plan. Levels must be related to site conditions after site strip.

to exist m.h.
cover 95 72
invert 93 30

from garage

stack over on conc slab built in

gas boiler

utility    kitchen    study

F.F.L 96·80

joist span

clks    feature archway    vertical spindle balustrade    lounge
ceiling 19 pbd + skim to lounge ceiling

entrance hall

2no 178x102 rsj bolted together with tube spacers on 50 wide x 300 long x 15 th ms seating padstones as shown

dining    porch

GROUND FLOOR PLAN

© *Design & Materials*

**Ref: P2612**

**180 sq.m. 1937 sq.ft.**
**(exc. garage)**

garage side elevation     rear elevation     side elevation

This large house with a half-hip roof has a country feel, and would make a splendid farmhouse in the South or West of England. If it is built in that role, then most farmers would want a door leading from the study or farm office to the utility room and back door, and of course this is easily arranged.

Notice that the en-suite bathroom is just as large and well fitted as the main bathroom: this is a new trend, and sometimes the en-suite facilities are larger and more luxurious than the others - which is logical if you consider who is paying for the new home.

The porch roof is supported with gallows brackets, and it is important that these are made from really heavy section timber and should not look skimped. If you have chosen your front door before the gallows brackets are made, a good carpenter should be able to match the style of the door in chamfers or flutings on the brackets.

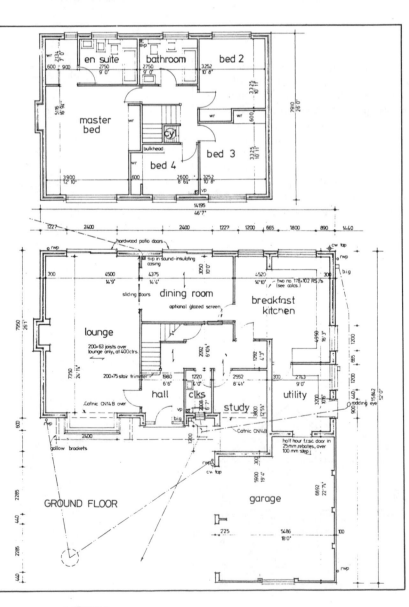

©P.S.S.

**Ref: W1269**

**185 sq.m.    1991 sq.ft.**

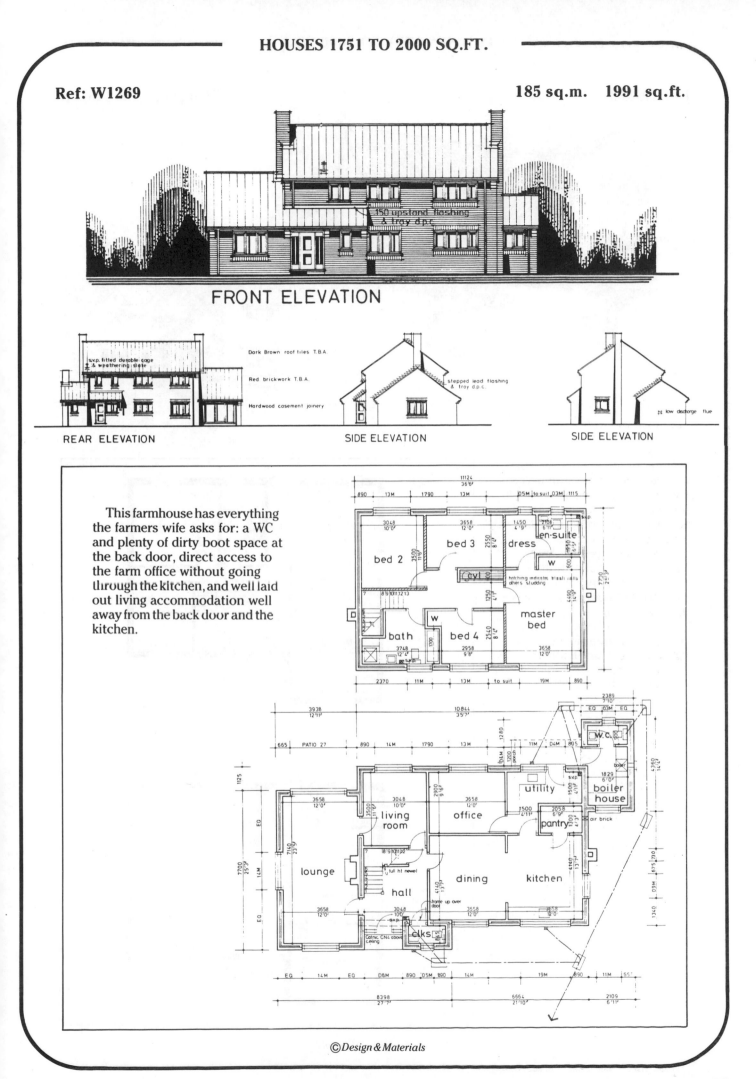

FRONT ELEVATION

REAR ELEVATION

SIDE ELEVATION

SIDE ELEVATION

This farmhouse has everything the farmers wife asks for: a WC and plenty of dirty boot space at the back door, direct access to the farm office without going through the kitchen, and well laid out living accommodation well away from the back door and the kitchen.

©Design & Materials

**Ref: 96273**

**176 sq.m.    1900 sq.ft.**

A house with a period feel that was designed to be built in the Tudor style but which looks equally well when constructed in stone with appropriate detailing.

This home has been built many times, often with the utility room amalgamated with the kitchen to permit an Aga stove to be installed using a flue in the fireplace chimney, with the breakfast area moved to the window in the side wall.

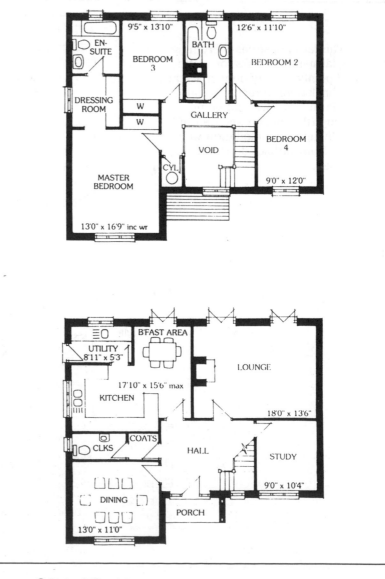

# Designs for Houses 1501 to 1750 sq. ft.

All new homes of this size and smaller must have the external appearance of a scaled down version of a larger home in the same style, with the windows, doors and other features at an appropriate size.

This leads to consideration of integral garages. These are rarely an attractive looking feature in a house of this size, but they are often unavoidable when the home is to be built on a narrow site. In this case the choice of garage door is one of the most important decisions to be made, and fortunately the range of styles available is now very wide. In terms of price per square foot the garage doors are the cheapest elements in the cost of the envelope of the house, and this is definitely not an area for cost savings.

Houses in this size range are usually laid out with a separate dining room and often a small study. If these are not required the other rooms can be correspondingly larger, giving it the feel of a bigger property. This will be enhanced by increasing the height of the ground floor rooms from the usual 8'3" to 9'.

First floor layouts invariably include a small en suite shower room for the master bedroom as well as the family bathroom. The other bedrooms are invariably as equal in size as the shape of the house permits, but it is sometimes more logical to have a second bedroom as large as possible at the expense of the other two. Decisions of this sort depend on family requirements.

**Ref: 96107**

**143 sq.m.    1540 sq.ft.**

A four square English rural home in the Tudor style, complete with a plinth, jettied first floor and traditional style timbering and roof. It is shown as built, with a panelled front door, although a door in the Tudor style would have been more appropriate.

The appearance of houses in this style involves four major colours – the bricks, the tiles, the render and the beams. Today the rendering and beams will almost certainly be black and white, and it is very important that the roof tiles and the brickwork should compliment the whole, so that there are not going to be any conflicts between the colours. (Having said that, the original Tudor houses of the 15th century had blue or red paint to the beams and ochre coloured plasterwork. It is doubtful if the planners would like that now – or your neighbours!)

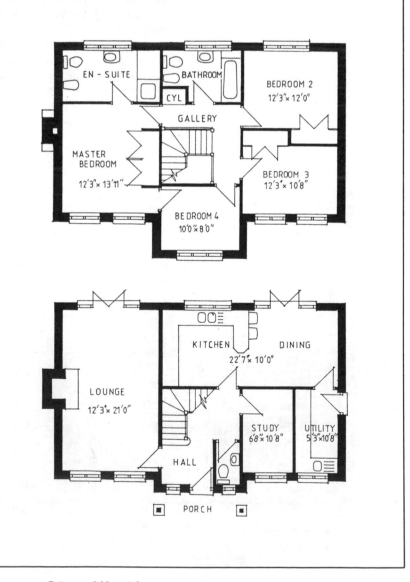

**Ref: 96266**

**158 sq.m.    1700 sq.ft.**
**(exc. garage)**

A pleasant house with rooms of a generous size, but at only 43 feet overall width it can fit on a suburban plot as all the windows to principle rooms face front and back.

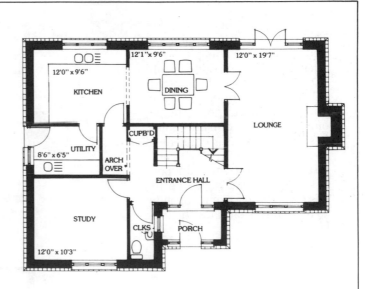

12'1" x 9'6"    12'0" x 19'7"

12'0" x 9'6"

KITCHEN    DINING    LOUNGE

CUPB'D

8'6" x 6'5"    UTILITY    ARCH OVER    ENTRANCE HALL

STUDY    CLKS    PORCH

12'0" x 10'3"

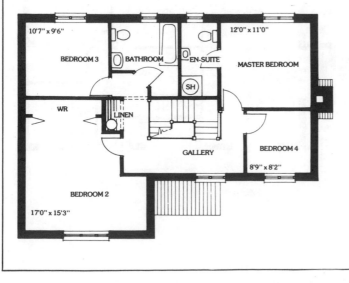

10'7" x 9'6"    12'0" x 11'0"

BEDROOM 3    BATHROOM    EN-SUITE    MASTER BEDROOM

SH

WR    LINEN

GALLERY    BEDROOM 4

8'9" x 8'2"

BEDROOM 2

17'0" x 15'3"

**Ref: 96147**

**148 sq.m.    1598 sq.ft.**

Outline planning consent for a building plot often stipulates a traditional steep roof pitch and often that the roof ridge should not be higher than the roofs of neighbouring properties. If you want to build an imposing home on a plot that has conditions like this on the planning consent, you will have to build with a restricted span to the main roof to keep down the ridge line. In this case the maximum span is 23 ft., and this dictates the layout.

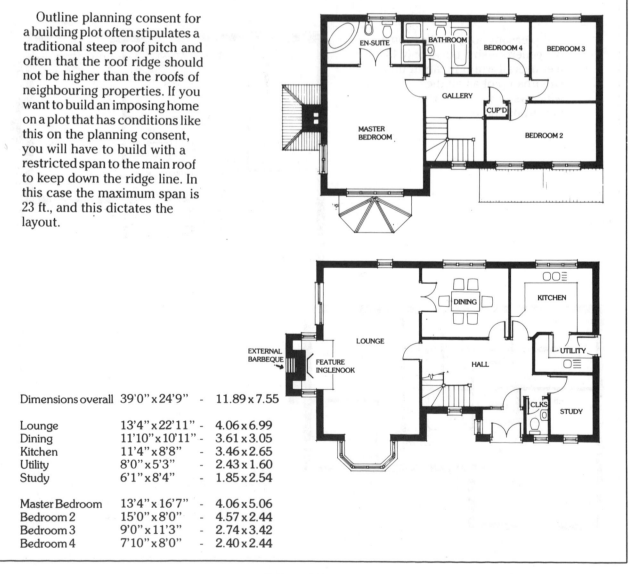

| | | | |
|---|---|---|---|
| Dimensions overall | 39'0" x 24'9" | - | 11.89 x 7.55 |
| | | | |
| Lounge | 13'4" x 22'11" | - | 4.06 x 6.99 |
| Dining | 11'10" x 10'11" | - | 3.61 x 3.05 |
| Kitchen | 11'4" x 8'8" | - | 3.46 x 2.65 |
| Utility | 8'0" x 5'3" | - | 2.43 x 1.60 |
| Study | 6'1" x 8'4" | - | 1.85 x 2.54 |
| | | | |
| Master Bedroom | 13'4" x 16'7" | - | 4.06 x 5.06 |
| Bedroom 2 | 15'0" x 8'0" | - | 4.57 x 2.44 |
| Bedroom 3 | 9'0" x 11'3" | - | 2.74 x 3.42 |
| Bedroom 4 | 7'10" x 8'0" | - | 2.40 x 2.44 |

**Ref: 96168**

**148 sq.m.  1600 sq.ft.**

This four bedroom home of only 1600 sq.ft. appears far larger than it is, and is shown built in two different styles.

| | | |
|---|---|---|
| Floor Area (exc. garage) | 1600 sq.ft. | 148 sq.m. |
| Dimensions overall | 35'11" x 25'3" | 10.95 x 7.70 |
| Lounge | 12'6" x 23'5" | 3.80 x 7.14 |
| Dining | 10'0" x 11'0" | 3.04 x 3.34 |
| Kitchen | 11'0" x 13'2" | 3.34 x 4.01 |
| Utility | 11'0" x 7'0" | 3.34 x 2.12 |
| Master Bed | 11'0" x 10'4" | 3.34 x 3.16 |
| Bed 2 | 12'6" x 12'2" | 3.80 x 3.70 |
| Bed 3 | 11'0" x 13'0" | 3.34 x 3.94 |
| Bed 4 | 12'6" x 11'0" | 3.80 x 3.34 |

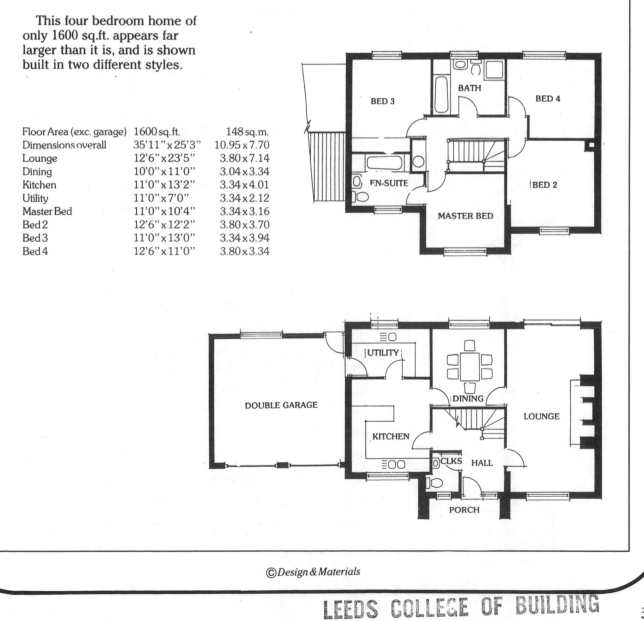

© *Design & Materials*

**Ref: S371**

**141 sq.m.    1517 sq.ft.**
**(exc. garage)**

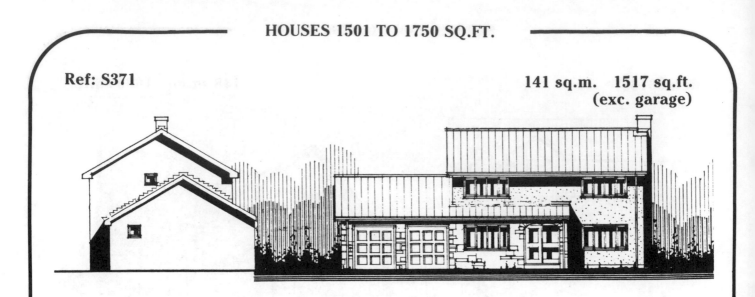

The master bedroom suite in this four bedroom home has a very large 'walk in' wardrobe, and this is a feature which is gaining in popularity.

The garage is 18'4" wide, which just permits two single garage doors instead of one double door. How much better this looks!

REAR ELEVATION

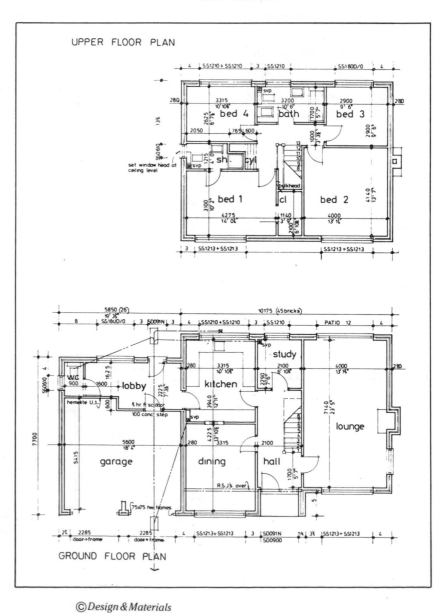

UPPER FLOOR PLAN

GROUND FLOOR PLAN

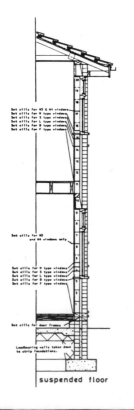

suspended floor

**Ref: W1207**

**140 sq.m.  1506 sq.ft.**
**(exc. garage)**

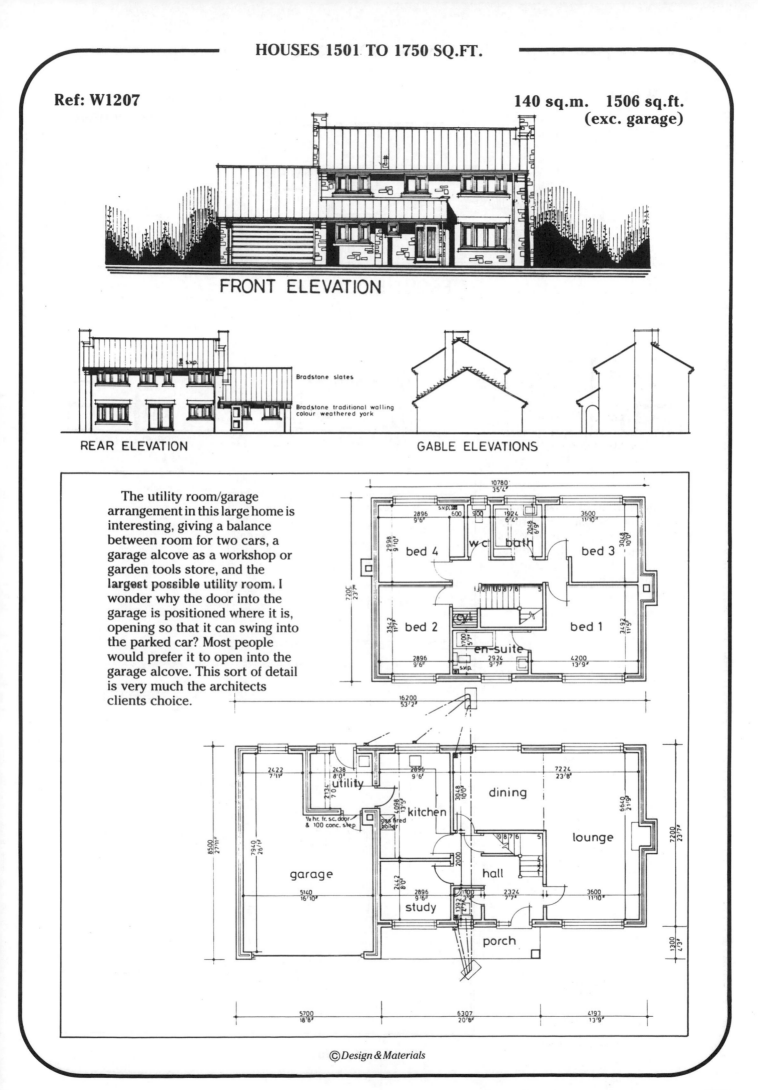

FRONT ELEVATION

REAR ELEVATION

Bradstone slates

Bradstone traditional walling
colour weathered york

GABLE ELEVATIONS

The utility room/garage arrangement in this large home is interesting, giving a balance between room for two cars, a garage alcove as a workshop or garden tools store, and the largest possible utility room. I wonder why the door into the garage is positioned where it is, opening so that it can swing into the parked car? Most people would prefer it to open into the garage alcove. This sort of detail is very much the architects clients choice.

bed 4

wc   bath

bed 3

bed 2

Cyl

bed 1

en-suite

utility

kitchen

dining

lounge

hall

garage

study

porch

*©Design & Materials*

**Ref: W1211**

**140 sq.m.  1506 sq.ft.**
**(exc. garage)**

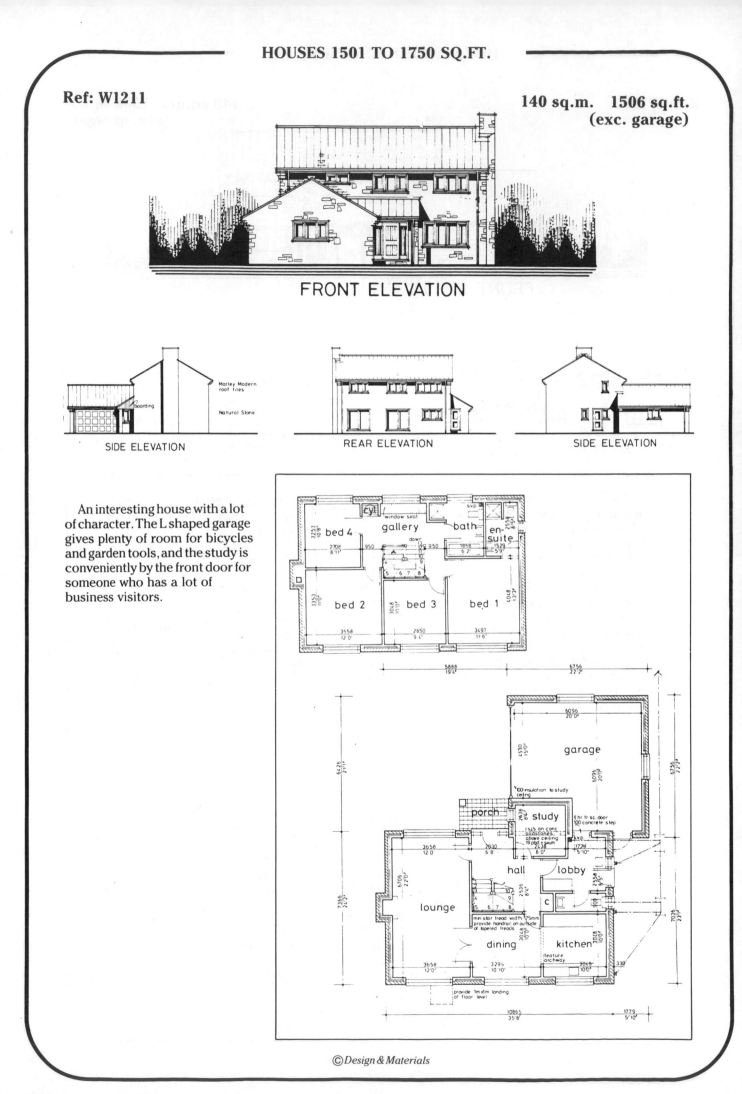

FRONT ELEVATION

SIDE ELEVATION

Marley Modern roof tiles

boarding

Natural Stone

REAR ELEVATION

SIDE ELEVATION

An interesting house with a lot of character. The L shaped garage gives plenty of room for bicycles and garden tools, and the study is conveniently by the front door for someone who has a lot of business visitors.

**Ref: S420**

**161 sq.m.   1733 sq.ft.**
**(exc. garage)**

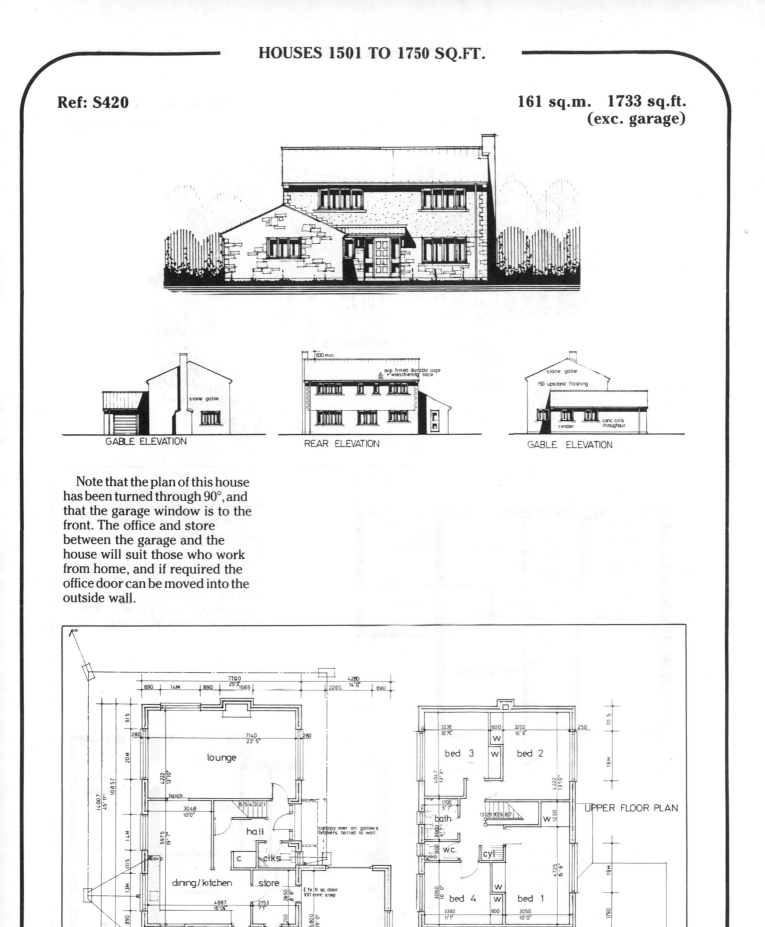

GABLE ELEVATION

REAR ELEVATION

GABLE ELEVATION

Note that the plan of this house has been turned through 90°, and that the garage window is to the front. The office and store between the garage and the house will suit those who work from home, and if required the office door can be moved into the outside wall.

GROUND FLOOR PLAN

UPPER FLOOR PLAN

**Ref: 96141**

**139 sq.m.    1500 sq.ft.**
**(inc. garage)**

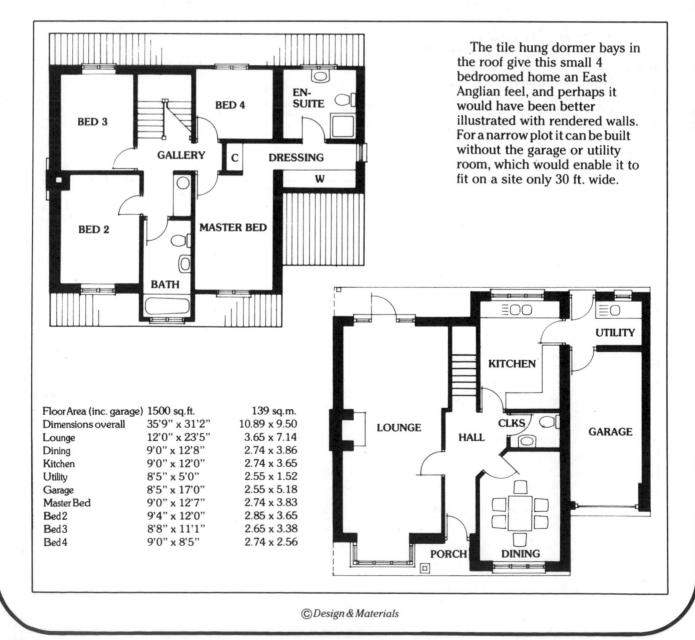

The tile hung dormer bays in the roof give this small 4 bedroomed home an East Anglian feel, and perhaps it would have been better illustrated with rendered walls. For a narrow plot it can be built without the garage or utility room, which would enable it to fit on a site only 30 ft. wide.

| | | |
|---|---|---|
| Floor Area (inc. garage) | 1500 sq.ft. | 139 sq.m. |
| Dimensions overall | 35'9" x 31'2" | 10.89 x 9.50 |
| Lounge | 12'0" x 23'5" | 3.65 x 7.14 |
| Dining | 9'0" x 12'8" | 2.74 x 3.86 |
| Kitchen | 9'0" x 12'0" | 2.74 x 3.65 |
| Utility | 8'5" x 5'0" | 2.55 x 1.52 |
| Garage | 8'5" x 17'0" | 2.55 x 5.18 |
| Master Bed | 9'0" x 12'7" | 2.74 x 3.83 |
| Bed 2 | 9'4" x 12'0" | 2.85 x 3.65 |
| Bed 3 | 8'8" x 11'1" | 2.65 x 3.38 |
| Bed 4 | 9'0" x 8'5" | 2.74 x 2.56 |

© Design & Materials

**Ref: PN674**

**142 sq.m.     1530 sq.ft.**

At 1530 square feet this design is the smallest of the Rectory range of Potton homes, but is an imposing house which is equally well suited to a site fronting a village street, or to a large garden. The classically proportioned rooms, with double doors to the drawing room, will be appreciated by those who value the elegance of a less hurried way of life.

Potton base this design on a rectory at Papplewick which was the original fictional scene for D.H. Lawrence's novel 'The Virgin and the Gypsy'. However building a Papplewick design home does not guarantee involvement in elemental relationships, nor make them compulsory.

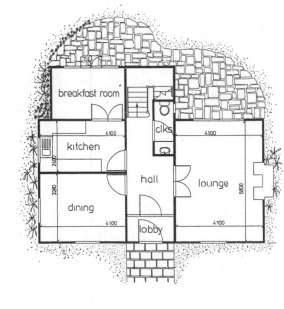

©*Potton*

**Ref: PN672**

**148 sq.m.    1580 sq.ft.**

This is a very popular variation on the design PN671 on page 400, to which has been added an integral garage and an additional bedroom. As shown here some space has been taken up at the back of the garage to provide a utility room, but for those who value storage space in the garage this can be dispensed with.

The right choice of garage door for a property like this is always most important, and to some extent this will depend on where the house is to be built. The range of garage doors available is very wide, and a choice should be made after considering all the options very carefully indeed. As always, it is important that the decision is made after you have seen actual doors of the sort that are of interest, and not from catalogues.

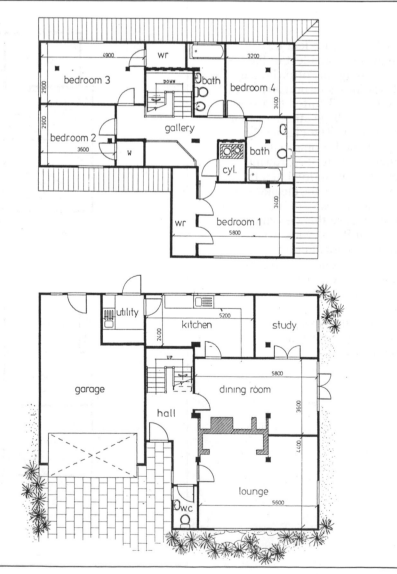

©Potton

**Ref: PN681**

**144 sq.m.   1550 sq.ft.**
**(exc. conservatory)**

An aisle frame house that can be built with or without the conservatory shown on the drawing here. The square rooms provide generous accommodation in a relatively small building, which looks significantly larger than it really is due to the combination of brickwork and exposed timbers.

The stairs are lit by a window on the landing and bath, and there is room for a small writing desk or sewing table on the landing which gives a spacious feel to the first floor of this compact home.

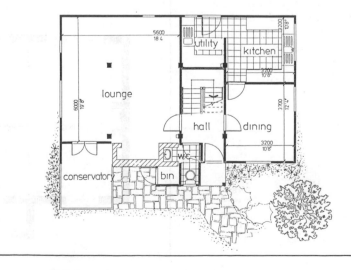

**Ref: 96174**

**147 sq.m.    1582 sq.ft.**

Another house that stands 'Four square to the wind' and which was originally built in the Cotswolds. This accounts for the stone heads and sills to the windows, as well as the exposed rafter feet under the eaves.

Again a design where there is room on the first floor landing for a desk and filing cabinet or perhaps for a sewing table.

It is shown here with the chimney breast wholly within the gable wall: if the planners will permit it to be moved outside it will give much more room in the lounge.

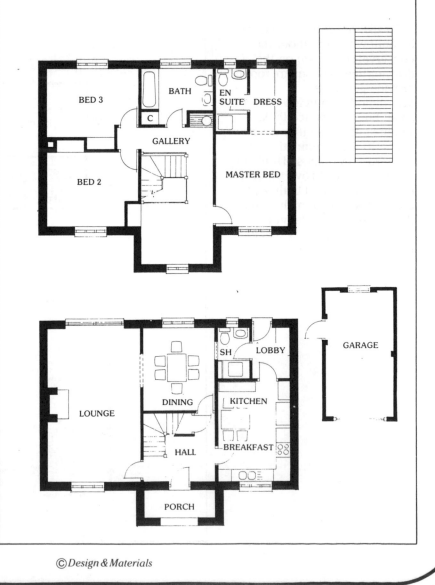

| Floor Area | 1582 sq.ft. | 147 sq.m. |
|---|---|---|
| Dimensions overall | 35'4" x 28'10" | 10.78 x 8.79 |
| Lounge | 13'0" x 22'0" | 3.96 x 6.70 |
| Dining | 10'0" x 11'6" | 3.04 x 3.50 |
| Kitchen/Breakfast | 10'0" x 14'6" | 3.04 x 4.45 |
| Master Bed | 10'0" x 13'0" | 3.04 x 3.96 |
| Bed 2 | 13'0" x 10'6" | 3.96 x 3.20 |
| Bed 3 | 13'0" x 9'6" | 3.96 x 2.90 |

© Design & Materials

**Ref: 96140**

142 sq.m.   1531 sq.ft.
(exc. garage)

A home with all the features that are usually expected with a 4 bedroom layout – a small study, ground floor cloakroom and two bathrooms. The utility room suited the owner, but these days it is more usual to dispense with the utility room in order to have a larger kitchen, usually because the family want a circular kitchen table in the middle of the room.

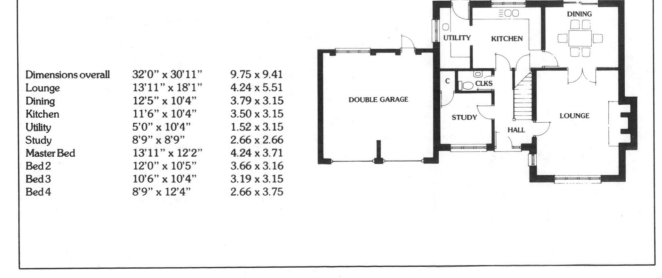

| Dimensions overall | 32'0" x 30'11" | 9.75 x 9.41 |
| Lounge | 13'11" x 18'1" | 4.24 x 5.51 |
| Dining | 12'5" x 10'4" | 3.79 x 3.15 |
| Kitchen | 11'6" x 10'4" | 3.50 x 3.15 |
| Utility | 5'0" x 10'4" | 1.52 x 3.15 |
| Study | 8'9" x 8'9" | 2.66 x 2.66 |
| Master Bed | 13'11" x 12'2" | 4.24 x 3.71 |
| Bed 2 | 12'0" x 10'5" | 3.66 x 3.16 |
| Bed 3 | 10'6" x 10'4" | 3.19 x 3.15 |
| Bed 4 | 8'9" x 12'4" | 2.66 x 3.75 |

**Ref: W1272**

**149 sq.m.    1603 sq.ft.**

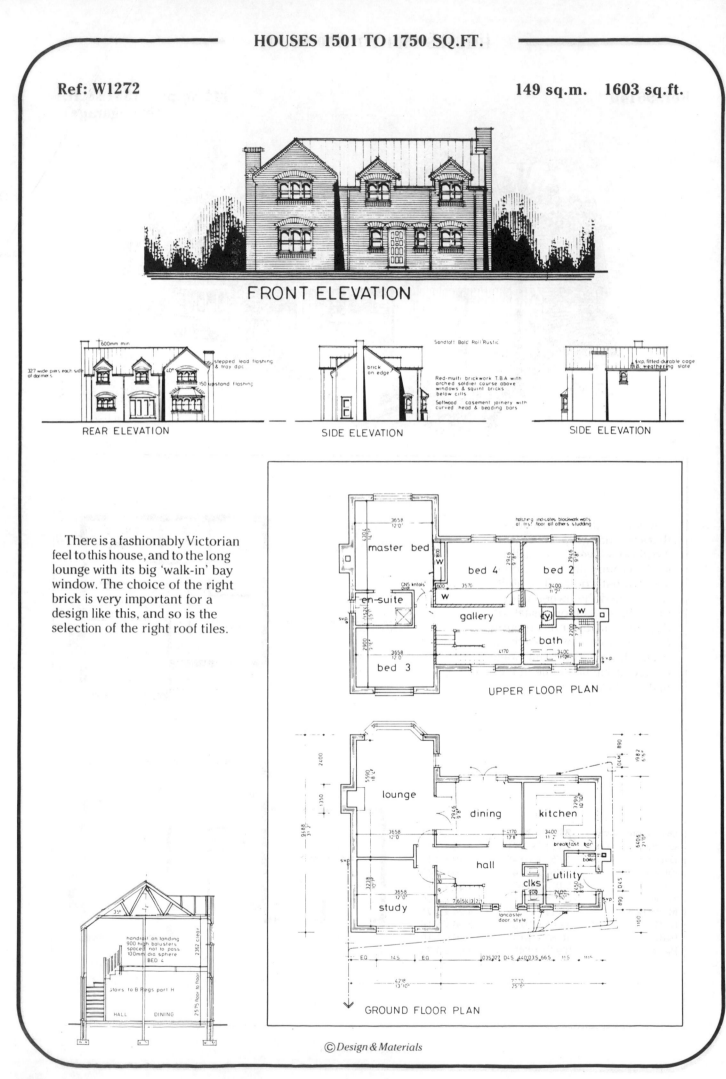

FRONT ELEVATION

REAR ELEVATION

SIDE ELEVATION

SIDE ELEVATION

There is a fashionably Victorian feel to this house, and to the long lounge with its big 'walk-in' bay window. The choice of the right brick is very important for a design like this, and so is the selection of the right roof tiles.

UPPER FLOOR PLAN

GROUND FLOOR PLAN

**Ref: PP2711**

**155 sq.m.   1668 sq.ft.
(exc. garage)**

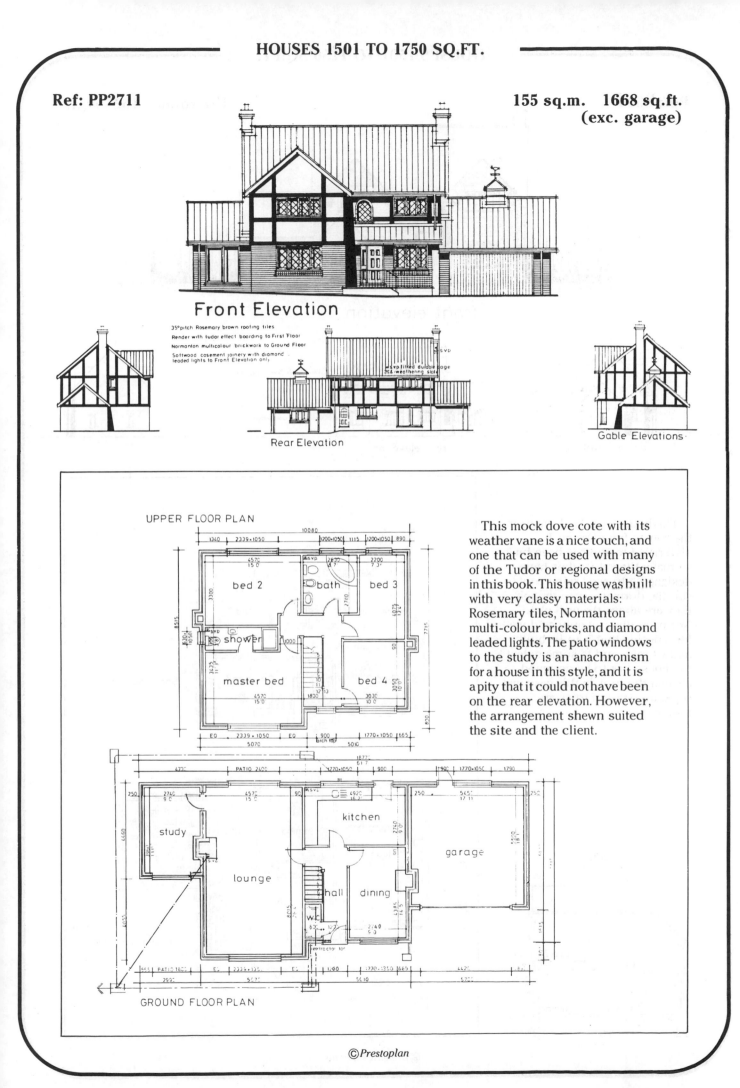

## Front Elevation

35°pitch Rosemary brown roofing tiles

Render with tudor effect boarding to First Floor

Normanton multicolour brickwork to Ground Floor

Softwood casement joinery with diamond
leaded lights to Front Elevation only)

Rear Elevation

Gable Elevations

UPPER FLOOR PLAN

bed 2

bath

bed 3

shower

master bed

bed 4

GROUND FLOOR PLAN

study

kitchen

lounge

garage

hall

dining

w.c.

This mock dove cote with its weather vane is a nice touch, and one that can be used with many of the Tudor or regional designs in this book. This house was built with very classy materials: Rosemary tiles, Normanton multi-colour bricks, and diamond leaded lights. The patio windows to the study is an anachronism for a house in this style, and it is a pity that it could not have been on the rear elevation. However, the arrangement shewn suited the site and the client.

©*Prestoplan*

313

**Ref: S524**

**151 sq.m.   1625 sq.ft.**

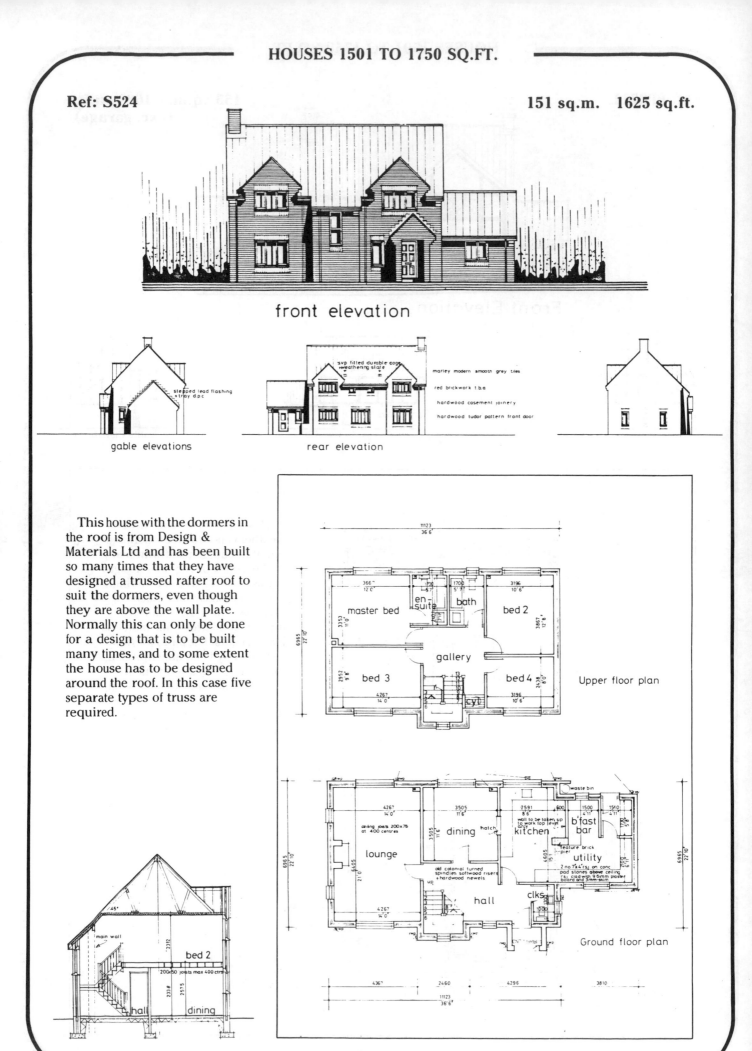

front elevation

gable elevations

rear elevation

svp fitted durable eage
+ weathering slate

stepped lead flashing
+ tray d.p.c

marley modern smooth grey tiles

red brickwork t.b.a

hardwood casement joinery

hardwood tudor pattern front door

This house with the dormers in the roof is from Design & Materials Ltd and has been built so many times that they have designed a trussed rafter roof to suit the dormers, even though they are above the wall plate. Normally this can only be done for a design that is to be built many times, and to some extent the house has to be designed around the roof. In this case five separate types of truss are required.

Upper floor plan

master bed
en-suite
bath
bed 2
gallery
bed 3
bed 4
cyl

Ground floor plan

lounge
dining
kitchen
b'fast bar
utility
hall
clks
waste bin

ceiling joists 200x75 at 400 centres

old colonial turned spindles softwood risers + hardwood newels

wall to be taken up to work top level

feature brick pier

2 no 7x4"rsj on conc pad stones above ceiling rsj clad wgth 9.5mm plaster board and 3mm skim

bed 2

main wall

hall            dining

45°

200x50 joists max 400 ctrs

**Ref: P2630**

**161 sq.m.    1733 sq.ft.**

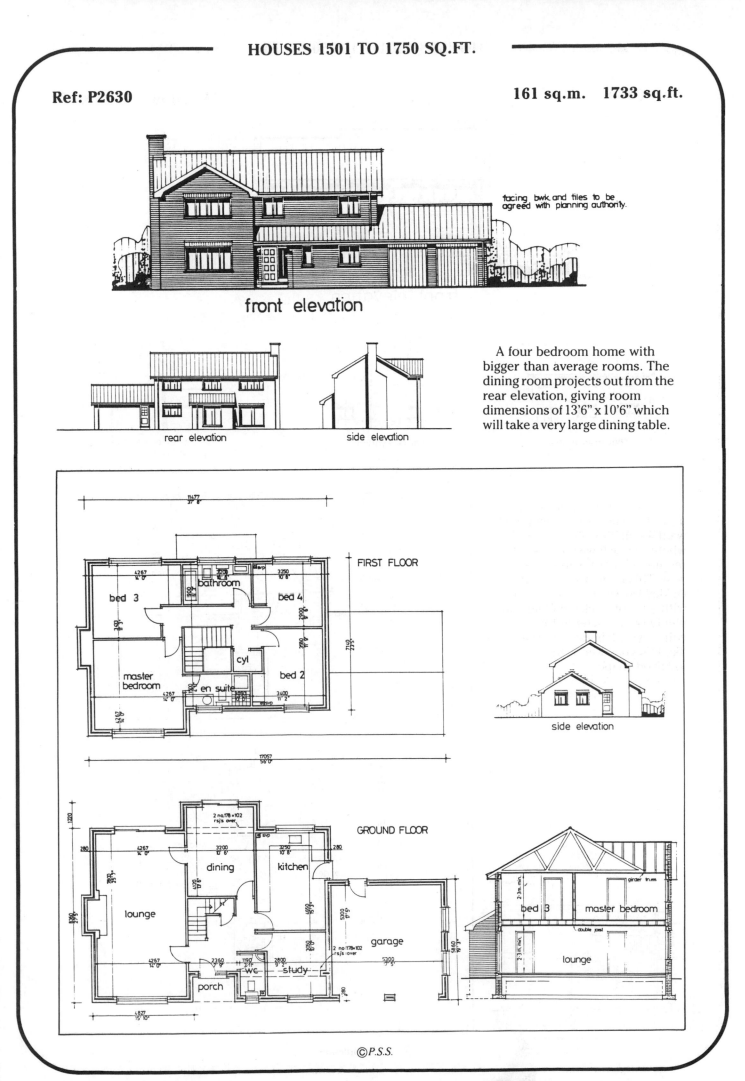

front elevation

facing bwk. and tiles to be
agreed with planning authority.

rear elevation

side elevation

A four bedroom home with bigger than average rooms. The dining room projects out from the rear elevation, giving room dimensions of 13'6" x 10'6" which will take a very large dining table.

FIRST FLOOR

bed 3

bathroom

bed 4

cyl

master bedroom

en suite

bed 2

side elevation

GROUND FLOOR

dining

kitchen

lounge

garage

bed 3

master bedroom

lounge

wc

study

porch

©P.S.S.

**Ref: C389**

**148 sq.m.   1593 sq.ft.**

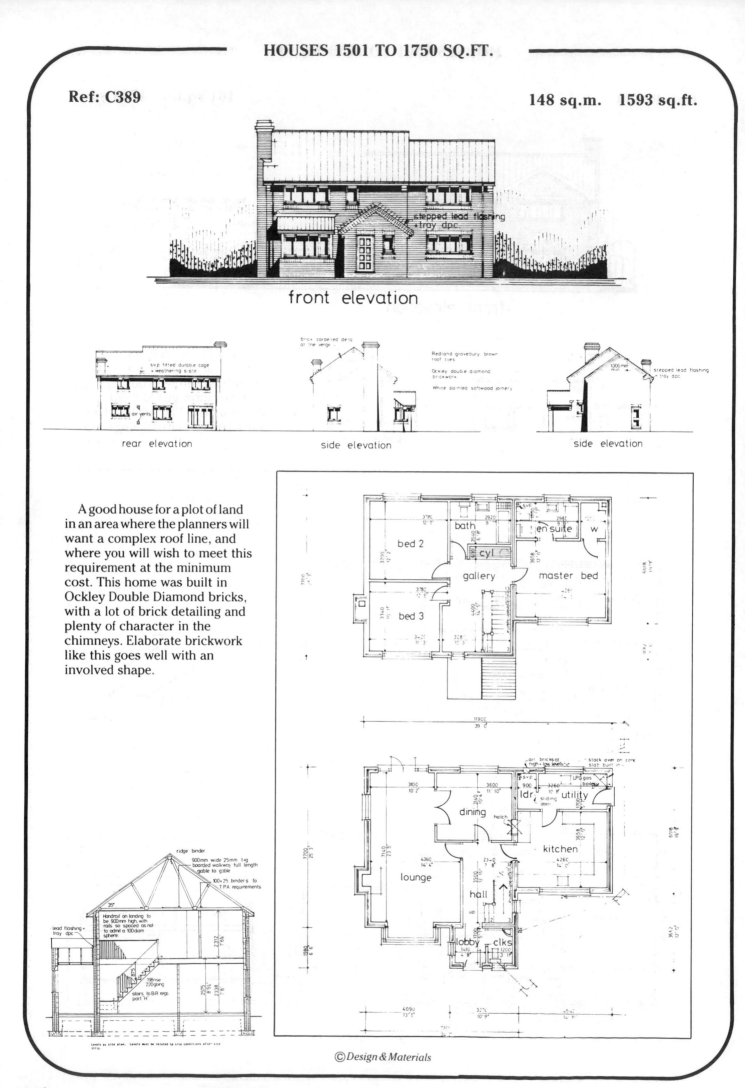

front elevation

rear elevation

side elevation

side elevation

brick corbelled detail at the verge

Redland grovebury brown roof tiles

Ockley double diamond brickwork

White painted softwood joinery

svp fitted durable cage + weathering slate

air vents

stepped lead flashing + tray dpc

1000mm min

stepped lead flashing + tray dpc

A good house for a plot of land in an area where the planners will want a complex roof line, and where you will wish to meet this requirement at the minimum cost. This home was built in Ockley Double Diamond bricks, with a lot of brick detailing and plenty of character in the chimneys. Elaborate brickwork like this goes well with an involved shape.

bed 2

bath

en suite

w

cyl

gallery

master bed

bed 3

ridge binder

900mm wide 25mm t+g boarded walkway full length gable to gable

100×25 binders to T P A requirements

Handrail on landing to be 900mm high, with rails so spaced as not to admit a 100 diam sphere.

lead flashing + tray dpc

stairs to B.R regs part 'H'

ldr

utility

dining

hatch

kitchen

lounge

hall

up

lobby

clks

air bricks at high + low levels

stack over on conc slab built in

LPG gas boiler

sliding door

**Ref: P2647**

**161 sq.m.    1733 sq.ft.**

A half-timbered house with the inglenook fireplace and huge outside chimney breast that matches the period style. The hall and first floor landing are very large and give an air of distinction to the interior. Double doors from the hall into the lounge add to this.

The house is shewn with no division at all between the kitchen and the dining room, and the arrangement of the floor joists to the first floor above enables any sort of non-structural divider to be used to separate the two areas - or a conventional wall can be built! The choice is yours.

The details of the staircase are always important in a house of this style, especially when there is room on the landing for furniture and a window seat. In recent years the staircase manufacturers have revived many of the Victorian newel and balustrade designs, and there is now a wide choice of both modern and period options. Of course, if you want a Tudor staircase to match your Tudor style home this will be something of a challenge, but it can be done!

rear elevation 1·100

side

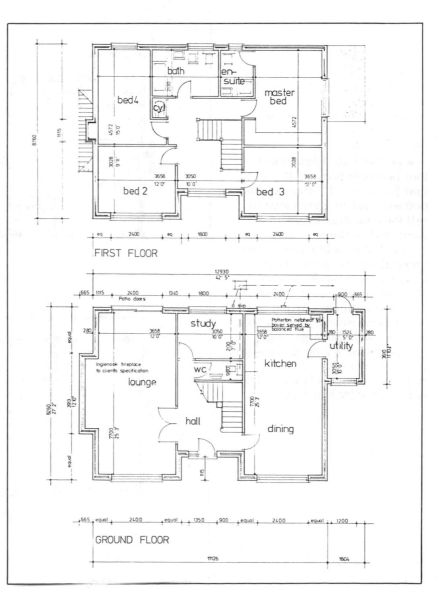

FIRST FLOOR

GROUND FLOOR

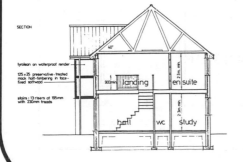

SECTION

**Ref: P2744**

**140 sq.m.  1506 sq.ft.**
**(exc. garage)**

front elevation

rear elevation

garage side elevation

side elevation

A perfectly straightforward four bedroom home of the sort that builders call "estate agents houses" - estate agents love to sell them because everyone wants to buy them.

The first floor box room is an unusual feature in a home like this, and would make a small study or sewing room if desired.

With no windows in one side wall this house can be built on a 50ft plot with the large single garage shewn. If a double garage with a fourteen foot door is required the width of the building is increased by four feet.

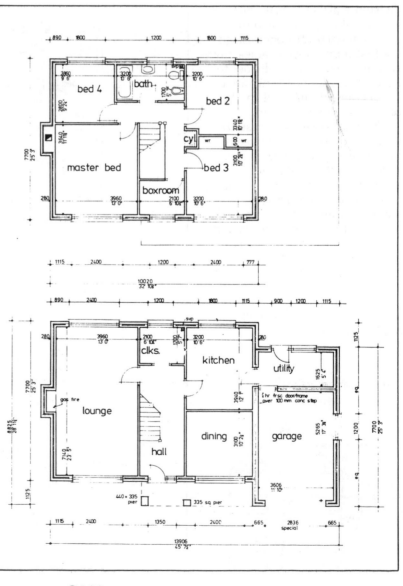

**Ref: W1176**

**152 sq.m. 1636 sq.ft.**
**(exc. garage)**

The storey height window to the stair well is a key feature in this house, which has an interesting layout. Besides having a bathroom that is bigger than the smaller bedrooms, it also has the only access to the dining room through the kitchen. If required it would be simple to turn one bathroom into two, one en suite and one for the family and guests, and a door can easily be provided between the dining room and the hall.

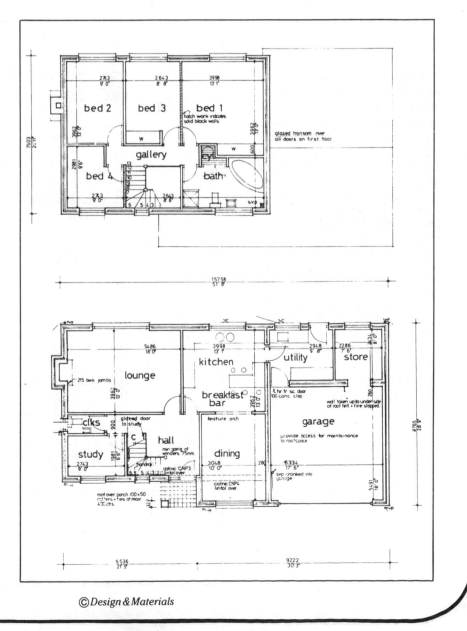

**Ref: P3065**

**140 sq.m.   1506 sq.ft.**
**(exc. garage)**

REAR   ELEVATION

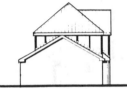

GARAGE  SIDE  ELEVATION

SIDE  ELEVATION

A nice simple house of 1600 sq.ft. which will be very cost effective to build. If constructed in a part of the country where gable ends are more usual than hip roofs, it can be built with two small gables over the first floor windows.

The layout illustrated has only one bathroom, which is unusual these days. However, as the roof construction does not depend on support from any of the first floor partition walls, the bedroom arrangements can be altered to suit the requirements of the family building this new home.

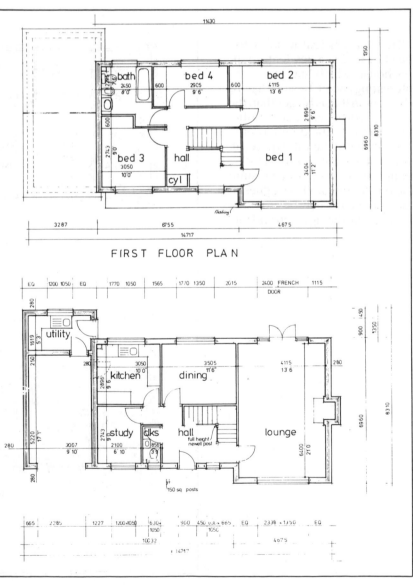

FIRST FLOOR PLAN

**Ref: S477**

**147 sq.m.    1582 sq.ft.**
**(exc. garage)**

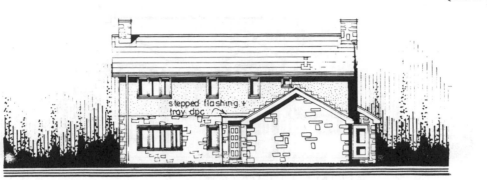

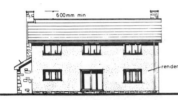

REAR ELEVATION

Double Roman tile
Somerset Red

150 upstand flashing
& tray d.p.c.

gables & plinth work
Bradstone reconstructed stone

stepped lead flashing
& tray dpc

GABLE ELEVATIONS

stepped flashing +
tray dpc

This very compact house has the unusual feature of a front entrance set across the angle of an L shaped hall, which helps it to have a very interesting and convenient ground floor layout. In spite of this it is a very straightforward building to construct and has been built many times since D & M first introduced this design in 1979.

It can be built without the garage if required, which enables the study to have a large window looking to the front.

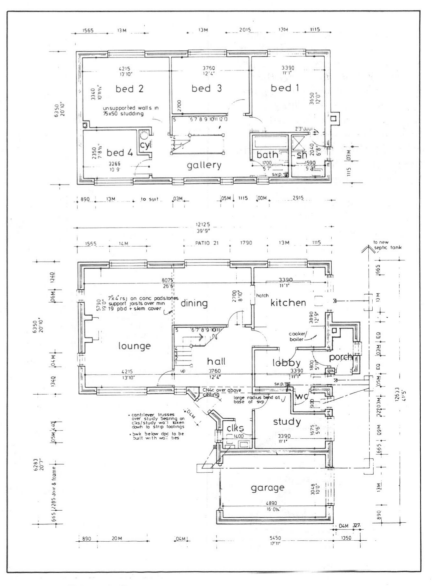

**Ref: S532**

**148 sq.m.   1593 sq.ft.**

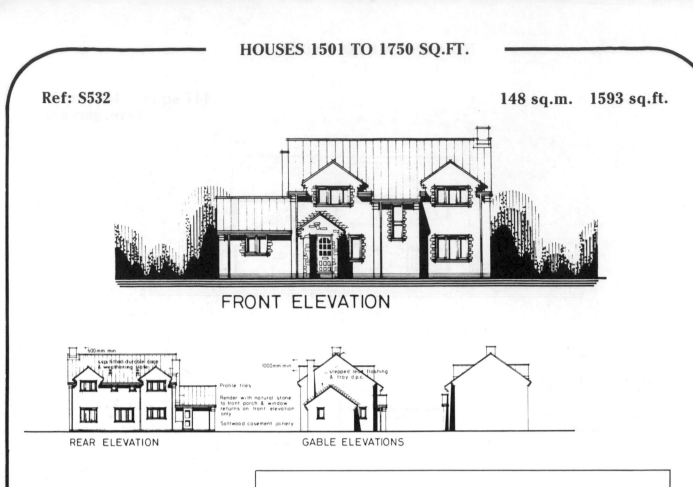

FRONT ELEVATION

REAR ELEVATION

GABLE ELEVATIONS

Another variant of a popular design for rural areas. The large and well lit hall gives this house a very spacious feel, and the kitchen end of the house can be rearranged in many different ways providing that the brick pier between the kitchen and utility room is retained, as this supports the joists which support the bedroom external walls above.

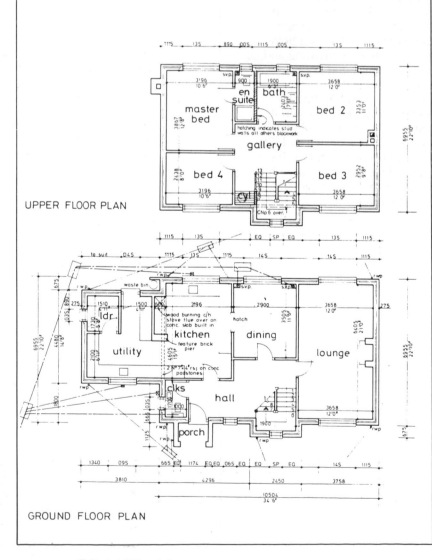

UPPER FLOOR PLAN

GROUND FLOOR PLAN

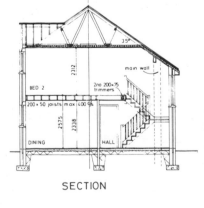

SECTION

**Ref: 96120**

**151 sq.m.   1624 sq.ft.**

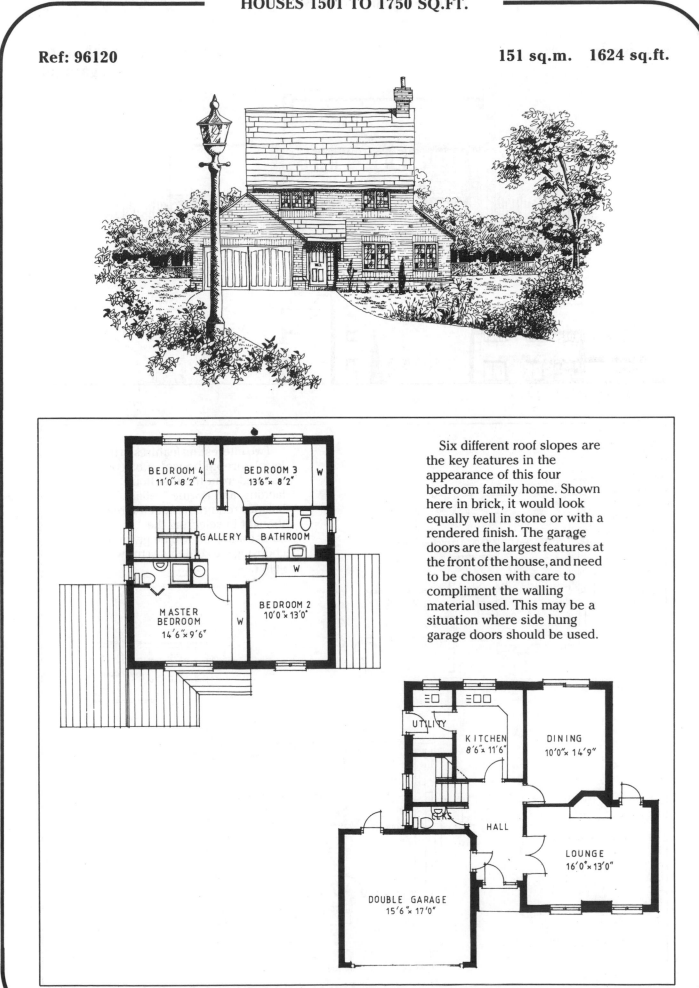

Six different roof slopes are the key features in the appearance of this four bedroom family home. Shown here in brick, it would look equally well in stone or with a rendered finish. The garage doors are the largest features at the front of the house, and need to be chosen with care to compliment the walling material used. This may be a situation where side hung garage doors should be used.

BEDROOM 4
11'0" × 8'2"

BEDROOM 3
13'6" × 8'2"

GALLERY

BATHROOM

MASTER BEDROOM
14'6" × 9'6"

BEDROOM 2
10'0" × 13'0"

UTILITY

KITCHEN
8'6" × 11'6"

DINING
10'0" × 14'9"

HALL

CLKS

LOUNGE
16'0" × 13'0"

DOUBLE GARAGE
15'6" × 17'0"

**Ref: W945**

**140 sq.m.  1506 sq.ft.**
**(exc. garage)**

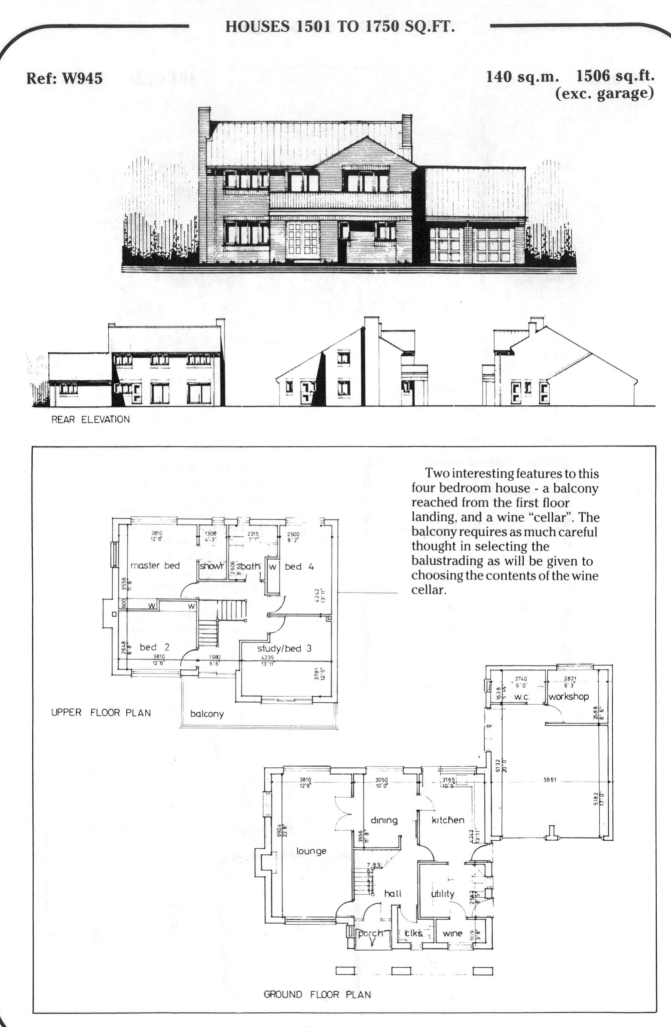

REAR ELEVATION

Two interesting features to this four bedroom house - a balcony reached from the first floor landing, and a wine "cellar". The balcony requires as much careful thought in selecting the balustrading as will be given to choosing the contents of the wine cellar.

UPPER FLOOR PLAN

GROUND FLOOR PLAN

© *Design & Materials*

**Ref: C335**

**154 sq.m.   1657 sq.ft.**

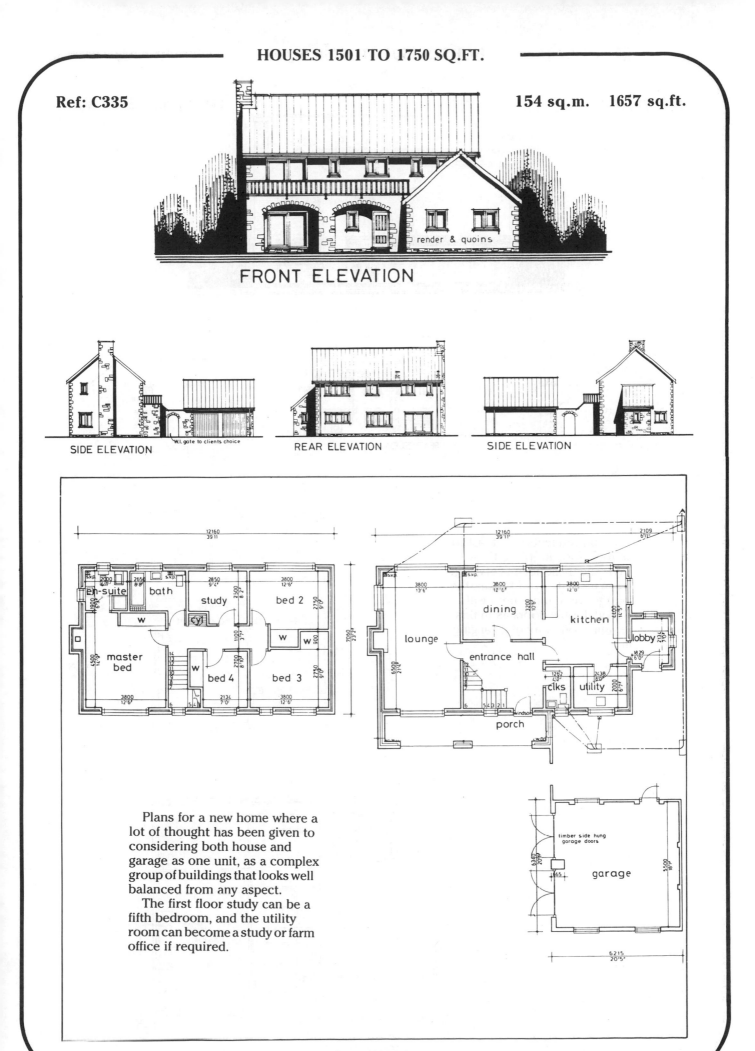

FRONT ELEVATION

render & quoins

SIDE ELEVATION

W.I. gate to clients choice

REAR ELEVATION

SIDE ELEVATION

Plans for a new home where a lot of thought has been given to considering both house and garage as one unit, as a complex group of buildings that looks well balanced from any aspect.

The first floor study can be a fifth bedroom, and the utility room can become a study or farm office if required.

**Ref: W1029**

**146 sq.m.    1571 sq.ft.**

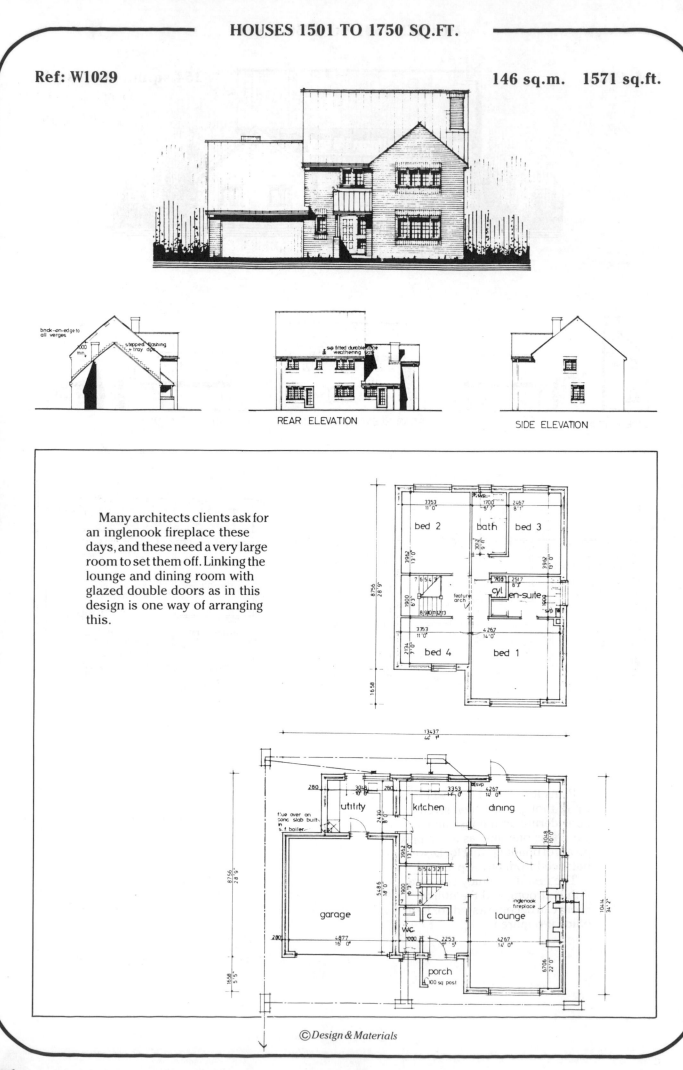

REAR ELEVATION

SIDE ELEVATION

Many architects clients ask for an inglenook fireplace these days, and these need a very large room to set them off. Linking the lounge and dining room with glazed double doors as in this design is one way of arranging this.

© *Design & Materials*

**Ref: P2711**

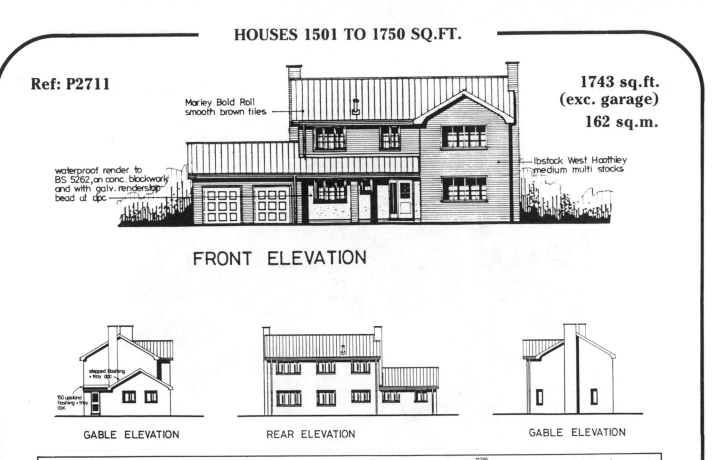

Marley Bold Roll smooth brown tiles

waterproof render to BS 5262, on conc. blockwork and with galv. renderstop bead at dpc

Ibstock West Hoathley medium multi stocks

## FRONT ELEVATION

GABLE ELEVATION

stepped flashing + tray dpc

150 upstand flashing + tray dpc

REAR ELEVATION

GABLE ELEVATION

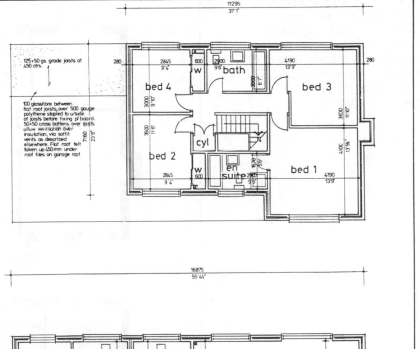

A house with Georgian sash windows to the front, and modern side hung casement windows at the back and sides. An arrangement of this sort needs careful consideration, and in this case it requires accepting that there will be two different types of window in the lounge.

Note that the inside wall of the front porch is to be rendered. This was common fifty years ago, but is unusual now. It is certainly a good way to lighten the appearance of a house that has a canopy over the front door, and emphasises the entrance in a useful way.

125×50 gs grade joists at 450 ctrs.

100 glassfibre between flat roof joists, over 500 gauge polythene stapled to u/side of joists before fixing pl board. 50×50 cross battens over joists allow ventilation over joists insulation, via soffit vents as described elsewhere. Flat roof felt taken up 450mm under roof tiles on garage roof

11295 / 37'1"

2845 / 9'4" · 600 · 2300 / 9'6" · bath · 4190 / 13'9" · 280

w · bed 4 · 3000 / 9'10" · bed 3 · 3650 / 11'10"

bed 2 · 3650 / 11'8" · cyl · 4100 / 13'5"

w · 600 · en suite · 2300 / 9'6" · bed 1 · 4190 / 13'9"

2845 / 9'4"

7160 / 23'6"

16875 / 55'4½"

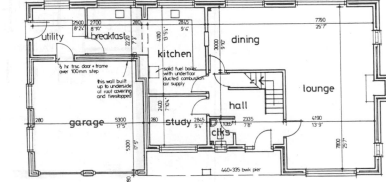

2500 / 8'2" · 2700 / 8'10" · 280 · 2845 / 9'4" · 7790 / 25'7"

utility · breakfast · 4100 / 13'5" · dining · 3000 / 9'10"

kitchen

½ hr frsc door + frame over 100mm step

this wall built up to underside of roof covering and firestopped

solid fuel boiler with underfloor ducted combustion air supply

lounge

hall

garage · 5300 / 17'5" · 280 · study · 2845 / 9'4" · cths · 2335 / 7'8" · 4190 / 13'9"

5300 / 17'5"

280 · 440×335 bwk pier

8360 / 27'5"

7800 / 25'7"

**Ref: 96204**

**139 sq.m.    1500 sq.ft.**

A Victorian style home with the garage disguised with ornamental side hung doors. The distinctive style of the upper floor windows, typical of the turn-of-the-century, is another example of the attention to detail.

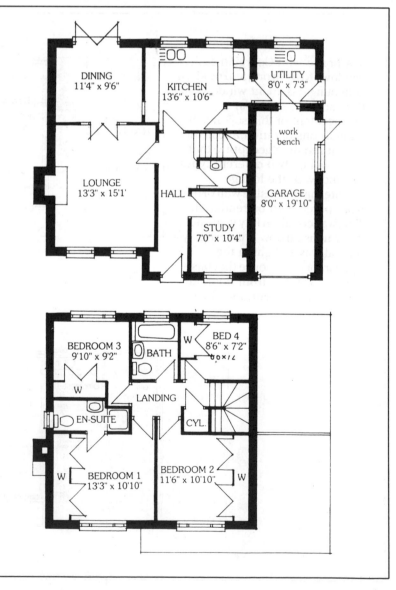

DINING
11'4" x 9'6"

KITCHEN
13'6" x 10'6"

UTILITY
8'0" x 7'3"

work bench

LOUNGE
13'3" x 15'1"

HALL

GARAGE
8'0" x 19'10"

STUDY
7'0" x 10'4"

BEDROOM 3
9'10" x 9'2"

BATH

W

BED 4
8'6" x 7'2"

W

LANDING

EN-SUITE

CYL.

BEDROOM 1
13'3" x 10'10"

BEDROOM 2
11'6" x 10'10"

W

W

W

**Ref: 96129**

**149 sq.m.    1600 sq.ft.**

This is a village street house: modest in size, wider than it is deep, and with an authentic regional or period style. In this case the stone label mouldings over the windows, the flat roof to the porch and the tabling at the top of the gables were all designed to match other houses in a village street near Stamford, and succeeded in this very well indeed.

Inside this home the room layout is uncompromisingly modern, with a dining hall, a small study and a hobbies room for each partner to have their own den. Note the interesting shape to the first floor gallery which has its own window and can be used for a multitude of purposes.

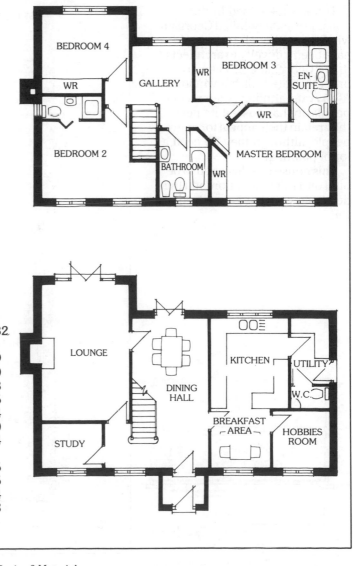

| | | | |
|---|---|---|---|
| Dimensions overall | 41'1" x 30'7" | - | 12.53 x 9.32 |
| Lounge | 11'6" x 18'0" | - | 3.50 x 5.49 |
| Dining Hall | 10'0" x 20'0" | - | 3.05 x 6.10 |
| Study | 8'0" x 6'0" | - | 2.44 x 1.83 |
| Kitchen | 10'0" x 12'0" | - | 3.05 x 3.66 |
| Breakfast Area | 7'6" x 8'0" | - | 2.29 x 2.44 |
| Utility | 5'0" x 8'6" | - | 1.52 x 2.60 |
| Hobbies Room | 7'6" x 7'8" | - | 2.29 x 2.34 |
| Master Bedroom | 15'4" x 12'0" | - | 4.67 x 3.66 |
| Bedroom 2 | 11'6" x 10'0" | - | 3.50 x 3.05 |
| Bedroom 3 | 12'0" x 7'8" | - | 3.66 x 2.34 |
| Bedroom 4 | 11'6" x 10'9" | - | 3.50 x 3.28 |

**Ref: W867**

**140 sq.m.   1506 sq.ft.**

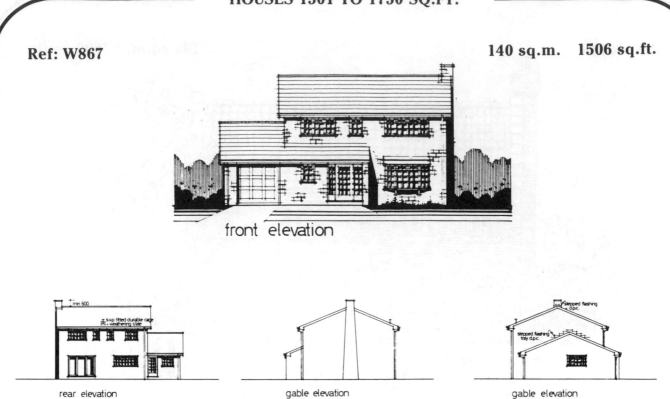

front elevation

rear elevation

gable elevation

gable elevation

The windows used in this house are usually called Georgian windows, although they would have been a novelty to architects in the Georgian era. They are properly called 'full bar windows'. At any rate, although their recent popularity has passed its peak, they retain their appeal for many people, although they do need a lot of painting!

This house was designed to be built on a raft foundation, and the detail shews what is involved in this.

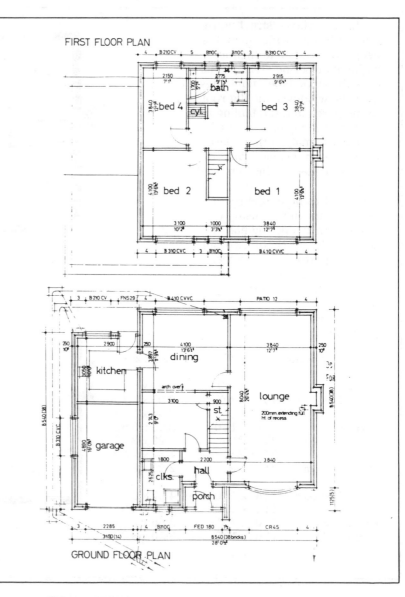

FIRST FLOOR PLAN

bed 4   bath   cyl   bed 3

bed 2   bed 1

GROUND FLOOR PLAN

kitchen   dining

garage   lounge

st

clks   hall   porch

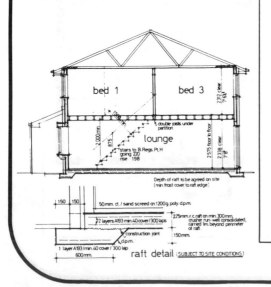

bed 1   bed 3

lounge

raft detail (SUBJECT TO SITE CONDITIONS)

**Ref: C380**

**142 sq.m.    1528 sq.ft.**

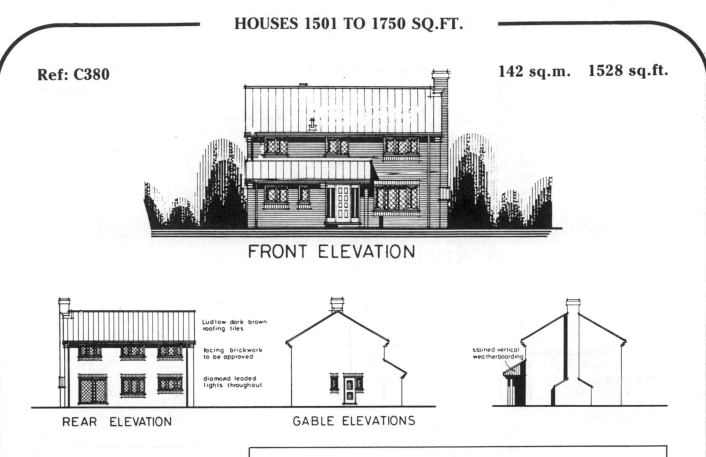

FRONT ELEVATION

Ludlow dark brown roofing tiles

facing brickwork to be approved

diamond leaded lights throughout

REAR ELEVATION        GABLE ELEVATIONS

Diamond leaded lights throughout are a feature of this 3/4 bedroom home, which has a first floor layout that enables a fourth bedroom to be used as a dressing room if desired. I always thought the point of a dressing room was that it could be as untidy as you wish, while the bedroom remains immaculate! Once you get used to this it must be difficult to dispense with the dressing room and have to keep the bedroom tidy.

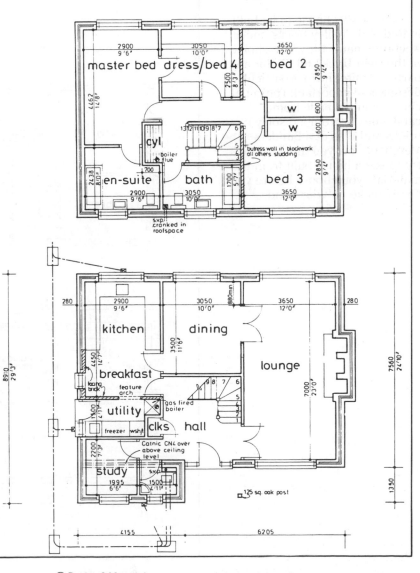

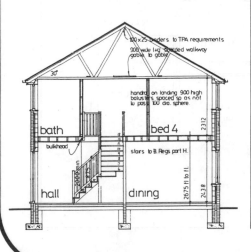

**Ref: C340**

**157 sq.m.  1689 sq.ft.
(exc. garage)**

FRONT ELEVATION

REAR ELEVATION

SIDE ELEVATION

SIDE ELEVATION

An imposing house to be built in Redland Chailey bricks under Anchor Senator tiles. The choice of the right brick and tile for any particular site and for a particular design, is so important. The initial choice can be made from catalogues or from a display of bricks and tiles at a Builders Merchants, but you should always try to see a house built from the materials you choose before you finally make up your mind.

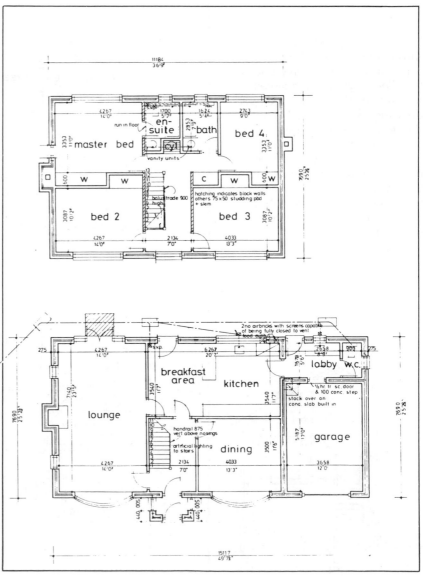

**Ref: P2677**

**141 sq.m.    1517 sq.ft.**
**(exc. garage)**

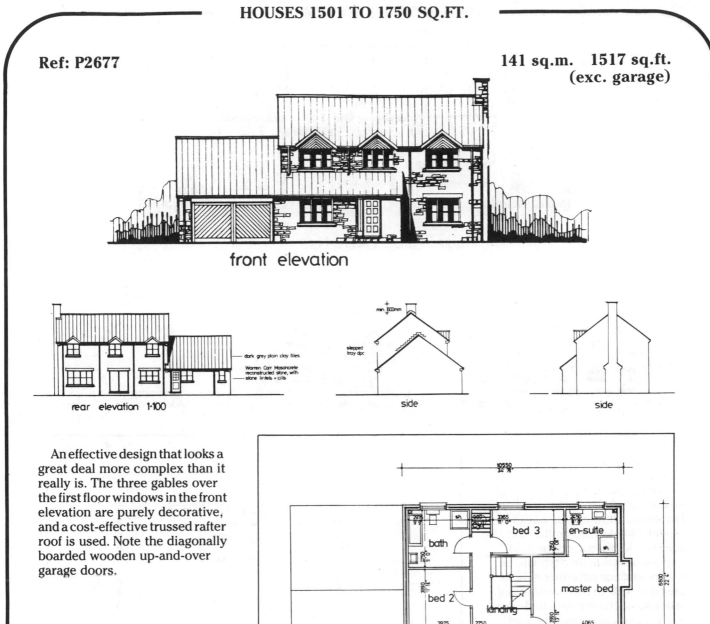

front elevation

rear elevation 1·100

dark grey plain clay tiles

Warren Carr Masoncrete reconstructed stone, with stone lintels + cills

min. 600mm

stepped tray dpc

side

side

An effective design that looks a great deal more complex than it really is. The three gables over the first floor windows in the front elevation are purely decorative, and a cost-effective trussed rafter roof is used. Note the diagonally boarded wooden up-and-over garage doors.

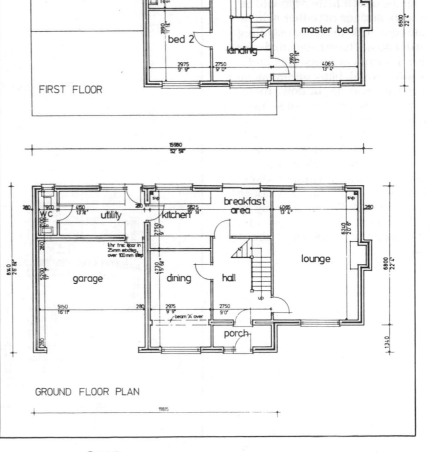

FIRST FLOOR

bath

bed 3

en-suite

sh

bed 2

landing

master bed

GROUND FLOOR PLAN

WC

utility

kitchen

breakfast area

garage

dining

hall

lounge

porch

1 hr frsc floor in 25mm robotics, over 100mm step

beam 'A' over

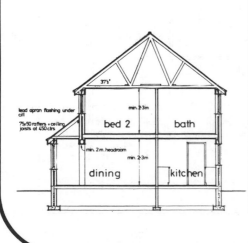

lead apron flashing under cill

75/50 rafters + ceiling joists at 450 ctrs

min. 2·3m

bed 2

bath

min. 2 m. headroom

min. 2·3m

dining

kitchen

**Ref: P2795**

**142 sq.m.    1528 sq.ft.**

FRONT ELEVATION

SIDE ELEVATION

stepped flashing
+ tray d.p.c.

brickwork eaves, detailing

waterproof render
to B.S. 5262

facing brick plinth
galv. renderstop bead at d.p.c.

facing brickwork Westbrick no. 31
warm red multi rustics

rear elevation 1·100

side elevation

A house in the Cotswold style. The kitchen is interesting, with an 'island' stove. A stove in this position does not meet the NHBC requirement that there should be a work surface on either side of the cooker, so that pans of boiling water do not have to be lifted over the floor in case they spill and scald any cat, baby or comatose husband who may be down there. For this reason the plan shows one work surface extended round to the stove, and it should really be shewn on the other side as well. This rather defeats the object of having a feature cooker like this, but, as your new house is not being built speculatively by a developer, the NHBC inspector is unlikely to be too strict about this.

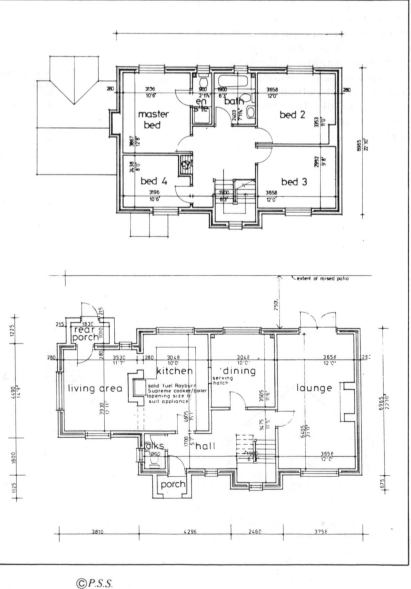

**Ref: W1295**

**141 sq.m.    1517 sq.ft.**
**(exc. garage)**

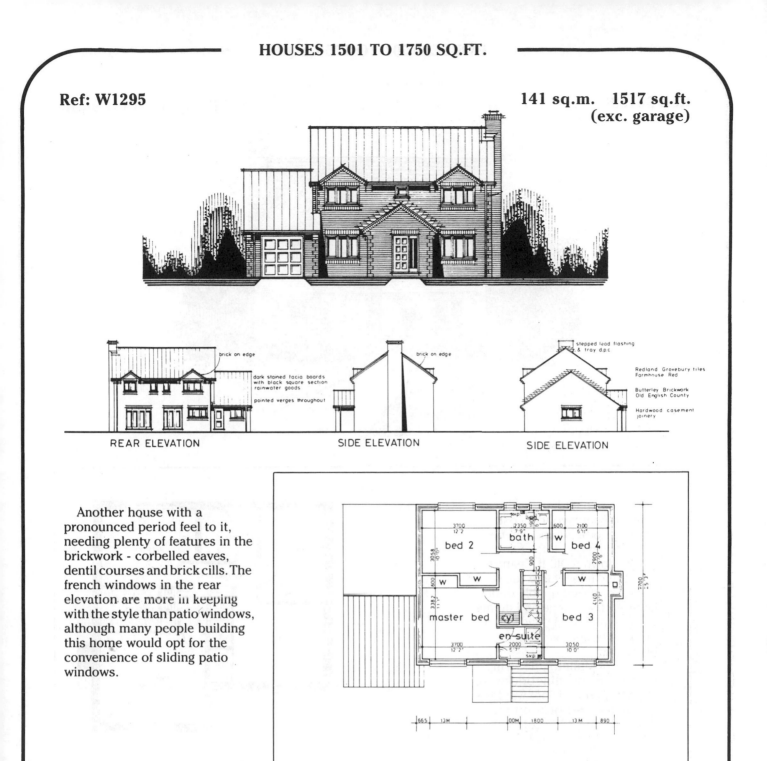

REAR ELEVATION          SIDE ELEVATION          SIDE ELEVATION

brick on edge

dark stained facia boards
with black square section
rainwater goods

pointed verges throughout

brick on edge

stepped lead flashing
& tray d.p.c

Redland Grovebury tiles
Farmhouse Red

Butterley Brickwork
Old English County

Hardwood casement
joinery

Another house with a pronounced period feel to it, needing plenty of features in the brickwork - corbelled eaves, dentil courses and brick cills. The french windows in the rear elevation are more in keeping with the style than patio windows, although many people building this home would opt for the convenience of sliding patio windows.

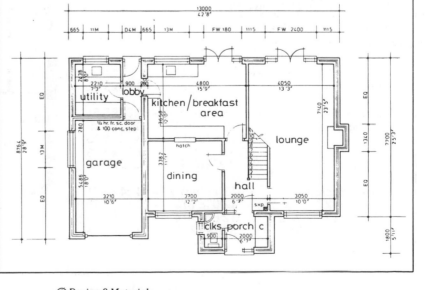

**Ref: 96128**

**142 sq.m.  1531 sq.ft.**

This compact house with a conventional layout is cost effective to build and can be constructed on plots of any widths down to 40 ft. Features shown include a large recessed fireplace, glazed double doors between the lounge and dining room, a small study, and lots of built in cupboards in the bedrooms.

The brick plinth, the string course of contrasting brickwork above the ground floor windows and the feature brickwork under the eaves provide a lot of character at a modest cost, but care should be taken in the choice of bricks to give this effect.

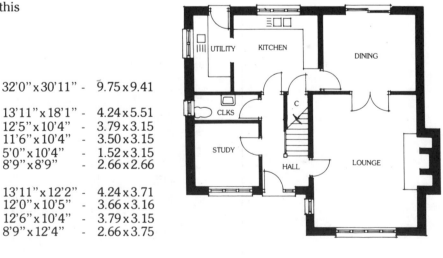

| | | |
|---|---|---|
| Dimensions overall | 32'0" x 30'11" - | 9.75 x 9.41 |
| Lounge | 13'11" x 18'1" - | 4.24 x 5.51 |
| Dining | 12'5" x 10'4" - | 3.79 x 3.15 |
| Kitchen | 11'6" x 10'4" - | 3.50 x 3.15 |
| Utility | 5'0" x 10'4" - | 1.52 x 3.15 |
| Study | 8'9" x 8'9" - | 2.66 x 2.66 |
| Master Bedroom | 13'11" x 12'2" - | 4.24 x 3.71 |
| Bedroom 2 | 12'0" x 10'5" - | 3.66 x 3.16 |
| Bedroom 3 (inc WR) | 12'6" x 10'4" - | 3.79 x 3.15 |
| Bedroom 4 (inc WR) | 8'9" x 12'4" - | 2.66 x 3.75 |

© *Design & Materials*

**Ref: 96207**

**145 sq.m.   1555 sq.ft.**

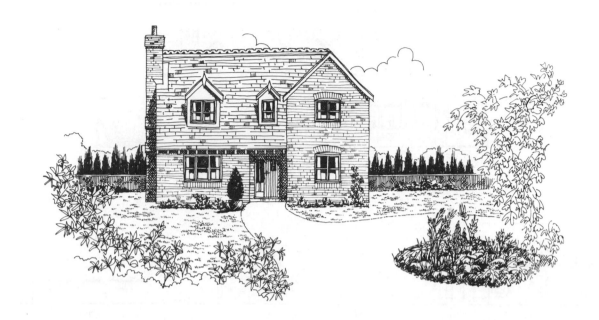

A pleasant four bedroom house in the Victorian style which is often called the Railway Cottage style. The originals date from the years of the great railway engineers who would contract with the local builders to build them for railway staff at isolated junctions for about £60 each. Today the originals make very high prices, and this replica will be equally valuable on the right site.

| | | | |
|---|---|---|---|
| Lounge | 13'0" x 15'4" | - | 3.96 x 4.67 |
| Dining | 10'6" x 9'7" | - | 3.20 x 2.93 |
| Kitchen/B'fast | 21'4" x 9'0" | - | 6.50 x 2.74 |
| Utility | 7'11" x 6'8" | - | 2.41 x 2.03 |
| Study | 7'11" x 10'10" | - | 2.41 x 3.29 |
| | | | |
| Master Bedroom | 11'5" x 11'11" | - | 3.48 x 3.62 |
| Bedroom 2 | 13'0" x 10'10" | - | 3.96 x 3.31 |
| Bedroom 3 | 10'6" x 9'2" | - | 3.20 x 2.79 |
| Bedroom 4 | 11'0" x 9'0" | - | 3.35 x 2.74 |

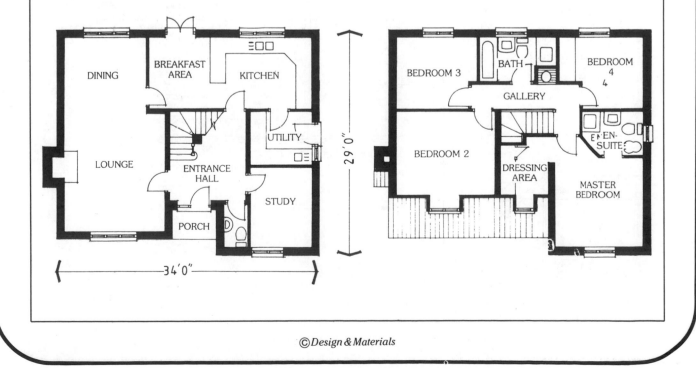

**Ref: S475**

**156 sq.m. 1679 sq.ft.**
**(exc. garage)**

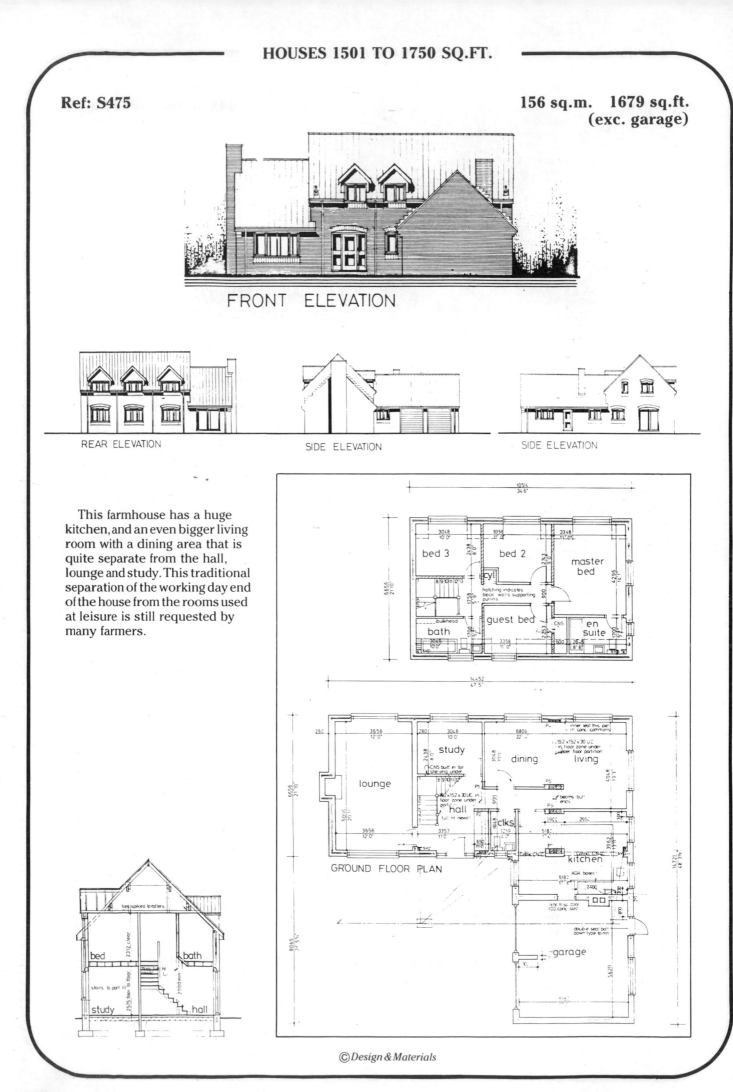

FRONT ELEVATION

REAR ELEVATION

SIDE ELEVATION

SIDE ELEVATION

This farmhouse has a huge kitchen, and an even bigger living room with a dining area that is quite separate from the hall, lounge and study. This traditional separation of the working day end of the house from the rooms used at leisure is still requested by many farmers.

GROUND FLOOR PLAN

**Ref: C315**

162 sq.m.   1743 sq.ft.

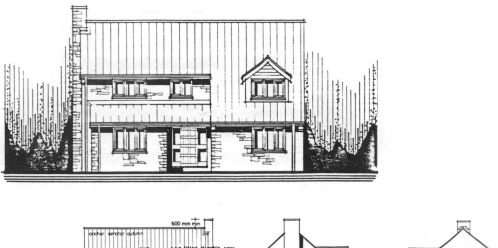

REAR ELEVATION          SIDE ELEVATIONS

The section drawing of this four bedroom house shews how the complex looking roof of this house is based on a simple rectangle of trussed rafters, with the dormer above the wall plate. If this can be arranged easily then the cost savings are significant, and the money saved can either be used to reduce the total budget or else spent on more expensive features elsewhere.

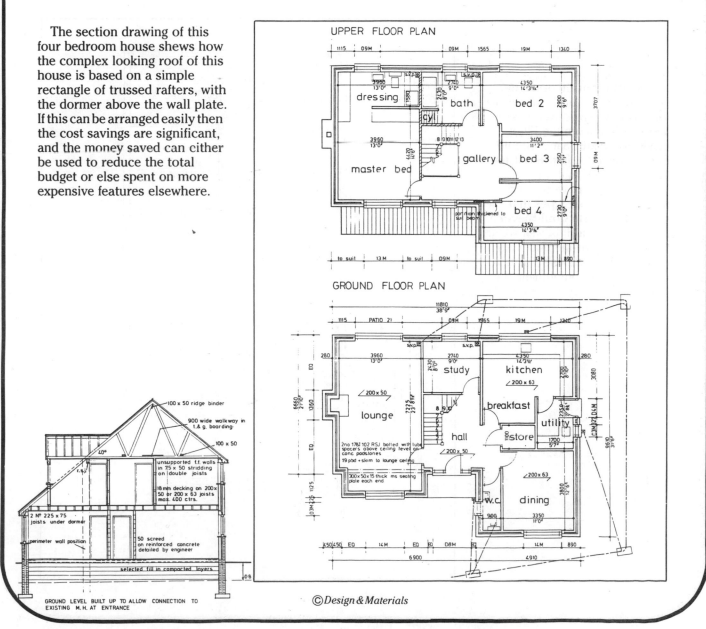

UPPER FLOOR PLAN

dressing    bath    bed 2

cyl

master bed    gallery    bed 3

bed 4

GROUND FLOOR PLAN

study    kitchen

lounge    breakfast

hall    store    utility

w.c.    dining

100 x 50 ridge binder

900 wide walkway in t.& g. boarding

100 x 50

40°

unsupported f.f. walls in 75 x 50 stridding on double joists

18 mm decking on 200 x 50 or 200 x 63 joists max. 400 ctrs.

2 N° 225 x 75 joists under dormer

perimeter wall position

50 screed on reinforced concrete detailed by engineer

selected fill in compacted layers

GROUND LEVEL BUILT UP TO ALLOW CONNECTION TO EXISTING M.H. AT ENTRANCE

© *Design & Materials*

**Ref: W1224**

**161 sq.m.   1733 sq.ft.**

FRONT ELEVATION

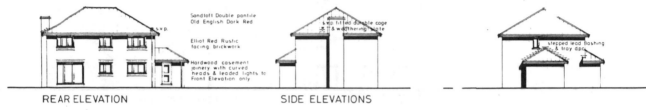

Sandtoft Double pantile
Old English Dark Red

Elliot Red Rustic
facing brickwork

Hardwood casement
joinery with curved
heads & leaded lights to
Front Elevation only

s.v.p. fitted durable cage
& weathering plate

stepped lead flashing
& tray d.p.c.

REAR ELEVATION          SIDE ELEVATIONS

A lot of careful thought has gone into choosing the materials for this new home: Red Rustic facing bricks from the Elliot brickyard, under Sandtoft Old English pantiles. In the last few years the brick and tile manufacturers have revived many of their old types that they probably thought would never be made again, and it is well worth while looking at them all very carefully. In this house the choice of bricks is to compliment the hardwood joinery as well as the tiles.

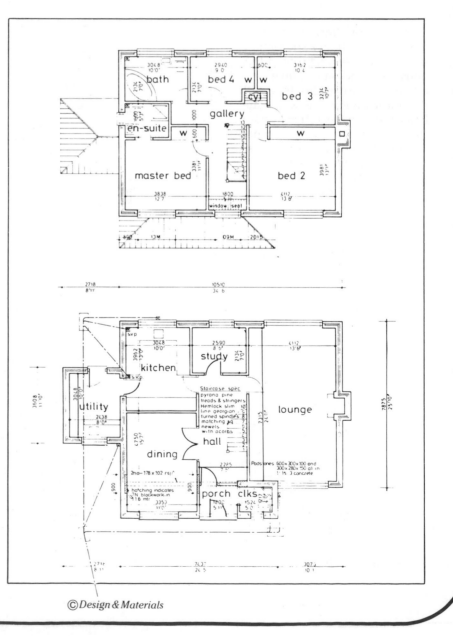

© Design & Materials

**Ref: P2778**

148 sq.m.   1593 sq.ft.

front elevation

side elevation

rear elevation

side elevation

A house in an Essex style with a tile hung projecting bay to one of the front bedrooms. The study at the rear is really quite separate from the rest of the house, giving the privacy from everyday living that is needed by many people who work at home.

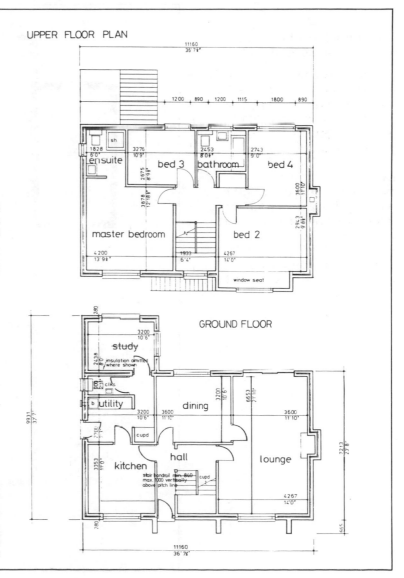

UPPER FLOOR PLAN

ensuite

bed 3

bathroom

bed 4

master bedroom

bed 2

window seat

GROUND FLOOR

study

utility

dining

hall

kitchen

lounge

341

**Ref: 96200**

**142 sq.m.    1526 sq.ft.**

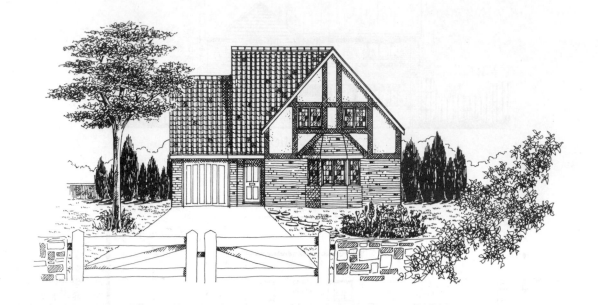

A compact four bedroom
home for a small garden plot.

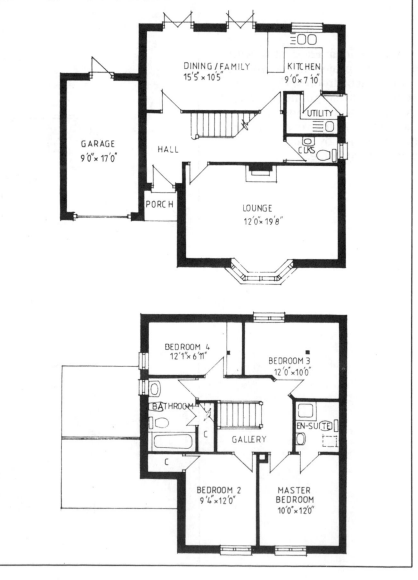

© *Design & Materials*

# *Designs for Houses Under 1500 sq. ft.*

A two storey home of under 1500 sq. ft. can be classified as either a cottage, designed to conform to a traditional local style, or else designed to project the image of a larger property. In this section we are concerned with the latter category.

Whether a modest home is in a neo Georgian, neo Tudor, Victorian, regional or post modern style, the size of windows and other features have to reflect the proportions of larger examples of their type, and this may require careful consideration. Small houses require windows that are in proportion to their overall size, and in particular any porch or portico must not seem inappropriate. Decorative features, such as any half timbering or use of contrasting brickwork, should be used to make the property appear larger than it really is, and any dormer window set in a roof should be modest in size. Garages are best detached whenever practicable, and possibly linked to the main building by a wall or other feature so that the two units together appear larger than the total of their areas.

Designing the internal layouts of homes of this size must start with a conscious decision on the number of rooms required. The fewer they are, the larger they can be. Consideration of this will inevitably lead to debating whether there should be a single large living room, or smaller but separate lounges and dining rooms. Another issue will be whether there is a real need for a utility room, and the way in which space can be saved in the hall and landing areas. With under 1500 sq. ft. available the number of options are severely restricted, and most of them are shown on the pages that follow.

**Ref: 96205**

**128 sq.m.    1376 sq.ft.**

This house has elements of a number of different styles which the architectural purest might find incongruous, but it will fit in well in a road of homes built in the 1920's. The portico over the front door was the owners choice, and there is now a huge variety of these classical style porticos available in modern materials. Alternatively a more restrained porch could be built in brick to match the other brick features.

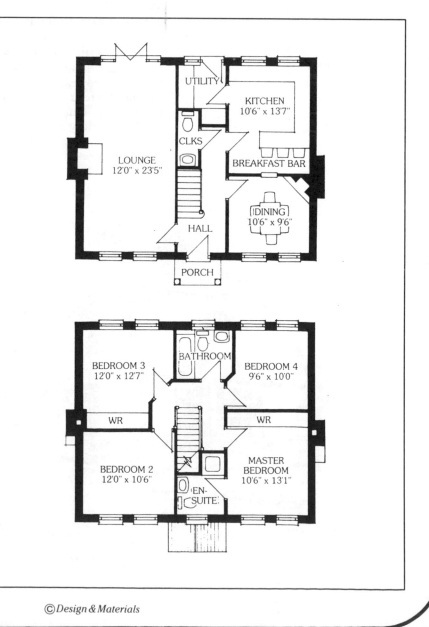

**Ref: 96178**

**110 sq.m.    1197 sq.ft.**

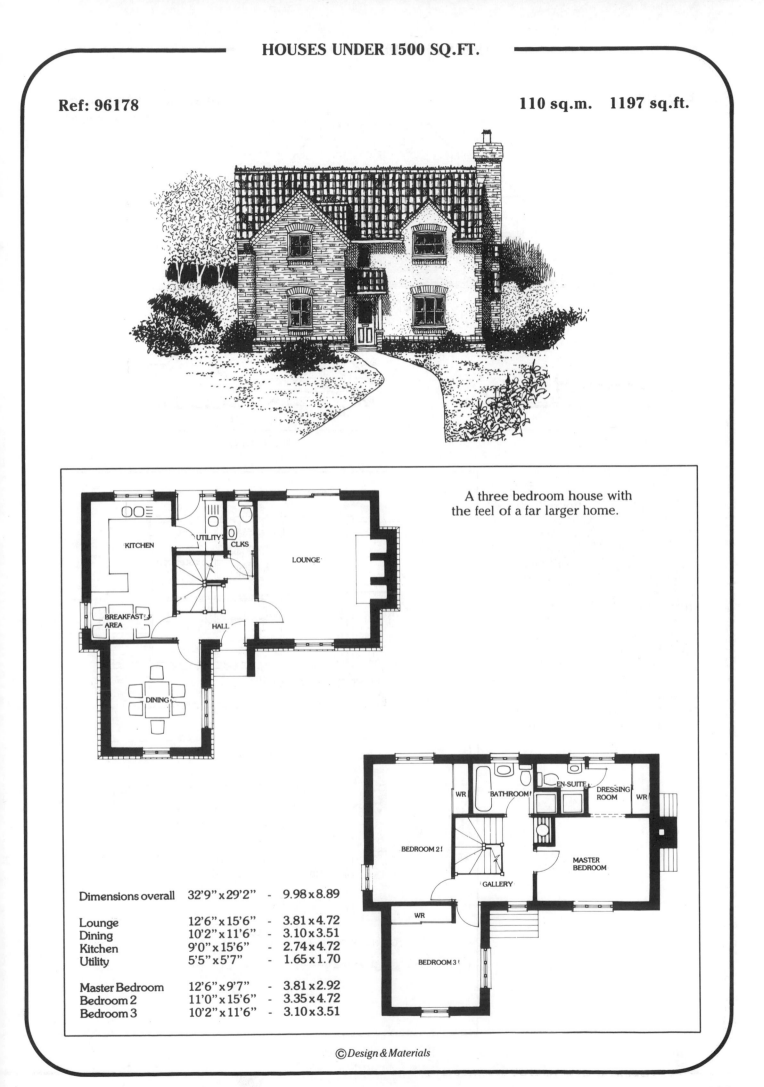

A three bedroom house with
the feel of a far larger home.

| Dimensions overall | 32'9" x 29'2" | - | 9.98 x 8.89 |
|---|---|---|---|
| Lounge | 12'6" x 15'6" | - | 3.81 x 4.72 |
| Dining | 10'2" x 11'6" | - | 3.10 x 3.51 |
| Kitchen | 9'0" x 15'6" | - | 2.74 x 4.72 |
| Utility | 5'5" x 5'7" | - | 1.65 x 1.70 |
| Master Bedroom | 12'6" x 9'7" | - | 3.81 x 2.92 |
| Bedroom 2 | 11'0" x 15'6" | - | 3.35 x 4.72 |
| Bedroom 3 | 10'2" x 11'6" | - | 3.10 x 3.51 |

© *Design & Materials*

**Ref: 96268**

**130 sq.m.   1400 sq.ft.**
**(exc. garage)**

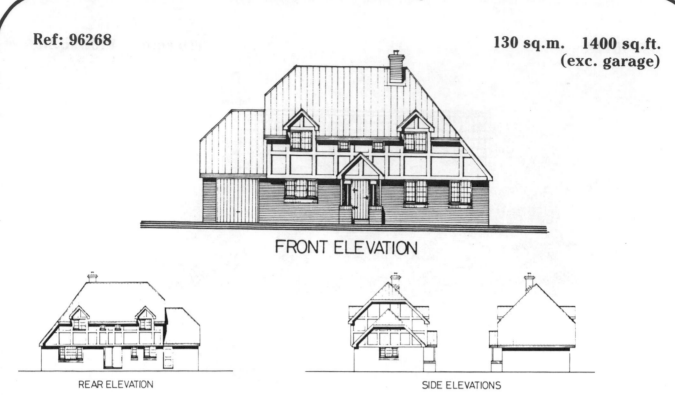

FRONT ELEVATION

REAR ELEVATION

SIDE ELEVATIONS

The depth of this house from front to back has again been kept at under 25 sq ft to conform to the concern of some county design guides that tudor houses should stick to genuine tudor dimensions, at any rate in village street situations.

The layout shown provides for a cloakroom at the back door, which is very popular with those who live in the country. It will be seen that by moving the kitchen to the back of the house this same cloakroom can open into the hall, which is more popular in urban situations.

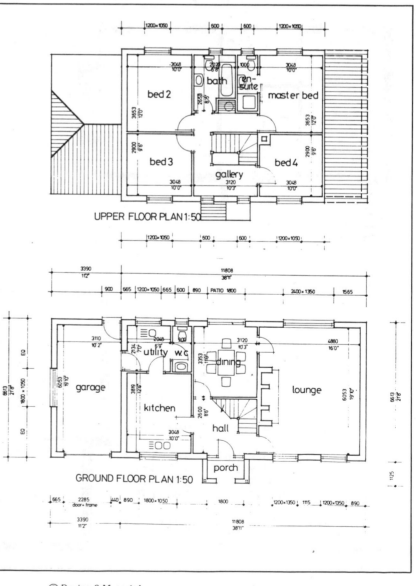

UPPER FLOOR PLAN 1:50

GROUND FLOOR PLAN 1:50

**Ref: 96269**

**121 sq.m.    1300 sq.ft.**
**(exc. garage)**

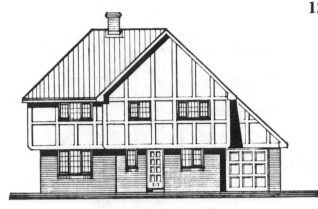

FRONT ELEVATION

The layout of this 1300 sq.ft. house provides good size rooms. Measuring only 22 sq.ft. from front to back, this design is very useful for areas like the Cotswolds where the planners often insist on a modest depth to match existing cottages, but it has all the feel of a larger property.

REAR ELEVATION

SIDE ELEVATION

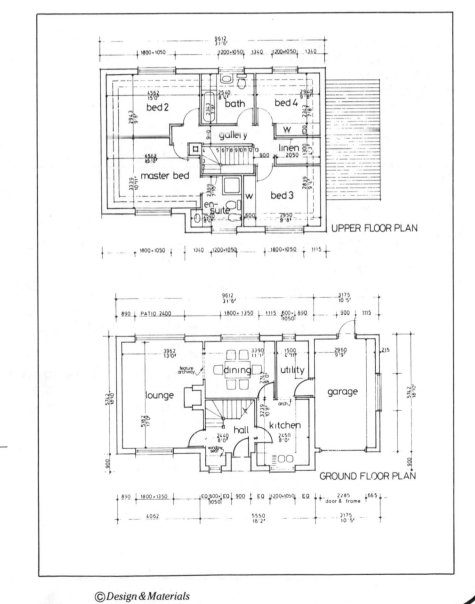

UPPER FLOOR PLAN

GROUND FLOOR PLAN

**Ref: 96270**

**111 sq.m.  1199 sq.ft.**
**(exc. garage)**

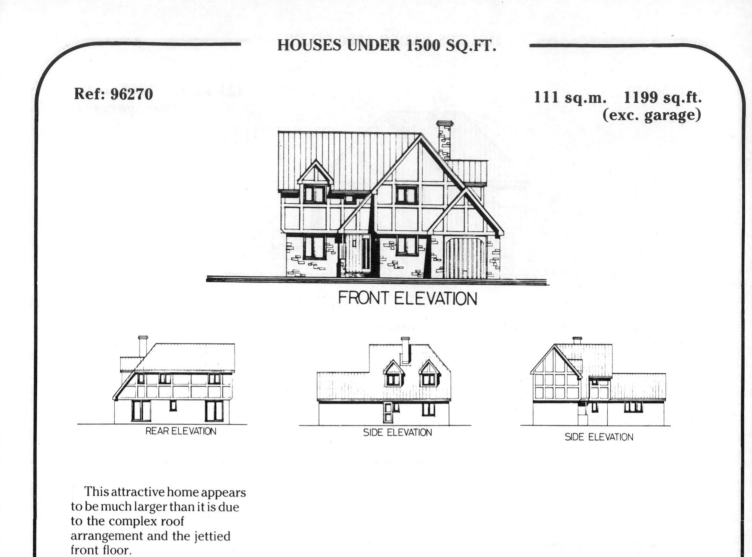

FRONT ELEVATION

REAR ELEVATION

SIDE ELEVATION

SIDE ELEVATION

This attractive home appears to be much larger than it is due to the complex roof arrangement and the jettied front floor.

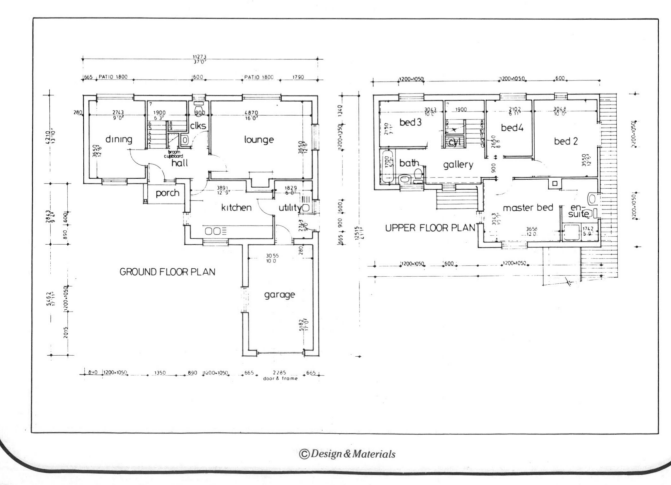

GROUND FLOOR PLAN

UPPER FLOOR PLAN

**Ref: 96267**

**139 sq.m.   1500 sq.ft.**

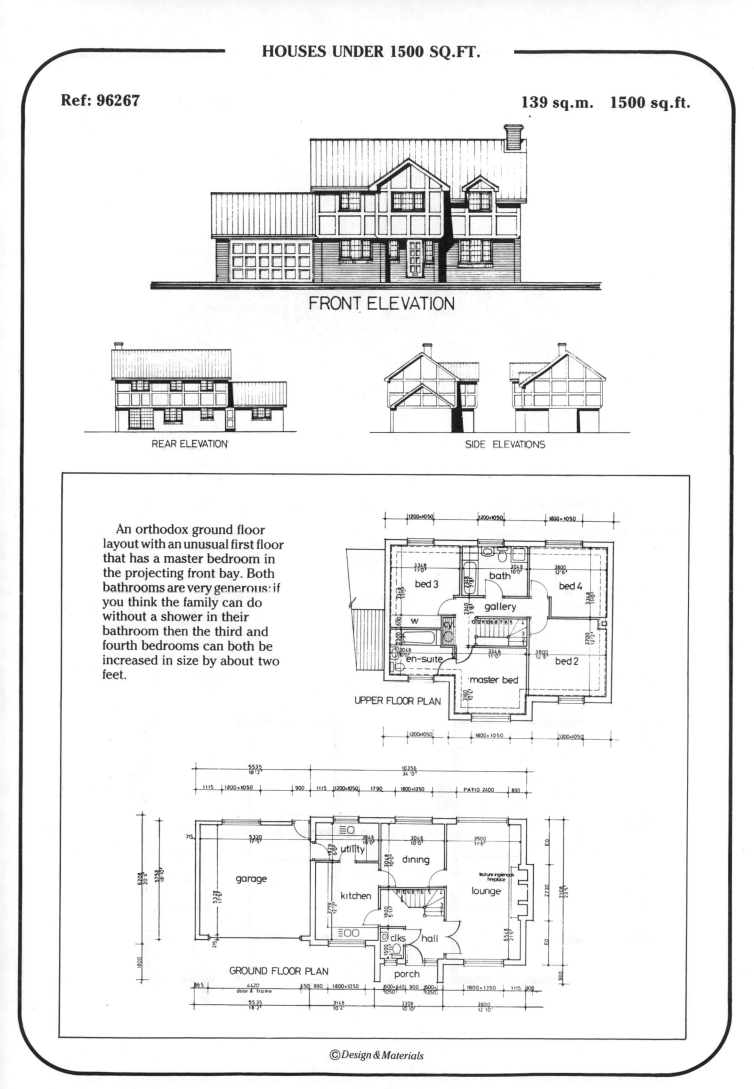

FRONT ELEVATION

REAR ELEVATION

SIDE ELEVATIONS

An orthodox ground floor layout with an unusual first floor that has a master bedroom in the projecting front bay. Both bathrooms are very generous: if you think the family can do without a shower in their bathroom then the third and fourth bedrooms can both be increased in size by about two feet.

UPPER FLOOR PLAN

GROUND FLOOR PLAN

**Ref: 96258**

**128 sq.m.    1380 sq.ft.**

A modest four bedroom home which has some interesting features. The separate utility room with its serving hatch through to the dining area in the lounge is unusual: serving hatches are now out of fashion, although no doubt they will reappear in due course. The cloakroom at the front door is unusually large for a house of this size, and is designed to permit a pram to be stored in it.

| Dimensions overall | 26'0" x 36'1" | - | 7.93 x 11.00 |
|---|---|---|---|
| Lounge | 12'0" x 16'0" | - | 3.66 x 4.88 |
| Dining | 10'0" x 11'0" | - | 3.05 x 3.35 |
| Kitchen | 10'0" x 9'3" | - | 3.05 x 2.82 |
| Utility | 6'0" x 5'3" | - | 1.83 x 1.60 |
| Master Bedroom | 10'0" x 12'0" | - | 3.05 x 3.66 |
| Bedroom 2 | 10'0" x 10'0" | - | 3.05 x 3.05 |
| Bedroom 3 | 12'0" x 8'5" | - | 3.66 x 2.57 |
| Bedroom 4 | 12'0" x 8'0" | - | 3.66 x 2.44 |

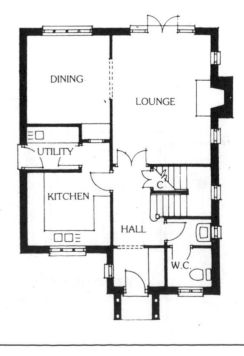

**Ref: 96183**

**106 sq.m.    1142 sq.ft.**

A cottage for a site in Sussex where the outline planning consent stipulated a maximum size of 1200 sq.ft. The owner really wanted a larger home, and this design was drawn in the hope of gaining approval to extend it at a later date. If this is granted, the access to the new wing will be under lintels built into a gable wall in the positions shown.

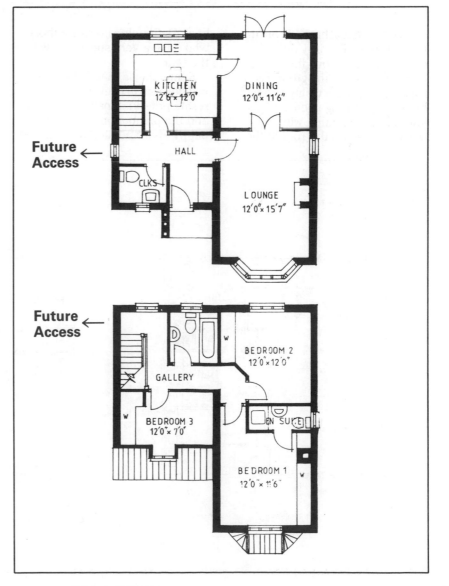

©Design & Materials

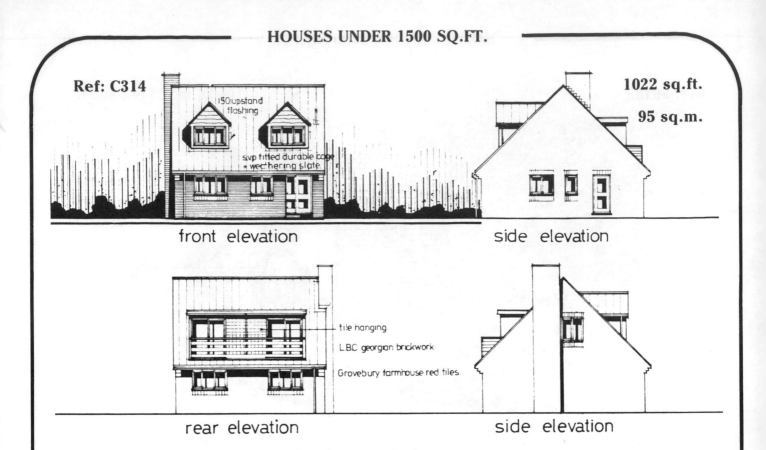

**Ref: C314**

150 upstand flashing

svp fitted durable cope + weathering slate

front elevation

**1022 sq.ft.**

**95 sq.m.**

side elevation

tile hanging

LBC georgian brickwork

Grovebury farmhouse red tiles

rear elevation

side elevation

A very unusual home. From the front it looks like any other dormer cottage, but the bedrooms are on the ground floor together with the utility room. A big lounge/dining room and the kitchen are upstairs, with a balcony set into the roof at the back. Definitely a house for those who have a very special view to the rear.

Remember a house like this will not appeal to everyone, so its resale potential may be limited, and the planners may not be happy about a balcony set in the roof in many areas. Still, a home with special character for a special site, and what fun to live in if you don't mind stairs.

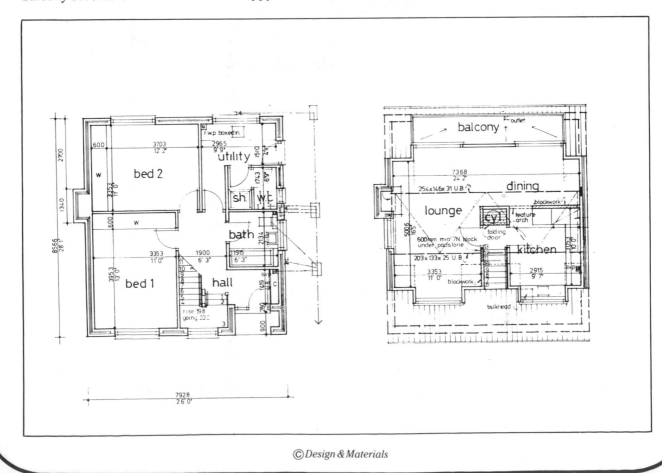

**Ref: PN675**

**119 sq.m.   1285 sq.ft.**

This design is the only two storey house in Potton's Shire range of homes, and is built with walling panels and not the aisle frames with which the company is usually associated. It is available with either a single or double garage, and here the single garage version is shown in the illustration with the larger double garage home illustrated in the plan.

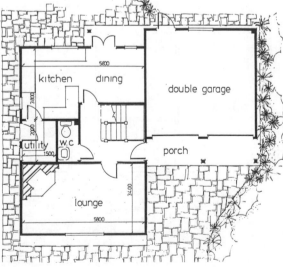

**Ref: W1312**

**124 sq.m.   1334 sq.ft.**

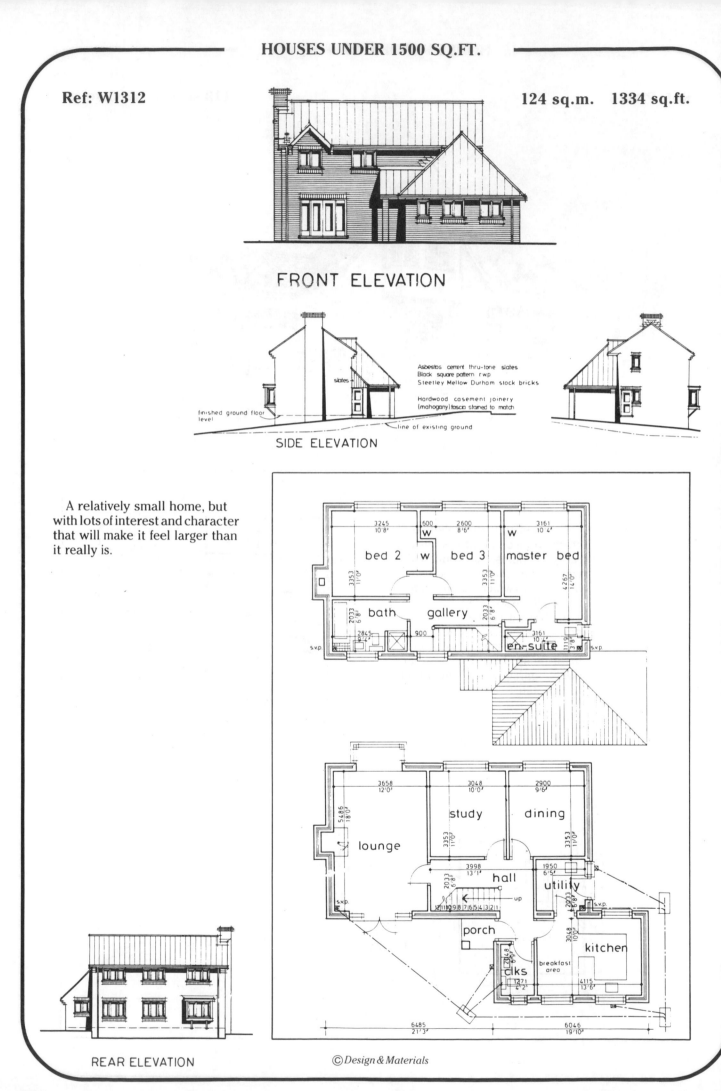

FRONT ELEVATION

SIDE ELEVATION

Asbestos cement thru-tone slates
Black square pattern rwp
Steetley Mellow Durham stock bricks

Hardwood casement joinery
(mahogany) fascia stained to match

A relatively small home, but with lots of interest and character that will make it feel larger than it really is.

REAR ELEVATION

© *Design & Materials*

**Ref: P2735**

**106 sq.m.    1141 sq.ft.**

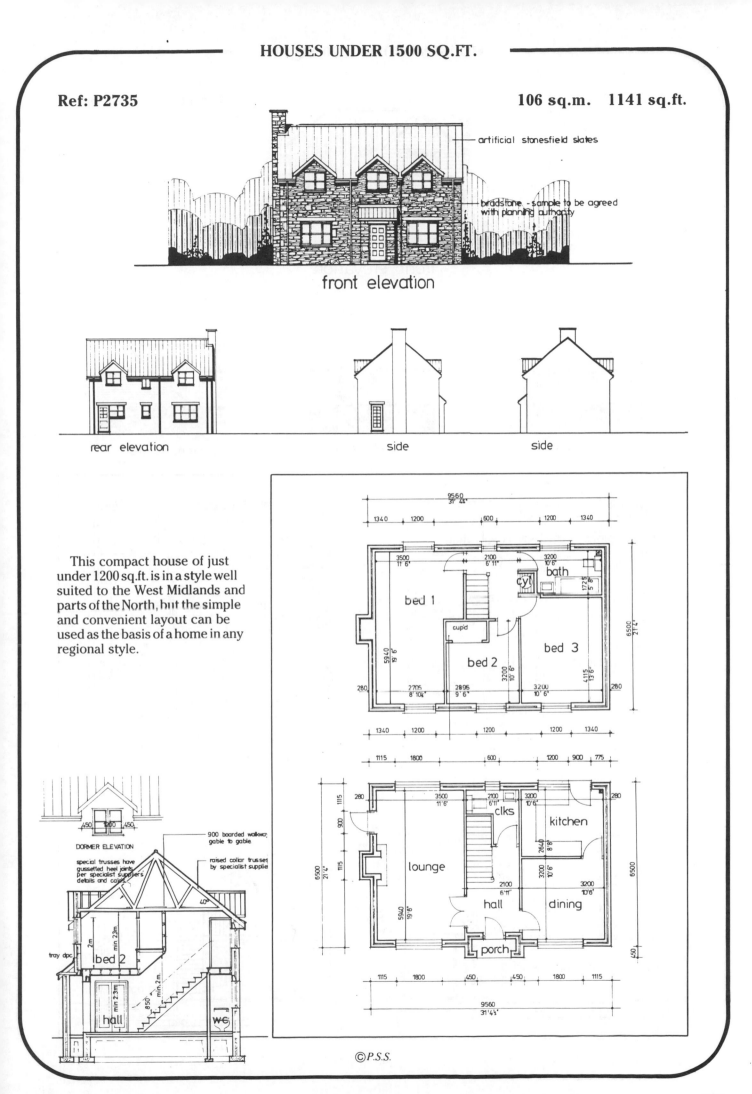

artificial stonesfield slates

bradstone - sample to be agreed with planning authority

front elevation

rear elevation

side

side

This compact house of just under 1200 sq.ft. is in a style well suited to the West Midlands and parts of the North, but the simple and convenient layout can be used as the basis of a home in any regional style.

DORMER ELEVATION

special trusses have gussetted heel joints per specialist suppliers details and calcs

900 boarded walkway gable to gable.

raised collar trusses by specialist supplier

bed 2

hall

WC

tray dpc

9560
31' 4½"

1340   1200   600   1200   1340

3500
11' 6"

2100
6' 11"

3200
10'6"

bath

cyl

bed 1

cup'd

bed 2

bed 3

6500
21' 4"

5940
19' 6"

3200
10' 6"

1725
5' 8"

4115
13' 6"

280

2705
8' 10½"

2895
9' 6"

3200
10' 6"

280

1340   1200   1200   1200   1340

1115   1800   600   1200   900   775

1115

280

3500
11' 6"

2100
6' 11"

3200
10'6"

280

900

clks

kitchen

1115

lounge

2640
8'8"

6500
21' 4"

5940
19' 6"

hall

2100
6' 11"

3200
10' 6"

dining

3200
10'6"

6500

porch

450

1115   1800   450   450   1800   1115

9560
31'4½"

©P.S.S.

**Ref: P2548**

**136 sq.m.   1463 sq.ft.**

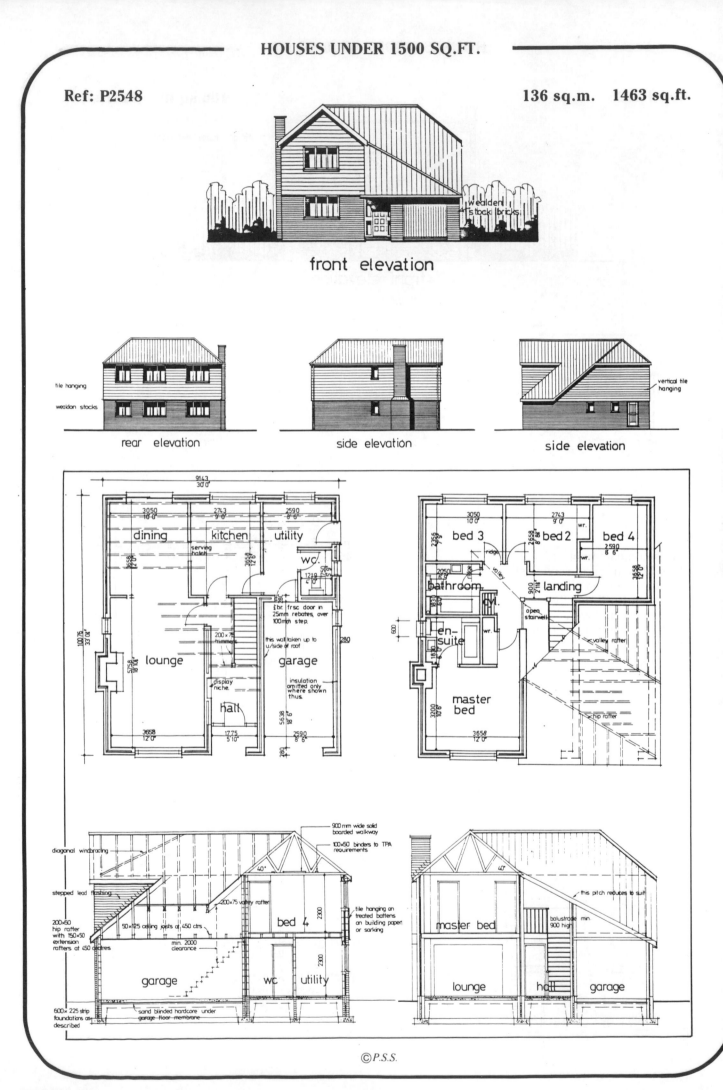

front elevation

rear elevation

side elevation

side elevation

**Ref: 96142**

**133 sq.m.    1438 sq.ft.**

The Swannington house was drawn for a rural site in the North Country, where a property such as this is said to 'stand square' and is not expected to blend into a gentle landscape. Very carefully considered brick features are essential to this style, and here we have the house built on a high plinth, brick arches over the windows, a stringer course at first floor level and elaborate feature brickwork under the tiles.

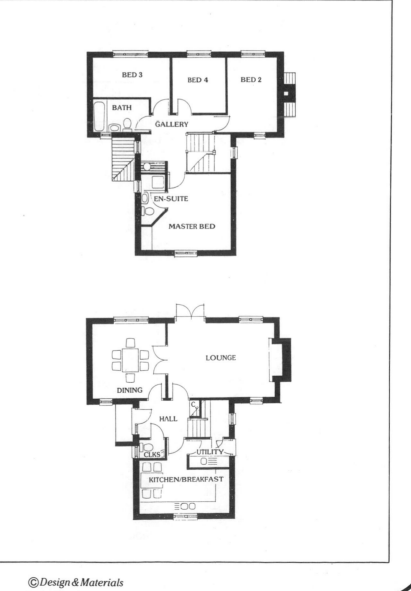

| Floor Area | 1438 sq.ft. | 133 sq.m |
|---|---|---|
| Dimensions overall | 32'8'' x 34'8'' | 9.94 x 10.5€ |
| Lounge | 18'0'' x 13'0'' | 5.48 x 3.96 |
| Dining | 12'6'' x 13'0'' | 3.81 x 3.96 |
| Kitchen/Breakfast | 15'0'' x 7'9'' | 4.57 x 2.35 |
| Master Bed | 15'0'' x 13'0'' | 4.57 x 3.95 |
| Bed 2 | 8'4'' x 13'0'' | 2.54 x 3.96 |
| Bed 3 | 13'0'' x 7'1'' | 3.96 x 2.16 |
| Bed 4 | 8'10'' x 9'9'' | 2.69 x 2.96 |

**Ref: W1283**

**134 sq.m.    1442 sq.ft.**

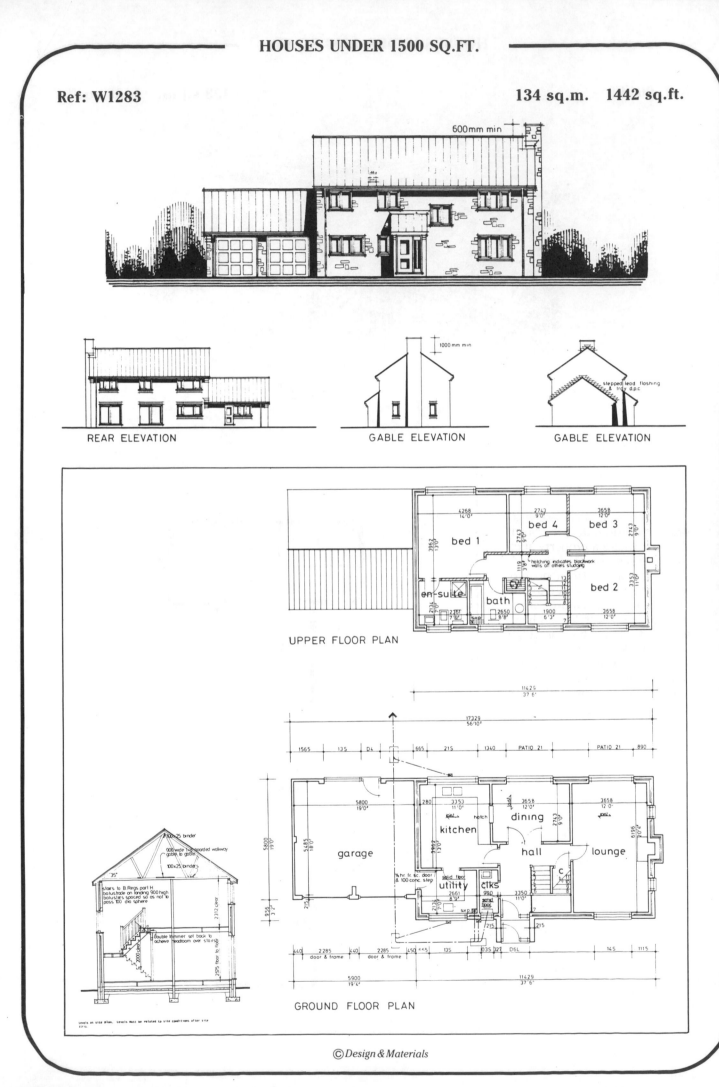

REAR ELEVATION

GABLE ELEVATION

GABLE ELEVATION

UPPER FLOOR PLAN

bed 1

bed 4

bed 3

bed 2

en-suite

bath

GROUND FLOOR PLAN

garage

kitchen

dining

hall

lounge

utility

ctks

© *Design & Materials*

**Ref: P2730**

**139 sq.m. 1496 sq.ft.**

— Redland Regent Mk II tiles or similar; colour to be agreed

— retaining wall

original ground level

rear elevation  gable elevation  side elevation

stepped flashing + tray dpc at roof abutment

Half timbering comes in many styles, and it is important to make sure that the style adopted for a new home is in what is called the "local architectural idiom". The half timbering shewn in the drawing would not suit every situation, but can be adapted if required. The local planners will readily advise on the characteristics of the traditional style, and this is easily arranged.

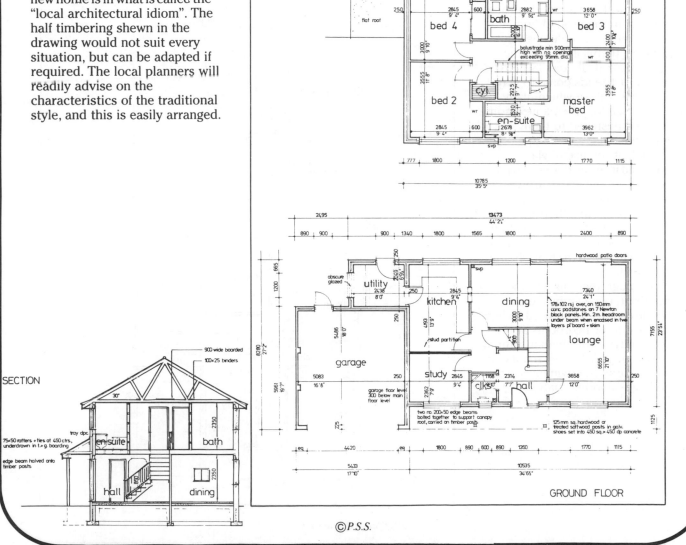

SECTION

GROUND FLOOR

© P.S.S.

**Ref: C351**

131 sq.m.   1410 sq.ft.
(exc. garage)

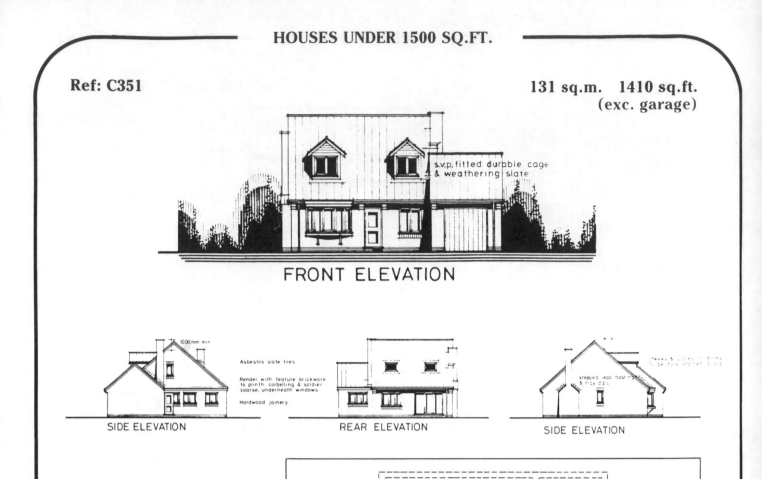

FRONT ELEVATION

SIDE ELEVATION

Asbestos slate tiles

Render with feature brickwork
to plinth, corbelling & soldier
coarse, underneath windows

Hardwood joinery

REAR ELEVATION

SIDE ELEVATION

A dormer bungalow with a number of interesting features. To start with the master bedroom suite is on the ground floor, so that a retired couple need not concern themselves with the upper floor at all except when the family or friends come to stay. This is a feature which many clients ask for when a new home is being designed to their requirements.

Look at the use of glass panelled internal doors, two pairs of them double doors, to give the feel of a much larger property, and to ensure that there is plenty of light in the hall. The landing will also be light and airy thanks to the window at the half landing on the stairs.

Although there are dormers to the front, two sloping velux windows have been used to light the first floor bedrooms at the rear, and this will give substantial cost savings. Whether or not you like these sloping windows in the ceiling is another matter.

**Ref: C412**

**85 sq.m.    914 sq.ft.**
**(exc. garage)**

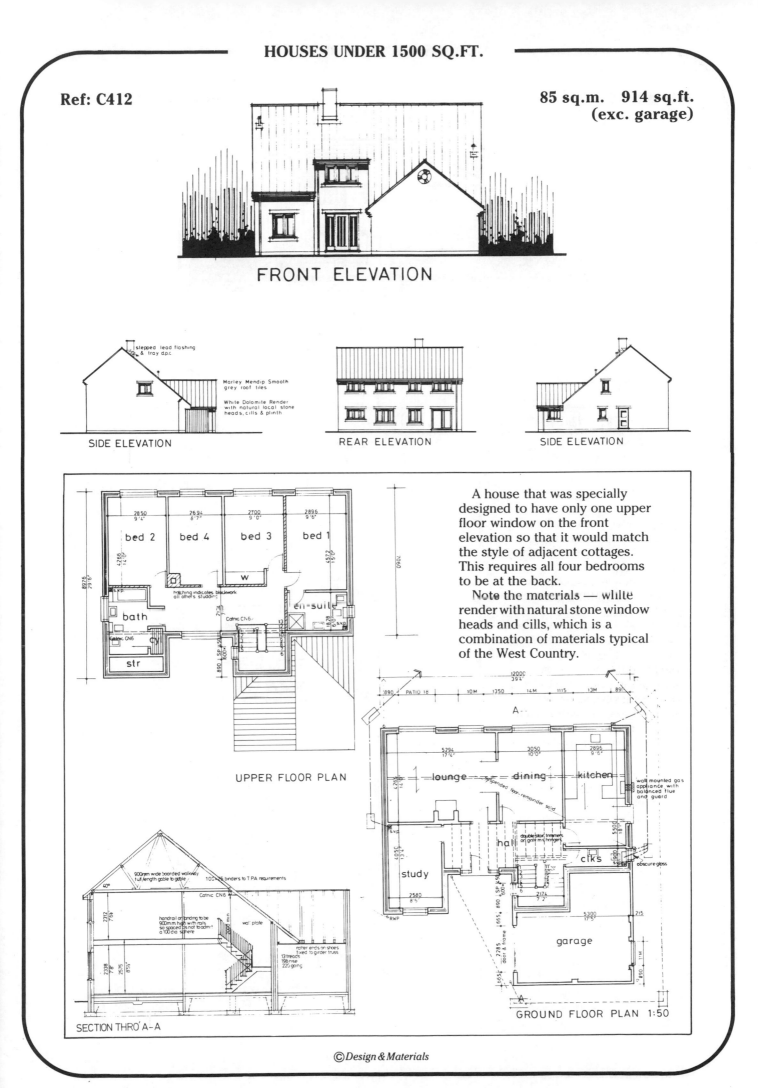

FRONT ELEVATION

stepped lead flashing
& tray d.p.c.

Marley Mendip Smooth
grey roof tiles

White Dolomite Render
with natural local stone
heads, cills & plinth

SIDE ELEVATION

REAR ELEVATION

SIDE ELEVATION

A house that was specially
designed to have only one upper
floor window on the front
elevation so that it would match
the style of adjacent cottages.
This requires all four bedrooms
to be at the back.

Note the materials — white
render with natural stone window
heads and cills, which is a
combination of materials typical
of the West Country.

UPPER FLOOR PLAN

bed 2    bed 4    bed 3    bed 1

bath

str

en-suite

w

GROUND FLOOR PLAN 1:50

lounge    dining    kitchen

study

hall

clks

garage

SECTION THRO' A-A

**Ref: W1150**

**128 sq.m.  1377 sq.ft.**

FRONT ELEVATION

REAR ELEVATION

Marley Bold Rolled
Old English dark red

L.B.C. Regency brickwork to
groundfloor with painted common
brickwork to upper floor

Softwood casement joinery
dark stained

SIDE ELEVATIONS

s.v.p. fitted durable cage
& weathering slate

stepped lead flashing
& tray d.p.c

brick on edge

floor level

A compact home with the crisp feel that comes from the combination of brick, render and a gable roof.

The drainage arrangements have been left on the plans, as there is a special combined system with both rainwater and foul drainage taken into the same main drain. The usual arrangement is for rainwater — called surface water — to be taken to soakaways or into a completely separate drain. The local authority advises on what is required in any particular area.

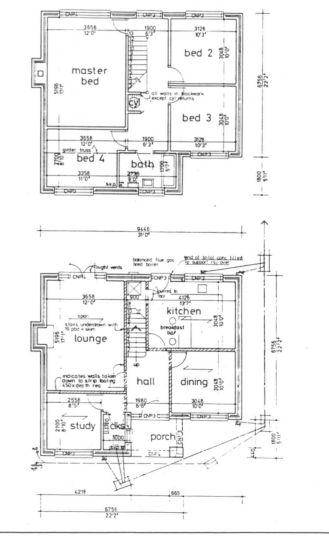

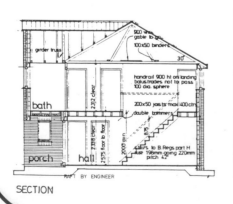

SECTION

**Ref: W1287**

**134 sq.m.   1442 sq.ft.**

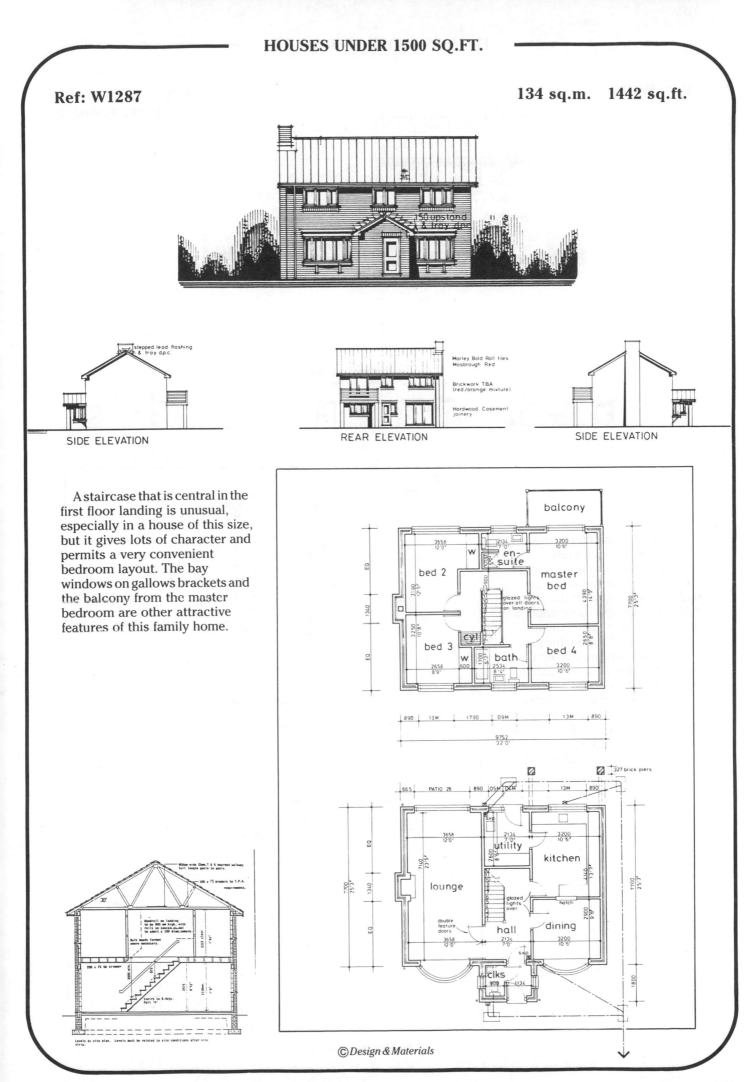

SIDE ELEVATION

stepped lead flashing
& tray d.p.c.

REAR ELEVATION

Marley Bold Roll tiles
Mosbrough Red

Brickwork T.B.A.
(red/orange mixture)

Hardwood Casement
joinery

SIDE ELEVATION

A staircase that is central in the first floor landing is unusual, especially in a house of this size, but it gives lots of character and permits a very convenient bedroom layout. The bay windows on gallows brackets and the balcony from the master bedroom are other attractive features of this family home.

balcony

bed 2

w

en-suite

master bed

glazed lights over all doors on landing

bed 3

cyl

w

bath

bed 4

lounge

utility

kitchen

hall

dining

clks

**Ref: W1061**

**110 sq.m.   1184 sq.ft.
(exc. garage)**

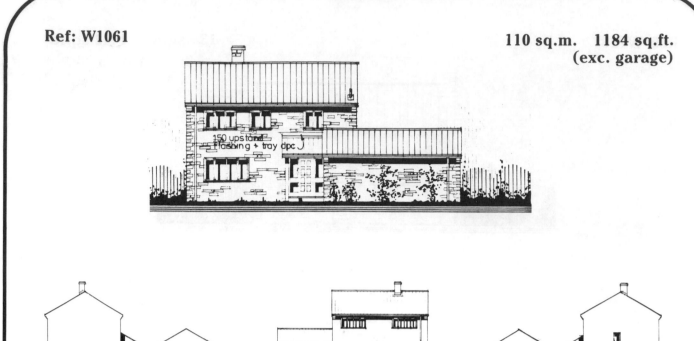

This plan is an interesting example of a design prepared to meet a situation where a garage and a close boarded large gate had to be allowed for in the total scheme of things. The garage door, which is a non-standard width of twelve feet, and the gate were certain to be very prominent features, and so were specified to be diagonally boarded as shewn. They were stained to be a perfect match with the stained windows and doors of the new house, and definitely added to the appearance of the buildings in a very satisfactory way.

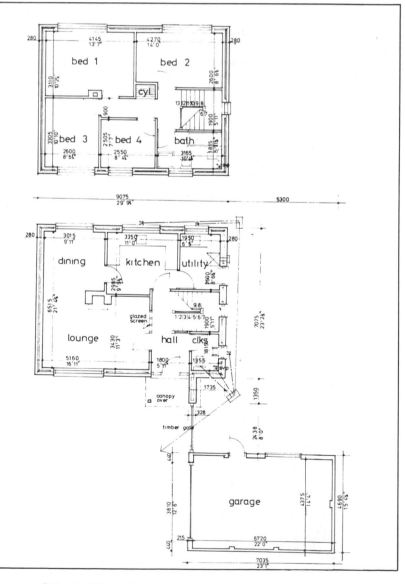

© *Design & Materials*

**Ref: P2621**

**1194 sq.ft.
(exc. garage)
111 sq.m.**

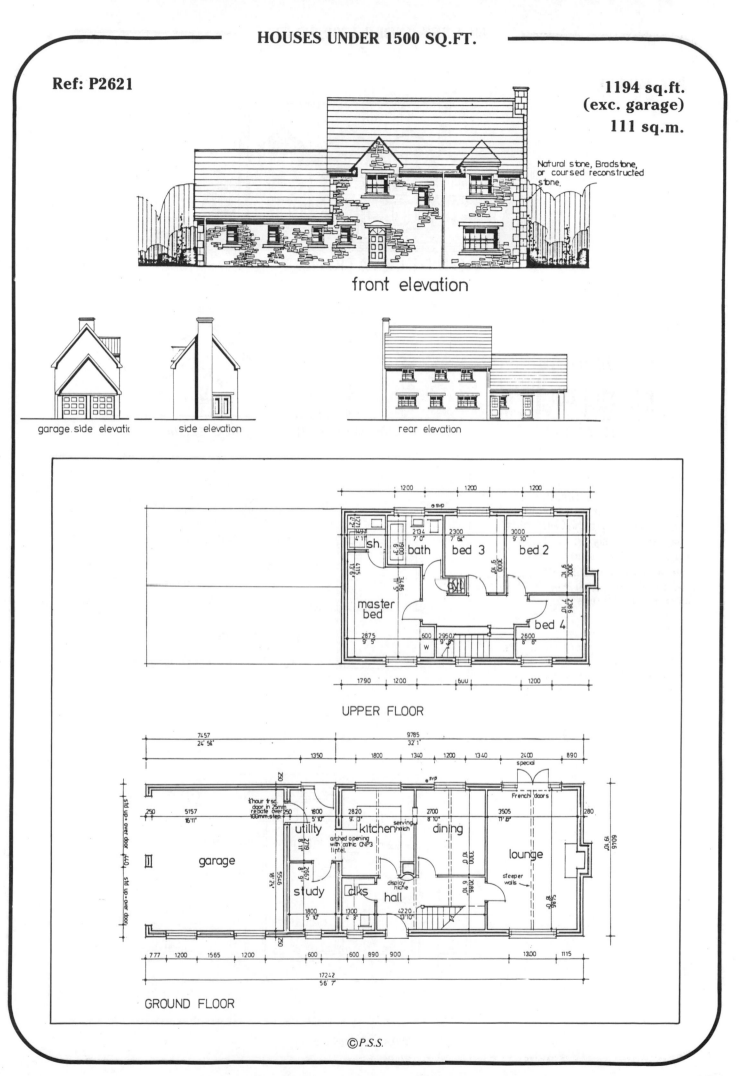

Natural stone, Bradstone, or coursed reconstructed stone.

front elevation

garage side elevation

side elevation

rear elevation

UPPER FLOOR

sh.

bath

bed 3

bed 2

master bed

bed 4

W

GROUND FLOOR

garage

utility

kitchen

dining

study

clks

hall

lounge

French doors

serving hatch

arched opening with gothic GNP3 lintel.

display niche

sleeper walls

**Ref: W1349**

**124 sq.m.   1334 sq.ft.**

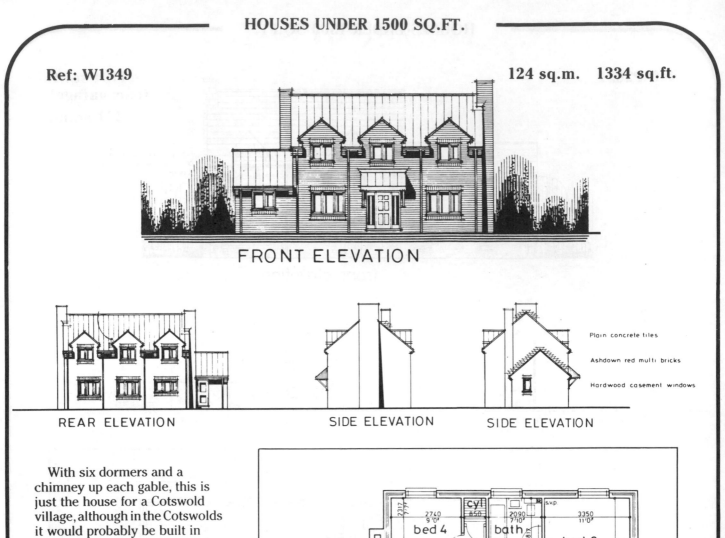

FRONT ELEVATION

REAR ELEVATION          SIDE ELEVATION          SIDE ELEVATION

Plain concrete tiles

Ashdown red multi bricks

Hardwood casement windows

With six dormers and a chimney up each gable, this is just the house for a Cotswold village, although in the Cotswolds it would probably be built in stone. The style is now very fashionable on "village street" plots, and looks well with leaded lights to the windows.

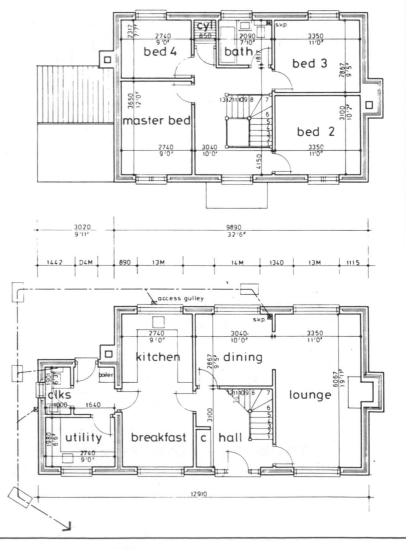

**Ref: P2590**

114 sq.m.   1227 sq.ft.

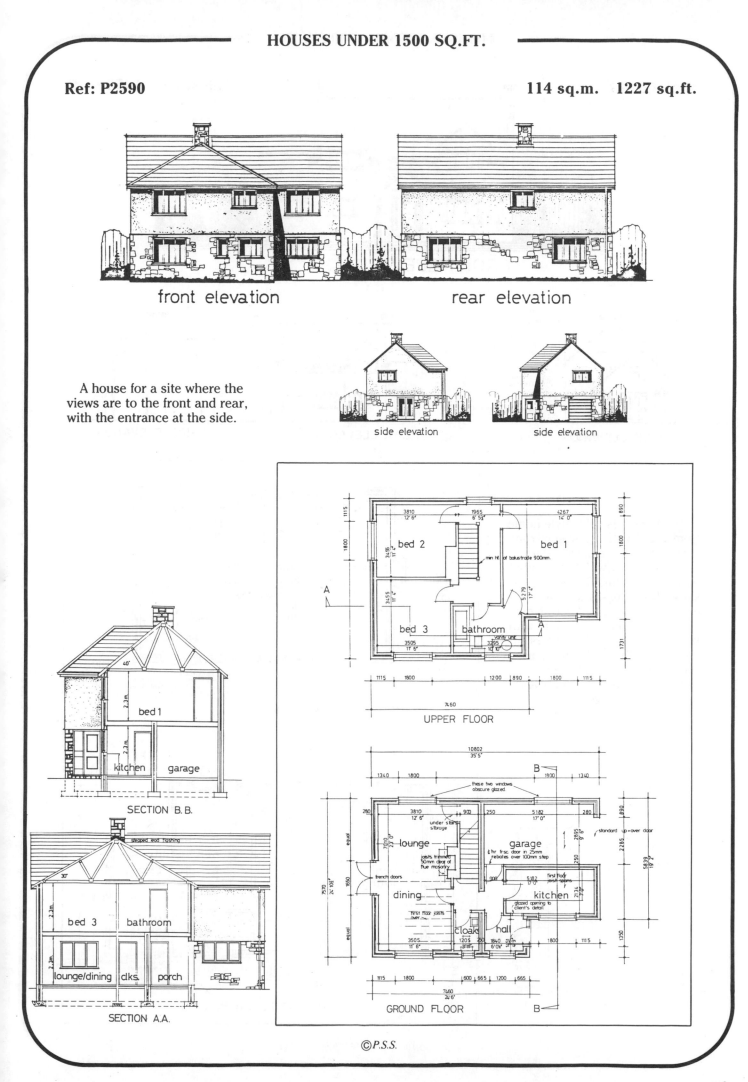

front elevation

rear elevation

A house for a site where the views are to the front and rear, with the entrance at the side.

side elevation

side elevation

SECTION B.B.

bed 1

kitchen   garage

SECTION A.A.

bed 3   bathroom

lounge/dining   dks.   porch

UPPER FLOOR

bed 2   bed 1

bed 3   bathroom

GROUND FLOOR

lounge   garage

dining   kitchen

cloaks   hall

©P.S.S.

**Ref: C414**

**135 sq.m.   1453 sq.ft.**

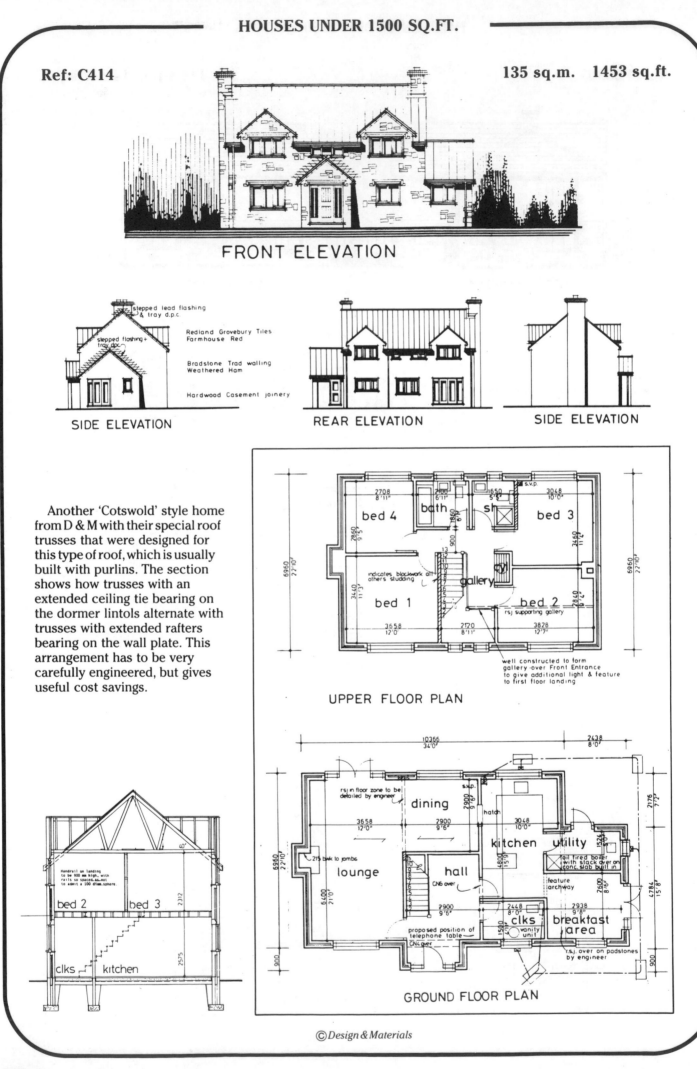

FRONT ELEVATION

stepped lead flashing & tray d.p.c.

stepped flashing + tray dpc

Redland Grovebury Tiles Farmhouse Red

Bradstone Trad walling Weathered Ham

Hardwood Casement joinery

SIDE ELEVATION

REAR ELEVATION

SIDE ELEVATION

Another 'Cotswold' style home from D & M with their special roof trusses that were designed for this type of roof, which is usually built with purlins. The section shows how trusses with an extended ceiling tie bearing on the dormer lintols alternate with trusses with extended rafters bearing on the wall plate. This arrangement has to be very carefully engineered, but gives useful cost savings.

UPPER FLOOR PLAN

bed 4

bath

sh

bed 3

bed 1

gallery

bed 2

indicates blockwork all others studding

rsj supporting gallery

well constructed to form gallery over Front Entrance to give additional light & feature to first floor landing

GROUND FLOOR PLAN

dining

kitchen

utility

lounge

hall

breakfast area

clks

rsj in floor zone to be detailed by engineer

215 bwk to jambs

hatch

oil fired boiler with stack over on donc. slab built in

feature archway

vanity unit

proposed position of telephone table

r.s.j. over on padstones by engineer

Handrail on landing to be 900 mm high, with rails so spaced as not to admit a 100 diam. sphere.

bed 2

bed 3

clks

kitchen

© Design & Materials

**Ref: 96271**

**102 sq.m.    1100 sq.ft.**
**(exc. garage)**

## FRONT ELEVATION

SIDE ELEVATION                REAR ELEVATION

Those building a house under 1200 square feet usually want it to look as large as possible, and this four bedroomed home achieves this with its complex roof and neo-tudor 'jetting' or projecting wall to the front floor. The garage has a useful storage or workshop bay, and in every way this home is a quart in a pint pot.

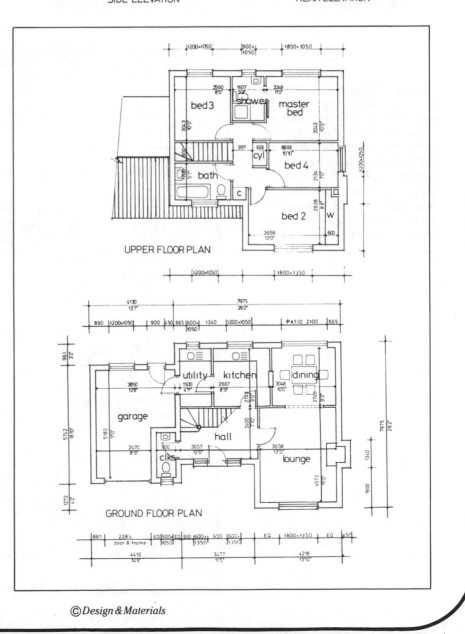

UPPER FLOOR PLAN

GROUND FLOOR PLAN

**Ref: S504**                    **130 sq.m.    1399 sq.ft.**

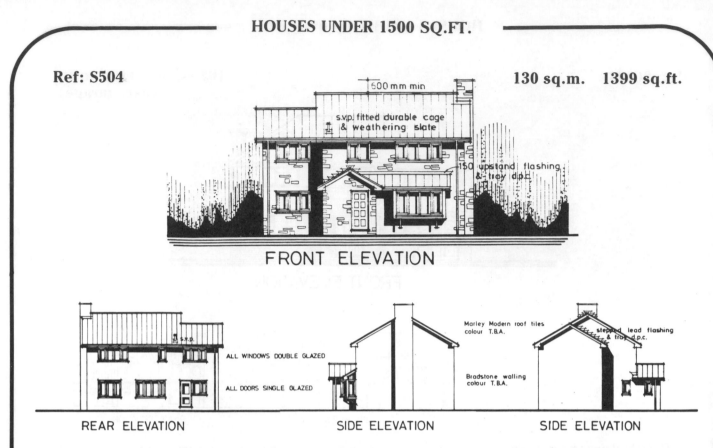

FRONT ELEVATION

REAR ELEVATION                    SIDE ELEVATION                    SIDE ELEVATION

ALL WINDOWS DOUBLE GLAZED

ALL DOORS SINGLE GLAZED

Marley Modern roof tiles colour T.B.A.

Bradstone walling colour T.B.A.

stepped lead flashing & tray d.p.c.

A really big dining kitchen is the key feature of this three bedroom home, together with a large L shaped lounge. The note of the materials reads "colour TBA". This is architects' shorthand for "to be agreed", and suggests that there was an argument about this with the planners, and that consent was granted subject to this matter being resolved before the walls were built up!

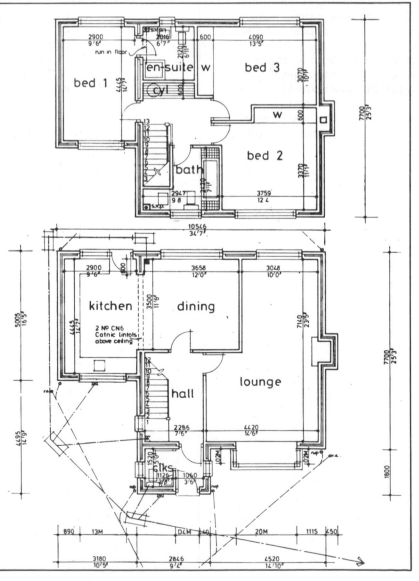

**Ref: P2617**

**124 sq.m.   1334 sq.ft.**

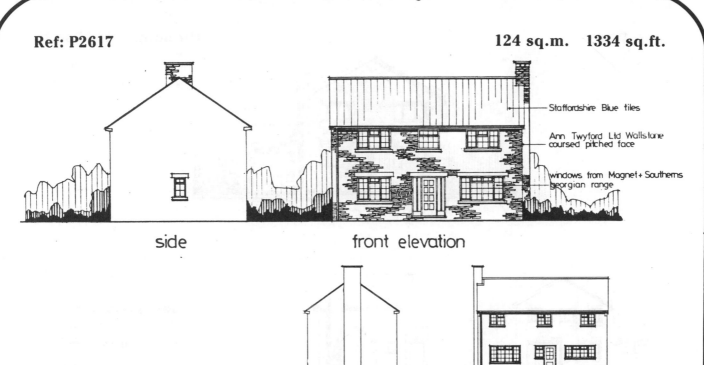

side

front elevation

- Staffordshire Blue tiles
- Ann Twyford Ltd Wallstone coursed pitched face
- windows from Magnet + Southerns Georgian range

side

rear elevation

A large three bedroom home that could be built with four bedrooms if required. The large area of landing outside the door to the master bedroom is quite large enough for a desk and chair, and can be used as a study for childrens homework or anything else.

The materials specification is for artificial stone walls under Staffordshire blue tiles, all chosen to suit the surroundings.

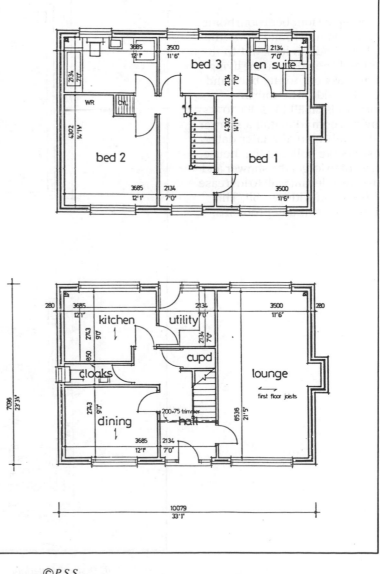

**Ref: W1031**

**107 sq.m.  1173 sq.ft.**

FRONT ELEVATION

REAR ELEVATION

SIDE ELEVATIONS

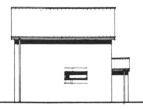

A compact four bedroom home for a site with all round views: the kitchen windows look out to the front and one side, and the living room looks out to the back and the other side. The fourth bedroom is small in order to provide room to install a shower in the bathroom at a later date: most people building this house will want to forget the shower and move the relevant wall to increase the bedroom width to 8ft. This will not present any problems.

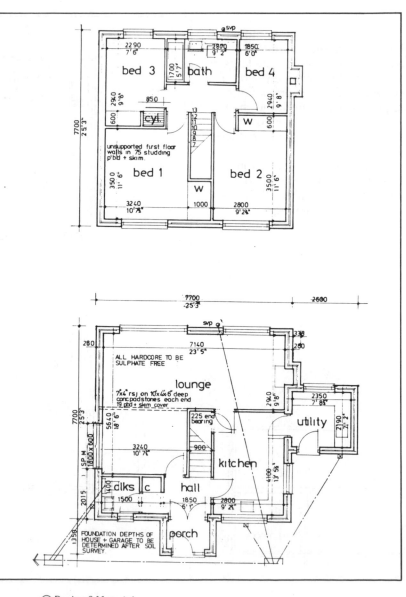

**Ref: C361**

**127 sq.m.    1374 sq.ft.**

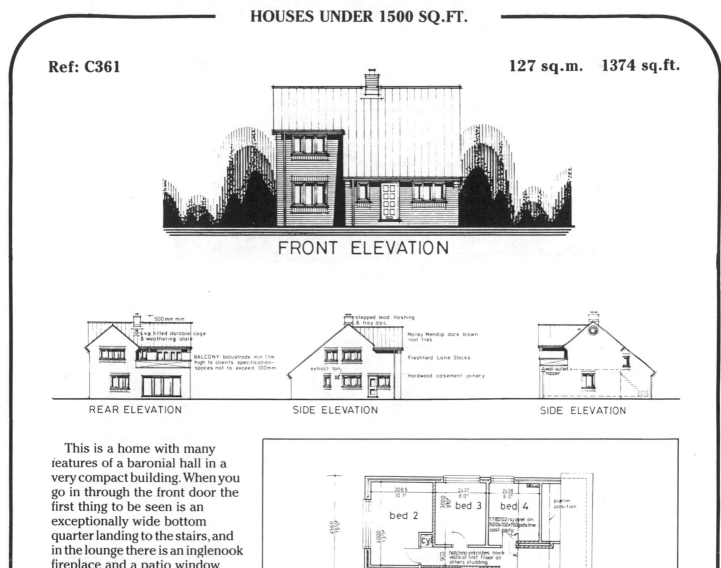

FRONT ELEVATION

REAR ELEVATION          SIDE ELEVATION          SIDE ELEVATION

This is a home with many features of a baronial hall in a very compact building. When you go in through the front door the first thing to be seen is an exceptionally wide bottom quarter landing to the stairs, and in the lounge there is an inglenook fireplace and a patio window nearly twelve feet wide. French windows to the master bedroom lead onto a balcony. You will see that no details are shewn of the balcony railings, except for a note that they will conform to the Building Regulations. If you can get Planning Consent for a 'blank cheque' specification like this it is very useful, as a decision on the balustrade can be postponed until you are actually standing on the balcony and can make up your mind what you want when you have got the feel of it all.

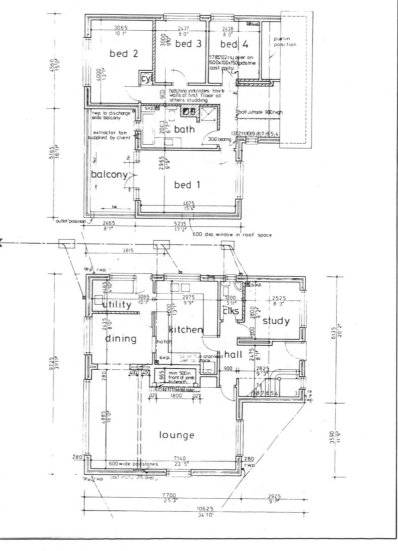

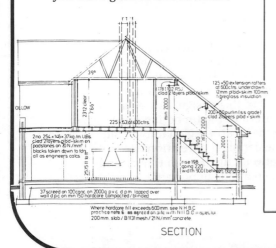

SECTION

© *Design & Materials*

**Ref: C508**

**130 sq.m.    1399 sq.ft.**

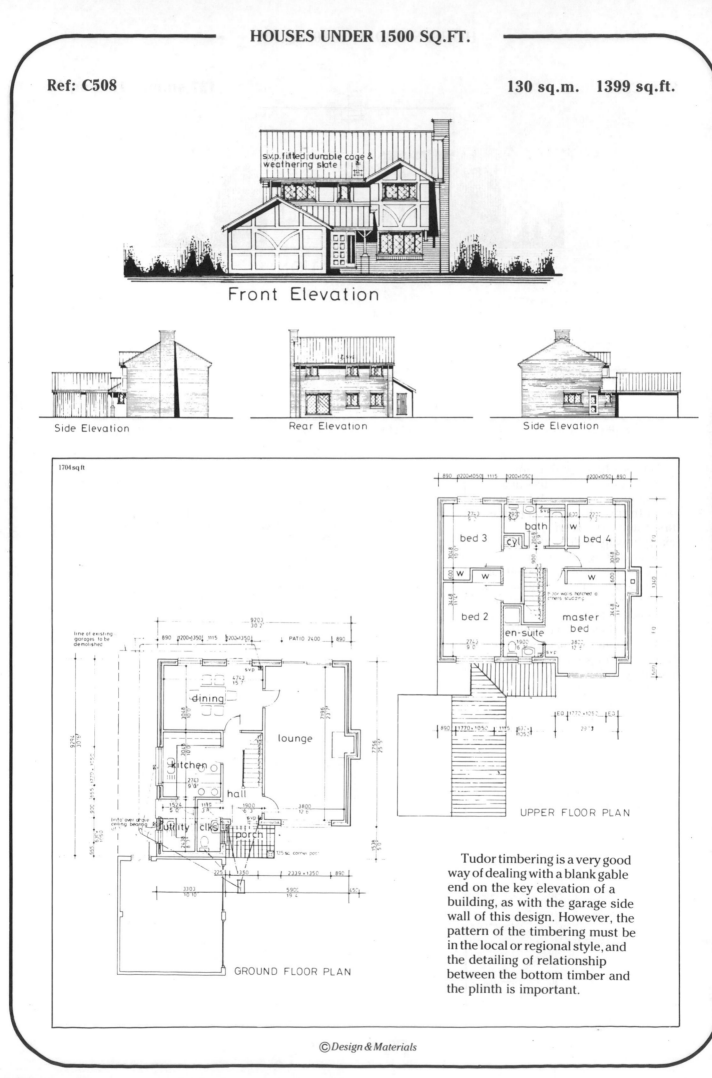

s.v.p. fitted durable cage & weathering slate

Front Elevation

Side Elevation

Rear Elevation

Side Elevation

1704 sq ft

line of existing garages to be demolished

dining

kitchen

hall

utility    clks    porch

lintol over above ceiling bearing

125 sq corner post

GROUND FLOOR PLAN

lounge

PATIO 2400

svp

bed 3    bath    w    bed 4

cyl

w    w    w

bed 2    master bed

en-suite

svp

UPPER FLOOR PLAN

Tudor timbering is a very good way of dealing with a blank gable end on the key elevation of a building, as with the garage side wall of this design. However, the pattern of the timbering must be in the local or regional style, and the detailing of relationship between the bottom timber and the plinth is important.

© Design & Materials

**Ref: W1208**

**125 sq.m.  1345 sq.ft.**

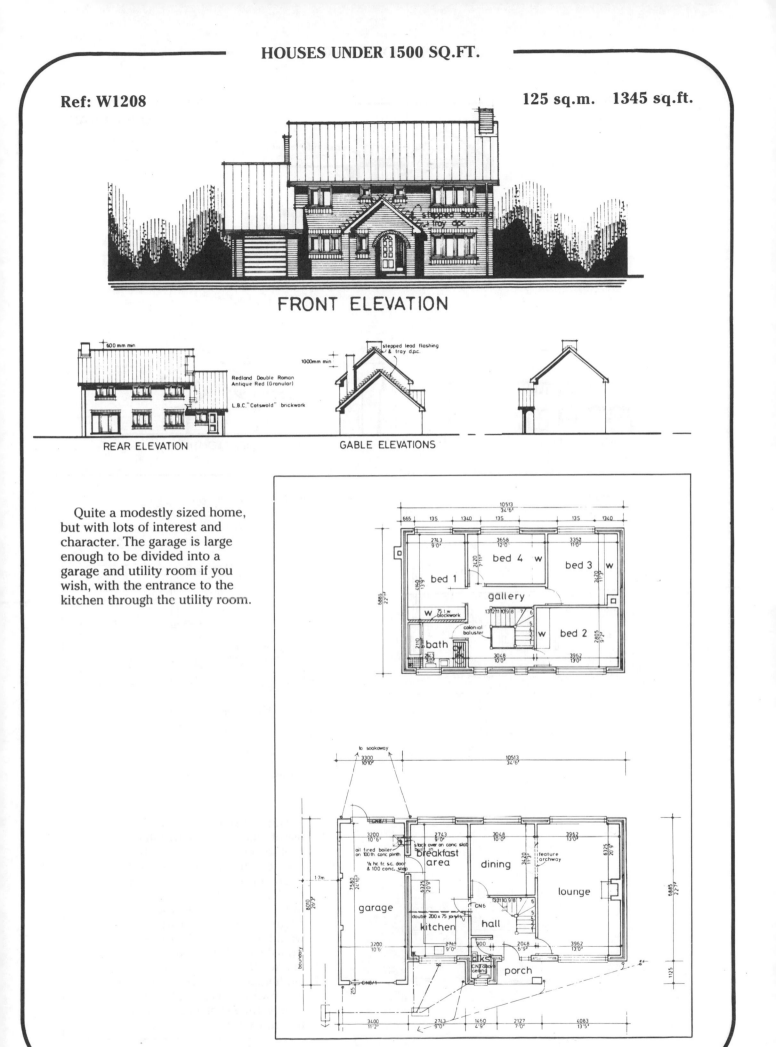

FRONT ELEVATION

600 mm min

Redland Double Roman
Antique Red (Granular)

L.B.C. "Cotswold" brickwork

1000mm min

stepped lead flashing
& tray d.p.c.

REAR ELEVATION

GABLE ELEVATIONS

Quite a modestly sized home, but with lots of interest and character. The garage is large enough to be divided into a garage and utility room if you wish, with the entrance to the kitchen through the utility room.

**Ref: P2808**

**136 sq.m. 1463 sq.ft.**
**(inc. garage)**

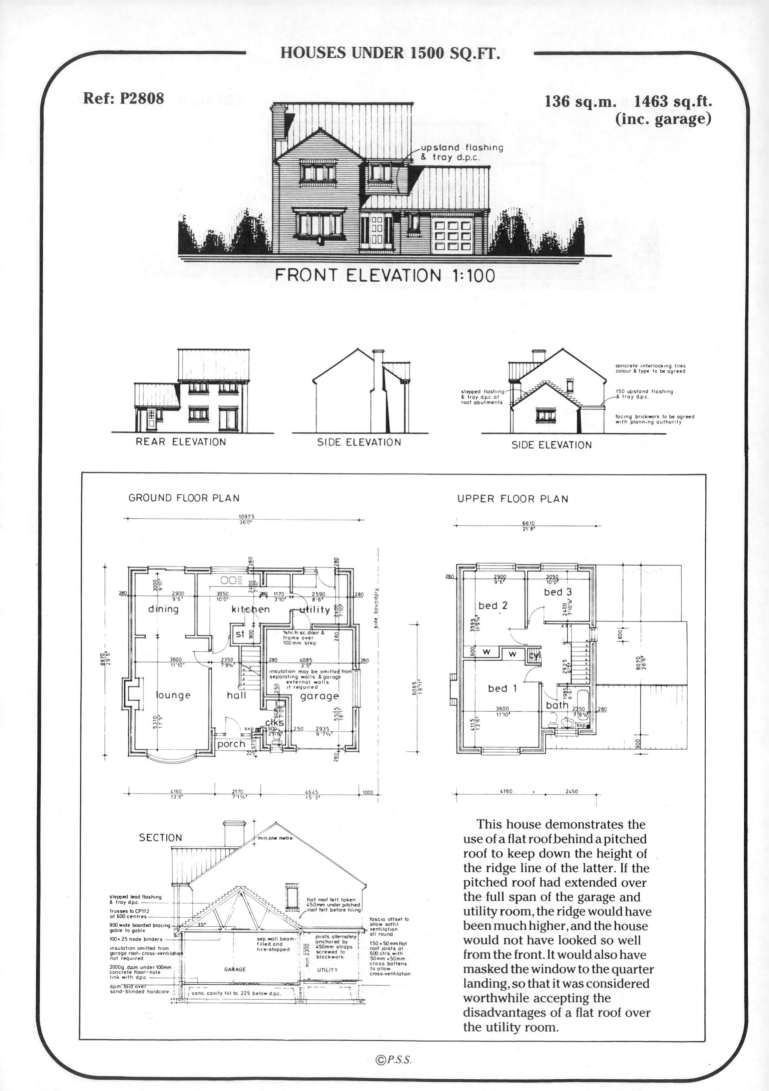

upstand flashing
& tray d.p.c.

## FRONT ELEVATION 1:100

REAR ELEVATION

SIDE ELEVATION

SIDE ELEVATION

concrete interlocking tiles
colour & type to be agreed

stepped flashing
& tray d.p.c. at
roof abutments

150 upstand flashing
& tray d.p.c.

facing brickwork to be agreed
with planning authority

### GROUND FLOOR PLAN

dining
kitchen
utility
st
lounge
hall
garage
cl'ks
porch

½ hr. fr. sc. door &
frame over
100 mm step

insulation may be omitted from
separating walls & garage
external walls
if required

### UPPER FLOOR PLAN

bed 2
bed 3
w   w   cy
bed 1
bath

### SECTION

min. one metre

stepped lead flashing
& tray d.p.c.

trusses to CP112
at 600 centres

900 wide boarded bracing
gable to gable

100 × 25 node binders

insulation omitted from
garage roof—cross-ventilation
not required

2000g d.p.m. under 100mm
concrete floor—note
link with d.p.c.

d.p.m. laid over
sand-blinded hardcore

GARAGE

sep. wall beam-
filled and
fire-stopped

joists alternately
anchored by
450mm straps
screwed to
blockwork

flat roof felt taken
450mm under pitched
roof felt before tiling

fascia offset to
allow soffit
ventilation
all round

150 × 50mm flat
roof joists at
600 ctrs. with
50mm × 50mm
cross battens
to allow
cross-ventilation

UTILITY

conc. cavity fill to 225 below d.p.c.

This house demonstrates the use of a flat roof behind a pitched roof to keep down the height of the ridge line of the latter. If the pitched roof had extended over the full span of the garage and utility room, the ridge would have been much higher, and the house would not have looked so well from the front. It would also have masked the window to the quarter landing, so that it was considered worthwhile accepting the disadvantages of a flat roof over the utility room.

**Ref: S509**

**114 sq.m.   1227 sq.ft.**

FRONT ELEVATION

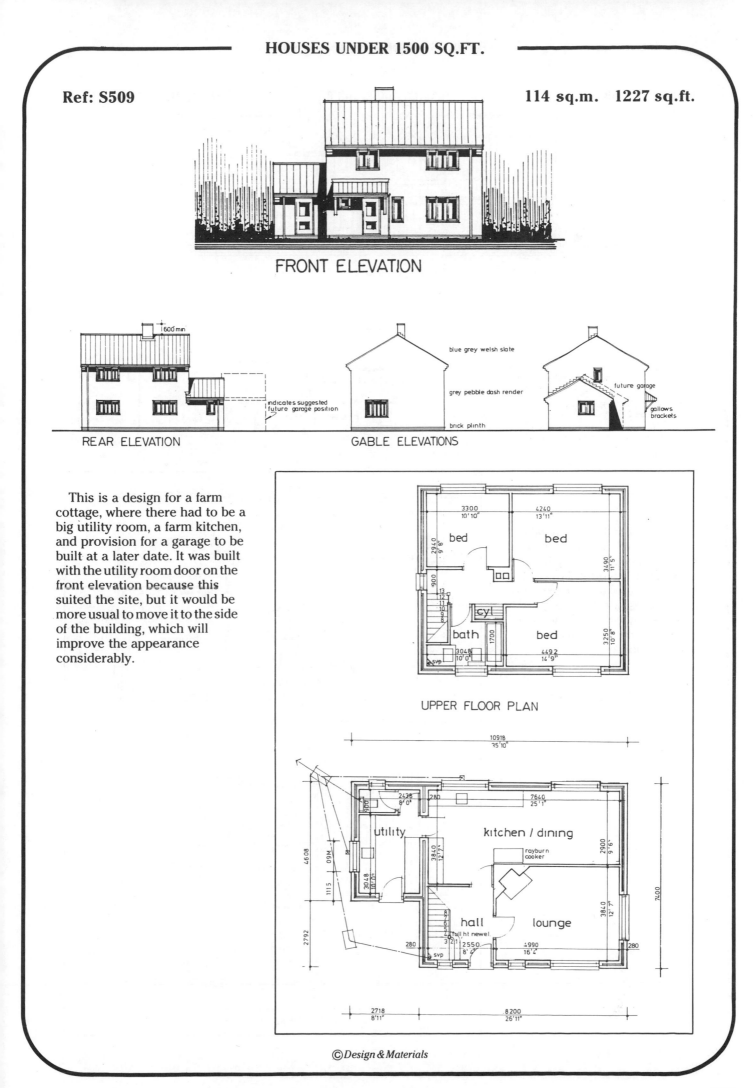

REAR ELEVATION

GABLE ELEVATIONS

blue grey welsh slate

grey pebble dash render

brick plinth

1600 min

indicates suggested future garage position

future garage

gallows brackets

This is a design for a farm cottage, where there had to be a big utility room, a farm kitchen, and provision for a garage to be built at a later date. It was built with the utility room door on the front elevation because this suited the site, but it would be more usual to move it to the side of the building, which will improve the appearance considerably.

UPPER FLOOR PLAN

bed
3300
10'10"
2940
9'8"
900

bed
4240
13'11"
3490
11'5"

13 12 11 10 9 8

cyl

bath
3048
10'0"
svp
1700

bed
4492
14'9"
3250
10'8"

utility

kitchen / dining
7640
25'1"
2900
9'6"

rayburn cooker

hall

lounge
4990
16'4"
3840
12'7"

10918
35'10"

4608

09M

1115

2792

2436
8'0"

280

3840
12'7"

3048
10'0"

280
svp

2550
8'

tall ht newel

2718
8'11"

8200
26'11"

7400

**Ref: P2799**

**131 sq.m.   1410 sq.ft.**

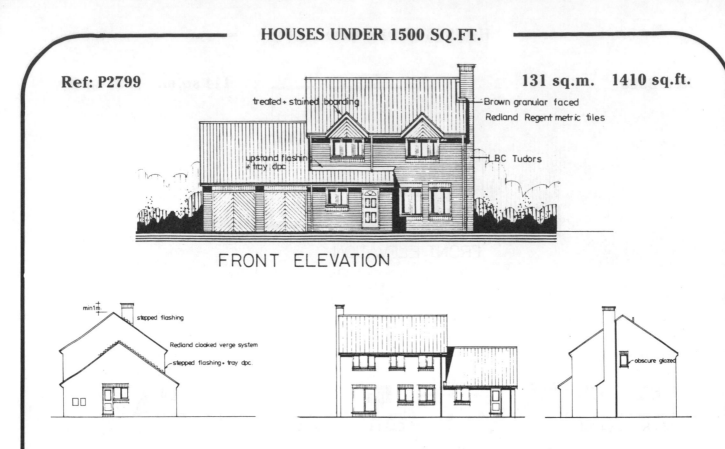

FRONT ELEVATION

A compact and economical four bedroom house with a large double garage and a very large utility room behind it. This is a layout that appeals to those who run a business in the country and whose family cars, and the loads that they carry, are more than usually important.

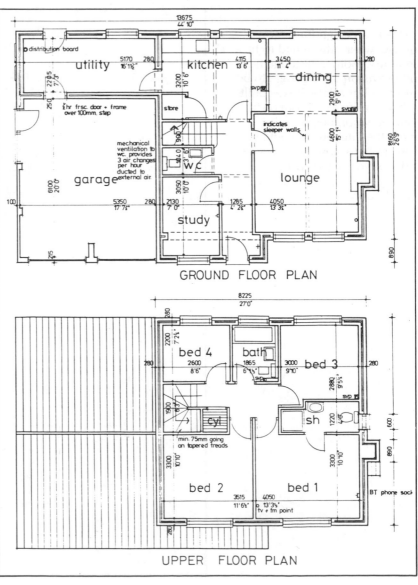

GROUND FLOOR PLAN

UPPER FLOOR PLAN

©P.S.S.

**Ref: W1302**

**127 sq.m.  1367 sq.ft.
(exc. garage)**

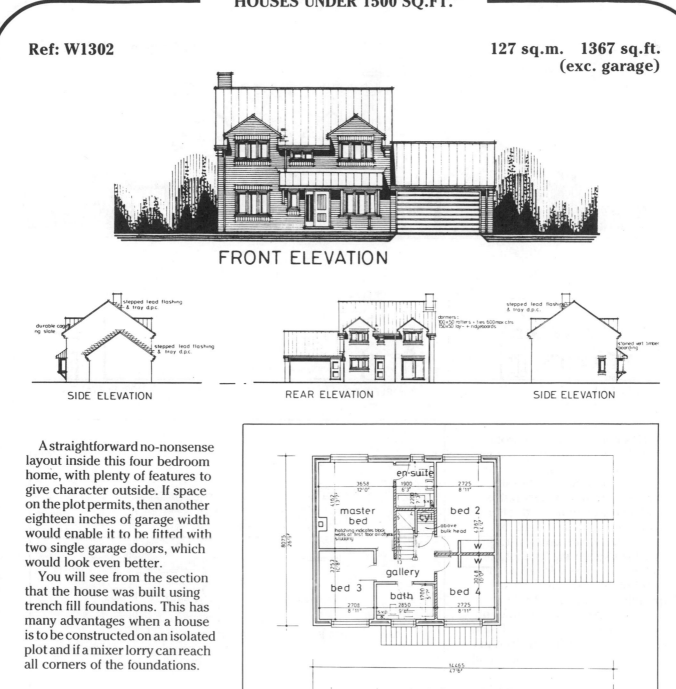

## FRONT ELEVATION

SIDE ELEVATION

REAR ELEVATION

SIDE ELEVATION

A straightforward no-nonsense layout inside this four bedroom home, with plenty of features to give character outside. If space on the plot permits, then another eighteen inches of garage width would enable it to be fitted with two single garage doors, which would look even better.

You will see from the section that the house was built using trench fill foundations. This has many advantages when a house is to be constructed on an isolated plot and if a mixer lorry can reach all corners of the foundations.

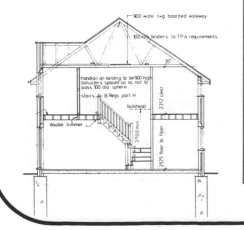

**Ref: C413**

**135 sq.m.   1453 sq.ft.**

REAR ELEVATION

SIDE ELEVATION

stepped lead flashing
& tray d.p.c.

Redland Grovebury Tiles
Farmhouse Red

Bradstone Trad walling
Weathered Ham

Hardwood Casement joinery

SIDE ELEVATION

This house in the Cotswold style has a layout which is now very popular. It is also very cost effective to build, as the gable features are purely decorative and an ordinary trussed rafter roof can be used with all the consequent cost savings. The trick is to keep the level of the gable window heads below the level of the wall plate. This permits a flat ceiling to the bedroom. Move the windows up in the strictly traditional style and you are necessarily involved in sloping ceilings, purlin roofs - and extra cost!

The off-set kitchen/breakfast area arrangement is interesting, and inevitably the breakfast area will become a family room if small children live in the home. It is just big enough for this, and french windows are shewn in this room. They can be replaced with an ordinary window if they are not appropriate.

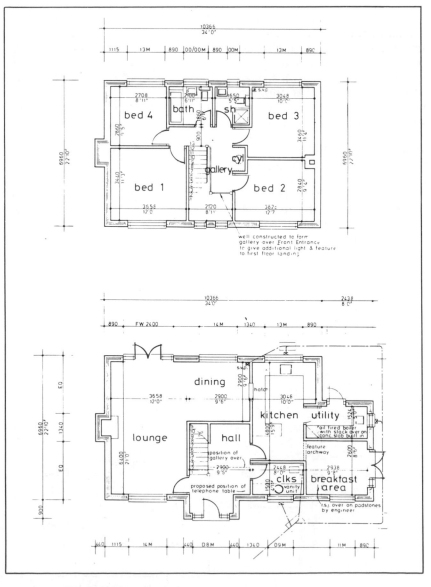

# Cottage Style Homes

The dictionary defines a cottage as a small rural dwelling, but as generally used the term has a narrower meaning than this. For most people it is a house – a bungalow is never a cottage – which is in a distinctive local style and which is essentially unpretentious. A cottage is designed to fit into the village street or to blend into the landscape, and does not draw attention to itself. This is completely different from the small houses elsewhere in this book which are often described as 'appearing larger than it' or 'having the authority of a larger property'. As used today, the word cottage often implies inverted snobbery, and a premium value per square foot. Image is all!

The cottage look is achieved by identifying the essence of the local style – or the perceived local style – and emphasising its essentials. If the village street houses built 200 years ago had 40° pitch roofs, stone slates in diminishing courses, a ratio of frontage to depth of 2.5 to 1 and small porches at off-set front doors, then this is copied in today's new cottage. Add windows in the right style, ledge braced doors, reclaimed bricks and period style pointing to the brickwork. Finish with a garden fence that matches the others in the village that have seemingly been there for ever, and you have a cottage.

One advantage of building in a cottage style is that use can be made of space saving layouts which would be less acceptable in a small house. In particular a front porch can lead straight into a living room, and a cottage style staircase can be in a living room or even in the kitchen instead of in the hall. The sloping ceiling in a bathroom becomes a delightful period feature and features that are less than ergonomic become charmingly quaint!

The biggest obstacle to achieving the cottage look is the motor car. Just as village streets were not laid out for car parking, local cottages were not built with garages. A new cottage with an integral garage having a 7ft x 7ft up-and-over door will completely spoil the most carefully designed front elevation. If a garage facing the road is absolutely unavoidable, and it often is, it is preferable to recess the front wall slightly, and to provide side hung doors that suggest a pony and trap within. A detached garage to the rear of the main building is preferable, and should be given as much character as possible. A stable door at the side of a garage will help: a metal panel door at the front will certainly not!

Chimneys are a feature that helps to define a local cottage style. Does the chimney breast project outside, or inside into the room. How high does it reach, and how is it finished? Your neighbours and visitors may not realise how much thought and research has gone into designing your chimney, but it will be a key element in their appreciation of how perfect a cottage you have built!

**Ref: 96182**

**122 sq.m.    1310 sq.ft.**

A cottage for a site in a National Park where all new homes had to be in the style of the existing buildings.

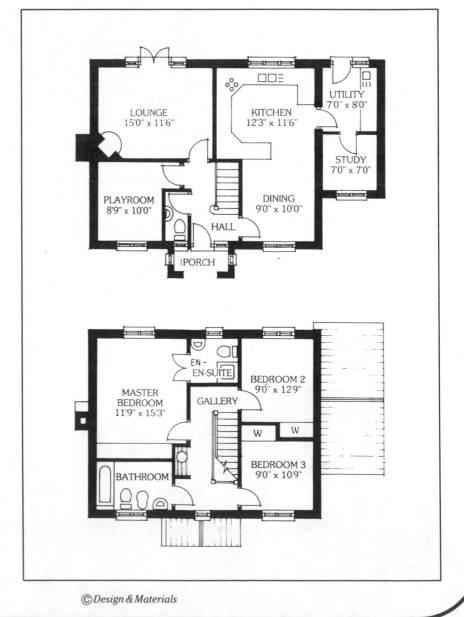

LOUNGE
15'0" x 11'6"

KITCHEN
12'3" x 11'6"

UTILITY
7'0" x 8'0"

PLAYROOM
8'9" x 10'0"

DINING
9'0" x 10'0"

STUDY
7'0" x 7'0"

HALL

PORCH

EN-SUITE

MASTER BEDROOM
11'9" x 15'3"

GALLERY

BEDROOM 2
9'0" x 12'9"

W    W

BATHROOM

BEDROOM 3
9'0" x 10'9"

**Ref: 95101**

**121 sq.m.    1306 sq.ft.**

A country cottage which is traditional in its external appearance but which has an impressive modern layout, with a through drawing room, a large hall and a kitchen with a connecting breakfast room. The first floor has a gallery above the hall and a small en-suite bathroom to the master bedroom. If the occupants of the master bedroom feel that by paying for the property they qualify for the larger bathroom, this can easily be arranged!

*Dimensions overall*
*44'6" x 20'10" - 13.5 x 6.3*
*Lounge*
*11'0" x 19'0" - 3.3  x  5.7*
*Dining*
*10'0" x 9'0" - 3.0 x 2.7*
*Study*
*9'0" x 6'3"   - 2.7  x 1.9*
*Kitchen*
*9'0" x 12'6" - 2.7 x 3.8*
*Breakfast Room*
*10'0" x 6'2" - 3.0 x 1.8*
*Utility*
*5'9" x 6'6"  - 1.7 x 1.9*
*Master Bedroom*
*9'0" x 11'6" - 2.7  x  3.5*
*Bedroom 2*
*11'0" x 9'8" - 3.3 x 2.9*
*Bedroom 3*
*11'0" x 9'0" - 3.3 x 2.7*
*Bedroom 4*
*9'0" x 7'3"  - 2.7  x 2.2*

**Ref: 96256**

**188 sq.m.   2025 sq.ft.**

A straightforward four bedroom home in a village style common throughout the south and midlands in the last century.

Architectural purists would say that the porch to the front door is inappropriate when combined with the exposed rafter feet and the arched window heads, but it reflects what the owners wanted rather than the text book, and none the worst for that. The proportions and room layouts would be perfect if you wanted to build this home in a neo Georgian style.

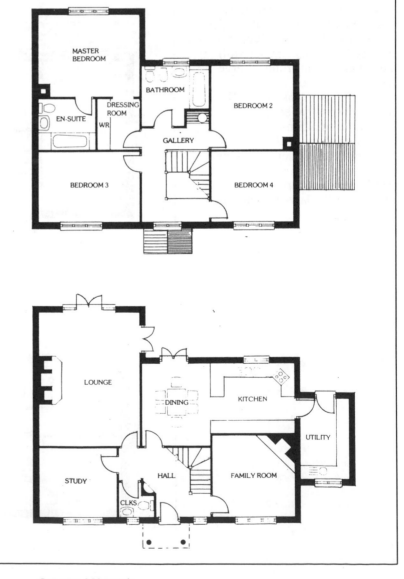

© *Design & Materials*

**Ref: 96136**

**129 sq.m.    1388 sq.ft.**

A cottage style design for an area where the County Design Guide called for village homes to have a maximum depth of 25 ft. with chimneys on gable walls. This interesting layout complied with both these requirements, and also met the owners wish for a living room with views to both front and rear.

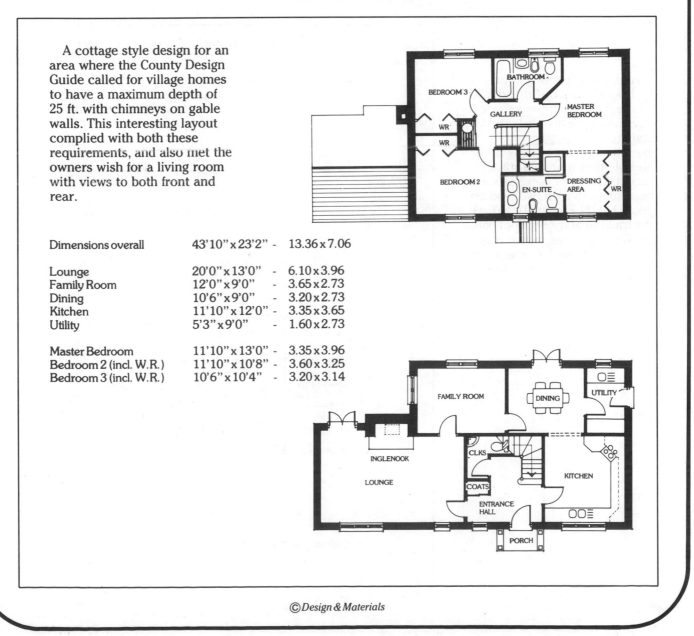

| Dimensions overall | 43'10" x 23'2" | - | 13.36 x 7.06 |
|---|---|---|---|
| Lounge | 20'0" x 13'0" | - | 6.10 x 3.96 |
| Family Room | 12'0" x 9'0" | - | 3.65 x 2.73 |
| Dining | 10'6" x 9'0" | - | 3.20 x 2.73 |
| Kitchen | 11'10" x 12'0" | - | 3.35 x 3.65 |
| Utility | 5'3" x 9'0" | - | 1.60 x 2.73 |
| Master Bedroom | 11'10" x 13'0" | - | 3.35 x 3.96 |
| Bedroom 2 (incl. W.R.) | 11'10" x 10'8" | - | 3.60 x 3.25 |
| Bedroom 3 (incl. W.R.) | 10'6" x 10'4" | - | 3.20 x 3.14 |

**Ref: S582**

**120 sq.m.   1291 sq.ft.**

FRONT ELEVATION

stepped lead flashing
& tray d.p.c

Marley Modern
Smooth Brown Tiles

Bradstone T.B.A.

Hardwood casement
joinery

GABLE ELEVATION

REAR ELEVATION

GABLE ELEVATION

A nice conventional four bedroom house of 1310 sq.ft., where the decision was made to have an impressive hall and a stairwell with a gallery above even though this cut down the size of other rooms to some extent. The front porch is shewn here supported on two wooden posts, but the essential is to have the traditional style of front porch in your local area, which may involve dwarf walls, or an open porch gable, or other features.

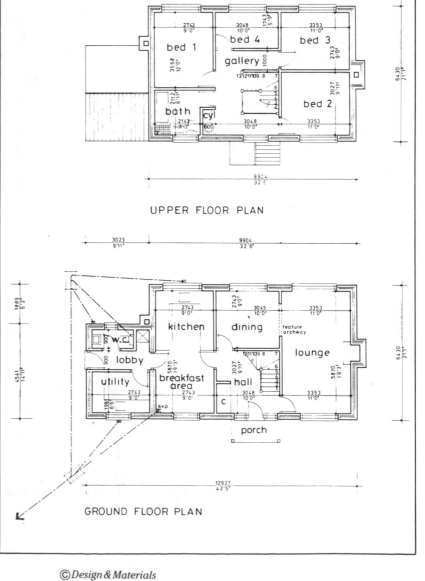

UPPER FLOOR PLAN

GROUND FLOOR PLAN

# COTTAGE STYLE HOMES

**Ref: C432**

**154 sq.m.   1657 sq.ft.**

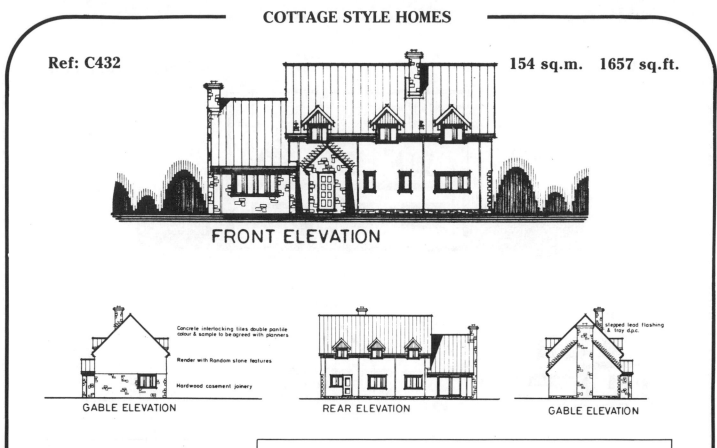

FRONT ELEVATION

GABLE ELEVATION

Concrete interlocking tiles double pantile colour & sample to be agreed with planners

Render with Random stone features

Hardwood casement joinery

REAR ELEVATION

stepped lead flashing & tray d.p.c.

GABLE ELEVATION

A house in the Cotswold style with a mix of render and natural stone for the walls. A note on the drawing says that the tile type and colour were to be agreed with the planners, and the choice will have had to be made very carefully to suit the walling style. The dormer gables are shewn with timber infill panels, but they could have been built in masonry if required as they rise directly from loadbearing walls. This would have needed a narrow pillar of masonry at the side of each window.

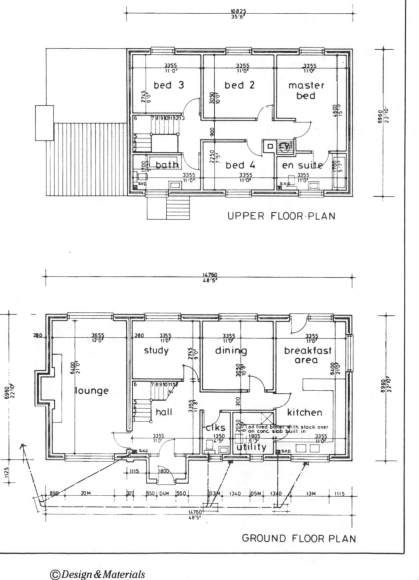

UPPER FLOOR PLAN

GROUND FLOOR PLAN

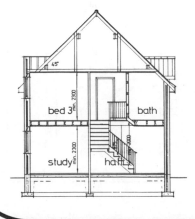

# COTTAGE STYLE HOMES

**Ref: W960**

**150 sq.m.    1614 sq.ft.**

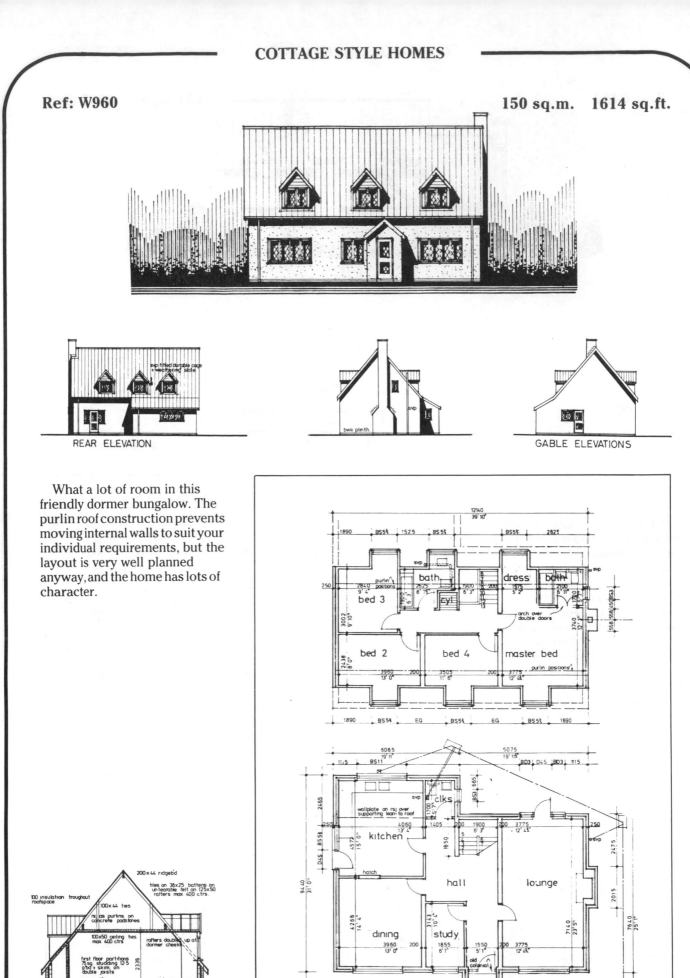

REAR ELEVATION

GABLE ELEVATIONS

What a lot of room in this friendly dormer bungalow. The purlin roof construction prevents moving internal walls to suit your individual requirements, but the layout is very well planned anyway, and the home has lots of character.

bed 3

bath

dress

bath

cyl

bed 2

bed 4

master bed

arch over double doors

purlin positions

clks

kitchen

hall

lounge

dining

study

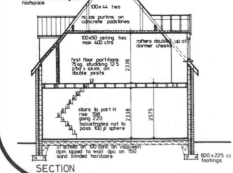

SECTION

© *Design & Materials*

# COTTAGE STYLE HOMES

**Ref: S541**

**94 sq.m.  1011 sq.ft.**

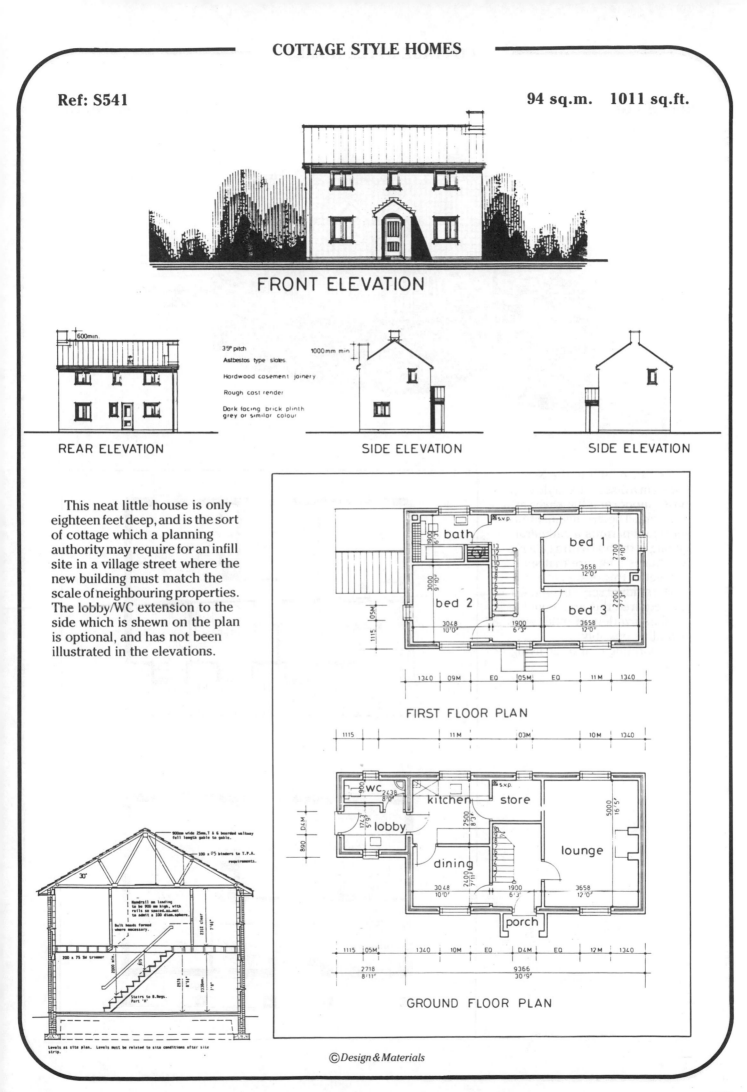

FRONT ELEVATION

REAR ELEVATION

35° pitch

Astbestos type slates.

Hardwood casement joinery

Rough cast render

Dark facing brick plinth
grey or similar colour

SIDE ELEVATION

SIDE ELEVATION

This neat little house is only
eighteen feet deep, and is the sort
of cottage which a planning
authority may require for an infill
site in a village street where the
new building must match the
scale of neighbouring properties.
The lobby/WC extension to the
side which is shewn on the plan
is optional, and has not been
illustrated in the elevations.

FIRST FLOOR PLAN

bath

bed 1

bed 2

bed 3

GROUND FLOOR PLAN

wc

lobby

kitchen

store

dining

lounge

porch

**Ref: 96110**

**143 sq.m.   1542 sq.ft.**

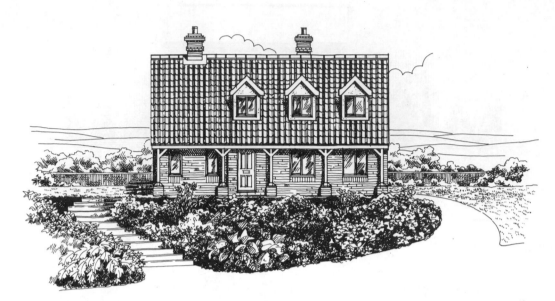

A cottage built in the New Forest in a distinctive style with posts supporting the eaves at the front. The arrangement of the stairs permits a cathedral ceiling to the hall with a gallery, and this is a feature that suits the feel of this design.

The study is very small, and if not required this area could be used in a variety of other ways, including possibly incorporating it into the living room.

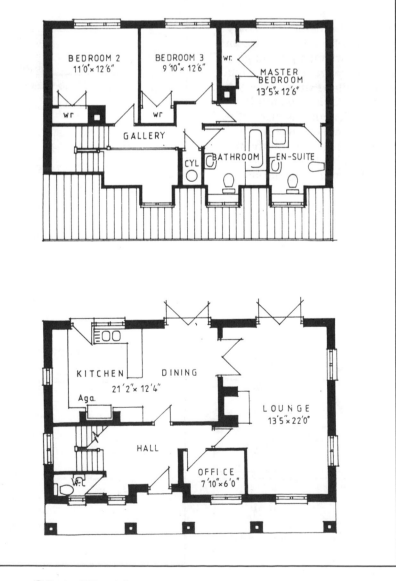

© *Design & Materials*

**Ref: 96106**

**153 sq.m.    1650 sq.ft.**

A straightforward country cottage of the sort that is found from one end of the country to the other, but with an internal layout to suit todays living patterns. There are side windows to light the front porch, but the hall relies on borrowed light from the window above the stairs. One way of enhancing this is to use glazed double doors to the lounge and dining room.

The porch, wc and storage at the back door is very appropriate to a country life style, but of course it can be built at a later stage if required.

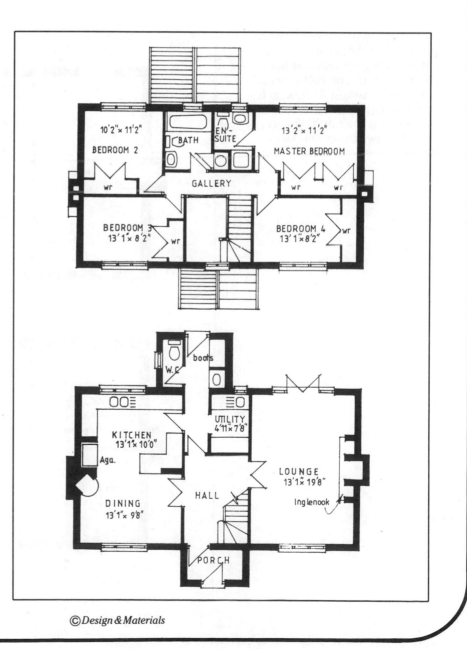

**Ref: 96186**

**119 sq.m.    1283 sq.ft.**

A traditional thatched cottage for a site in the West Country. Thatch is expensive, and the more compact the cottage the less it will cost. At 31 ft. x 26 ft. this home will cost up to £8000 to thatch in reed or £7000 in wheat straw. Either will last a lifetime.

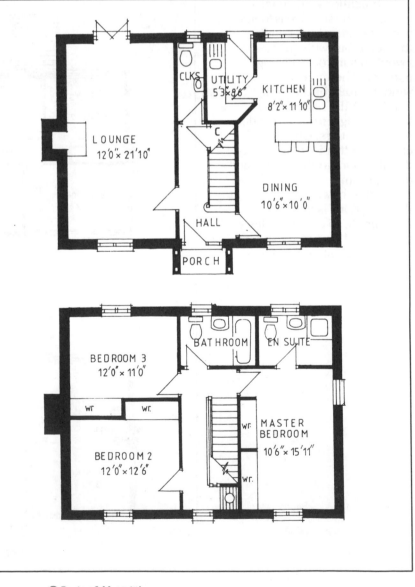

**Ref: 96259**

**101 sq.m.   1092 sq.ft.**
**(exc. garage)**

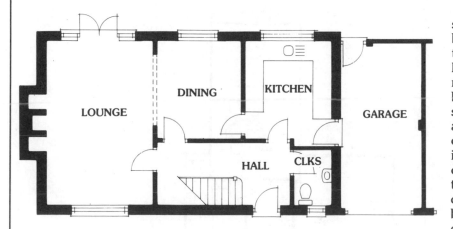

This thatched cottage has a simple layout, and of course can be built without the garage. New thatch is very attractive and will last a lifetime, but its use will require discussions with the building inspector at an early stage, leading to a possible application for the relaxation of certain building regulations. It is important that the builder collaborates closely with the thatcher over details of the roof construction, and it is usually best to employ firms who can demonstrate recent experience of building thatched homes.

The room layout, with the stairs running along the front wall, is interesting and can be used even if this cottage is built in more conventional materials.

| Dimensions overall | 32'2" x 19'10" | 9.81 x 6.04 |
|---|---|---|
| Lounge | 11'6" x 18'0" | 3.50 x 5.48 |
| Dining | 8'10" x 10'10" | 2.70 x 3.30 |
| Kitchen | 9'4" x 10'10" | 2.84 x 3.30 |
| Master Bed | 9'5" x 10'6" | 2.87 x 3.20 |
| Bed 2 | 9'10" x 9'10" | 3.00 x 3.00 |
| Bed 3 | 7'6" x 9'10" | 2.30 x 3.00 |
| Bed 4 | 8'6" x 7'10" | 2.59 x 2.38 |

**Ref: PN662**

**132 sq.m.    1425 sq.ft.**

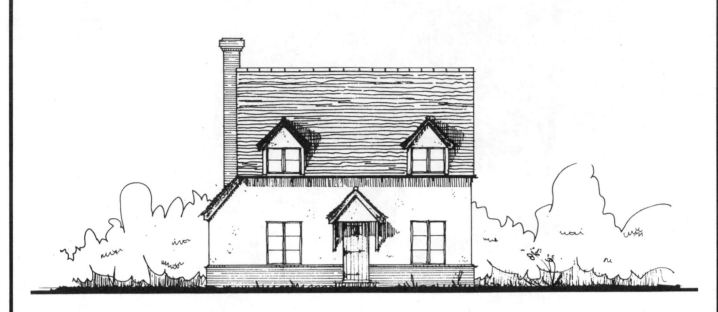

A design for a simple country cottage that will be acceptable to the planners almost everywhere while inside it has modern amenities and far larger rooms than would be guessed from its external appearance. Aisle frame construction for small homes like this results in some surprising positions for the frame posts, as in the study or the main bathroom in this design. These posts provide a character and period feel which you either love or hate: happily for Potton it is popular in rural areas to the extent that it is becoming a cult!

| | | |
|---|---|---|
| *Living Room* | *4.2 x 5.8* | *13'9" x 19'0"* |
| *Dining Room* | *3.7 x 3.3* | *12'2" x 10'10"* |
| *Kitchen* | *3.7 x 3.2* | *12'2" x 10'6"* |
| *Study* | *2.4 x 3.5* | *7'10" x 11'6"* |
| *Bedroom 1* | *3.3 x 5.8* | *10'10" x 19'0"* |
| *Bedroom 2* | *3.8 x 3.3* | *12'6" x 10'10"* |
| *Bedroom 3* | *2.5 x 3.6* | *8'2" x 11'10"* |

# COTTAGE STYLE HOMES

**194 sq.m.   1653 sq.ft.**

A home with an open plan kitchen/dining room/family room. This is now a more popular arrangement than the open plan lounge/dining room/kitchen of the 60's, although once children living in this country home get involved in homework or their own hobbies the family room is likely to gain its own dividing wall and a door that can be fully closed.

| Dimensions overall | 31'8" x 41'6" | - | 9.66 x 12.65 |
|---|---|---|---|
| Lounge | 13'11" x 18'1" | - | 4.25 x 5.51 |
| Family Room | 12'0" x 10'0" | - | 3.66 x 3.05 |
| Dining/Kitchen | 24'6" x 10'4" | - | 7.48 x 3.15 |
| Utility | 5'0" x 10'4" | - | 1.52 x 3.15 |
| Study | 8'0" x 8'9" | - | 2.44 x 2.67 |
| Master Bedroom | 13'11" x 12'2" | - | 4.25 x 3.71 |
| Bedroom 2 | 12'0" x 10'5" | - | 3.67 x 3.17 |
| Bedroom 3 (incl. W.R.) | 12'6" x 10'4" | - | 3.79 x 3.15 |
| Bedroom 4 (incl. W.R.) | 8'6" x 12'4" | - | 2.60 x 3.75 |

**Ref: 96203**

**139 sq.m.   1500 sq.ft.**

A cottage with dormer windows to all the first floor rooms except for the master bedroom, which has it's window in the gable end. The design was drawn for a very small plot in a conservation area, and used handmade bricks under clay pantiles. This was expensive, but the cost of meeting a planners choice of materials in this situation is usually more than balanced by the high value of the finished property.

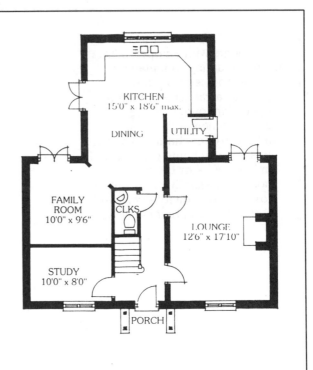

KITCHEN
15'0" x 18'6" max.

DINING          UTILITY

FAMILY ROOM
10'0" x 9'6"        CLKS

                        LOUNGE
                        12'6" x 17'10"

STUDY
10'0" x 8'0"

PORCH

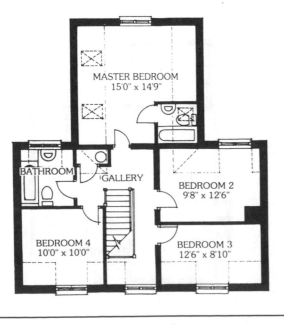

MASTER BEDROOM
15'0" x 14'9"

BATHROOM        GALLERY

                BEDROOM 2
                9'8" x 12'6"

BEDROOM 4
10'0" x 10'0"

        BEDROOM 3
        12'6" x 8'10"

**Ref: 96189**

**154 sq.m.    1660 sq.ft.**

This unusual cottage has an open plan ground floor layout with a huge central fireplace, a study, and a shower room by the back door for someone with a very muddy open air lifestyle. The stairs lead to a conventional three bedroom upper floor. At 1660 sq.ft. this is not a small home, but can be scaled down if required.

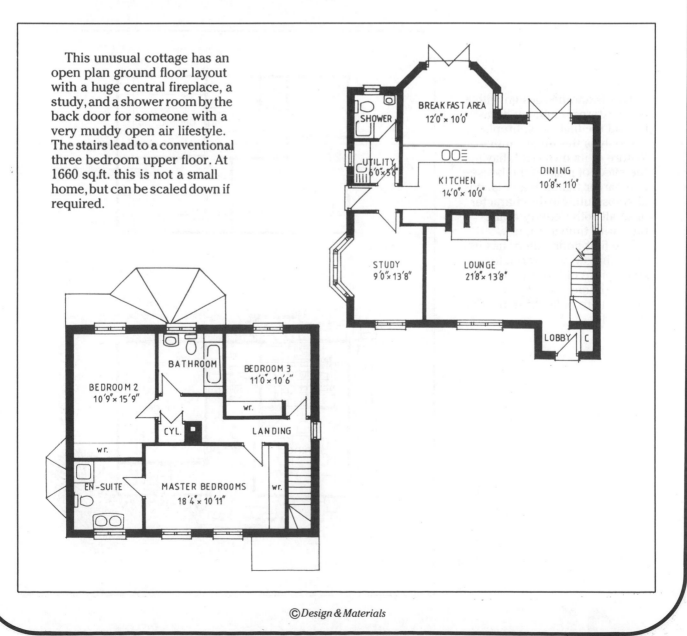

SHOWER

UTILITY
6'0" × 5'8"

BREAK FAST AREA
12'0" × 10'0"

DINING
10'8" × 11'0"

KITCHEN
14'0" × 10'0"

STUDY
9'0" × 13'8"

LOUNGE
21'8" × 13'8"

LOBBY    C

BATHROOM

BEDROOM 2
10'9" × 15'9"

BEDROOM 3
11'0" × 10'6"

wr.

CYL.    LANDING

wr.

EN-SUITE    MASTER BEDROOMS
18'4" × 10'11"    wr.

© *Design & Materials*

397

**Ref: PN669**

**101 sq.m.　1430 sq.ft.**

This is another design with a huge external chimney breast behind the Inglenook fireplace. Not only is this an attractive feature in its own right, having the effect of making the house look larger than it really is, it is also absolutely in the character of small 16th Century homes built with timber frames.

The first floor gallery has its own window, with room for a small piece of furniture below, and the home has all the feel and atmosphere of larger houses in this style.

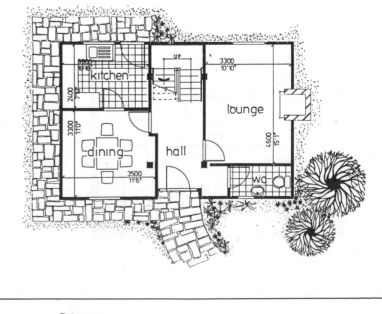

*©Potton*

**Ref: PN668**

**111 sq.m.    1290 sq.ft.**

This half timbered cottage has an interesting angled hall which permits a small study in the ground floor layout. The hall is well lit by a window on the half landing of the stairs, and the whole property has a feel of a much larger home.

If a home to this design is to be built on a narrow site the building regulations will probably require that the windows in the end walls are moved into the front and back elevations. This does not present any problems at all, and the dormer windows that will then be required for bedrooms one and two will add further interest to the appearance of this attractive cottage.

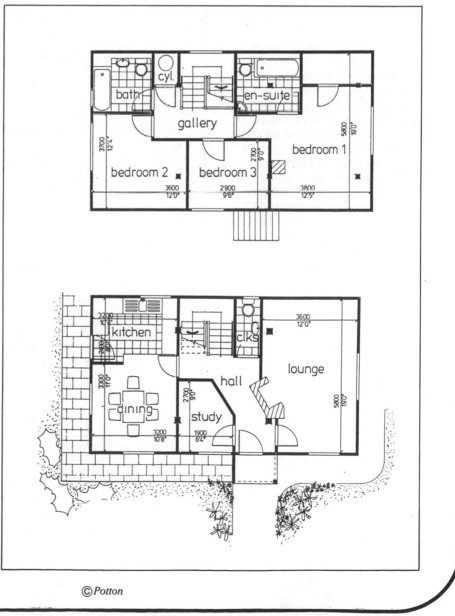

© *Potton*

**Ref: PN671**

**148 sq.m.    1580 sq.ft.**

This three bedroom house has an interesting layout and can be accommodated on a very narrow plot as none of the key windows look out to the sides. The stairs are well lit, with windows in both the hall and the gallery above, and this gives a spacious feel on entering the front door. The long thin kitchen is essentially a cooks workshop with little room for anything else, so the ground floor layout shown is for a family that prefers not to eat in the kitchen.

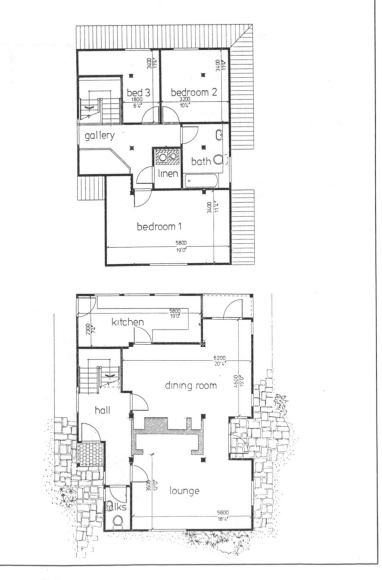

© *Potton*

# COTTAGE STYLE HOMES

**132 sq.m.    1420 sq.ft.**

This is another versatile design concept for an aisle frame house which has a large number of variants. The version shown, which Potton know as Caxton A, has a very interesting ground floor room layout with an angled fireplace in the lounge. Other variants provide for the large Inglenook fireplace which is so popular with those who build a Potton home. It is a particularly economical house to build.

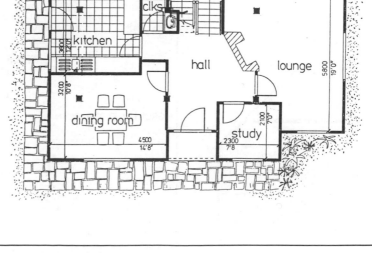

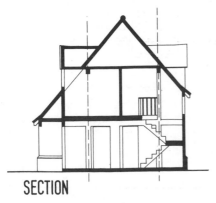

SECTION

©Potton

# COTTAGE STYLE HOMES

**Ref: W1123**

**118 sq.m.   1270 sq.ft.**

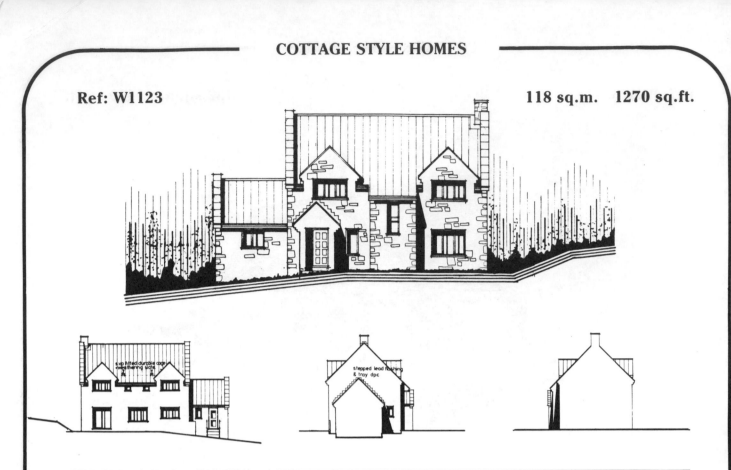

This country home was built on a very special site in the Peak District of Derbyshire, and the design incorporates all the stone features that are typical of the area, and which the planners invariably require. In the Peak National Park, as in all National Parks, all planning applications are considered at great length by a number of interested bodies, and obtaining a consent is invariably a lengthy process.

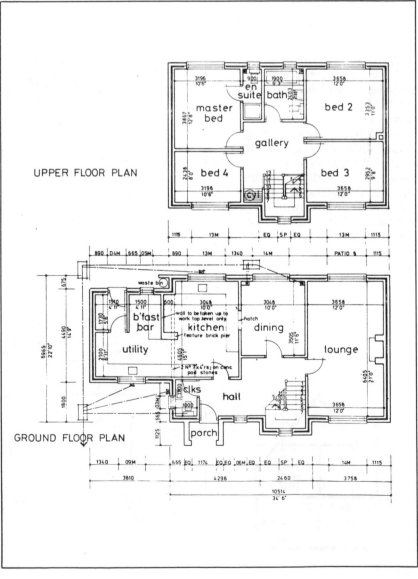

UPPER FLOOR PLAN

master bed

en suite

bath

bed 2

gallery

bed 4

bed 3

GROUND FLOOR PLAN

b'fast bar

kitchen

utility

dining

lounge

clks

hall

porch

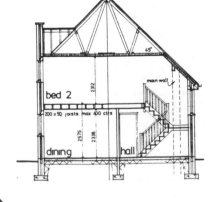

bed 2

dining

hall

# COTTAGE STYLE HOMES

**Ref: S484**

**163 sq.m.    1754 sq.ft.**

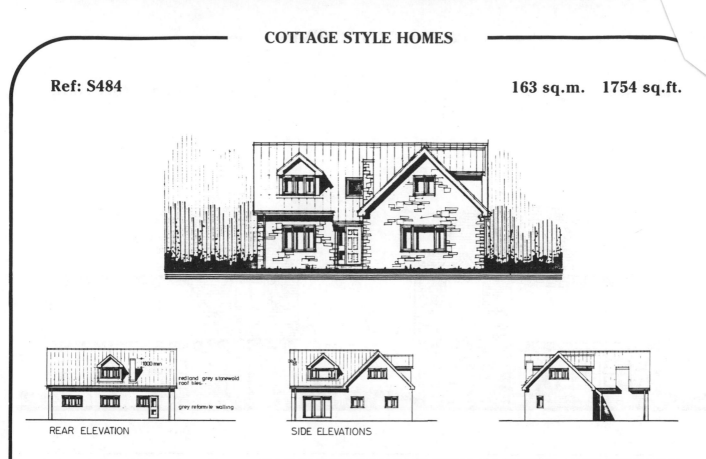

REAR ELEVATION

redland grey stonewold
roof tiles.

grey reformite walling

SIDE ELEVATIONS

This dormer bungalow has a great deal more accommodation than its compact appearance may suggest. The layout shewn in the plan has a large lobby at the back door with a shower and WC to suit a farmer. This is easily rearranged to give a bathroom leading off the ground floor bedroom, making it very suitable for an elderly person.

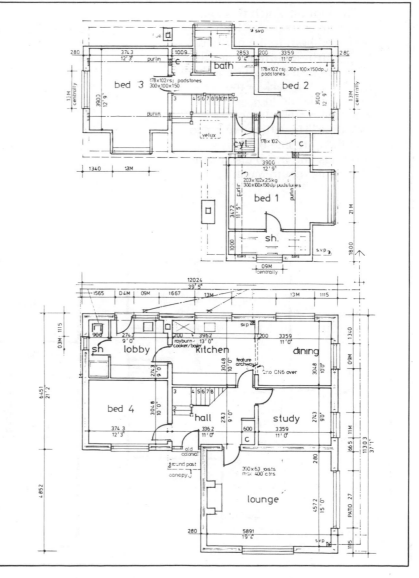

**Ref: PN652**

**146 sq.m.    1570 sq.ft.**

The plot on which this four bedroom cottage was built is bordered both to the north and the south by main roads, and the planners insisted that both the front and the back of the building should look as if they were the main entrance elevation. This attractive home was the outcome of many meetings and much discussion about this requirement.

| | |
|---|---|
| Living Room | 5.7 x 4.7 |
| Dining Room | 3.4 x 4.5 |
| Kitchen | 3.1 x 4.5 |
| Utility | 2.4 x 2.3 |
| Bedroom 1 | 3.9 x 3.7 |
| Bedroom 2 | 3.2 x 2.8 |
| Bedroom 3 | 3.5 x 2.7 |
| Bedroom 4/Study | 2.2 x 2.7 |

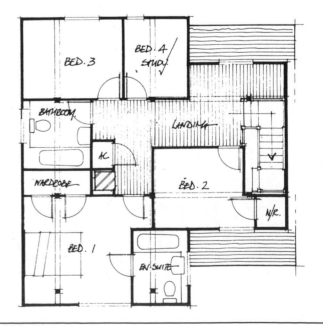

© Potton

**Ref: PN677**

**152 sq.m.    1640 sq.ft.**

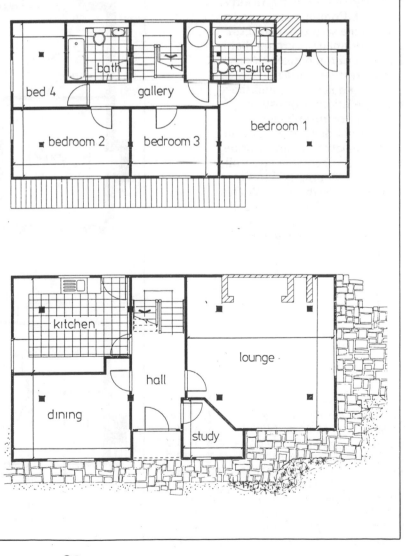

This attractive home is one of the most popular of Potton's aisle frame houses, combining a period external appearance with an internal layout appropriate to todays living patterns.

Note that the plan shows the fireplace and chimney in the rear wall of the lounge, while the artists sketch shows it in the gable end wall and with the whole cottage built to the opposite hand. All the plans in this book can be built in mirror image in this way, and whether or not to ask for your plans to be drawn to one hand or the other deserves very careful consideration when relating a design to your plot.

© *Potton*

**Ref: 95102**

125 sq.m.    1350 sq.ft.

A four bedroom cottage property which will fit on a forty foot plot. Compact and economical to build – look how all the drainage is grouped at one side of the house – it has many prestige features including a large hall and the separate utility room so essential for rural living.

The right dormer window in the front elevation can easily be moved into the gable end wall, enabling a double bed to be situated facing the window. This is also possible in the second bedroom, and this offers small cost savings if building to a tight budget.

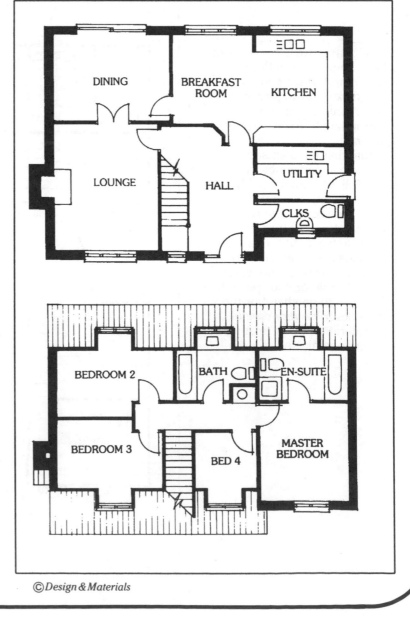

| Dimensions overall | 35'0" x 26'10" | - | 10. 6 x 8.1 |
|---|---|---|---|
| Lounge | 12'0" x 14'8" | - | 3.6 x 4.4 |
| Dining | 13'6" x 10'0" | - | 4.1 x 3.0 |
| Breakfast room | 9'0" x 10'7" | - | 2.7 x 3.2 |
| Kitchen | 10'0" x 12'6" | - | 3.0 x 3.8 |
| Utility | 10'0" x 6'0" | - | 3.0 x 1.8 |
| Master Bedroom | 10'0" x 11'6" | - | 3.0 x 3.8 |
| Bedroom 2 | 13'6" x 8'0" | - | 4.1 x 2.4 |
| Bedroom 3 | 12'0" x 8'0" | - | 3.6 x 2.4 |
| Bedroom 4 | 7'3" x 6'3" | - | 2.2 x 1.9 |

© Design & Materials

# *Bungalows Under 1500 sq. ft.*

Most small bungalows in Britain are simple rectangles with 30% pitch roofs, and there are plenty of examples of them in the pages that follow. For many people they represent an ideal, and they want nothing better. However, in recent years there has been a move to building more complex structures, even when it is only putting a false gable onto a simple roof, or projecting the wall of a room forward of the bungalow by a metre or so. Small bungalows are usually built to a strict budget, but the cost of providing interesting design features like this is very little compared with the total project cost, and will make a very real difference to the appearance and value of the property.

Room layouts for small bungalows are generally determined by the principal view, and there is little opportunity for variety. Designers find that people who want a compact bungalow invariably have a very clear idea of what they want. However, if you have an open mind there are plenty of options to choose from in the following pages.

If at all possible avoid having an integral garage: a detached garage linked to the bungalow by a wall will add character and may also be cheaper to build.

**Ref: 96223**

**125 sq.m.    1344 sq.ft.**

A three bedroom bungalow built as a retirement home with a particularly large master bedroom.

| | | | |
|---|---|---|---|
| Lounge | 16'0" x 12'0" | - | 4.88 x 3.65 |
| Dining (max) | 11'0" x 11'0" | - | 3.35 x 3.35 |
| Kitchen (max) | 13'0" x 11'6" | - | 3.96 x 3.50 |
| Utility | 6'1" x 6'3" | - | 1.86 x 1.90 |
| Master Bedroom | 11'6" x 20'0" | - | 3.50 x 6.10 |
| Bedroom 2 | 11'6" x 10'0" | - | 3.50 x 3.04 |
| Bedroom 3/Study | 11'3" x 10'0" | - | 3.42 x 3.04 |

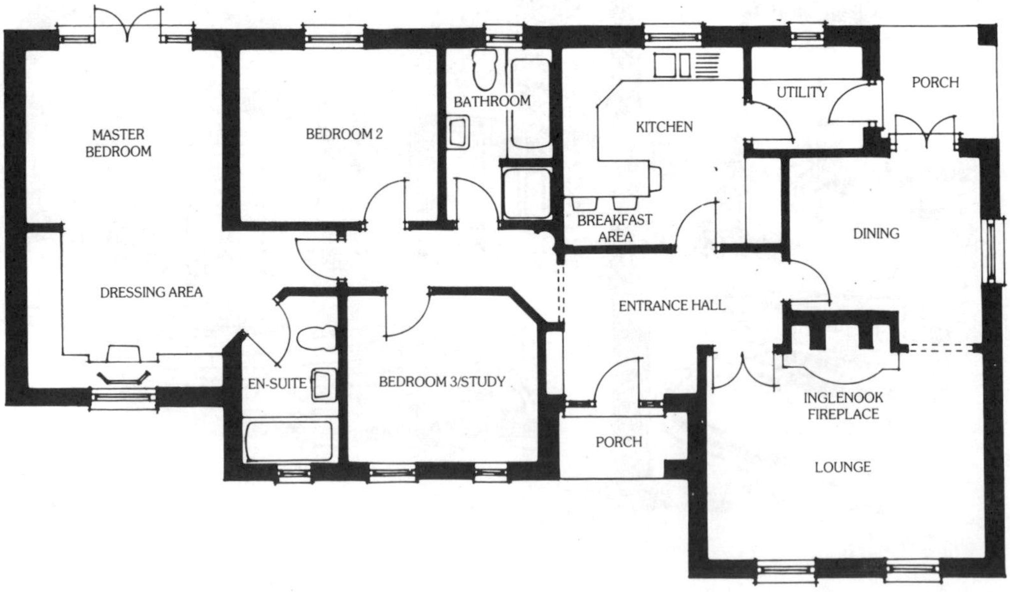

**Ref: 96216**

**120 sq.m.    1288 sq.ft.**

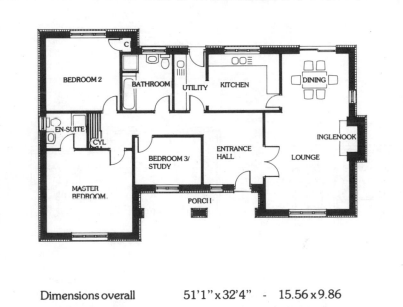

A bungalow with the feel of a property that is a lot larger than its 1288 sq.ft., with potential for rooms in the roof. There is space for a stairway in the hall, and the necessary framing to the roof timbers to enable the stairs to be installed can be arranged very easily when the bungalow is being built. If it is left until a later date its likely to be difficult and expensive.

| Dimensions overall | 51'1" x 32'4" | - | 15.56 x 9.86 |
|---|---|---|---|
| Lounge/Dining (max) | 13'9" x 24'6" | - | 4.20 x 7.46 |
| Kitchen | 11'11" x 9'0" | - | 3.62 x 2.74 |
| Utility | 5'3" x 9'0" | - | 1.60 x 2.74 |
| Master Bedroom | 14'0" x 13'0" | - | 4.26 x 3.96 |
| Bedroom 2 | 12'0" x 11'6" | - | 3.65 x 3.50 |
| Bedroom 3/Study | 10'9" x 7'6" | - | 3.27 x 2.28 |

# BUNGALOWS UNDER 1500 SQ.FT.

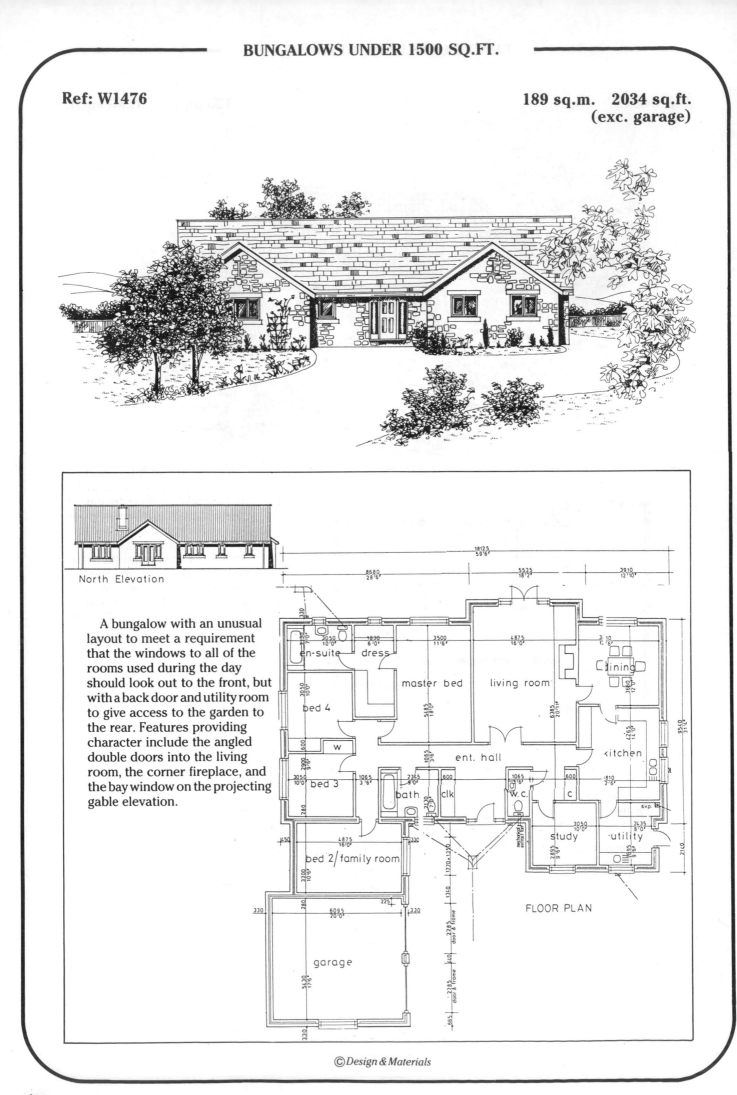

North Elevation

A bungalow with an unusual layout to meet a requirement that the windows to all of the rooms used during the day should look out to the front, but with a back door and utility room to give access to the garden to the rear. Features providing character include the angled double doors into the living room, the corner fireplace, and the bay window on the projecting gable elevation.

FLOOR PLAN

en-suite  dress  master bed  living room  dining  bed 4  w  kitchen  bed 3  bath  clk  ent. hall  w.c.  c  study  utility  bed 2/ family room  garage

**Ref: 96133**

**106 sq.m.    1147 sq.ft.**

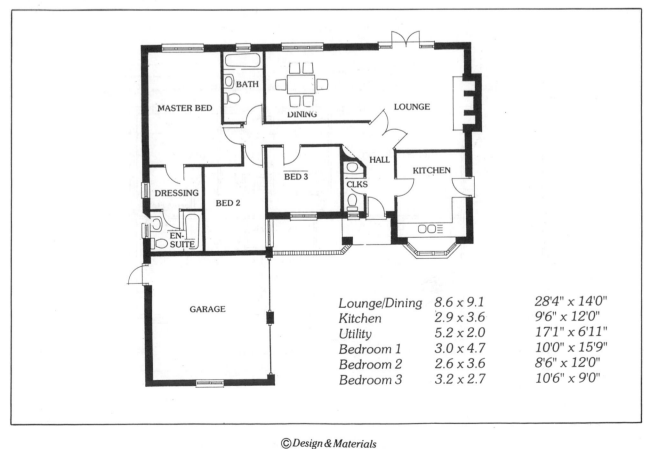

This bungalow can be built with or without the garage, which gives the option of moving the window in bedroom 2 into the front elevation.

| | | |
|---|---|---|
| Lounge/Dining | 8.6 x 9.1 | 28'4" x 14'0" |
| Kitchen | 2.9 x 3.6 | 9'6" x 12'0" |
| Utility | 5.2 x 2.0 | 17'1" x 6'11" |
| Bedroom 1 | 3.0 x 4.7 | 10'0" x 15'9" |
| Bedroom 2 | 2.6 x 3.6 | 8'6" x 12'0" |
| Bedroom 3 | 3.2 x 2.7 | 10'6" x 9'0" |

**Ref: S379**

**128 sq.m.   1377 sq.ft.**
**(exc. garage)**

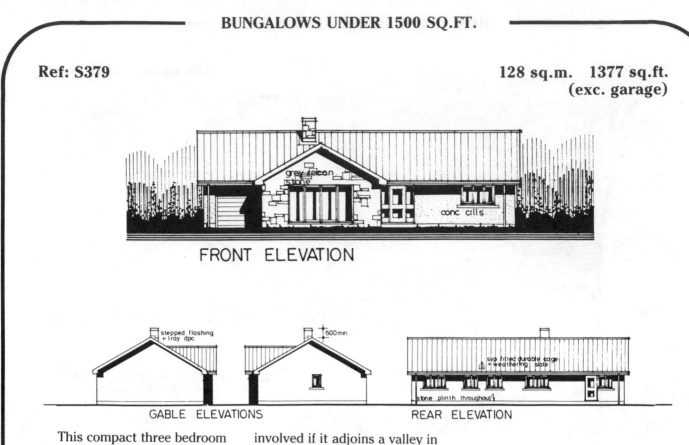

FRONT ELEVATION

GABLE ELEVATIONS

REAR ELEVATION

This compact three bedroom bungalow has the garage door hidden away at the side of a projecting gable, which is the ideal arrangement for a garage door that has to be on the front of the building. By putting the lounge fireplace on the kitchen wall the chimney can be taken straight up through the roof ridge, avoiding the complicated work involved if it adjoins a valley in the roof. In this position it can also accommodate another flue from a solid fuel stove in the kitchen.

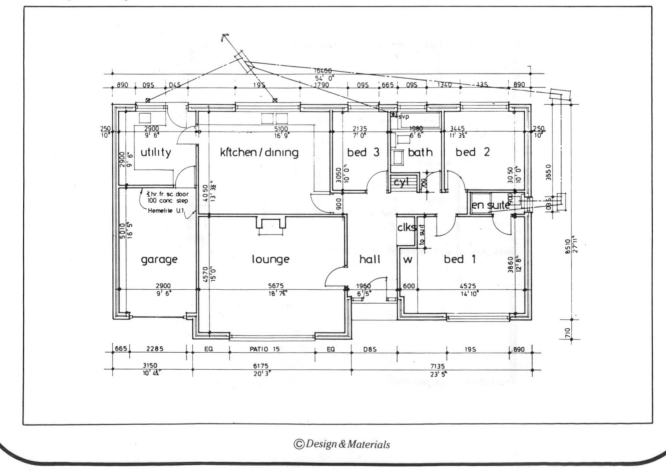

**Ref: W1279**

**118 sq.m.    1270 sq.ft.**

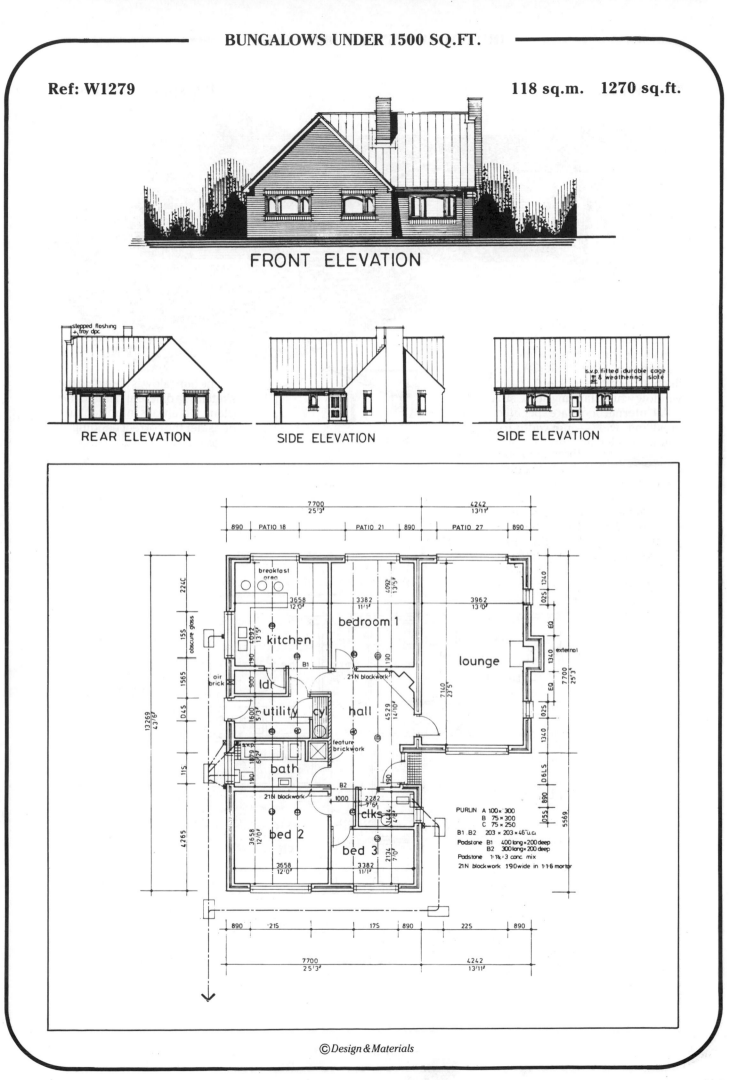

FRONT ELEVATION

REAR ELEVATION

SIDE ELEVATION

SIDE ELEVATION

breakfast area

kitchen

bedroom 1

lounge

ldr

utility    cyl    hall

feature brickwork

bath

clks

bed 2

bed 3

PURLIN   A 100 × 300
         B  75 × 300
         C  75 × 250
B1 B2    203 × 203 × 46 u.c.
Padstone B1   400 long × 200 deep
         B2   300 long × 200 deep
Padstone 1:1½:3 conc mix
21N blockwork 190 wide in 1:1:6 mortar

21N blockwork

© Design & Materials

413

**Ref: W1309**

**120 sq.m.   1291 sq.ft.**

If the best view from a new home is to the front, why not have the kitchen at the front so that the housewife can enjoy it while washing up? After all, she is more likely to want to look out of the window while standing at the sink.

All internal doors are specified at 900mm wide — the width to suit a wheelchair.

SIDE ELEVATION

The bungalow is shown in the sketch to a different hand to the plans. It is always important to consider the correct handing for a design.

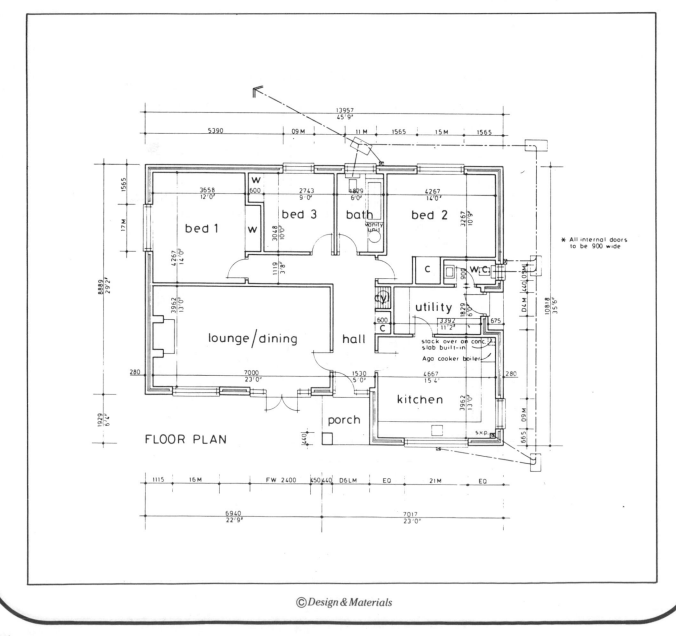

FLOOR PLAN

bed 1

bed 3

bath

bed 2

lounge/dining

hall

utility

kitchen

porch

\* All internal doors to be 900 wide

**Ref: W892**

**113 sq.m.    1216 sq.ft.**
**(exc. garage)**

A four bedroom bungalow with an integral garage to fit on a narrow plot. The garage is over twenty three feet long, so there is plenty of room to divide it to fit a hobbies room or garden store into it at the back.

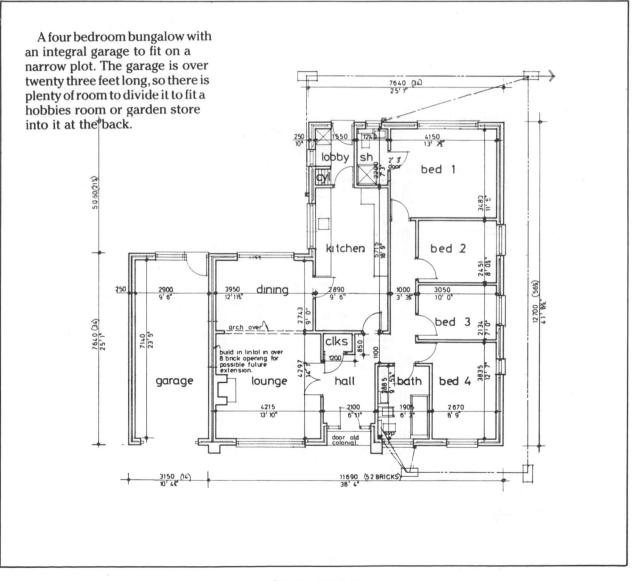

© *Design & Materials*

**Ref: C404**

**113 sq.m.  1216 sq.ft.**
**(exc. garage)**

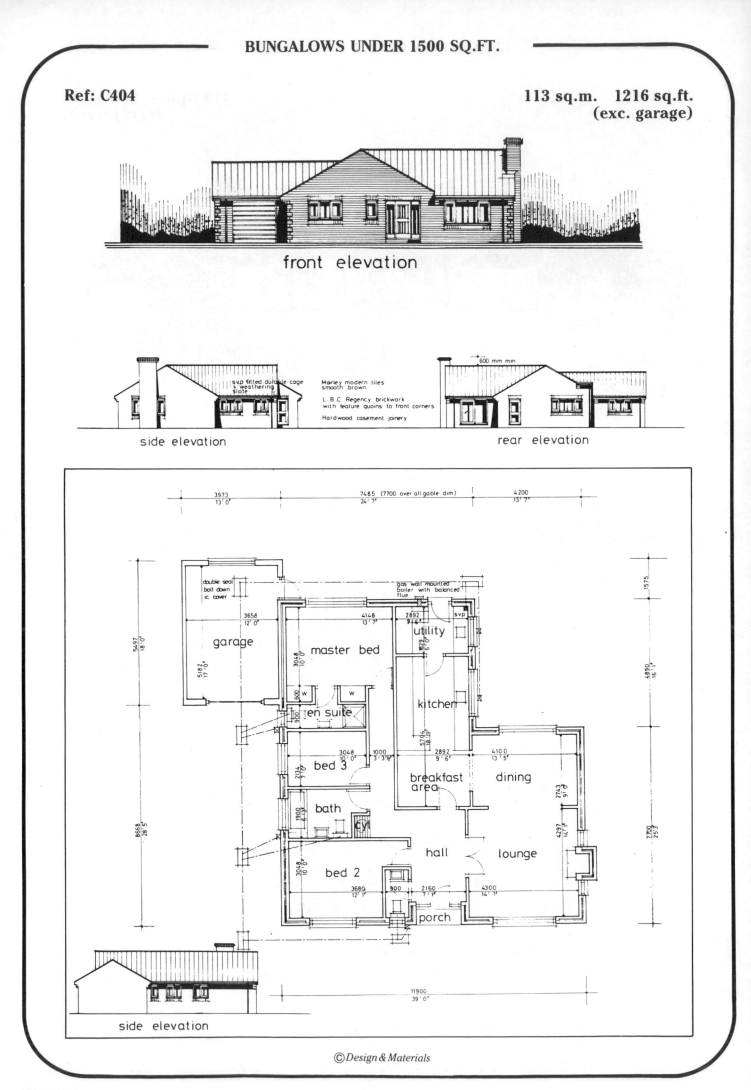

front elevation

side elevation

rear elevation

s.v.p fitted durable cage
+ weathering
slate

Marley modern tiles
smooth brown

L.B.C. Regency brickwork
with feature quoins to front corners

Hardwood casement joinery

600 mm min

garage

master bed

utility

kitchen

en suite

bed 3

breakfast area

dining

bath

cyl

hall

lounge

bed 2

porch

double seal
bolt down
ic cover

gas wall mounted
boiler with balanced
flue

side elevation

**Ref: W1229**

**112 sq.m.    1205 sq.ft.**
**(exc. garage)**

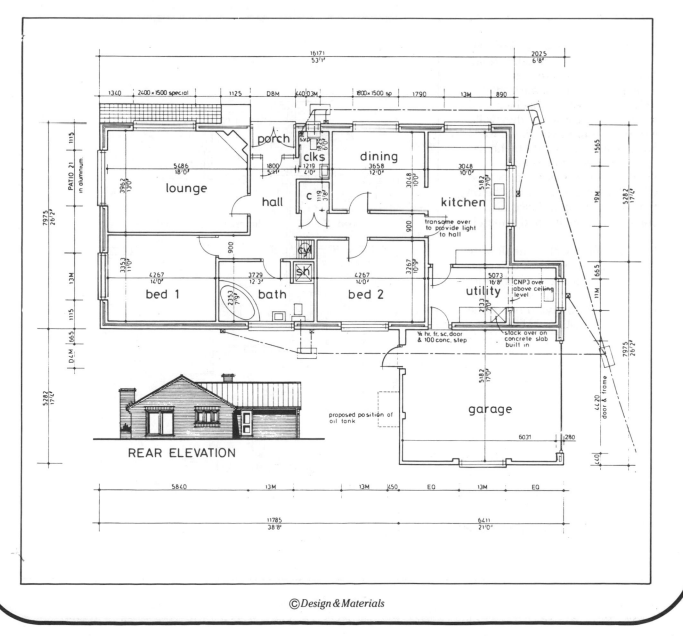

REAR ELEVATION

**Ref: W1089**

**106 sq.m.   1141 sq.ft.**

A stone bungalow with box bay windows on the front elevation. These will dominate the appearance of the home from the front, and deserve special attention. Presumably they will be made in hardwood, and the corner timbers should be heavy enough to be chamfered or finished in some other decorative way. The gallows brackets below the windows should also be substantial and finished to match other features.

The angled wall at the door to the master bedroom is different, and helps to make the hall more interesting. Alternatively it can be straightened to give room in the hall for a telephone table.

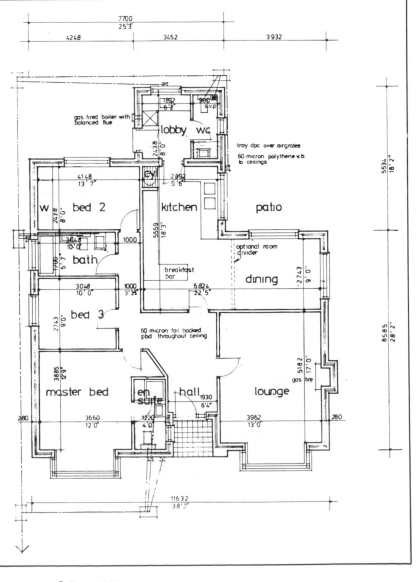

**Ref: W976**

**131 sq.m.   1410 sq.ft.**
**(exc. garage and workshop)**

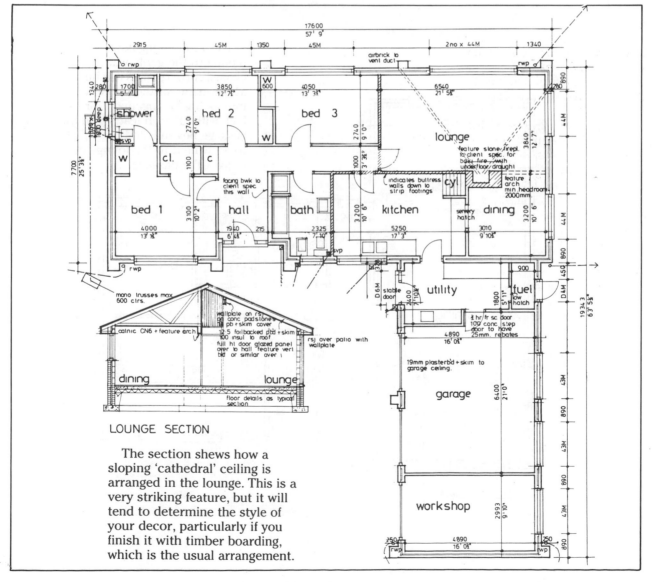

## LOUNGE SECTION

The section shews how a sloping 'cathedral' ceiling is arranged in the lounge. This is a very striking feature, but it will tend to determine the style of your decor, particularly if you finish it with timber boarding, which is the usual arrangement.

**Ref: W881**

**110 sq.m.   1184 sq.ft.**

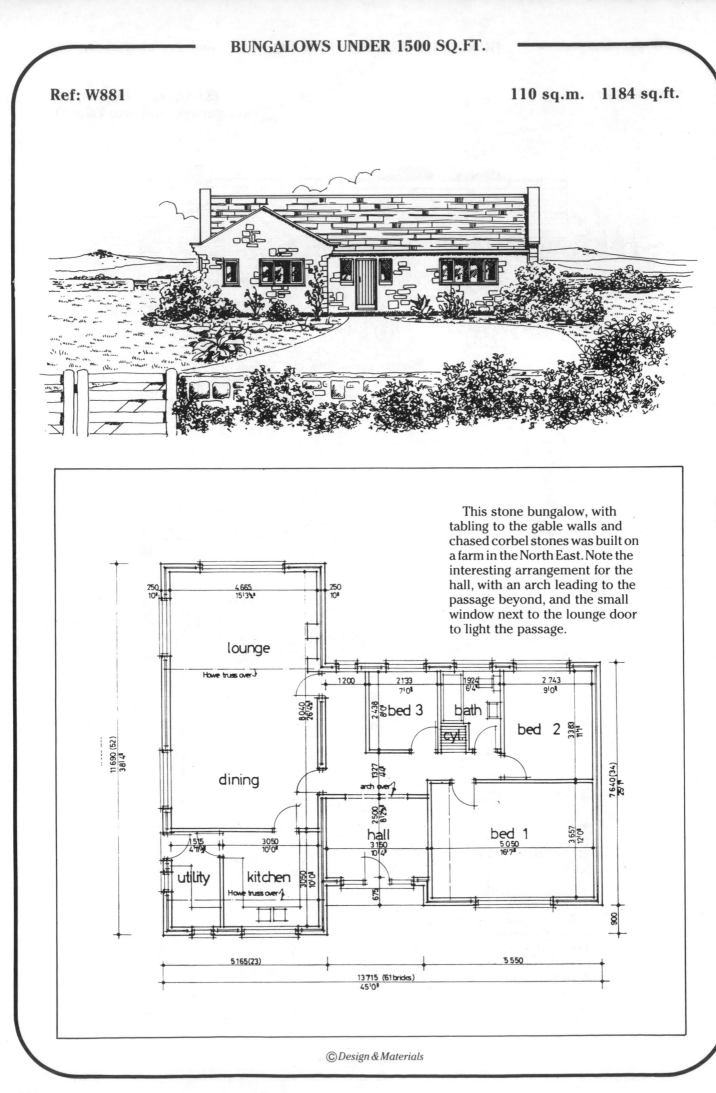

This stone bungalow, with tabling to the gable walls and chased corbel stones was built on a farm in the North East. Note the interesting arrangement for the hall, with an arch leading to the passage beyond, and the small window next to the lounge door to light the passage.

lounge

Howe truss over

dining

utility

kitchen

Howe truss over

bed 3

bath

cyl

bed 2

arch over

hall

bed 1

**Ref: W1187**

**109 sq.m.    1173 sq.ft.**

A farm bungalow where the back door will be in constant use and the front entrance used only rarely. The bathroom is at the opposite end of the building from the main bedroom, which groups all the drainage at one end. It can easily be moved between any two of the bedrooms which will probably be thought to be more convenient.

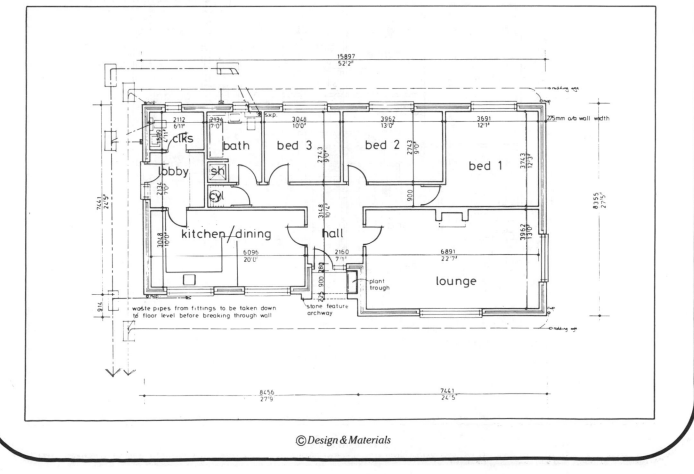

**Ref: W1177**

**98 sq.m.   1054 sq.ft.**
**(exc. garage)**

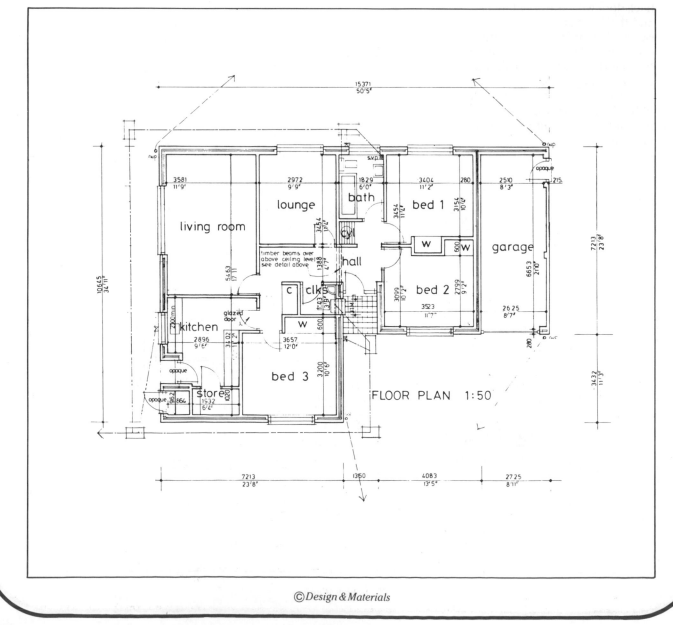

FLOOR PLAN 1:50

living room

lounge

bath

bed 1

garage

kitchen

hall

cyl

hall

store

bed 3

bed 2

clk

c

w

w

w

timber beams over
above ceiling level
see detail above

glazed
door

opaque

opaque

opaque

s.v.p.

15371
50'5"

3581
11'9"

2972
9'9"

1829
6'0"

3404
11'2"

280

2510
8'3"

215

3454
11'4"

3154
10'4"

3454
10'4"

1388
4'7"

5463
17'11"

34.02
11'2"

2896
9'6"

3657
12'0"

3200
10'6"

3099
10'2"

2799
9'2"

3523
11'7"

2625
8'7"

280

6653
21'10"

7213
23'8"

3432
11'3"

10645
34'11"

7213
23'8"

1350
4'5"

4083
13'5"

2725
8'11"

1932
6'4"

962

864

1120

600

600

600

2300min
7'7"

**Ref: S496**

**111 sq.m. 1194 sq.ft.**

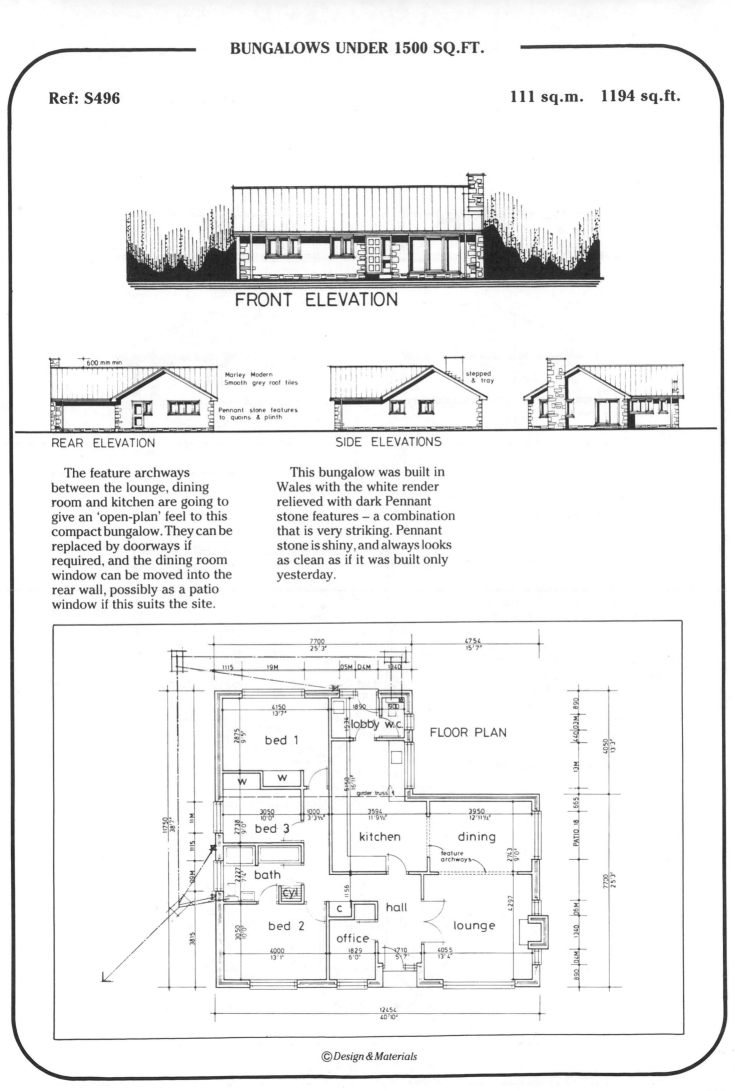

FRONT ELEVATION

600 mm min

Marley Modern
Smooth grey roof tiles

Pennant stone features
to quoins & plinth

REAR ELEVATION

stepped
& tray

SIDE ELEVATIONS

The feature archways between the lounge, dining room and kitchen are going to give an 'open-plan' feel to this compact bungalow. They can be replaced by doorways if required, and the dining room window can be moved into the rear wall, possibly as a patio window if this suits the site.

This bungalow was built in Wales with the white render relieved with dark Pennant stone features – a combination that is very striking. Pennant stone is shiny, and always looks as clean as if it was built only yesterday.

FLOOR PLAN

bed 1

lobby w.c.

bed 3

kitchen          dining

feature
archways

bath

cyl

c          hall

bed 2                    lounge

office

girder truss

**Ref: P2561**

**87 sq.m.   936 sq.ft.**

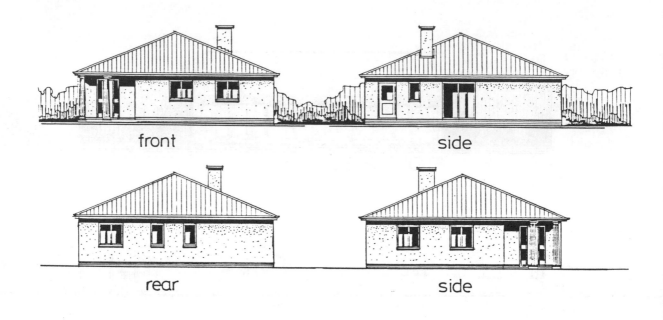

front

side

rear

side

Square bungalows were popular between the wars, and have not been built since. I wonder why? They are economical to build, to heat, and are very compact. At any rate, this example will suit an infill plot in a road of homes built fifty years ago and not look out of place in any way.

The sauna adjacent to the two bathrooms was specified by the client for whom this bungalow was designed. It is very imporant to give expert consideration to the ventilation of a sauna like this which is part of the structure of the building, and not simply free standing in the corner of a large bathroom.

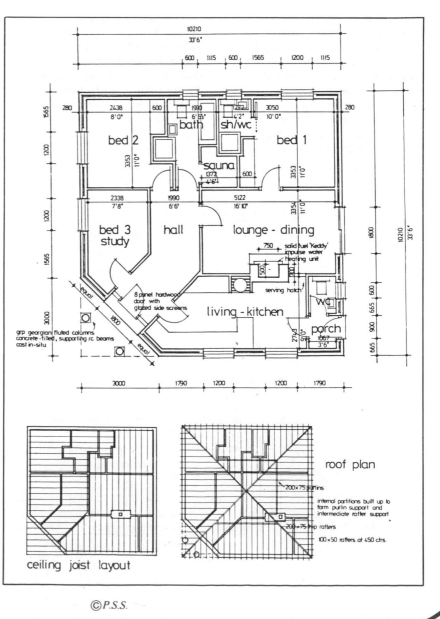

# BUNGALOWS UNDER 1500 SQ.FT.

**Ref: W1297**

**89 sq.m. 958 sq.ft.**
**(exc. garage)**

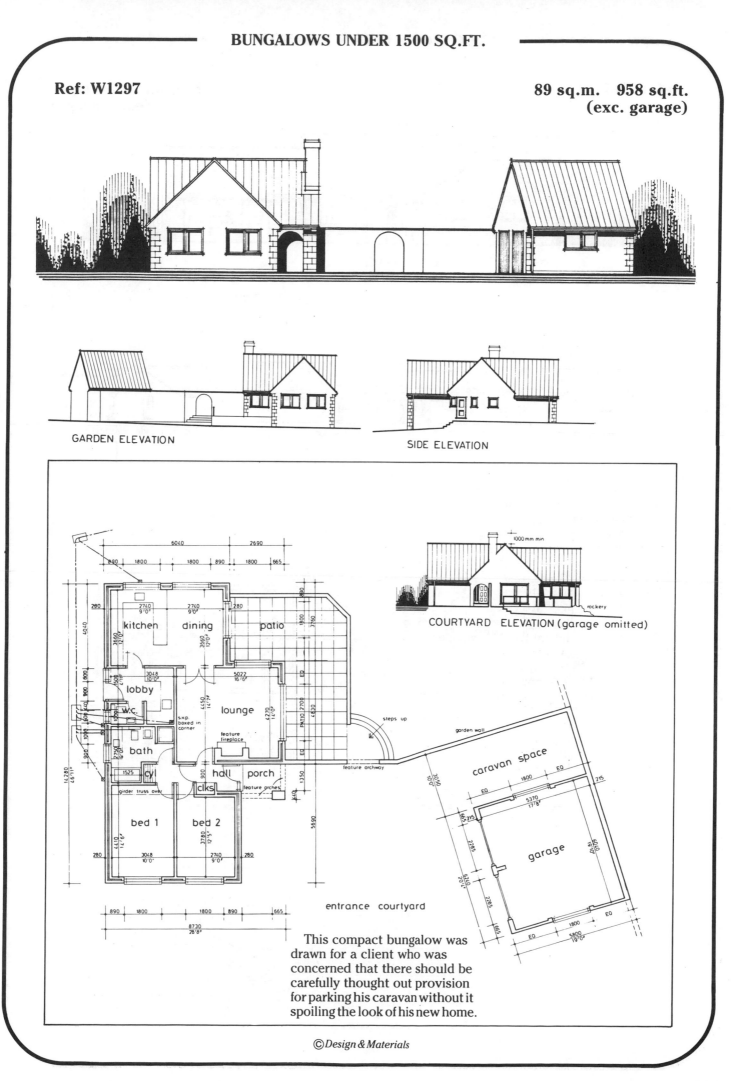

GARDEN ELEVATION

SIDE ELEVATION

COURTYARD ELEVATION (garage omitted)

entrance courtyard

This compact bungalow was drawn for a client who was concerned that there should be carefully thought out provision for parking his caravan without it spoiling the look of his new home.

**Ref: P2789**

**118 sq.m.   1270 sq.ft.**
**(exc. garage)**

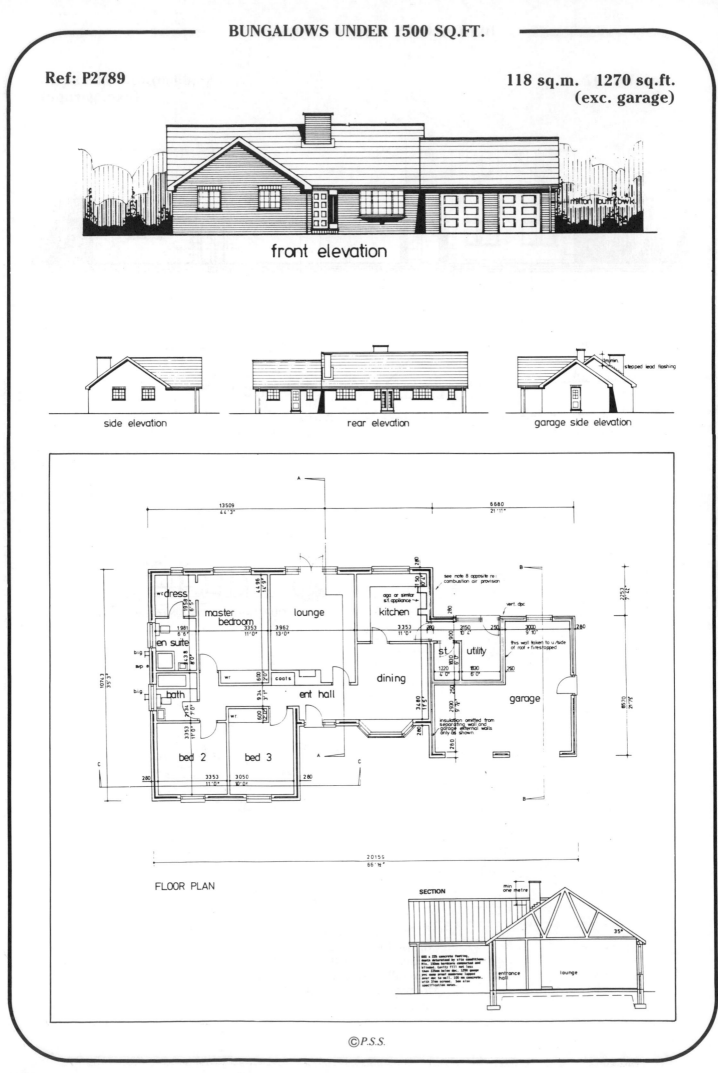

front elevation

side elevation

rear elevation

garage side elevation

FLOOR PLAN

SECTION

©P.S.S.

**Ref: P2553**

**136 sq.m.    1463 sq.ft.**

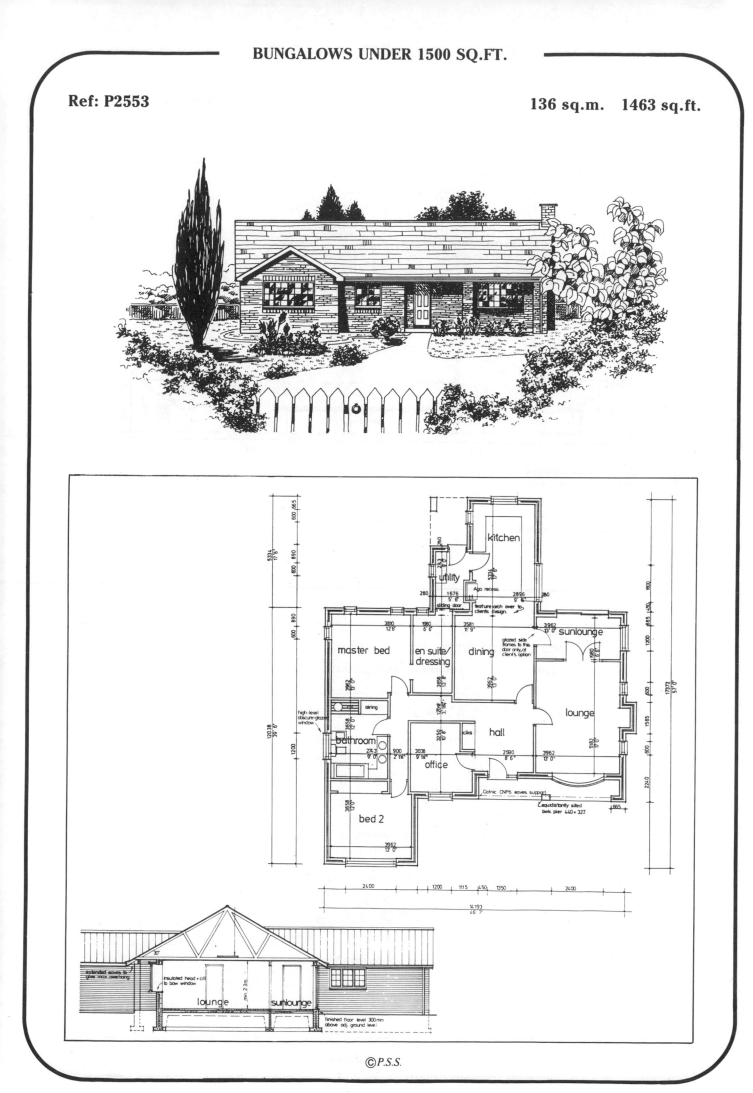

**Ref: 1474**                    **120 sq.m.    1291 sq.ft.**

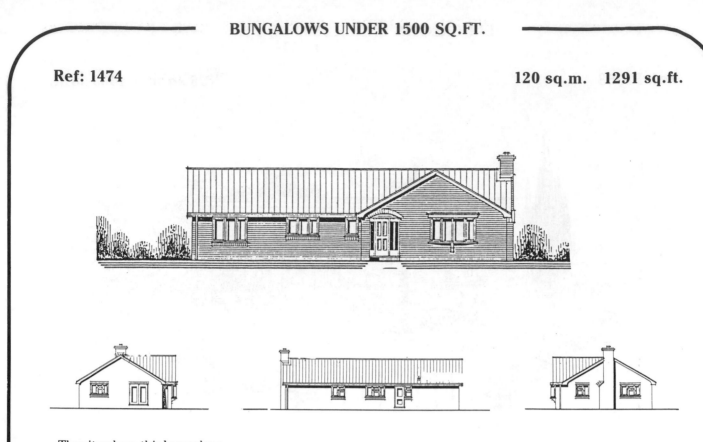

The site where this bungalow was built had both the access and key views at the front, with little to see at the rear or at either side. This unusual layout of rooms was to meet the clients requirements.

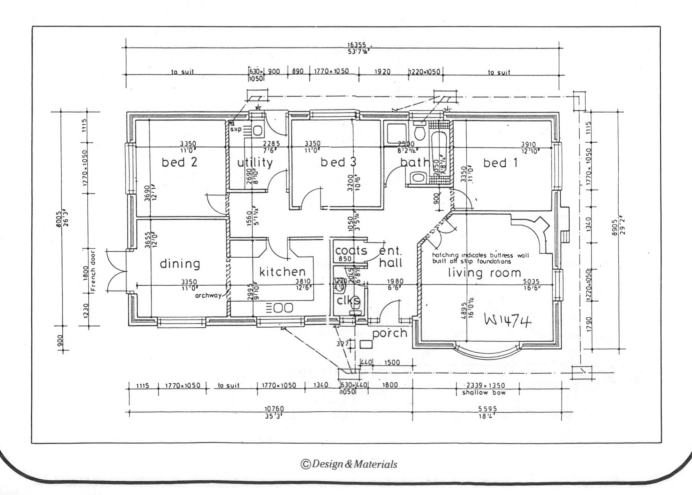

**Ref: W1025**

**116 sq.m.    1250 sq.ft.**

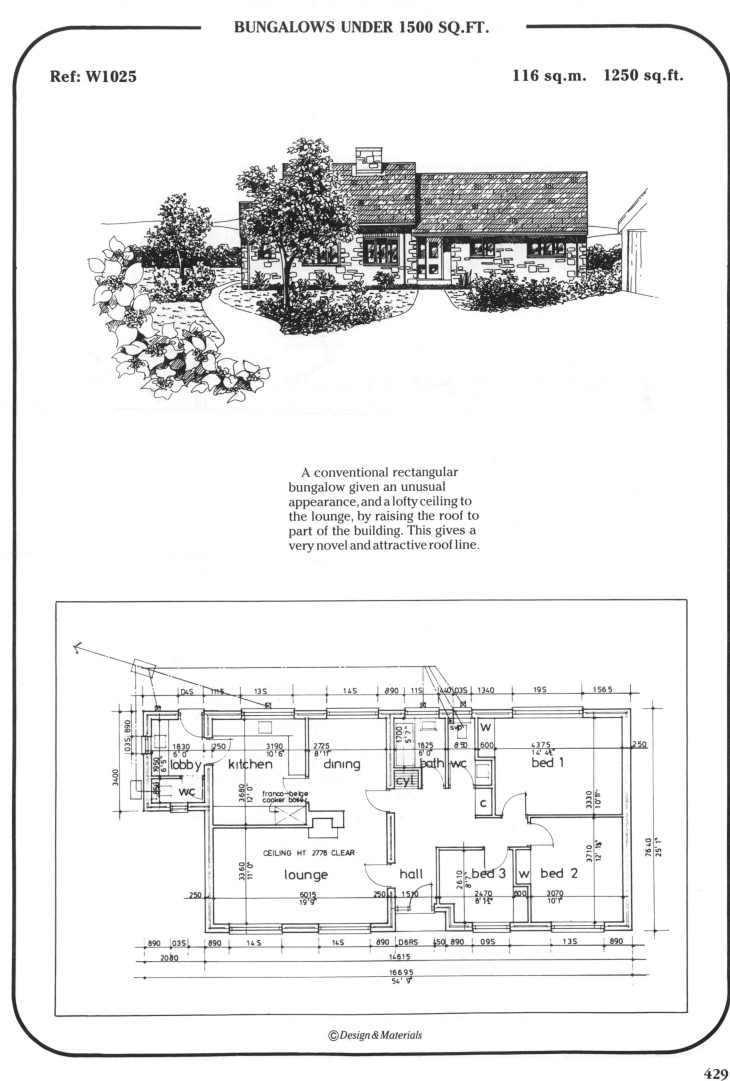

A conventional rectangular bungalow given an unusual appearance, and a lofty ceiling to the lounge, by raising the roof to part of the building. This gives a very novel and attractive roof line.

**Ref: C336**

**112 sq.m.    1205 sq.ft.**

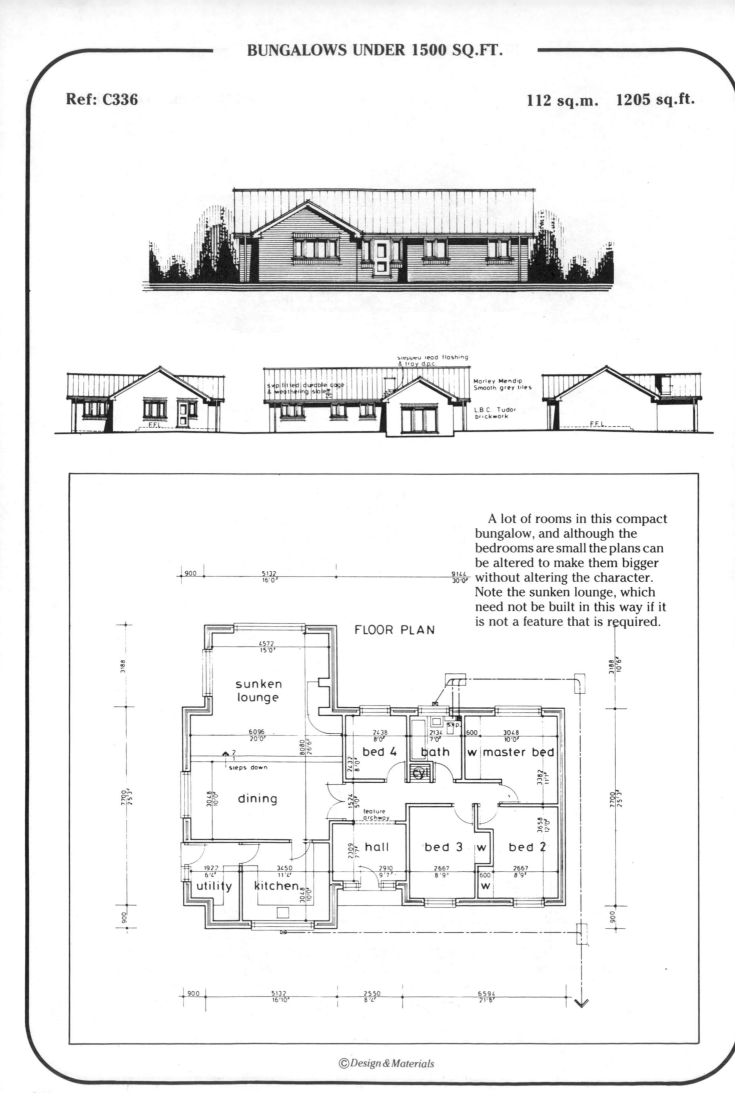

A lot of rooms in this compact bungalow, and although the bedrooms are small the plans can be altered to make them bigger without altering the character. Note the sunken lounge, which need not be built in this way if it is not a feature that is required.

FLOOR PLAN

sunken lounge

dining

steps down

utility    kitchen

feature archway

hall

bed 4    bath    w    master bed

cyl

bed 3    w    bed 2

w

stepped lead flashing & tray d.p.c.

svp fitted durable dage & weathering slate

Marley Mendip Smooth grey tiles

L.B.C. Tudor brickwork

F.F.L.

© Design & Materials

# Bungalows Over 1500 sq. ft.

Although larger bungalows provide more design opportunities than those under 1500 sq. ft., most people commissioning a designer to prepare plans already have a very clear idea of what they want. This is invariably a new home with a conventional appearance and a standard room layout: bungalow builders are not nearly as adventurous as house builders!

A really large bungalow is only suited to a large plot. A two storey house can occupy the full width of the site on which it is built and look very attractive, but a large single storey property must have plenty of space around it. If this is not possible, consider building two storeys. If your interest in bungalows is because you wish to avoid having stairs, then consider a lift of some sort. This is now a practical proposition and will not cost a fortune these days.

The external character of a bungalow is largely determined by the roof pitch, which is traditionally either 30° or 35°. A steeper pitch of roof, or a lower 22.5° roof for a ranch style home is often more interesting, although a decision on this will depend on adjacent buildings.

With the right site, a design for a large bungalow has to be considered together with the landscaping: garden and building must be complementary to each other, and ideally designed together. Internally, large bungalows provide opportunities for striking design features, sometimes involving changes of level. Glazed screens or other ways of providing vistas across two rooms can give a special character very cheaply, and most individual designs for larger single storey homes are drawn with a specific interior design theme in mind as well as carefully planned landscaping. The home, the furnishings and the garden all conform to a specific concept.

Integral garages should be avoided if possible, and if a detached garage can be built at an angle to the bungalow, and perhaps linked to it with a wall or wrought iron gate, the development becomes a group of structures and is visually much more interesting. Clever garden design, with any paving or patio planned on a generous scale will add to the effect. Beware skimpy terraces or narrow paths: they will make the property look smaller. A big patio, with wide walls and wide paths will make it look larger.

**Ref: 96156**

**292 sq.m.    3137 sq.ft.**

A large bungalow which has many of the features of homes in the eastern states of the USA. The low level windows to the front elevation, emphasised by deep reveals, are typical American features. So is the concept of stepping through the front door to have a view right through the living area with an array of impressive columns between the hall and the lounge. Note that the dining area floor is raised above the general floor level.

There is space in the roof for a hobbies room or study, with various possible arrangements for stairs. The probable choice will be an exposed open tread stairway on the wall opposite the fireplace in the lounge.

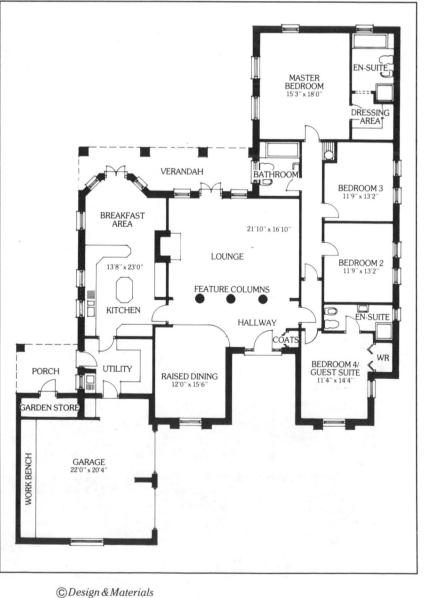

© *Design & Materials*

**Ref: 96157**

**347 sq.m.   3737 sq.ft.**

Another large bungalow which owes a lot to American design ideas. Look how the garage on the right has windows and a bay which makes it look part of the living accommodation, and enhances the prestige of the home when seen from the road. This is not unusual in the States, but rarely seen here. As with the design opposite there are feature columns and a raised dining area, and every bedroom has an en suite shower room.

The space in the roof can be used for a study or workroom, with a number of optional arrangements for a stairway.

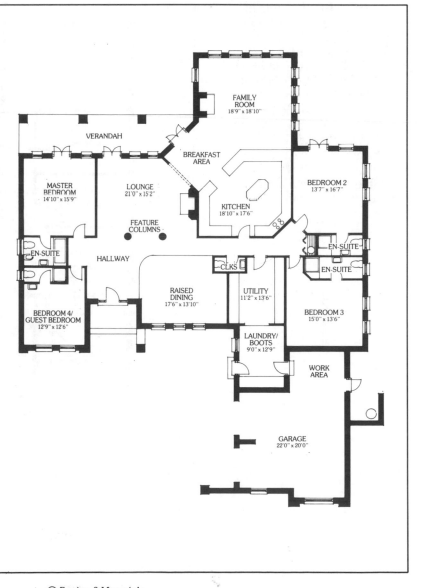

FAMILY ROOM
18'9" x 18'10"

VERANDAH

BREAKFAST AREA

MASTER BEDROOM
14'10" x 15'9"

LOUNGE
21'0" x 15'2"

BEDROOM 2
13'7" x 16'7"

KITCHEN
18'10" x 17'6"

FEATURE COLUMNS

EN-SUITE

EN-SUITE

EN-SUITE

HALLWAY

CLKS

BEDROOM 4/ GUEST BEDROOM
12'9" x 12'6"

RAISED DINING
17'6" x 13'10"

UTILITY
11'2" x 13'6"

BEDROOM 3
15'0" x 13'6"

LAUNDRY/ BOOTS
9'0" x 12'9"

WORK AREA

GARAGE
22'0" x 20'0"

**Ref: 96134**

**146 sq.m.    1577 sq.ft.**

A bungalow that has lots of character with deep small pane windows, a sunken lounge and an unusual shape to the entrance hall. It is typical of many single storey houses built in the USA, and does not conform to any specific British style. This is definitely a design concept to be checked out with the planners at an early stage, but in many areas it would be acceptable, and much admired by those who like something different.

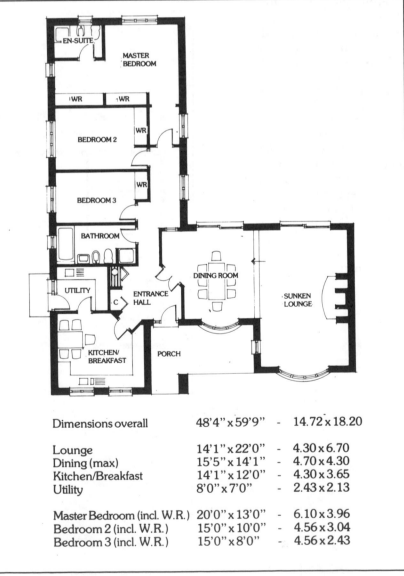

| Dimensions overall | 48'4" x 59'9" | - | 14.72 x 18.20 |
|---|---|---|---|
| Lounge | 14'1" x 22'0" | - | 4.30 x 6.70 |
| Dining (max) | 15'5" x 14'1" | - | 4.70 x 4.30 |
| Kitchen/Breakfast | 14'1" x 12'0" | - | 4.30 x 3.65 |
| Utility | 8'0" x 7'0" | - | 2.43 x 2.13 |
| Master Bedroom (incl. W.R.) | 20'0" x 13'0" | - | 6.10 x 3.96 |
| Bedroom 2 (incl. W.R.) | 15'0" x 10'0" | - | 4.56 x 3.04 |
| Bedroom 3 (incl. W.R.) | 15'0" x 8'0" | - | 4.56 x 2.43 |

**Ref: 95104**

**204 sq.m.   2193 sq.ft.**
**(with upper floor)**

A bungalow which has a generous three bedroom layout on the ground floor, and which can be extended with another three bedrooms in the roof if required. The piping and wiring to the first floor can be easily and cheaply provided to the first floor when the property is built so that the accommodation in the roof is provided with the minimum of trouble at a later stage.

Only one of the dormers faces the front, and if necessary it can be moved into the side wall. In some circumstances this would enable the upper floor to be provided as 'permitted development' in circumstances where planning consent was for a single storey dwelling only, although tactics of this sort require the best advice available. (Permitted development is not usually possible when there is any change in a *front* elevation).

CONVERSION WITH DORMER WINDOWS

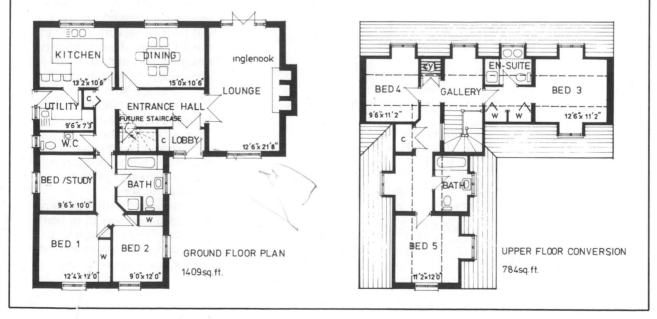

KITCHEN 13'2" x 10'6"

DINING 15'0" x 10'6"

inglenook

LOUNGE

UTILITY 9'6" x 7'3"

C

ENTRANCE HALL

FUTURE STAIRCASE

W.C

C LOBBY

BED/STUDY 9'6" x 10'0"

BATH

12'6" x 21'8"

BED 1 12'4" x 12'0"

W

BED 2 9'0" x 12'0"

W

GROUND FLOOR PLAN

1409 sq.ft.

BED 4 9'6" x 11'2"

EN-SUITE

GALLERY

BED 3 12'6" x 11'2"

W   W

C

BATH

BED 5 11'2" x 12'0"

UPPER FLOOR CONVERSION

784 sq.ft.

© *Design & Materials*

**Ref: 96220**

**262 sq.m.   2815 sq.ft.**

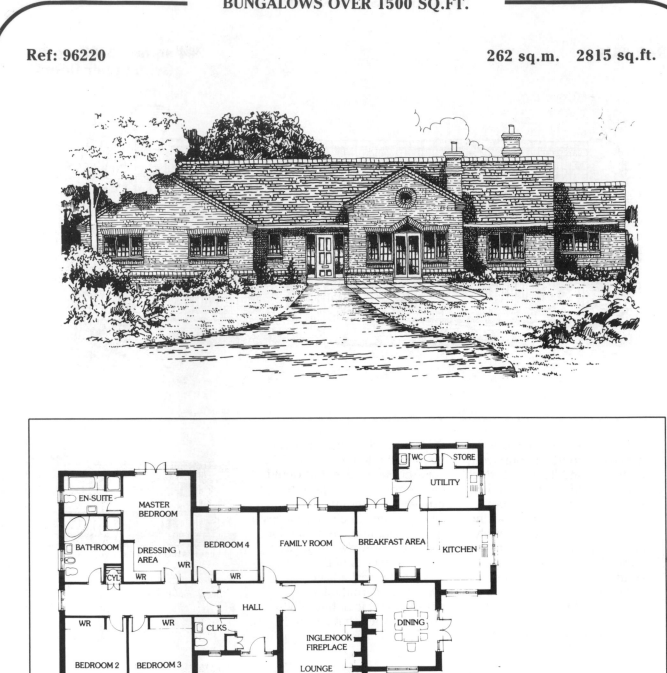

| Dimensions overall | 82'2" x 50'6" | - | 25.04 x 15.38 |
|---|---|---|---|
| Lounge | 15'0" x 24'0" | - | 4.57 x 7.31 |
| Dining | 13'0" x 16'0" | - | 3.96 x 4.87 |
| Breakfast/Kitchen (max) | 25'0" x 15'0" | - | 7.62 x 4.56 |
| Family Room | 18'0" x 13'0" | - | 5.48 x 3.96 |
| Utility | 15'0" x 7'5" | - | 4.56 x 2.25 |
| Master Bedroom (incl. Dressing Room) | 13'0" x 20'0" | - | 3.96 x 6.10 |
| Bedroom 2 (incl. W.R.) | 12'0" x 16'0" | - | 3.65 x 4.87 |
| Bedroom 3 (incl. W.R.) | 12'0" x 16'0" | - | 3.65 x 4.87 |
| Bedroom 4 (incl. W.R.) | 12'0" x 13'0" | - | 3.65 x 3.96 |

Very large bungalows like this were not uncommon in the 60's, but their popularity waned in the 70's when the first county design guides appeared and proclaimed "a presumption against single storey construction". Twenty years later the design guides have been so undermined by successful planning appeals that really big single storey homes are again getting approval in some circumstances, although they are still a long way from being popular. The exception is in Eire, where this splendid home will be really appreciated.

**Ref: 96219**

**152 sq.m.    1632 sq.ft.**

A three bedroom home for a large plot, with rooms of above average size. Large bungalows with a wide frontage like this must have a large plot, as they are rarely attractive when cramped, while the same property with plenty of room around it will look splendid.

| | | | |
|---|---|---|---|
| Dimensions overall | 64'5" x 30'2" | - | 19.63 x 9.20 |
| Lounge | 13'0" x 24'8" | - | 3.96 x 7.51 |
| Dining | 10'0" x 10'0" | - | 3.04 x 3.04 |
| Kitchen | 15'0" x 10'0" | - | 4.57 x 3.04 |
| Utility | 6'0" x 8'0" | - | 1.82 x 2.44 |
| Master Bedroom (incl. W.R.) | 12'0" x 15'4" | - | 3.65 x 4.67 |
| Bedroom 2 (incl. W.R.) | 14'9" x 9'0" | - | 4.49 x 2.74 |
| Bedroom 3 (incl. W.R.) | 11'2" x 9'0" | - | 3.40 x 2.74 |
| Bedroom 4 | 9'0" x 10'9" | - | 2.74 x 3.26 |

**Ref: 96221**

**144 sq.m.    1558 sq.ft.**

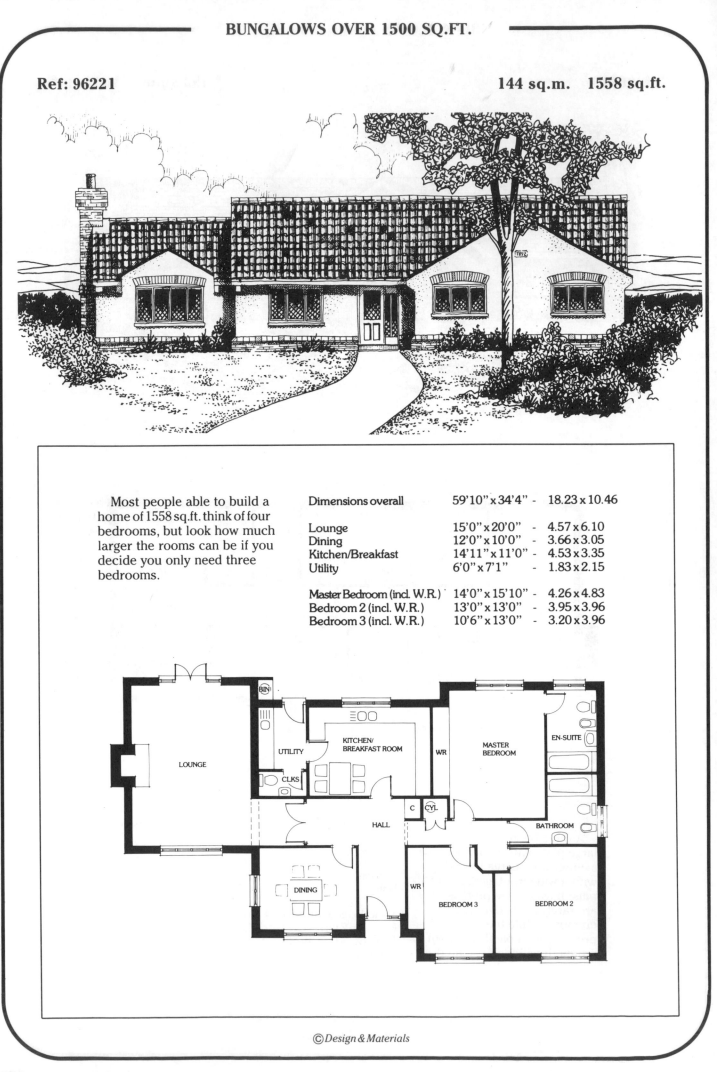

Most people able to build a home of 1558 sq.ft. think of four bedrooms, but look how much larger the rooms can be if you decide you only need three bedrooms.

| Dimensions overall | 59'10" x 34'4" | - | 18.23 x 10.46 |
|---|---|---|---|
| Lounge | 15'0" x 20'0" | - | 4.57 x 6.10 |
| Dining | 12'0" x 10'0" | - | 3.66 x 3.05 |
| Kitchen/Breakfast | 14'11" x 11'0" | - | 4.53 x 3.35 |
| Utility | 6'0" x 7'1" | - | 1.83 x 2.15 |
| Master Bedroom (incl. W.R.) | 14'0" x 15'10" | - | 4.26 x 4.83 |
| Bedroom 2 (incl. W.R.) | 13'0" x 13'0" | - | 3.95 x 3.96 |
| Bedroom 3 (incl. W.R.) | 10'6" x 13'0" | - | 3.20 x 3.96 |

**Ref: 96214**

**144 sq.m.    1550 sq.ft.**

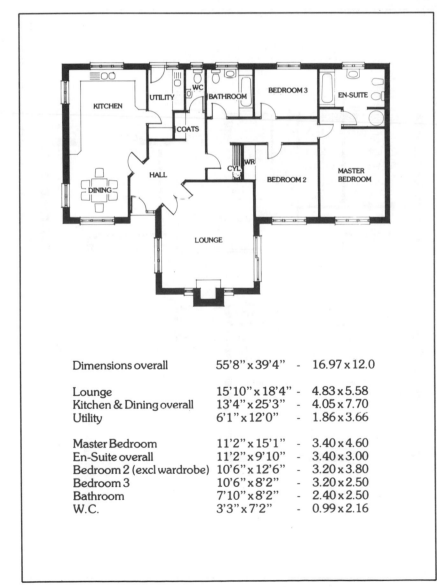

A bungalow with a central lounge that projects from the front elevation. Homes with this sort of layout are often built with a chimney breast to the front like this, presumably because the owners want to enjoy the view from the side windows, or because they instinctively feel a fireplace should be on the opposite side of the room to the door. Those who pay the piper call the tune, but I would have preferred to see it on one of the side walls.

| | | |
|---|---|---|
| Dimensions overall | 55'8" x 39'4" - | 16.97 x 12.0 |
| Lounge | 15'10" x 18'4" - | 4.83 x 5.58 |
| Kitchen & Dining overall | 13'4" x 25'3" - | 4.05 x 7.70 |
| Utility | 6'1" x 12'0" - | 1.86 x 3.66 |
| Master Bedroom | 11'2" x 15'1" - | 3.40 x 4.60 |
| En-Suite overall | 11'2" x 9'10" - | 3.40 x 3.00 |
| Bedroom 2 (excl wardrobe) | 10'6" x 12'6" - | 3.20 x 3.80 |
| Bedroom 3 | 10'6" x 8'2" - | 3.20 x 2.50 |
| Bathroom | 7'10" x 8'2" - | 2.40 x 2.50 |
| W.C. | 3'3" x 7'2" - | 0.99 x 2.16 |

**Ref: 96119**

**146 sq.m.    1569 sq.ft.**

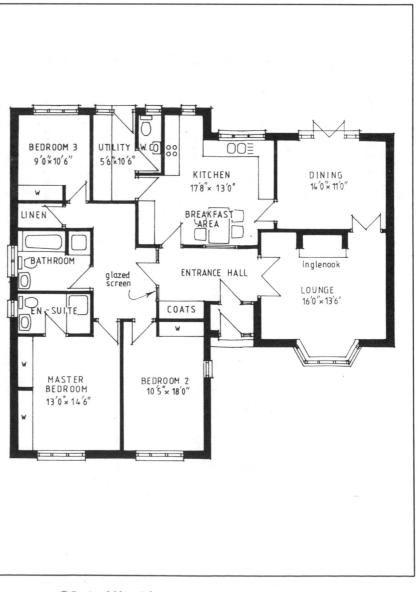

This bungalow is a good deal larger than it looks, and provides generous three bedroom accommodation with plenty of living space. Architectural purests would say that the Inglenook fireplace is totally inappropriate to a bungalow, but houses are for living in, and if an Inglenook fireplace is what you want, have it by all means. The planning acts only apply to the outside appearance of a property, and this well proportioned bungalow has restrained appearance that would be acceptable to the planners anywhere.

BEDROOM 3
9'0"×10'6"

UTILITY
5'6"×10'6"

W.C.

KITCHEN
17'8"× 13'0"

DINING
14'0"× 11'0"

LINEN

BREAKFAST AREA

BATHROOM

Inglenook

glazed screen

ENTRANCE HALL

LOUNGE
16'0"× 13'6"

EN-SUITE

COATS

MASTER BEDROOM
13'0"× 14'6"

BEDROOM 2
10'5"× 18'0"

**Ref: PN670**

**140 sq.m.    1505 sq.ft.**

This three bedroomed bungalow from Potton is typical of the company's Shire range of timber framed homes to be built with wall panel construction. They vary in size from 935 to 1785 square feet, and are remarkably cost effective to build. The styling can be varied within limits, and adapted to suit regional design requirements in all parts of the country.

All the Shire bungalows have high levels of insulation built into the wall panels, and are very energy efficient.

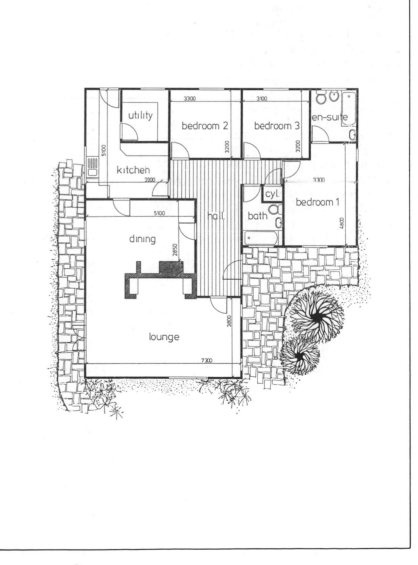

©Potton

**Ref: C135**

**158 sq.m.   1700 sq.ft.**

Bungalows with full length verandahs are very popular in Ireland and parts of Wales, and have a very attractive period feel. The detail design of the pillars and of any arches that link them together is very important, and is shewn here in dark masonry to set off the rendered walls.

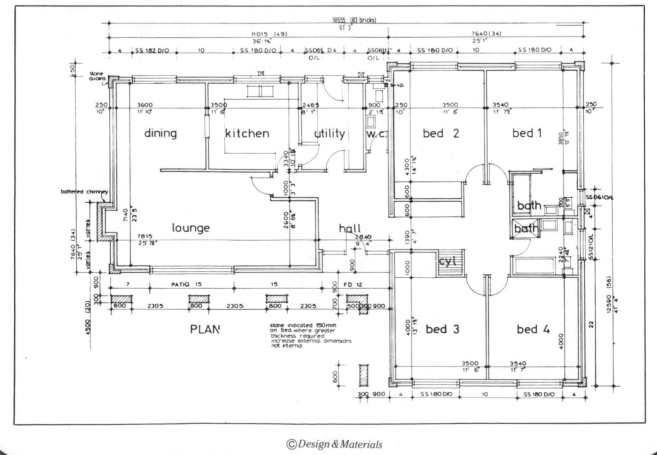

PLAN

stone indicated 150mm on bed. where greater thickness required increase external dimensions not internal

**Ref: S425**

**140 sq.m.   1506 sq.ft.**

A three bedroom layout for a bungalow in a very popular style. The accommodation can easily be re-arranged to provide an extra bedroom, which can also double as a study.

A large patio window set centrally in a gable end as shown here always looks attractive when in the rear elevation, to be seen from the garden, but invariably looks awkward in the front of the building. I have never been able to understand why this is!

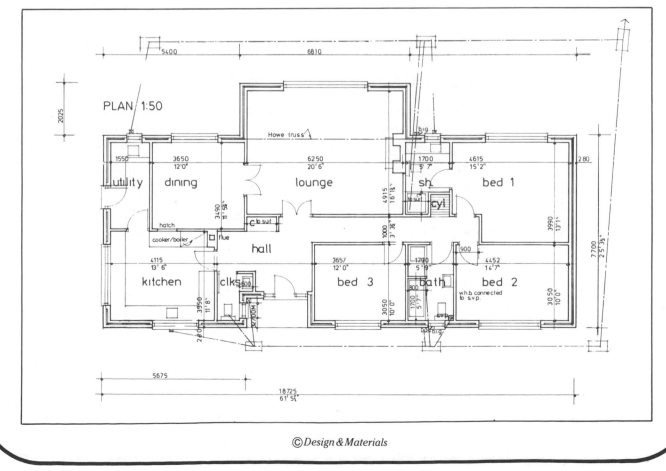

**Ref: W887**                                                    **142 sq.m.    1528 sq.ft.**

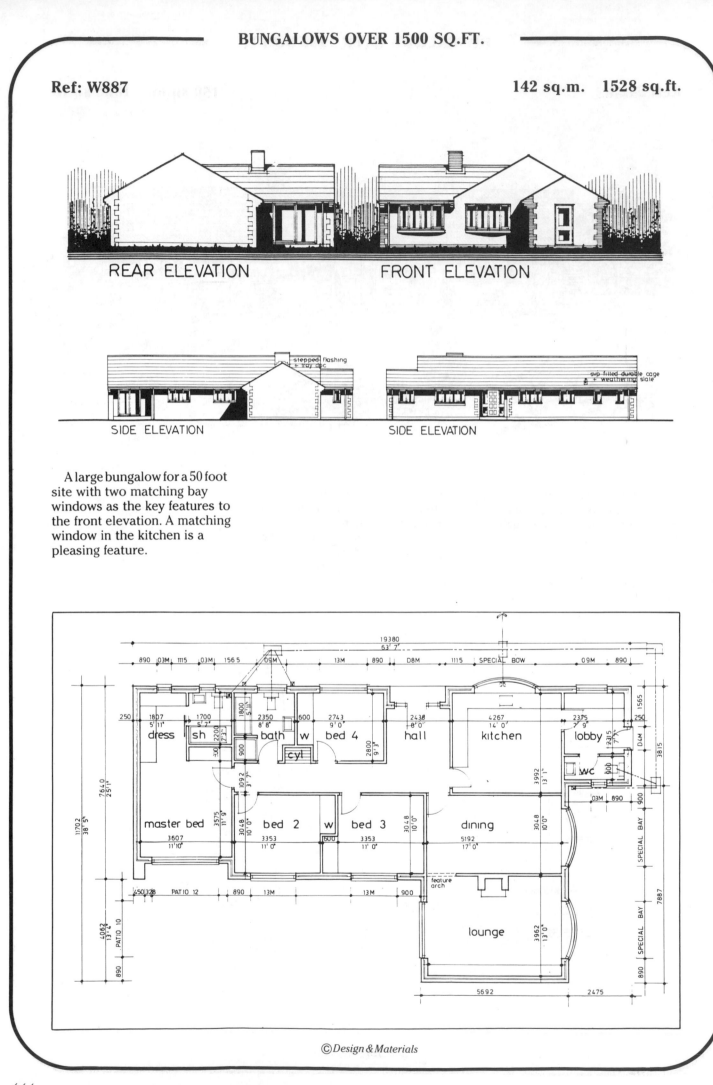

REAR ELEVATION          FRONT ELEVATION

SIDE ELEVATION          SIDE ELEVATION

A large bungalow for a 50 foot
site with two matching bay
windows as the key features to
the front elevation. A matching
window in the kitchen is a
pleasing feature.

# BUNGALOWS OVER 1500 SQ.FT.

**Ref: W1188**

**154 sq.m.   1657 sq.ft.**
**(exc. garage)**

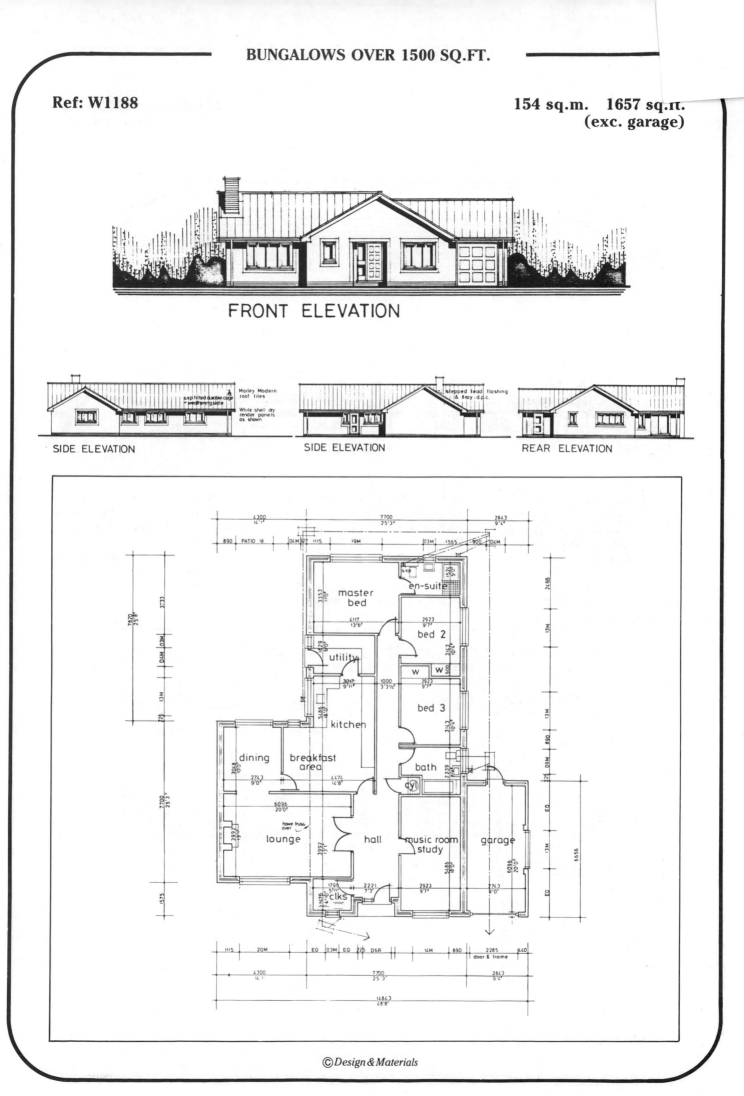

FRONT ELEVATION

SIDE ELEVATION

SIDE ELEVATION

REAR ELEVATION

s.v.p fitted durable cage
weathering slate

Marley Modern
roof tiles

White shell dry
render panels
as shown

stepped lead flashing
& tray d.p.c.

master bed

en-suite

bed 2

utility

w   w

bed 3

kitchen

dining   breakfast area

bath

cyl

lounge   hall   music room study   garage

clks

howe truss over

**Ref: W1104**

**191 sq.m.   2055 sq.ft.**
**(exc. garage)**

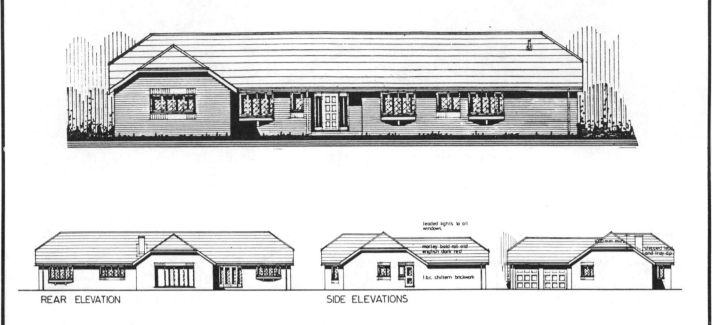

REAR ELEVATION                    SIDE ELEVATIONS

This large bungalow with its half hip roof, bay windows and leaded lights has a very gracious feel to it, and needs a beautifully landscaped large garden to set it off. The garage wing can be dispensed with if a detached garage is preferred, but it must be said that the lower garage roof adds complexity and interest to the roof line. If it is not to be built then the relationship of the detached garage to the main building needs very careful consideration.

The inglenook fireplace offers all sorts of scope for imaginative decor, and the lounge floor can be dropped to give more ceiling height, particularly if the lounge is extended. If this is done then the inglenook is probably best changed for a classical fireplace, and this will not present any problem.

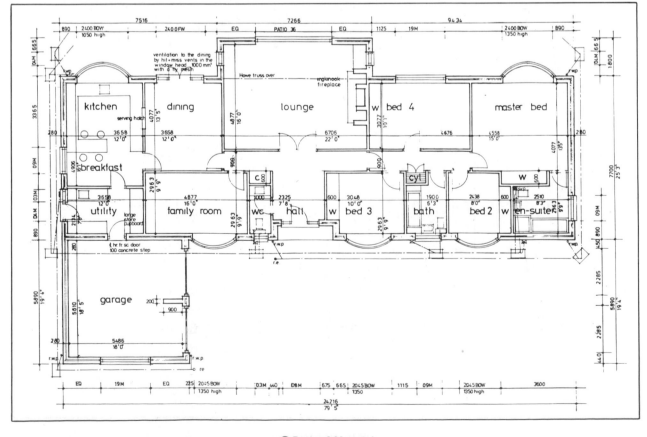

**Ref: W946**

**240 sq.m.   2583 sq.ft.**

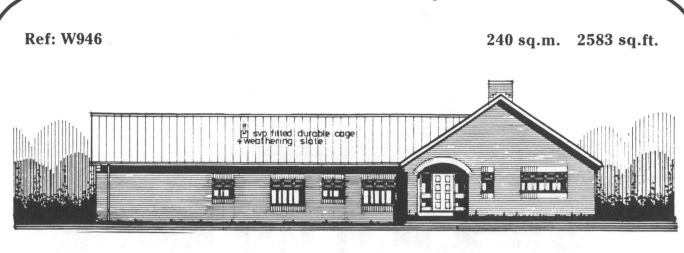

This bungalow is on two levels and has some interesting features. The large hall and kitchen area have a room height of 8'6", but there are steps down to the lounge and to the bedroom wing which have rooms that are 10'4" high. The lounge is thirty feet long by twenty six feet wide, so that it carries this height with ease and is a most elegant room. The plant trough at the side of the steps up to the dining area gives a special opportunity to the house plant enthusiast.

The master bedroom suite is huge, with a sunken bath as a feature in the bedroom itself, and french windows leading out onto a patio. Of course, if this arrangement does not suit you, a

SIDE ELEVATIONS

more conventional bathroom can be arranged and still leave a very big bedroom.

The other two double bedrooms each have a door into the guest bathroom - an arrangement which is unusual but very logical.

A bungalow of this size is normally built on a site with a large garden and it is important

that its design features should be complemented by really imaginative landscaping and the careful choice of the right walling materials. Handmade bricks under a plain tile roof will look particularly effective, especially if squint bricks are used for external window cills and regional brick features are used at the eaves and verge.

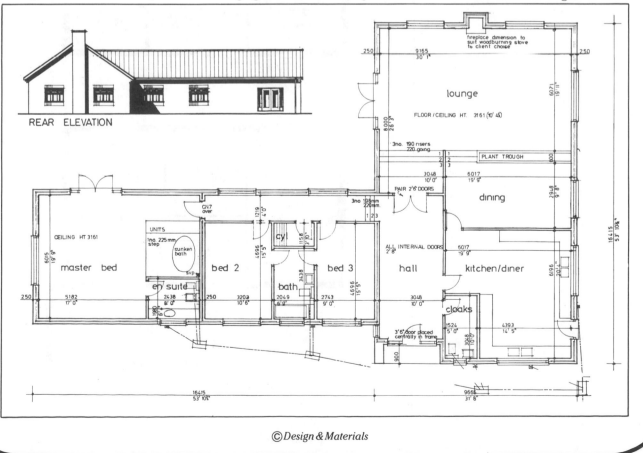

REAR ELEVATION

**Ref: 96193**

**141 sq.m.    1520 sq.ft.**

A bungalow from Wales, with rendered walls under a slate roof.

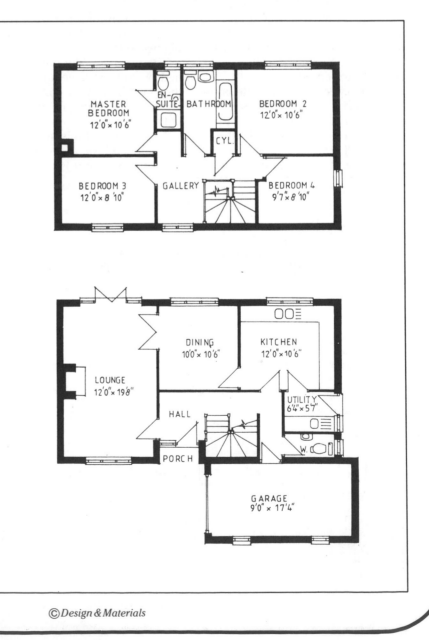

**Ref: 96201**

**152 sq.m.    1640 sq.ft.**

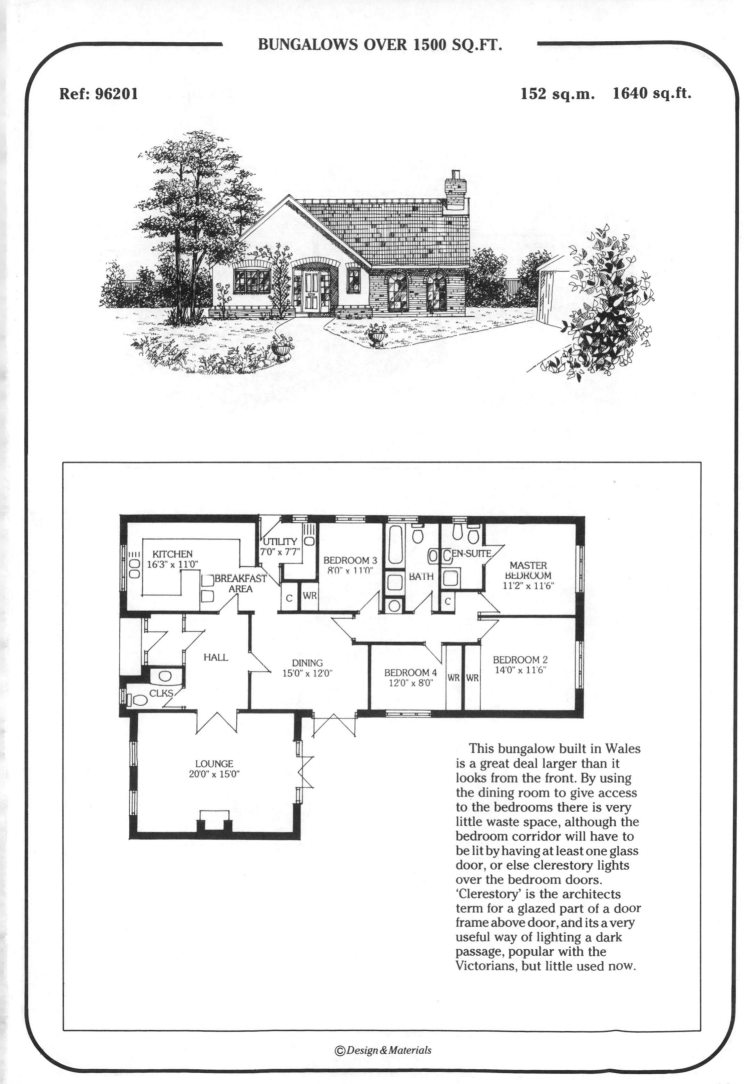

**KITCHEN**
16'3" x 11'0"

**BREAKFAST AREA**

**UTILITY**
7'0" x 7'7"

**BEDROOM 3**
8'0" x 11'0"

**EN-SUITE**

**BATH**

**MASTER BEDROOM**
11'2" x 11'6"

C    WR

C

**HALL**

**DINING**
15'0" x 12'0"

**BEDROOM 4**
12'0" x 8'0"

WR   WR

**BEDROOM 2**
14'0" x 11'6"

**CLKS.**

**LOUNGE**
20'0" x 15'0"

This bungalow built in Wales is a great deal larger than it looks from the front. By using the dining room to give access to the bedrooms there is very little waste space, although the bedroom corridor will have to be lit by having at least one glass door, or else clerestory lights over the bedroom doors. 'Clerestory' is the architects term for a glazed part of a door frame above door, and its a very useful way of lighting a dark passage, popular with the Victorians, but little used now.

**Ref: 1333**

**213 sq.m.   2292 sq.ft.**

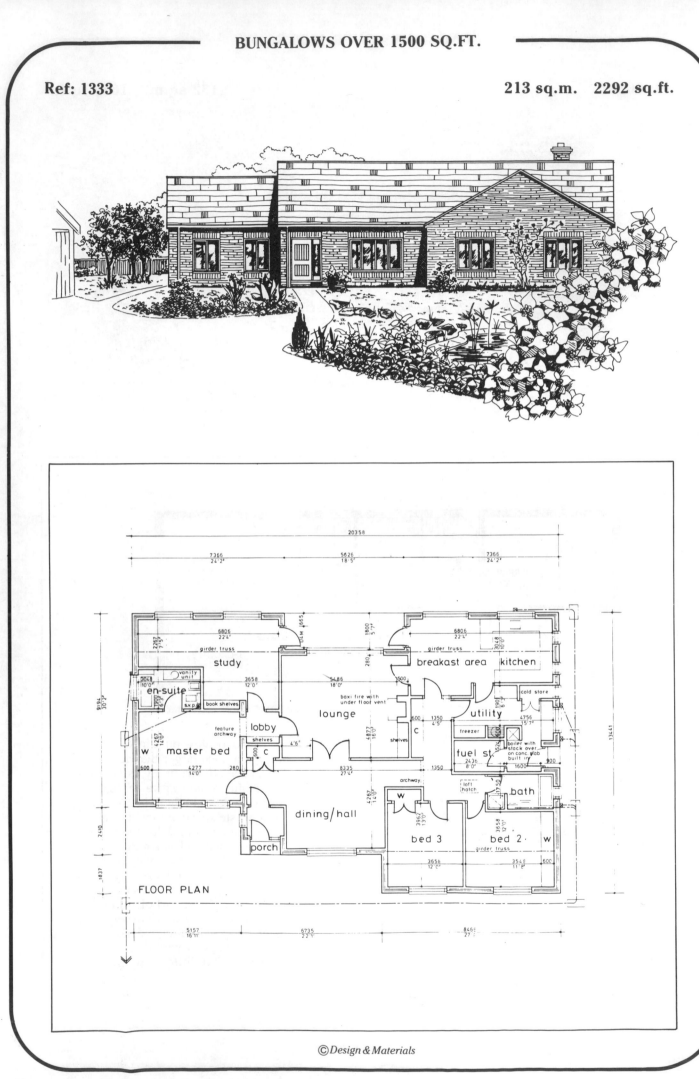

FLOOR PLAN

**Ref: S377**

**168 sq.m.    1808 sq.ft.**
**(exc. garage)**

This bungalow has four exceptionally large bedrooms, and this is a feature that some people building a new home particularly value. Another feature is the hobbies room behind the garage, linked to the central heating system and with plenty of windows to give good light.

The remainder of the layout is conventional, except that the plan is drawn with an outside WC next to the cloakroom off the hall. If this is not required then the space can be used to double the size of the cloakroom, giving room for a cloaks cupboard, golf bags and all the other things for which a large cloakroom makes such a convenient store.

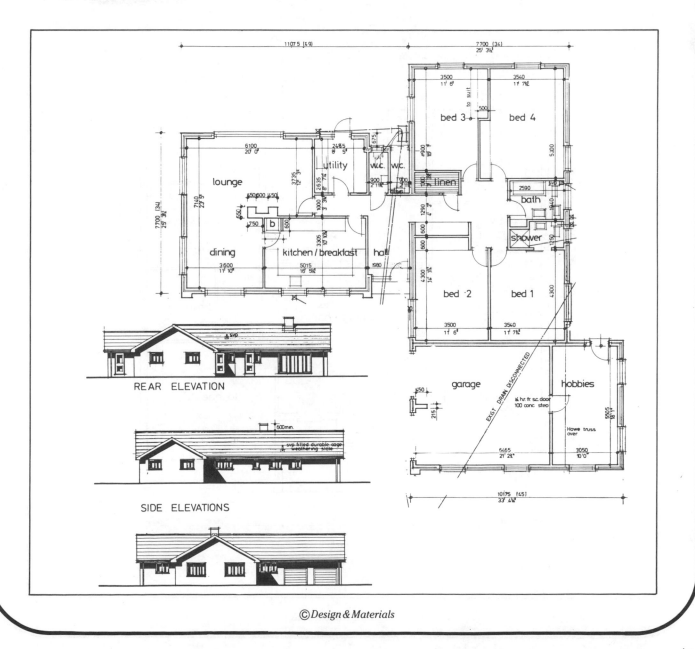

REAR ELEVATION

SIDE ELEVATIONS

© Design & Materials

**Ref: S404**

**170 sq.m.   1829 sq.ft.
(inc. garage)**

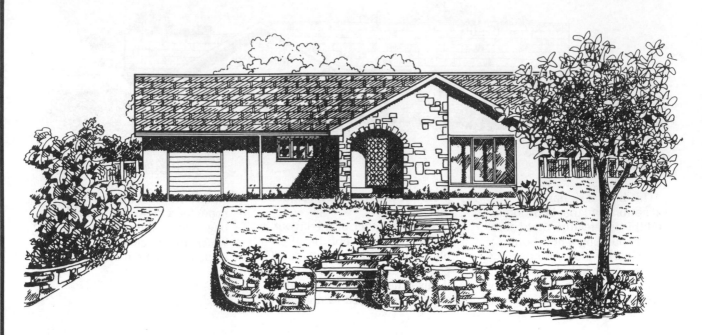

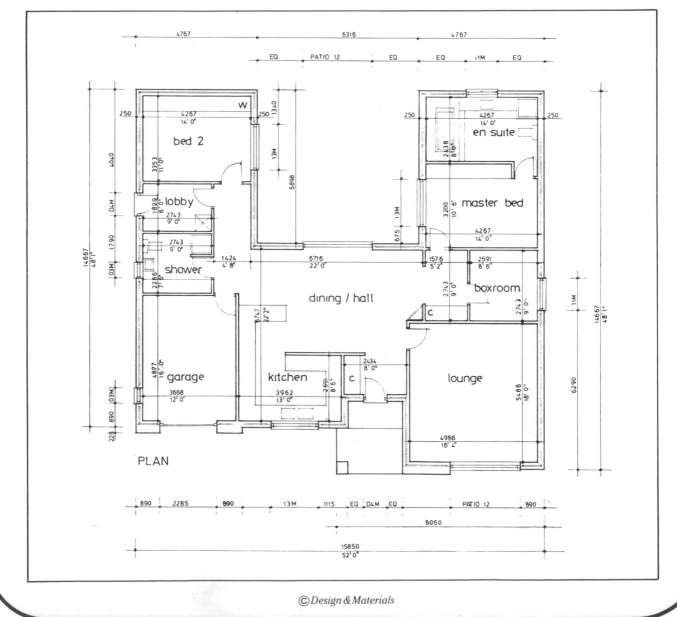

PLAN

**Ref: S528**

**158 sq.m.   1700 sq.ft.**

In most large homes the master bedroom suite is as far away from the living accommodation as possible, usually at the end of a bedroom corridor. In this five bedroom bungalow it is right in the centre of things. The choice is yours.

Note the outside store in the angle by the utility room window. This unusual feature was for a particular client, and most people interested in this design will want the boiler moved and the utility room rearranged to use this space in some other way.

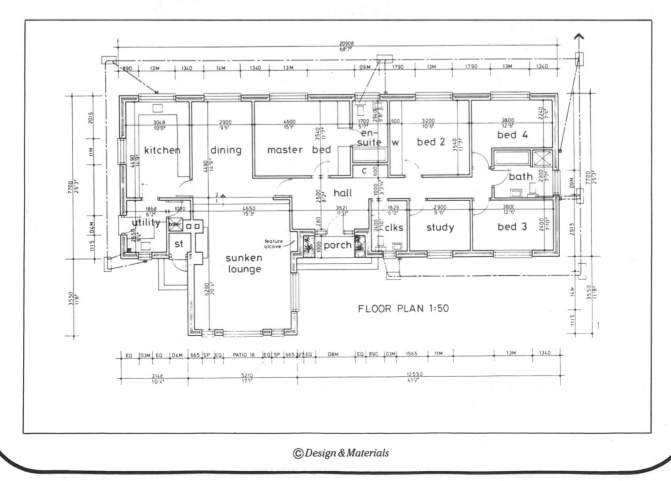

FLOOR PLAN 1:50

**Ref: C433**

**159 sq.m.   1711 sq.ft.**
**(inc. garage)**

## FLOOR PLAN

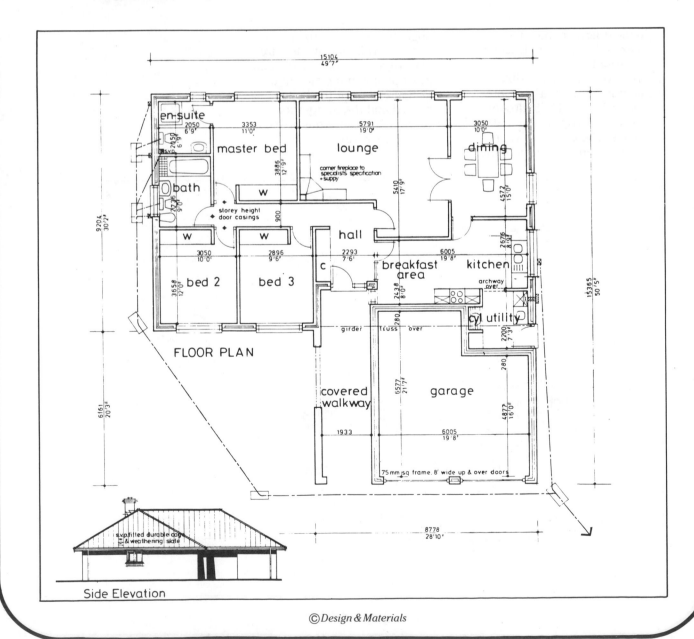

15104
49'7"

en-suite

2050
6'9"

3353
11'0"

5791
19'0"

3050
10'0"

master bed

lounge

dining

3886
12'9"

corner fireplace to
specialists specification
+ suppy

5410
17'9"

4577
15'0"

bath

w

storey height
door casings

900

hall

2676
8'9"

w

w

c

2293
7'6"

breakfast
area

kitchen

3050
10'0"

2896
9'6"

6005
19'8"

archway
over

3658
12'0"

bed 2

bed 3

2638
8'0"

cyl utility

2200
7'3"

9204
30'2"

280

girder truss over

280

covered
walkway

6577
21'7"

garage

4877
15'0"

15365
50'5"

6161
20'3"

1933

6005
19'8"

75mm sq frame. 8' wide up & over doors

8778
28'10"

Side Elevation

s.v.p. fitted durable caa
& weathering slate

© Design & Materials

**Ref: W1318**

**179 sq.m.   1926 sq.ft.**
**(exc. garage)**

This large bungalow has some very interesting features. No fewer than five of the rooms have more than four walls, and this gives an excitingly different feel to the home as soon as the visitor steps through the porch into the dining hall with its off-set doors into the lounge.

In spite of the complex shape the whole of the roof is supported on the external walls, so that rooms can be rearranged just as you wish. In particular, the utility room area can become a cloakroom with access to the entrance porch if required, and of course the garage doors can be moved to either the front or the rear.

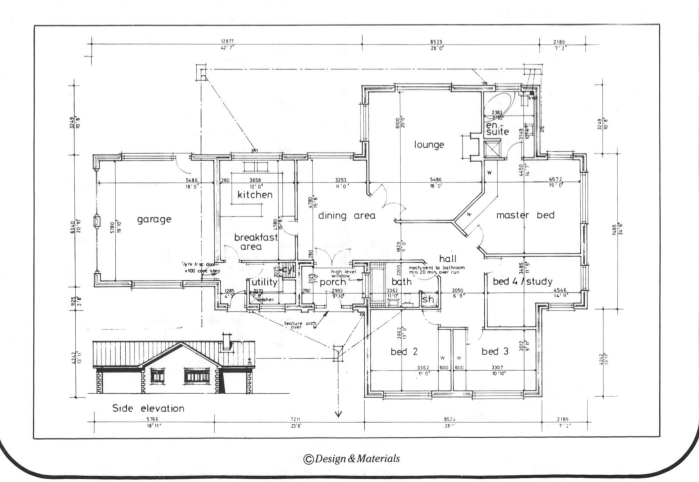

Side elevation

**Ref: 95103**

**198 sq.m.   2127 sq.ft.**

A large bungalow for a site which need only be 60 ft. wide, although the more room there is round it, the better it will look. There are no windows in the rear elevation, as when originally built this was not considered appropriate as there was an old barn behind the house. It would be perfectly easy to change this window arrangement to enjoy a view to the rear on a different site.

The bungalow is illustrated with a 22½ pitch roof. In areas where planners are likely to require a steeper roof pitch it must be remembered that this will restrict the overhang of the eaves, and make a significant change to the appearance of the property.

*Dimensions overall*
*52'0" x 65'5"  -  15.8 x 19.9*
*Lounge  15'0" x 22'0"  -  4.5 x 6.7*
*Family Room  12'0" x 14'0"  -  3.6 x 4.2*
*Kitchen/Breakfast*
*16'0" x 12'0"  -  4.8 x 3.6*
*Utility  5'9" x 8'5"  -  1.7 x 2.5*
*Dining  10'0" x 12'0"  -  3.0 x 3.6*
*Master Bedroom (incl W.R)*
*14'11" x 17'10"  -  4.5 x 5.4*
*Bedroom 2 (incl. W. R.)*
*10'0" x 13'0"  -  3.0 x 3.9*
*Bedroom 3 (incl. W. R.)*
*12'0" x 12'0"  -  3.6 x 3.6*
*Bedroom 4 (incl. W. R.)*
*10'0" x 12'0"  -  3.0 x 3.6*

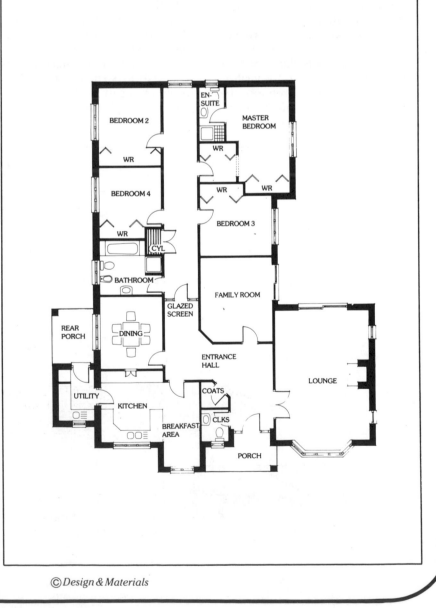

© *Design & Materials*

# *Further Information*

Building for yourself is all about managing a complex project. Management, so the experts tell us, is all about obtaining and using information. This is particularly important for those who intend to build for themselves. Time spent in reading the consumer guides and text books before you start, going to shows and exhibitions, and particularly finding opportunities to meet other selfbuilders is time very well spent. The costs involved will be recouped many times. Making yourself an expert on how others go about buying building plots and building homes on them can easily save you 5% on the total project costs. For a new home costing £80,000 this would be a saving of £4,000.

This does not mean that you have to learn about every technicality, but rather that you need to know what is going to be required, the best way to find the right people to get the job done, how to make arrangements with them, and where to get further advice and help if it is required. The various organisations and companies listed on the following pages can help with both the general information that you will require and with technical matters. They all have literature which explains exactly what they can offer. Collecting their publications and learning from them is the essential first step in building for yourself.

## COMPANIES WHOSE DESIGNS ARE FEATURED IN THIS BOOK

Full sets of drawings for the plans in this book may be obtained from the copyright holders. Drawings for some of the designs are only available as part of a more comprehensive service, for which details are available on request. The copyright holders are identified at the bottom of relevant pages. The plans may not be reproduced by any means for any purpose without the permission of the copyright holders

DESIGN AND MATERIALS LIMITED,
LAWN ROAD INDUSTRIAL ESTATE, CARLTON IN LINDRICK,
WORKSOP, NOTTS S81 9LB
Phone    01909 730333
Fax       01909 731201

POTTON LIMITED, WILLOW ROAD, POTTON,
BEDS SG19 2PP.
Phone    01767 260348
Fax       01767 261800

PRESTOPLAN LIMITED, FOUR OAKS ROAD,
WALTON SUMMIT CENTRE, PRESTON, PR5 8AS
Phone    01772 627373
Fax       01772 62757

PLAN SALES SERVICES LIMITED,
LAWN ROAD INDUSTRIAL ESTATE, CARLTON IN LINDRICK,
WORKSOP, NOTTS. S81 9LB
Phone    01909 733927
Fax       01909 730201

## FURTHER INFORMATION

For further information call the numbers listed and ask for details of services available for those who are building a new house or bungalow.   A detailed enquiry is best made after studying the literature which is available.

### BOOKS, MAGAZINES, VIDEOS

Book 'BUILDING YOUR OWN HOME,  Murray Armor, published Ebury.
Companion volume to Plans for Dream Homes, order form on page 285 of this book

Book 'HOME PLANS',  Murray Armor, published Dents.
Companion volume to Plans for Dream Homes, order form on page 285 of this book

Book 'PRACTICAL HOUSEBUILDING', Matthews, Dents
Construction techniques for selfbuilders

Book 'COLLINS COMPLETE DIY MANUAL', Collins.
The standard DIY guide

Books 'FIND and BUY A BUILDING PLOT',
Speer and Dade, Dents
'GET PLANNING PERMISSION',
Speer and Dade, Dents
Excellent guides to buying land and planning matters

FURTHER SELFBUILD BOOK LISTS FROM RYTON BOOKS, 01909 591652

Magazine 'BUILD IT'. Monthly.
Subscriptions 0181 286 3000

Magazine 'INDIVIDUAL HOMES'. Monthly.
Subs 01527 836600

Magazine 'DIY MAGAZINE'. Monthly.
Subs 01908 371981

Video 'THE HOUSE THAT MUM AND DAD BUILT'.
0171 833 4152

Video 'BUILD IT YOURSELF'.
01782 638339

### AGENCIES PROVIDING SERVICES TO INDIVIDUAL BUILDERS AND SELFBUILDERS

INDIVIDUAL HOUSEBUILDERS ASSOCIATION.
01753 621277
Provide lists of package companies etc

THE ASSOCIATION OF SELFBUILDERS.  0188 958 4221 or 0116 270 8843
Run by selfbuilders for selfbuilders

ROYAL INSTITUTE OF BRITISH ARCHITECTS (RIBA).
0171 580 5533
Leaflets and Lists of local architects

ASSOCIATED SELF BUILD ARCHITECTS.   0800 387310
Details of architects who specialise in selfbuild clients

ROYAL TOWN PLANNING INSTITUTE.  0171 636 9107
Lists of planning consultants

PLANNING INSPECTORATE · ENGLAND   0117 987 8754
                                                      WALES        0122 282 5493
                                                      SCOTLAND  0131 244 5657
                                                      N.IRELAND  01232 244710
Appeal forms and booklets

THE BRITISH CEMENT ASSOCIATION  01344 762676
Useful booklets on foundations, cellars etc,

THE GLASS AND GLAZING FEDERATION  00127 781 0882
Glass options, glazing techniques, conservatories

CONSERVATORY ASSOCIATION  01480 458278
Specialist advice on conservatories

SOLAR TRADES ASSOCIATION  01208 873518
Solar energy information

NATIONAL ENERGY FOUNDATION  01908 501908
Energy saving information and the SAP rating

TIMBER RESEARCH & DEVELOPMENT ASSOCIATION.
001494 563091
Publications on timber frame construction

TIMBER AND BRICK INFORMATION COUNCIL
01923 778136
Leaflets on timber frame construction and lists of manufacturers

THE BUILDING RESEARCH ESTABLISHMENT 01923 894040
Wide variety of publications on problems of all sorts. Also sell advice. A good place to start if you are looking at a problem site.

DISABLED LIVING FOUNDATION 0171 289 6111
General advice and contacts for specialist advice

H M LAND REGISTRY 0171 917 8888
Will identify owners of registered land titles

BRICK DEVELOPMENT ASSOCIATION 01344 885651
Information on bricks and brickwork

THE CLAY PIPE DEVELOPMENT ASSOCIATION 01494 791456
Advice on design of drains etc

NATIONAL RADIOLOGICAL PROTECTION BOARD 01235 831600
Leaflets on Radon

THATCHING ADVISORY SERVICES 01256 880282
Thatched roofs

COMMISSION FOR THE NEW TOWNS 01908 692692
Plots in the New Towns, including Milton Keynes

LANDBANK SERVICES 01734 618002
Plot finding service

NATIONAL LAND FINDING AGENCY 01371 876875
Plot finding service

BRADFORD & BINGLEY BUILDING SOCIETY 0800 252993
Guide to selfbuild mortgages

## AGENCIES PROVIDING SERVICES TO SELFBUILD GROUPS, INCLUDING COMMUNITY GROUPS

THE COMMUNITY SELFBUILD AGENCY. 0171 415 7092
The key agency for advice. Useful publications.

THE NATIONAL FEDERATION OF HOUSING ASSOCIATIONS. 0171 278 6571
Advice and formal registration for selfbuild groups

ROYAL INSTITUTE OF BRITISH ARCHITECTS (RIBA). 0171 580 5533
Information on grants for feasibility studies

THE HOUSING CORPORATION. 0171 393 2000
Information for those sponsoring community groups

THE WALTER SEGAL TRUST. 0171 388 9582
Unique timber frame system and special group structures

THE YOUNG BUILDERS TRUST 01730 266766
Selfbuild schemes for young people.

CHISEL HOUSING COOPERATIVE 0181 768 2036
'Selfbuild for rent' schemes

CONSTRUCTIVE INDIVIDUALS 01904 625300
Consultancy services for low cost group schemes

## EXHIBITIONS AND COURSES

THE BUILDING CENTRE,
First class permanent exhibition on six floors at 26 Store St, London, near Goodge St underground station. The Building Bookshop is in the same building.

BUILD IT EXHIBITIONS 0181 286 3000
Annual Selfbuild exhibition in London and roadshows throughout the country, with seminars and advice centres

THE INDIVIDUAL HOMES SHOW 01527 836 600
Annual Individual Homes Exhibition at the NEC with seminars and advice centres

IDEAL HOMES EXHIBITION
Hardy annual at Earls Court every March. Some selfbuild.

CONSTRUCTIVE INDIVIDUALS 01904 625300
Courses of all sorts for Selfbuilders

CENTRE FOR ALTERNATIVE TECHNOLOGY 01654 702400
Ecologically friendly selfbuild courses and exhibition

FINDHORN FOUNDATION 01309 690311
Ecologically friendly selfbuild courses etc. near Elgin in Scotland

BRITISH GYPSUM 0115 984 4844
DIY courses on dry plastering techniques

KNAUFF UK LTD 01795 424499
DIY courses on dry plastering techniques

## INSURANCES AND WARRANTIES

DMS SERVICES 01909 591652
Insurances for Individual Builders and Selfbuilders for new properties

VULCAN INSURANCE 01622 671747
Insurances for renovations and conversions

THURCROFT INSURANCE 01709 540348
Arrange to convert selfbuild insurances to householders insurances when the project is finished

FRASER MILLER 01483 797948
Insurances for selfbuild groups

NHBC 01494 434477, or for N.IRELAND 0232 683131
The NHBC building warranty

ZURICH CUSTOMBUILD 01252 522000
The Zurich Custombuild warranty

## COMPANIES WITH PARTICULARLY USEFUL LITERATURE OR ADVISORY SERVICES

BUTTERLEY BRICK LIMITED (alias Hanson Brick) 01773 570570
Bricks and brickwork, paver bricks.

REDLAND TILES LIMITED 01737 242488
Tiles and tiling

RICHARD BURBIDGE LIMITED 01691 655131
Staircases and balustrading etc

PILKINGTON GLASS LIMITED 01744 28882
Advice on glass, and particularly insulating glass

FLYGT LIMITED 0115 940 0444
Pumps to solve drainage problems

CONDER PRODUCTS LIMITED 01962 863577
Septic tanks, Cess Pools, Pumps, and advice on them

CLEARWATER SYSTEMS 01373 858090
Mini sewage systems for individual homes

HEPWORTH BUILDING PRODUCTS LIMITED 01226 763561
Useful booklets on drainage

CAMAS BUILDING PRODUCTS 01335 372222
Reconstituted stone products

# BUILDERS RISKS INSURANCES
# FOR THOSE BUILDING ON THEIR OWN LAND

**NORWICH UNION**

The Norwich Union is able to offer an insurance package for those who are building for their own occupation private dwellings of traditional construction with or without the help of builders or sub-contractors. It does not apply to the extension, alteration, repair or renovation of existing buildings. This affords Contract Works, Public Liability and Employers' Liability cover and automatically includes the interest of any Mortgagee. Cover is provided in one policy document, summarised as follows. This description of insurance must be regarded only as an outline. The policy is a legal document and as such defines the insurance in precise terms. A specimen copy of the policy form is available on request.

## CONTRACT WORKS

| | |
|---|---|
| Cover | "All Risks" of loss or damage to: |
| | (a) the new building whilst under construction and materials for incorporation therein |
| | (b) plant, tools, equipment, temporary buildings and caravans. |
| Sum insured | The full rebuilding cost of the property, excluding the value of the land. |
| Including | (a) your own and hired plant, tools and equipment used in connection with the work up to a total sum insured of £2000 (can be increased if required). |
| | (b) Employees personal effects and tools whilst on the site up to a sum insured of £330 any one employee in accordance with standard Building Industry/Union agreements. |
| | (c) Architects, Surveyors and other fees necessarily incurred in rebuilding following loss or damage. |
| | (d) the cost of removing debris following any claim. |
| Excluding | (a) the first £50 of each and every claim for loss or damage to employees personal effects or tools. |
| | (b) the first £500 of each and every other loss. |

## EMPLOYERS LIABILITY (compulsory by law)

| | |
|---|---|
| Cover | Your legal liability for death or bodily injury to employees, including labour only sub-contractors, arising out of the building work. |
| Limit | £10,000,000 each occurrence. |
| Including | Legal costs and expenses in defending any claim. |
| Note | A Certificate of Insurance will be provided, and must by law be displayed on site. |

## PUBLIC LIABILITY

| | |
|---|---|
| Cover | Your legal liability to members of the public, (including sub-contractors working on the site not classed as employees) for death, bodily injury or damage to property, arising out of the building work. |
| Limit | £1,000,000 any one loss. (Can be increased if required) |
| Including | Legal costs and expenses in defending any claim. |
| Excluding | The first £250 of any claim for damage to property. |

| | |
|---|---|
| PERIOD | From the commencement date you specify (which should be no earlier than the date you complete the proposal form) up to completion of the building work, subject to a maximum of 24 months. Extensions to this period may be available on payment of an additional premium. There is no refund for early completion. |
| THE POLICY | Will be sent direct to you by DMS Services Ltd. on behalf of the Insurance Company. |
| THE PREMIUM | £6.24 per 1,000 on the rebuilding cost of the property. (Minimum £80,000). This is a total rate for all the cover set out above, subject to submission of the completed proposal form overleaf. and includes insurance premium tax at 2½%. Proposal forms should be accompanied by cheques for the relevant premium made out to DMS Services Ltd. |

| Rebuilding Cost Up to £ | Premium £ | Rebuilding Cost Up to £ | Premium £ | Rebuilding Cost Up to £ | Premium £ |
|---|---|---|---|---|---|
| 80,000 | 499.20 | 110,000 | 686.40 | 160,000 | 998.40 |
| 85,000 | 530.40 | 120,000 | 748.80 | 170,000 | 1060.80 |
| 90,000 | 561.60 | 130,000 | 811.20 | 180,000 | 1123.20 |
| 95,000 | 592.80 | 140,000 | 873.60 | 190,000 | 1185.60 |
| 100,000 | 624.00 | 150,000 | 936.00 | 200,000 | 1248.00 |

Over £200,000 @ £6.24 per £1000

| | |
|---|---|
| TAX | The scale of premiums shown in this prospectus and proposal are inclusive of Insurance Premium Tax at 2½% and are only valid while the rate of tax remains at this level. DMS Services Ltd. will advise on revised premiums should the rate of tax change. |

**IMPORTANT** The above terms only apply:
(a) up to 31st December 1996. Amended terms may be necessary for proposal forms completed after that date.
(b) to risks in Mainland Great Britain only. Proposals from N. Ireland are quoted individually and special excesses may apply. Phone 01909 591652 or fax 01909 591031 for a quotation. Proposals cannot be accepted from Eire.
(c) Where there is no abnormal exposure to risk of floods, storm damage or vandalism.

## THE AGENCY
The Agency is DMS Services Ltd., a company which provides specialised insurance services to those building on their own. The proposal form overleaf should be completed and sent to the agency with a cheque for the premium payable to DMS Services Ltd.

---

**D.M.S. Services Ltd., Orchard House, Blyth, Worksop, Notts. S81 8HF.**
**Phone 01909 591652    Fax 01909 591031**

1996

Agency: DMS Services Ltd    Agency Reference: 50GA59    Policy No.

# Proposal – BUILDING OWN PRIVATE DWELLING
## The Insurer: Norwich Union Fire Insurance Society Limited

**NORWICH UNION**

| Name of Proposer MR/MRS/MISS | Phone No. |

Full Postal Address
..................................................................................................................................................
............................................................................................. Postcode ...............................

Address of property to be erected
..................................................................................................................................................
..................................................................................................................................................

| Name and address of any interested party – eg Bank or Building Society | Commencing date of insurance |
| ................................................................................................ | |
| ................................................................................................ | ........................... |

**Important** – Please give a definite answer to each question (block letters) or tick appropriate boxes

|  | Yes | No | If "Yes" please give details |
|---|---|---|---|
| 1. Have you made any other proposal for insurance in respect of the risk proposed? | ☐ | ☐ | |
| 2. Has any company or underwriter declined your proposal? | ☐ | ☐ | |
| 3. Have you ever been convicted of (or charged but not yet tried with) arson or any offence involving dishonesty of any kind (eg fraud, theft, handling stolen goods)? | ☐ | ☐ | |

4. Will the property be

(a) a completely new structure and not an extension, conversion or restoration of an existing building?  ☐ ☐   (If "No" please refer to DMS Services Ltd.) Phone 01909 591652

(b) of conventional construction, either in loadbearing masonry, or with a timber frame, and built to drawings approved under the requirements of the Building Regulations as meeting the requirements of the regulations in full?  ☐ ☐

(c) occupied as your permanent residence on completion?  ☐ ☐   (If "No" please refer to DMS Services Ltd.) Phone 01909 591652

5. (a) Will the total value of plant, tools, equipment and temporary buildings, whether hired or owned on site at any one time exceed £2,000. If so see page 6 of the prospectus for the additional premium required (cover for plant on site can be altered at any time while the policy is in force)  ☐ ☐

Contractors plant hired in with operators, such as excavators, need not be included if proposers are wholly satisfied the hirers insurances cover all risks. However if cover is required on such machines phone DMS Services on 01909 591652

6. Is there any abnormal exposure to risk of flooding, storm damage or vandalism?  ☐ ☐

7. State estimated value of building work on completion at builder price for reinstatement.  £ _____

It is important that this sum is the cost of a professional building firm rebuilding the entire dwelling should it be completely destroyed just prior to completion. This will be the limit of indemnity for item (A) of the Contract Works section, and payments of premium on a lesser figure will result in any contracts works claim being proportionately reduced. Please discuss with DMS Services Ltd if in any doubt.

8. Material facts – state any other material facts here. Failure to do so could invalidate the policy. A material fact is one which is likely to influence an insurer in the assessment and acceptance of the proposal. If you are in any doubt as to whether a fact is material it should be disclosed to the insurer.

If work on site has started certify here that there have been no incidents on site which would have given rise to a claim

**Note:** 1. You should keep a record (including copies of letters) of all information supplied to the insurer for the purpose of entering into the contract.
2. A copy of this proposal form will be supplied by the Insurer on request.
3. Please note that the details you are asked to supply may be used to provide you with information about other products and services which the Norwich Union Group can offer.

**Declaration** To be completed in all cases
I desire to insure with the Insurer in the terms of the Policy used in this class of Insurance. I declare that the above statements and particulars are true to the best of my knowledge and belief and that I have not withheld any material information. I agree to give immediate notice to the insurer of any alteration to the circumstances described herein and that this proposal shall form the basis of the contract between us.

| Proposer's signature | Date |

Send completed form to DMS Services Ltd., Orchard House, Blyth, Worksop, Notts. S81 8HF, together with a cheque made payable to DMS Services Ltd. Any queries to DMS Services. Phone 01909 591652.

Norwich Union Fire Insurance Society Limited. Registered in England No. 99122. Registered Office: Surrey Street, Norwich NR1 3NS. Member of the Association of British Insurers. Member of the Insurance Ombudsman Bureau.

**HOME PLUS COVER**
Quotations will be provided for household insurances when the building approaches completion. If this is not required please tick box – ☐

1996

# BUILDERS RISKS INSURANCES
# FOR THOSE BUILDING ON THEIR OWN LAND

**NORWICH UNION**

The Norwich Union is able to offer an insurance package for those who are building for their own occupation private dwellings of traditional construction with or without the help of builders or sub-contractors. It does not apply to the extension, alteration, repair or renovation of existing buildings. This affords Contract Works, Public Liability and Employers' Liability cover and automatically includes the interest of any Mortgagee. Cover is provided in one policy document, summarised as follows. This description of insurance must be regarded only as an outline. The policy is a legal document and as such defines the insurance in precise terms. A specimen copy of the policy form is available on request.

## CONTRACT WORKS

**Cover** — "All Risks" of loss or damage to:
(a) the new building whilst under construction and materials for incorporation therein
(b) plant, tools, equipment, temporary buildings and caravans.

**Sum insured** — The full rebuilding cost of the property, excluding the value of the land.

**Including**
(a) your own and hired plant, tools and equipment used in connection with the work up to a total sum insured of £2000 (can be increased if required).
(b) Employees personal effects and tools whilst on the site up to a sum insured of £330 any one employee in accordance with standard Building Industry/Union agreements.
(c) Architects, Surveyors and other fees necessarily incurred in rebuilding following loss or damage.
(d) the cost of removing debris following any claim.

**Excluding**
(a) the first £50 of each and every claim for loss or damage to employees personal effects or tools.
(b) the first £500 of each and every other loss.

## EMPLOYERS LIABILITY (compulsory by law)

**Cover** — Your legal liability for death or bodily injury to employees, including labour only sub-contractors, arising out of the building work.

**Limit** — £10,000,000 each occurrence.

**Including** — Legal costs and expenses in defending any claim.

**Note** — A Certificate of Insurance will be provided, and must by law be displayed on site.

## PUBLIC LIABILITY

**Cover** — Your legal liability to members of the public, (including sub-contractors working on the site not classed as employees) for death, bodily injury or damage to property, arising out of the building work.

**Limit** — £1,000,000 any one loss. (Can be increased if required)

**Including** — Legal costs and expenses in defending any claim.

**Excluding** — The first £250 of any claim for damage to property.

**PERIOD** — From the commencement date you specify (which should be no earlier than the date you complete the proposal form) up to completion of the building work, subject to a maximum of 24 months. Extensions to this period may be available on payment of an additional premium. There is no refund for early completion.

**THE POLICY** — Will be sent direct to you by DMS Services Ltd. on behalf of the Insurance Company.

**THE PREMIUM** — £6.24 per 1,000 on the rebuilding cost of the property. (Minimum £80,000). This is a total rate for all the cover set out above, subject to submission of the completed proposal form overleaf. and includes insurance premium tax at 2½%. Proposal forms should be accompanied by cheques for the relevant premium made out to DMS Services Ltd.

| Rebuilding Cost Up to £ | Premium £ | Rebuilding Cost Up to £ | Premium £ | Rebuilding Cost Up to £ | Premium £ |
|---|---|---|---|---|---|
| 80,000 | 499.20 | 110,000 | 686.40 | 160,000 | 998.40 |
| 85,000 | 530.40 | 120,000 | 748.80 | 170,000 | 1060.80 |
| 90,000 | 561.60 | 130,000 | 811.20 | 180,000 | 1123.20 |
| 95,000 | 592.80 | 140,000 | 873.60 | 190,000 | 1185.60 |
| 100,000 | 624.00 | 150,000 | 936.00 | 200,000 | 1248.00 |

Over £200,000 @ £6.24 per £1000

**TAX** — The scale of premiums shown in this prospectus and proposal are inclusive of Insurance Premium Tax at 2½% and are only valid while the rate of tax remains at this level. DMS Services Ltd. will advise on revised premiums should the rate of tax change.

**IMPORTANT** The above terms only apply:
(a) up to 31st December 1996. Amended terms may be necessary for proposal forms completed after that date.
(b) to risks in Mainland Great Britain only. Proposals from N. Ireland are quoted individually and special excesses may apply. Phone 01909 591652 or fax 01909 591031 for a quotation. Proposals cannot be accepted from Eire.
(c) Where there is no abnormal exposure to risk of floods, storm damage or vandalism.

## THE AGENCY

The Agency is DMS Services Ltd., a company which provides specialised insurance services to those building on their own. The proposal form overleaf should be completed and sent to the agency with a cheque for the premium payable to DMS Services Ltd.

**D.M.S. Services Ltd., Orchard House, Blyth, Worksop, Notts. S81 8HF.**
**Phone 01909 591652   Fax 01909 591031**

Agency: DMS Services Ltd     Agency Reference: 50GA59     Policy No.

# Proposal – BUILDING OWN PRIVATE DWELLING
## The Insurer: Norwich Union Fire Insurance Society Limited

**NORWICH UNION**

Name of Proposer                            Phone No.
MR/MRS/MISS

Full Postal Address
......................................................................................................
...................................................................... Postcode ...........................

Address of property to be erected
......................................................................................................
......................................................................................................

Name and address of any interested party – eg Bank or Building Society
......................................................................................................
......................................................................................................

Commencing date
of insurance
..........................

**Important** – Please give a definite answer to each question (block letters) or tick appropriate boxes

| | Yes | No | If "Yes" please give details |
|---|---|---|---|
| 1. Have you made any other proposal for insurance in respect of the risk proposed? | ☐ | ☐ | |
| 2. Has any company or underwriter declined your proposal? | ☐ | ☐ | |
| 3. Have you ever been convicted of (or charged but not yet tried with) arson or any offence involving dishonesty of any kind (eg fraud, theft, handling stolen goods)? | ☐ | ☐ | |

4. Will the property be

(a) a completely new structure and not an extension, conversion or restoration of an existing building? ☐ ☐   (If "No" please refer to DMS Services Ltd.) Phone 01909 591652

(b) of conventional construction, either in loadbearing masonry, or with a timber frame, and built to drawings approved under the requirements of the Building Regulations as meeting the requirements of the regulations in full? ☐ ☐

(c) occupied as your permanent residence on completion? ☐ ☐   (If "No" please refer to DMS Services Ltd.) Phone 01909 591652

5. (a) Will the total value of plant, tools, equipment and temporary buildings, whether hired or owned on site at any one time exceed £2,000. If so see page 6 of the prospectus for the additional premium required (cover for plant on site can be altered at any time while the policy is in force) ☐ ☐   Contractors plant hired in with operators, such as excavators, need not be included if proposers are wholly satisfied the hirers insurances cover all risks. However if cover is required on such machines phone DMS Services on 01909 591652

6. Is there any abnormal exposure to risk of flooding, storm damage or vandalism? ☐ ☐

7. State estimated value of building work on completion at builder price for reinstatement. £   It is important that this sum is the cost of a professional building firm rebuilding the entire dwelling should it be completely destroyed just prior to completion. This will be the limit of indemnity for item (A) of the Contract Works section, and payments of premium on a lesser figure will result in any contracts works claim being proportionately reduced. Please discuss with DMS Services Ltd if in any doubt.

8. Material facts – state any other material facts here. Failure to do so could invalidate the policy. A material fact is one which is likely to influence an insurer in the assessment and acceptance of the proposal. If you are in any doubt as to whether a fact is material it should be disclosed to the insurer.   If work on site has started certify here that there have been no incidents on site which would have given rise to a claim

**Note:** 1. You should keep a record (including copies of letters) of all information supplied to the insurer for the purpose of entering into the contract.
2. A copy of this proposal form will be supplied by the Insurer on request.
3. Please note that the details you are asked to supply may be used to provide you with information about other products and services which the Norwich Union Group can offer.

**Declaration** To be completed in all cases
I desire to insure with the Insurer in the terms of the Policy used in this class of Insurance. I declare that the above statements and particulars are true to the best of my knowledge and belief and that I have not withheld any material information. I agree to give immediate notice to the insurer of any alteration to the circumstances described herein and that this proposal shall form the basis of the contract between us.

Proposer's signature                              Date

Send completed form to DMS Services Ltd., Orchard House, Blyth, Worksop, Notts. S81 8HF, together with a cheque made payable to DMS Services Ltd. Any queries to DMS Services. Phone 01909 591652.
Norwich Union Fire Insurance Society Limited. Registered in England No. 99122. Registered Office: Surrey Street, Norwich NR1 3NS. Member of the Association of British Insurers. Member of the Insurance Ombudsman Bureau.

**HOME PLUS COVER**
Quotations will be provided for household insurances when the building approaches completion. If this is not required please tick box – ☐

1996